Microprocessors/
Microcomputers/
System Design

TEXAS INSTRUMENTS ELECTRONICS SERIES

Microprocessors/ Microcomputers/ System Design

William D. Simpson, MSEE, Staff Consultant

Gerald Luecke, MSEE, Manager of Technical
Product Development

Don L. Cannon, PhD., Staff Consultant

David H. Clemens, Staff Consultant

Texas Instruments Learning Center
and
The Engineering Staff of Texas Instruments Incorporated

McGraw-Hill Book Company

New York   St. Louis   San Francisco   Auckland
Bogotá   Singapore   Johannesburg   London
Madrid   Mexico   Montreal   New Delhi
Panama   São Paulo   Hamburg
Sydney   Tokyo   Paris

Acknowledgement:

Many members of the engineering and marketing staff of Texas Instruments Incorporated have contributed previously authored materials for the content of this book. The contributions, which are significant but are too numerous to identify individually, have been edited and combined with original authored material into the present book written by the Texas Instruments Learning Center and its staff consultants.

A final review and edit was done by the 9900 Family marketing and engineering staffs.

Design and artwork by:
Schenck, Plunk & Deason

Library of Congress Cataloging in Publication Data
Texas Instruments Incorporated. Learning Center.
   Microprocessors/microcomputers/system design.
   (Texas Instruments electronics series)
   Includes index.
   1. Microprocessors.   2. Microcomputers.   3. TMS9900
family (Computer)   4. System design.   I. Simpson,
William D.   II. Texas Instruments Incorporated.
III. Title
QA76.S.T49   1980   001.6'4'04   79-24390
ISBN   0-07-063758-X

TABLE OF CONTENTS

TABLE OF CONTENTS

TABLE OF CONTENTS

TABLE OF CONTENTS

TABLE OF CONTENTS

TABLE OF CONTENTS

TABLE OF CONTENTS

## CHAPTER 1

Basic Decisions
In System Design

INTRODUCTION

Texas Instruments has developed and is manufacturing a family of microprocessor products and systems based on the architecture of its 990 minicomputer. The purpose of this book is to present enough factual information about the 9900 and the family of devices and systems surrounding it to serve not only as a guide for deciding to use the 9900 in an application, but also as the primary reference for design and programming activities. The book is much more than a data book or a collection of application notes. It contains basic concepts, presents methods and techniques, and most important of all, shows how the architecture of the 9900, substantially superior to other microprocessor architectures, can be translated into cost effective applications.

The time investment you make in learning how to use the 9900 will inevitably produce substantial benefits because your designs will be advanced well beyond other microprocessor systems; they will be expandable, flexible, easily upgraded and will not be obsolescent. The capital investment in programming systems will bring powerful computing equipment and software tools to your design team that will have them out-distancing the competition in a very short time.

In reading this book, you will see the 9900 product as more than a single microprocessor. You will find a family of processors, peripherals, boards, minicomputers and systems all based on a single architectural concept called *memory-to-memory architecture.* It is this basic principle which, when fully understood at the fundamental level, will help you understand why and how the 9900 can be used to implement outstanding products. In addition, you will see why Texas Instruments has made the commitment to the continued support of the 9900 family in both hardware and software. New microprocessors and peripheral devices will retain and complement the basic architectural features—the 16-bit word length, the instruction set, the I/O techniques. etc. Texas Instruments software support goes beyond the standard assembler, editor, linker and PROM programmer software. New design tools such as POWER BASIC and PASCAL are now available. These powerful software products bring structured programming disciplines into focus and help you to attain an advanced programming capability.

All in all, the book is a collection of useful factual material which should be of substantial benefit to anyone considering designing with microprocessors. For those who have very limited exposure to designing with semiconductor products, the next few sections will be helpful because the theme of "more functions at lower cost" is demonstrated. These ideas lead to the basic philosophy that designing with *standard hardware* — semiconductor LSI products which are *programmable* — is the most economical procedure, and should be carefully considered for *every* new electronic product.

THE IMPACT OF SEMICONDUCTORS

In the short thirty years since the invention of the transistor (the first semiconductor device to exhibit amplification), there have been more inventions and more scientific and engineering accomplishments than in all time previous. The field of digital electronics (especially computers) has been the greatest contributor of new products for these accomplishments and, therefore, has become one of the most rapidly growing industries. Manufacturers of semiconductor components (transistors, integrated circuits, microprocessors and memories) have been providing the building blocks, and the equipment manufacturers have been taking advantage of the opportunity by developing the most sophisticated systems that are economically feasible.

In his keynote address to the 1977 National Computer Conference, Mark Shepherd, Chairman of the Board of Texas Instruments, made the following points:

"Until 1971, the semiconductor industry was in the circuits business. Semiconductor circuits, complex though they were, constituted only a fraction of an entire system. The one-chip calculator developed in 1971 was the first significant complete system. Since then many calculators and watches have been developed where the entire system function is accomplished by one or a few semiconductor chips. These were custom chips because the technology did now allow any reserve computing power for other applications.

"The semiconductor industry has now entered an era where the entire system function of an end product can be accomplished by a few semiconductor chips, or a single chip, with enough versatility to permit adaptation to many different applications through the programming.

"This change carries enormous implications for the system designer. 1) The lead time for system implementation is shortened because no special chip development is required. 2) The development cost will be low because it will be limited to software (which may be executed in hardware). 3) The required degree of electronic sophistication on the part of the user is much less. To achieve these advantages the system designer must be prepared to use standard products produced in large volume rather than custom devices.

"The functional equivalent of a medium-scale computer *(Figure 1-1)* cost $30,000 in the early 1960s. Its cost equivalent has now dropped to $4,000 and is projected to be at less than $100 by 1985, penetrating the personal cost threshold. As this is accomplished, greater challenges will be encountered in the cost of sales, service, and maintenance, requiring that we learn to incorporate self-diagnostic and self-repair functions into our systems."

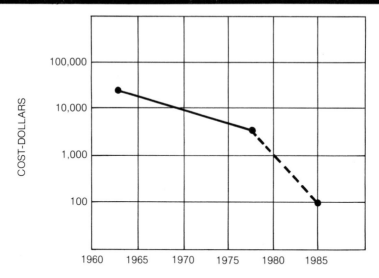

Figure 1-1. *Cost of Medium Scale Computer*
(M. Shepherd, 1977 NCC)

The cost of the hardware components for a typical digital system has been decreasing
with time because new and more powerful semiconductor devices have been developed.
Equally important is the fact that the development cost for the typical digital system
hardware has also been decreasing. *Figure 1-2* illustrates how impressive this cost
reduction has been. Contrast the figures of 7-8 *million* dollars in the early fifties with 8-9
thousand dollars in the late seventies; digital system development cost has been reduced
by a factor of *one thousand* in a period of 25 years! An extension of this trend indicates
that typical system hardware development cost will be approximately $1,000 by 1985.

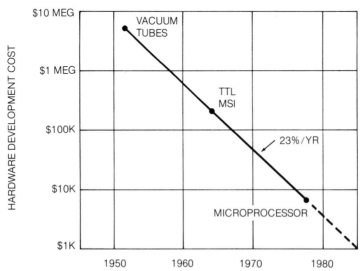

Figure 1-2. *Typical Digital System Hardware Development Cost at OEM Manufacturer*

How has this been accomplished? *Figure 1-3* shows what has been happening. As the number of components per chip of silicon increases, the development cost for each chip also increases. For a semiconductor manufacturer, volume production is required to offset the development cost. Semiconductor devices are therefore being *batched fabricated* — a few hundred, a few thousand per chip — and this means lower cost per *active element group* or AEG. (An AEG is defined as a logic gate, flip-flop, or a memory cell.)

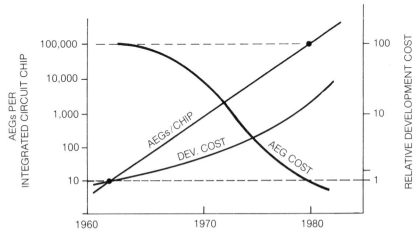

Figure 1-3. Evolution of Semiconductor Technology

Figure 1-4 shows the chronology of semiconductor device development. An AEG in the early 1950's consisted of one or two transistors, several resistors, a capacitor or two, and some area of a printed circuit board to hold the parts together as an assembly. Early integrated circuits contained about 10 AEG's. Then medium scale integration achieved up to 100 AEG's per chip and large scale integration reached 1,000 AEG's per chip.

At this point (the late 1960's), the semiconductor technologists had apparently reached an impasse. If they continued to increase the number of AEG's per chip the high degree of specialization would preclude volume production, and the benefits of LSI would be lost. In fact, the only area in which LSI appeared to be feasible was in memories — primarily read/write memories now called RAM's. Read only memories (ROM's) and programmable read only memories (PROM's) were not required until later (as you will see). But the semiconductor technologists continued their thrust toward greater numbers of AEG's per chip, focusing primarily on memory products.

There was one other product which appeared to be feasible (in 1970) — a single-chip calculator. Here was an opportunity to stretch the imagination to greater degrees of achievement. At the producibility level of about 1,000 AEG's per chip, all of the functions of a microcomputer could be built on one chip — and the application certainly had the required volume potential. So *custom* LSI found a niche in the form of the hand-held calculator.

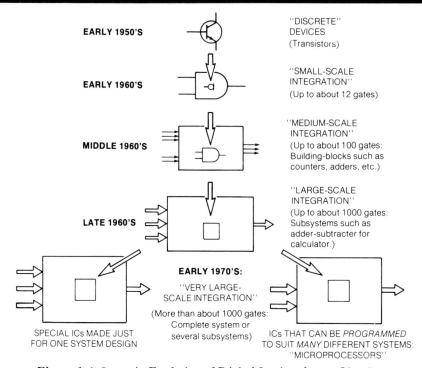

Figure 1-4. Stages in Evolution of Digital Semiconductor Circuitry.
(G. McWhorter, Understanding Digital Electronics, Texas Instruments Inc., Dallas, Texas, 1978)

From the very beginning the designers of the single chip microcomputer envisioned new and varied applications of this device, so it was made with a ROM for instructions and RAM for data. It was *programmable,* at least it was "mask programmable." And as we witness the growth of this segment of the semiconductor market, we see a host of dedicated applications for single chip microcomputers such as controllers for microwave ovens, sewing machines, and other appliances.

By designing a "standard" chip that could be *programmed* to do a variety of jobs, semiconductor technologists repeated the step taken by the inventors of the first programmable machine — the first computer — in the late 1940's. The first digital computer was a *stored program* digital calculating machine. Programming provided versatility and variety of applications. Similarly, programmable single chip, LSI semiconductor devices — microcomputers — gave LSI variety of applicability.

The next logical step in the evolution of LSI was the design of the general purpose microprocessor, a computer CPU on a chip. By interfacing the microprocessor to a memory — a set of chips arranged to provide as much storage as needed — one can build larger, more powerful microcomputers which can replace special purpose hardwired logic. In fact, general purpose hardware that is *programmable* provides *multichip* applicability of LSI technology.

With this breakthrough in the concept of LSI application, the semiconductor technologists have been motivated to continue to increase the number of AEG's per device. *Figure 1-5* projects the growth of AEG's per chip to over 10^6 by 1985 — a level sufficient for a single chip 32-bit microcomputer. The 16-bit microprocessor and 4K RAM require about 50,000 AEG's. RAM's of 16K and 64K bits requiring up to 100,000 AEG's are not unrealistic extensions of the trends; they are real products rapidly moving into the marketplace. New advances are being made in semiconductor process technology to achieve the packing densities needed for the future. As *Figure 1-5* indicates, optical techniques for defining regions and interconnections reach a resolution limit at about 10^5 AEG's. E-beam and X-ray technology will be required to further increase component density.

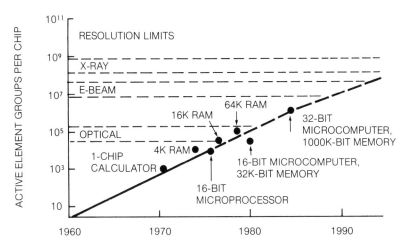

Figure 1-5. *Semiconductor Chip Complexity*
(M. Shepherd, 1977 NCC)

The impact of programmable semiconductor devices is shown in *Figure 1-6.* Prior to 1972, semiconductor devices were designed as *circuits.* Now they are being designed as *systems* or at least subsystems. As the number of AEG's/chip continues its rise, driving down the cost of CPU and memory devices, unlimited opportunity is being created for an unbelievable variety of new products.

Figure 1-7 shows that a dramatic change is anticipated in the rate of AEG cost reduction with time due to the impact of microprocessors. Functions (AEG's) costing $1.00 in 1966 were obtained for around *5 cents* in 1976. In fact, the cost per AEG is projected to be less than *a tenth of a cent* by 1985.

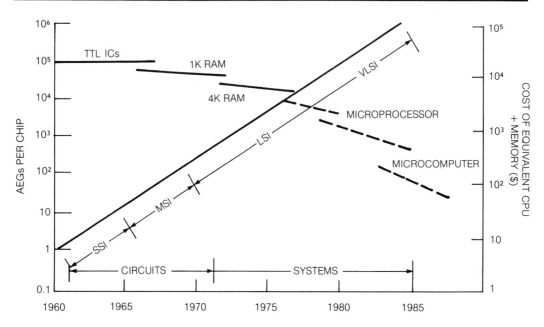

Figure 1-6. *Distributed Semiconductor Power*

(M. Shepherd, 1977 NCC)

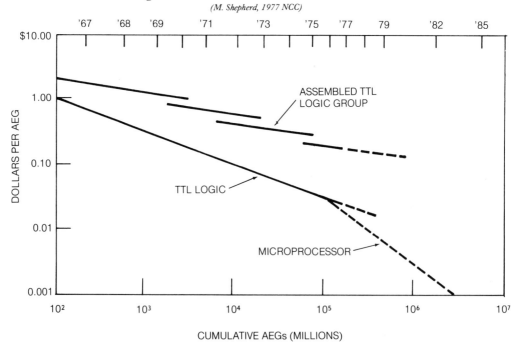

Figure 1-7. *Cost Per AEG for TTL and Microprocessor*

(M. Shepherd, 1977 NCC)

Memory costs (on a per bit basis) are diminishing, too. Following the projected trends for the cost of AEG's, RAM cost is forecast to be less than .05 cents per bit by 1982 (*Figure 1-8*). The need for various memory types has now been established. Programs for microcomputers are stored in non-volatile memories such as ROM's, PROM's and EPROM's. ROM's are mask programmable by the manufacturer and are best suited for high volume applications. PROM's are programmable after the devices are completely packaged. Either the manufacturer, the distributor or the user may store the desired program (or data) in a PROM. PROM's are suited for medium volume to low volume applications. EPROM's are erasable and so find use during prototyping and development cycles. They are also used in applications where software must be periodically changed, upgraded, or modified in any way. Other memory technologies such as CCD's (charge coupled device) and bubbles will be used for mass storage requirements where speed is not critical.

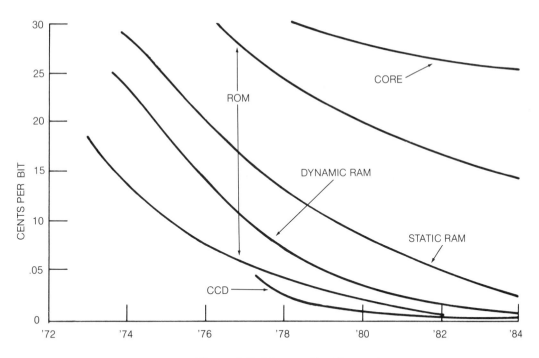

Figure 1-8. *Memory Cost Comparison*

(M. Shepherd, 1977 NCC)

The effect of modern semiconductor technology has been to alter the roles of the component manufacturer and the OEM (original equipment manufacturer). Component manufacturers are continuing to produce batch-fabricated semiconductor products. But the economic benefit — the low cost per AEG — of batch fabricated semiconductor devices with high functional density cannot be realized except through applications which are program controlled. The component manufacturer must therefore provide programming support via PDS's (program development systems) and software products to enable the OEM to develop applications programs. Thus increased development cost of high functional density devices is found not only in improved process technology and in the design of LSI masks, but also in the attendant software support products. And volume production is required to offset these costs.

The role of the OEM is undergoing a corresponding shift. Component costs and the assembly cost of hardware have been sharply reduced. *Table 1-1* demonstrates the evolutionary steps in hardware costs. The cost improvement ratio of each step as compared with the previous step is dramatic: overall, it is 600:1.

Table 1-1. System Cost Reduction

EVOLUTIONARY STEP	COMPONENTS TO ASSEMBLE	TOTAL COST	
		COMPONENTS + ASSEMBLY COST	COST IMPROVEMENT RATIO
DISCRETES	20000-30000	6000-9000	—
IC'S (GATES & FLIP FLOPS)	350-500	600-900	10:1
IC'S + MSI	125-150	250-450	2,5:1
MICROPROCESSORS	7-10	120-190	2:1
MICROCOMPUTERS	1	6-12	12:1

While hardware costs are decreasing, the software costs, as a percentage of the overall design effort, are increasing. *Figure 1-9* illustrates the relationship of hardware to software costs in product development and the change in emphasis. In the 1950's computers were only used in large-scale business and scientific applications. OEM's had no opportunity to use computing power in their systems. When minicomputers were introduced in the 1960's, OEM's found applications in process control and small business EDP functions, and therefore had to provide some special programs for their use. With the advent of microprocessors in the 1970's, the software component of the development cost increased further, and this trend can easily be forecast into the 1980's — less than 25% of the development cost of most products will be for hardware.

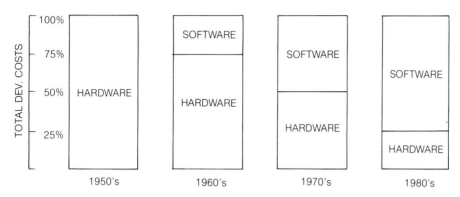

Figure 1-9. Increasing % of Software Development Cost

Development costs are changing — becoming more software oriented — and this has a strong impact on overall product cost. In any product design, the development cost is amortized over some production quantity, and this affects the price of the product. But developing *software* to achieve any design goal is less expensive than developing *hardware* to do the same thing. Therefore, the *total* development cost for "equivalent systems" is decreasing (perhaps by as much as 15-20% per year).

The development of *programmable semiconductors* has been a major accomplishment equivalent in importance to the inventions of the transistor, the integrated circuit, and the stored program computer.

The trends appear to be well established. The number of AEG's per chip will be increasing by at least *75% per year* for at least another two decades. As a result, AEG cost will decline by about *50% per year* and RAM cost per bit will decline by about *20% per year.* The computing power of LSI devices will increase while the price will continue to decrease. The impact will be felt in all walks of life.

APPLICATIONS OF PROGRAMMABLE SEMICONDUCTORS

The application of programmable semiconductors can be considered as an extension of the application of computers. All applications of LSI semiconductor devices are as computers because microprocessors, microcomputers and programmable LSI peripheral chips are *programmed* to perform the special functions required for each application. All the elements of a computer — ALU, control, memory and I/O — are present.

As the price of computing power decreases, the number of applications increases. The number of computers of any given type being applied is inversely proportional to the cost (*Figure 1-10*). As of 1976 there were relatively few systems in the $100-$10000 range. But microcomputers are changing this. Applications are being found in new designs of digital electronic systems, in products previously using electro-mechanical devices, and in new products which previously were not economically feasible.

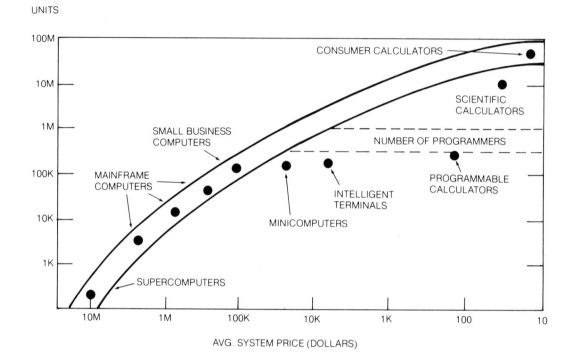

Figure 1-10. *U.S. Installed Computer Base—1976*
(M. Shepherd, 1977 NCC)

While some people may feel that the number of computers cannot exceed the number of "programmers" (approximately one million according to *Figure 1-10*), it is evident that all designers of products which use microcomputers will acquire the necessary programming skills to achieve the desired end product results.

SINGLE CHIP MICROCOMPUTER APPLICATIONS

Single chip microcomputers are being used in the small, dedicated, high volume applications such as calculators, microwave ovens, and general appliance controllers. As the computing power of single chip devices increases, the range of applications will obviously expand. Early devices contained about 1K bytes of memory. New devices with 2K bytes of ROM for instructions and small amounts (256 bytes) of RAM for data have been built and designed into more complex applications. One example is a terminal controller using the TMS 9940 microcomputer with one support chip; this is described in Chapter 8.

MULTI-CHIP MICROCOMPUTER APPLICATIONS

The application areas which involve the greatest number of designers and programmers by far are those using a multi-chip approach — a microprocessor, memory sized to the application, and peripheral interface devices. Limitations are much less in multi-chip systems than for single chip microcomputers. Designs can be accomplished using the general purpose microcomputer boards which have been designed to be applied to a variety of end products. Or the designer can start with individual LSI devices and build a special microcomputer for each application.

The list of applications for microprocessors is long and continues to grow. But a few of the representative areas are these:

Instrumentation
Test Equipment
Industrial Process Control
Point-of-sale Terminals
Cash Registers
Typewriter/Word Processing Equipment
CRT Terminals
Vending Machines
TV Games
Automobile Engine Ignition Controllers
General Automotive Products
CB Equipment
Communications Controllers
Educational Toys
Personal Computers
Special Dedicated EDP Functions

In each application standard programmable semiconductor LSI devices are used to sense input information, process the information according to special procedures (algorithms), and send information to external devices for display, printing, physical control devices, etc. Obviously the need for interface circuits is great. They cover specific functions such as A/D converters, D/A converters, transducers, and special display drivers, etc., as well as standard digital circuits for buffering, multiplexing, latching, etc. *Figure 1-11* shows conceptually how the elements of the microcomputer are arranged for any application.

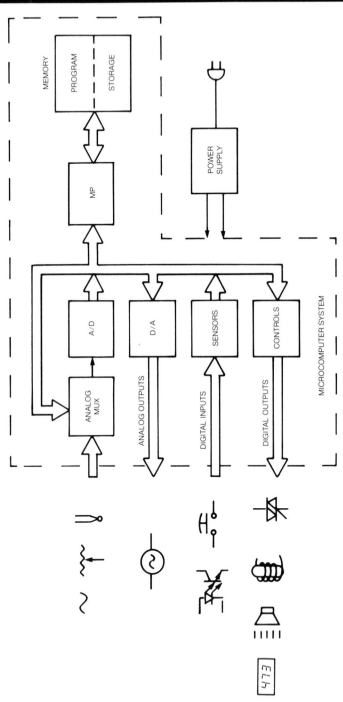

Figure 1-11. *Microprocessor Applications in Process Control Systems*

BUILDING A MICROPROCESSOR BASED SYSTEM

Given an application idea, how does one proceed toward designing a product in which a microprocessor is the central control device? The design steps may be diagrammed in great detail, but the most important steps are these.

1. System Specifications — The system requirements include electrical specifications for each input and output, timing details, and overall performance logic.

2. Division into small subsystems — By defining small, easily managed tasks, the hardware and software requirements can be measured, and design can be scheduled.

3. Decisions for hardware and software — This is the appropriate design point at which the tradeoff between hardware and software solutions for each task is evaluated. For economy, the best solution may appear to be software, but there may be a penalty in performance.

4. Hardware and software design — Here the two design activities may be carried out in parallel. The microcomputer parts are assembled on one or more breadboards and tested for signal flow. Software is developed using a software development system (a computer with appropriate peripherals and programs). Software testing may be done to provide algorithm functionality.

5. System integration — Ultimately, the hardware must be tested under program control. At this point the programs must be loaded into the system memory (usually PROM or EPROM) for testing. Often special logic analyzers and other computer based diagnostic tools are needed to debug the complete system (see the description of the AMPL system in Chapters 2 and 7).

It is clear from the foregoing list of steps that a thorough understanding of the hardware components and a knowledge of programming is required to design with microprocessors and microcomputers. But this is not difficult to acquire. By learning the names of standard building blocks and software packages, you will have taken a major step toward understanding what you read about them.

Basic Hardware Components

Since the hardware for digital systems is being standardized, the basic elements and their functions can easily be studied. Comparisons of similar devices from various manufacturers must be made and design tradeoffs evaluated. Here are the basic building blocks, what they do, and how they are used.

Microprocessor or CPU

This fundamental chip contains the Arithmetic and Logic Unit (ALU) which basically performs addition and comparisons between two numbers. Temporary storage registers are available to hold numbers (called operands) and addresses (memory location numbers) which identify or point to instructions and data. Sometimes the ALU is used to calculate addresses by arithmetic operations on certain register contents. The microprocessor must also contain timing and control circuitry to direct all activities in an orderly step-by-step procedure. The actual control functions are determined by decoding and executing instructions. Instruction execution is a special type of operation on information which comes from memory. The memory stores numerical values which may be interpreted by the processor in one of two ways. Either the number is an instruction, which will direct the sequence of operations over the next few clock cycles, or it is data to be operated upon either arithmetically or logically.

Memory

The main memory of a microcomputer holds the program and data for the system. Because semiconductor RAM devices are volatile (that is, all data is lost when power is removed), it is desirable to use ROM devices (Real Only Memory or non-volatile memory) for the program and RAM for data. ROM devices are programmed (information stored in the cells) by means of a metalization pattern or mask at the time of chip fabrication. Programmable read only memories (PROM's) may be programmed by the manufacturer or the user because information is stored by burning small metalic fuse links via the application of electric current. Programming is performed on the device after it has been packaged. EPROM's are non-volatile read-only memories which may be *erased,* usually via the application of ultraviolet light. These devices are especially useful in prototyping and system development during which program changes are frequent.

Memory devices are designed for cascading so that any size memory may be obtained by adding more devices. Capacities of 4K bits per chip are common; devices with 64K bits per chip are not far away.

Input/Output

For the input and output function — interfacing the microprocessor-memory combination to the "outside world" — usually consists of a variety of devices including programmable LSI devices. Examples of interface requirements are as follows:

1. For communication of digital information over a pair of wires, conversion from 8-bit bytes (parallel) to single bits sent in sequence (serial) is required. The I/O device must receive a number of bits, hold them in a register and then shift them serially to a transmission line. The reverse procedure, serial to parallel conversion, must be performed for receiving information from the transmission line. Since the clock rates, start and stop characters, and "handshaking" requirements can be complex in communications networks, the protocol is designed into the TMS 9902 and TMS 9903 programmable communications controllers.

2. Man-machine interfacing may consist of arrays of switches and indicators or may be performed via a terminal such as a teletype (TTY) or a video display terminal (VDT). Arrays of switches are connected to microcomputers via multiplexers. The address bus may be used to select one of the switches for sampling at any given moment. Addressable latches are useful in supplying on-off data to arrays of indicators. The address bus is again used to select one specific display device (a single lamp) to be turned on (or off) in a given computer cycle. Terminal interfacing can be accomplished via a serial data interface such as the TMS 9902 (see Chapter 8 — example using the TM 990/100M board).

3. The broad category of analog (continuously variable) inputs and outputs requires converters (A/D and D/A) to obtain digital information on the computer side of the interface. Input signals from transducers or output signals to actuators (positioners) require this type of conversion.

Connecting the I/O devices to the CPU and addressing them may present problems in some microcomputer systems. The 9900 solves the problem by providing two types of general purpose I/O. Memory mapped I/O allows a set of memory addresses to identify the I/O devices (as though they were words of memory), while the communications register unit (CRU) provides a separate I/O port specially designed to interface single bit devices, communications devices, standard computer peripherals, etc. Unique to the 9900 architecture, the CRU interface is a powerful and versatile I/O technique; it is easily utilized via the special LSI peripheral supports circuits (such as the TMS 9901, 2, and 3, and the TIM 9905 and 6).

The rules for interconnecting the various elements of the microcomputer include loading specifications and signal level limitations. In observing these rules the designer will occasionally use a few standard devices to reduce loading or perform level shifting. Generally, the addition of such devices is an insignificant part of the overall design. (Details for hardware interfacing are given in Chapter 4.)

PROGRAMMING FOR MICROCOMPUTERS

The writing of programs — often called software development — is the companion activity to hardware breadboarding and testing in computer systems. But software is substantially more flexible than hardware because it consists primarily of *ideas,* documented in strings of characters on a page, or in 1's and 0's in a memory. In fact, until a program is actually loaded into a memory, it is truly a set of ideas on paper, hence the contrasting name, *software.*

In developing the individual hardware components of a microcomputer, designers usually subdivide the activities into small, easily managed tasks. These tasks are performed sequentially by one designer or simultaneously by several members of a design team. The same is true of software design. Small, easily defined and understood sub-programs are given as individual assignments to the programmers on the design team.

The disciplines for programming are set up so that each sub-program stands alone, yet couples to the other sub-programs in a harmonious manner. But the overall plan begins at the top (a program to handle all sub-programs) and expands to several lower levels (a "Christmas tree" of programs). This is known as "top-down programming", and it is a form of structured programming.

The term *structured programming* means that discipline in programming in which each program module implements an algorithm with a single entry point, a single exit point and a definitive result for each possible input. Each module must contain its own buffer area so that it cannot alter procedures or data of other modules. (In some cases common buffers are allowed, but complex rules for their use are needed.)

How is programming done? What equipment is needed? And what support can you get from a microcomputer manufacturer? First, there is a preparation phase in which the designer and/or programmer must become familiar with the instruction set and the architectural elements of the microcomputer selected for the design. The second phase involves writing selected short program segments to gain insight into the memory requirements and the execution speed of various sub-programs. Then the main body of the program may be developed.

Writing programs means writing code; writing program steps which must be executed in sequence. Usually these steps are written in a mnemonic language which uses one to four letters as operation codes, and strings of other characters to designate the operand (the number to be operated upon). These program steps must be translated and "assembled" into a set of 1's and 0's — the machine language executable by the microcomputer — by a special program development computer.

The programmer writes the program on paper. Then he enters the program steps via a keyboard into the program development system (PDS), and directs the PDS to "assemble" the instruction into machine code. The output from the PDS is a set of numbers which represent the program steps, and a listing of the input and output codes.

Obviously the PDS uses some special programs (software) for performing the tasks outlined. The programmer writes *source code* statements, submits them to the PDS via a program called the *editor,* then uses the *assembler* program to produce *object code* — the machine code used by the microcomputer. Errors in the program statements are printed along with the object code listing. Errors are corrected by editing the source code (via the editor) and resubmitting it to the assembler.

After a number of program modules are complete, a set of two or more may be "linked" together as a single program. This is done by submitting object code programs to the *linker.* The output from the linker is a single program which may be loaded into the microcomputer.

The list of support software is just beginning.

The following outline of software products describes the program development cycle further.

Program development software
    Editor — for entering and changing source code
    Assembler — for conversion from symbols and mnemonics into machine code
    Linker — for connecting several programs into one
    PROM programmer — for loading numbers (programs) into PROMs

Program testing software
    Debug routines — for testing programs
    AMPL system software — for testing programs and the interaction with the
        hardware

Software available for use with user programs
    Monitor — for checking status of all program modules
    Executive — for overall control
    Operating system — for operating peripheral devices
    Library (utility) programs — for performing special mathematical conversions
        and calculations
    High level language software for program development
        PASCAL — for structured programming
        POWER-BASIC — for ease of programming in BASIC language
        FORTRAN — for general computer problem solving

This partial list of software is intended as a categorical outline which should indicate the level of support one finds in the areas of software development. To comprehend the value of any or all of these software products, you must work with them and develop a few programs for microcomputers.

The obvious difficulty with software evaluation is that few designers can afford the capital investment for a large PDS to properly evaluate each of the alternative paths for software development. But Texas Instruments has developed a variety of program development systems. Some of these are very economical and readily available. They were designed specifically for product and programming evaluation and for initial design.

You will find descriptions and approximate prices for each PDS in Chapter 2.

WHICH MICROPROCESSOR OR MICROCOMPUTER TO USE

You may be convinced that designing with programmable semiconductors is the best design philosophy, and you may be attempting to evaluate the various products on the market. But a significant decision point has been reached: "which microprocessor or microcomputer is best for my application?" The selection of the proper device is based on many factors, some of which are not related to architecture or instruction execution speed.

Selection of a microcomputer or microprocessor usually means selection of one primary vendor (and sometimes one or more second sources) who manufactures the product and the compatible peripheral devices. It also means the purchase of a program development system designed especially for the specific microprocessor. Selection of one device means a commitment to using that device for future designs. Changing to another microprocessor is costly both in hardware and in the development of programming skills.

Selection criteria for a microprocessor may be summarized as follows:

1. The microprocessor must be versatile so that it can be used in many applications.

2. The vendor must provide a comprehensive set of support and peripheral circuits.

3. One PDS should serve the programming activity for a significant period of time.

4. The cost of the devices and the PDS must be economically attractive.

5. The performance of the microprocessor must be sufficient to meet the design goals.

EVOLUTION OF MEMORY-TO-MEMORY ARCHITECTURE

All things change with time, and computers are no exception. An evolutionary process has been at work in computer design since the beginning. Early machines were designed

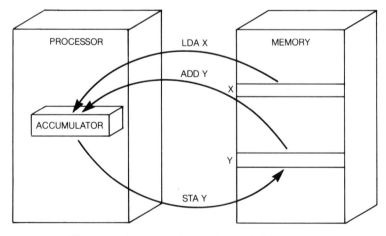

Figure 1-12. Single Accumulator Architecture

around a single accumulator which served as the focal point of most of the instructions. Steps such as load the accumulator (LDA), add to the accumulator (ADD), and store the accumulator (STA) were common in programs written for such machines. (The instruction mnemonics used here are simply illustrative and are not intended to be identified with any specific computer or microprocessor.) But there was a fundamental limitation—the bottleneck effect of forcing all transactions to be performed via a single accumulator *(Figure 1-12)*.

As circuit elements became less expensive, especially through the introduction of integrated circuits, multiple accumulator architectures emerged *(Figure 1-13)*. A and B accumulators were the focal points of expanded instruction sets which allowed loading either accumulator (LDA, LDB), adding to either accumulator (ADA, ADB), and storing either accumulator (STA, STB). With this design came the increased use of an accumulator for holding the address of an operand, adding flexibility and power to the instruction set and to the architecture.

It should be clear at this point that the instructions, the dictionary of words used by a computer to implement the ideas of the programmer, are as much a part of the architectural fabric as the registers, the control unit or the bus structure. In fact, by implementing instructions as strings of microinstructions stored in an on-chip control ROM, microprocessor designers have created the opportunity for increasing instruction set power through microprogramming.

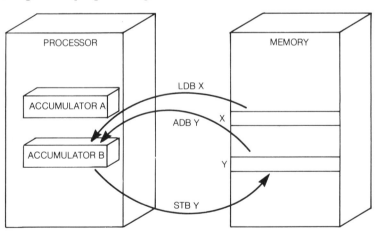

Figure 1-13. Multiple Accumulator Architecture

The next major step in the architectural evolution was the design of machines based on a set of general registers which could be used as accumulators for numerical operations or for storage of operand addresses *(Figure 1-14)*. The expanded capabilities allowed increased flexibility not only in arithmetic functions but also, and more importantly, in the generation of operand addresses via indirect addressing, and indexed addressing.

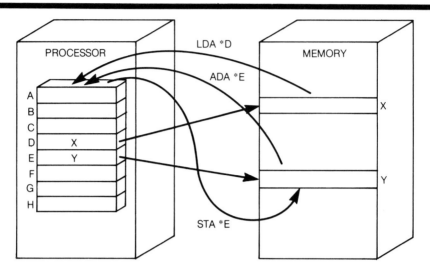

Figure 1-14. *General Register Architecture*

Perhaps it is well to digress for a moment and explain these terms. Indirect addressing allows a register to serve as a pointer to identify specific elements in a table or an array of data *(Figure 1-15)*. Instructions for an arithmetic operation may be used over and over, with the pointer (or pointers) being adjusted to access different values for each pass. In indexed addressing, the instruction contains a base value while an index register holds the displacement value *(Figure 1-16)*. The base value locates the table, and the index register contains the number of the element in the table (one, two, three, etc.). The base value must be added to the contents of the index register to obtain the actual memory address.

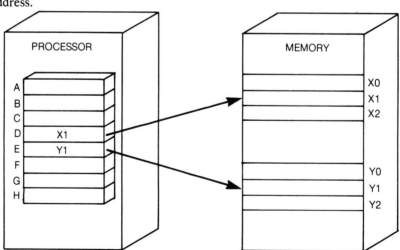

Registers D and E contain the addresses of operands X1 and Y1. D and E may be incremented to address sequential elements in tables.

Figure 1-15. *Indirect Addressing*

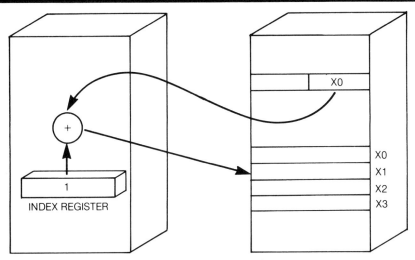

X0 is the address of the first element in the table.

X1 is obtained by adding X0 to the 1 in the index register.

The index register may be incremented to address sequential entries in the table.

Figure 1-16. Indexed Addressing

The general register architectures were made economically feasible by the expanded capabilities of integrated circuits through the technological advancements of Medium scale integration (MSI) and large scale integration (LSI) *(Figure 1-17)*. As more and more circuits were implemented on a chip, it became feasible to expand from two accumulators, to a general register file, to the general register file on a single LSI microprocessor chip.

In discussing LSI, one must not fail to recognize that the single most important impact of LSI is in the development of memories. More bits per unit area of silicon means higher capacity and lower cost, generally without sacrificing speed. The advent of microprocessors was the natural evolutionary step in the utilization of memory for a greater variety of logic and control applications.

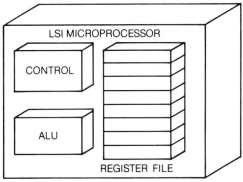

Figure 1-17. LSI Microprocessor

In looking toward the future of memories and microprocessors, the technologists see the implementation of an ever increasing number of memory cells and microprocessor calculation and control functions on an ever-shrinking area of silicon *(Figure 1-18)*. Registers and memory cells are virtually identical in their implementation at this point, so the words *register* and *memory* no longer connote high speed and low speed storage. In fact, memory speed is rapidly approaching register speed *(Figure 1-19)*.

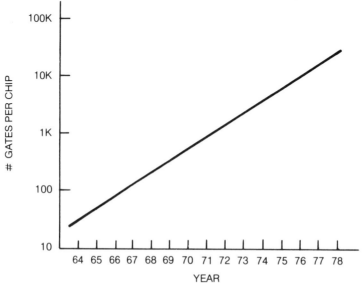

Figure 1-18. Trend in Gates per Chip

In view of this convergence of memory speed and register speed, the architects of the 990 minicomputer (from which the 9900 is derived) envisioned an architecture in which the instructions are written with respect to *memory words* rather than *registers*. The architectural concept, called memory-to-memory architecture, was the basis for a new computer design in which all memory reference instructions operate on one or two words of memory and store the result before going on to the next instruction.

There were actually two major reasons for developing such an architecture. First, since all instructions would reference words of memory and complete their cycles by placing results in memory, there would be no requirement for register-save operations in a multitask or interrupt processing environment. Second, while this approach might at first be slightly slower in some cases, the architects envisioned that the technological evolution would continue to narrow the gap between register speed and memory speed, and in the long run this minor disadvantage would vanish.

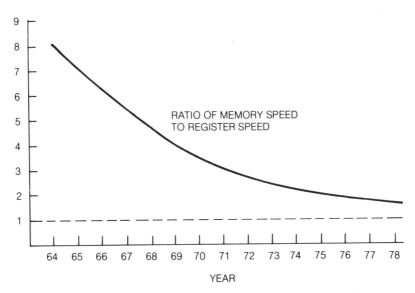

Figure 1-19. Ratio of Memory Speed to Register Speed

Another important advantage of this new architecture, often overlooked, appears to be an even stronger and more important justification for the development of this radical departure from conventional computer architectures. When one instruction can identify two memory words or operands, perform an operation, and store the result in memory, it will replace common sequences such as LDA, ADA, STA found in the instruction sequences of all accumulator-based machines. Furthermore, a single instruction can access additional memory words for use in addressing operands and can even increment pointers and employ index registers all as a part of its execution sequence. If a single instruction can do all this, then the writing of instruction sequences, programming, must be substantially easier. Fewer lines of code are required. (In data manipulation and address computation sequences, the reduction is typically 3:1.) Support software, such as monitors, executives, and operating systems can be smaller, easier to use and understand, and will consume less memory.

For these reasons, benchmarks written to compare the 9900 architecture with conventional register file based microprocessors show the advantage of the 9900's memory-to-memory architecture in three important categories: the number of bytes of memory required, execution speed, and the number of instructions written to accomplish a given task *(Figure 1-20)*. The 9900 comes out ahead in all three categories.

	Program memory requirements (bytes)				Assembler statements				Execution time (microseconds)			
	9900	A	B	C	9900	A	B*	C	9900	A	B	C
Input/output handler	24	38	28	17	9	14	17	7	71	154	79	49
Character search	22	24	20	18	8	10	9	8	661	1636	760	808
Computer go to	12	12	17	14	5	5	11	8	98	352	145	145
Vector addition: $A_N \leftarrow B_N = C_N(16)$	20	30	29	46	5	14	20	22	537	2098	1098	1866
Vector addition: $A_N \rightarrow B_N = C_N(8)$	20	32	23	40	5	15	14	22	537	2108	738	936
Shift right 5 bits	10	6	19	20	3	3	12	9	22	56	137	81
Move block	14	18	16	34	4	9	9	16	537	1750	1262	2246
Totals	122	160	152	189	39	70	92	92	2464	8154	4219	6131

Figure 1-20. Benchmark Comparison of 9900 vs. Other Microprocessors

One final note about architecture. Memory-to-memory architecture and instructions in the 9900 do not sacrifice the concept of "registers" as they are conceived in the architectures with general register organizations. The general "register file" is conceptually retained as a block of sixteen words of memory *(Figure 1-21)*. Over two thirds of the instructions in the 9900 refer in one way or another to this "register file" in much the same way as prior architectures referenced the general register file in the CPU. Thus, base addresses, subroutine linkage and interrupt save operations can all be accomplished via the "register-file-in-memory" concept.

By using memory for the register file, the advanced memory-to-memory architecture allows new programming flexibility. There is a way to identify *multiple register files* in 9900 based systems *(Figure 1-22)*. Each basic process can have its own set of "registers." *There is no limit (except memory size) to the number of "registers" available* for use in programming the functions of a particular application.

The memory-to-memory architecture of the 990 and 9900 products is clearly revolutionary and innovative. Programming effort for the 9900 is typically less than half that for any other microprocessor currently available because the instructions operate on words of memory and store results automatically. This means not only that programs consume less memory, but execution speed (for the 16-bit processors) is faster than that of other processors.

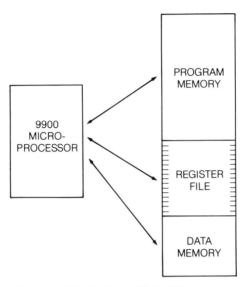

Figure 1-21. Register File in Memory

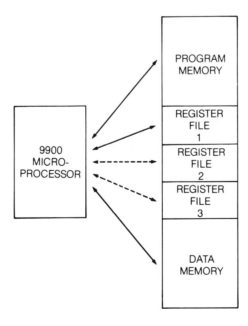

Figure 1-22. Multiple Register Files in Memory

GETTING UP TO SPEED ON MICROPROCESSORS

By now you may be convinced that this book contains a great amount of information about microprocessors and microcomputers, but you may feel that you are not as well prepared to understand it as you would like to be. This section has the answer. Here are the steps you should take to learn about microprocessors and microcomputers. The knowledge gained will help you in all new designs and will be especially helpful in designing with the 9900 family of processors and peripherals.

Few people have had the opportunity to learn about microcomputers in college. In fact, schools and colleges exist primarily to teach you *how to learn*, and not to teach you everything you need to know to do a particular job. Your effectiveness in performing any job is directly related to your willingness to acquire new specialized knowledge in your particular field. This book will serve as one source of specialized knowledge in the field of microcomputers, but it is focused on the 9900 family. And you may require additional education in this field before achieving a full understanding of the material presented.

It may be that knowledge of MOS and I²L technologies is needed for a clearer understanding of interfacing techniques. Basic computer fundamentals, such as storage of data and programs and the sequential operations may be an area you would like to study. It could be that you feel a need to improve your understanding of programming and the concepts of building programs via the modular approach. The list of specialized areas within the field of microcomputer technology can be quite long.

Technology advances so rapidly today that it seems virtually impossible to keep up, much less catch up. But you can do both, and without spending an inordinate amount of time. To acquire specialized knowledge in any field, you should devote 30 minutes a day to reading books or periodicals which contain the information you need. Advising you on the implementation of such a program is not the intent of this section. You know where you are and where you are going. What you need is a clear path or plan of action to achieve the goal: the acquisition of specialized knowledge about microprocessors and microcomputers.

The first step is to find authoritative texts on the various subjects in the field. This chapter contains a bibliography of texts and periodicals from which to begin your search for new information. Get your hands on these books and articles. Review them for general content and readability, then decide which ones are best suited to your needs. Set up a plan to read one or more of these books in a definite period of time, devoting a *scheduled*, uninterrupted period of 30 minutes a day to this program. Take notes while you are reading and (if the book belongs to you) underline the information which is especially important to you.

As you are getting up to speed, you will become aware of certain periodicals that contain articles most directly suited to your background and experience. Subscribe to one or more of these or be sure to obtain each issue as it is published so that you are not only reading about fundamentals, but current topics, the latest improvements in devices and systems.

Set up the goal, the plan of action; and then, above all, form the habit of reading for 30 minutes a day. Few people can set up such a plan, and fewer still can continue to execute it for long periods of time. But if you persist, you can learn, not just one, but *all* facets of design with microprocessors and microcomputers, and in time you will achieve the success you desire.

BIBLIOGRAPHY

Books

Altman, L., *Microprocessors*, Electronics Book Series, McGraw-Hill, 1975

Bartree, T. C., I. L. Lebow, and I. S. Reed, *Theory and Design of Digital Machines,* McGraw-Hill, 1969

Bibbero, R., *Microprocessors in Instruments and Control,* John Wiley, 1977

Blakeslee, Thomas R., *Digital Design with Standard MSI and LSI,* John Wiley, 1973

Gear, C. William, *Computer Organization and Programming*, McGraw-Hill, 1969

Greenfield, Joseph D., *Practical Digital Design Using IC's,* John Wiley, 1977

Hansen, P.B., *The Architecture of Concurrent Programs,* Prentice-Hall, Inc., 1977

Hansen, P.B., *Operating System Principles,* Prentice-Hall, Inc., 1973

Knuth, D. E. *The Art of Computer Programming, VOL I, Fundamental Algorithms*, 2nd Edition, Addison-Wesley, 1973.

Knuth, D.E. *The Art of Computer Programming, VOL II, Semi-Numerical Algorithms,* Addison-Wesley, 1969

Knuth, D.E. *The Art of Computer Programming, VOL III, Sorting and Searching,* Addison-Wesley, 1973.

Luecke, G., J. Mize, W. Carr, *Semiconductor Memory Design and Application,* McGraw-Hill, 1973

Malrino, A., *Digital Computer Electronics,* McGraw-Hill, 1977

McWhorter, G., *Understanding Digital Electronics,* Texas Instruments Learning Center, 1976

Morris, R. L., J. D. Miller, *Designing with TTL Intergrated Circuits*, McGraw-Hill, 1971

Norris, B., *Power Transmission and TTL Integrated-Circuit Applications,* McGraw-Hill, 1977

Silver, G., *Computer Algorithms and Flowcharting,* McGraw-Hill, 1975

Sloan, M.E., *Computer Hardware and Organization,* Science Research Associates, Inc., 1976

Solomon, L., *Getting Involved with Your Own Computer; A Guide for Beginners,* Ridley Enslow Publishing, 1977

Soucek, B., *Microprocessors and Microcomputers,* John Wiley, 1976

Torrero, E., *Microprocessors, New Directions for Designers,* Electronic Design, Hayden, 1975

Wester, John G. and William D. Simpson, *Software Design for Microprocessors,* Texas Instruments Learning Center, 1976

Williams, Gerald E., *Digital Technology,* Science Research Associates, Inc., 1977

Zaks, R., *Microprocessors: From Chips to Systems,* Sybex, 1977

Staff of the Texas Instruments Learning Center, *Understanding Solid-State Electronics, 3rd Edition,* Texas Instruments Learning Center, 1978

ARTICLES

Barna, Arpad, and Dan I. Porat, *"Integrated Circuits in Digital Electronics",* John Wiley, 1973

Reid-Green, K.S., *"A Short History of Computing",* Byte, Vol. 3, No. 7, July 1978

Special Issue on Microelectronics, *"Scientific American",* Vol. 237, No. 3, September 1977

Electronic Business, *"New Rules in an Old Game",* Vol. 18, No. 6, June 1978

LIST OF PERIODICALS TO BE MONITORED

ACM Computing Surveys, The Survey and Tutorial Journal of the Association for Computing Machinery, ACM, Inc., Mt. Royal and Guilford Avenues, Baltimore, MD 21202

EDN, Cahners Publishing Co., 270 St. Paul St., Denver, Colorado 80206

Electronics, McGraw-Hill Inc., 1221 Avenue of the Americas, New York, N.Y. 10020

Electronics Design, Hayden Publishing Co., 50 Essex St., Rochelle Park, N.J. 07662

IEEE Spectrum, The Institute of Electrical and Electronics Engineers, Inc., 345 East 47 Street, New York, N.Y. 10017

Interface Age, McPheters, Wolfe & Jones, 16704 Marquardt Avenue, Cerritos, CA 90701

CHAPTER 2
Product
Selection Guide

THE 9900 FAMILY — WHAT IS IT?

The 9900 Family is a compatible set of microprocessors, microcomputers, microcomputer modules, and minicomputers. It is supported with peripheral devices, development systems, and software. It provides a designer with a system solution having built-in protection against technological obsolescence. The family features true software compatibility, I/O bus compatibility and price/performance ratios which encompass a wide range of applications. The family is designed with a unique flexible architecture to allow technological changes to be easily incorporated while minimizing the impact these changes have on an overall system design.

FAMILY OVERVIEW

THE HARDWARE FAMILY

Figure 2-1 is a diagram of the 9900 Family members. The spectrum of microprocessors and microcomputer products available in a variety of formats is shown in *Figures 2-2* and *2-3*. In the first part of *Figure 2-1,* the microprocessors or microcomputers are combined with microcomputer support components *(Figure 2-3)* to form systems. These systems also include I/O interface, read-only and random access memory, and additional support components such as timing circuits and expanded memory decode .

The family also includes microcomputer board modules containing the 9900 microprocessors and peripheral components *(Figure 2-4).* As shown in the second part of *Figure 2-1,* these modules can be used for product evaluation, combined for system development or applied directly as end equipment components.

When applications require minicomputers, completely assembled units can be purchased and installed. The software will be fully compatible with any associated microprocessor and microcomputer system. *Figure 2-5* gives a brief overview of the minicomputers.

These three levels of compatible hardware — the TMS9900 family parts, the TM990 microcomputer modules, and the 990 minicomputers — provide the flexibility to obtain an optimum match with the user's system application.

THE SOFTWARE AND DEVELOPMENT SYSTEMS SUPPORT

New products cannot be made without design, development, test and debug. Development support for all of the levels is shown in *Figure 2-1,* including:

     A. Product documentation
     B. Software (or firmware)
     C. Software development systems
     D. Prototyping systems.

Software and development and prototyping systems are outlined in *Figure 2-6.*

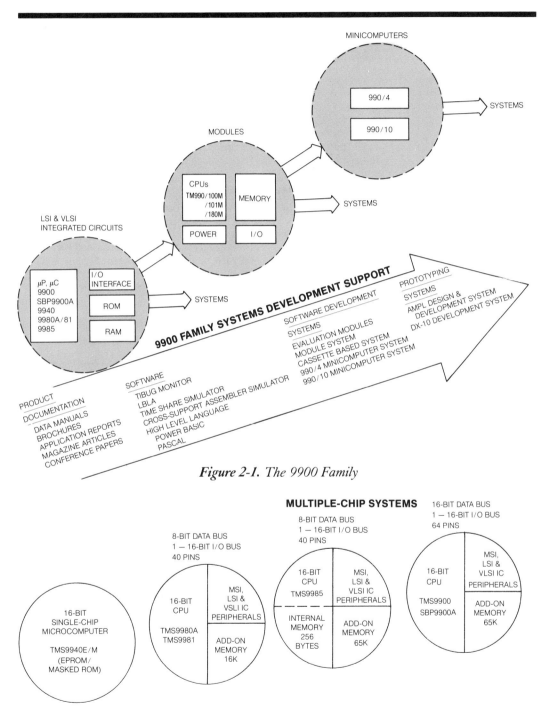

Figure 2-1. *The 9900 Family*

MULTIPLE-CHIP SYSTEMS

Figure 2-2. *9900 Family CPUs*

CPU's	
TMS9900	NMOS 16-Bit Microprocessor, 64 Pins
TMS9900-40	Higher Frequency Version 9900
SBP9900A	I²L Extended Temperature Range 9900
TMS9980A/ 9981	40-Pin, NMOS 16-Bit Microprocessor with 8-Bit Data Bus. 9981 has XTAL Oscillator
TMS9985	40-Pin, NMOS 16-Bit Microprocessor with Single 5V Supply and 256-Bits of RAM
TMS9940E	40-Pin, NMOS Single Chip Microcomputer, EPROM Version
TMS9940M	40-Pin, NMOS Single Chip Microcomputer, Mask Version

PERIPHERAL DEVICES			
TMS9901	Programmable Systems Interface	TMS9914	GPIB Adapter
TMS9901-40	Higher Frequency Version of 9901	TMS9915	Dynamic RAM Controller Chip Set
TMS9902	Asynchronous Communications Controller	TMS9916	92K Magnetic Bubble Memory Controller
TMS9902-40	Higher Frequency Version of 9902	TMS9922	250K Magnetic Bubble Controller
TMS9903	Synchronous Communications Controller	TMS9923	250K Magnetic Bubble Controller
TMS9904	4-Phase Clock Driver	TMS9927	Video Timer/Controller
TMS9905	8 to 1 Multiplexer	TMS9932	Combination ROM/RAM Memory
TMS9906	8-Bit Latch	SBP9960	I/O Expander
TMS9907	8 to 3 Priority Encoder	SBP9961	Interrupt-Controller/Timer
TMS9908	8 to 3 Priority Encoder w/Tri-State Outputs	SBP9964	SBP9900A Timing Generator
TMS9909	Floppy Disk Controller	SBP9965	Peripheral Interface Adapter
TMS9911	Direct Memory Access Controller		

ADD-ON MEMORY

ROMS

TMS4700—1024 X 8
*TMS4710—1024 X 8
TMS4732—4096 X 8
SBP8316—2048 X 8
SBP9818—2048 X 8

*Character Generator—ASCII

**PROMS

SN74S287— 256 X 4
SN74S471— 256 X 8
SN74S472— 512 X 8
SN74S474— 512 X 8
SN74S476—1024 X 4
SN74S478—1024 X 8 △

△Equivalent to
   SN74S2708

**Also available
   in 54 series

EPROMS

TMS2508   —1024 X 8
TMS2708   —1024 X 8
TMS27L08 —1024 X 8
TMS2516   —2048 X 8
TMS2716   —2048 X 8
TMS2532   —4096 X 8

DYNAMIC RAMS

TMS4027—4096 X 1
TMS4050—4096 X 1
TMS4051—4096 X 1
TMS4060—4096 X 1
TMS4116—16,384 X 1
TMS4164— 65,536 X 1

STATIC RAMS

TMS4008	—1024 X 8	TMS4043-2	— 256 X 4
TMS4016	—2048 X 8	TMS4044	—4096 X 1
TMS4033	—1024 X 1	TMS40L44	—4096 X 1
TMS4034	—1024 X 1	TMS4045	—1024 X 4
TMS4035	—1024 X 1	TMS40L45	—1024 X 4
TMS4036-2	— 64 X 8	TMS4046	—4096 X 1
TMS4039-2	— 256 X 4	TMS40L46	—4096 X 1
TMS4042-2	— 256 X 4	TMS4047	—1024 X 4
		TMS40L47	—1024 X 4

Figure 2-3. Microcomputer Support Components

MICROCOMPUTER MODULES	
TM990/100M	Microcomputer, 1-4K EPROM
TM990/101M	Microcomputer, 1-4K ROM, 1K-2K RAM
TM990/101M-10	Microcomputer, 1-4K ROM, 1K-2K RAM, Evaluation POWER BASIC®
TM990/180	Microcomputer, (8-Bit Data Bus), 1-2K ROM, 256-1K RAM
TM990/189	Microcomputer, University Microcomputer Module
TM990/201	Memory Expansion Module, 4K-16K ROM, 2K-8K RAM
TM990/206	Memory Expansion Module, 4K-8K RAM
TM990/301	Microterminal
TM990/302	Software Development Module
TM990/310	I/O Expansion Module
TM990/401*	TIBUG® Monitor in EPROM
TM990/402*	Line-by-Line Assembler in EPROM
TM990/450*	Evaluation POWER BASIC® —8K Bytes in EPROM
TM990/451*	Development POWER BASIC—12K Bytes in EPROM
TM990/452*	Development POWER BASIC Software Enhancement—4K Bytes in EPROM
TM990/501-521	Chassis, Cable and Power Supply Accessories

*FIRMWARE

Figure 2-4. TM990 Board Modules and Software Support

Software is provided in EPROM (firmware) to operate with the assembled microcomputer modules. It is provided on either "floppy" diskette or on disk pack for use with the minicomputers, and is distributed on magnetic tape for use on in-house computing equipment.

In addition to the development systems available directly from Texas Instruments, a Fortran-IV cross-support package with assembler and simulator is provided by TI for those desiring to use in-house computing equipment. GE, National-CSS and Tymeshare provide similar capabilities on a timeshared basis.

POWER BASIC and PASCAL software systems have just been introduced and will continue to be expanded in the future.

Hardware and software for development and production use is available in appropriate system sizes to support individual designers as well as large design teams.

CS990/4	• A 990/4 Minicomputer with 4K words of RAM
	• Expanded memory controller with 4K words of RAM
	• 733 ASR ROM Loader
	• 733 ASR Data Terminal
	• Necessary chassis, power supply, and packaging

FS990/4	• Model 990/4 Minicomputer with 48K bytes of parity memory in a 13-slot chassis with programmer panel and floppy disk loader/self-test ROM
	• Model 911 Video Display Terminal (1920 character) with dual port controller
	• Dual FD800 floppy disk drives
	• Attractive, office-style single-bay desk enclosure
	• Licensed TX990/TXDS Terminal Executive Development System Software with one-year software subscription service

FS990/10	• Model 990/10 Minicomputer with 64K bytes of error-correcting memory and mapping in a 13-slot chassis with programmer panel and floppy disk loader/self-test ROM
	• Model 911 Video Display Terminal (1920 character) with dual port controller
	• Dual FD800 floppy disk drives
	• Attractive, office-style single-bay desk enclosure
	• Licensed TX990/TXDS Terminal Executive Development System Software with one-year software subscription service

DS990/10	• Model 990/10 Minicomputer with mapping, 128K bytes of error-correcting memory in a 13-slot chassis with programmer panel and disk loader ROM
	• Model 911 Video Display Terminal (1920 character) with dual-port controller
	• Licensed copy of DX10 Operating System on compatible disk media, with one-year software subscription service
	• DS10 disk drive featuring 9.4M bytes of formatted mass storage, partitioned into one 4.7M-byte-fixed disc and a 5440-type removable 4.7M-byte top-loading disk cartridge
	Options:
	One additional DS10 disk drive with 9.4M bytes of formatted mass storage, in deskmount, rackmount, or quietized pedestal version

Figure 2-5. 990 Minicomputers

PRODUCT DOCUMENTATION

9900 Family Systems Design and
       Data Book
9900 Software Design Handbook
TM990 System Design Handbook
990 Computer Family Systems Handbook
Product Data Manuals
Product User's Guides
Product Brochures
Application Notes
Application Sheets

SOFTWARE AND FIRMWARE

TM990/401	TIBUG Monitor in EPROM
TM990/402	Line-by-Line Assembler in EPROM
TMSW101MT	ANSI-Fortran Cross-Support Assembler, Simulator and ROM Utility
TM990/450	Evaluation POWER BASIC —8K Bytes in EPROM
TM990/451	Development POWER BASIC — 12K Bytes in EPROM
TM990/452	Development POWER BASIC Software Enhancement Package — 4K Bytes in EPROM
TMSW201F/D	Configurable POWER BASIC in FS990 Diskette
TMSW301F/D	TIPMX — TI PASCAL Executive Components Library

SOFTWARE DEVELOPMENT		SUPPORT SOFTWARE
TM990/302	Software Development Module	Edit, Assembler, Load, Debug, PROM Programming
TM990/40DS	Software Development system for TMS9940 Microcomputer	Assembler, Debug Monitor, Trial-in-System Emulator, PROM Programmer
CS990/4	Single User Software Development System (Cassette Based), uses PX990 software.	Text Editor, Assembler, Linking Loader, Debug Monitor, PROM Programmer
FS990/4	Software Development system (Floppy Disk)	Source Editor, Assembler, Link Editor, PROM Programmer
FS990/10	Software Development System (Floppy Disk)	Same as 990/4, expandable to DS System
DS990/10	Disk Based 990/10 with Macro Assembler	Source Editor, Link Editor, Debug, Librarian, and High-Level Language such as FORTRAN, BASIC, PASCAL, and COBOL

MICROPROCESSOR PROTOTYPING LAB FOR DESIGN AND DEVELOPMENT

AMPL	FS990 with video display and dual floppy diskettes includes TX990/TXDS system software — Text Editor, Assembler, and Link Utility — and has an in-circuit Emulator Module and a Logic-State Trace Module for proposed system emulation and analysis.

TIMESHARE SYSTEMS

GE, NCSS, Tymeshare	Assembler, Simulator, ROM Utilities

Figure 2-6. *The 9900 Family Software and Development Systems*

TYPICAL APPLICATIONS

The range of applications for microprocessors and microcomputers expands each day; *Figure 2-7* provides a broad scope of the applications extending from those that can be satisfied with single-chip microcomputers to those requiring high performance multichip systems. The market tends to be characterized by lower performance, high volume single-chip systems, and higher performance, low volume multichip systems.

As shown in *Figure 2-7*, the spectrum of applications is satisfied throughout by 9900 Family members. The single-chip 16-bit microcomputer, the TMS 9940, is used where there is large volume, because it has the lowest cost, yet achieves outstanding performance. At the other end are the system with the 16-bit TMS 9900 and SBP 9900A CPUs, the specially designed family peripherals, and add-on memory. For maximum system performance, the bit slice SN74S481 units are available. For in-between performance limits there are the 16-bit CPUs using 8-bit data buses. The TMS 9980A/81 has lower cost, and the TMS 9985 will accommodate larger memory for extended applications. Both processors use the more economical 40-pin package. Applications in the low and medium performance range include simple instruments, computer peripherals, cash registers and controls for manufacturing.

At the higher performance end, a myriad of products that are emulating many computer-like functions — data terminals, point-of-sale terminals, data acquisition systems, process control systems, military systems — are all gaining performance at lower cost by using microprocessor multichip systems.

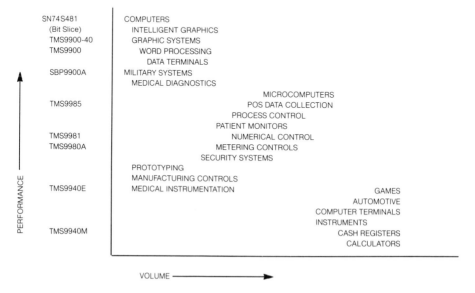

Figure 2-7. Application Spectrum

Figure 2-8 details further the applications for single-chip and multiple-chip systems.

SINGLE-CHIP MICROCOMPUTER	MULTIPLE-CHIP SYSTEMS	
Gas Pump Control	Video Controllers	CPU's-Microcomputer
Alarm Systems	Telephone Switching	Computer Peripherals
Paging Systems	Word Processing Equipment	Intelligent Terminals
Sorters	Manufacturing Material Handlers	Tape Drive Controls
Vending Machines	Electronic Musical Instruments	Graphic Terminals
Microwave Ovens	Small Business/Financial Systems	Communications Network
Appliance Control	Factory Automation	Communications Processing
Power Tools	Instrumentation	Data Concentration
Utility Meter Monitoring	Data Acquisition	Input Terminals
Environmental Controls	Machine Controls	General Purpose Terminals
Automotive	Medical Equipment	
Games	Security Systems	
Cryptography	Machine Tool Controls	
Process Controls		
Navigation Equipment		
Metering Controls		

Figure 2-8. Applications

HARDWARE SELECTION

To reduce the range of detail which must be considered in a given system design, it is often possible to make a definite choice between the three hardware design levels; designing with individual components, designing with prefabricated modules, and designing with minicomputer subsystems. The criteria upon which this choice is based include the number of units to be manufactured per design, complexity of design, performance requirements, special feature requirements, microprocessor system design expertise available, and the importance placed on product introduction — the time to the market place. General tendencies of these decisions are known although the particular choice may be skewed by other considerations. Here are a number of examples.

In terms of production volume, users tend to incorporate minicomputers in their designs up to a volume of 50 to 100 identical systems per year. They tend to use prefabricated modules if the volume is below 500 to 2000 systems per year, and for higher volume, they tend to develop from the component level right from the start. Simple systems may not be able to stand the cost of a minicomputer at any volume, while even at much higher volumes, performance requirements may force the utilization of a disk-based minicomputer. When system specifications require special features, this often forces the use of modules even at low volumes. However, the need for maintenance capability may force the use of minicomputers or prefabricated modules for system construction at extremely large volumes. A firm with expert microprocessor design teams would tend to maximize its value-added by designing from the component level, while a firm without hardware designers would look for completely prefabricated systems.

Finally, product introduction priorities often call for a compromise approach because of an urgent need to get a product to market ahead of competition. It is often ideal to enter the market with prefabricated systems and switch to in-house fabrication as the system is accepted and sales volume builds.

THE COMPONENT ROUTE: CPU

In the beginning your product selection decisions are tied entirely to the central processor. A very real danger at this point is choosing a processor which is not optimum for the design. Either the cost will be greater than desired, or the processor will not quite meet the required performance. In the TMS9900 Family, each processor is uniquely tuned to its applications environment while maintaining a common architecture, input/output system and instruction set. This commonality allows a simple move up or down the performance scale with a minimum of redesign *(See Figure 2-9)*.

The single packaged CPUs divide into microprocessors and a microcomputer. The TMS 9940 microcomputer is available either with EPROM or with mask programmable ROM.

Microprocessors	*Microcomputer*
TMS9900 TMS9980A/81	TMS9940 E/M
TMS9900-40 TMS9985	
SBP9900A	

The basic architecture of each is shown in *Figure 2-10*.

CRITERIA	SYSTEM CHOICE	FAMILY PRODUCTS USED
HIGHEST PERFORMANCE	MULTIPACKAGE	1. TMS9900, SBP9900A 2. Microcomputer peripherals for I/O 3. TIM9904 for clock 4. ROM, EPROM 5. RAM
TRADEOFF FOR BEST COST AT PERFORMANCE REQUIRED	A. MINIMUM PACKAGES	1. TMS9980A/81 (with clock) 2. Microcomputer peripherals for I/O 3. Combined ROM & RAM
	B. MINIMUM PACKAGES	1. TMS9985 (with clock and RAM) 2. Microcomputer peripherals for I/O 3. ROM
LOWEST COST	SINGLE PACKAGE	1. TMS9940 Microcomputer with on board I/O, Clock, ROM & RAM, Timer

Figure 2-9. Cost/Performance Trade-off

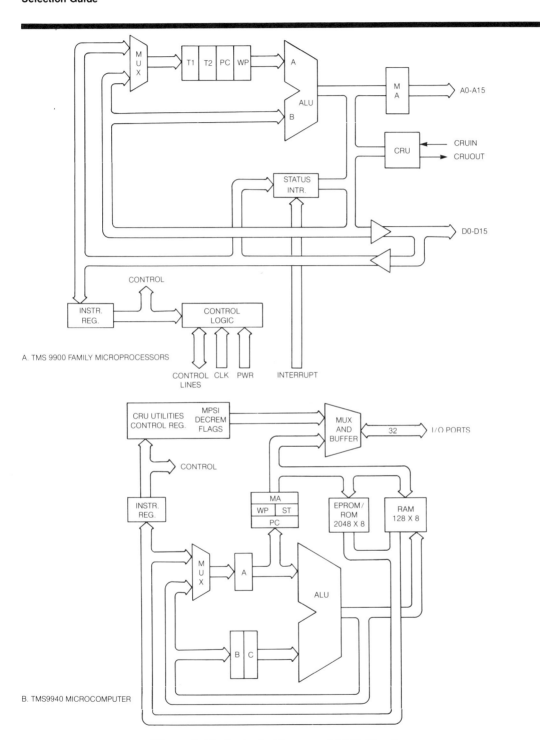

Figure 2-10. Basic Architecture of 9900 Family

CPU Selection

Selecting a CPU for an application requires a study of the CPU characteristics to see which one fits best. *Figure 2-11* provides key characteristics of the 9900 Family CPUs as well as a bit-slice version (SN54/74S481) for the ultimate in performance.

FEATURE \ DEVICE	SN54S481 SN74S481 Note 1	SBP9900A	TMS9900/ TMS9900-40	TMS9980A/ TMS9981	TMS9985	TMS9940E/M
Number of bytes addressable	65K	65K	65K	16K	65K 256 on chip	2K EPROM/128 RAM 2K 128 RAM/128 RAM
Number of Interrupts	16	16	16	5	5	4
Number of Pins	48/chip	64	64	40	40	40
Power Supply Requirements	+5	Resistor Programmable Note 2	+12, ±5	+12, ±5	+5	+5
Technology	Schottky TTL	I²L	NMOS	NMOS	NMOS	NMOS
Environmental (Temperature, °C)	−55 to 125	−55 to 125	0 to 70	0 to 70	0 to 70	0 to 70
Clock Rate	10MHz	3MHz	3.3MHz/4MHz	10MHz	5MHz	5MHz
Relative Thruput	6	0.9	1.0/1.3	0.6	0.65−0.8 Note 3	1.2
Number of Address Bus Lines	15	15	15	14	16	Note 4
Number of Data Bus Lines	16	16	16	8	8	Note 4
Clock	SN54S124	SN54LS124	TIM9904	On Chip	On Chip	On Chip

Note 1 : Based on four slices microcoded to duplicate TMS9900.
Note 2: Voltage for the SBP9900A is 1.5 to 30 volts with a series resistor.
Note 3: Relative thruput is 0.65 with off-chip RAM and 0.8 with on-chip RAM.
Note 4: No external memory or data bus. 32 general purpose I/O pins 10 of which provide 256 bit CRU I/O expansion if desired.

Figure 2-11. Key Characteristics of 9900 Family CPUs

Figure 2-12 provides, in a "quick look" format, four specifications of the family members that are usually important to all applications — the directly addressable memory, the data bus length, the operating temperature, and the package size.

Figure 2-13 plots the relative thruput of the 9900 Family microprocessors and microcomputers. The thruput, estimated by calculating execution times for a given benchmark program, is plotted relative to the performance of the TMS9900. 30% more thruput is obtained using the TMS9900-40. The thruput of the SBP9900A is 90% of the TMS9900. Both of these processors operate with a full 16-bit data bus and are in 64-pin packages. As mentioned previously, ultimate performance is obtained by using a bit-slice microprocessor. A relative thruput of six is shown for four SN54/74S481 bit-slice packages microcoded to duplicate a TMS9900.

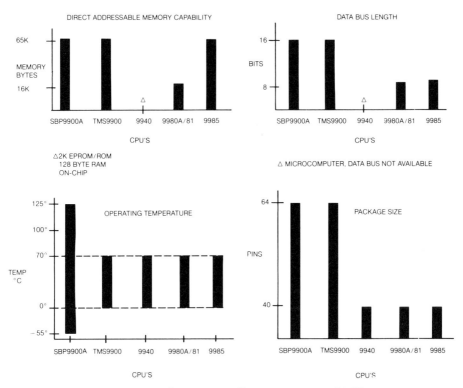

Figure 2-12. "Quick Look" at 9900 Family CPU's

Cost reduction can be realized via 40-pin packaging. This is accomplished by changing the external operating configuration to an 8-bit format even though the internal processor is a 16-bit processor. This causes a reduction in thruput — the thruput of the 9980A/81 and 9985 is reduced to 60% to 80% of the TMS9900 — because a byte organized memory is required and the number of memory accesses will obviously be increased. The advantage, of course, is that family software can be used even though the 8-bit configuration is used. Note that the 9940 microcomputer thruput is 20% *greater* than the TMS9900. Excellent performance is obtained from this single-chip microcomputer.

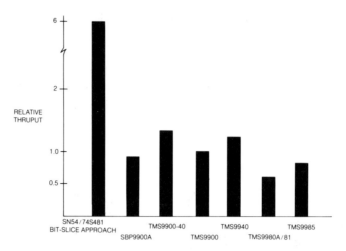

Figure 2-13. Thruput of 9900 Family CPU'S

The 9980A/81 is designed for the lowest system cost for full family performance while the 9985 spans the link between microprocessor and microcomputer by offering RAM memory on board.

Flexible I/O

The TMS9900 provides non-multiplexed parallel I/O and memory control for maximum performance when needed, with full 16-bit address and data bus. It also has a separate serial bus to allow use of minimum cost, maximum funtionality peripherals for relatively slow I/O processes which will tolerate the reduced speed. This is the Communications Register Unit, CRU.

Family Members Fitted to the Application

The TMS9980A/81 and the TMS9985 multiplex the data bus for reduced cost and package size at some sacrifice in performance. The TMS9940 is the least expensive approach for those applications which will tolerate the limitations of a single-chip. It provides full computer capabilities, albeit of a limited range, on a single integrated circuit. By not taking the address and data bus off-chip, buffer time delays are eliminated resulting in higher performance within a limited memory range (2K EPROM/ROM, 128 bytes RAM). For those applications requiring better temperature or reliability performance than that available from NMOS processors, the SBP9900A provides the same sophisticated processor functions as the TMS9900 over military and industrial temperature and specification ranges.

Interrupt Flexibility

The 9900 Family provides fully prioritized, vectored interrupts as well as software vectored interrupts for maximum flexibility.

The Component Route: Peripherals

Microcomputer component peripherals perform functions that assist the CPU in a microprocessor or microcomputer system. Data communications through serial data links in a synchronous or asynchronous mode; parallel input and output interfaces for general purpose I/O, instrument communications, direct memory access or mass storage control; and display control and memory expansion and control are some of the present peripheral functions provided as shown below.

FAMILY UNITS—INTERFACING TECHNIQUES	
Serial I/O for Data Communications	
Asynchronous Communications Controller	TMS9902
4 MHz Version	TMS9902-40
Synchronous Communications Controller	TMS9903
Parallel I/O	
General Purpose	
Programmable Systems Interface	TMS9901
4 MHz Version	TMS 9901-40
I/O Expander	SBP9960
Interrupt—Controller/Timer	SBP9961
Instrument Communications	
General Purpose Interface Bus Adapter	TMS9914
Direct Memory Access	
Direct Memory Access Controller	TMS9911
Mass Storage	
Floppy Disk Controller	TMS9909
CRT Display (Memory Mapped I/O)	
Video Timer/Controller	TMS9927
Memory	
Combination ROM/RAM Memory	TMS9932
Memory Control	
Dynamic RAM Controller Chip Set	
Refresh Timing Controller	TIM9915A
Memory Timing Controller	TIM9915B
Multiplexer/Latch	TIM9915C
FAMILY UNITS—SUPPORT LOGIC	
Four-Phase Clock Driver	TIM9904
8 to 1 Multiplexer	TIM9905
8-Bit Latch	TIM9906
8 to 3 Priority Encoder	TIM9907
8 to 3 Priority Encoder W/Three State Outputs	TIM9908

Significant progress has been made in implementing these important functions in high-functional-density designs for the 9900 Family. This integration will continue in the future. It provides cost-effective package substitutions for multiple standard TTL units. The result is reduced assembly costs and materials, increased reliability, and shorter time from design to production.

As the key features of the microcomputer component peripherals are reviewed, note these points: (1) Many of the peripherals units are as complex or even more complex than the CPUs they support; (2) Many of the peripheral units are designed to be *programmable* providing outstanding flexibility to vary their use in system applications. Such design trends reinforce the systems concept of the future—that standard hardware will be used but varied in use by software; (3) Family units will drive two TTL loads, allowing direct interface to low-power Schottky, standard TTL, and even standard Schottky circuits, eliminating the need for many special purpose peripherals which do little else than provide this interface.

Interface Techniques

A computer must be controlled by a person or another machine to be useful. It must be programmed to accept inputs, process data, and give results as outputs. It will do only what it is programmed to do (barring malfunction). Output results must be acted upon otherwise the computer manipulations are worthless. Peripheral components form the required systematic interface between the computer and the outside world and range in functional capability from the general purpose to highly specialized units.

The interface of a microcomputer or microprocessor system to external inputs and outputs is by serial or parallel data lines. Two parallel and two serial techniques are used. The parallel techniques include direct memory access and CPU controlled I/O. The serial techniques include asynchronous and synchronous serial I/O. A final technique called interrupt is used to alert the processor of a change in external conditions.

Serial I/O for Data Communications

Serial I/O for data communications is handled through the TMS9902 and TMS9903. The TMS9902 and TMS9902-40 are for asynchronous serial data that is established around the RS232C protocol and the TMS9903 is for synchronous data, designed for any high-speed communications protocol. CPU control of these devices, as shown in *Figure 2-14* via the Communications Register Unit, allows their construction in small, plug-compatible packages.

Parallel I/O

GENERAL PURPOSE

General purpose parallel I/O and interrupt control along with an on-chip timer are provided by the TMS9901 and TMS9901-40, as shown in *Figure 2-14*. The same functions are served in I²L for extended temperature range operation by the SBP9960 and SBP9961.

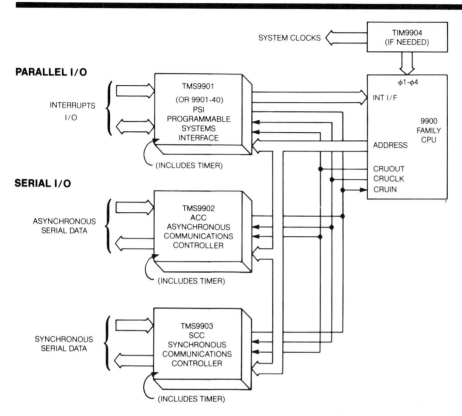

Figure 2-14. Microcomputer Component Peripherals for I/O Interface

A significant advantage of the 9900/9901 parallel I/O interface through the CRU is the ability to transfer fields of from 1 to 16 bits of data as inputs or outputs under the command of one instruction and to modify this structure from instruction to instruction. Additionally, use of the CRU allows implementation of multiple functions in the TMS9901.

MEMORY-MAPPED

Since the CRU is essentially a time-division multiplexed serial port, speed critical applications may require a faster parallel technique. Memory-mapping, the treatment of a parallel I/O port as if it were a memory location, provides this technique. With the memory-to-memory architecture of the 9900 Family, direct manipulation of such an I/O port is practical. The dual-TTL drive of the 9900 Family allows economical construction of memory-mapped I/O ports using standard TTL or LS (Low-Power Schottky) components.

GPIB—GENERAL PURPOSE INTERFACE BUS

In 1975 the IEEE defined a very precise electrical and mechanical protocol designated the IEEE 488 Interface Bus, or commonly known as a General Purpose Interface Bus (GPIB). This protocol allows direct connection of instruments and processors supplied by various manufacturers. The TMS9914 General Purpose Interface Bus Adapter either directly, or under software control, adapts all the capabilities of the GPIB to a microprocessor bus including talker, listener, controller and control passer. This is a general purpose component and will work quite well with any microprocessor, although it is complemented by the speed and power of the 9900 Family.

DMA—DIRECT MEMORY ACCESS

Many I/O devices can be made more effective if transfer rates can be increased beyond the 8 microseconds required for a typical memory-mapped transfer. The GPIB mentioned above, for instance, allows data transfers at rates up to a million bytes per second. The TMS9911 Direct Memory Access Controller allows low cost implementation of two such super high speed ports. The TMS9911 itself is controlled by the CPU via the CRU bus, until one of the DMA channels takes control long enough to process a DMA transfer (either single or block) between I/O port and memory.

FLOPPY DISK

For those applications requiring more storage space than is convenient or economical in a microcomputer, a mass storage device is needed. Floppy disk units provide the benefits of fast access, reliable mass storage using a portable, easily stored media. Interfacing these units to microprocessors is greatly simplified by the TMS9909 Floppy Disk Controller. This device will control up to four floppy disk units using standard or minifloppies, single, double, or triple density, hard or soft sectors. It is also capable of full IBM compatibility (including double-sided, double density at the *same* time). This is a general purpose component and will work quite well with any microprocessor. It is a memory-mapped device and will also interface easily to a DMA controller such as the TMS9911. The TMS9909 can be programmed for:

  1. Data encoding formats
  2. Number and type of diskette drives
  3. Stepper motor control rates
  4. Number of sectors and tracks

It can perform the following functions:

  1. Step to any track on the diskette
  2. Format tracks (set initial conditions on diskette)
  3. Read and write diskette data
  4. Send status to the host system

CRT CONTROL

The TMS9927 video timer/controller is a memory-mapped device which contains all of the logic necessary to generate all the timing signals for display of video data on CRT monitors, standard or not, and interlaced or not.

This video timer/controller has nine 8-bit registers used for programming; seven for horizontal and vertical formatting and two for the cursor character and address. All the functions for generating the timing signals for video data display are programmable:

1. Characters per row
2. Data rows per frame
3. Raster scans per data row
4. Raster scans per frame

All timing functions are implemented on the chip except the dot generation and dot counting which operate at video frequency. A character generator and shift register are used to shift out video data. The control registers can be loaded by the microprocessor or from PROM. This is a general purpose part for use with any microprocessor.

MEMORY

Contained in the microcomputer component peripherals is a unit for memory expansion, the TMS9932, a combination ROM/RAM memory unit with 1920 bytes of ROM and 128 bytes of RAM. It contains the same key features that characterize the 9900 Family support memory.

MEMORY CONTROL

The TIM9915 chip set consists of 3 packages, a 16-pin Refresh Timing Controller (TIM9915A), a 16-pin Memory Timing Control (TIM9915B), and a 28-pin Multiplexer/Latch with tri-state outputs (TIM9915C). *This chip set becomes the complete packaged set for 4K to 64K of dynamic RAM memory, and provides all the timing and control signals necessary to interface dynamic RAM memory and make it appear as static RAM.*

Clock and Support Logic

Four-Phase Clock Generator/Driver

Microprocessor and microcomputer systems require clock generators and drivers for the timing control of the system. The TMS9904 is such a unit. An oscillator which can be crystal or inductance controlled provides the basic timing source. Four high-level clock phases provide the 9900 microprocessor timing. Four additional TTL-level clocks can be used to time memory or other control functions in a 9900 system.

Support Logic

Common TTL MSI peripherals included in the 9900 Family of microcomputer components are:

TIM9905	8 to 1 Multiplexer
TIM9906	8-Bit Latch
TIM9907	8 to 3 Priority Encoder
TIM9908	8 to 3 Priority Encoder w/Tri-State Outputs

The reason, of course, is that they are standard units for accomplishing the following tasks:

1. Parallel-to-Serial Conversion
2. Multiplexing from N-lines to one line
3. Providing multiple data selectors
4. Providing bus interface from multiple sources
5. Encoding 10 line decimal to 4 line BCD
6. Encoding 8 lines to 3 lines

All units are fabricated using standard low-power Schottky TTL technology in 16-pin packages. They have tri-state output drivers to interface directly with a system bus and are fully compatible with all TTL interfaces.

Cost Effectiveness of NMOS LSI Peripherals

Figure 2-15 clearly demonstrates the cost effectiveness of the specially designed CRU microcomputer component peripherals. The replacement of large numbers of less complex packages provides a significant reduction in cost due to simplified design, layout, assembly and testing, besides the reduced material costs.

In addition, there are major contributions to improving the reliability of the system just by reducing the number of packages and the associated solder connections and assembly connections external to the IC.

FUNCTION	UNIT USED	SSI AND MSI PACKAGES REPLACED
INTERRUPTS AND I/O	TMS9901	23
ASYNCHRONOUS SERIAL COMMUNICATIONS	TMS9902	45
SYNCHRONOUS SERIAL COMMUNICATIONS	TMS9903	100

Figure 2-15. System Package Reduction Using Microcomputer Component Peripherals.

CRU Interface

In the features for the 9900 Family, the Communications Register Unit interface provides:

1. The most cost effective I/O for low and medium speed peripherals via the instruction driven serial data link.
2. Completely separate address space.
3. A choice of transferring fields of 1 to 16 bits per instruction.

The CRU serial data link is an effective mechanism for operation-per-instruction I/O. The CRU interface is simpler and therefore less expensive than memory-mapped I/O. In applications where there are many I/O transfers of one or two bits, the CRU serial data link provides execution times that are better than for memory-mapped I/O, which always transfers 8 or 16 bits at a time.

One way of demonstrating the cost effectiveness of the CRU is shown in *Figure 2-16* Package pins per function are less using the CRU interface and the 9900 Family units. Thus, costs are saved over memory-mapping in implementing the example I/O functions shown.

FUNCTION	CRU PINS	MEMORY MAPPED PINS
8-Bit Output	16 (TIM9906)	24
UART	18 (TMS9902)	24-40
USRT	20 (TMS9903)	24-40

Figure 2-16. CRU vs Memory Mapped I/O — Package Pins Required Per Function

THE COMPONENT ROUTE: MEMORY

Semiconductor memory is the most natural storage media to add to a 9900 system. It has fast access times, an interface that is completely compatible with the microprocessor or microcomputer, and high-density storage per package. The semiconductor industry offers a broad spectrum of storage media products in support of microprocessors. These products encompass dynamic and static random access memory (DRAM and SRAM), mask programmable read-only memory (ROM), fused-link programmable read-only memory (PROM), and erasable programmable read-only memory (EPROM).

Read-Only Memory: Costs and Flexibility

Figure 2-17 shows the characteristics of read-only memories and their cost per bit vs. design flexibility. Mask programmable read-only memory is lowest cost per bit but also has no flexibility. It is used for high volume production after a design is proved to be correct and no changes are expected. PROMs have excellent performance and have more flexibility because programming is done after they are manufactured. However, once programmed they cannot be changed. PROMs cost somewhat more than ROMs because they use more real estate. EPROM has much more flexibility because design changes are done quickly and because it is reuseable, but EPROM costs more to manufacture than ROM or PROM because it is eraseable. EAROM is also indicated in *Figure 2-17*. This is really "read mostly" memory, because it can be erased in a relatively short period of time (microseconds), but once programmed again, it acts like fixed storage. EAROMs as a practical product are still a bit in the future. The flexibility of EPROMs is well worth the added cost. This is especially true when used as a prototyping tool.

A. READ-ONLY MEMORY CHARACTERISTICS

	ROM	PROM	EPROM	EAROM
COST (RANK)	1	2	3	4
PROGRAM TIME	WEEKS	MINUTES	MINUTES	MICROSECONDS
SETUP CHARGE	YES	NO	NO	NO
REUSABILITY	NO	NO	YES	YES
SPEED	FAST	VERY FAST	MEDIUM	SLOW

B. READ-ONLY MEMORY COST/BIT VS FLEXIBILITY

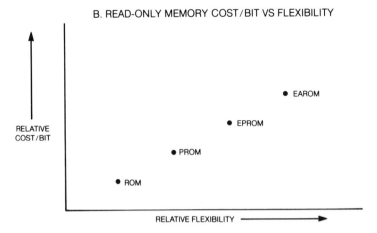

Figure 2-17. Read-Only Memory Overview

THE COMPONENT ROUTE: MISCELLANEOUS COMPONENTS

Included in the full support of the 9900 Family and other types of microprocessors as well is the large array of SSI, MSI, linear and interface integrated circuits that are used to couple the microprocessor to all types of system units.

Some of these units are for the transformation of input signal levels to levels acceptable by the microprocessor. Others boost the power output of output signal pins so that solenoids, relays, large networks of memory address lines. or large capacitive loads can be driven properly.

Many manufacturers support such components with data books and application notes. This information is readily available by writing to the manufacturer. For example, correspondence and inquiries to Texas Instruments about such components can be directed to:

Texas Instruments Incorporated
P.O. Box 225012, M/S 308
Dallas, Texas 75265
(214) 238-2011

As the increased integration continues more and more support circuits are being incorporated into one package, therefore, special attention should be paid to such circuits because they can save a great deal of design and assembly time and most likely have a lower initial cost than the complement of components they replace.

THE MODULAR ROUTE: MICROCOMPUTER MODULES

TM9900 microcomputer modules are preassembled, pre-tested, ready-to-use combinations of 9900 Family components which are available to meet the needs of the microprocessor and microcomputer system designers.

An overview of the TM990 microcomputer module product line, divided into the product series, is shown in *Figure 2-18*. A summary of the type of products is shown in *Table 2-1*. This serves as an example of the wide variety of products available to the designer to begin a microprocessor evaluation or an initial design. The series ranges from microcomputers to expansion boards for memory and I/O, to software support in read-only memory (EPROM), to the accessories required to interconnect the modules. System and software development are of particular importance to the beginner in microprocessors because of the need to get started without excessive capital expenditures. For this reason, a low-cost terminal and a module of I/O and memory is included in the microcomputer modules to use in software and system development. Even firmware in the form of a monitor, a line-by-line assembler, and pre-programmed software in BASIC are provided as an example of the type software support that is needed for microprocessor systems development. These are included in the microcomputer module series because they are closely tied to software and system development.

100 Series — MICROCOMPUTERS

100M — 1, 2, 3	16-bit word 2K to 8K Bytes EPROM	512 to 4K Bytes RAM (± Monitor)
101M — 1, 2, 3	16-bit word 2K to 8K Bytes EPROM	2K to 4K Bytes RAM (± Monitor)
180M — 1, 3	8-bit bytes 2K to 4K Bytes EPROM	512 to 1K Bytes RAM (± Monitor)
189	4K to 6K Bytes EPROM	1K to 2K Bytes RAM (+ Symbolic Assembler, Terminal)

200 Series — MEMORY EXPANSION

201 — 41, 42, 43	8K — 32K bytes EPROM	4K to 16K Bytes SRAM
203A		16K to 64 Bytes DRAM
206 — 41, 42		8K to 16K Bytes SRAM

300 Series — I/O, I/O — MEMORY EXPANSION

301	Low Cost Terminal for Address and Data Display
302	Makes Software Development System with 100M or 101M
310	Expands I/O

400 Series — FIRMWARE

401 — 1, 2	Monitors for 100M, 101M or 180M
402 — 1, 2	Line-by-Line Assembler for 100M, 101M or 180M
450 — 1, 2	BASIC Programs for Program Development

500 Series — ACCESSORIES

501, 521	Chassis, Cable and Power Supply Accessories for Program and System Development.

Table 2-1. Example of Microcomputer Modules

The Application

Microcomputer modules are for the system designer who wants to:

1. Apply and evaluate a 9900 Family microcomputer without taking the time for all the engineering, planning, assembly and testing needed to design and assemble the equivalent microcomputer system.
2. Free himself from design details to concentrate on speeding an end product to market.
3. Expand memory of an existing 9900 Family system.
4. Assemble a low-cost software development system to edit, assemble, load and debug programs for PROMs.
5. Expand a university course with low-cost hands-on hardware.
6. Evaluate POWER BASIC programs and apply them to microcomputer systems.

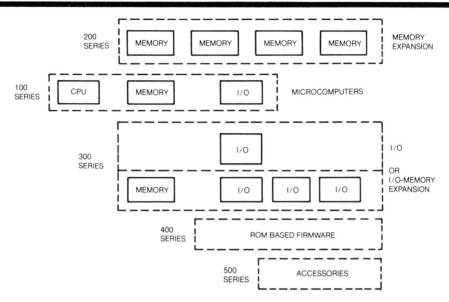

Figure 2-18. TM990 Microcomputer Module Series

A Special Product — A Learning Tool

Many would-be users of microprocessors have a difficult time getting started because of the initial cost of development·systems. They need a microcomputer to be able to understand the function of all of the parts of a system. They need a terminal to develop programs and they need outputs to be able to readily recognize correct program solutions.

An example of such a product in the microcomputer module series is the TM990/189 University Board. It is designed as a learning tool for the engineer, student or hobbyist. It aids in the instruction of microcomputer fundamentals, machine and assembly language programming and microcomputer interfacing. An ASC II type terminal is built right on the board and along with a symbolic assembler it provides the means for program development. Such programs can drive Light Emitting Diodes right on the module, or a ceramic speaker, or output lines that can interface to other output devices. If desirable, a program for a specific application can be developed using such a module, and then the module used in the actual application.

Analog I/O Expansion

There is a need when interfacing between analog and digital signals to have modules that provide the conversion from analog to digital and digital to analog. Several manufacturers are supplying products that complement microprocessors and microcomputers to make them easy to use. Such devices are readily available from the appropriate distributors.

The Minicomputer Route

For large system applications in which the computer system is a small portion of total system costs, use of prepackaged OEM minicomputers as system components provides a number of advantages. A full complement of system and applications software is readily available for immediate use on the machine, including assemblers, linkers, editors, operating systems, high-level languages, a variety of utility packages, many applications packages, etc.

With a family concept such as the 9900 Family, Texas Instruments Digital Systems Group, for example, manufactures two minicomputers which are compatible with the TMS9900. The first is the 990/4 minicomputer which uses the TMS9900 as its central processing unit. It utilizes the CRU for control of peripheral devices making this system directly compatible with the 9900 Family. The second minicomputer implements the CPU in TTL, maintaining upward compatibility with the 9900 Family. This unit, the 990/10 uses a DMA peripheral device interface called TILINE™ for control of high speed peripherals such as magnetic tape units and moving head disk drives, and provides extended addressing capability.

Support documentation and applications information for people desiring to use such components is readily available from the manufacturer of such equipment.

A Selection Process

Criteria for selecting a microprocessor, microcomputer, microcomputer component peripheral, or a minicomputer for a system application are listed in *Figure 2-19*. System performance, cost, reliability, and delivery may also depend on the vendor that designs and supports the products used.

MPU ARCHITECTURE

    Word Size
    Number of Instructions
    Address Bus Length
    Data Bus Length
    I/O Bus Length
    Clock Rate
    Benchmark Performance
      (Selected Functions)
    Arithmetic Capability
      Multiply
      Divide

I/O CAPABILITY AND PERIPHERAL CIRCUITS

    Parallel I/O

      How Many Bits
      Data Rate
      Programmability
      Drive Required

    Serial I/O

      Asynchronous
      Synchronous
      Baud Rate
      EIA
      Current Loop

    Timers and Event Counters

      Interval
      Max Count

    Interrupts

      Number
      Masking

    DMA

      Channels
      Chaining Required

    Other Interfaces

      Floppy Disk
      Analog
      Keyboard
      CRT
      Tape

MPU (other specifications)

    Package
    Temperature Range
    Supply Voltages
    Power Consumption
    Special Reliability
    Unit Costs
      (Selected Volumes)

System Environmental

    Supply Voltages
    Temperature Range
    Power Consumption
    Special Reliability
    Special Size

Support

    Technical Documentation
    Hardware Development Support
      Emulators
      Testers
      Evaluation Modules

Software

    Assemblers
    Text Editors
    Simulators
    Utilities
    Application Libraries
    High-level language

Software Development

    Systems
      Cross-Support
      Dedicated

Figure 2-19. Selection Criteria for Microprocessor, Microcomputer Systems

Vendor Selection

One way of evaluating a vendor is to make a list of items similar to the selection criteria for system components. Some of the same items from this list, especially in the support area, can be included. Additional items for consideration are shown in *Figure 2-20.*

DOCUMENTATION	CREDIBILITY
Product	Reputation
Support Systems	Investment
Applications	Financial Status
MANUFACTURING CAPABILITY	CUSTOMER SUPPORT
Facilities	Application Engineers
Product Levels	Distribution
Backlog	Hot Lines

Figure 2-20. Vendor Criteria

Setting weights for each item and summing these for individual vendors allows a direct comparison. The total number accumulated for each vendor establishes a vendor rating.

9900 FAMILY SOFTWARE AND DEVELOPMENT SYSTEMS

IMPORTANCE OF SOFTWARE

As described in Chapter 1 *(Figure 1-9),* the term software is used to describe the programs and documented ideas which allow small amounts of general purpose hardware (microprocessors, memory, peripherals) to replace large amounts of special purpose hardware. The costs for software are becoming a much larger percentage of the total system development cost. These costs are primarily incurred prior to production of a system. For large volume systems the share of these one-time costs attributed to each unit is small since the total software costs are divided by a very large number. Correspondingly, when the volume of units produced is low, the software cost per unit will be quite high. This factor, coupled with a lack of familiarity, has led many users to underestimate software development costs.

Since software now commands 80% of the design effort of complete systems, and since many software tasks are common to the industry, the level of software support from a vendor can have tremendous impact on total system design cost. Perhaps more importantly, availability of a wide variety of system and application software packages can drastically shorten design time and speed the product to market.

SOFTWARE DEVELOPMENT SYSTEMS

Development of software requires equipment — program or software development systems. As a system designer makes a decision to use a microprocessor or microcomputer, all design avenues seem to focus on software development. Questions naturally arise, "How can I do software 'breadboarding' and program testing?", "How can I arrive at a final program and be assured that it is correct?" and "Can it be done economically"?

Figure 2-21 illustrates cost versus capability for each of the program development systems that support the 9900 Family. Lower cost systems tend to have lower capability. The choice of a program development system depends on many factors. Some examples are: (1) *Capital Status* — capital availability determines whether a firm can consider the sophisticated emulator systems which boost designer productivity. (2) *Equipment on Hand* — availability of a terminal, line printer, or EPROM programmer or other useable equipment would likely reduce the required level of investment. (3) *Equipment Longevity* — How long the equipment will be used may allow division of the cost of the equipment over several projects. (4) *System Complexity* — Highly complex applications often require the best development tools possible; therefore, the most sophisticated system is required or the job can't be done. (5) *Production quantities* — High volume applications can more easily bear the cost of top-of-the-line development equipment; the corresponding increase in productivity made possible by this equipment, increases design efficiency. (6) *In-House Computer Capability* — Availability of in-house computer support makes development via timeshare cross-support an efficient alternative.

A brief description of the program development systems follows:

Program Development Systems

1. TM990/189—   University Board. (Price: less than $250) This board provides an inexpensive means of evaluating the 9900 Family and learning about microprocessors in general. It comes with a debug monitor and assembler. Key features include full alphanumeric keyboard; display via 10 seven-segment digits; 16-bit parallel, RS232, TTY, and audio cassette interface; and a tutorial text and hardware reference manual.

2. TM990/100M—   Microcomputer with line-by-line assembler
   TM990/301—   Microterminal for programming (combined price: less than $500)

(Figure 2-22). These components are described in detail in Chapter 3. Basic program benchmarks may be written and tested with the 9900 microcomputer. A terminal such as 743 KSR may be connected to the board and additional development software used. (This technique is described in Chapter 8).

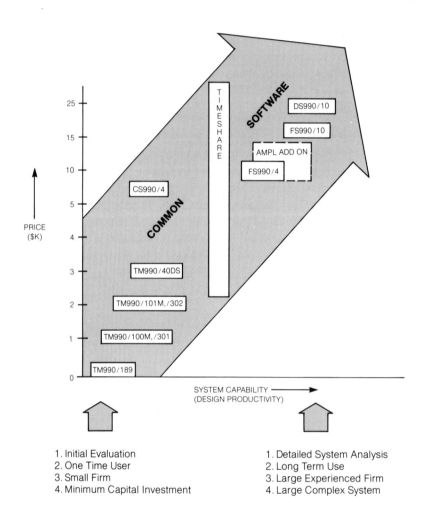

Figure 2-21. Cost vs. System Capability for 9900 Family Program Development Systems

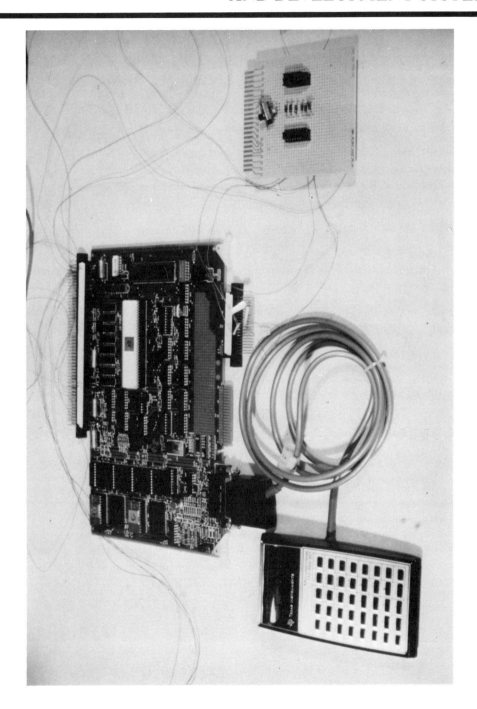

Figure 2-22. TM990/100M Microcomputer with TM990/301 Microterminal

3. TM990/302— Microcomputer board (price: less than $600)

Software is on the board in the form of EPROM devices for editor, assembler, linker, debugger, and EPROM programmer functions. A terminal and one or two cassette recorders are needed to complete a very powerful, yet very low cost program development system. The /302 is a companion to (or extension of) the TM990/100M or /101M board *(Figure 2-23)*.

4. TM990/40DS— TMS9940 development system (price: less than $2800) containing an EPROM programmer for the TMS9940E, Debug Monitor, Assembler and Trial In-System Emulation; the /40DS provides development capability and emulation of most of the TMS9940's operations *(Figure 2-24)*.

5. CS990/4— 990/4 minicomputer with a 733 ASR dual cassette terminal (price: less than $6000) *(Figure 2-25)*.

Program development software is available on cassettes to perform every task outlined previously.

6. FS990/4— 990/4 minicomputer, terminal, and dual floppy disk storage unit (price: less than $12,000) *(Figure 2-26)*.

Complete program development system with peripheral add-on capacity.

7. FS990/AMPL— Same as FS990 but with AMPL hardware and software added (price: less than $20,000) *(Figure 2-27)*.

The primary advantage of the AMPL system is the complete hardware debugging capability via the AMPL software and 9900 emulator and trace functions.

8. FS990/10— 990/10 minicomputer *(Figure 2-28)*, terminal, and dual floppy disk storage unit (base system starts at $15,000).

Complete program development system which can be upgraded to include moving-head disk mass storage. AMPL is available as an option.

9. DS990/10— 990/10 minicomputer *(Figure 2-29)*, terminal, moving head-disk mass storage with complete multi-user system software (base system starts at $25,000). Supports Macro-Assembler, FORTRAN, BASIC, PASCAL and COBOL.

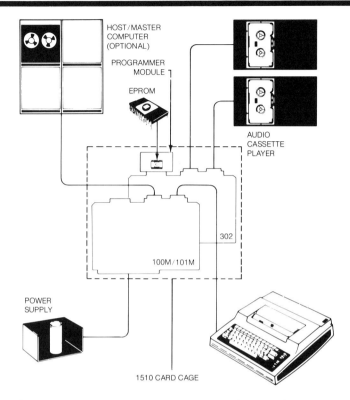

Figure 2-23. TM990/302 Program Development System

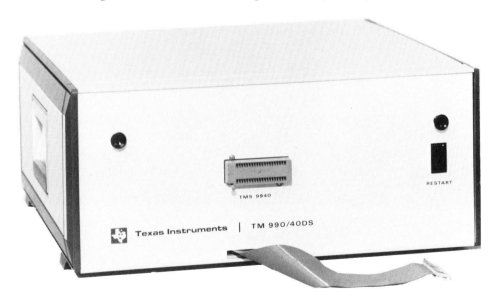

Figure 2-24. TM990/40DS cables and card chassis

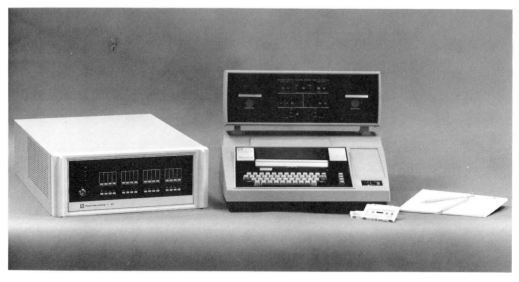

Figure 2-25. CS 990/4 Software System

911 VIDEO DISPLAY
TERMINAL

810 LINE PRINTER

FD800 FLOPPY
DISC UNIT

PROGRAMMER PANEL
(990/4 CPU WITH
MINIMUM OF 48K
BYTES OF MEMORY)

*Figure 2-26. FS990 Software Development System
(with optional printer)*

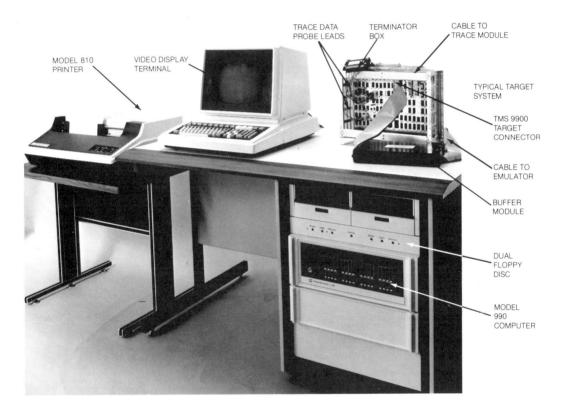

Figure 2-27. Typical AMPL Microprocessor Prototyping Laboratory

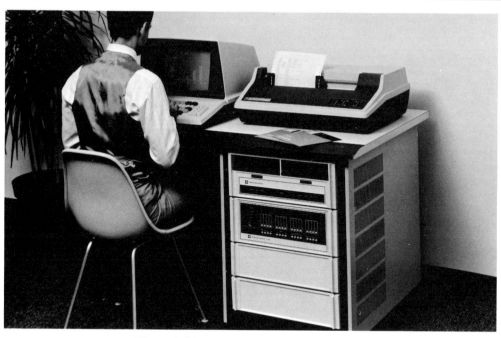

Figure 2-28. *FS990/10 Minicomputer System*

Figure 2-29. *DS990/10 Minicomputer System*

Which Program Development System to Use

The choice of a program development system requires evaluation of an application's specific requirements. The lowest cost system (TM 990/100M board and /301 microterminal) will allow a very basic level of programming, and is suitable for writing short routines to test algorithms or evaluate execution speed. Since labels are not allowed and there is no editing program to help add or delete program steps, programming is relatively difficult.

By adding the TM990/302 Software Development Module (with the TM990/100M or 101M) programming becomes much easier. An editor program helps you modify the program steps, the assembler allows labels, and the other elements—debug, EPROM programmer, relocating loader, and I/O handlers—add substantial programming flexibility. A programmer might well evaluate this system as being an order of magnitude better than the /100M board alone. It is best suited for one designer working on a single prototype.

But there are limitations to the /302. The system depends on cassette recorders for storage of development software and user programs. And cassettes are slow. The number of times per day that a programmer can make a change in his program, process it through the system, and test the results is generally in the range of three to five.

The number of program change cycles per day can be increased by purchasing a CS990 system. This digital cassette based software development system, being more versatile, can increase daily program iterations to about ten. Two or three programmers can use a single system comfortably.

The FS990/4 system uses floppy disk storage to further improve flexibility. Daily program iterations can be over 20. Because program turnaround is fast, a single FS990 system is often used by several programmers.

By adding AMPL hardware and software the FS990 system can be upgraded to an AMPL prototyping system. Hardware testing may be performed under program control.

The chart shown in *Figure 2-30* shows the different levels of sophistication of program development systems that can be used with each 9900 CPU.

SELECTED PROCESSOR	TMS9900/ SBP9900A	TMS9980A/ TMS9981	TMS9985	TMS9940
MINIMUM SYSTEM	TM990/100M TM990/101M TM990/302	TM990/189 TM990/180	TM990/185	TM990/140
MEDIUM SYSTEM	CS990/4	CS990/4	CS990/4	TM990/40DS
LARGE SYSTEM	FS990/4 AMPL FS990/10	FS990/4 AMPL FS990/10	FS990/4 AMPL FS990/10	FS990/4 AMPL FS990/10
MAXIMUM CAPABILITY	DS990/10	DS990/10	DS990/10	DS990/10
TIMESHARE TMSW101MT GE, NCSS, Tymeshare	X X	X X	X X	X X

Figure 2-30. Program Development Systems for Each 9900 Family CPU

Timeshare

Timeshare users approach software development in one of two ways. Either they purchase and install the TMSW101MT cross-support package on an in-house computer, or they lease access to a similar package on a commercial timeshare system such as GE TERMINET, NCSS, and TYMSHARE. Both approaches provide a 9900 cross-assembler compatible with the FS990 prototype development system. Both also provide a simulator and ROM utility. In-house users often interface the ROM utility directly to EPROM programmers. Otherwise several printout formats are available to match standard ROM and PROM order techniques.

The timeshare approach provides high-level development capability at minimum initial cost. It does, however, incur large operating costs, especially when using commercial systems.

SUPPORT SOFTWARE AND FIRMWARE

The program development systems and the 9900 Family of components are supported by a full line of software. The chart shown in *Figure 2-31* summarizes the capability of the program development system software.

PROGRAM STEP		CROSS-SUPPORT TMSW101MT	TM990/302	TM990/40DS	PX990	TX990	FS990 AMPL	DX990 W/AMPL
EDIT		X	X		X	X	X	X
ASSEMBLE		X	X	X	X	X	X	MACRO
LINK		X			X	X	X	X
LOAD		CREATES LOAD MODULE	X	X	X	X	X	X
DEBUG		X	X	X	X	X	X	X
EMULATOR				X			X	X
LOGIC TRACE							X	X
SIMULATOR		X						
READ-ONLY MEMORY	ROM	X				X	X	X
PROGRAM-MING	PROM	X	X	X	X	X	X	X

Figure 2-31. 9900 Family Software Development System Capabilities

Additional software and firmware are as follows:

TM990/401 — TIBUG Monitor

The TMS990/401 TIBUG Monitor is a comprehensive, interactive debug monitor in EPROM included in the basic price of the TM990 CPU modules. TIBUG includes 13 user commands plus six user accessible utilities and operates with 110, 300, 1200 and 2400 baud terminals. The basic TIBUG functions include:

1. Inspect/change the following: CRU, memory locations, program counter, workspace pointer, status register, workspace registers.
2. Execute user programs under breakpoint in single or multiple steps.

TM990/402 — Line-by-Line Assembler (LBLA)

TM990/402 is a line-by-line assembler which is supplied pre-programmed in EPROM for immediate system use. By allowing the entry of instructions in mnemonic form and performing simple address resolution calculations with a displacement range of $+254$ to -256 bytes, the assembler is an extremely powerful tool for assembly language input of short programs or easy patching of long programs.

POWER BASIC High-Level Language

POWER BASIC, an easy-to-use extension of the original BASIC language, is highly suitable for the majority of industrial control applications. It greatly simplifies the solution of complex system problems and eliminates unnecessary design details.

POWER BASIC can be used for a general system implementation language as well as for information processing. It is also versatile enough to solve problems in real-time control of events while improving programmer efficiency in implementing complex algorithms.

The performance of POWER BASIC is outstanding — 2 to 3 times faster than any existing 8-bit microcomputer-oriented BASIC. In effect, you get minicomputer performance at microcomputer cost.

Other advantages of POWER BASIC include:

Full string processing capability
Multidimensional arrays
13-digit arithmetic accuracy
Automatic minimum memory configuration

POWER BASIC language interpreters are available in economical yet versatile packages shown in *Table 2-2.*

Table 2-2. POWER BASIC Firmware

PART NO.	MEDIA	NAME	DESCRIPTION
TM990/450	EPROM device kit	Evaluation POWER BASIC	Reduced memory version (8K byte) designed to offer evaluation tools for exploring POWER BASIC applications.
TM990/101M-10	*TM990/101M		ROM kit executes standalone on TM990/100M, 101M modules.
TM990/451	EPROM device kit	Development POWER BASIC	Expanded memory version (12K byte) providing capability for design, development, and debug of POWER BASIC programs. Executes on TM990/201 or 302 module interfaced with TM990/100M, 101M CPU modules.
TM990/452	EPROM device kit	Enhancement of Development POWER BASIC Software Package	Provides EPROM programming, dual audio cassette handling, and I/O utilities for TMS990/302.
TMSW201F	FS990 diskette	Configurable POWER BASIC	Fully expanded version including complete diskette file support and a configurator program which reduces the size of POWER BASIC programs for execution.

*Contained in TM990/101M Module

PASCAL High-Level Language

TIPMX Executive Components Library in PASCAL

TIPMX is a configuration of software processes that provides executive functions such as multitask priority scheduling, interrupt servicing, and inter-process communication. It relieves the programmer of the necessity to develop these processes. TIPMX also supports, but is not limited by, PASCAL data structures and program structures.

A tailored TIPMX is configured by selecting desired processes from a library of system and run-time support modules. These processes are link-edited to form a supervisory nucleus which is loaded into EPROM memory to enhance its speed, efficiency and reliability.

PASCAL, FORTRAN or Assembly Language processes then execute under the auspices of this tailored TIPMX executive.

CHAPTER 3

A First Encounter:
Getting Your Hands on a 9900

PURPOSE

Remember the common saying, "What you've always wanted to know about subject X, but were always afraid to try." The same applies, and probably especially so, to persons who have contact with the world of digital electronics; who have heard about computers and minicomputers and even operated them; who have seen and experienced the advances made in the functional capabilities and low cost of digital integrated circuits by owning and operating handheld calculators; who have worked around and even built electronic equipment; who have heard about microprocessors and their amazing capabilities — but have not tried them.

If you are one of these people, this chapter is for you, for in it we want to help you try out a microprocessor, work it together, operate it, have success with it. In this way we hope to demonstrate that microprocessor systems are not that difficult to use. That, even though they require an understanding of a new side of electronic system design — "software" — if a base of understanding is established, and if an engineering approach is followed, there is no need to fear getting involved.

So that's the purpose of this first encounter — to get your hands on a 9900 microprocessor system and operate it.

WHERE TO BEGIN

It would be very easy to be satisfied with a paper example for a first encounter, however, it has been demonstrated that a great deal more is learned by actually having the physical equipment and doing something with it. Therefore, this first encounter example requires that specific pieces of equipment be purchased.

However, the purchase is not to be in vain. The first encounter has been chosen so that is may be followed with more extensive applications described in Chapter 8. Applications that will help to bring understanding of the 9900 microprocessor system to the point that actual control applications, akin to automating an assembly line, can be implemented. Outputting control of ac and dc voltage for motors or solenoids and producing controlled logic level signals are examples. In this way, useful outcomes are being accomplished, the equipment is being expanded, and problem solutions are demonstrated. At all times, of course, the base foundation of knowledge about microprocessor systems is growing.

To get underway then, purchase the following items from your industrial electronics distributor that handles Texas Instruments Incorporated products.

Quantity	Part #	Description
1	TM990/100M-1 (Assembly No. 999211-0001) (see *Figure 3-1*)	TMS9900 microcomputer module with TIBUG monitor in two TMS 2708 EPROM's and EIA or TTY serial I/O jumpers option.
1	TM990/301 (see *Figure 3-2*)	Microterminal
1	TIH431121-50 or Amphenol 225-804-50 or Viking 3VH50/9N05 or Elco 00-6064-100-061-001	100 pin, 0.125″ c-c, wire-wrap PCB edge connector (or equivalent solder terminal unit)
1	TIH421121-20 or Viking 3VH20/1JND5	40 pin, 0.1″ c-c, wire-wrap PCB edge connector (or equivalent solder terminal unit)

In addition, some small electronic parts to interconnect the light emitting diode displays that will be used will be needed. These are listed later on so you may want to continue to read further before purchasing the module and microterminal so that all necessary parts can be obtained at the same time.

WHAT YOU HAVE

In *Figure 3-3* is shown a generalized computer system, it has a CPU (central processing unit) which contains an arithmetic and logic unit (ALU), all the control and timing circuits, and interface circuits to the other major parts. It has a memory unit. It has some peripheral units for inputting data such as tape machines, disk memories, terminals and keyboards. It has output units such as printers, CRT screens, tape machines, disk memories.

The TM990/100M-1 microcomputer shown in *Figure 3-1* is a miniature version of this computer system as shown in *Figure 3-4.* It has a CPU centered around the TMS9900 microprocessor, a memory unit — in this case a random access memory (RAM) and a read only memory (ROM). It does not have the input/output units indicated in *Figure 3-3* but it does have circuitry (TMS9901, 9902) for interface to such units. The TMS9901 will handle parallel input/output data and single bit addressed data as will be shown in this first encounter. The TMS9902 handles serial input/output data interface either through an EIA R5232 interface or a TTY interface. A more complete interconnection of the components of the microcomputer is shown in the block diagram of *Figure 3-5.* The physical position of these units on the board is identified in *Figure 3-1.*

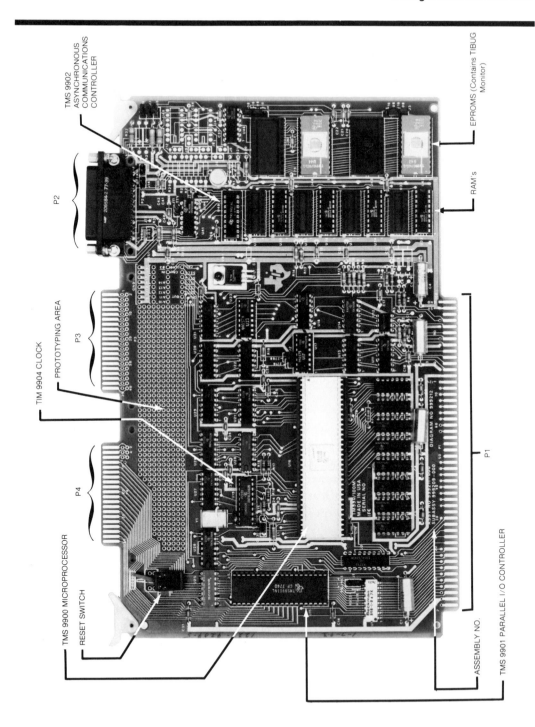

Figure 3-1. TM 990/100M-1 Microcomputer

Figure 3-2. TM 990/301 Microterminal

Just think, a complete microcomputer with: **1)** 256 16-bit words of random access memory to hold program steps and program data, expandable to 512 words; **2)** 1024 16-bit words of read only memory which contains pre-programmed routines (TIBUG Monitor) that provides the steps necessary for the TM990/100M-1 microcomputer to accept input instructions and data and to provide output data. This ROM capability can be expanded to 4096 words to provide program flexibility; **3)** input/output interface that can handle 16 parallel lines expandable to 4096 and an interface for serial characters of 5-8 bits at a programmable data rate; **4)** an input terminal to input the sequence of steps to solve a problem — the program.

GETTING IT TOGETHER

Of course, in order to operate the microprocessor system, it must be put together. It must be interconnected.

What function will it perform? The first encounter application is shown in *Figure 3-6.* The microcomputer will be used to provide basic logic level outputs to turn on and off, in sequence, light emitting diode segments of a 7 segment numeric display element, the TIL303. This will demonstrate the "software" techniques used to provide dc logic levels at the I/O interface which through proper drivers can later be used to control solenoids, motors, relays, lights, etc.

In the first encounter application, the microterminal shown in *Figure 3-2* will be used to input the instructions and data required to perform the function.

Recall that a light emitting diode (LED) is made of semiconductor material and emits light when a current is passed through it in the correct direction. Each segment of the 7-segment display is a separate LED. Four segments of the display will turn on in the sequence f, b, e, c at a slow or a fast rate depending on the position of a switch, as shown in *Figure 3-6.* Each segment will first be turned on, then a short delay, then off, then a short delay. The sequence is continued with the next segment; proceeding around through 4 segments and then starting over again. The rate is varied by changing the delay in the sequence. The switch position controls the delay.

A 7-segment display is used because of its ready availability and its dual-in-line package. Only 4 of the segments will be programmed into the sequence although driver capability will be provided for 6 segments. This allows flexibility for the person doing the first encounter to experiment on their own to include the remaining 2 segments. A next step would be to provide an additional driver. In this way all 7 segments of the display can be included.

Here's what's required to provide the segment display. *Figure 3-7* shows the integrated circuit driver package for the LED segments, the SN74H05N. The physical package and a schematic are shown. It contains 6 open collector inverters, each capable of "sinking" 20 ma. A 14- or 16-pin dual-in-line socket is required. A wire-wrap one is shown. However, it could be a solder terminal unit just as well.

Figure 3-8 shows the 7-segment display physical package and schematic and a 14- or 16-pin DIP socket for interconnection. 100 ohm resistors for limiting current through the LEDs are also required.

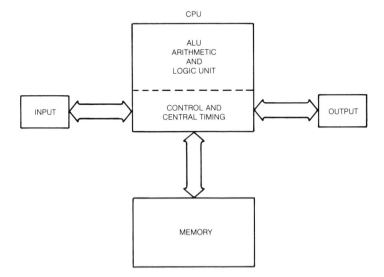

Figure 3-3. Generalized Computer

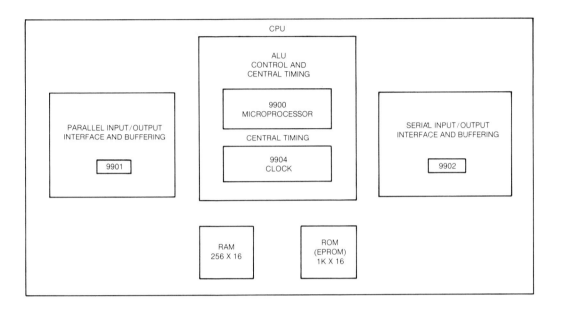

Figure 3-4. Miniature Computer System on TM 990/100M-1 Module

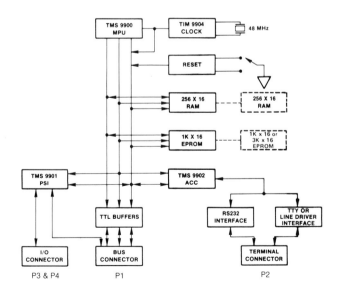

Figure 3-5. TM 990/100M-1 Block Diagram

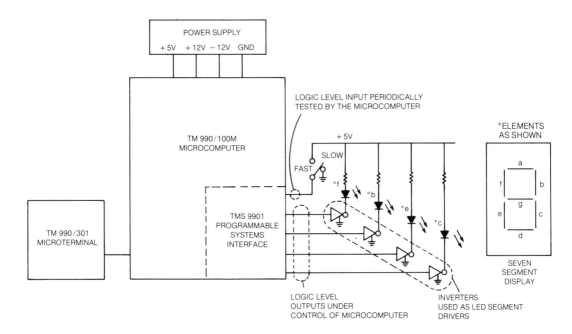

Figure 3-6. The First Encounter Task

All of the components of *Figure 3-7* and *3-8* are wired together on a separate printed circuit board as shown in *Figure 3-9*. The Radio Shack #276-152 board provides individual plated surfaces around holes to make it easy to anchor components and to interconnect all components with wire-wrap. J4, the 40 pin wire-wrap PCB edge connector accepts the edge connections of P4 on the TM990/100M-1 board shown in *Figure 3-1*. After wiring this connector, put a piece of tape across the top of this connector so that it is correctly oriented before the board is plugged in; or the same can be done here as for P_1 discussed a little later. Note also on *Figure 3-1* that there is an area on the 990/100M-1 board for prototyping. The components of *Figure 3-9* may be wired in this area rather than using a separate printed circuit board. Using a separate board allows this area to be used for more permanent components for a specific dedicated application of the 990/100M module.

A. SN74H05N
SIX INVERTER
DRIVERS
14 PIN PLASTIC PKG.

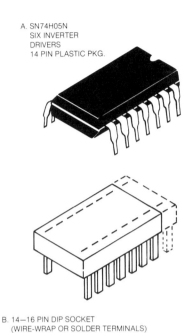

B. 14—16 PIN DIP SOCKET
(WIRE-WRAP OR SOLDER TERMINALS)

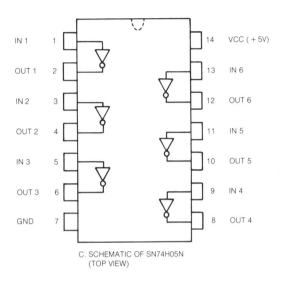

IN 1	1		14	VCC (+ 5V)	
OUT 1	2		13	IN 6	
IN 2	3		12	OUT 6	
OUT 2	4		11	IN 5	
IN 3	5		10	OUT 5	
OUT 3	6		9	IN 4	
GND	7		8	OUT 4	

C. SCHEMATIC OF SN74H05N
(TOP VIEW)

COMPONENT PARTS

1 — SN 74H05N HEX DRIVER
(EACH DRIVER CAPABLE OF SINKING 20 MA.)

1 — 14 OR 16 PIN DIP SOCKET
(RADIO SHACK # 276-1993, 94)
(TI # 811604 M&C — 16 PIN WIRE-WRAP)

Figure 3-7. LED Driver Parts

TOP VIEW
A.   TIL303 7 SEGMENT NUMERICAL DISPLAY

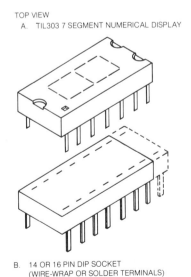

B.   14 OR 16 PIN DIP SOCKET
(WIRE-WRAP OR SOLDER TERMINALS)

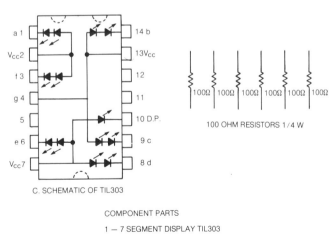

C. SCHEMATIC OF TIL303

COMPONENT PARTS

1 — 7 SEGMENT DISPLAY TIL303

1 — 14 OR 16 PIN DIP PACKAGE
(C-811604 M&C — 16 PIN WIRE WRAP)
(RADIO SHACK — 276 — 1993, 94)

6 — 100 OHM RESISTORS, 1/4 W

Figure 3-8. Segment Display Parts

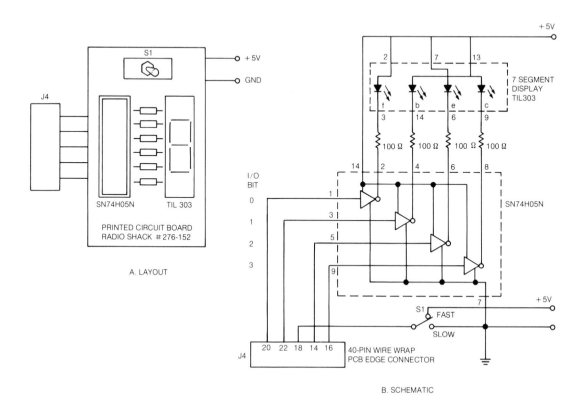

Figure 3-9. The Output Board

Following is a complete list of the parts, tools and supplies required. This is the list that was referred to earlier. Check carefully that all necessary parts are purchased.

PARTS LIST

A.   *Microcomputer*

      1 — TM990/100M-1   TMS9900 Microcomputer module with TIBUG minitor in two TMS 2708 EPROM's and EIA or TTY serial I/O jumper option.

B.   *Terminal*

      1 — TM990/301   Microterminal

C.   *Output*

1 — Hex LED Driver	SN74H05N
1 — 7 Segment Display	TIL303
2 — 14 or 16 Pin Dip Sockets	TI wire-wrap; 16 Pin — C-811604 M&C; Radio Shack wire-wrap; 14 Pin 276-1993; 16 Pin 276-1994
6 — 100 ohm Resistors, ¼ W	
1 — Switch, Toggle or Slide, SPST or DPST	
1 — J4, 40 pin, 0.1″ c-c, wire-wrap	TIH421121-20
PCB Edge Connector (or equiv. solder terminal unit)	Viking 3VH20/1JND5
1 — Printed Circuit Board	Radio Shack #276-152

D.   *Bus Connector* (Use for Power in First Encounter)

1 — J1, 100-pin, 0.125″ c-c, wire-wrap	TIH431121-50
PCB Edge Connector (or equiv. solder terminal unit)	AMPHENOL 225-804-50 Viking 3VH50/9N05 Elco 00-6064-100-061-001

E.   *Power Supplies — Regulated*

Voltage	Regulation	Current
+ 5V	±3%	1.3A
+ 12V	±3%	0.2A
− 12V	±3%	0.1A

F.   *Tools*

Wire-wrap connector tool	Soldering Iron
Wire-wrap disconnecting tool	
Wire stripper (30 G)	Long-nose pliers
	Diagonal cutter
	VOM, DVM, DMM

G.   *General Supplies*

Wire (30 G Kynar)
Solder
Plugs and jacks for power supply connections

Note the power supplies required, the voltages, currents, and regulation. Assure that there is a common ground between all units.

(Electronic shops or laboratories might have available individual LEDs, therefore, *Figure 3-10* is provided in case this alternate method of display is chosen. The necessary drivers and resistors are identified. The necessary substitutions can be made on *Figure 3-9*.)

After wiring the output board, what remains is to supply power to the board. This is accomplished through P1 on the 990/100M-1 board. *Figure 3-11* shows how the edge connector is wired to supply power. Be careful to use the correct pins as numbered on P1 on the board; *these pin numbers may not correspond to the number on the particular edge connector used.* Label the top side of the edge connector "TOP" and the bottom "TURN OVER." This will prevent incorrect connection of power to board. Wire the connector pins so that the top and bottom connections on the board are used to supply power, e.g., 1 & 2 for ground; 3 & 4 for $+5V$; 73 & 74 for $-12V$; and 75 & 76 for $+12V$. Plugs or jacks may be placed on the end of the power supply wires to make easy interface. With both the P1 and P4 connectors and the output board wired, the total system is ready for interconnection.

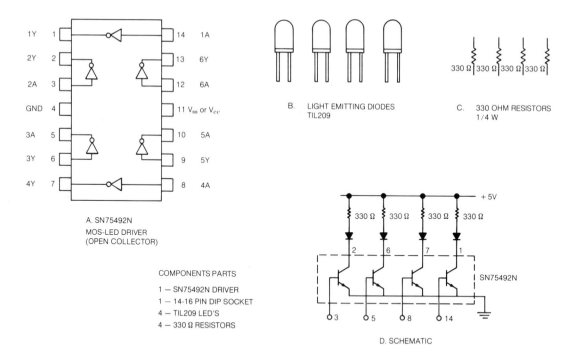

Figure 3-10. Alternative LED Output Display

UNPACKING AND CHECKING THE MICROCOMPUTER (TM990/100M-1)

It is very important to realize that the microcomputer module has MOS (metal-oxide-semiconductor) integrated circuits on it. These circuits are particularly sensitive to static charge and can be damaged permanently if such charge is discharged through their internal circuitry. Therefore, make sure to ground out all body static charge to workbench, table, desk or the like before handling the microcomputer board or any components that go onto it.

After unpacking the TM990/100M-1 module from its carton and examining it for any damage due to shipping, compare it to *Figure 3-12* to determine the correct location of all parts. Additional detail is available in the user's guide shipped with the board. Make sure that EPROM TIBUG Monitor (TM990/401-1) units are in the U42 and U44 positions on the board. Make sure that the RAM integrated circuits are in the U32, 34, 36, and 38 positions.

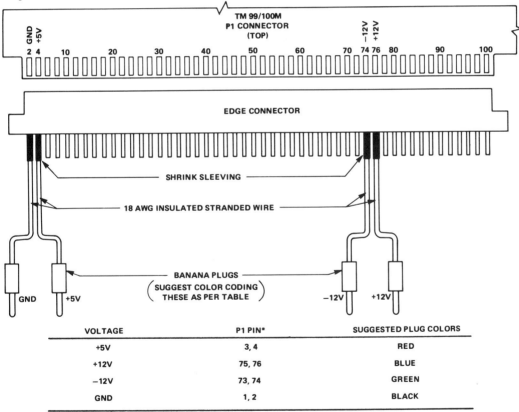

VOLTAGE	P1 PIN*	SUGGESTED PLUG COLORS
+5V	3, 4	RED
+12V	75, 76	BLUE
−12V	73, 74	GREEN
GND	1, 2	BLACK

*ON BOARD, ODD-NUMBERED PADS ARE DIRECTLY BENEATH EVEN-NUMBERED PADS.

Figure 3-11. *Power Supply Hookup for 990/100M-1 Microcomputer*

CAUTION: Before connecting the power supply to P1, use a volt-ohmmeter
to verify that correct voltages are present as shown in Figure 3-11.

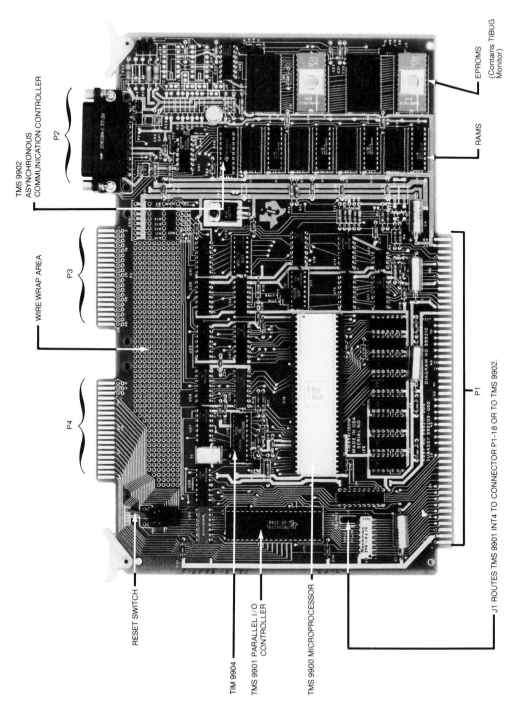

Figure 3-12. TM 990/100M-1 Module as Shipped

Compare the board to *Figure 3-12 & 3-13*. Make sure that the jumpers are in the following positions:

Jumper	Position	Jumper	Position
J1	P1-18	J4	08, 08
J2	2708	J7	EIA
J3	08, 08	J11	OPEN

They assure that memory locations are identified correctly and that the microterminal interfaces correctly.

CONNECTING THE MICROTERMINAL TM990/301

The microterminal *(Figure 3-2)* should be examined to verify there is no damage due to shipment. It will be connected to the microcomputer through P2 on *Figure 3-12*. Jumpers J13, J14, and J15 must be installed on the TM990/100M-1 board in order to supply power to the microterminal. Using the extra jumpers provided, short pins on the board at J13, J14, and J15 *(Figure 3-13)*. Attach the plug on the microterminal cable to the P2 connector on the board.

OPERATING THE MICROCOMPUTER

Check once more that all wiring is correct for the output board *(Figure 3-9)*, the power connector *(Figure 3-11)* and the jumpers, then follow these steps:

Step 1 Begin with connectors to P1 or P4 disconnected

Step 2 Turn on power supplies and verify that all voltages are correct at the connector for P1. Turn off power supplies.

Step 3 Connect the power supply connector to P1. Make sure edge connector has the word "TOP" showing. Turn on $-12V$ supply first, then $+12V$, then $+5V$.

Step 4 Verify the voltages of $+5V$, $-12V$, and $+12V$ on the board printed wiring connections near the edge of the board between P2 and P3. Adjust power supplies or verify trouble if these are not correct.

Step 5 Verify the voltages of these terminals:

J13	$+5V$
J14	$+12V$
J15	$-12V$

If these are incorrect, correct the problem.

Step 6 Turn off power supplies. With the top edge of connector for P4 in correct position, connect output board to P4, turn on power supplies in same sequence as before, $-12V$, $+12V$, $+5V$.

The total setup should now look like *Figure 3-14* and the microcomputer is now ready to perform the task; all that's required is to tell it what to do.

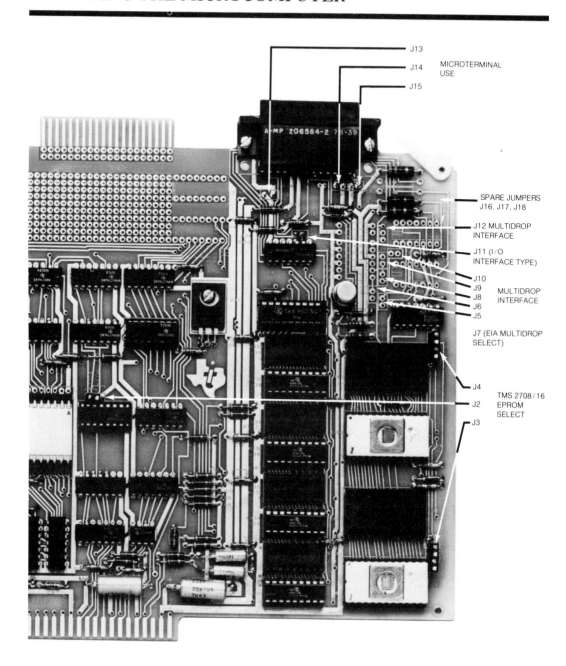

Figure 3-13. Jumpers used on TM 990/100M-1 Board for Option Selection

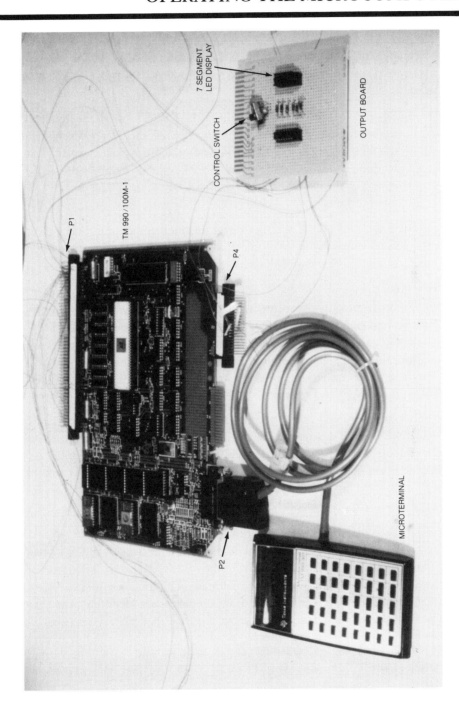

TELLING THE MICROCOMPUTER WHAT TO DO

The microcomputer is told what to do through the microterminal keyboard. This is shown in *Figure 3-15*. Initial conditions are necessary so *Step 7* starts everything at an initial point.

Step 7   *Figure 3-1* and *Figure 3-12* identify the RESET switch. Switch it all the way to the right (facing the toggle). Now depress the CLR (clear) key on the microterminal. Nothing will be on the display but to verify that it is working, press several of the number keys. The numbers pressed will appear in the display. Now press the CLR key again on the microterminal.

As we depress selected keys on the microterminal, the microcomputer is being given instructions — a step by step sequence of things to do to perform the first encounter task. The microcomputer is being *programmed* to do a job.

In order for the microcomputer to do its task according to the instructions given, it must also do many things dictated by other instructions that are stored in sequence in the TIBUG Monitor read-only memory (ROM). The program that performs the first encounter task is stored in the random access memory of the microcomputer and used in sequence. As a result, as the microcomputer accomplishes the task for which it is programmed, it performs each of the steps dictated by the "main program" in the RAM and by TIBUG in ROM.

There are only a few keys used on the microterminal for the first encounter. Identify these on *Figure 3-15* and on the microterminal. Three of these are: EMA (enter memory address) is used to display a specific memory address and give the user the ability to change the contents of that location. EMD (enter memory data) changes the contents of the memory location and EMDI (enter memory data and increment) changes the contents of the memory location and advances the address by two.

Note that *Figure 3-15* identifies the information given by the display. There are two banks of 4 digits each that are displayed. The left 4 digits display the address register (memory address) and the right 4 digits display the data in the data register (data to be stored in memory, being read from memory, or being operated on by the microcomputer). It is of no concern at the moment but both of these 4 digit registers are identifying the value of their data in hexadecimal code. Suffice it to say at this time that each hexadecimal digit represents 4 bits of data for a number that has a value represented by 16 bits. Each hexadecimal digit can have at any one time an alphanumeric value of any one of the following: 0, 1, 2, 3, 4, 5, 6, 7, 8, 9, A, B, C, D, E, F. The decimal value of these numbers are shown in *Figure 3-16* as they occur in the place value position of the 4 bit display. Hexadecimal numbers will be identified with a subscript of 16 in the text, e.g., $02E0_{16}$ or 0100_{16} whenever there is need to avoid confusion.

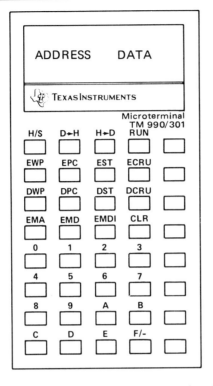

The display of the microterminal is divided into two 4 hexadecimal digit banks. The left bank displays address register information and the right bank displays data registers.

Figure 3-15. Microterminal Keyboard and Display

Every program starts at a particular place in the RAM memory. The first encounter program will start at memory location identified by the hexadecimal address FE00. This is a 16 bit address which in machine code looks like this: 1111 1110 0000 0000 (F = 15; E = 14; 0 = 0; 0 = 0) and from *Figure 3-16* has a decimal value of 61,440 + 3584 + 0 + 0 = 65,024. The program starts at memory location 65,024.

To start the sequence of instruction steps for out first encounter, the starting address is entered and the EMA (enter memory address) key is depressed on the microterminal. This is program *Step 2* in *Step 8.* To help verify the steps the display data is also recorded.

Step 8		**Display**	
KEYSTROKES		ADDRESS	DATA
0. CLR		—	—
1. F/– E 0 0			FE00
2. EMA		FE00	XXXX (X = Don't care)
3. 0 2 E 0		FE00	02E0

This keystroke at Step 3 is a hexadecimal code — an instruction — that is telling the microcomputer to load a register with data. The data, however, is at the next address location. Therefore, with the next keystroke [EMDI] (enter memory data and increment), the instruction 02E0 is stored at address location FE00 and the next memory address for an instruction is brought into the display by incrementing (advancing) the FE00 address by 2 (the reason for advancing by 2 will become clear as more is learned about the 9900 microprocessor).

Step 9

KEYSTROKE	ADDRESS	DATA
4. [EMDI]	FE02	XXXX

MSB   **LSB**

		16^3			16^2			16^1			16^0	
BITS	0 1 2 3			4 5 6 7			8 9 10 11			12 13 14 15		
	HEX	**DEC**		**HEX**	**DEC**		**HEX**	**DEC**		**HEX**	**DEC**	
	0	0		0	0		0	0		0	0	
	1	4 096		1	256		1	16		1	1	
	2	8 192		2	512		2	32		2	2	
	3	12 288		3	768		3	48		3	3	
	4	16 384		4	1 024		4	64		4	4	
	5	20 480		5	1 280		5	80		5	5	
	6	24 576		6	1 536		6	96		6	6	
	7	28 672		7	1 792		7	112		7	7	
	8	32 768		8	2 048		8	128		8	8	
	9	36 864		9	2 304		9	144		9	9	
	A	40 960		A	2 560		A	160		A	10	
	B	45 056		B	2 816		B	176		B	11	
	C	49 152		C	3 072		C	192		C	12	
	D	53 248		D	3 328		D	208		D	13	
	E	57 344		E	3 584		E	224		E	14	
	F	61 440		F	3 840		F	240		F	15	

To convert a number from hexadecimal, add the decimal equivalents for each hexadecimal digit. For example, $7A82_{16}$ would equal in decimal $28,672 + 2,560 + 128 + 2$. To convert decimal to hexadecimal find the nearest number in the above table less than or equal to the number being converted. Set down the hexadecimal equivalent then subtract its decimal number from the original decimal number. Using the remainder(s), repeat this process. For example:

$$31,362_{10} = 7000_{16} + 2690_{10}$$
$$2,690_{10} = A00_{16} + 130_{10}$$
$$130_{10} = 80_{16} + 2_{10}$$
$$2_{10} = 2_{16}$$

```
        7000
        A00
        80
        2
      7A82₁₆
```

Figure 3-16. *Place Value of Hexadecimal Digits in Significant Bit Positions*

Program *Step 4* of operating *Step 9* shows this. Memory location identified by address FE02 is now ready for the data that will be put into the register identified by the instruction 02E0 at location FE00. The data is FF20.

	KEYSTROKE	ADDRESS	DATA
5.	F F 2 0	FE02	FF20
6.	EMDI	FE04	XXXX

Program *Step 6* has now advanced to the next memory location which is awaiting the next instruction which is keystroked in by program *Step 7*.

	KEYSTROKE	ADDRESS	DATA
7.	0 2 0 1	FE04	0201

Step 10

Continue now to program steps through the end of the program. Note how the address memory location advances by 2 each time EMDI is pressed. This is how the program will be followed when it is run. The starting address FE00 will be loaded into the program counter. The program counter will then count by 2 and advance the microcomputer through each program step as the instructions are completed.

	KEYSTROKE	ADDRESS	DATA
8.	EMDI	FE06	XXXX
9.	F E 2 E	FE06	FE2E
10.	EMDI	FE08	XXXX
11.	0 2 0 C	FE08	020C
12.	EMDI	FE0A	XXXX
13.	0 1 2 0	FE0A	0120
14.	EMDI	FE0C	XXXX
15.	1 D 0 0	FE0C	*1d00
16.	EMDI	FE0E	XXXX
17.	0 6 9 1	FE0E	0691
18.	EMDI	FE10	XXXX
19.	1 E 0 0	FE10	1E00
20.	EMDI	FE12	XXXX
21.	0 6 9 1	FE12	0691
22.	EMDI	FE14	XXXX
23.	1 D 0 1	FE14	*1d01
24.	EMDI	FE16	XXXX
25.	0 6 9 1	FE16	0691
26.	EMDI	FE18	XXXX
27.	1 E 0 1	FE18	1E01
28.	EMDI	FE1A	XXXX
29.	0 6 9 1	FE1A	0691
30.	EMDI	FE1C	XXXX
31.	1 D 0 2	FE1C	*1d02

*As displayed on 301 Terminal

Keystroke	Address	Data
32. EMDI	FE1E	XXXX
33. 0 6 9 1	FE1E	0691
34. EMDI	FE20	XXXX
35. 1 E 0 2	FE20	1E02
36. EMDI	FE22	XXXX
37. 0 6 9 1	FE22	0691
38. EMDI	FE24	XXXX
39. 1 D 0 3	FE24	*1d03
40. EMDI	FE26	XXXX
41. 0 6 9 1	FE26	0691
42. EMDI	FE28	XXXX
43. 1 E 0 3	FE28	1E03
44. EMDI	FE2A	XXXX
45. 0 6 9 1	FE2A	0691
46. EMDI	FE2C	XXXX
47. 1 0 E F	FE2C	10EF
48. EMDI	FE2E	XXXX
49. 1 F 0 4	FE2E	1F04
50. EMDI	FE30	XXXX
51. 1 3 0 5	FE30	1305
52. EMDI	FE32	XXXX
53. 0 2 0 3	FE32	0203
54. EMDI	FE34	XXXX
55. F F F F	FE34	FFFF
56. EMDI	FE36	XXXX
57. 0 6 0 3	FE36	0603
58. EMDI	FE38	XXXX
59. 1 6 F E	FE38	16FE
60. EMDI	FE3A	XXXX
61. 0 4 5 B	FE3A	*045b
62. EMDI	FE3C	XXXX
63. 0 2 0 3	FE3C	0203
64. EMDI	FE3E	XXXX
65. 3 F F F	FE3E	3FFF
66. EMDI	FE40	XXXX
67. 0 6 0 3	FE40	0603
68. EMDI	FE42	XXXX
69. 1 6 F E	FE42	16FE
70. EMDI	FE44	XXXX
71. 0 4 5 B	FE44	*045b
72. EMDI	FE46	XXXX

Step 11

All the program steps are now entered. It remains to run the program, that is, send the microcomputer through its sequenced steps to determine if it will accomplish the task.

Recall, that the system must be set to the initial conditions and to the starting point. This means that the system must start at memory address FE00 because that is where the first instruction is located.

Inside the microcomputer there is a register (a temporary storage location for 16 bits) that always contains the address of an instruction. It was previously noted that as the memory location of instructions was incremented by 2 as the program was entered, so also will the program counter be incremented by 2 by the microcomputer to go to the next instruction. Therefore, the initial conditions are accomplished by loading the program counter with the address location FE00. This is accomplished by an EPC key on the microterminal. The EPC (enter program counter) key changes the value of the program counter. It will enter into the program counter the value that is in the data register of the microterminal display.

The DPC (display program counter) key on the microterminal is depressed to determine if the correct value has been entered into the program counter because it displays the current value of the program counter.

The RUN key is depressed to begin execution of the program starting with the address in the program counter.

To run the program, go through *Steps 1* thru *5.*

KEYSTROKE	ADDRESS	DATA
1. CLR	—	—
2. F/− E 0 0	—	FE00
3. EPC	—	FE00
4. DPC	—	FE00
5. RUN	—	run

VOILA!

The first encounter task is being accomplished. Switching the toggle switch will change the rate of the segment display.

Under program control output logic levels on a set of output lines have been set to a "1", held for a time, set to a "0", held for a time, etc. in a particular sequence. The delay between "1s" and "0s" also is under program control. Such output levels then have been interfaced to driver circuits to accomplish a given task — in this case lighting LED segments of a display.

Step 12

To stop the program, depress H/S . The RESET switch on the microcomputer could also be pressed. (However, in doing so, to return to the program, go through the initial five steps of running the program at the end of operating *Step 10*.) The program may be started again by depressing RUN after it was halted by H/S .

Step 13

If for some reason the first encounter task is not being accomplished after completing *Step 10*, the program can be checked by entering FE00, the beginning address and depress EMA . The contents of memory and the instruction at FE00 will be displayed. Each memory location can then be examined by depressing EMDI and reading the display. In this manner, the program can be examined for an error. When the error is located, the correct data can be entered as it was in the original program and EMD is pressed. The program can then be run by returning to the initial sequence of operating *Step 11*.

The program may be entered at any valid address by entering the address and pressing EMA and then proceeding step by step with EMDI . There is no need to go back to the beginning address each time.

HOW WAS IT DONE?

The question naturally arises — how was this task accomplished by the microcomputer, and more importantly, how was the task taken from idea to the actual program? How does one know what to tell the microcomputer to do?

Of course, this will take a great deal of study of this book and much operation of systems, starting with the TM990/100M-1 microcomputer. The way the *idea* is turned into a *program* for the first encounter is covered in the remaining part of this chapter. This is a good foundation for building knowledge of the 9900 microprocessor, applying the 990/100M microcomputer to many other tasks, and understanding the use of the 9900 in solving other types of problems.

BACK TO BASICS

The process of understanding how the task was taken from idea to instructions for the microcomputer begins by returning to some basic concepts to assure that these are understood.

Recall that *Figure 3-4* identified the functional blocks of our microcomputer. The central processing unit includes the 9900 microprocessor. Examining *Figure 3-5* further and the functional block diagram of *Figure 3-17* shows that the 990/100M microcomputer is bus oriented. Recall that a bus is one or more conductors running in parallel which are used for sending information. The 9900 microprocessor sends an address to memory, to identify data required, on the 15-bit address bus. It receives data from memory on a 16-bit data bus. It should be noted that the same 15-bit address bus goes to the input/output interface units. The address bus is used either to send an address to *memory* or an address to *input/output*, not both at the same time. When the signal $\overline{\text{MEMEN}}$ is a logic low, the address bus is for memory. If the address bus is not for memory then it can be used by I/O. When the address is for I/O, the selection of which lines will be inputs or outputs is under control of the 9900.

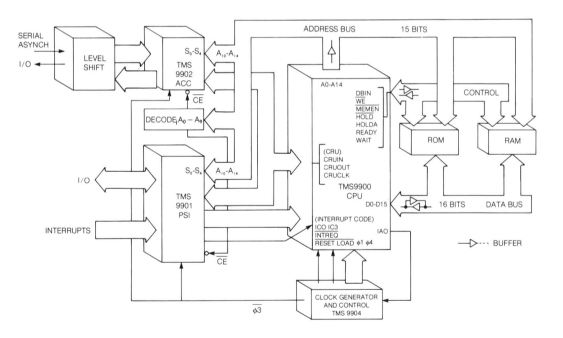

Figure 3-17. *Functional Diagram of TM 990/100M-1 Microcomputer*

Therefore, lines to accept data as input, or to deliver output data are selected by address bits in the same fashion that address bits locate data in a memory.

Examination of the architecture of the 9900 microcomputer in *Figure 3-18* reveals, as in *Figure 3-17,* the address bus, the data bus, signals for the CRU (the Communications Register Unit is an I/O interface for the 9900 architecture), signals for interrupt, control signals and master timing signals. Each of these are external signals. Further examination of internal parts is required to expand on more basic concepts, with emphasis on the ones that are used for the first encounter task.

REGISTERS

Recall that a register is a temporary storage unit for digital information. Inside the 9900 there are these types of registers: a memory address register, a source data register (data register), an instruction register, an interrupt register, some auxiliary registers like T_1 and T_2, and the registers that will be most applicable to the first encounter — the program counter, the workspace register, the status register and a shift register used as part of the hardware to select the input and output terminals. Additional parts include: **1)** the ALU — it is the arithmetic and logic unit that performs arithmetic functions, logic and comparisons. **2)** Multiplexers that direct the data over the correct path as a result of signals from the control ROM and control circuitry. **3)** Timing circuits so that all operations are synchronized by the master timing.

Every time a piece of information is required to be stored in memory or retrieved (fetched) from memory, the memory must be told where the data is located or to be located. The memory address register holds the address to be put on the address bus for this purpose.

Data fetched from memory is received either by the source data register and distributed by the 9900 microprocessor as required, or by the instruction register when it is an instruction. The instruction is decoded and transmitted to the control ROM which sequences through microinstructions previously programmed into the control ROM to execute the instruction. The instruction might be "Increment register 1 by two". Instruction steps take the data from register 1 to the ALU which adds "2" and returns the data to register 1.

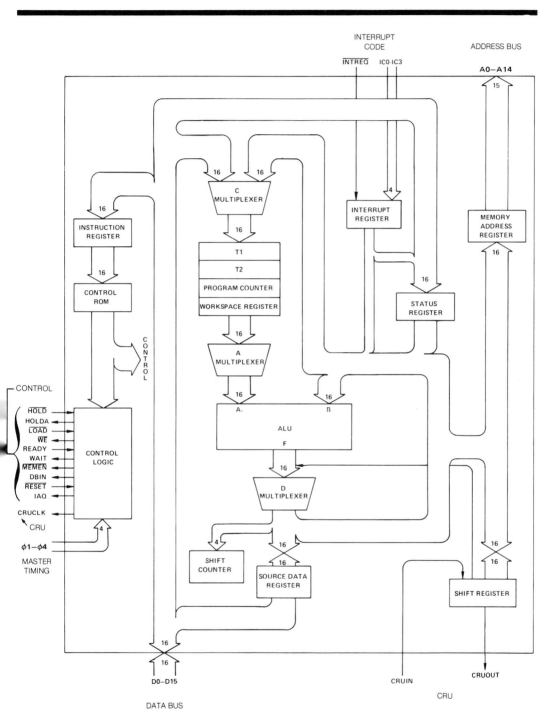

Figure 3-18. *Architecture of 9900 Microprocessor*

Two registers of significant concern for the first encounter task are the status register and the workspace register. The status register is just what the name implies. The 9900 microprocessor continually checks on how things are going (the status) by following instructions that command it to check various bits of the status register. *Figure 3-19* shows the bits of the status register.

0	1	2	3	4	5	6	7	8	9	10	11	12	13	14	15
ST0	ST1	ST2	ST3	ST4	ST5	ST6			not used (=0)			ST12	ST13	ST14	ST15
L>	A>	=	C	O	P	X							Interrupt Mask		

Figure 3-19. Status Register

Each bit of the first 7 bits is concerned with identifying that a particular operation or event has or has not occurred as shown here.

BIT	PURPOSE	BIT	PURPOSE
0	Logical Greater Than	4	Overflow
1	Arithmetic Greater Than	5	Parity
2	Equal	6	XOP
3	Carry	12-15	Interrupt Mask

The last 4 bits are concerned with the interrupt signals and a priority code associated with the interrupts.

The first encounter uses bit 2, the "equals" status bit to change the time delay in the LED sequence.

WORKSPACE

The workspace register is the same as the other registers, but it is used in a special way. As the 9900 microprocessor and the microcomputer step through program instructions, there is a need to have more registers than those available on the 9900. Instead of providing these registers in the 9900, a file of registers is set up in memory and a reference to this file saved in the workspace register. One of the rules in setting up this file is that it will always contain 16 registers in 16 contiguous (one following another in sequence) memory words. The workspace register on the 9900 is called the workspace pointer because, as shown in *Figure 3-20*, it contains the address of the first memory word in the contiguous register file, referred to for the application of the 9900 and in this book as "workspace registers" or just "workspace". The register file can be located anywhere within RAM that seems appropriate. In the total available memory space, there are certain reserved spaces for RAM, others for ROM, and others for special instructions. Therefore, the register file can only be set up in certain portions of memory. So, where 0200_{16} to $021E_{16}$ are the 16 locations shown in *Figure 3-20a*, with the workspace pointer being 0200_{16}, the file could have started at 0300_{16} and extended to $031E_{16}$ as long as these are allowable locations in the overall memory matrix. The workspace pointer would contain 0300_{16} in the second case.

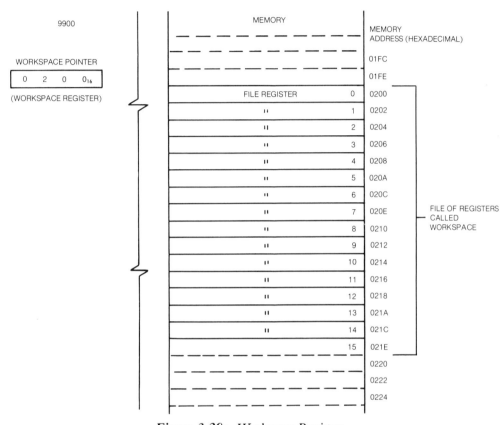

Figure 3-20a. Workspace Registers

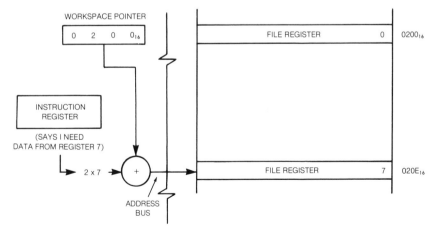

Figure 3-20b. Locating Specific Register

To locate a specific register in the workspace file, the 9900 microprocessor adds the register number to the workspace pointer address to obtain the address of the specific register in the file that is required. (It actually adds 2R, where R is the register number, so that the addresses advance by even numbers. The odd number addresses are used when the word contents are to be processed in 8-bit bytes.) For example, if register 7 contains the information required by the 9900 microprocessor, then the address 020E in *Figure 3-20a* is obtained by adding 14 to the workspace pointer at 0200_{16}. This is shown in *Figure 3-20b.* In like fashion, if the workspace pointer contained 0300_{16}, then adding 14 to 0300_{16} gives $030E_{16}$ the address of register 7, the 7th register down in the file.

Recall that to accomplish the first encounter task, logic levels on output lines had to be set to a "1" or a "0" in order for the LED drivers to turn on or turn-off the LED segment respectively. Recall, also, that the particular output lines could be selected. To understand how this is done, refer to *Figure 3-21*. This figure is divided into three bounded regions; the TMS 9900, Memory, and the TMS 9901. The output line from the 9900 microprocessor that will do the setting is the line "CRUOUT." It is coupled to the TMS 9901, the programmable systems interface.

The TMS 9901 contains more functional parts to handle the interrupt code and interrupt input signals but for now the part that is important is that shown in *Figure 3-21.* The portion shown is a demultiplexer. The data appearing at CRUOUT is strobed by CRUCLK into latches feeding the output pins. The particular latch and the particular output line is selected by the code that exists on the select bit lines S_0, S_1, S_2, S_3, and S_4, which, as shown in *Figure 3-21*, are the address lines A_{10} through A_{14}. The code on S_0 through S_4, and the CRU logic selects the output latch and line that is to be set. The "1" or "0" on CRUOUT does the setting. The latching occurs when CRUCLK strobes the data in.

SBZ AND SBO INSTRUCTIONS

Enough basics have now been covered to begin understanding several of the important instructions for the first encounter task. *Figure 3-21* will again be used and will be followed from left to right and top to bottom starting with the upper left corner. At a particular step in the program, controlled by the program counter, the instruction address (the bit contents of the program counter) is sent to memory over the address bus to obtain the instruction. Memory is read and the instruction is received by the 9900 on the data bus and placed in the instruction register. Via the control ROM and the control logic, the instruction is interpreted as an SBO instruction — "set CRU bit to one." The 9900 is designed so that it generates the correct S_0-S_4 address for the TMS9901 that selects the output line to be set to a "1" by the instruction. However, as indicated in *Figure 3-21,* first an ALU operation must occur before the correct address is obtained. The ALU adds the contents of one of the registers in the file, workspace register 12 (WR12), to a portion of the instruction, SBO. This portion of the SBO instruction is identified as DISP (meaning displacement) in *Figure 3-21.* It identifies the specific line to be used in the 9901 for the output. Eight bits are used for the signed displacement (7 and a sign). Bits 3 through 14 are used from the workspace register 12.

After the ALU operation, the address is sent out on the address bus. Because the $\overline{\text{MEMEN}}$ line is not active, this tells the 9901 that the address is for I/O. All 15 address bits are there; however, only A_3 through A_{14} are used for the effective CRU address. A_{10} through A_{14} provide S_0 through S_4 for the 9901, while bits A_0 through A_9 are used for decoding additional I/O as shown in *Figure 3-17.* A_0, A_1, and A_2 are set to zero for all CRU data transfer operations.

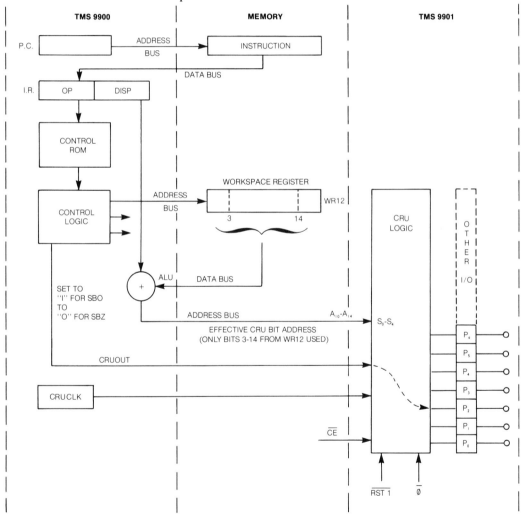

Figure 3-21. *CRU Concept — Single Bit Output SBO or SBZ on CRUOUT.*

I/O SELECTION

The codes required on S_0 through S_4 that select a specific output or input in the 9901 are shown in *Figure 3-22*. To make it convenient, the P_0 line will be used for bit zero of the output or input, P_1 for bit one, P_2 for bit 2, P_3 for bit 3 and P_4 for bit 4. Therefore, to select the line for P_0, the code on S_0 through S_4 must be 1 0000. Rather than starting at select bit 0, the output sequence is started at select bit 16. Adding 32_{10} (base ten) to the contents of the file register 12 accomplishes this. This is 10_{16} in Hex code times two, to shift it into bits 3 through 14.

What do the contents of register 12 indicate? They identify the particular 9901 used. Referring back to *Figure 3-17*, it is noted that several I/O units are connected to the address bus of the microcomputer TM990/100M-1. In order for the decoder to activate the correct $\overline{CE}$ signal to enable the right I/O, a base address is assigned to each I/O unit. The software base address for the 9901 on the microcomputer is 0100_{16}. The hardware base address is 0080_{16}.

Figure 3-23 summarizes the ALU operation. Workspace register 12 contains the software base address of the 9901 on board the microcomputer. The signed displacement of $+10_{16}$ is located in the instruction register as part of the SBO instruction. These two pieces are added together by the ALU and the result placed in the address register. Note that the ALU uses only the bits from 3 to 14 of the software base address to get the hardware base address, adds the displacement, and that the effective CRU address is bits 0 through 14. Bit 15 becomes a "don't care" bit.

SELECT BIT	S_0	S_1	S_2	S_3	S_4	INPUTS	OUTPUTS
0	0	0	0	0	0		
15	0	1	1	1	1		
16	1	0	0	0	0	P_0IN	P_0OUT
17	1	0	0	0	1	P_1IN	P_1OUT
18	1	0	0	1	0	P_2IN	P_2OUT
19	1	0	0	1	1	P_3IN	P_3OUT
20	1	0	1	0	0	P_4IN	P_4OUT
21	1	0	1	0	1	P_5IN	P_5OUT
22	1	0	1	1	0	P_6IN	P_6OUT
23	1	0	1	1	1	P_7IN	P_7OUT
24	1	1	0	0	0	P_8IN	P_8OUT
25	1	1	0	0	1	P_9IN	P_9OUT
26	1	1	0	1	0	P_{10}IN	P_{10}OUT
27	1	1	0	1	1	P_{11}IN	P_{11}OUT
28	1	1	1	0	0	P_{12}IN	P_{12}OUT
29	1	1	1	0	1	P_{13}IN	P_{13}OUT
30	1	1	1	1	0	P_{14}IN	P_{14}OUT
31	1	1	1	1	1	P_{15}IN	P_{15}OUT

Figure 3-22. I/O Selection in TMS 9901

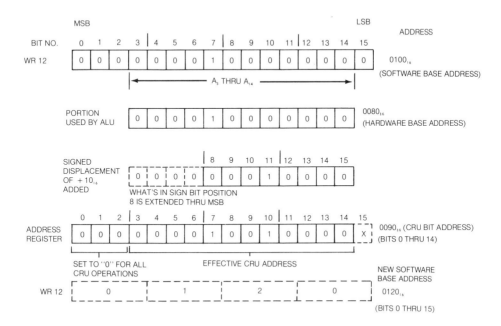

Figure 3-23. Generating the Output Line Address for the 9901

Recall that the software base address assigned to the 9901 is 0100_{16} but this is to be changed by the added displacement of 10_{16}. If all of WR 12 were used, the sum would be 0110_{16}. Because the signed displacement addition occurs with bit 15 neglected, the effective CRU address sent to the 9901 for bits A_0 through A_{14} is 0090_{16}, the hardware base address of 0080_{16} plus the 10_{16} displacement. Had bit 15 not been neglected, the sum would appear as shifted over one bit position or 0120_{16}.

Additional displacement will have to be added to the 10_{16} displacement to obtain the correct code for P_1, P_2 and P_3 shown in *Figure 3-22*. To be able to add a displacement of "0" for the zero bit, 1 for the one bit, 2 for the two bit, 120_{16} is used as the software base address in workspace register 12 right from the start.

From the past discussion, it should be quite clear now that one of the 32 outputs or inputs can be selected by including this information with the SBO instruction, and that a particular 9901 (if there were more than one) is selected by programming the correct base address into the workspace register 12.

Referring back to *Figure 3-21*, a SBZ — "Set CRU bit to Zero" — instruction is the same as the SBO instruction except that the output latch is now set to a "0" rather than a "1". Note in particular in both of these instructions that only one bit is set at a time. An instruction must be included for each bit to be set when using SBO and SBZ.

TB INSTRUCTION

Besides setting logic levels on output pins, an additional system requirement for the first encounter task is to receive an input on an input line. One way of accomplishing this is to have the 9900 microprocessor look at a selected input line, bring the information present at a specified time into the 9900 and then examine the information, or test it, to determine if the information was a "1" or a "0". The TB instruction, "Test CRU Bit", accomplishes bringing the information into the 9900. Subsequent instructions are added to determine if the information was a "1" or a "0".

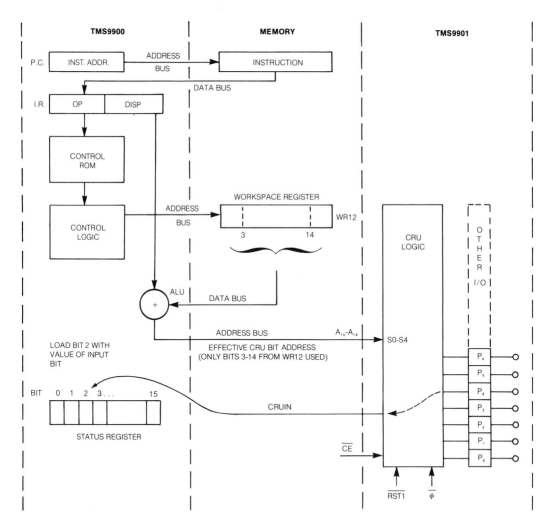

Figure 3-24. CRU Concept-Single Bit TB Input on CRUIN

The selection of the particular line in the I/O unit is the first concern. *Figure 3-24* shows that this is done in the same way as just explained for the SBO and SBZ instructions. The same portions of the 9901 are used as for the SBO or SBZ instructions except now these portions are a data selector. Data is selected from one of multiple input lines and sent to the 9900 microprocessor along the CRUIN line. The value of the information on the line is placed in bit 2 position of the status register. As discussed previously for the status register, instructions must follow the TB instruction that will examine bit 2 of the status register to determine what to do if this bit is a "1" and what to do if it is a "0". Conditional jump instructions are used to make the decision based on the value of the data. Note again that this is done one bit at a time.

Accomplishing a TB instruction requires that a base address be given for the particular input or output line desired. This hardware base address adjusted to a software base address is placed in workspace register 12. With the TB instruction, a displacement is given that identifies the particular line which needs to be sampled. This again is the same as for SBO. The line selected provides data straight through to the CRUIN line — there are no latches, as with the output data.

Thus, the basic concepts studied have shown the means of getting data to the output and bringing data in from an input — one bit at a time. They have shown how data is located, read, transferred, stored, and operated on arithmetically. With this, it should be possible now to get the first encounter idea into a sequence of steps — a program for the microcomputer to follow.

IDEA TO FLOWCHART

Bringing the idea from concept to program begins with a concept level diagram as shown in *Figure 3-25*. It has been decided that the microcomputer is to do the first encounter task; turn on and off 4 lights in sequence, with a time delay between each light activation.

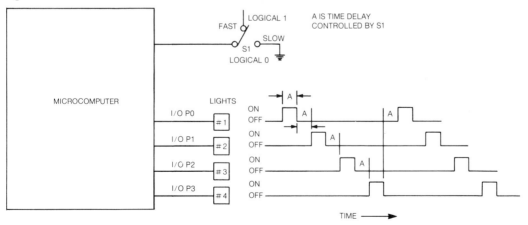

Figure 3-25. Concept Level Diagram

The time delay is to be under control of an external switch.

Understanding the basic concepts of the microcomputer led to the discussion that output lines could be selected and set to standard TTL logic levels to control drivers that would light the lights. In like fashion, a standard TTL logic level signal could be brought to the microcomputer as an input and examined. With this information, a decision could be made to vary the time delay. If the input is a "1," the lights would go on and off at a fast sequence. If the input is a "0," the sequence rate would be slow.

Obviously, other mechanical decisions also were made, such as:

1) The lights would be segments of a 7 segment light emitting diode numerical display because of the compatible packaging and ease of availability.

2) The microcomputer output pins, I/O identification and light number to 7 segment display segment were set as follows:

990/100M	9901 I/O	Light No.	Display Segment	Note
P_4 Connector				
20	P_0	1	f	
22	P_1	2	b	
14	P_2	3	e	
16	P_3	4	c	
18	P_4			to S_1

(These pin identifications are obtained from the schematics in the TM990/100M User's Guide and data sheet information on the TIL303.)

The microterminal TM990/301 was selected as the unit to use for communication with the microcomputer because of its low cost and ease of use. Terminals such as a TTY and a 743 KSR can be used and an application shown in Chapter 8 takes up this type interface.

FLOWCHARTS

The problem solution proceeds from concept to program by constructing a well defined flowchart to follow in an organized fashion while generating the sequence of steps required for the microcomputer to complete the task. *Figure 3-26* is such a flowchart of the first encounter task.

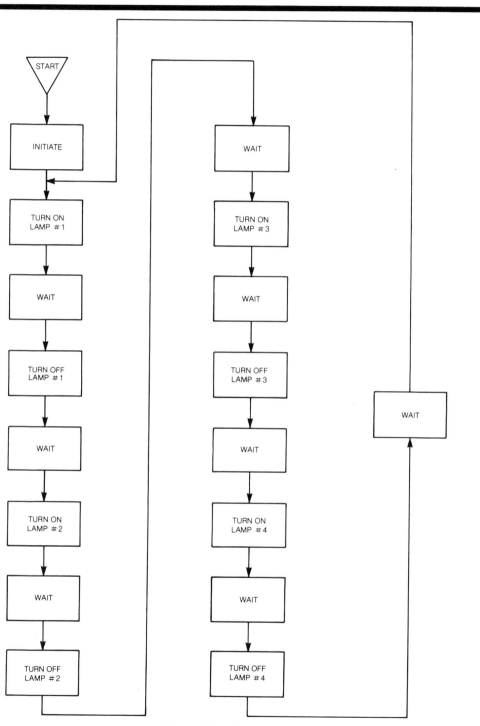

Figure 3-26. *Flowchart*

From START, which requires initial conditions, and a signal to begin — INITIATE — the task is diagrammed. Each light is turned on, the time delay occurs, the light is turned off, the time delay occurs, the next light is turned on, etc. The sequence continues until all lights have been turned on and off and the program begins again.

WAIT Subroutine

Note the time delay is identified as WAIT and it occurs over and over again in the sequence. Because of this, separate steps will be written for this sequence only one time rather than repeating it over and over in the program. In this manner, the main sequence of steps, the main program, can be directed to this identified set of steps, called a subroutine, by an instruction. The main program is then said to branch to the subroutine until it completes the steps in the subroutine, then it returns to the main program.

In simpler terms, the WAIT block of the flowchart requires a given number of program steps, say X. WAIT occurs 8 times in the flowchart. Instead of rewriting the X steps 8 times in the program, the X steps are written once, given the name WAIT, and referred to 8 times.

Because WAIT is a subroutine, a separate flowchart *(Figure 3-27)* is generated for it. In addition, the time delay is to be varied by the switch S_1, therefore, different steps are followed if the switch is "on" with a value of a logical "1" or "off" with a value of a logical "0". Note that when the subroutine WAIT is encountered, the first thing that occurs is to find out the position of the switch. Is it a logical "1" or a logical "0?" A decision is made on the basis of what is found. "Yes, the switch is on," (logical "1") makes the time delay short and the sequence fast. "No, the switch is off," (logical "0") makes the time delay long and the sequence slow.

There are a number of ways to provide a time delay. This flowchart uses one of the simplest — load a register with a number, keep subtracting one (decrementing) from the number until the number is zero. The number of cycles it takes to get the number to zero times the time for each cycle is the time delay. Larger numbers, longer counts, provide longer delays.

Each arm of the flowchart contains the same type of sequence, loading the number; decrementing; checking for zero; if not zero, jumping back and decrementing again; if zero, returning to the main program. Note that in the flowchart there is a branch decision and a branch decision with a jump back or a loop. The program runs in this loop until it comes to a condition where it can get out of the loop or "exit from the loop."

Subroutine Jump

Special things happen when a subroutine such as WAIT is encountered in the main program. *Figure 3-28* diagrams the steps. The main program has executed from *Step 1* to *Step 5*. At *Step 6*, the computer encounters the instruction telling it to branch to subroutine A and do subroutine A. Therefore, in order to return to the correct location in the main program after executing the subroutine, the branch instruction at *Step 6* also tells the computer to remember the address of *Step 7*.

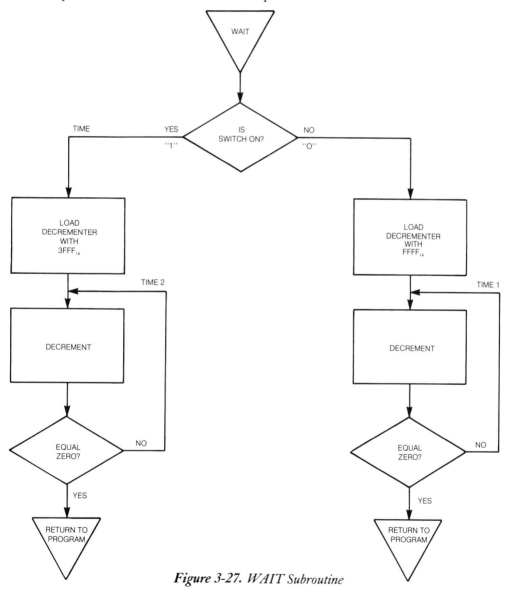

Figure 3-27. WAIT Subroutine

The subroutine is executed through *Step A-8.* Whereupon the computer encounters an instruction at *Step A-9* that tells it to return to the *Step 7* address which it remembered at *Step 6.* In this fashion, each subroutine can be executed and program control returned to the main program. Of course, there are branches that can occur from a subroutine to another subroutine but the principle is the same.

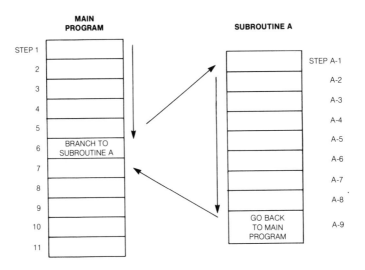

Figure 3-28. *Branch to Subroutine*

The instruction from the TM990/100M microcomputer instruction set that accomplishes the branch to a subroutine is called *Branch* and *Link.* This is called a "subroutine jump" instruction and will be identified by the letters BL and some additional information that tells the location of the address of the first instruction of the subroutine. In addition, recall that a register file is to be set up for general registers. Well, register 11 of this file (WR 11) is the storage place used to remember the main program address that is returned to after executing the subroutine.

The return instruction from the subroutine used is called an unconditional branch instruction. It is identified by *Branch.* Since the contents of register 11 must be returned to the program counter to return from a subroutine, this instruction will be identified as B*11. Note that the file register 11 must be reserved for this use by the programmer, otherwise its contents are likely to be changed at the wrong time and the computer misled into a wrong sequence.

A Loop Within the WAIT Subroutine

Within the WAIT subroutine is another common reoccurring concept — a loop. However, before examining this program sequence further, it would be beneficial to clearly understand the meaning of the blocks in the flow charts. The general meaning of the most commonly used blocks is shown in *Figure 3-29.* There is a symbol for the entry to or exit from a program (or for an off-page connection). This is identified with an appropriate symbol or label — START and STOP in this example. Rectangles identify operations. Inside the rectangle is an appropriate abbreviated statement to describe the operation. Decisions are identified with a diamond. Since programmed logic occurs in sequence, these blocks are relatively simple. A two-state decision answers a question of yes or no, true or false, etc. A three-state decision answers a comparison question of greater than, equal to, or less than (of course, there could be further mixtures of these). So decision blocks have appropriate questions identifying them.

In the WAIT subroutine of *Figure 3-27,* the first decision is "Is the switch ON?," and the consequences have already been discussed. The second decision has the question "The quantity examined — is it equal to zero?" Within this program sequence, if the quantity is not equal to zero, then the program goes through the same path again.

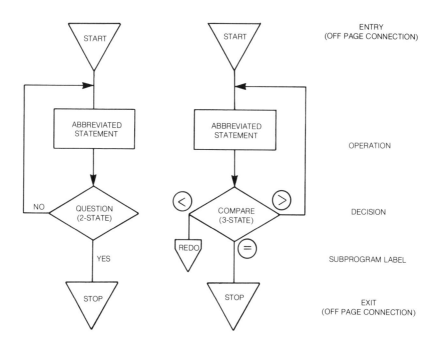

Figure 3-29. Common Flow Chart Blocks

The program loop is accomplished by a branch instruction from the instruction set called a conditional jump instruction. The conditional jump causes the microcomputer program to branch to a specified program step depending on the condition of certain bits in the status register. Recall in *Figure 3-19* that the status bits were identified and that the "equals bit" — bit 2 — was going to be used to change the time delay sequence. Therefore, the decision block in the program is really asking, "Is bit 2 of the status register set to a "1"?"

The status bit 2 is set to 1 by the program step before the decision block in *Figure 3-27* — the decrement step. An instruction *Decrement (by One)* causes a named file register to have one subtracted from its contents, comparison of the result to zero and the setting of the appropriate status bits (0-4) of the status register. When the register contents are equal to zero, the "equals" status bit (2) will be set to a "1".

When the status bit 2 is not set to a "1", the program must return to the decrement instruction and subtract one again from the register. JNE (label) is the conditional jump instruction that will be used to accomplish the loop. It is activated by the "equals bit" being "0". The program will jump to a point ahead of the decrement step which will be identified with an appropriate label. In the program this label must be included with the JNE *(Jump if not equal)* instruction.

A similar type of conditional jump instruction is used to answer the question of the switch in the first decision block of the WAIT subroutine. However, in this case, *Jump if Equal* (JEQ (label)), with the appropriate label will be used. Now the conditional jump will occur if the equal bit is set to a "1". Recall, this is the type instruction previously referred to that must follow the TB instruction so that the status bit can be examined and a decision made.

The number of steps in the decrement block is now the only remaining portion of the subroutine which has not been discussed.

LOADING A REGISTER FOR THE TIME DELAY

Assume that the switch is "ON" in the WAIT routine. A logical "1" is the input to the microcomputer. The TB instruction identifies the logical "1" and it sets the equals bit 2 of the status register to a "1" as previously described. The JEQ instruction jumps to a selected (labeled) instruction which loads a selected file register with a number, $3FFF_{16}$. As a 16 bit binary number, it is 0011 1111 1111 1111. No jump occurs in the program if the switch is inputting a logical "0". The program just proceeds to the next step.

Well, how does the data get loaded into the selected file register? Simply enough with a load instruction which is one of the data transfer instructions. *Load Immediate* (file register number), $3FFF_{16}$ will tell the microcomputer to load the hexadecimal number $3FFF_{16}$ into the selected register. What actually happens is that two memory words must be used for this instruction. The first word provides the operation code and register number and the second word the operand or data to be operated on. For the addressing mode used for the *Load Immediate* instruction, the word following the instruction LI 3, will contain the data to be put into register 3, $3FFF_{16}$. The programmer must remember that a memory word location $(PC + 2)$ is used for the $3FFF_{16}$ data when the instruction is located at PC.

Following on then, new data is placed into the same register by a new *Load Immediate* instruction. For example, for a longer time delay, the file register R3 is loaded with $FFFF_{16}$. The instruction LI 3, $FFFF_{16}$ accomplishes this.

WHERE DOES THE PROGRAM START?

Most of the information is now in hand to write the program. The question is, "Where does the program start"? Recall that when the program was entered into the microcomputer through the microterminal, $FE00_{16}$ was chosen as the starting memory location. How was this decided?

The first step in the decision is to determine what words are available in memory — what addresses can be used.

Figure 3-30 is reproduced from the TM 990/100M Users Guide. There are address locations from 0000_{16} to $FFFE_{16}$ for 65,536 bytes (8-bit pieces), or 32,768 16-bit word locations. This is commonly called the address space. Word address locations move by an increment of 2, byte locations by 1. The incrementing of the program counter by 2 was previously noted. This is the reason.

Recall that the TM 990/100M microcomputer has 256 16-bit words of RAM into which the program is going to be placed and it also has 1024 16-bit words of ROM, or EPROM in this case. The EPROM is the TIBUG monitor that provides the necessary pre-programmed instructions that were referred to for accepting input and output data.

The 256 words of RAM occupy address space from $FE00_{16}$ to $FFFE_{16}$ as shown in *Figure 3-30*. The EPROM address space is from 0000_{16} through $07FE_{16}$ which is address space that is dedicated for this purpose and not available for change by the first encounter program. Notice that within this space are interrupt and XOP vectors. These are of no concern at this time.

Since not all the available memory sockets are filled, address space from 0800_{16} through $FDFE_{16}$ does not have memory cells — it is unpopulated.

It would seem that all the address spaces in RAM from $FE00_{16}$ to $FFFE_{16}$ are available. However, as shown in *Figure 3-30,* 40 words of RAM must be reserved for use by the TIBUG monitor and additional space is necessary for interrupts. Thus, the available space is from $FE00_{16}$ to $FF66_{16}$.

Obviously, some analysis of the possible length of the program in number of steps must be made, as well as some estimate of the number of file register blocks of 16 (workspaces) that will be used. This will determine whether adequate address space is available or whether additional memory space must be populated.

The first encounter assumptions are as follows:

1. The program will be less than 96 steps long — 96 words or 192 bytes.

2. Only one workspace will be required. (16 contiguous words)

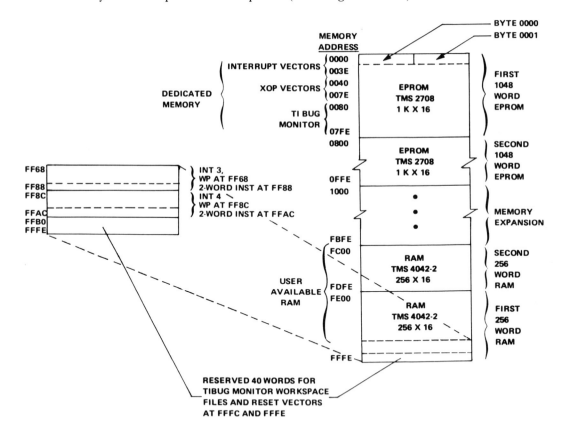

Figure 3-30. Memory Map

On this basis, the starting address of the program is chosen as $FE00_{16}$. The workspace file register could have been chosen to start at 16 words away from $FF66_{16}$. However, since there is plenty of space, it is placed at $FF20_{16}$, leaving the room from $FE00_{16}$ to $FF1E_{16}$ as the space for the program (144 words).

WRITING THE PROGRAM

Refer now to the flowchart in *Figure 3-26* as the basis for writing the program. To help in the organization of the program, a form shown in *Table 3-1* will be used. Note that it has a column for addresses, for machine code, for a label, for the assembly language statement and for comments. Each of these columns will be filled in as needed as the program is developed. Not all columns will have an entry when the program is complete. The machine code will be the last column completed. Of particular importance, especially for later references, or reference by another programmer, will be the comments column. Keep referring to *Table 3-1* after each program step to note the comments and see the program develop.

Figure 3-26 indicates that the first step in the program is to be an initializing statement. The location of the file register (workspace) used must be identified by loading the workspace pointer with the address $FF20_{16}$. The program must at all times know where the file registers are in memory for it will use these registers for obtaining data or addresses.

Reference to Chapter 5 and 6 shows there is a load instruction for the workspace pointer, LWPI, *Load Workspace Pointer Immediate.* Recall that the immediate addressing requires two words. Therefore, *Step 1* of the program at address $FE00_{16}$ is shown as:

Step	A	MC	L	ASSY LANG.
1	FE00			LWPI >FF20

and *Step 2* has the operand to be loaded. The greater than ($>$) sign identifies the data as hexadecimal.

The program must be able to branch to the subroutine WAIT when that routine is called by the program. Therefore, the starting address of the WAIT subroutine must be loaded into a file register which then will be referenced when the address is needed. *Step 3* of the program accomplishes this with a *Load Immediate* instruction and register 1 is chosen to hold the address. Note that the program address is incrementing by two. *Step 3* is:

Step	A	MC	L	ASSY. LANG
3	FE04			LI 1,>XXXX

Note that the specific address cannot be put in at this time — not until the location is known. *Step 4* is the step for loading the operand.

Recall that a reference needs to be established for the particular 9901 I/O interface unit to be used by the microcomputer. This was referred to as the CRU base address for the chosen 9901. Register 12 of the file register is the one that must contain the CRU base address, therefore, it must be loaded with 0120_{16}, the software base address of the 9901 in the TM990/100M microcomputer. Step 5 of the program is for this purpose.

Step	A	MC	L	Assy. Lang.
5	FE08			LI 12, >0120

Again *Step 6* must be added because of the immediate addressing.

All initial conditions are now complete and the flowchart now moves to the start of the light sequence. Light #1 must be turned on. Recall from *Figure 3-25* that light #1 is connected to I/O output 0 (P_0). Therefore, I/O-0 on the 9901 must be set to a "1". This is accomplished with the SBO instruction of *Step 7*. Recall, this instruction was previously discussed in detail. *Step 7* looks like this:

Step	A	MC	L	Assy. Lang.
7	FE0C		BEGIN	SBO 0

Note that this instruction is labeled BEGIN. This is done because the program will jump back to this address location after the complete sequence of the first encounter task is completed. The label BEGIN provides an easy reference to this location.

WAIT SUBROUTINE CALL

The first encounter task as defined now requires the light #1 be held on for the time delay represented by the subroutine WAIT. Therefore, the program must be directed to the first address of the subroutine. This first address is contained in the file register 1 (workspace register 1) because *Step 3* and *Step 4* accomplished this.

Recall the discussion on the WAIT subroutine (*Figure 3-28*). The main program must be directed to the subroutine (the main program "calls" the subroutine) but it must also remember where it is in the main program so it can return to the correct location. The *Branch and Link* to register 1 of *Step 8* accomplishes this.

Step	A	MC	L	Assy. Lang.
8	FE0E			BL *1

At the same time the address of the next step in the program, *Step 9* is being saved in register 11.

However, note that there is a new symbol in the assembly language instruction. The asterisk (*) means that an indirect addressing mode is used. That means that file register 1 (WR1) does not contain operand information but contains the *address* of an operand to be used for further processing. That is exactly what has been put into register 1 — the address of the first instruction of the WAIT subroutine. Therefore, an indirect addressing mode is used.

Why is that important? When the machine code for an instruction is constructed a little later (this will be done by hand but normally it would be done by a computer under control of a program called an assembler), an identifying code for the addressing mode must be used in the format for each instruction.

Figure 3-31 shows how the 16 bits of the machine code are arranged for the various types of instructions. Much more discussion of these formats is contained in Chapters 5 and 6. For the purpose here, format 6 is the one of particular interest for the *Branch and Link* instruction. Note that for format 6 the first 10 bits are for the operation code, bits 10 and 11 are a T_s field, and bits 12 thru 15 are an S field for identifying the address of the source information. Note that the code for T_s defines the addressing mode for the instruction. 01 will be entered in this field for bits 10 and 11 for the *Branch and Link* instruction because this is the code for indirect addressing. 0001 will be the code for the S field because register 1 contains the source address.

RETURN FROM WAIT SUBROUTINE

The end of the subroutine will return the microcomputer to the main program at *Step 9* because this is the address saved in register 11. *Step 9,* according to the flowchart of *Figure 3-26*, must now turn light #1 off. The instruction is:

Step	*A*	*MC*	*L*	*Assy. Lang.*
9	FE10			SBZ 0

Since I/O port 0 was set to a "1" in order to turn the light on, now it is set to a "0" to turn the light off.

Time delay subroutine WAIT is called for again for the next step and again the *Branch and Link* instruction is used. Thus, *Step 10 is:*

Step	*A*	*MC*	*L*	*Assy. Lang.*
10	FE12			BL *1

Upon return from the WAIT subroutine light #2 is turned on, the WAIT routine occurs, light #2 is turned off, the WAIT routine occurs and the process continues until light #4 is turned off and the time delay is complete. These steps are shown in *Table 3-1* and carry the program through *Step 22*.

The program will return to *Step 23* after the time delay. The flowchart indicates a return to the beginning of the sequence. Recall that this was labeled BEGIN. Therefore, *Step 23* is a jump instruction that jumps the program back to the address of the instruction labeled BEGIN. The assembly language instruction is simple enough:

Step	A	MC	L	Assy. Lang.
23	FE2C			JMP BEGIN

This instruction is called an unconditional jump instruction because there are no decisions involved — just the direction to "go to" a specified place. There is no return instruction address saved in register 11 and no testing of status bits.

All the program steps in the flowchart of *Figure 3-26* are now complete. What remains is to define the steps in the subroutine WAIT. *Figure 3-27* is used for this purpose.

WAIT SUBROUTINE

The address at *Step 24*, FE2E$_{16}$, is the one that must be loaded into register 1 at *Step 3* because it is the first instruction of the subroutine. The flowchart identifies this step as a decision block. Is the switch on for a logical "1" or is it off for a logical "0"?
The input line must be tested to determine this. A TB instruction, examining I/O pin P$_4$, is used for this purpose. This instruction is *Step 24*:

Step	A	MC	L	Assy. Lang.
24	FE2E			TB 4

This is the *Test Bit* instruction discussed previously. Recall that when the input line is tested by the instruction it sets the "equals" bit, bit 2 of the status register to the value of the input.

In order to make the decision called for in the flowchart, an instruction that examines bit 2 of the status register must follow. This will be a conditional jump instruction because if the status bit is a "1", the time delay is to be the shortest and the sequence fast. Correspondingly, the sequence would be slow and the time delay long for a status bit 2 of "0". Chapters 5 and 6 identify the jump instructions. JEQ is the one selected which says that the program will jump to a new location if the "equals" bit is set to a "1", otherwise, the program will continue on to the next step. The instruction is:

Step	A	MC	L	Assy. Lang.
25	FE30			JEQ TIME

Convenient labels have been placed on the flowchart of *Figure 3-27*. The branch jumped to in *Step 25* is labeled TIME. This branch will be executed in a moment. For now, assume that the "equals" bit is set to "0" and the program continues. The next step is to load a register so that it can be decremented to produce the time delay. In this branch, this must be the largest value for the longest delay and the slowest sequence. Another file register must be selected. Register 3 is chosen and the load instruction is as follows:

Step	A	MC	L	Assy. Lang.
26	FE32			LI 3, >FFFF

This is the same as previous *Load Immediate* instructions and another word must be allowed for the value to be loaded. Thus, *Step 27* at FE34.

One must now be subtracted from the value. There is an instruction called *Decrement (by one)* and, of course, it must tell what value to be decremented. In this case, the contents of R3. Thus, *Step 28* is:

Step	A	MC	L	Assy. Lang.
28	FE3		TIME1	DEC 3

The flowchart shows the decrement as an operation. In addition, as mentioned previously, *the value in register 3 is compared to zero* and the greater than, equal, carry or overflow status bits are set accordingly. This is found in the discussion on the instructions in Chapter 5 and 6.

The decision that follows is made on the basis again of examining the "equals" bit. The flow chart shows that if the "equals" bit is not set, the program will loop back and be decremented again as previously discussed. Therefore, a label, TIME 1, is placed on the instruction at FE36 to tell the program the location of the jump.

The jump occurs this time if the "equals" bit is not set, using the instruction *Jump if Not Equal*, and looks like:

Step	A	MC	L	Assy. Lang.
29	FE38			JNE TIME1

When the file register has been decremented to zero, the equals bit will be set and the program is ready to return to the main program. Recall that register 11 contains the address (location) for the return. The branch instruction used for the return is Branch and *Step 30* is:

Step	A	MC	L	Assy. Lang.
30	FE3A			B *11

Note this again is an indirect addressing mode.

TIME BRANCH

The only remaining portion of the flowchart that must be programmed is the TIME branch.

In this branch, the time delay is shorter to make the sequence faster. R3, the same register, is loaded with a smaller value, $3FFF_{16}$. Again a *Load Immediate* instruction shown in *Step 31* is used.

Step	A	MC	L	Assy. Lang.
31	FE3C		TIME	LI3, >3FFF

This step is labeled with TIME, and will be the location jumped to from *Step 25*. *Step 32* is the extra word required.

The register must again be decremented, therefore, the instruction is the same type as *Step 28*. However, the label for the location to jump to is now TIME2. *Step 33* is:

Step	A	MC	L	Assy. Lang.
33	FE40		TIME2	DEC 3

The same jump instruction is used in this branch as for *Step 29* except the label is now TIME 2. Therefore, *Step 34* is:

Step	A	MC	L	Assy. Lang.
34	FE42			JNE TIME2

When the equals bit is set, the program must return to the main program as with the other branch. The same return instruction as *Step 30* is used, as shown in *Step 35*.

Step	A	MC	L	Assy. Lang.
35	FE44			B *11

The total program is now complete in assembly language. It is shown in *Table 3-1.*

TABLE 3-1
ASSEMBLY LANGUAGE PROGRAM

Table 3-1. Assembly Language Program.

(Source Code Statements)

Step	Hex Address	Hex Machine Code	Label	Op Code	Operand	Comments.
1.	FE00			LWPI	>FF20	Load workspace pointer
2.	FE02					with $FF20_{16}$
3.	FE04			LI	1, >FE2E	Load R1
4.	FE06					with 1st Address of WAIT
5.	FE08			LI	12, >0102	Load R12
6.	FE0A					with base address of 9901, 0120_{16}
7.	FE0C		BEGIN	SBO	0	Set I/O P_0 (segment f) equal to one
8.	FE0E			BL	*1	Branch to address in R1 (saves next address in R11)
9.	FE10			SBZ	0	Set I/O P_0 (segment f) equal to zero
10.	FE12			BL	*1	Branch to address in R1 (saves next address in R11)
11.	FE14			SBO	1	Set I/O P_1 (segment b) equal to one
12.	FE16			BL	*1	Branch to address in R1
13.	FE18			SBZ	1	Set I/O P_1 equal to zero
14.	FE1A			BL	*1	Branch to address in R1
15.	FE1C			SBO	2	Set I/O P_2 (segment e) equal to one
16.	FE1E			BL	*1	Branch to address in R1
17.	FE20			SBZ	2	Set I/O P_2 equal to zero
18.	FE22			BL	*1	Branch to address in R1
19.	FE24			SBO	3	Set I/O P_3 (segment c) equal to one
20.	FE26			BL	*1	Branch to address in R1
21.	FE28			SBZ	3	Set I/O P_3 to equal to zero
22.	FE2A			BL	*1	Branch to address in R1
23.	FE2C			JMP	BEGIN	Jump to BEGIN
24.	FE2E		WAIT	TB	4	Test I/O P_4 for a "1" or a "0"
25.	FE30			JEQ	TIME	If equals bit is set ("1"), jump to TIME
26.	FE32			LI	3, >FFFF	Load R3
27.	FE34					with $FFFF_{16}$
28.	FE36		TIME1	DEC	3	Decrement R3
29.	FE38			JNE	TIME1	Jump to TIME 1 if equals bit is not set
30.	FE3A			B	*11	Return to main program (by way of R11)
31.	FE3C		TIME	LI	3, >3FFF	Load R3
32.	FE3E					with $3FFF_{16}$
33.	FE40		TIME2	DEC	3	Decrement R3
34.	FE42			JNE	TIME2	Jump to TIME 2 if equals bit is not set
35.	FE44			B	*11	Return to main program (by way of R11)

WRITING THE MACHINE CODE

Normally the next step in programming (shown in *Table 3-2*) would be done by
a computer as mentioned previously. However, in order to demonstrate what an
Assembler Program would do and because the program input to the TM990/100M
microcomputer is through the microterminal, which requires the machine code, it will be
a good exercise to demonstrate how to develop the machine code. If this is of no interest,
this portion of the discussion can be bypassed and a jump made to the summary.

As mentioned previously in *Figure 3-31*, there is a set format for the 16 bits of machine
code that must be generated for each instruction. The formats used for the first
encounter task are shown in *Figure 3-32* for reference. Each instruction has an operation
code (OP CODE) and then additional information is required in the various fields of the
format. A complete discussion of the format for each instruction can be found in Chapter
6. *Figure 3-33* lists the instructions used in the first encounter.

The same programming form will be used as before which is summarized to this point in
Table 3-1. The machine code will be filled in and several other changes made and the
result will be the final program of *Table 3-2*. As before, continue to refer to *Table 3-2* as
the machine code is developed.

IMMEDIATE INSTRUCTIONS

The coding begins at *Step 1*. LWPI is an immediate instruction. Therefore, the format 8
of *Figure 3-32* is used. There are two words to this instruction; the second one containing
the immediate value to be loaded. In the first word, the op code occupies bits 0 through
10; register numbers, where the immediate value is going to be placed, occupy bits 12
thru 15. Bit 11 is not used. The op code is obtained from *Figure 3-33* for the LWPI
instruction. The filled out instruction would look like this.

		0 1 2 3	4 5 6 7	8 9 10 11	12 13 14 15
Binary	—	0 0 0 0	0 0 1 0	1 1 1 0	0 0 0 0
Op Code	—	0	2	E	0
Machine Code	—	0	2	E	0

LWPI is a special case of format 8. Bits 11-15 are not used and as such could contain
anything. They are don't care conditions. Therefore, the machine code is 02E0. This
is entered into *Table 3-2* on the same line as LWPI as *Step 1*. *Step 2* is the immediate
value FF20, therefore, the machine code is $FF20_{16}$.

FORMAT (USE)

	0	1	2	3	4	5	6	7	8	9	10	11	12	13	14	15
1 (ARITH)	OP CODE		B	T_D			D				T_S		S			
2 (JUMP)	OP CODE						SIGNED DISPLACEMENT°									
3 (LOGICAL)	OP CODE					D				T_S		S				
4 (CRU)	OP CODE					C				T_S		S				
5 (SHIFT)	OP CODE					C						W				
6 (PROGRAM)	OP CODE										T_S		S			
7 (CONTROL)	OP CODE									NOT USED						
8 (IMMEDIATE)	OP CODE									NU		W				
	IMMEDIATE VALUE															
9 (MPY, DIV,XOP)	OP CODE						D			T_S		S				

KEY

B = BYTE INDICATOR
   (1 = BYTE, 0 = WORD)
T_D = D ADDR. MODIFICATION
D = DESTINATION ADDR.
T_S = S ADDR. MODIFICATION

S = SOURCE ADDR.
C = XFR OR SHIFT LENGTH (COUNT)
W = WORKSPACE REGISTER NO.
° = SIGNED DISPLACEMENT OF − 128 TO + 127 WORDS
NU = NOT USED

Figure 3-31. Instruction Formats

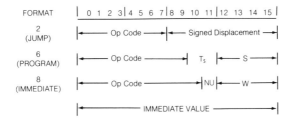

FORMAT	0 1 2 3 4 5 6 7 8 9 10 11 12 13 14 15
2 (JUMP)	◄─── Op Code ───► ◄─── Signed Displacement ───►
6 (PROGRAM)	◄─── Op Code ───► T_S ◄─ S ─►
8 (IMMEDIATE)	◄─── Op Code ───►NU◄─ W ───►
	◄─────── IMMEDIATE VALUE ───────►

NOTES:

T_S = SOURCE ADDRESS MODIFICATION
S = SOURCE ADDRESS
W = WORKSPACE (FILE) REGISTER NO.
NU = NOT USED

SIGNED DISPLACEMENT CAN BE
− 128 TO + 127 WORDS

CODES FOR T_S FIELD	ADDRESSING MODE
00	REGISTER
01	INDIRECT
10	INDEXED (S OR D ≠ 0)
10	SYMBOLIC (DIRECT, S OR D = 0)
11	INDIRECT WITH AUTO INCREMENT

Figure 3-32. Formats used for First Encounter

In like fashion, the instructions at *Step 3* and *Step 5* are immediate instructions, use the same format, and are coded with the appropriate register numbers. *Step 4* and *Step 6* are the immediate values to be loaded.

Note, however, that when the program was first prepared, the first address of the WAIT subroutine was not known. Now, it is known. It is substituted for the XXXX in *Table 3-1* at Step 3. Thus, the address of *Step 24*, FE2E is placed after the "greater than" symbol.

The op code for LI is 0200_{16} and since register 1 is used for *Step 3*, the machine code is 0201_{16} while for *Step 5* it is 020C because register 12 is being loaded. The machine code for *Step 4* is the value $FE2E_{16}$ and for *Step 6* it is 0120_{16}.

INSTRUCTIONS SBO, SBZ

The instruction SBO at *Step 7* uses a different format. This is format 2 in *Figure 3-32*. It has the op code in bits 0 through 7 and the signed displacement that was discussed previously when the 9901 I/O unit program was examined. Recall that the CRU base address was arranged so that the bit number is the value that is put in for the signed displacement.

The op code for SBO from *Figure 3-33* is $1D00_{16}$ and with the first bit being zero, the machine code is:

	0 1 2 3	4 5 6 7	8 9 10 11	12 13 14 15
Binary —	0 0 0 1	1 1 0 1	0 0 0 0	0 0 0 0
Op Code —	1	D	0	0
Machine Code —	1	D	0	0

MNEMONIC	HEX OP CODE	FORMAT	RESULT COMPARE TO ZERO	INSTRUCTION
LWPI	02E0	8	N	LOAD IMMEDIATE TO WORKSPACE POINTER
LI	0200	8	N	LOAD IMMEDIATE
BL	0680	6	N	BRANCH AND LINK (WR11)
B	0440	6	N	BRANCH
DEC	0600	6	Y	DECREMENT (BY ONE)
SBO	1D00	2	N	SET CRU BIT TO ONE
SBZ	1E00	2	N	SET CRU BIT TO ZERO
TB	1F00	2	N	TEST CRU BIT
JEQ	1300	2	N	JUMP EQUAL (ST2 = 1)
JMP	1000	2	N	JUMP UNCONDITIONAL
JNE	1600	2	N	JUMP NOT EQUAL (ST2 = 0)
			(ST2 = 0)	

Figure 3-33. Instructions used for First Encounter.

The other SBO instructions can be machine coded accordingly using the appropriate bit number. Therefore, *Step 11* is $1D01_{16}$, *Step 15* is $1D02_{16}$ and *Step 19* is $1D03_{16}$.

Similarly, using the op code of $1E00_{16}$ for the SBZ instructions and the appropriate bit number, *Step 9* is $1E00_{16}$, *Step 13* is $1E01_{16}$, *Step 17* is $1E02_{16}$, and *Step 21* is $1E03_{16}$.

INSTRUCTION BL

Now *Step 8* brings in another new format. For the BL instruction, it is format 6. Bits 0 thru 9 contain the op code. Bits 12 through 15 are the address of the source data. Ts is a field that modifies the source address and it contains the two bits that code the addressing mode that is being used. Recall BL *1 uses indirect addressing. Therefore, from *Figure 3-32* Ts would be 01 for these 2 bits. It's important to remember that this modifies the op code into a different number for the machine code as shown below.

		0 1 2 3	4 5 6 7	8 9 10 11	12 13 14 15
Op Code	—	0	6	8	0
Binary	—	0 0 0 0	0 1 1 0	1 0 0 0	0 0 0 0
T_s				0 1	
S	—				0 0 0 1
Machine Code— (Binary)	—	0 0 0 0	0 1 1 0	1 0 0 1	0 0 0 1
Machine Code— (Hex)	—	0	6	9	1

Thus, the machine code is 0691_{16} and can be placed in *Step 8, 10, 12, 14, 16, 18, 20* and *22*, since register 1 is used in each case.

MISCELLANEOUS INSTRUCTIONS

Because the jump instructions fall into a class that needs special discussion, the remaining instructions will be coded first.

Step 26 and *Step 31* are LI instructions like Step 3 and Step 5 — the code is 0203_{16} in this case because register 3 is being used. Don't forget the values of $FFFF_{16}$ for *Step 27* and $3FFF_{16}$ for *Step 32*.

The TB instruction has an op code of $1F00_{16}$ and a format 2. It is just like the SBO and SBZ so that the bit must be used for the displacement. Bit 4 causes a displacement of 4, therefore, the machine code is $1F04_{16}$. This is *Step 24*.

A branch instruction similar to BL, but does not save the next address in register 11, is the instruction B. It is using the contents of register 11 for a return to the main program. The op code for B is 0440_{16}. It uses an indirect addressing mode so $T_S = 01$ and S is 1011 for register 11. The machine code results as follows:

		0 1 2 3	4 5 6 7	8 9 10 11	12 13 14 15
Op Code	—	0	4	4	0
		0 0 0 0	0 1 0 0	0 1 0 0	0 0 0 0
T_S	—			0 1	
S	—				1 0 1 1
Machine Code (Binary)	—	0 0 0 0	0 1 0 0	0 1 0 1	1 0 1 1
Machine Code (Hex)	—	0	4	5	B

It is entered at *Step 30* and *35.*

The only remaining instruction besides the jump instructions is the decrement instruction DEC. From *Figure 3-33* the op code is 0600_{16} and the format is 6. Register 3 is being used, therefore, S is 0011. The addressing mode is a register mode so T_S is 00 and there is no modification of the op code. The machine code is then 0603_{16} for *Step 28* and *33.*

Jump Instructions

Jump instructions use format 2 of *Figure 3-32* which has an op code for bits 0 through 7 and a signed displacement in bits 8 through 15. The signed displacement means the number of program addresses that the program must move to arrive at the required address. For example, let

A_J = present address of jump instruction
A_D = destination address of jump instruction

then,

    1.) $A_J + 2 \text{ DISP} = A_D$

since the program moves by increments of 2.

However, for the 9900 microprocessor in the TM990/100M microcomputer, the jump instruction signed displacement must be calculated from the address following the address of the jump instruction or $A_J + 2$. Therefore, equation **(1)** becomes,

    2.) $(A_J + 2) + 2 \text{ DISP} = A_D$

Solving for DISP, gives

    3.) $\dfrac{A_D - (A_J + 2)}{2} = \text{DISP}$

Recall that in preparing the program of *Table 3-1* labels were used for instructions so that easy reference could be made to the desired destination address for a jump instruction. *Step 23* at $FE2C_{16}$ is the first jump instruction. The destination is the label BEGIN which is located at address $FE0C_{16}$. Applying equation (3) gives (in Hex)

4.) $DISP = \dfrac{FE0C - (FE2C + 2)}{2}$

5.) $DISP = \dfrac{FE0C - FE2E}{2}$

Now,

$$\begin{array}{r} FE0C \\ -\,FE2E \\ \hline -\,0022_{16} \end{array}$$

Therefore,

6.) $DISP = \dfrac{-22}{2} = -11_{16}$

This means that in the jump instruction the program moves back 11_{16} steps or 17 decimal steps.

Now, since this is a negative number, a two's complement must be used for the code, thus

$$\begin{array}{lr} & -\,0011 \\ \text{COMPLEMENT} & FFEE \\ \text{ADD ONE} & +\,0001 \\ \hline \text{2'S COMPLEMENT} & FFEF \end{array}$$

Now, only the 8 least significant bits are used along with the op code of *Figure 3-33*. JMP of *Step 23* has an op code of 1000_{16}. Therefore, the machine code is:

		0 1 2 3	4 5 6 7	8 9 10 11	12 13 14 15
Op Code	—	1	0	0	0
Displacement	—			E	F
Machine	—	1	0	E	F
Code					

This machine code is entered at *Step 23*.

Step 25 has a JEQ instruction. A_J is $FE30_{16}$. The instruction says to jump to TIME which has an address of FE3C at *Step 31*, therefore, $A_D = FE3C$. Applying equation (3) gives, again in hexadecimal;

$$DISP = \frac{FE3C - FE32}{2} = \frac{10}{2} = 5_{16}$$

JEQ has an op code of 1300 and the machine code then becomes:

	0 1 2 3	4 5 6 7	8 9 10 11	12 13 14 15
Op Code —	1	3	0	0
Displacement —			0	5
Machine Code—	1	3	0	5

Step 25 then has 1305 as the machine code.

The remaining jump instructions, JNE at *Steps 29* and *34* have an op code of 1600_{16}. Calculating the displacement from *Step 29* to *Step 28* and from *Step 34* to *Step 33*, obviously is -02_{16}. The complement of -02 is FFFD and the twos complement is FFFE. Thus the machine code is:

	0 1 2 3	4 5 6 7	8 9 10 11	12 13 14 15
Op Code —	1	6	0	0
Displacement —			F	E
Machine Code—	1	6	F	E

Even though the labels jumped to for *Steps 29* and *34* are different, the displacement is the same and, therefore, the machine code entered at these steps is the same, $16FE_{16}$.

TABLE 3-2

Every step is now coded and the program is complete. This is the program that was entered into the microcomputer via the terminal to accomplish the first encounter task.

Only one comment remains. If the *Table 3-1* program were run on a computer under the direction of an assembler program, certain symbols used for directives to the assembler would have to be used. The $ symbol could have been used to indicate the fact that a displacement is to be made from the jump instruction address which was identified in equation (3) as A_J. The instruction then would contain the $ symbol followed by the necessary displacement in hexadecimal. For this reason the instructions at *Step 23, 25, 29,* and *34* would have looked as follows:

Step	A	MC	L	Assy. Lang.
23	FE2C	10EF		JMP $-17
25	FE30	1305		JEQ $+5
29	FE38	16FE		JNE $-2
34	FE42	16FE		JNE $-2

SUMMARY

It has been a long discussion. However, a great deal of material has been covered and many basic concepts developed. The facts and procedures presented should provide a solid foundation for expanding an understanding of the 9900 Family of microprocessors and microcomputer component peripherals and the microcomputers which use it. Hopefully, enough examples have been presented with the first encounter task that with a minimum of effort, new real applications of the TM990/100M board can be implemented. A few simple ones that can be implemented immediately with the present setup would be:

A. Wire-up the necessary drivers and resistors to drive all seven-segments of the display and write a new program to make the numbers 1, 2, 3, 4, 5, 6, 7, 8, 9, 0 come up in sequence.

B. Write a program that uses the 7 segment display numbers so that they spell a word when read up-side down.

Maybe more memory will be required, but that is easy to add to the TM990/100M.

The next step is to implement the logic levels at the output pins into real applications of controlling dc and ac voltages for control applications. An extended application in Chapter 8 using this same TM990/100M board setup shows how this can be done. Persons interested can follow right into this application example to gain more insight into the details of the 9900 family of components explained in detail in the following chapters.

TABLE 3-2:
ASSEMBLY LANGUAGE PROGRAM

Table 3-2. *Assembly Language Program.*

(With Machine Code)

Step	Hex Address	Hex Machine Code	Label	Op Code	Operand	Comments.
1.	FE00	02E0		LWPI	>FF20	Load workspace pointer
2.	FE02	FF20				with FF20$_{16}$
3.	FE04	0201		LI	1, >FE2E	Load R1
4.	FE06	FE2E				with 1st address of WAIT
5.	FE08	020C		LI	12, >0102	Load 12
6.	FE0A	0120				With base address of 9901, 0120$_{16}$
7.	FE0C	1D00	BEGIN	SBO	0	Set I/O P$_0$ (segment f) equal to one
8.	FE0E	0691		BL	*1	Branch to address in R1, (saves next address in R11)
9.	FE10	1E00		SBZ	0	Set I/O P$_0$ (segment f) equal to zero
10.	FE12	0691		BL	*1	Branch to address in R1 (saves next address in R11)
11.	FE14	1D01		SBO	1	Set I/O P$_1$ (segment b) equal to one
12.	FE16	0691		BL	*1	Branch to address in R1
13.	FE18	1E01		SBZ	1	Set I/O P$_1$ equal to zero
14.	FE1A	0691		BL	*1	Branch to address in R1
15.	FE1C	1D02		SBO	2	Set I/O P$_2$ (segment e) to one
16.	FE1E	0691		BL	*1	Branch to address in R1
17.	FE20	1E02		SBZ	2	Set I/O P$_2$ equal to zero
18.	FE22	0691		BL	*1	Branch to address in R1
19	FE24	1D03		SBO	3	Set I/O P$_3$ (segment c) equal to one
20.	FE26	0691		BL	*1	Branch to address in R1
21.	FE28	1E03		SBZ	3	Set I/O P$_3$ equal to zero
22.	FE2A	0691		BL	*1	Branch to address in R1
23.	FE2C	10EF		JMP	BEGIN	Jump to BEGIN
24.	FE2E	1F04	WAIT	TB	4	Test I/O P$_4$ for a "1" or a "0"
25.	FE30	1305		JEQ	TIME	If equals bit is set ("1"), jump to TIME
26.	FE32	0203		LI	3, >FFFF	Load R3
27.	FE34	FFFF				with FFFF$_{16}$
28.	FE36	0603	TIME 1	DEC	3	Decrement R3
29.	FE38	16FE		JNE	TIME1	Jump to TIME1 if equals bit is not set
30.	FE3A	045B		B	*11	Return to main program (by way of 11)
31.	FE3C	0203	TIME	LI	3, >3FFF	Load R3
32.	FE3E	3FFF				with 3FFF$_{16}$
33.	FE40	0603	TIME 2	DEC	3	Decrement R3
34.	FE42	16FE		JNE	TIME2	Jump to TIME2 if equals bit is not set
35.	FE44	045B		B	*11	Return to main program (by way of R11)

CHAPTER 4

Hardware Design: Architecture and Interfacing Techniques

INTRODUCTION

Describing the 9900 system from a hardware standpoint clearly requires detailed descriptions of a large number of design features as well as the interaction between the 9900 and peripheral circuits. In this chapter, material is arranged to develop a 9900 system from the viewpoint of the 9900 microprocessor chip. In the architecture section, the concepts of instruction fetch and decode, the memory-to-microprocessor bus structures, and memory partitioning (the use of volatile and non-volatile memories) are explained. Other topics include descriptions of the registers on the microprocessor chip and the working registers, the concept of memory-to-memory architecture, timing and descriptions of interface signals.

A special section covers memory in detail, especially the controls and timing, multichip memory structure, static and dynamic RAM, and DMA (direct memory access).

Following the architecture and memory sections are sections devoted to the instruction set, design considerations for input/output techniques especially in CRU development, the interrupt structure and electrical requirements.

A special section devoted to the unique features of the single chip microcomputer, the TMS9940, is included at the end of the chapter.

Information in this chapter flows from the most basic fundamentals to an understanding of the more complex design features of the 9900 and the chip family. When very specific and detailed information regarding pin assignments and speed is given, the TMS9900 device specifications are used.

The 9900 family of 16-bit microprocessors includes several device types each aimed at a specific market segment. The same basic architecture and instruction set are maintained throughout. Consider first the single-chip microprocessor which consists of an ALU (arithmetic and logic unit), a few registers, and instruction handling circuitry (*Figure 4-1*). There is no memory on the chip for instructions and data so it must be interfaced to memory devices, usually RAM for data (and instructions which must be modified) and ROM, PROM, or EPROM for instructions (*Figure 4-2*). It is often desirable to store instructions in a non-volatile memory to eliminate the requirement for loading the program into memory immediately following application of power. This is especially important in dedicated applications where the program is fixed and power off-on cycles are common occurrences.

The microprocessor is connected to memory devices and external input/output (I/O) devices via sets of signals or busses (*Figure 4-2*). An address bus selects a word of memory. The contents of this word will be transferred to or from the microprocessor via the data bus. Control signals required to effect the transfer of information between the microprocessor and the memory are grouped into a control bus.

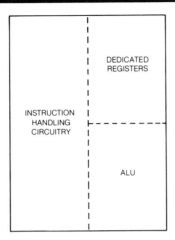

Figure 4-1. The 9900 Microprocessor

The interface to external devices (I/O) may be accomplished by using the address, data and control busses. This technique is known as parallel I/O or memory mapped I/O because data is transferred in parallel and the I/O devices occupy locations in the memory address space.

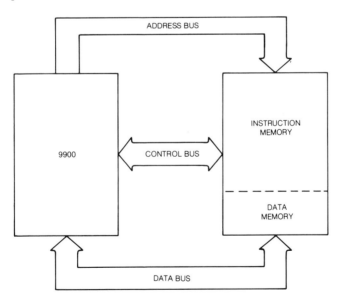

Figure 4-2. 9900 Microprocessor and Memory

The extension of parallel I/O is direct memory access (DMA). External hardware is employed to act as a separate special purpose processor for transferring large blocks of contiguous memory words to or from an external device (such as a disc memory). Once such a transfer is set up (via a string of instructions in the program), the DMA controller automatically synchronizes the transfer of data between the external device and memory, sharing the buses timewise with the microprocessor.

The 9900 architecture includes one other important I/O technique. Designed primarily for single bit I/O transfers, the communications register unit (CRU) provides a powerful alternative to parallel, memory mapped I/O (*Figure 4-3*). The address bus is used to select one of 4096 individual input or output bits in the CRU address space. During the execution of one of the single bit CRU instructions, the processor transfers one bit in or out. Multiple bit instructions are also available which provide for transfer of up to sixteen bits via a single CRU operation.

This chapter describes primarily the basic TMS9900 16-bit microprocessor.

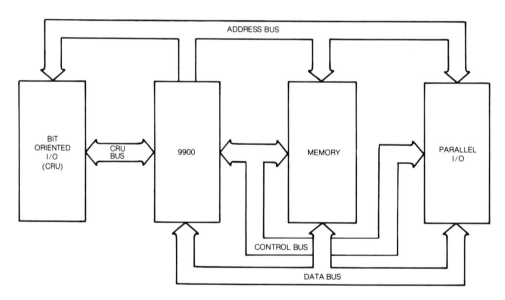

Figure 4-3. 9900 Bus Architecture

An overview is given here to establish design paths for microprocessor systems. Listed below are the processors in the 9900 family.

Device	Technology	Description
TMS 9900	N-MOS	16-bit CPU 3 MHz
TMS 9900-40	N-MOS	16-bit CPU 4 MHz
SBP 9900A	I²L	16-bit CPU −55° to 125°C
TMS 9980A/81	N-MOS	16-bit CPU 40-pin package
TMS 9985	N-MOS	16-bit CPU 40-pin package
TMS 9940	N-MOS	16-bit CPU with 2 k on-chip ROM

General purpose applications are designed around the TMS9900 device. The same is true for systems with severe environmental specs; however, a transition to the SBP9900A is made after the design is complete and the software completely debugged. The TMS9980A/81 and the TMS9985 are used where the 40-pin package is advantageous and a slightly slower speed is acceptable. The TMS9940 is a single-chip microcomputer for small special purpose controllers.

At the end of this chapter there is detailed design data for application of the LSI (large scale integration) peripheral support circuits in the 9900 family which are available for use in the 9900 microprocessor-based systems. But in order to read and understand the data presented in this chapter and in this book, an understanding of the basic fundamentals of microprocessors is needed.

ARCHITECTURE

Basic Microprocessor Chip

The 9900 is an advanced 16-bit LSI microprocessor with minicomputer-like architecture and instructions. It is easy to understand and easy to use. Consider first the microprocessor device itself (*Figure 4-4*). Operations are carried out with a set of dedicated registers, an ALU, and instruction handling circuits. As clock signals are applied, the processor will fetch an instruction word from a memory (external to the chip), will execute it, fetch another instruction, execute it and so on. In each case the instruction is saved in an instruction register (IR) on the chip. The decode circuit sets up the appropriate controls based on the content of the instruction register for a multi-step execution phase. A memory address register (MAR) is used to hold address information on the address bus. The ALU and the other registers perform their specified functions during the execute phase of the instruction cycle.

Microprocessor Registers

There are three registers on the 9900 chip which are the key architectural features of the microprocessor (*Figure 4-5*). They are the workspace pointer (WP), the program counter (PC), and the status register (ST).

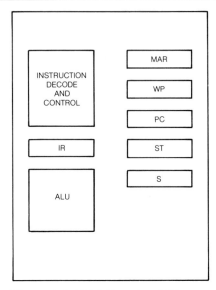

Figure 4-4. 9900 Functional Elements

Workspace Pointer

The general purpose registers for the 9900 are implemented as blocks of memory called workspaces. A workspace consists of 16 contiguous words of memory, but are general registers to the user. The workspace pointer on the 9900 chip holds the address of the first word in the workspace. After initializing the content of the WP at the beginning of a program (or subprogram), the programmer may concentrate on writing a program using the registers to hold data words or to address data elsewhere in memory.

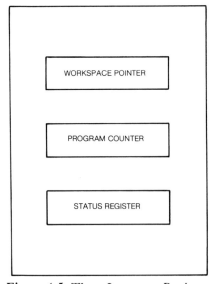

Figure 4-5. Three Important Registers

Program Counter

The program counter (PC) in the 9900 is used in the conventional way to locate the next instruction to be executed. As each instruction is executed, the program counter is incremented to the next consecutive word address. Because word addresses are even numbers in the 9900, the program counter is incremented by two in order to address sequential instructions. If the instruction to be executed occupies two or three memory words, the program counter will be incremented to generate sequential (even) addresses to access the required number of words. At the end of execution the PC is incremented to the next even address which is the location of the next instruction. If the instruction to be executed is a jump or branch instruction, the program counter is loaded with a new address and program execution continues starting with the instruction at that location in memory.

Figure 4-6 shows the program counter pointing to (addressing) instruction words in the program. Starting with location (x) the instructions are performed in sequence until a jump is encountered at (y). Processing resumes sequentially starting at location (z) which was the address specified by the jump instruction to be placed in the program counter.

Status Register

The status register (ST) is the basis for decision making during program execution. Individual bits of the ST are set as flags as the result of instructions. They may thereafter be tested in the execution of conditional jump instructions. *Figure 4-7* shows the status register and its flag bits.

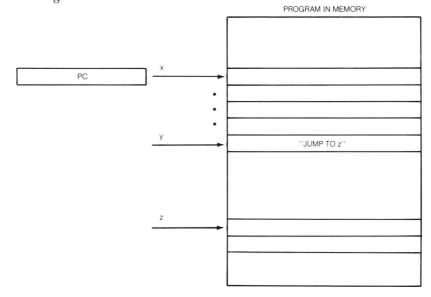

Figure 4-6. Program Counter Operation

0	1	2	3	4	5	6	7	8	9	10	11	12	13	14	15
L>	A>	=	C	O	P	X			RESERVED				INTERRUPT MASK		

Bit	Function
0	Logical "Greater Than"
1	Arithmetic "Greater Than"
2	Equal
3	Carry
4	Overflow
5	Parity
6	XOP Instruction Being Executed
12-15	Interrupt Mask

Figure 4-7. Status Register

The first three bits are set as a result of comparisons. Some instructions identify two operands (numbers) to be compared. If the first is greater than the second, the "greater than" bit should be set. In the 9900 there are two such conditions. First, the logical-greater-than bit considers 16-bit words as positive integers and the comparison is made accordingly. Second, the arithmetic-greater-than bit is set as the result of a comparison of two numbers which are considered in two's complement form. For example: consider the numbers A and B below as the numbers in the compare instruction C A, B:

$$A \quad 1000 \quad 1110 \quad 1100 \quad 0101$$

$$B \quad 0110 \quad 1010 \quad 1100 \quad 1101$$

If they are 16-bit positive integers, it is clear from the most significant bits (MSB) that A is greater than B, and the logical-greater-than bit of the status register should be set to one. But as two's complement numbers, A is negative (MSB = 1) and B is positive. Therefore the arithmetic-greater-than bit must be made zero (A is not greater than B). Since the processor has no way of knowing how the designer has used the memory words for data (integers or two's complement), two status bits must be provided for decision making. The designer can select the appropriate conditional jump instruction (testing status bit 0 or 1) because he knows what the data format is.

Status bit 2, the equal bit, is set if the two words compared are equal.

In many instructions, only one number is involved or a new number is determined as the result of an arithmetic operation. For these instructions status bits 0, 1 and 2 are set as the result of comparisons against zero; that is, if the single number or answer obtained is greater than zero or equal to zero.

MEMORY-TO-MEMORY ARCHITECTURE

The 9900 family of processors employs memory-to-memory architecture in the execution of instructions. Memory-to-memory architecture is that computer organization and instruction set which enables direct modification of memory data via a single instruction. That is, a single instruction can fetch one or two operands from memory, perform an arithmetic or logical operation, and also store the result in memory. In doing so, some of the on-chip registers are used as temporary buffers in much the same manner as an accumulator is used in other systems. But instructions to load an accumulator and store the accumulator are rarely necessary in memory-to-memory architecture. A single 9900 instruction (arithmetic or logical) does the work of two or more instructions in other systems.

Figure 4-8 describes the technique used by the 9900 to locate words in memory as "registers" in the workspace. Additional information is included for reference purposes. Registers 1-15 may be used for indexing (see the description of this addressing mode in Chapter 5 and 6). Register 0 may be used for a shift count. Registers 11 and 13-15 are used for subroutine techniques. Register 12 is a base value for CRU instructions. These special uses of the workspace registers are stated here as an initial evaluation of the register set. Program control and CRU instructions make use of the contents of registers 11-15; therefore, programmers and systems designers must be aware that while use of these registers is not restricted to their special functions, they should be used with caution in performing other functions.

The use of these workspaces in an actual application is best described in the Software Design chapter. But the step-by-step execution of the instructions is of concern in hardware design because of the execution speed and the techniques for handling interrupts.

Instruction cycles in the 9900 require memory access not only for the instruction words but also for operand addresses and actual operands (or numbers to be operated upon.) A simple add instruction requires at least four memory cycles: one to fetch the instruction, two to access the two numbers to be added, and one to store the result. As will be explained in detail later in this chapter, the execution of an add instruction may require as many as eight memory cycles (because of the addressing mode.) The execution steps are not the same for all instructions. There is, in fact, substantial variation of execution steps within any one instruction due to addressing. Tables and charts are provided in this chapter to explain the execution time of each instruction.

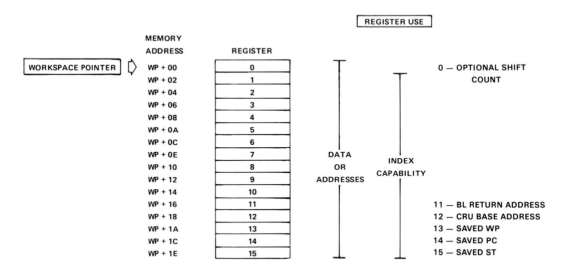

Figure 4-8. 9900 Workspace Registers

There is one additional concept regarding microprocessor and memory interfacing to be introduced at this time: it is the way in which data is stored in the memory. *Figure 4-9* shows the bit numbering for a general 16-bit data word or instruction. Instructions and 16-bit data words are always located at even addresses. Since the memory is byte addressable, even and odd bytes are the left and right half words in the 16-bit memory organization and have even or odd addresses respectively. Memories for the TMS9900 and SBP9900A contain 16 bits per word, while the other processors in the family use 8-bit memory structures. But all use the same addressing concept: a 16-bit address describing a 64k-byte address space.

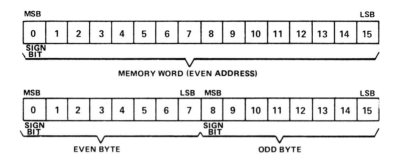

Figure 4-9. Word and Byte Formats

CONTEXT SWITCHING

One of the more important advantages of the workspace architecture of the
9900 is the fact that "register save and restore" operations are greatly simplified. In any
interrupt processing system, provisions must be made to perform an orderly transition
into a new program segment in response to an interrupt. In other microprocessor
systems, the first few instructions of an interrupt service routine perform the steps of
saving register contents in memory, and then loading new values into the registers.

In the 9900, an interrupt cycle starts with a hardware operation to save the contents of
the three key registers, the WP, PC and ST. In addition, the WP and PC must be loaded
with new numbers. *Figures 4-10* and *4-11* show an example of the technique. Prior to the
interrupt, the WP locates the workspace (pointing to 0800), the PC locates the current
instruction (pointing to 0100), and the ST contains the status as a result of the execution
of the current instruction (e.g., 4000). At the end of execution, the processor tests for an
interrupt condition and finding it, performs a *context switch* as follows.

Step 1. The new WP value is fetched from the appropriate interrupt vector location in
the first 32 words of memory. This identifies the location of the workspace assigned to
the interrupt service routine.

Step 2. The current values of the WP, PC and ST registers are stored in the new
workspace — ST in R15, PC in R14, WP in R13 in that order. After this, the new PC
value is fetched from memory (the second location of the two-word interrupt vector) and
loaded into the PC.

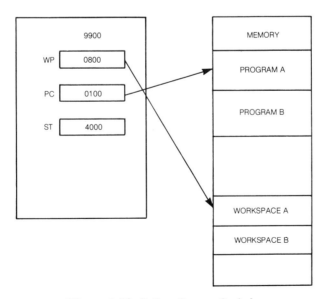

Figure 4-10. Before Context Switch

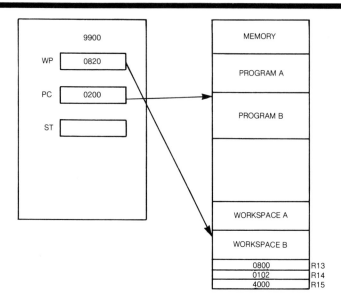

Figure 4-11. After Context Switch

Step 3. With the context switch completed, processing resumes with the first instruction in the interrupt service routine.

Processing continues in this mode until, at the end of the interrupt routine, an RTWP instruction is encountered. A "reverse" context switch now occurs to return to the previous program. Since R13, 14 and 15 contain the control register contents for the previous program, they are now transferred to the CPU which loads them into the WP, PC and ST. Processing resumes from the point at which the interrupt occurred.

The obvious advantage of context switching is the reduced register-save register-restore operations required by microprocessors in an interrupt environment. The context switch is also used as a subroutine technique. This is described in Chapters 5 and 6, but the important fact is that context switching is, to the designer, a single step, when in fact several steps are performed by the microprocessor.

MEMORY

The 9900 is easily interfaced to any of the standard types of semiconductor memory devices. Texas Instruments provides masked ROMs, field-programmable ROMs (PROMs), and erasable PROMs (EPROMs) for non-volatile program and data storage. RAMs are available in sizes from a 64 x 8 static RAM to the 64K dynamic RAMs for use as a temporary program and data storage. 9900-compatible memory devices are listed in Chapter 2.

MEMORY ORGANIZATION

The 9900 instructions build a 16-bit address word which describes a 64K x 8 bit address space. A memory map for the 9900 is shown in *Figure 4-12*.

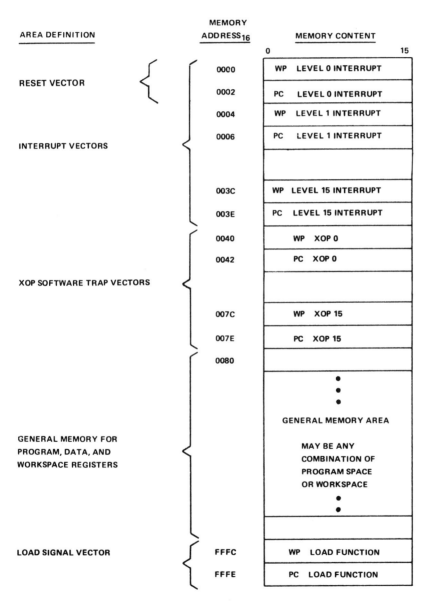

Figure 4-12. TMS 9900 Dedicated Memory Addresses

RESET Vector

The first two memory words are reserved for storage of the RESET vector. The RESET vector is used to load the new WP and PC whenever the CPU RESET signal occurs. The first word contains the new WP, which is the starting address of the RESET workspace. The second word contains the new PC, which is the starting address of the RESET service routine.

Interrupt Vectors

The next thirty memory words, 0004_{16} through $003E_{16}$ are reserved for storage of the interrupt transfer vectors for levels 1 through 15. Each interrupt level uses a word for the workspace pointer (WP) and a word for the starting address of the service routine (PC). If an interrupt level is not used within a system, then the corresponding two memory words can be used for program or data storage.

Software Trap Vectors

The next thirty-two memory words, 0040_{16} through $007E_{16}$, are used for extended-operation software trap vectors. When the CPU executes one of the 16 extended operations (XOPs), the program traps through the corresponding vector. Two words are reserved for each trap vector, with one word for the WP and one word for the PC. If an XOP instruction is not used, the corresponding vector words can be used for program or data storage.

LOAD Vector

The last two memory words $FFFC_{16}$ and $FFFE_{16}$ are reserved for the LOAD vector, with one word for the WP and one word for the PC. The LOAD vector is used whenever the CPU LOAD signal is active (low).

Transfer Vector Storage

The transfer vectors can be stored either in ROM or RAM, but either the RESET or LOAD vector should be in non-volatile memory and should point to a program in non-volatile storage to ensure proper system start-up. The restart routine should initialize any vector which is in RAM. The program can then manipulate the RAM-based vectors to alter workspace assignments or service routine entry points, while ROM-based vectors are fixed and cannot be altered.

MEMORY CONTROL SIGNALS

The 9900 uses three signals to control the use of the data bus and address bus during memory read or write cycles. Memory enable ($\overline{\text{MEMEN}}$) is active low during all memory cycles.

Data bus in (DBIN) is active high during memory read cycles and indicates that the CPU has disabled the output data buffers.

Write enable ($\overline{\text{WE}}$) is active low during memory write cycles and has timing compatible with the read/write (R/$\overline{\text{W}}$) control signal for many standard RAMs.

Memory Read Cycle

Figure 4-13 illustrates the timing for a memory read machine cycle with no wait states. At the beginning of the machine cycle, $\overline{\text{MEMEN}}$ and DBIN become active and the valid address is output on A0-A14. D0-D15 output drivers are disabled to avoid conflicts with input data. $\overline{\text{WE}}$ remains high for the entire machine cycle. The READY input is sampled on $\phi 1$ of clock cycle 1, and must be high if no wait states are desired. Data is sampled on $\phi 1$ of clock cycle 2, and set-up and hold timing requirements must be observed. A memory-read cycle is never followed by a memory-write cycle, and D0-D15 output drivers remain disabled for at least one additional clock cycle.

Memory Write Cycle

Figure 4-14 illustrates the timing for a memory write machine cycle with no wait states. $\overline{\text{MEMEN}}$ becomes active, and valid address and data are output at the beginning of the machine cycle. DBIN remains inactive for the complete cycle. $\overline{\text{WE}}$ goes low on $\phi 1$ of clock cycle 1 and goes high on $\phi 1$ of clock cycle 2, meeting the address and data set-up and hold timing requirements for the static RAMs listed in Chapter 2. For no wait states, READY must be high during $\phi 1$ of clock cycle 1.

Read/Write Control with DBIN

In some memory systems, particularly with dynamic RAMs, it may be desirable to have READ and WRITE control signals active during the full memory cycle. *Figure 4-15* shows how the WRITE signal can be generated. Note that DBIN is high *only* for READ cycles; therefore, $\overline{\text{MEMEN}}$ can be NORed with DBIN to yield a WRITE signal which is high only during memory write operations.

Slow Memory Control

Although most memories operate with the 9900 at the full system speed, some memories cannot properly respond within the minimum access time determined by the system clock. The system clock could be slowed down in order to lengthen the access time but the system through-put would be adversely affected since non-memory and other memory reference cycles would be unnecessarily longer. The READY and WAIT signals are used instead to synchronize the CPU with slow memories. The timing for memory-read and memory-write cycles with wait states is shown in *Figures 4-16* and *4-17*.

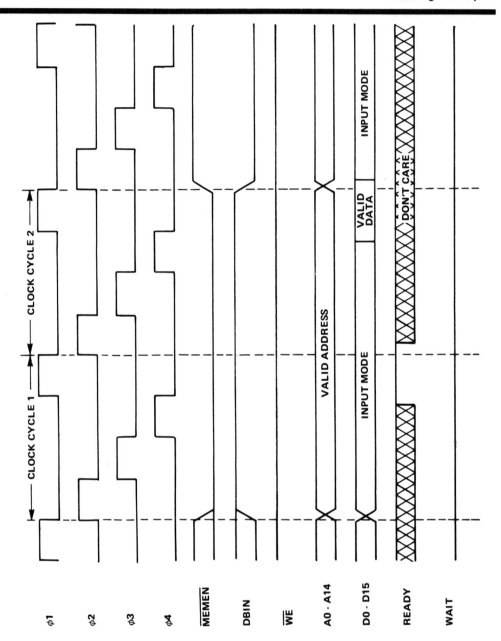

Figure 4-13. Memory-Read Cycle Timing

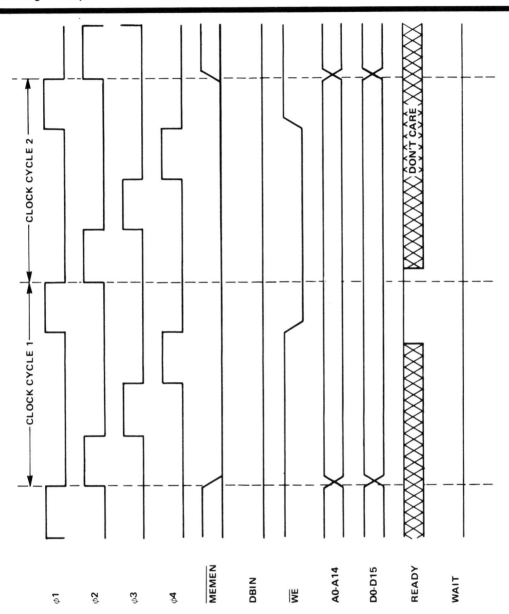

Figure 4-14. *Memory-Write Cycle Timing*

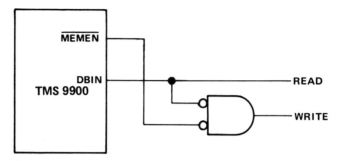

Figure 4-15. Read/Write Control Using $\overline{MEMEN}$ and DBIN

The READY input is tested on $\phi 1$ of clock cycle 1 of memory-read and memory-write cycles. If READY = 1, no wait states are used and the data transfer is completed on the next clock cycle. If READY = 0, the processor enters the wait state on the next clock cycle and all memory control, address, and data signals maintain their current levels. The WAIT output goes high on $\phi 3$ to indicate that a wait state has been entered. While in the wait state, the processor continues to sample READY on $\phi 1$, and remains in the wait state until READY = 1. When READY = 1 the processor progresses to clock cycle 2 and the data transfer is completed. WAIT goes low on $\phi 3$. It is important to note that READY is only tested during $\phi 1$, of clock cycle 1 of memory-read and memory-write cycles and wait states, and the specified set-up and hold timing requirements must be met; at any other time the READY input may assume any value. The effect of inserting wait states into memory access cycles is to extend the minimum allowable access time by one clock period for each wait state.

Wait State Control

Figure 4-18 illustrates the connection of the WAIT output to the READY input to generate one wait state for a selected memory segment. The address decode circuity generates an active low signal $(\overline{SLOMEM} = 0)$ whenever the slow memory is addressed. For example, if memory addresses 8000_{16} — $FFFE_{16}$ select slow memory, $\overline{SLOMEM} = A0$. If one wait state is required for all memory, WAIT may be connected directly to READY, causing one wait state to be generated on each memory-read or memory-write machine cycle. Referring again to *Figures 4-16* and *4-17* note that the WAIT output satisfies all of the timing requirements for the READY input for a single wait state. The address decode signal is active only when a particular set of memory locations has been addressed. *Figure 4-19* illustrates the generation of two wait states for selected memory by simply delaying propagation of the WAIT output to the READY input one clock cycle with a D-type flip-flop. The rising edge of $\phi 2TTL$ is assumed to be coincident with the falling edge of the $\phi 2$ clock input to the TMS 9900.

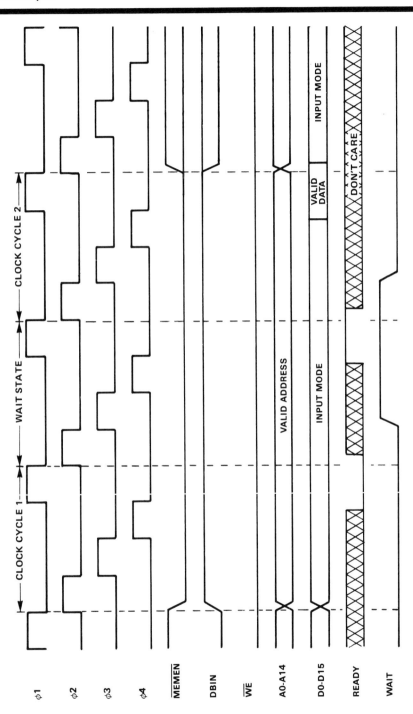

Figure 4-16. *Memory-Read Cycle With One Wait State*

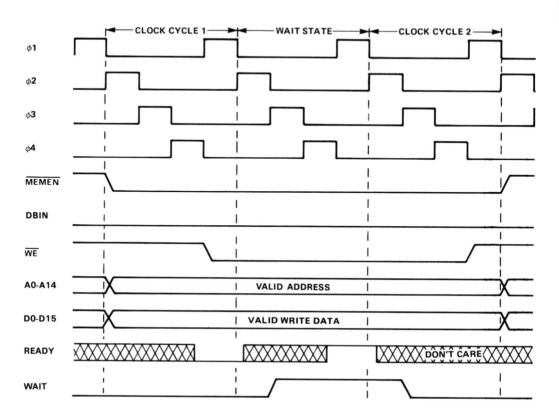

Figure 4-17. Memory-Write Cycle With One Wait State

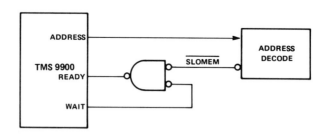

Figure 4-18. Single Wait State for Slow Memory

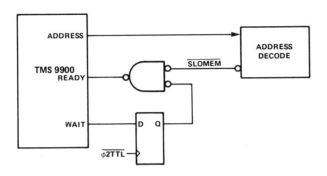

***Figure 4-19.** Double Wait States for Slow Memory*

Memory Access Time Calculation

Maximum allowable memory access time for the TMS 9900 can be determined with the aid of *Figure 4-20*. Memory control and address signals are output on $\Phi 2$ of clock cycle 1, and are stable 20 ns (t_{PLH}, t_{PHL}) afterwards. Data from memory must be valid 40 ns (t_{su}) before the leading edge of $\Phi 1$ during clock cycle 2. Therefore, memory access time may be expressed by the equation:

$$t_{acc} \leq (1.75 + n)\, t_{cy} - t_{PLH} - t_r - t_{su}$$

where n equals the number of wait states in the memory-read cycle. Assigning worst-case specified values for t_{PLH} (20ns), t_r (12ns), and t_{su} (40 ns), and assuming 3 MHz operation:

$$t_{acc} \leq \frac{(1.75 + n)}{0.003} - 72 \text{ ns}$$

Access time is further reduced by address decoding, control signal gating, and address and data bus buffering, when used. Thus, for a known access time for a given device, the number of required wait states can be determined.

For example, a TMS 4042-2 RAM has a 450 nanosecond access time and does not require any wait states. A TMS 4042 has a 1000 nanosecond access time and requires two wait states. Propagation delays caused by address or data buffers should be added to the nominal device access time in order to determine the effective access time.

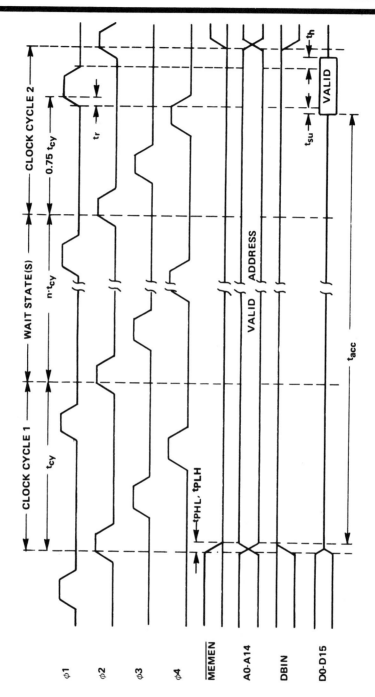

Figure 4-20. Memory Access Timing Calculation

STATIC MEMORY

Static RAMs and PROMs are easily interfaced to the 9900. A 9900 memory system using the TMS 4042-2 256 X 4 static RAM and the TMS 2708 1K X 8 EPROM is shown in *Figure 4-21*.

Address

The most-significant address bit, A0, is used to select either the EPROMs or the RAMs during memory cycles. When A0 is low, the EPROMs are selected, and when A0 is high, the RAMs are selected. Address lines A1 through A4 are not used since the full address space of the TMS 9900 is not required in the example. The lower address bits select internal RAM or EPROM cells. Other memory systems can fully decode the address word for maximum memory expansion.

Control Signals

Since DBIN is also used to select the EPROMs during memory-write cycles, the EPROMs cannot inadvertently be selected and placed into output mode while the CPU is also in the output mode on the data bus. $\overline{\text{MEMEN}}$ is used to select the RAMs during either read or write cycles, and $\overline{\text{WE}}$ is used to select the read/write mode. DBIN is also used to control the RAM output bus drivers.

The 9900 outputs $\overline{\text{WE}}$ three clock phases after the address, data, and $\overline{\text{MEMEN}}$ are output. As a result, the address, data, and enable-hold times are easily met. $\overline{\text{WE}}$ is enabled for one clock cycle and satisfies the minimum write pulse width requirement of 300 nanoseconds. Finally, $\overline{\text{WE}}$ is disabled one clock phase before the address, data, and other control signals and meets the TMS 4042-2 50-nanosecond minimum data and address hold time.

Loading

The loads on the CPU and memory outputs are well below the maximum rated loads. As a result no buffering is required for the memory system in *Figure 4-21*. The TMS 4042-2 and the TMS 2708 access times are low enough to eliminate the need for wait states, and the CPU READY input is connected to V_{cc}.

The minimum high-level input voltage of the TMS 2708 is 3 volts while the maximum high-output voltage for the TMS 9900 is 2.4 volts at the maximum specified loading. For the system in *Figure 4-21*, the loads on the CPU and memory outputs are well below the maximum rated load. At this loading, the TMS9900 output voltage exceeds 3 volts, so pull-up resisters are not needed.

There are many other Texas Instruments static memories compatible with the TMS 9900. Most memory devices do not require wait states when used with the TMS 9900 at 3 MHz.

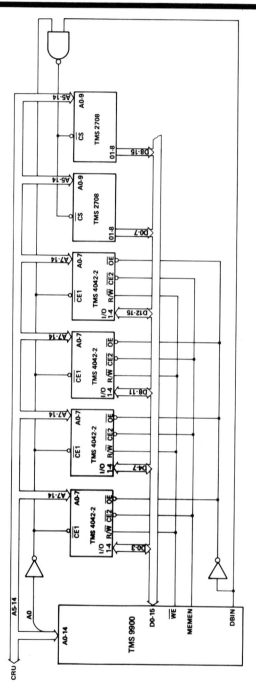

Figure 4-21. TMS 9900 Static Memory System

DYNAMIC MEMORY

Memory applications requiring large bit storage can use 4K, 16K or 64K dynamic memories for low cost, low power consumption, and high bit density. TMS 9900 systems requiring 4K words or more of RAM, can economically use the 4096-bit TMS 4051, the 16,384-bit TMS 4116, or any of the other dynamic RAMs covered in Chapter 2.

Refresh

The dynamic RAMs must be refreshed periodically to avoid the loss of stored data. The RAM data cells are organized into a matrix of rows and columns with on-chip gating to select the addressed bit. Refresh of the 4K RAM cell matrix is accomplished by performing a memory cycle of each of the 64 row addresses every 2 milliseconds or less. The 16K RAM has 128 row addresses. Performing a memory cycle at any cell on a row refreshes all cells in the row, thus allowing the use of arbitrary column address during refresh.

Refresh Modes

There are several dynamic memory refresh techniques which can be used for a TMS 9900 system. If the system periodically accesses at least one cell of each row every 2 milliseconds, then no additional refresh circuitry is required. A CRT controller which periodically refreshes the display, illustrates this concept.

Refresh control logic is included wherever the system cannot otherwise ensure that all rows are refreshed every 2 milliseconds. The dynamic memory in such TMS 9900 systems can be refreshed in the block, cycle stealing, or transparent mode.

Block Refresh.

The block mode of refresh halts the CPU every 2 milliseconds and sequentially refreshes each of the rows. The block technique halts execution for a 128 (4K) or 256 (16K) clock cycle periods every 2 milliseconds. Some TMS 9900 systems cannot use this technique because of the possibility of slow response to priority interrupts or because of the effect of the delay during critical timing or I/O routines.

Cycle Stealing.

The cycle stealing mode of refresh "steals" a cycle from the system periodically to refresh one row. The refresh interval is determined by the maximum refresh time and the number of rows to be refreshed. The 4K dynamic RAMs have 64 rows to be refreshed every 2 milliseconds and thus require a maximum cycle stealing interval of 31.2 microseconds.

A cycle stealing refresh controller for the TMS 4051 4K dynamic RAM is shown in *Figure 4-22*. The refresh timer generates the refresh signal (RFPLS) every 30 microseconds. The refresh request signal (RFREQ) is true until the refresh cycle is completed. The refresh grant signal (RFGNT) goes high during the next CPU clock cycle in which the CPU is not accessing the dynamic memory. The refresh memory cycle takes two clock cycles to complete after RFGNT is true. During the second clock cycle, however, the CPU can attempt to access the dynamic memory since the CPU is not synchronized to the refresh controller. If the CPU does access memory during the last clock cycle of the refresh memory cycle, the refresh controller makes the memory not-ready for the remainder of the refresh memory cycle, and the CPU enters a wait state during this interval. The dynamic memory row address during the refresh memory cycle is the output of a modulo-64 counter. The counter is incremented each refresh cycle in order to refresh the rows sequentially.

The dynamic memory timing controller generates the proper chip enable timing for both CPU and refresh initiated memory cycles. The timing controller can be easily modified to operate with other dynamic RAMs.

Since the TMS 9900 performs no more than three consecutive memory cycles, the refresh request will be granted in a maximum of three memory cycles. Some systems may have block DMA, which uses $\overline{\text{HOLD}}$. RFREQ can be used in such systems to disable HOLDA temporarily in order to perform a refresh memory cycle if the DMA block transfer is relatively long (greater than 30 microseconds). The cycle stealing mode "steals" clock cycles only when the CPU attempts to access the dynamic memory during the last half of the refresh cycle. Even if this interference occurs during each refresh cycle, a maximum of 64 clock cycles are "stolen" for refresh every 2 milliseconds.

Transparent Refresh.

The transparent refresh mode eliminates this interference by synchronizing the refresh cycle to the CPU memory cycle. The rising edge of $\overline{\text{MEMEN}}$ marks the end of a memory cycle immediately preceding a non-memory cycle. The $\overline{\text{MEMEN}}$ rising edge can initiate a refresh cycle with no interference with memory cycles. The refresh requirement does not interfere with the system throughput since only non-memory cycles are used for the refresh cycles. The worst-case TMS 9900 instruction execution sequence (all divides) will guarantee the complete refresh of a 4K or 16K dynamic RAM within 2 milliseconds.

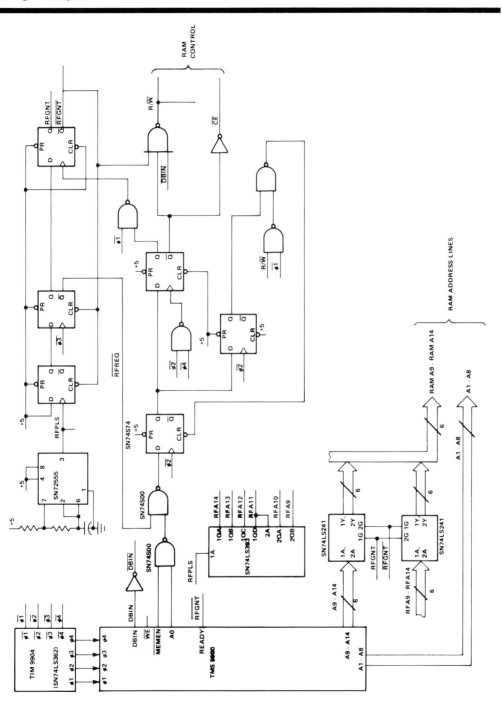

Figure 4-22. Cycle-Stealing Dynamic RAM Refresh for TMS 4051

While the transparent refresh mode eliminates refresh-related system performance degradation, the system power consumption can be higher since the RAMs are refreshed more often than required. As many as one-half of the CPU machine cycles can be refresh cycles, resulting in multiple refresh cycles for each row during the refresh interval. This situation can be corrected by adding a timer to determine the start of the refresh interval and an overflow detector for the refresh row counter. When every row has been refreshed during an interval, the refresh circuit is disabled until the beginning of the next interval. Since each row is refreshed only once, the system power consumption is reduced to a minimum.

Direct memory access using $\overline{\text{HOLD}}$ should guarantee that sufficient non-memory cycles are available for refresh during large block transfers. An additional refresh timer can be used to block HOLDA in order to provide periodic refresh cycles.

BUFFERED MEMORY

The TMS 9900 outputs can drive approximately two standard TTL inputs and 200 picofarads. Higher capacitive loads may be driven, but with increased rise and fall times. Many small memory systems can thus be directly connected to the CPU without buffer circuits. Larger memory systems, however, may require external bipolar buffers to drive the address or data buses because of increased loading. Texas Instruments manufactures a number of buffer circuits compatible with the TMS 9900. The SN74LS241 noninverting-octal buffer with three-state outputs is an example of a buffer circuit.

A TMS 9900 memory system with address and data bus buffering is shown in *Figure 4-23*. The system consists of sets of four 256 X 4 memory devices in parallel to provide the 16-bit data word. The four sets of four devices provide a total of 1024 words of memory. The memory devices can be the TMS 4042-2 NMOS static RAM.

The SN74S412 octal buffer/latch is designed to provide a minimum high-level output voltage of 3.65 V. Buffered TMS 9900 memory systems containing the TMS 4700 ROM or the TMS 2708 EPROM, for example, require input voltages in excess of the output voltages of many buffer circuits. The SN74S412 can be used to buffer the memories without the pull-up resistors needed for buffers.

MEMORY PARITY

Parity or other error detection/correction schemes are often used to minimize the effects of memory errors. Error detection schemes such as parity are used to indicate the presence of bad data, while error correction schemes correct single or multiple errors.

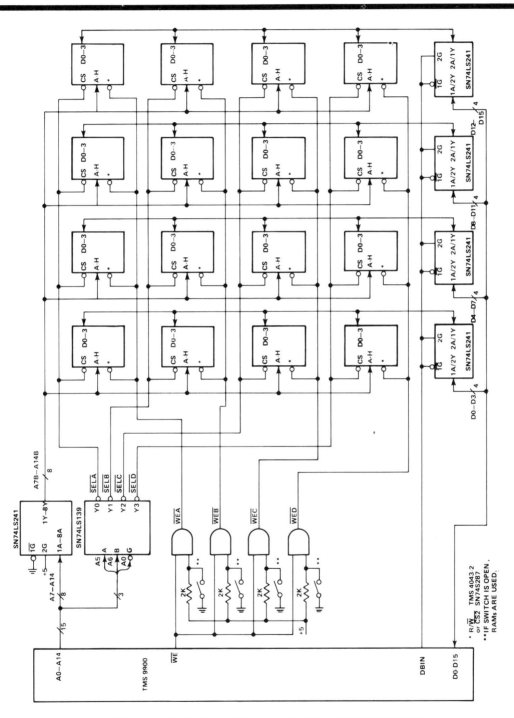

Figure 4-23. Buffered Memory with Mixed PROM/ROM

The SN74LS280 parity generator/checker can be used to implement memory parity in a TMS 9900 system. The system in *Figure 4-24* uses two SN74LS280 circuits to generate and to check the odd-memory parity. During memory write cycles, the generated parity bit is output to bit D16 of the memory. During memory read cycles, the parity is checked and an interrupt, $\overline{\text{PARERR}}$, is generated if the parity is even.

It should be noted that the faulty memory word will have already been used by the CPU as an op code, address, or data before the interrupt is generated. This can cause trouble in determining the exact location of the error. For example, an error in bit 8 of the CLR op code will cause the CPU to branch unconditionally. When the interrupt is serviced, there would then be no linkage to the part of the program at which the error occurred. A diagnostic routine can often isolate such errors by scanning the memory and checking parity under program control. Such a parity error in the diagnostic itself can be extremely difficult to isolate.

An external address latch clocked at IAQ can be used to retain program linkage under the above circumstances. When the parity error is detected, the address latch is frozen, thus pointing to the address of the instruction during which the parity error occurred.

Memory Layout

It is generally advantageous to lay out memory devices as arrays in the system. The advantages are twofold. First, positioning the devices in an orderly fashion simplifies identification of a particular memory element when troubleshooting. Second, and most important, layout of memory arrays simplifies layout, shortens interconnections, and generally allows a more compact and efficient utilization of board space. Crosstalk between adjacent lines in memory arrays is minimized by running address and data lines parallel to each other, and by running chip enable signals perpendicular to the address lines.

Memory devices, particularly dynamic RAMs generally require substantially greater supply currents when addressed than otherwise. It is therefore important that all power and ground paths be as wide as possible to memory arrays. Furthermore, in order to avoid spikes in supply voltages, it is advisable to decouple supply voltages with capacitors as close as possible to the pins of the memory devices. As an example, a system containing a 4K x 16-bit array of TMS 4051s should contain one 15 μF and one 0.05 μF capacitor for each set of four memory devices; with the large capacitors decoupling V_{DD}, and the small capacitors decoupling V_{BB}.

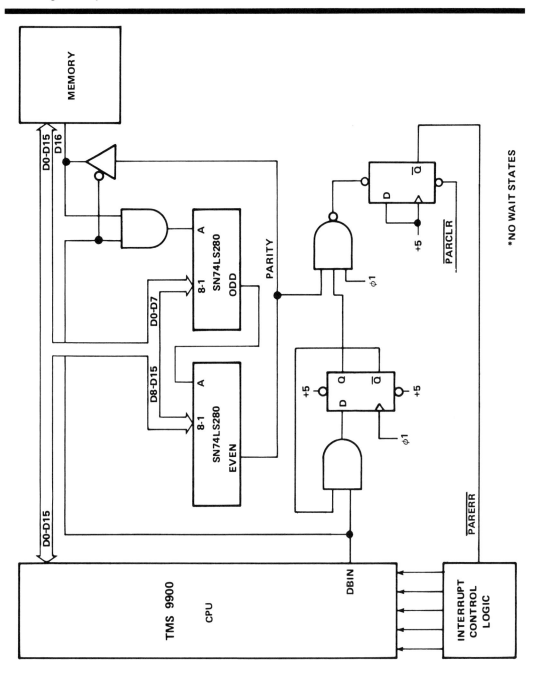

Figure 4-24. Memory Parity Generator Checker

INSTRUCTION EXECUTION

Execution time for an instruction is a function of the clock frequency, the number of clock cycles, the number of memory accesses and the number of wait states if required for slower memories. The following tables list the number of clock cycles required to execute each instruction if no wait states are required. The number of memory accesses is also given so that the extra clock cycles can be calculated for the number of wait states required. A wait state is entered when the ready signal from the memory does not go high within one clock period after initiation of a memory cycle. For example: The clock frequency for the TMS 9900 is 3 MHz. From the calculation of maximum access time for no wait states, the memory access time must be less than 512 ns. One wait state (of 333 ns duration) will be required for memories with access times between 512 ns and 845 ns, two wait states will be required if the access time is between 845 ns and 1.178 μ sec, and so on.

Timing

From *Figure 4-25,* the first execution time table, an add instruction (A) using direct register addressing for both operands requires 14 clock cycles if there are no wait states required. For other addressing modes, the number of clock cycles increases to a maximum of 30. If the memory requires one wait state per access, an additional four clock periods will be required since there are four memory cycles in the execution of an add instruction. For the TMS 9900 running at 3 MHz, 14 clock periods will take 4.667 microseconds; 30 clock periods will take 10.0 microseconds. The number of memory cycles is from 4 up to 8 depending upon addressing mode (3 to 7 for compare, C). Use the tables in the following manner. Assuming one wait state, a clock frequency of 3 MHz, and an instruction with complex addressing, the tables can be used to determine the execution time for the instruction

A *R1, @ LIST

is 26 clock cycles for fetch and execution and 6 clock cycles for wait states, or 32 x .333 microseconds which is 10.667 microseconds.

Figures 4-26, 27 and *28* give the rest of the execution time data, always by number of clock cycles (assuming no wait states) and memory cycles.

INSTRUCTIONS A, C†, S, SOC, SZC, MOV

	Destination Address	Source Address				
		R	*R	*R +	@LIST	@TABLE (R)
Clock Cycles	R	14	18	22	22	22
	*R	18	22	26	26	26
	*R +	22	26	30	30	30
	@LIST	22	26	30	30	30
	@TABLE (R)	22	26	30	30	30
Memory Cycles	R	4	5	6	5	6
	*R	5	6	7	6	7
	*R +	6	7	8	7	8
	@LIST	5	6	7	6	7
	@TABLE (R)	6	7	8	7	8
†Memory Cycles for C instr.	R	3	4	5	4	5
	*R	4	5	6	5	6
	*R +	5	6	7	6	7
	@LIST	4	5	6	5	6
	@TABLE (R)	5	5	6	7	6

Figure 4-25.

INSTRUCTIONS: AB, CB††, SB. SOCB, SZCB, MOVB

	Destination Address	Source Address				
		R	*R	*R +	@LIST	@TABLE (R)
Clock Cycles	R	14	18	20	22	22
	*R	18	22	24	26	26
	*R +	20	24	26	28	28
	@LIST	22	26	28	28	28
	@TABLE (R)	22	26	28	28	28
Memory Cycles	R	4	5	6	5	6
	*R	5	6	7	6	7
	*R +	6	7	8	7	8
	@LIST	5	6	7	6	7
	@TABLE (R)	6	7	8	7	8
††Memory Cycles for CB instr.	R	3	4	5	4	5
	*R	4	5	6	5	6
	*R +	5	6	7	6	7
	@LIST	4	5	6	5	6
	@TABLE (R)	5	6	7	6	7

Figure 4-26.

INSTRUCTIONS LDCR, STCR

LDCR

	Addressing Mode	Bit Count, C															
		1	2	3	4	5	6	7	8	9	10	11	12	13	14	15	0
Clock Cycles	R	22	24	26	28	30	32	34	36	38	40	42	44	46	48	50	52
	*R	26	28	30	32	34	36	38	40	42	44	46	48	50	52	54	56
	*R +	28	30	32	34	36	38	40	42	46	48	50	52	54	56	58	60
	@LIST	30	32	34	36	38	40	42	44	46	48	50	52	54	56	58	60
	@TABLE (R)	30	32	34	36	38	40	42	44	46	48	50	52	54	56	58	60
Memory Cycles	R	3								3							
	*R	4								4							
	*R +	5								5							
	@LIST	4								4							
	@TABLE (R)	5								5							

STCR

	Addressing Mode	Bit Count, C															
		1	2	3	4	5	6	7	8	9	10	11	12	13	14	15	0
Clock Cycles	R	42	42	42	42	42	42	42	44	58	58	58	58	58	58	58	60
	*R	46	46	46	46	46	46	46	48	62	62	62	62	62	62	62	64
	*R +	48	48	48	48	48	48	48	50	66	66	66	66	66	66	66	68
	@LIST	50	50	50	50	50	50	50	52	66	66	66	66	66	66	66	68
	@TABLE (R)	50	50	50	50	50	50	50	52	66	66	66	66	66	66	66	68
Memory Cycles	R	4								4							
	*R	5								5							
	*R..	6								6							
	@LIST	5								5							
	@TABLE (R)	6								6							

Figure 4-27.

Instruction	Clock Cycles					Memory Cycles				
	R	*R	*R+	@LIST,	@TABLE (R)	R	*R	*R+	@LIST	@TABLE (R)
ABS MSB = 0	12	16	20	20	20	2	3	4	3	4
MSB = 1	14	18	22	22	22	3	4	5	4	5
B	8	12	16	16	16	2	3	4	3	4
BL	12	16	20	20	20	3	4	5	4	5
BLWP	26	30	34	34	34	6	7	8	7	8
CLR	10	14	18	18	18	3	4	5	4	5
DEC	10	14	18	18	18	3	4	5	4	5
DECT	10	14	18	18	18	3	4	5	4	5
INC	10	14	18	18	18	3	4	5	4	5
INCT	10	14	18	18	18	3	4	5	4	5
INV	10	14	18	18	18	3	4	5	4	5
NEG	12	16	20	20	20	3	4	5	4	5
SETO	10	14	18	18	18	3	4	5	4	5
SWPB	10	14	18	18	18	3	4	5	4	5
XOP	36	40	44	44	44	8	9	8	9	8
XOR	14	18	22	22	22	4	5	6	5	6

Figure 4-28.

CYCLIC OPERATION

An example of a machine cycle sequence is illustrated in *Figure 4-29*. For an add
instruction the machine cycles alternate between memory cycles and ALU cycles. The
first cycle is always a memory read cycle to fetch the instruction and the second is always
an ALU cycle to decode the instruction. Each machine cycle requires two clock cycles,
thus the 7 machine cycles shown for the add instruction require 14 clock cycles.

A R1, R2

1	Memory Read	Instruction Fetch
2	ALU	Decode Opcode
3	Memory Read	Fetch (WR1)
4	ALU	Set Up
5	Memory Read	Fetch (WR2)
6	ALU	Addition
7	Memory Write	Store Result in WR2 and Increment PC

Figure 4-29. Machine Cycles for an Add Instruction

The 9900 performs its functions under control of a 4-phase clock and, fundamentally, performs instruction fetch and execution cycles. *Figure 4-30* illustrates the step-by-step procedure the 9900 uses to execute an add instruction. From previous cycles, the workspace pointer has been loaded with the number 0800, and the program counter contains the number 0100.

Step 1. The first step in any instruction cycle is to fetch the instruction. This is accomplished by gating the content of the program counter into the memory address register. The output of the memory address register is the address bus which is connected to the memory. In this case, word number 0100 is read from the memory and placed in the instruction register on the 9900 chip. From this point, the ones and zeros of the instruction register control the sequence of microcode stored in the microcontrol read only memory on the 9900 chip. These microsteps become the execution phase of the instruction.

Step 2. At this point, the microcontrol shifts to the execution of an add instruction; the first operand must be obtained from memory. In order to do this, the workspace pointer and a portion of the instruction word (the source operand register number) are added together via the ALU and placed in the memory address register.

Step 3. The address 0802 is the result (in this example), and being supplied to the memory produces on the data bus the content of memory word 0802 which is the binary equivalent of 25. This number must be stored in a temporary register on the 9900 chip, in this case the T1 register.

Step 4. Now a second operand must be fetched. Again the workspace pointer is added to the content of that portion of the instruction word which is the destination register identifier. The sum of these two is 0804 for register two, and this number is placed in memory address register and goes out on the address bus.

Step 5. Memory word 0804 is read and the number 10 is brought into the 9900 chip. The register which stores the second operand is called the source data register or S register.

Step 6. At this point the two operands have been loaded into registers on the 9900 chip and may be added by the ALU to produce the result. Register T1 containing 25 is added to the register S which contains 10 and the sum, 35, replaces the 10 in the S register and is placed on the data bus via the S register.

Step 7. The address bus still contains the number 0804 which was the address of the second operand and is the location in memory where the result is to be stored. So at this point in the cycle, a memory write cycle is initiated and the binary equivalent of 35 is stored in memory location 0804. At the conclusion of this memory cycle the program counter is incremented by two to point to the next sequential memory word, which is the instruction to be executed next.

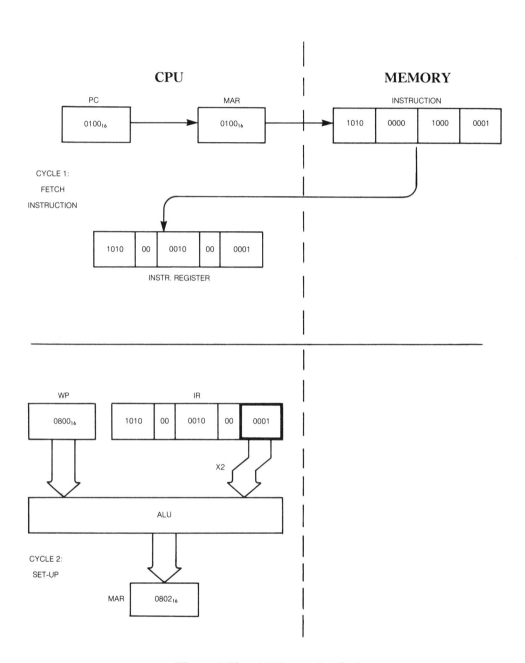

Figure 4-30a. Add Instruction Cycle

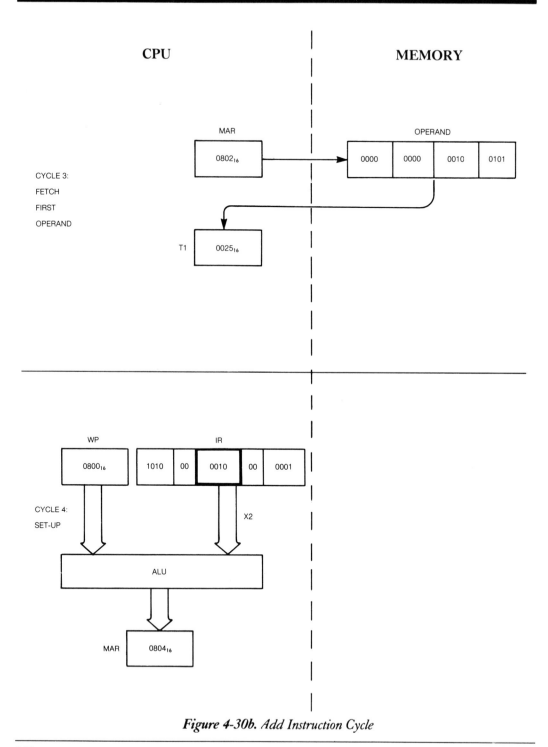

Figure 4-30b. *Add Instruction Cycle*

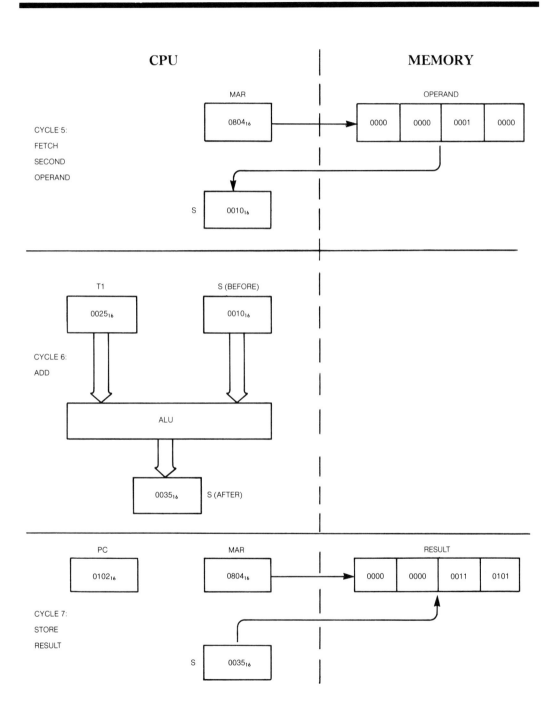

***Figure 4-30c.** Add Instruction Cycle*

After all steps have been done, the processor checks to see if there is any pending interrupt operations to be performed and, if not, fetches the next instruction and the cycle continues. In the event that an interrupt signal were present, the processor would proceed to the appropriate interrupt service routine and continue execution from that point. Interrupts are described in detail in a special section of this chapter.

Each operation performed by the 9900 consists of a sequence of machine cycles. In each machine cycle the processor performs a data transfer with memory or with CRU and/or an arithmetic or logical operation internally with the ALU. A detailed discussion of the machine cycles for each instruction is included at the end of the chapter.

Each ALU machine cycle is two clock cycles long. In an ALU cycle no external data transfer occurs, but the ALU performs an arithmetic or logical operation on two operands contained internally. The function of the memory read cycle is to transfer a word of data contained in the memory to the processor. An ALU operation may be performed during the memory read cycle. Memory read cycles are a minimum of two clock cycles long. The memory write cycle is identical to the memory read cycle except that data is written rather than read from memory.

Each CRU output machine cycle is two clock cycles long. In addition to outputting a bit of CRU data, an ALU operation may also be performed internally. The CRU input cycle is identical to the CRU output cycle except that one bit of data is input rather than output.

Machine Cycle Limits

Table 4-1 lists information which will be useful for system design. The maximum number of consecutive memory-read cycles is used to calculate the maximum latency for the TMS 9900 to enter the hold state since the hold state is only entered from ALU, CRU input, or CRU output machine cycles. The minimum frequency of consecutive memory/non-memory cycle sequences occurs when the DIV instruction is executed. This number is used to ensure that the refresh rate meets specifications when the transparent-refresh mode described in the memory section is used since memory is refreshed in this mode each time an ALU or CRU cycle follows a memory cycle. *Figure 4-31* shows the logic to generate a pulse for each memory access cycle. Consecutive cycle timing is shown in *Figure 4-32.*

Table 4-1. *Machine Cycle Limits*

	MINIMUM	MAXIMUM
Consecutive Memory Read Cycles	1	3
Consecutive Memory Write Cycles	1	1
Consecutive ALU Cycles	1	51
Consecutive CRU Cycles	1	16

Frequency of Consecutive memory/non-memory cycle pairs (used for transparent refresh)	**5 pairs** (64 machine cycles during DIV.)

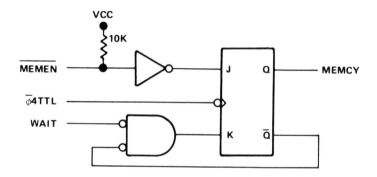

Figure 4-31. *Memory Cycle Pulse Generation*

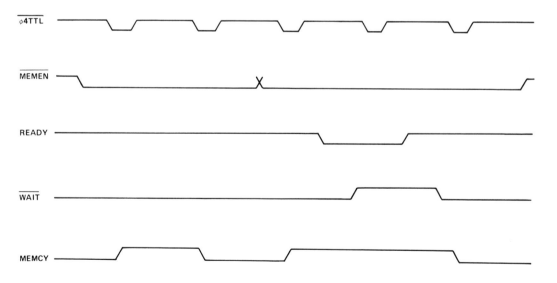

Figure 4-32. *Memory Cycle Pulse Timing*

INPUT/OUTPUT

The 9900 has three I/O modes: direct memory access (DMA), memory mapped, and communications register unit (CRU). This multi-mode capability enables the designer to optimize a 9900 I/O system to match a specific application. One or all modes can be used, as shown in *Figure 4-33*.

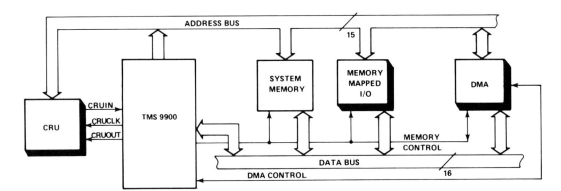

- COMMUNICATIONS REGISTER UNIT - CRU
- MEMORY MAPPED I/O
- DIRECT MEMORY ACCESS - DMA

Figure 4-33. 9900 I/O Capability

Direct Memory Access

DMA is used for high-speed block data transfer when CPU interaction is undesirable or not required. The DMA control circuitry can be relatively complex and expensive when compared to other I/O methods. However, a special interface device, the TMS 9911, is available for DMA control.

The 9900 controls CRU-based I/O transfers between the memory and peripheral devices. Data must pass through the CPU during these program-driven I/O transfers, and the CPU may need to be synchronized with the I/O device by interrupts or status-bit polling.

Some I/O devices, such as disk units, transfer large amounts of data to or from memory. Program driven I/O can require relatively large response times, high program overhead, or complex programming techniques. Consequently, direct memory access (DMA) is used to permit the I/O device to transfer data to or from memory without CPU intervention. DMA can result in a high I/O response time and system throughput, especially for block data transfers. The DMA control circuitry is somewhat more expensive and complex than the economical CRU I/O circuitry and should therefore be used only when required.

The 9900-based DMA can occur in the same modes as dynamic memory refresh: block, or cycle stealing. The block and cycle stealing modes, however, use the CPU $\overline{\text{HOLD}}$ capability and are more commonly used. The I/O device holds $\overline{\text{HOLD}}$ active (low) when a DMA transfer needs to occur. At the beginning of the next available non-memory cycle, the CPU enters the hold state and raises HOLDA to acknowledge the $\overline{\text{HOLD}}$ request. The maximum latency time between the hold request and the hold acknowledge is equal to three clock cycles plus three memory cycles. The minimum latency time is equal to one clock cycle. A 3-megahertz system with no wait cycles has a maximum hold latency of nine clock cycles or 3 microseconds and a minimum hold latency of one clock cycle or 0.3 microseconds.

When HOLDA goes high, the CPU address bus, data bus, DBIN, $\overline{\text{MEMEN}}$, and $\overline{\text{WE}}$ are in the high-impedance state to allow the I/O device to use the memory bus. The I/O device must then generate the proper address, data, and control signals and timing to transfer data to or from the memory as shown in *Figure 4-34.* Thus the DMA device has control of the memory bus when the TMS 9900 enters the hold state (HOLDA = 1), and may perform memory accesses without intervention by the microprocessor. Since DMA operations, in effect remove the 9900 from control while memory accesses are being performed, no further discussion is provided in this manual. Because the lines shown in *Figure 4-34* go into high impedance when HOLDA = 1, the DMA controller must force these signals to the proper levels. The I/O device can use the memory bus for one transfer (cycle-stealing mode) or for multiple transfers (block mode). At the end of the DMA transfer, the I/O device releases $\overline{\text{HOLD}}$ and normal CPU operation proceeds. The 9900 $\overline{\text{HOLD}}$ and HOLDA timing are shown in *Figure 4-35.*

Memory Mapped I/O

Memory mapped I/O permits I/O data to be addressed as memory with parallel data transfer through the system data bus. Memory mapped I/O requires a memory bus compatible interface; that is, the device is addressed in the same manner as a memory, thus the interface is identical to that of memory. *Figure 4-36* shows a memory mapped I/O interface with eight latched outputs and eight buffered inputs. In using memory mapped I/O for output only, care must be taken in developing the output device strobe to ensure it is not enabled during the initial read of the memory address, since the 9900 family of processors first reads, then writes data to a memory location in write operations. This can be effectively accomplished by using the processor write control signal $\overline{\text{WE}}$ in decoding the output address.

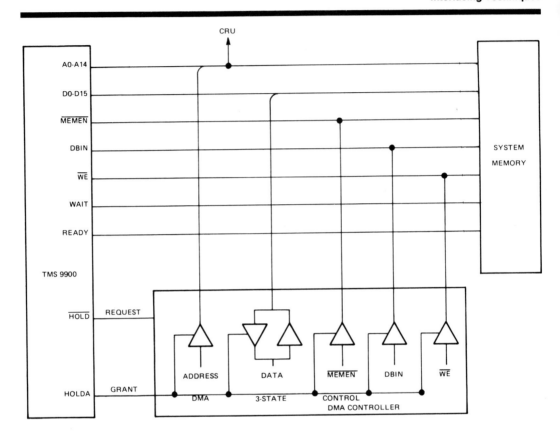

Figure 4-34. DMA Bus Control

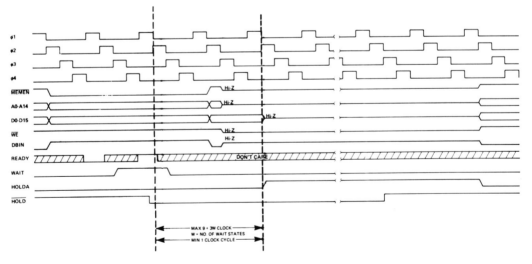

Figure 4-35. $\overline{HOLD}$ and HOLDA Timing

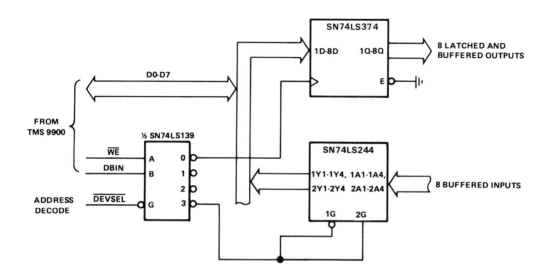

Figure 4-36. 8-Bit Memory Mapped I/O Interface

COMMUNICATION REGISTER UNIT (CRU)

CRU I/O uses a dedicated bit addressable interface for I/O. The CRU instructions permit transfer of one to sixteen bits. The CRU interface requires fewer interface signals than the memory interface and can be expanded without affecting the memory system. In the majority of applications, CRU I/O is superior to memory mapped I/O as a result of the powerful bit manipulation capability, flexible field lengths, and simple bus structure.

The CRU bit manipulation instructions eliminate the masking instructions required to isolate a bit in memory mapped I/O. The CRU multiple-bit instructions allow the use of I/O fields not identical to the memory word size, thus permitting optimal use of the I/O interface. Therefore, the CRU minimizes the size and complexity of the I/O control programs, while increasing system throughput.

The CRU does not utilize the memory data bus. This can reduce the complexity of printed circuit board layouts for most systems. The standard 16-pin CRU I/O devices are less expensive and easier to insert than larger, specially designed, memory mapped I/O devices. The smaller I/O devices are possible as a result of the bit addressable CRU bus which eliminates the need for multiple pins dedicated to a parallel-data bus with multiple control lines. System costs are lower because of simplified circuit layouts, increased density, and lower component costs.

CRU Interface

The interface between the 9900 and CRU devices consists of address bus lines A0-A14, and the three control lines, CRUIN, CRUOUT, and CRUCLK as shown in *Figure 4-33*. A0-A2 indicate whether data is to be transferred and A3-A14 contain the address of the selected bit for data transfers; therefore, up to 2^{12} or 4,096 bits of input and 4,096 bits of output may be individually addressed. CRU operations and memory-data transfers both use A0-A14; however, these operations are performed independently, thus no conflict arises. The $\overline{\text{MEMEN}}$ line may be used to distinguish between CRU and memory cycles.

CRU Interface Logic

CRU based I/O interfaces are easily implemented using either CRU peripheral devices such as the TMS 9901 or the TMS 9902, or TTL multiplexers and addressable latches, such as the TIM 9905 (SN74LS251) and the TIM 9906 (SN74LS259). These I/O circuits can be easily cascaded with the addition of simple address decoding logic.

TTL Outputs. The TIM 9906 (SN74LS259) octal-addressable latch can be used for CRU outputs. The latch outputs are stable and are altered only when the CRUCLK is pulsed during a CRU output transfer. Each addressable latch is enabled only when addressed as determined by the upper address bits. The least-significant address bits (A12-A14) determine which of the eight outputs of the selected latch is to be set equal to CRUOUT during CRUCLK, and shown in *Figure 4-37*.

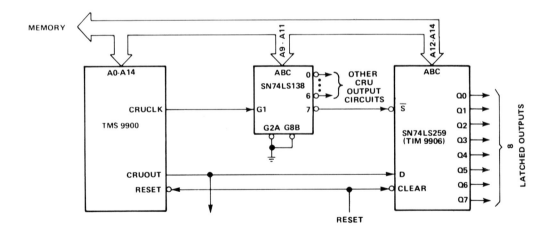

Figure 4-37. Latched CRU Interface

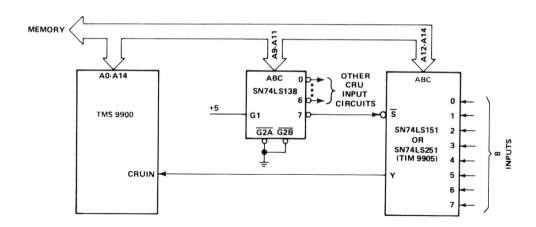

Figure 4-38. Multiplexer CRU Interface

TTL Inputs. The SN74LS151 and TIM 9905 (SN74LS251) octal multiplexers are used for CRU inputs as shown in *Figure 4-38*. The multiplexers are continuously enabled with CRUIN equal to the addressed input. The TIM 9905 should be used for larger systems since its three-state outputs permit simple "wire-ORing" of parallel-input multiplexers.

Expanding CRU I/O

A CRU interface with eight inputs and eight outputs is shown in *Figure 4-39* using the TMS 9901. An expanded interface with 16 inputs and 16 outputs is shown in *Figure 4-40* using TTL devices. The CRU inputs and outputs can be expanded up to 4096 inputs and 4096 outputs by decoding the complete CRU address. Larger I/O requirements can be satisfied by using memory mapped I/O or by using a CRU bank switch, which is set and reset under program control. When reset, the lower CRU I/O bank is selected, and when set, the upper CRU I/O bank is selected. In actual system applications, however, only the exact number of interface bits required need to be implemented. It is not necessary to have a 16-bit CRU output register to interface a 10-bit device.

CRU Machine Cycles

Each CRU operation consists of one or more CRU output or CRU input machine cycles, each of which is two clock cycles long. As shown in *Table 4-2*, five instructions (LDCR, STCR, SBO, SBZ, TB) transfer data to or from the 9900 with CRU machine cycles, and five external control instructions (IDLE, RSET, CKOF, CKON, LREX) generate control signals with CRU output machine cycles.

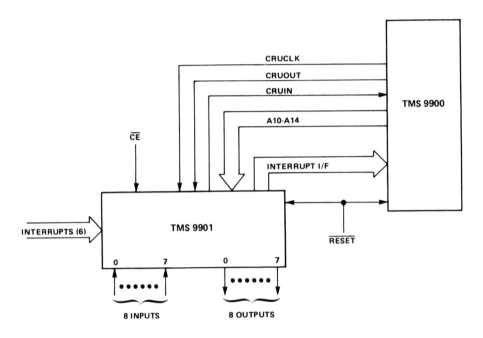

Figure 4-39. 8-Bit CRU Interface

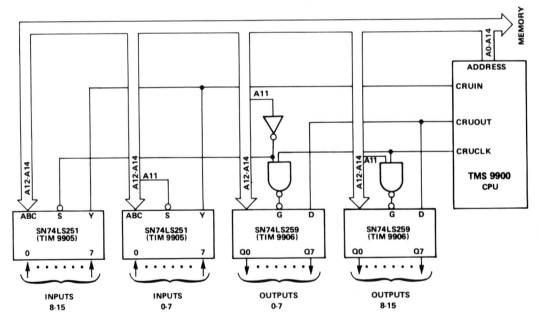

Figure 4-40. 16-Bit CRU Interface

Table 4-2. Instructions Generating CRU Cycles

INSTRUCTION	NUMBER OF CRU CYCLES	TYPE OF CRU CYCLES	A0-A2	DATA TRANSFER
LDCR	1-16	Output	0 0 0	Yes
STCR	1-16	Input	0 0 0	Yes
SBO	1	Output	0 0 0	Yes
SBZ	1	Output	0 0 0	Yes
TB	1	Input	0 0 0	Yes
IDLE	1	Output	0 1 0	No
RSET	1	Output	0 1 1	No
CKOF	1	Output	1 0 1	No
CKON	1	Output	1 1 0	No
LREX	1	Ouput	1 1 1	No

Figure 4-41 shows the timing for CRU *output* machine cycles. Address (A0-A14) and data (CRUOUT) are output on $\phi2$ of clock cycle 1. One clock cycle later, the 9900 outputs a pulse on CRUCLK for ½ clock cycle. Thus, CRUCLK can be used as a strobe, since address and data are stable during the pulse. Referring again to *Table 4-2,* it is important to note that output data is transferred only when A0-A2 = 000. Otherwise, no data transfer should occur, and A0-A2 should be decoded to determine which external control instruction is being executed. These external control instructions may be used to perform simple control operations. The generation of control strobes for external instructions and a data transfer strobe (OUTCLK) is illustrated in *Figure 4-42*. If none of the external control instructions is used, A0-A2 need not be decoded for data transfer since they will always equal 000.

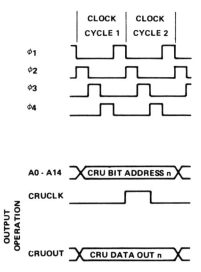

Figure 4-41. CRU Output Machine Cycle Timing

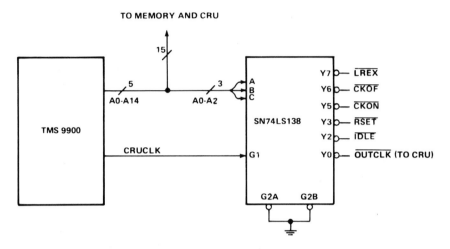

Figure 4-42. CRU Control Strobe Generation

The timing for CRU *input* machine cycles is shown in *Figure 4-43*. The address is output at the beginning of the first clock cycle. The CRUIN data input is sampled on $\phi 1$ of clock cycle 2. Thus, CRU input is accomplished by simply multiplexing the addressed bit onto the CRUIN input. A0-A2 will always be 000, and may be ignored. CRU input machine cycles cannot be differentiated from ALU cycles by external logic, thus no operations (such as clearing interrupts) other than CRU input should be performed during CRU input machine cycles.

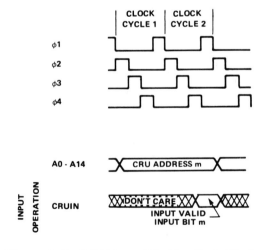

Figure 4-43. CRU Input Machine Cycle Timing

CRU Data Transfer

In order to transfer data from a memory location to an external latch in the Communications Register Unit, or to transfer data from a CRU multiplexer to memory, special instructions must be used. The CRU instructions are:

SBO	Set bit to one (output)
SBZ	Set bit to zero (output)
TB	Test bit (input)
LDCR	Load n bits to CRU (output)
STCR	Receive n bits from CRU (input)

These instructions always use the address bus to identify the bit or bits to be transferred, but they make the actual transfer of data over the dedicated CRU lines, CRUIN and CRUOUT. Addressing of the CRU bits is accomplished by adding a portion of the instruction word to a CRU base address register. The use of such a base address technique allows one program segment to service any number of identical I/O devices. For example: five TMS 9902's each with its own assigned base address can be operated from a single program, provided the base address register is properly set at the beginning. In the 9900, workspace register 12 is the CRU software base address register. All CRU instructions use the contents of this register in addressing individual CRU bits.

The CRU hardware base address is defined by bits 3-14 of the current WR12 when CRU data transfer is performed. Bits 0-2 and bit 15 of WR12 are ignored for CRU address determination.

For single-bit CRU instructions (SBO, SBZ, TB), the address of the CRU bit to or from which data is transferred is determined as shown in *Figure 4-44*. Bits 8-15 of the machine code instruction contain a signed displacement. This signed displacement is added to the CRU hardware base address (bits 3-14 of WR12). The result of this addition is output on A3-A14 during the CRU output or the CRU input machine cycle.

For example, assume the instruction "SBO 9" is executed when WR12 contains a value of 1040_{16}. The machine code for "SBO 9" is $1D09_{16}$ and the signed displacement is 0009_{16}. The CRU hardware base address is 0820_{16} (bits 0-2 and bit 15 are ignored). Thus, the effective CRU bit address is $0820_{16} + 0009_{16} = 0829_{16}$, and this value is output on A0-A14 during the CRU output machine cycle.

As a second example, assume that the instruction TB $- 32$ is executed when $WR12 = 100_{16}$. The effective CRU address is 80_{16}. (CRU hardware base) $+ FFEO_{16}$ (signed displacement) $= 60_{16}$. Thus, the TB $- 32$ instruction in this example causes the value of the CRU input bit at address 60_{16} to be transferred to bit 2 of the status register. This bit is tested in the execution of the JEQ or JNE instructions; if it is a one, the PC will be loaded with a new value (JEQ instruction).

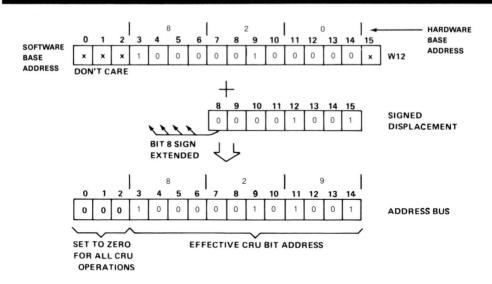

Figure 4-44. TMS 9900 Single-Bit CRU Address Development

LDCR Instruction

The LDCR may transfer from 1 to 16 bits of output data with each instruction. Output of each bit is performed by a CRU output machine cycle; thus, the number of CRU output machine cycles performed by an LDCR instruction is equal to the number of bits to be transferred.

As an example, assume that the instruction "LDCR @600,10" is executed, and that WR12 = 800_{16} and the memory word at address 600 contains the bit pattern shown in *Figure 4-45*. In the first CRU output machine cycle the least significant bit of the operand (a) is output on CRUOUT. In each successive machine cycle the address is incremented by one and the next least-significant bit of the operand is output on CRUOUT, until 10 bits have been output. It is important to note that the CRU base address is unaltered by the LDCR instruction, even though the address is incremented as each successive bit is output.

STCR Instruction

The STCR instruction causes from 1 to 16 bits of CRU data to be transferred into memory. Each bit is input by a CRU input machine cycle.

Consider the circuit shown in *Figure 4-46*. The CRU interface logic multiplexes input signals m-t onto the CRUIN line for addresses 200_{16}-207_{16}. If WR12 = 400_{16} when the instruction "STCR @ 602,6" is executed, the operation is performed as shown in *Figure 4-47*. At the end of the instruction, the six LSBs of memory byte 602 are loaded with m-r. The upper bits of the operand are forced to zero.

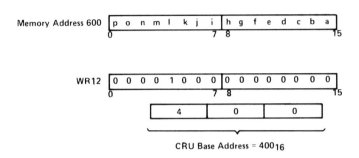

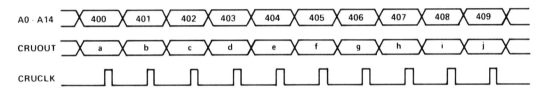

Figure 4-45. Multiple-Bit CRU Output

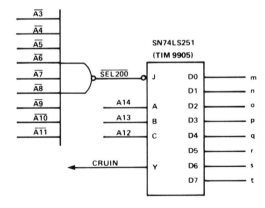

Figure 4-46. Example CRU Input Circuit

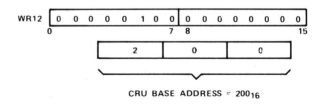

CRU BASE ADDRESS = 200_{16}

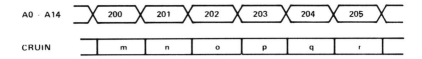

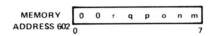

Figure 4-47. Multiple-Bit CRU Input

CRU Paper Tape Reader Interface

CRU interface circuits are used to interface data and control lines from external devices to the 9900. This section describes an example interface from a paper tape reader.
The paper tape reader is assumed to have the following characteristics:

1. It generates a TTL-level active-high signal (SPROCKET HOLE) on detection of a sprocket hole on the paper tape.

2. It generates an 8-bit TTL active-low data which stays valid during SPROCKET HOLE = 1.

3. It responds to a TTL-level active-high command (Paper Tape RUN) signal by turning on when PTRUN = 1 and turning off when PTRUN = 0.

Figure 4-48 illustrates the circuitry to interface the reader to the CRU. The interface is selected when $\overline{PTRSEL}$ = 0; $\overline{PTRSEL}$ is decoded from the A0-A11 address outputs from the 9900. Thus, the output of the SN74LS251 is active only when $\overline{PTRSEL}$ = 0; otherwise, the output is in high impedance and other devices may drive CRUIN. The data inputs are selected by A12-A14 and inverted, resulting in active high data input on CRUIN. The positive transition of SPROCKET HOLE causes $\overline{PTRINT}$ to go low. $\overline{PTRINT}$ is the active low interrupt from the interface. $\overline{PTRINT}$ is set high, clearing the interrupt, whenever a CRU output machine cycle is executed and the address causes $\overline{PTRSEL}$ to be active. When a one is output, $\overline{PTRUN}$ is set, enabling the reader, and the reader is disabled when a zero is output to the device. Thus, any time $\overline{PTRUN}$ is set or reset, the interrupt is automatically cleared.

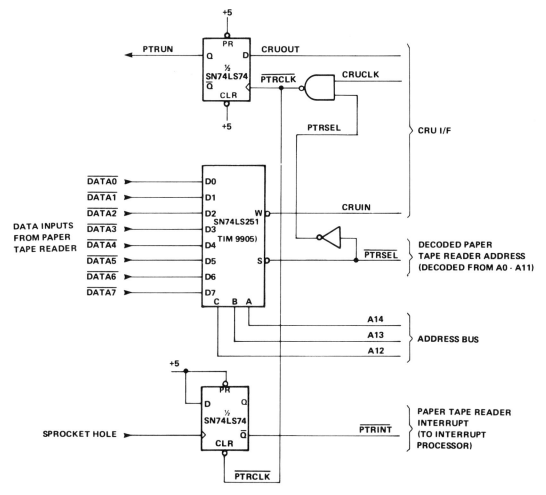

Figure 4-48. Paper Tape Reader Interface

The software routine in *Figure 4-49* controls the paper-tape reader interface described above. It is a re-entrant procedure that can be shared by several readers. The assumptions are that:

1. Each reader has its own workspace which is set up on the trap location for that reader's interrupt.

2. The workspace registers are allocated as shown in *Figure 4-50.*

3. The CRU input bits 0-7 (relative to CRU base) are reader data. CRU output bit 0 controls PTRUN and clears the interrupt.

4. The most significant byte of R9 = End of File Code.

5. R10 = Overflow Count

6. R11 = Data Table Pointer Address.

The procedure has two entry points. It is entered by a calling routine at PTRBEG to start the reader and it returns control to that routine. It is entered at PTRINT via interrupt to read a character. The return in this case is to the interrupted program.

The control program may be used by any number of paper-tape reader interfaces, as long as each interface has a separate interrupt level and workspace. As each reader issues an interrupt, the 9900 will process the interrupt beginning at location PTRINT. However, the workspace unique to the interrupting device is used. The organization of memory to control two paper tape readers is shown in *Figure 4-50.* The interrupt-transfer vector causes the appropriate WP value to be loaded. In both cases PTRINT, the entry point for the control program, is loaded into the PC.

PTRINT	STCR	*R11, 8
	CB	*R11+, R9
	JEQ	PTREND
	DEC	R10
	JEQ	PTREND
PTRBEG	SBO	PTRUN
	RTWP	
PTREND	SBZ	PTRUN
	LI	R10, MAXCOUNT
	RTWP	

Figure 4-49. Paper Tape Reader Control Program

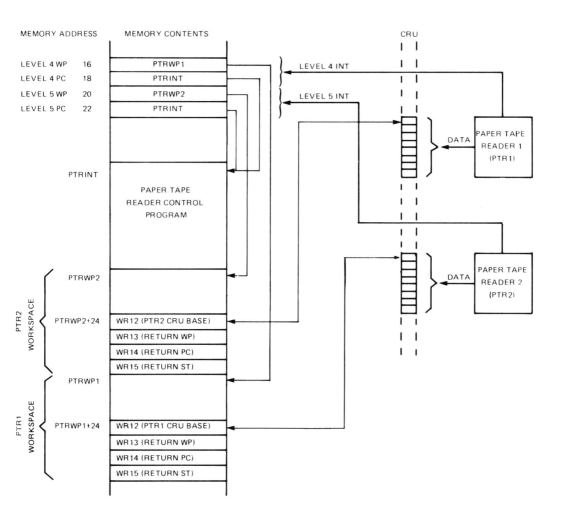

Figure 4-50. Software Configuration for Two Paper Tape Readers with Common Control Program

Burroughs SELF-SCAN Display Interface

This section describes a TMS9900 CRU interface to a Burroughs SELF-SCAN® panel display model SS30132-0070. The display panel has a 32-position, single-row character array with a repertoire of 128 characters.

The panel display operates in a serial-shift mode in which characters are shifted into the panel one at a time. Characters are shifted in right-to-left and can be shifted or backspaced left-to-right. A clear pulse erases the display.

The CRU display interface is shown in *Figure 4-51* and a display control subroutine is shown in *Figure 4-52.* The subroutine is called by one of two XOP instructions, XOP0 and XOP1. The calling routine passes the address and length of the output string in registers 8 and 9 of its workspace. The two XOP subroutines share the same workspace and perform the same function except that XOP1 clears the panel display first. The backspace feature is not used. The panel display is blanked during character entry.

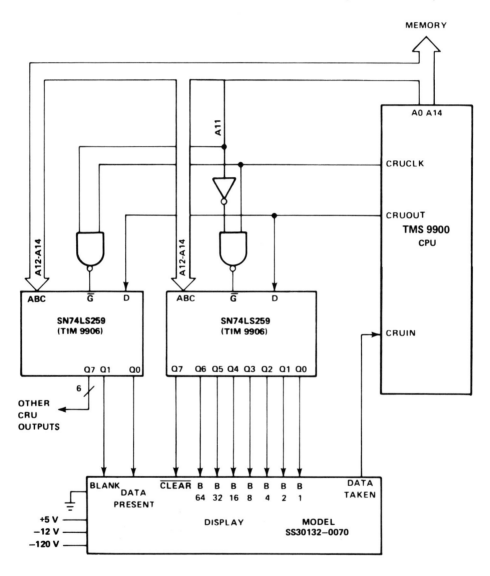

Figure 4-51. Display Control Interface

EIGHT	EQU	16	
NINE	EQU	18	
RXOP1	SBZ	7	Clear Panel
	LI	R1,11	
LOOP1	DEC	R1	Delay >67μsec
	JNE	LOOP1	
	SBO	7	
RXOP2	SBO	9	Blank Panel
	MOV	@EIGHT (13),1	Load Address (Old R8→R1)
	MOV	@NINE (13),2	Load Length (Old R9→R2)
LOOP2	LDCR	*1+,7	Output Char
	SBO	8	Data Present
WAIT	TB	0	Wait for Data Taken
	JEQ	Wait	
	SBZ	8	
	DEC	2	Decrement Count
	JNE	LOOP2	Loop Until Through
	SBZ	9	Unblank Panel
	RTWP		Return

Figure 4-52. Burroughs SELF-SCAN® Display Control Program

INTERRUPTS

The TMS 9900 provides fifteen maskable interrupt levels in addition to the $\overline{\text{RESET}}$ and $\overline{\text{LOAD}}$ functions. The CPU has a priority ranking system to resolve conflicts between simultaneous interrupts and a level mask to disable lower priority interrupts. Once an interrupt is recognized, the CPU performs a vectored context switch to the interrupt service routine. The $\overline{\text{RESET}}$ and $\overline{\text{LOAD}}$ functions are initiated by external input signals.

RESET

The $\overline{\text{RESET}}$ signal is normally used to initialize the CPU following a power-up. When active (low), the $\overline{\text{RESET}}$ signal inhibits $\overline{\text{WE}}$ and CRUCLK, places the CPU memory bus and control signals in a high-impedance state, and resets the CPU. When the $\overline{\text{RESET}}$ signal is released, the CPU fetches the restart vector from locations 0000 and 0002, stores the old WP, PC, and ST into the new workspace, resets all status bits to zero and starts execution at the new PC. The $\overline{\text{RESET}}$ signal must be held active for a minimum of three clock cycles. The $\overline{\text{RESET}}$ machine cycle sequence is shown in *Figure 4-53.*

A convenient method of generating the $\overline{\text{RESET}}$ signal is to use the Schmitt-triggered D-input of the TIM9904 clock generator. An RC network connected to the D-input maintains an active $\overline{\text{RESET}}$ signal for a short time immediately following the power-on, as shown in *Figure 4-54.*

CYCLE	TYPE	FUNCTION
*	*	Loop While Reset is Active
1	ALU	Set Up
2	ALU	Set Up
3	Memory	Fetch New WP, Move Status To T Reg, Clear Status
4	ALU	Set Up
5	Memory	Store Status
6	ALU	Set Up
7	Memory	Store PC
8	ALU	Set Up
9	Memory	Store WP
10	ALU	Set Up
11	Memory	Fetch New PC
12	ALU	Set Up MAR for Next Instruction

Figure 4-53. RESET Machine Cycles

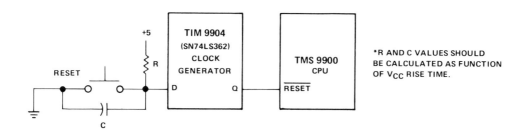

Figure 4-54. $\overline{RESET}$ Generation

LOAD

The $\overline{\text{LOAD}}$ signal is normally used to implement a restart ROM loader or front panel functions. When active (low), the $\overline{\text{LOAD}}$ signal causes the CPU to perform a non-maskable interrupt. The $\overline{\text{LOAD}}$ signal can be used to terminate a CPU idle state.

The $\overline{\text{LOAD}}$ signal should be active for one instruction period. Since there is no standard TMS 9900 instruction period, IAQ should be used to determine instruction boundaries. If the $\overline{\text{LOAD}}$ signal is active during the time that the $\overline{\text{RESET}}$ signal is released, the CPU will perform the $\overline{\text{LOAD}}$ function immediately after the $\overline{\text{RESET}}$ function is completed. The CPU performs the $\overline{\text{LOAD}}$ function by fetching the $\overline{\text{LOAD}}$ vector from addresses $FFFC_{16}$ and $FFFE_{16}$, storing the old WP, PC, and ST in the new workspace, and starting the $\overline{\text{LOAD}}$ service routine at the new PC, as shown in *Figure 4-55*.

An example of the use of the $\overline{\text{LOAD}}$ signal is a bootstrap ROM loader. When the $\overline{\text{LOAD}}$ signal is enabled, the CPU enters the service routine, transfers a program from peripheral storage to RAM, and then transfers control to the loaded program.

Figure 4-56 illustrates the generation of the $\overline{\text{LOAD}}$ signal for one instruction period.

CYCLE	TYPE	FUNCTION
1	ALU	Set Up
2	Memory Read	Fetch New WP
3	ALU	Set Up
4	Memory Write	Store Status
5	ALU	Set Up
6	Memory Write	Store PC
7	ALU	Set Up
8	Memory Write	Store WP
9	ALU	Set Up
10	Memory Read	Fetch New PC
11	ALU	Set UP MAR for Next Instruction

Figure 4-55. $\overline{LOAD}$ Machine Cycle Sequence

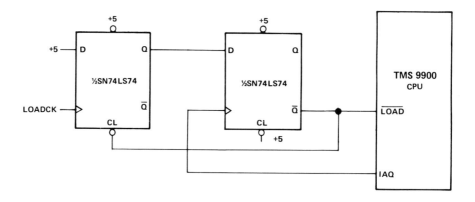

Figure 4-56. $\overline{LOAD}$ Generation

Basic Machine Cycle

The interrelationship between the $\overline{\text{LOAD}}$ and $\overline{\text{RESET}}$ signals and the general operation of the 9900 and execution of instructions may best be shown by the flow diagram in *Figure 4-57*. An orderly starting procedure involves the holding of the $\overline{\text{RESET}}$ line low when power is applied to the chip. After application of power and after the clock has begun to run, the internal instruction control circuitry checks to see if the $\overline{\text{RESET}}$ line is held low, and, if the answer is "yes", will stay in a loop as shown in the diagram. When the $\overline{\text{RESET}}$ line goes high, it is no longer active and a level zero interrupt is taken in which the $\overline{\text{RESET}}$ vector, the numbers to fill the workspace pointer and program counter registers, are fetched from memory locations zero and two. Furthermore, the previous values of the workspace pointer, program counter and status register are stored in the new workspace, although these values are random numbers immediately following power up. Following this, the interrupt mask is set to zero to mask all other interrupts.

The next decision is regarding the $\overline{\text{LOAD}}$ line. If this particular line is active, or low, then immediately there will be another context switch in which the $\overline{\text{LOAD}}$ vector will be brought in from the last two locations in memory, $FFFC_{16}$ and $FFFE_{16}$, and loaded into the workspace pointer and program counter respectively. If the $\overline{\text{LOAD}}$ is not active, the 9900 proceeds directly to an instruction acquisition cycle. In either case, the very next step is to fetch the instruction from the memory and execute it.

Following this, the program counter is updated and a sequence of checks made regarding the $\overline{\text{LOAD}}$, XOP, and interrupt conditions. First is the check for the $\overline{\text{LOAD}}$ line. If this is active, the $\overline{\text{LOAD}}$ context switch will occur. If not, there will be a test to see if the instruction just executed was an XOP or BLWP. If not, the interrupt request line will be checked. If there is not an interrupt request, and the last instruction was not an idle instruction, the machine may proceed to fetch the next instruction and continue.

In the event that the last instruction executed was an XOP or BLWP, the 9900 will ignore the interrupt request line and will proceed to fetch a new instruction. This insures that at least one instruction of a subprogram that is entered via a context switch will be executed before another context switch may occur, such as an interrupt. In the event that the interrupt request line is active following the execution of a normal instruction, a test is made to determine that the interrupt is valid, that is to say, "Is the interrupt mask set to allow this interrupt." If the interrupt is not allowed, the processor proceeds to fetch the next instruction. In the event that it is allowed, a context switch will be made and the interrupt vector from the appropriate locations in the first 32 words of memory will be fetched and the workspace pointer and program counter will be loaded with the new numbers. As a part of this context switch, the interrupt mask is set to a level one less than the interrupt just taken. This is to insure that no lower priority interrupt may occur during the servicing of the current interrupt cycle. Notice further that in this diagram that the logic is such that at least one instruction of any subprogram will be executed immediately following a context switch. The only exception to this is the simultaneous presence of $\overline{\text{RESET}}$ and $\overline{\text{LOAD}}$ signals. Finally, the idle instruction will suspend instruction execution in the 9900 until an interrupt, $\overline{\text{RESET}}$ or $\overline{\text{LOAD}}$ signal occurs.

MASKABLE INTERRUPTS

The TMS 9900 has 16 interrupt levels with the lower 15 priority levels used for maskable interrupts. The maskable interrupts are prioritized and have transfer vectors similar to the $\overline{\text{RESET}}$ and $\overline{\text{LOAD}}$ vectors.

Interrupt Service

A pending interrupt of unmasked priority level is serviced at the end of the current instruction cycle with two exceptions. The first instruction of a $\overline{\text{RESET}}$, $\overline{\text{LOAD}}$, or interrupt service routine is executed before the CPU tests the $\overline{\text{INTREQ}}$ signal. The interrupt is also inhibited for one instruction if the current instruction is a branch and load workspace pointer instruction (BLWP) or an extended operation (XOP). The one instruction delay permits one instruction to be completed before an interrupt context switch can occur. A LIMI instruction can be used as the first instruction in a routine to lock out higher priority maskable interrupts.

The pending interrupt request should remain active until recognized by the CPU during the service routine. The interrupt request should then be cleared under program control. The CRU bit manipulation instructions can be used to recognize and clear the interrupt request.

The interrupt context switch causes the interrupt vector to be fetched, the old WP, PC, and ST to be saved in the new workspace, and the new WP and PC to be loaded. Bits 12-15 of ST are loaded with a value of one less than the level of the interrupt being serviced. The old WP, PC, and ST are stored in the new workspace registers 13, 14, and 15. When the return instruction is executed, the old WP, PC, and ST are restored to the CPU. Since the ST contains the interrupt mask, the old interrupt level is also restored. Consequently, all interrupt service routines should terminate with the return instruction in order to restore the CPU to its state before the interrupt.

The linkage between two interrupt service routines is shown in *Figure 4-58* and the interrupt machine cycle sequence is shown in *Figure 4-59.*

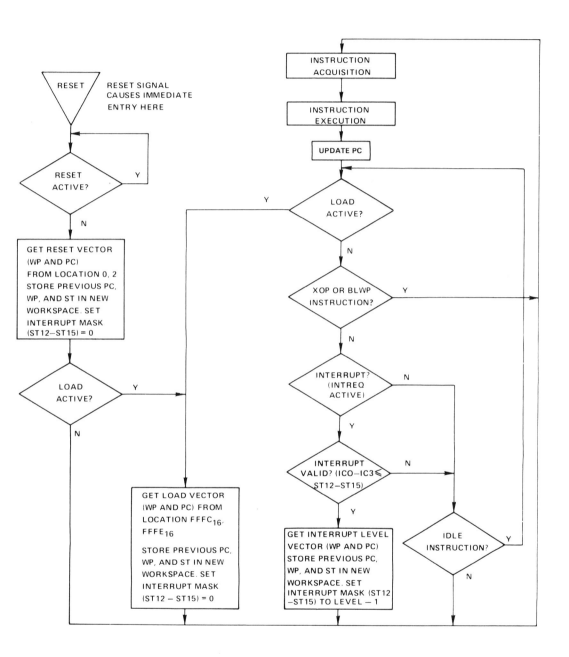

Figure 4-57. TMS 9900 CPU Flow Chart

Interrupt Signals

The TMS 9900 has five inputs that control maskable interrupts. The $\overline{\text{INTREQ}}$ signal is active (low) when a maskable interrupt is pending. If $\overline{\text{INTREQ}}$ is active at the end of the instruction cycle, the CPU compares the priority code on IC0 through IC3 to the interrupt mask (ST12-ST15). If the interrupt code of the pending interrupt is equal to or less than the current interrupt mask, the CPU executes a vectored interrupt; otherwise, the interrupt request is ignored. The interrupt priority codes are shown in *Table 4-3*. Note that the level-0 interrupt code should not be used for external interrupts since level 0 is reserved for RESET.

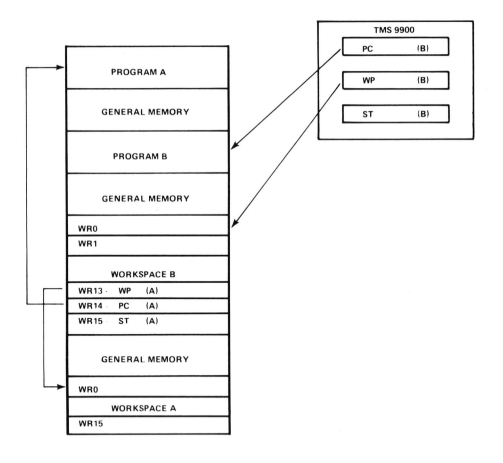

Figure 4-58. Interrupt Linkage

CYCLE	TYPE	FUNCTION
1	ALU	Set Up
2	Memory Read	Fetch New WP
3	ALU	Set Up
4	Memory Write	Store Status
5	ALU	Set Up
6	Memory Write	Store PC
7	ALU	Set Up
8	Memory Write	Store WP
9	ALU	Set Up
10	Memory Read	Fetch New PC
11	ALU	Set Up MAR for Next Instruction

Figure 4-59. Interrupt Processing Machine Cycle Sequence

Figure 4-60 illustrates the use of the TMS 9901 programmable system interface for generation of the interrupt code from individual interrupt input lines. The TMS 9901 provides six dedicated and nine programmable latched, synchronized, and prioritized interrupts, complete with individual enabling/disabling masks. Synchronization prevents transition of ICO-IC3 while the code is being read. A single-interrupt system with an arbitrarily chosen level-7 code is shown in *Figure 4-61*. The single-interrupt input does not need to be synchronized since the hardwired interrupt code is always stable.

Interrupt Masking

The TMS 9900 uses a four-bit field in the status register, ST12 through ST15, to determine the current interrupt priority level. The interrupt mask is automatically loaded with a value of one less than the level of the maskable interrupt being serviced. The interrupt mask is also affected by the load interrupt mask instruction (LIMI).

Since the interrupt mask is compared to the external interrupt code before an interrupt is recognized, an interrupt service routine will not be halted due to another interrupt of lower or equal priority unless a LIMI instruction is used to alter the interrupt mask. The LIMI instruction can be used to alter the interrupt-mask level in order to disable intervening interrupt levels. At the end of the service routine, a return (RTWP) restores the interrupt mask to its value before the current interrupt occurred.

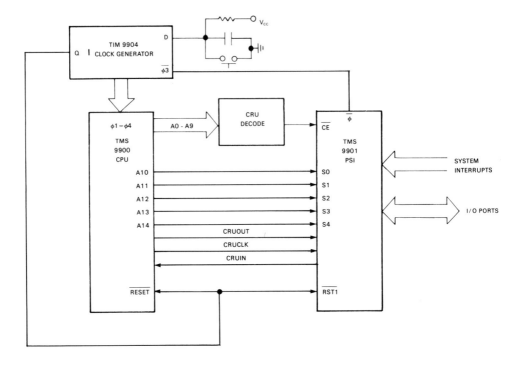

Figure 4-60. System With 15 External Interrupts

Table 4-3. Interrupt Priority Codes

Interrupt Level		Vector Location (Memory Address In Hex)	Device Assignment	Interrupt Mask Values To Enable Respective Interrupts (ST12 thru ST15)	Interrupt Codes IC0 thru IC3
(Highest priority)	0	00	Reset	0 through F*	0000
	1	04	External device	1 through F	0001
	2	08		2 through F	0010
	3	0C		3 through F	0011
	4	10		4 through F	0100
	5	14		5 through F	0101
	6	18		6 through F	0110
	·7	1C		7 through F	0111
	8	20		8 through F	1000
	9	24		9 through F	1001
	10	28		A through F	1010
	11	2C		B through F	1011
	12	30		C through F	1100
	13	34		D through F	1101
	14	38		E and F	1110
(Lowest priority)	15	3C	External device	F only	1111

*Level 0 can not be disabled.

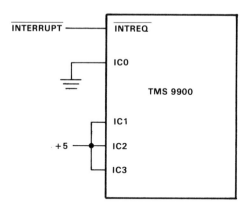

Figure 4-61. Single-Interrupt System

Note that the TMS 9900 actually generates the interrupt vector address using IC0-IC3 five clock cycles after it has sampled $\overline{\text{INTREQ}}$ and four clock cycles after it has compared the interrupt code to the interrupt mask in the status register. Thus, interrupt sources which have individual masking capability can cause erroneous operation if a command to the device to mask the interrupt occurs at a time when the interrupt is active and just after the TMS 9900 has sampled $\overline{\text{INTREQ}}$ but before the vector address has been generated using IC0-IC3.

The individual interrupt masking operation can be easily allowed if the masking instruction is placed in a short subroutine which masks all interrupts with a LIMI 0 instruction before individually masking the interrupt at the device, as shown in *Figure 4-62.*

INCORRECT

	XXX		
	SBO	0	SET MASK (INTERRUPT CAN OCCUR DURING SBO CAUSING ERRONEOUS
	YYY		OPERATION)

CORRECT

	XXX		
	BLWP	9	(WR9) = ADDRESS OF SBW
			(WR10) = ADDRESS OF SB1
	XXXX		
SB1	LIMI	0	CLEAR STATUS MASK TO INHIBIT INTERRUPTS
	MOV	@ 24 (13), 12	MOVE CRU BASE ADDRESS TO WR12
	SBO	0	SET MASK
	RTWP		RETURN
SBW	BSS	32	**SUBROUTINE WORKSPACE**

Figure 4-62. External Interrupt Clearing Routine

Interrupt Processing Example

The routine in *Figure 4-63* illustrates the use of the LIMI instruction as a privileged or non-interruptable instruction. The level-5 routine sets a CRU bit and then loops until a corresponding CRU bit is true. The first instruction in the routine is completed before a higher priority interrupt can be recognized. The LIMI instruction, however, raises the CPU priority level to level 0 in order to disable all other maskable interrupts. Consequently, the level-5 routine will run to completion unless a RESET signal or a LOAD signal is generated. At the end of the routine, the RTWP instruction restores the CPU to its state before the level-5 interrupt occurred.

Level 5	LIMI	0	Disable Maskable INTREQs
	SBO	ACK	Set CRU Output Bit
Loop	TB	RDY	Test CRU Input Bit
	JNE	LOOP	Loop Until Input True
	RTWP		Return

Figure 4-63. LIMI Instruction Routine

ELECTRICAL REQUIREMENTS

UNDERSTANDING THE ELECTRICAL SPECIFICATIONS

A description of the interface to the 9900 would be incomplete without a set of specifications for the electrical signals which perform the functions described in the previous sections. Each pin of the 9900 may be characterized with a set of minimum and maximum voltage and current levels. In many cases, the switching characteristics, the rate of transition from the high state to the low state is also important. The detailed electrical specifications for each of the processors in the 9900 family are given in the *Product Data* chapter. A brief statement about the basic concepts of device characterization and data sheet specification is of value to designers with limited exposure to microprocessor and semiconductor memory products.

Specifications are given in two ways. First, absolute maximum ratings are given which simply define the limits of stress which the chip can withstand without damage. *(Figure 4-64* shows the absolute maximum ratings for the TMS 9900.) The normal design specification is the recommended operating conditions table *(Figure 4-65)* which specifies power supply limits, signal voltage levels, and the operating temperature range. In reading these two tables it is necessary to read the explanatory notes, one of which points out that the absolute maximum power supply voltages are specified with respect to the chip substrate or V_{BB} (pin 1). In the normal operating conditions, all voltages are specified with respect to the V_{SS} or ground (pins 26, 40). The four voltages given, V_{BB}, V_{CC}, V_{DD}, and V_{SS} are not actually four power supplies, but three power supplies: $+5V$, $-5V$, and $+12V$, with V_{SS} being the ground or reference point.

ABSOLUTE MAXIMUM RATINGS OVER OPERATING FREE-AIR TEMPERATURE RANGE (UNLESS OTHERWISE NOTED)*

Supply voltage, V_{CC} (see Note 1)	-0.3 to 20 V
Supply voltage, V_{DD} (see Note 1)	-0.3 to 20 V
Supply voltage, V_{SS} (see Note 1)	-0.3 to 20 V
All input voltages (see Note 1)	-0.3 to 20 V
Output voltage (with respect to V_{SS})	-2 V to 7 V
Continuous power dissipation	1.2 W
Operating free-air temperature range	$0°C$ to $70°C$
Storage temperature range	$-55°C$ to $150°C$

*Stresses beyond those listed under "Absolute Maximum Ratings" may cause permanent damage to the device. This is a stress rating only and functional operation of the device at these or any other conditions beyond those indicated in the "Recommended Operating Conditions" section of this specification is not implied. Exposure to absolute-maximum-rated conditions for extended periods may affect device reliability.

NOTE 1: Under absolute maximum ratings voltage values are with respect to the most negative supply, V_{BB} (substrate), unless otherwise noted. Throughout the remainder of this section, voltage values are with respect to V_{SS}.

Figure 4-64. Absolute Maximum Ratings

RECOMMENDED OPERATING CONDITIONS

	MIN	NOM	MAX	UNIT
Supply voltage, V_{BB}	−5.25	−5	−4.75	V
Supply voltage, V_{CC}	4.75	5	5.25	V
Supply voltage, V_{DD}	11.4	12	12.6	V
Supply voltage, V_{SS}		0		V
High-level input voltage, V_{IH} (all inputs except clocks)	2.2	2.4	$V_{CC}+1$	V
High-level clock input voltage, $V_{IH(\phi)}$	$V_{DD}-2$		V_{DD}	V
Low-level input voltage, V_{IL} (all inputs except clocks)	−1	0.4	0.8	V
Low-level clock input voltage, $V_{IL(\phi)}$	−0.3	0.3	0.6	V
Operating free-air temperature, T_A	0		70	C

Figure 4-65. Recommended Operating Conditions

Input signals should be in the range from 2.2V to 6V (assuming V_{CC} is 5V) for the high level, the nominal design point being at 2.4V. Low level input voltage should be below 0.6V (but not less than −0.3V.) These specifications are not the same as the standard TTL specifications as far as the "worst case" design criteria are concerned. Care should be exercised when interfacing the 9900 with TTL circuits that loading of the TTL devices does not produce input voltages to the 9900 which are outside the specified range.

The clock signal voltages are substantially different from the TTL standard; however, the TMS 9904 is available to provide these signals.

The electrical characteristics specification, *Figure 4-66.* defines the current into or out of the 9900 chip at the operating voltage levels. The input current, I_I, is specified for four groups of input signals over a range of input voltages. For example, the input current for any input on the data bus (when reading data from the memory) is nominally ±50 microamps over the input voltage range from 0V to 5V (when V_{CC} is 5V). The current is negative (flowing out of the 9900) for low levels, and positive (into the 9900) for high levels. For "worst case" design the maximum values should be used.

Voltage specifications on the output pins show how the 9900 output devices drive external circuits. For the high level, V_{OH}, the voltage will be at least 2.4V but may go as high as 5V (V_{CC}) under the condition of output current of 0.4 mA. (Currents flowing out of the chip are shown as negative values.) When an output signal is at the low state, the output voltage, V_{OL}, will be no greater than 0.65V when the current flowing into the chip is 3.2 mA. Although the I-V characteristic of the output circuit is nonlinear, a second data point is given: if the current is 2 mA, the voltage will be no greater than 0.50V. These numbers tell the designer what the output drive circuit current sinking capability is. Two standard TTL loads (1.6 mA each) can be accommodated, but the V_{OL} level, as specified, may be as high as at 0.65V (the standard TTL specification for outputs is V_{OL} 0.4V.)

ELECTRICAL CHARACTERISTICS OVER FULL RANGE OF RECOMMENDED OPERATING CONDITIONS
(UNLESS OTHERWISE NOTED)

PARAMETER			TEST CONDITIONS	MIN	TYP[†]	MAX	UNIT
I_I	Input current	Data bus during DBIN	$V_I = V_{SS}$ to V_{CC}		± 50	± 100	μA
		WE, MEMEN, DBIN, Address bus, Data bus during HOLDA	$V_I = V_{SS}$ to V_{CC}		± 50	± 100	
		Clock	$V_I = -0.3$ to 12.6 V		± 25	± 75	
		Any other inputs	$V_I = V_{SS}$ to V_{CC}		± 1	± 10	
V_{OH}	High-level output voltage		$I_O = -0.4$ mA	2.4		V_{CC}	V
V_{OL}	Low-level output voltage		$I_O = 3.2$ mA			0.65	V
			$I_O = 2$ mA			0.50	
I_{BB}	Supply current from V_{BB}				0.1	1	mA
I_{CC}	Supply current from V_{CC}				50	75	mA
I_{DD}	Supply current from V_{DD}				25	45	mA
C_i	Input capacitance (any inputs except clock and data bus)		$V_{BB} = -5$, f = 1MHz, unmeasured pins at V_{SS}		10	15	pF
$C_{i(\phi 1)}$	Clock-1 input capacitance		$V_{BB} = -5$, f = 1MHz, unmeasured pins at V_{SS}		100	150	pF
$C_{i(\phi 2)}$	Clock-2 input capacitance		$V_{BB} = -5$, f = 1MHz, unmeasured pins at V_{SS}		150	200	pF
$C_{i(\phi 3)}$	Clock-3 input capacitance		$V_{BB} = -5$, f = 1MHz, unmeasured pins at V_{SS}		100	150	pF
$C_{i(\phi 4)}$	Clock-4 input capacitance		$V_{BB} = -5$, f = 1MHz, unmeasured pins at V_{SS}		100	150	pF
C_{DB}	Data bus capacitance		$V_{BB} = -5$, f = 1MHz, unmeasured pins at V_{SS}		15	25	pF
C_o	Output capacitance (any output except data bus)		$V_{BB} = -5$, f = 1MHz, unmeasured pins at V_{SS}		10	15	pF

[†] All typical values are at $T_A = 25°C$ and nominal voltages.
* D.C. Component of Operating Clock

Figure 4-66. Electrical Characteristics

The timing of the various signals on the TMS 9900 chip is shown in *Figure 4-67*. The fundamental propagation time from a clock phase pulse (leading edge) to the specified output is given as t_p and is typically 20 ns but is never more than 40 ns (worst case). The parameters t_{pLH} and t_{pHL} are the propagation delays from the appropriate clock signal to the low-to-high transition of the output (t_{pLH}) or the high-to-low transition of the output (t_{pHL}). For example, the WE signal makes its high-to-low transition 20 ns after $\phi 1$ clock, and makes a low-to-high transition 20 ns after the next $\phi 1$ clock. Most of the output signals make transitions 20 ns after the $\phi 2$ clock, and remain valid until the next 02 clock.

Additional information regarding design constraints based on the electrical specifications is given in the next section.

SWITCHING CHARACTERISTICS OVER FULL RANGE OF RECOMMENDED OPERATING CONDITIONS

PARAMETER		TEST CONDITIONS	MIN	TYP	MAX	UNIT
t_{PLH} or t_{PHL}	Propagation delay time, clocks to outputs	C_L = 200 pF		20		ns

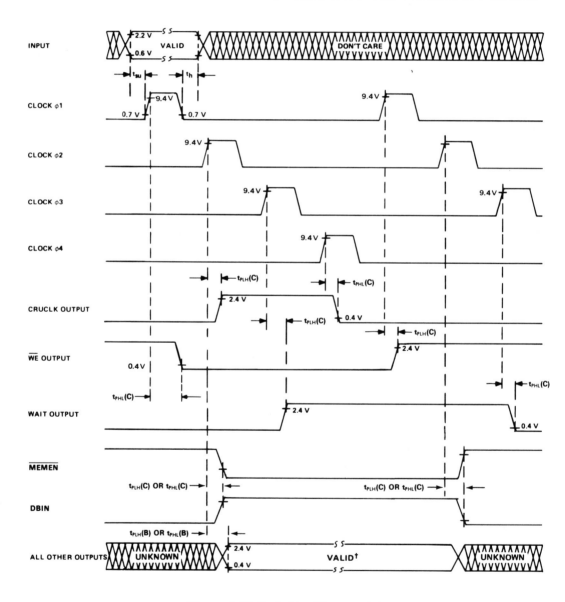

Figure 4-67. Switching Characteristics

DETAILED ELECTRICAL INTERFACE SPECIFICATIONS (TMS 9900)

This section reviews the TMS 9900 electrical requirements, including the system clock generation and interface signal characteristics.

TMS 9900 Clock Generation

The TMS 9900 requires a non-overlapping four-phase clock system with high-level MOS drivers. Additional TTL outputs are typically required for external signal synchronization or for dynamic memory controllers. A single-chip clock driver, the TIM 9904, can be used to produce these clock signals. An alternative clock generator uses standard TTL logic circuits and discrete components.

The TMS 9900 requires four non-overlapping 12V clocks. The clock frequency can vary from 2 to 3 Megahertz. The clock rise and fall times must not exceed 100 nanoseconds and must be 10 to 15 nanoseconds for higher frequencies in order to satisfy clock pulse width requirements. While the clocks must not overlap, the delay time between clocks must not exceed 50 microseconds at lower frequencies. The typical clock timing for 3 MHz is illustrated in *Figure 4-68.*

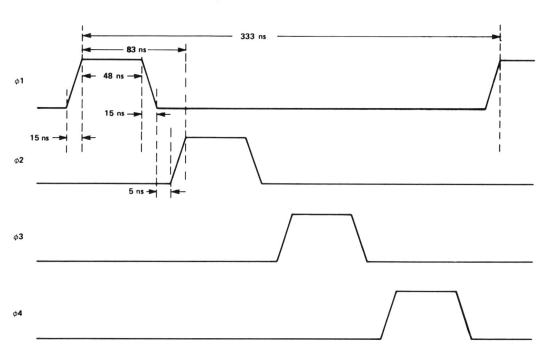

Figure 4-68. TMS 9900 Typical Clock Timing

TIM 9904 Clock Generator

The TIM 9904 (SN74LS362) is a single-chip clock generator and driver for use with the TMS 9900. The TIM 9904 contains a crystal-controlled oscillator, waveshaping circuitry, a synchronizing flip-flop, and quad MOS/TTL drivers as shown in *Figure 4-69*.

The clock frequency is selected by either an external crystal or by an external TTL-level oscillator input. Crystal operation requires a 16X input crystal frequency since the TIM 9904 divides the input frequency for waveshaping. For 3-megahertz operation, a 48-megahertz crystal is required. The LC tank inputs permit the use of overtone crystals. The LC network values are determined by the network resonant frequency:

$$ f \ = \ \frac{1}{2\pi\sqrt{LC}} $$

For less precise frequency control, a capacitor can be used instead of the crystal.

The external-oscillator input can be used instead of the crystal input. The oscillator input frequency is 4X the output frequency. A 12-megahertz input oscillator frequency is required for a 3-megahertz output frequency. A 4X TTL-compatible oscillator output (OSCOUT) is provided in order to permit the derivation of other system timing signals from the crystal or oscillator frequency source.

The oscillator frequency is divided by four to provide the proper frequency for each of the 4-clock phases. A high-level MOS output and an inverted TTL-compatible output is provided by each clock phase. The MOS-level clocks are used for the TMS 9900 CPU while the TTL clocks are used for system timing.

The D-type flip-flop is clocked by $\phi3$ and can be used to synchronize external signals such as a $\overline{RESET}$. The Schmitt-triggered input permits the use of an external RC network for power-on $\overline{RESET}$ generation. The RC values are dependent on the power supply rise time and should hold $\overline{RESET}$ low for at least three clock cycles after the supply voltages reach the minimum voltages.

All TIM 9904 TTL-compatible outputs have standard short circuit protection. The high-level MOS clock outputs, however, do not have short circuit protection.

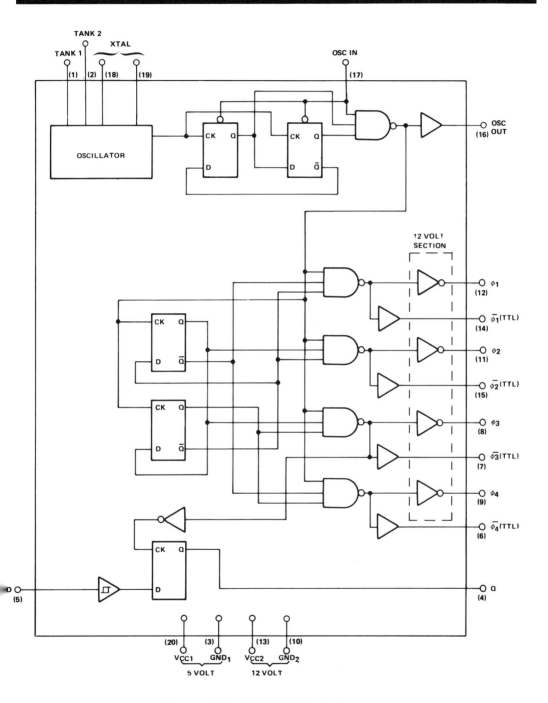

Figure 4-69. TIM 9904 Clock Generator

This driver uses inexpensive 2N3703s and 2N3704s and broad tolerance passive components. Resistor tolerances can be 10% with capacitor variations as much as 20% without affecting its performance noticeably. It shows very little sensitivity to transistor variations and its propagation times are largely unaffected by output capacitive loading. It produces rise times in the 10-12 ns region with fall times from 8-10 ns, driving 200 pF capacitive loads. Propagation times for this driver are such that it produces an output pulse that is wider than its input pulse. This driver can easily be used at 3 megahertz without special selection of components. It does have the disadvantage of taking nine discrete components per driver, but if assembly costs are prohibitive, these can be reduced by using two Q2T2222 and two Q2T2905 transistor packs. The Q2T2222 is basically four NPN transistors of the 2N2222 type while the Q2T2905 has four PNP, 2N2905 type transistors in single 14-pin dual-in-line packages. Thus, all four drivers can be built using two packages each of these quad packs.

TMS 9900 Signal Interfacing

The non-clock CPU inputs and outputs are TTL compatible and can be used with bipolar circuits without external pull-up resistors or level shifters. The TMS 9900 inputs are high impendance to minimize loading on peripheral circuits. The TMS 9900 outputs can drive approximately two TTL loads, thus eliminating the need for buffer circuits in many systems.

Switching Levels

The TMS 9900 input switch levels are compatible with most MOS and TTL circuits and do not require pull-up resistors to reach the required high-level input switching voltage. The TMS 9900 output levels can drive most MOS and bipolar inputs. Some typical switching levels are shown in *Table 4-4.*

Table 4-4. Switch Levels

SWITCHING LEVEL (V)	TMS 9900	TMS 2708	TMS 4042-2	SN 74XX	SN 74LSXX
V_{IH} min	2.2	3.0	2.2	2.0	2.0
V_{IL} max	0.6	0.65	0.65	0.8	0.7
V_{OH}^* min	2.4	3.7	2.2	2.4	2.7
V_{OL} max	0.5	0.45	0.45	0.5	0.5

*V_{OH} exceeds 2.4 V as shown in Figure 4-70.

It should be noted that some MOS circuits such as the TMS 4700 ROM and the TMS 2708 EPROM have a minimum high-level input voltage of 3 V to 3.3 V, which exceeds the TMS 9900 minimum high-level output voltage of 2.4 V. The TMS 9900 high-level output voltage exceeds 3.3 V; however, longer transition times as shown in *Figure 4-70* are required.

Loading

The TMS 9900 has high-impedance inputs to minimize loading on the system buses. The CPU data bus presents a *maximum* current load of ± 100 μA when DBIN is high. $\overline{\text{WE}}$, $\overline{\text{MEMEN}}$, and DBIN cause a *maximum* current load of ± 100 μA during HOLDA. Otherwise, the TMS 9900 inputs present a current load of only ± 10 μA. The data bus inputs have a 25-picofarad input capacitance, and all other non-clock inputs have a 15-picofarad input capacitance.

The TMS 9900 outputs can drive approximately two standard TTL loads. Since most memory devices have high-impedance inputs, the CPU can drive small memory systems without address or data buffers. If the bus load exceeds the equivalent of two TTL unit loads, external buffers are required.

The TMS 9900 output switching characteristics are determined for approximately 200 picofarads. Higher capacitive loads can be driven with degraded switching characteristics as shown in *Figure 4-71.*

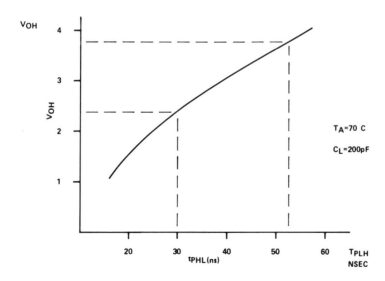

Figure 4-70. t_{PLH} *vs* V_{OH} *Typical Output Levels*

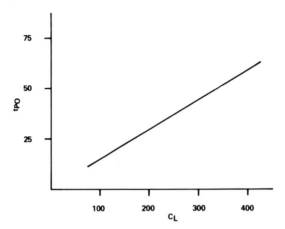

Figure 4-71. t_{PO} *vs Load Capacitance (Typical)*

Recommended Interface Logic

Many microprocessors and microcomputers such as the 9900 Family are compatible with the logic from any of the common TTL logic families. However, in many cases the low-power Schottky logic circuits, the 74LSXX series, are recommended for use in microprocessor systems because they have higher impedance inputs than standard TTL, allowing more circuits to be used without buffering. The 74LSXX gates also consume less power at similar switching speeds.

There are also a wide variety of bipolar support circuits which can be used. In fact, some are especially designed for microprocessor systems. Others which are particularly useful in many common applications have been dual symbolized to fit into microprocessor family support circuits.

Several very common bipolar circuits that are needed for address, data, and control bus applications are buffer circuits with three-state outputs. The three-state output allows these buffers to be used either as address drivers or as bidirectional data transceivers. Circuits such as the 74S241 or 74LS241 provide non-inverting octal buffers and circuits such as the 74S240 or 74LS240 provide inverting outputs. If a single circuit type is chosen for both functions, this can result in lower inventory and parts cost. The buffer switching times can be derated for larger capacitive loading as required.

System Layout

The pin assignments of the TMS 9900 are such that sets of signals (data bus, address bus, interrupt port, etc.) are grouped together. The layout of a printed circuit board can be simplified by taking advantage of these groups by locating associated circuitry (address buffers, interrupt processing hardware, etc.) as close as possible to the TMS 9900 interface. Shortened conductor runs result in minimal noise and compact and efficient utilization of printed circuit board area.

It is particularly important that the drivers for $\phi1-\phi4$ be located as close as possible to the inputs of the TMS 9900, since these signals have fast rise and fall times while driving fairly high capacitance over a wide voltage range. The 12 volt supply to the clock drivers should be decoupled with both high ($15\mu F$) and low ($0.05\mu F$) value capacitors in order to filter out high and lower frequency variations in supply voltage.

All voltage inputs to the TMS 9900 should be decoupled at the device. Particular attention should be paid to the $+5$ volt supply. All data and address lines are switched simultaneously. The worst-case condition occurs when all data and address signals switch to a low level simultaneously and they are each sinking 3.2 mA. It is thus possible for the supply current to vary nearly 100 mA over a 20 ns interval. Careful attention must be paid by the designer to avoid supply voltage spiking. The exact values for capacitors should be determined empirically, based on actual system layout and drive requirements.

TMS 9940 MICROCOMPUTER

The TMS9940 is a microcomputer chip in a 40-pin package which includes all of the elements of a computer, that is, memory, I/O and utilities in addition to ALU and control. Useful in a wide variety of dedicated control functions, it contains a 2k × 8 EPROM program memory and a 128 × 8 RAM for data, a 14 bit interval timer, and a multiprocessor system interface. Although the memory organization on chip is in 8 bit bytes, the instructions are the same 16-bit instructions of the 9900 family.

While most of the instructions are identical to the instruction set of the 9900, there are 68 instructions in the 9940 set (as opposed to 69 in the TMS9900) including three new ones. The differences in the instruction set are illustrated by the following list of instructions.

DCA	Decimal Correct for BCD add	⎫
DCS	Decimal Correct for BCD subtract	⎬ Added Instructions
LIIM	Load Interrupt mask	⎭
RSET	⎫	⎫
CKOF	⎬ (external instructions in 9900)	⎬ Deleted Instructions
CKON		⎭
LREX	⎭	
IDLE	Put processor into the idle state	⎬ Hardware in the 9940

The first three of the instructions in the above list are new instructions and are unique to the 9940 microcomputer. The DCA and DCS instructions perform decimal correct for BCD arithmetic. The LIIM instruction is a single word instruction to load the interrupt mask. (This instruction should be contrasted with the LIMI instruction of the 9900 set which performs the same function but occupies two memory words.) The idle instruction, an external instruction in the 9900 set, is now implemented in hardware. Four instructions in the list are not implemented in the 9940; they are external instructions in the 9900 set.

PIN ASSIGNMENTS AND FUNCTIONAL CONTROL .

One of the most extraordinary features of the TMS9940 is the I/O structure in which 32 pins of the 40-pin package are software assignable. That is, they do not perform single, predefined, hard-wired functions, but instead are under the control of the programmer in structuring input/output functions. *Table 4-5* lists the functions of four specific bits in the CRU which are called configuration bits. Because these four bits are assigned specific locations in the CRU output field and are therefore addressable and accessible via CRU output instructions, the pins of the package may be dynamically reassigned during program execution.

Table 4-5. Configuration Bit Functions

Configuration Bit	Function
0	External CRU expansion
1	Multiprocessor
2	Clock output for sync
3	Power down

Table 4-6 describes the way these four configuration bits assign the individual general-purpose I/O pins to specific functions. In effect, each of the pins may serve two or three functions, as described in the table. *Table 4-7* defines the functions of addressable CRU locations. The first 256 locations, addresses 000 through 0FF, are for external expansion of the general I/O to an additional 245 (256 less 11 used for expansion). It is important to note here that these 256 bits are two fields of 256 bits each, one for input and one for output. Addresses 100 through 17F are not used, and address 180 through 1DF are used internally.

Notice in *Table 4-7* that CRU addresses 183, 184, 185 and 186 locate the four configuration bits. It is via the setting or resetting of these individual bits that the I/O configuration is established.

Four other significant features should be pointed out.
One: The interrupt structure includes four levels of interrupt as opposed to the 16-level interrupt capability of the general 9900 microprocessor group.
Two: There is an on-chip timer, or event counter.
Three: 32 bits of CRU I/O are implemented on the chip. (Addresses 1E0-1EFF)
Four: A multiprocessor system interface is constructed as part of the CRU I/O.

INTERRUPTS

The four interrupt levels are shown in the table below.

Level 0	Reset	*Level 2*	Decrementer
Level 1	General Interrupt 1	*Level 3*	General Interrupt 2

Table 4-6. Configuration Bit Effects by Pin

Pin	Configuration bit 0 (CRU Expansion)	
	0	1
23	P0 (general I/O)	A1
24	P1	A2
25	P2	A3
26	P3	A4
27	P4	A5
28	P5	A6
29	P6	A7
30	P7	A8
18	P8	CRUIN
17	P9	CRUOUT
16	P10	CRUCLK

Pin	Configuration bit 1 (Multiprocessor)	
	0	1
14	P11	$\overline{TC}$ (Clock)
11	P12	TD (Data)

Pin	Configuration bit 2 (Sync)	
	0	1
15	P13	φ (Clock)

Pin	Configuration bit 3 (Power Down)	
	0	1
10	P14	$\overline{HLD}$
9	P15	$\overline{HLDA}$
8	P16	$\overline{IDLE}$

Table 4-7. Functions of CRU Address

CRU Addresses	Contents of R12	Input	Output
000-0FF	000-1FE	CRU Expansion	CRU Expansion
100-17F	200-2FE	NA	NA
180	300	Test for Interrupt 1	
181	302	Test for Decrementer Interrupt	Clear Decrementer
182	304	Test for Interrupt 2	
183	306		Set Configuration Bit 0
184	308		Set Configuration Bit 1
185	30A		Set Configuration Bit 2
186	30C		Set Configuration Bit 3
187-18F	30E-31E	NA	NA
190-19D	320-33A	Read Decrementer Value	Load Decrementer Value
19E	33C		TE (Timer/Event Cntr)
19F	33E		
1A0-1AF	340-35E	Read MPSI Value	Load MPSI Value
1B0-1BF	360-37E	Read Flag Register	Set Flag Register
1C0-1DF	380-3BE		Set I/O Direction for P0-P31
1E0-1FF	3C0-3FE	P0-P31 Input Data	P0-P31 Output Data

The 9940 implements interrupts using the same context switch concept of the 9900. Thus, the interrupt vectors for the four interrupt levels must be stored in the first 16 words of the 9940's program memory. As is described in a subsequent paragraph, the decrementer acts like a counter in an external piece of hardware in that after the contents of the circuit have been decremented to zero an interrupt signals the processor to perform a context switch and perform whatever function was programmed as the service routine for the decrementer. The reset, INT 1, and INT 2 interrupt signals are available to external hardware.

Since there is no $\overline{\text{INTREQ}}$ (interrupt request) signal input for the 9940, an interrupt input must be set and remain set until acknowledged. In fact, the acknowledgement of an interrupt must include instructions to reset holding flip-flops (if used) via CRU operations.

In the 9940, the interrupt input may be masked (as in all 9900 processors) but there are specific CRU bits which, if tested, will reveal pending interrupts which are not being serviced. Thus, the programmer may wish to mask interrupts but still be aware (via TB instructions to CRU locations 180, 181 and 182 as shown in *Table 4-7*) of the interrupt input status.

DECREMENTER

A timer/event counter is implemented on the 9940 chip to introduce interrupts after a predefined time period or number of events. A set of dedicated CRU addresses define the location of decrementer input and output registers. A value may be loaded into the decrementer via an LDCR instruction which loads CRU locations $190_{16} - 19D_{16}$. Likewise, the current value of the decrementer may be read via an STCR instruction identifying the same CRU field.

When the decrementer contents count down to zero, an interrupt is issued. The context switch thus activated automatically clears the interrupt request.

As a timer, the decrementer counts down at the rate of 1/30 of the oscillator frequency. With a clock frequency of 5 MHz, the time interval for counting is six microseconds.

As an event counter, the decrementer is first loaded with a value and it then counts down (one bit for each positive transition on pin 7) until it reaches zero. An interrupt is then issued.

CRU IMPLEMENTATION

One of the most important features of the 9940 is the manner in which the CRU is used to perform pin assignments and functional control as well as input and output. The major impact is that the external devices and some of the internal devices are under direct control of the programmer via CRU instructions. The major emphasis (see *Table 4-7*) is as follows.

> 32 bits of input — on-chip multiplexer
> 32 bits of output — on-chip flip-flops
> 32-bit register defining signal direction (in or out) for the assignable pins
> 16-bit flag register — may be written or read
> 14-bit "clock" register—for loading the decrementer
> 14-bit "read" register—for reading the decrementer
> 16-bit shift register for receiving instructions in a multiprocessor application, or
>   used for sending 16-bit information over the MPSI data line to other processors
> 14-bit decrementer (used as a timer or counter)
> 256-bit CRU expansion (input and output)

Pin assignments may be explained by showing the basic application concept, that of using the 32 bits of internal CRU. Here the only decision is one of signal direction. It is possible to set the configuration once during initialization and never change it. But this limits the total number of I/O signals to 32. It is permissible to change the signal direction of each pin as needed, thus obtaining full utilization of the 32 inputs and 32 outputs. The pins themselves (labelled P0-P31 in *Table 4-8*) serve as a dynamically configurable bidirectional CRU port. Data is addressed in the CRU address field 1E0 to 1FF. Direction control is established by writing a logical one for output or zero for input to the appropriate address(es) in the CRU field 1C0-1DF. Reading the addresses assigned for output is permissible and allows the program to interrogate or determine the status of the on-chip CRU output flip-flops

Functional assignments of the first 18 I/O signals may be accomplished as a "configuring" of the pins. As shown in *Table 4-8,* eighteen additional signals may pass through the pins corresponding to P0-P17. By setting configuration bit 0 for example, signals P0-P10 are no longer available to external hardware. Instead, the CRU expansion signals, A1-A8 and CRU controls, are available. Configuring may be accomplished by the following code.

LI R12,>200   Set CRU hardware base address at 100_{16}

SBO >83   Add 83_{16} to set CRU bit 183_{16}

(The LI instruction must set R12 to two times the hardware base address because the LSB is ignored.)

MULTIPROCESSOR SYSTEM INTERFACE (MPSI)

A two-wire communication technique is provided so that the 9940 may exchange 16-bit data and/or instructions with other CPU's in a multiprocessor application. This capability allows the RAM to be used as an instruction memory for short subprograms downloaded from another processor. Since the technique is based on the CRU concept, the 9940 will easily interface with the processors in the 9900 family. In order to use this feature, configuration bit 1 must first be set via

LI R12, >200
SBO >84

Then the information flows in from an external processor and is clocked by the external processor so that this operation is completely transparent to the CPU. The sender must interrupt the receiver to cause reading of the input word via

LI R12, > 340   Address the MPSI register

STCR @BUFF, 0   Store 16 bits in memory location BUFF

Refer to *Table 4-7* for CRU addresses of this and other functions.

To send data out over the MPSI the 9940 must first have configuration bit 1 set, and then it simply executes

LDCR @BUFF, 0

to send out 16 bits of data from memory location BUFF. The switch into and out of "send" status is automatic.

Table 4-8. TMS 9940 Configurable Pins

Pin Number	General I/O	CRU Address Data I/O	CRU Address for Direction Control	Alternate Function	Configuration Bit	CRU Address of Config. Bit
23	P0	1E0	1C0	A1	0	183
24	P1	1E1	1C1	A2	0	183
25	P2	1E2	1C2	A3	0	183
26	P3	1E3	1C3	A4	0	183
27	P4	1E4	1C4	A5	0	183
28	P5	1E5	1C5	A6	0	183
29	P6	1E6	1C6	A7	0	183
30	P7	1E7	1C7	A8	0	183
18	P8	1E8	1C8	CRUIN	0	183
17	P9	1E9	1C9	CRUOUT	0	183
16	P10	1EA	1CA	CRUCLK	0	183
14	P11	1EB	1CB	$\overline{TC}$	1	184
11	P12	1EC	1CC	TD	1	184
15	P13	1ED	1CD	$\overline{\phi}$	2	185
10	P14	1EE	1CE	$\overline{HLD}$	3	186
9	P15	1EF	1CF	$\overline{HLDA}$	3	186
8	P16	1F0	1D0	$\overline{IDLE}$	3	186
7	P17	1F1	1D1	EC	—	19E
6	P18	1F2	1D2			
5	P19	1F3	1D3			
4	P20	1F4	1D4			
3	P21	1F5	1D5			
2	P22	1F6	1D6			
1	P23	1F7	1D7			
31	P24	1F8	1D8			
32	P25	1F9	1D9			
33	P26	1FA	1DA			
34	P27	1FB	1DB			
35	P28	1FC	1DC			
36	P29	1FD	1DD			
38	P30	1FE	1DE			
39	P31	1FF	1DF			

SUMMARY

The 9940 is a powerful member of the 9900 family with execution techniques which are actually faster than the TMS9900. In fact, because of its higher speed clock (5 MHz) and a fast on-chip execution microcycle for register location, the average throughput is 20% faster than the standard 9900 devices. The assignability of the package pins via software adds a new dimension to microprocessor technology for improved flexibility and performance.

COMPLETE LISTING OF MACHINE CYCLES

In order to complete the description of instruction execution, the individual instruction execution cycles are given in this section. Each machine cycle consists of two or more clock cycles (depending upon addressing mode) as defined herein. (*Note:* These machine cycles apply equally to the TMS 9980A/81 microprocessor, with the exception of the memory cycle as detailed below.) The 9900 family machine cycles are divided into three categories described in the following paragraphs.

MACHINE CYCLES

ALU Cycle

The ALU cycle performs an internal operation of the microprocessor. The memory interface control signals and CRU interface control signals are not affected by the execution of an ALU cycle, which takes two clock cycles to execute.

Memory Cycle

The memory cycle primarily performs a data transfer between the microprocessor and the external memory device. Appropriate memory bus control signals are generated by the microprocessor as a result of a memory cycle execution. The memory cycle takes $2+W$ (where W is the number of wait states) clock cycles to execute.

In the TMS 9980A/81, which has an 8-bit data bus, the memory cycle is composed of two data transfers to move a complete 16-bit word. The TMS 9980A/81 memory cycle takes $4+2W$ (where W is the number of wait states) clock cycles to execute. For the TMS 9980A/81 the following machine cycle sequences replace the memory sequences used in the instruction discussion.

CYCLE			
1	Memory read/write	AB =	Address of most significant byte (A13 = 0)
		DB =	Most significant byte
2	Memory read/write	AB =	Address of least significant byte (A13 = 1)
		DB =	Least significant byte

CRU Cycle

The CRU cycle performs a bit transfer between the microprocessor and I/O devices. It takes two clock cycles to execute. The address of the CRU bit is set up during the first clock cycle. For an input operation the CRUIN line is sampled by the microprocessor during the second clock cycle. For an output operation the data bit is set up on the CRUOUT line at the same time the address is set up. The CRUCLK line is pulsed during the second clock cycle of the CRU output cycle. Please refer to the specific 99XX microprocessor data manual for timing diagrams.

The 9900 executes its operations under the control of a microprogrammed control ROM. Each microinstruction specifies a machine cycle. A microprogram specifies a sequence of machine cycles. The 9900 executes a specific sequence of machine cycles for a specific operation. These sequences are detailed on the following pages. The information can be used by the systems designers to determine the bus contents and other interface behavior at various instants during a certain 9900 operation. This description is maintained at the address bus (AD) and data bus (DB) levels.

9900 MACHINE CYCLE SEQUENCES

Most 9900 instructions execution consists of two parts: 1) the data derivation and 2) operation execution. The data derivation sequence depends on the addressing mode for the data. Since the addressing modes are common to all instructions, the data derivation sequence is the same for the same addressing mode, regardless of the instruction. Therefore, the data derivation sequences are described first. These are then referred to in appropriate sequence in the instruction execution description.

TERMS AND DEFINITIONS

The following terms are used in describing the instructions of the 9900:

TERM	DEFINITION
B	Byte Indicator ($1 = $ byte, $0 = $ word)
C	Bit count
D	Destination address register
DA	Destination address
IOP	Immediate operand
PC	Program counter
Result	Result of operation performed by instruction
S	Source address register
SA	Source address
ST	Status register
STn	Bit n of status register
SD	Source data register internal to the TMS 9900 microprocessor*
W	Workspace register
SRn	Workspace register n
(n)	Contents of n
Ns	Number of machine cycles to derive source operand
Nd	Number of machine cycles to derive destination operand
AB	Address Bus of the TMS 9900
DB	Data Bus of the TMS 9900
NC	No change from previous cycle

*Note: The contents of the SD register remain latched at the last value written by the processor unless changed by the ALU. Therefore, during all memory read or ALU machine cycles the SD register and hence the data bus will contain the operand last written to the data bus by the CPU or the results of the last ALU cycle to have loaded the SD register.

DATA DERIVATION SEQUENCE

Workspace Register

CYCLE	TYPE	DESCRIPTION
1	Memory read	AB = Workspace register address
		DB = Operand

Workspace Register Indirect

CYCLE	TYPE	DESCRIPTION
1	Memory read	AB = Workspace register address
		DB = Workspace register contents
2	ALU	AB = NC
		DB = SD
3	Memory read	AB = Workspace register content
		DB = Operand

Workspace Register Indirect Auto-Increment (Byte-Operand)

CYCLE	TYPE	DESCRIPTION
1	Memory read	AB = Workspace register address
		DB = Workspace register contents
2	ALU	AB = NC
		DB = SD
3	Memory write	AB = Workspace register address
		DB = (WRn) + 1
4	Memory read	AB = Workspace register contents
		DB = Operand

Workspace Register Indirect Auto-Increment (Word Operand)

CYCLE	TYPE	DESCRIPTION
1	Memory read	AB = Workspace register address
		DB = Workspace register contents
2	ALU	AB = NC
		DB = SD
3	ALU	AB = NC
		DB = SD
4	Memory write	AB = Workspace register address
		DB = (WRn) + 2
5	Memory read	AB = Workspace register contents
		DB = Operand

Symbolic

CYCLE	TYPE	DESCRIPTION
1	ALU	AB = NC
		DB = SD
2	ALU	AB = NC
		DB = SD
3	Memory read	AB = PC + 2
		DB = Symbolic address
4	ALU	AB = NC
		DB = 0000_{16}
5	Memory read	AB = Symbolic address
		DB = Operand

Indexed

CYCLE	TYPE	DESCRIPTION
1	Memory read	AB = Workspace register address
		DB = Workspace register contents
2	ALU	AB = NC
		DB = SD
3	Memory read	AB = PC + 2
		DB = Symbolic address
4	ALU	AB = PC + 2
		DB = Workspace register contents
5	Memory read	AB = Symbolic address + (WRn)
		DB = Operand

INSTRUCTION EXECUTION SEQUENCE

A, AB, C, CB, S, SB, SOC, SOCB, SZC, SZCB, MOV, MOVB, COC, CZC, XOR

CYCLE	TYPE	DESCRIPTION
1	Memory read	AB = PC
		DB = Instruction
2	ALU	AB = NC
		DB = SD
Ns	Insert appropriate sequence for source data addressing mode, from the data derivation sequences	(Note 1)
3 + Ns	ALU	AB = NC
		DB = SD
Nd	Insert appropriate sequence for destination data addressing mode from the data derivation sequences	(Note 2, 3)
4 + Ns + Nd	ALU	AB = NC
		DB = SD
5 + Ns + Nd	Memory write	AB = DA (Note 4)
		DB = Result

NOTES:

1) Since the memory operations of the 9900 microprocessor family fetch or store 16-bit words, the source and the destination data fetched for byte operations are 16-bit words. The ALU operates on the specified bytes of these words and modifies the appropriate byte in the destination word. The adjacent byte in the destination word remains unaltered. At the completion of the instruction, the destination word, consisting of the modified byte and the adjacent unmodified byte, is stored in a single-memory write operation.

2) For MOVB instruction the destination data word (16 bits) is fetched. The specified byte in the destination word is replaced with the specified byte of the source-data word. The resultant destination word is then stored at the destination address.

3) For MOV instruction the destination data word (16 bits) is fetched although not used.

4) For C, CB, COC, CZC instructions cycle $5 + N_s + N_d$ above is an ALU cycle with AB = DA and DB = SD.

MPY (Multiply)

CYCLE	TYPE	DESCRIPTION
1	Memory read	AB = PC
		DB = Instruction
2	ALU	AB = NC
		DB = SD
Ns	Insert appropriate data derivation sequence according to the source data (multiplier) addressing mode	
3 + Ns	ALU	AB = NC
		DB = SD
4 + Ns	Memory read	AB = Workspace register address
		DB = Workspace register contents
5 + Ns	ALU	AB = NC
		DB = SD
6 + Ns	ALU	AB = NC
		DB = Multiplier
7 + Ns		Multiply the two operands
	16 ALU	AB = NC
		DB = MSH of partial product
24 + Ns	Memory write	AB = Workspace register address
		DB = MSH of the product
25 + Ns	ALU	AB = DA + 2
		DB = MSH of product
26 + Ns	Memory write	AB = DA + 2
		DB = LSH of the product

DIV (Divide)

CYCLE	TYPE	DESCRIPTION
1	Memory read	AB = PC
		DB = Instruction
2	ALU	AB = NC
		DB = SD
Ns	Insert appropriate data derivation sequence according to the source data (divisor) addressing mode	
3 + Ns	ALU	AB = NC
		DB = SD
4 + Ns	Memory read	AB = Address of workspace register
		DB = Contents of workspace register
5 + Ns	ALU	(Check overflow)
		AB = NC
		DB = Divisor
6 + Ns	ALU	(Skip if overflow to next instruction fetch)
		AB = NC
		DB = SD
7 + Ns	Memory read	AB = DA + 2
		DB = Contents of DA + 2
8 + Ns	ALU	AB = NC
		DB = SD
9 + Ns	ALU	AB = NC
		DB = SD
	Divide sequence consisting of Ni cycles	AB = NC
	where $48 \leq Ni \leq 32$. Ni is data dependent	DB = SD
10 + Ns + Ni	ALU	AB = NC
		DB = SD
11 + Ns + Ni	Memory write	AB = Workspace register address
		DB = Quotient
12 + Ns + Ni	ALU	AB = DA + 2
		DB = Quotient
13 + Ns + Ni	Memory write	AB = DA + 2
		DB = Remainder

XOP

CYCLE	TYPE	DESCRIPTION
1	Memory read	AB = PC
		DB = Instruction
2	ALU	Instruction decode AB = NC
		DB = SD
Ns	Insert appropriate data derivation sequence according to the source data addressing mode	
3 + Ns	ALU	AB = NC
		DB = SD
4 + Ns	ALU	AB = NC
		DB = SA
5 + Ns	ALU	AB = NC
		DB = SD
6 + Ns	Memory read	AB = $40_{16} + 4 \times D$
		DB = New workspace pointer

CYCLE	TYPE	DESCRIPTION
7 + Ns	ALU	AB = NC
		DB = SA
8 + Ns	Memory write	AB = Address of WR11
		DB = SA
9 + Ns	ALU	AB = Address of WR15
		DB = SA
10 + Ns	Memory write	AB = Address of workspace register 15
		DB = Status register contents
11 + Ns	ALU	AB = NC
		DB = PC + 2
12 + Ns	Memory write	AB = Address of workspace register 14
		DB = PC + 2
13 + Ns	ALU	AB = Address of WR13
		DB = SD
14 + Ns	Memory write	AB = Address of workspace register 13
		DB = WP
15 + Ns	ALU	AB = NC
		DB = SD
16 + Ns	Memory read	AB = $42_{16} + 4 \times D$
		DB = New PC
17 + Ns	ALU	AB = NC
		DB = SD

CLR, SETO, INV, NEG, INC, INCT, DEC, DECT, SWPB

CYCLE	TYPE	DESCRIPTION
1	Memory read	AB = PC
		DB = Instruction
2	ALU	AB = NC
		DB = SD
Ns	Insert appropriate data derivation sequence according to the source data addressing mode	
3 + Ns	ALU	AB = NC
		DB = SD
4 + Ns	Memory write	AB = Source data address
		DB = Modified source data

Note: The operand is fetched for CLR and SETO although not used.

ABS

CYCLE	TYPE	DESCRIPTION
1	Memory read	AB = PC
		DB = Instruction
2	ALU	AB = NC
		DB = SD
Ns	Insert appropriate data derivation sequence according to the source data addressing mode	
3 + Ns	ALU	Test source data
		AB = NC
		DB = SD
4 + Ns	ALU	Jump to 5' + Ns if data positive
		AB = NC
		DB = SD

CYCLE	TYPE	DESCRIPTION
5 + ns	ALU	Negate source AB = NC DB = SD
6 + Ns	Memory write	AB = Source data address DB = Modified source data
5' + Ns	ALU	AB = NC DB = SD

X

CYCLE	TYPE	DESCRIPTION
1	Memory read	AB = PC DB = Instruction
2	ALU	AB = NC DB = SD
Ns	Insert the appropriate data derivation sequence according to the source data addressing mode	
3 + Ns	ALU	AB = NC DB = SD

Note: Add sequence for the instruction specified by the operand.

B

CYCLE	TYPE	DESCRIPTION
1	Memory read	AB = PC DB = Instruction
2	ALU	AB = NC DB = SD
Ns	Insert appropriate data derivation sequence according to the source data addressing mode	
3 + Ns	ALU	AB = NC DB = SD

Note: The source data is fetched, although it is not used.

BL

CYCLE	TYPE	DESCRIPTION
1	Memory read	AB = PC DB = Instruction
2	ALU	AB = NC DB = SD
Ns	Insert appropriate data derivation sequence according to the source data addressing mode	
3 + Ns	ALU	AB = NC DB = SD
4 + Ns	ALU	AB = Address of WR11 DB = SD
5 + Ns	Memory write	AB = Address of WR11 DB = PC + 2

Note: The source data is fetched although it is not used.

BLWP

CYCLE	TYPE	DESCRIPTION		
1	Memory read	AB	=	PC
		DB	=	Instruction
2	ALU	AB	=	NC
		DB	=	SD
Ns	Insert appropriate data derivation sequence according to the source data addressing mode			
3 + Ns	ALU	AB	=	NC
		DB	=	SD
4 + Ns	ALU	AB	=	Address of WR15
		DB	=	NC
5 + Ns	Memory write	AB	=	Address of workspace register 15
		DB	=	Status register contents
6 + Ns	ALU	AB	=	NC
		DB	=	PC + 2
7 + Ns	Memory write	AB	=	Address of workspace register 14
		DB	=	PC + 2
8 + Ns	ALU	AB	=	Address or workspace register 13
		DB	=	SD
9 + Ns	Memory write	AB	=	Address of workspace register 13
		DB	=	WP
10 + Ns	ALU	AB	=	NC
		DB	=	SD
11 + Ns	Memory read	AB	=	Address of new PC
		DB	=	New PC
12 + Ns	ALU	AB	=	NC
		DB	=	SD

LDCR

CYCLE	TYPE	DESCRIPTION		
1	Memory read	AB	=	PC
		DB	=	Instruction
2	ALU	AB	=	NC
		DB	=	SD
Ns	Insert appropriate data derivation sequence			
3 + Ns	ALU	AB	=	NC
		DB	=	SD
4 + Ns	ALU	AB	=	NC
		DB	=	SD
5 + Ns	ALU	AB	=	Address of WR12
		DB	=	SD
6 + Ns	ALU	AB	=	Address of WR12
		DB	=	SD
7 + Ns	Memory read	AB	=	Address of WR12
		DB	=	Contents of WR12
8 + Ns	ALU	AB	=	NC
		DB	=	SD
C	Shift next bit onto CRUOUT line. Enable CRUCLK. Increment CRU bit address on AB. Iterate this sequence C times, where C is number of bits to be transferred.	AB	=	Address + 2 Increments C Times
		DB	=	SD
9 + Ns + C	ALU	AB	=	NC
		DB	=	SD

STCR

CYCLE	TYPE	DESCRIPTION
1	Memory read	AB = PC
		DB = Instruction
2	ALU	AB = NC
		DB = SD
Ns	Insert appropriate data derivation sequence according to the source data addressing mode	
3 + Ns	ALU	AB = NC
		DB = SD
4 + Ns	Memory read	AB = Address of WR12
		DB = Contents of WR12
5 + Ns	ALU	AB = NC
		DB = SD
6 + Ns	ALU	AB = NC
		DB = SD
C	Input selected CRU bit. Increment CRU bit address. Iterate this sequence C times where C is the number of CRU bits to be input.	AB = Address + 2 C times
		DB = SD
7 + Ns + C	ALU	AB = NC
		DB = SD
8 + Ns + C	ALU	AB = NC
		DB = SD
C'	Right adjust (with zero fill) byte (if $C<8$) or word (if $8 < C < 16$).	AB = NC
		DB = SD
C'	$= \text{8-C-1 if } C \le 8$	
	$= \text{16-C if } 8 < C \le 16$	
9 + Ns + C + C'	ALU	AB = NC
		DB = SD
10 + Ns + C + C'	ALU	AB = NC
		DB = SD
11 + Ns + C + C'	ALU	AB = Source address
		DB = SD
12 + Ns + C + C'	Memory write	AB = Source address
		DB = I/O data

Note: For STCR instruction the 16-bit word at the source address is fetched. If the number of CRU bits to be transferred is ≤ 8, the CRU data is right justified (with zero fill) in the specified byte of the source word and source data word thus modified is then stored back in memory. If the bits to be transferred is > 8 then the source data fetched is not used. The CRU data in this case is right justified in 16-bit word which is then stored at the source address.

SBZ, SBO

CYCLE	TYPE	DESCRIPTION
1	Memory read	AB = PC
		DB = Instruction
2	ALU	AB = NC
		DB = SD
3	ALU	AB = NC
		DB = SD
4	Memory read	AB = Address of WR12
		DB = Contents of WR12
5	ALU	AB = NC
		DB = SD
6	CRU	Set CRUOUT = 0 for SBZ
		= 1 for SBO
		AB = CRU Bit Address
		Enable CRUCLK

TB

CYCLE	TYPE	DESCRIPTION
1	Memory read	AB = PC
		DB = Instruction
2	ALU	AB = NC
		DB = SD
3	ALU	AB = NC
		DB = SD
4	Memory read	AB = Address of WR12
		DB = Contents of WR12
5	ALU	AB = NC
		DB = SD
6	CRU	Set ST(2) = CRUIN
		AB = Address of CRU bit
		DB = SD

JEQ, JGT, JH, JHE, JL, JLE, JLT, JMP, JNC, JNE, JNO, JOC, JOP

CYCLE	TYPE	DESCRIPTION
1	Memory read	AB = PC
		DB = Instruction
2	ALU	AB = NC
		DB = SD
3	ALU	Skip to cycle #5 if TMS 9900 status satisfies
		the specified jump condition
		AB = NC
		DB = SD
4	ALU	AB = NC
		DB = Displacement value
5	ALU	AB = NC
		DB = SD

SRA, SLA, SRL, SRC

CYCLE	TYPE	DESCRIPTION
1	Memory read	AB = PC
		DB = Instruction
2	ALU	AB = NC
		DB = SD
3	Memory read	AB = Address of the workspace register
		DB = Contents of the workspace register
4	ALU	Skip to cycle #9 if C ≠ 0
		C = Shift count
		AB = NC
		DB = SD
5	ALU	AB = NC
		DB = SD
6	Memory read	AB = Address of WR0
		DB = Contents of WR0
7	ALU	AB = Source address
		DB = SD
8	ALU	AB = NC
		DB = SD
9		AB = NC
		DB = SD
C	Shift the contents of the specified workspace register in the specified direction by the specified number of bits. Set appropriate status bits.	
9 + C	Memory write	AB = Address of the workspace register
		DB = Result
10 + C	ALU	Increment PC
		AB = NC
		DB = SD

AI, ANDI, ORI

CYCLE	TYPE	DESCRIPTION
1	Memory read	AB = PC
		DB = Instruction
2	ALU	AB = NC
		DB = SD
3	ALU	AB = NC
		DB = SD
4	Memory read	AB = Address of workspace register
		DB = Contents of workspace register
5	Memory read	AB = PC + 2
		DB = Immediate operand
6	ALU	AB = NC
		DB = SD
7	Memory write	AB = Address of workspace register
		DB = Result of instruction

CI

CYCLE	TYPE	DESCRIPTION
1	Memory read	AB = PC
		DB = Instruction
2	ALU	AB = NC
		DB = NC
3	Memory read	AB = Address of workspace register
		DB = Contents of workspace register
4	ALU	AB = NC
		DB = SD
5	Memory read	AB = PC + 2
		DB = Immediate operand
6	ALU	AB = NC
		DB = SD
7	ALU	AB = NC
		DB = SD

LI

CYCLE	TYPE	DESCRIPTION
1	Memory read	AB = PC
		DB = Instruction
2	ALU	AB = NC
		DB = SD
3	ALU	AB = NC
		DB = SD
4	Memory read	AB = PC + 2
		DB = Immediate operand
5	ALU	AB = Address of workspace register
		DB = SD
6	Memory write	AB = Address of workspace register
		DB = Immediate operand

LWPI

CYCLE	TYPE	DESCRIPTION
1	Memory read	AB = PC
		DB = Instruction
2	ALU	AB = NC
		DB = SD
3	ALU	AB = NC
		DB = SD
4	Memory read	AB = PC + 2
		DB = Immediate operand
5	ALU	AB = NC
		DB = SD

LIMI

CYCLE	TYPE	DESCRIPTION
1	Memory read	AB = PC
		DB = Instruction
2	ALU	AB = NC
		DB = SD
3	ALU	AB = NC
		DB = SD
4	Memory read	AB = PC + 2
		DB = Immediate data

CYCLE	TYPE	DESCRIPTION
5	ALU	AB = NC
		DB = SD
6	ALU	AB = NC
		DB = SD
7	ALU	AB = NC
		DB = SD

STWP, STST

CYCLE	TYPE	DESCRIPTION
1	Memory read	AB = PC
		DB = Instruction
2	ALU	AB = NC
		DB = SD
3	ALU	AB = Address of workspace register
		DB = SD
4	Memory write	AB = Address of the workspace register
		DB = TMS 9900 internal register contents (WP or ST)

CKON, CKOF, LREX, RSET

CYCLE	TYPE	DESCRIPTION
1	Memory read	AB = PC
		DB = Instruction
2	ALU	AB = NC
		DB = SD
3	ALU	AB = NC
		DB = SD
4	CRU	Enable CRUCLK
		AB = External instruction code
		DB = SD
5	ALU	AB = NC
		DB = SD
6	ALU	AB = NC
		DB = SD

IDLE

CYCLE	TYPE	DESCRIPTION
1	Memory read	AB = PC
		DB = Instruction
2	ALU	AB = NC
		DB = SD
3	ALU	AB = NC
		DB = SD
4	CRU	Enable CRUCLK
		AB = Idle code
		DB = SD
5	ALU	AB = NC
		DB = SD
6	ALU	AB = NC
		DB = NC

RTWP

CYCLE	TYPE	DESCRIPTION
1	Memory read	AB = PC
		DB = Instruction
2	ALU	AB = NC
		DB = SD
3	ALU	WP + 30
4	Memory read	AB = Address of WR15
		DB = $Status_{OLD}$
5	Memory read	AB = Address of WR14
		DB = PC_{OLD}
6	Memory read	AB = Address of WR13
		DB = WP_{OLD}
7	ALU	AB = NC
		DB = SD

MACHINE-CYCLE SEQUENCE IN RESPONSE TO EXTERNAL STIMULI

RESET

CYCLE	TYPE	DESCRIPTION
1*	ALU	AB = NC
		DB = SD
2	ALU	AB = NC
		DB = SD
3	ALU	AB = 0
		DB = 0
4	Memory read	AB = 0
		DB = Workspace pointer
5	ALU	AB = NC
		DB = Status
6	Memory write	AB = Address of WR15
		DB = Contents of Status register
7	ALU	AB = NC
		DB = PC
8	Memory write	AB = Address of workspace register 14
		DB = PC + 2
9	ALU	AB = Address of WR13
		DB = SD
10	Memory write	AB = Address of workspace register 13
		DB = WP
11	ALU	AB = NC
		DB = SD
12	Memory read	AB = 2
		DB = New PC
13	ALU	AB = NC
		DB = SD

*Occurs immediately after $\overline{RESET}$ is released following a minimum 3 cycle $\overline{RESET}$

LOAD

CYCLE	TYPE	DESCRIPTION		
1*	ALU	AB	=	NC
		DB	=	SD
2	Memory read	AB	=	$FFFC_{16}$
		DB	=	Contents of $FFFC_{16}$
3	ALU	AB	=	NC
		DB	=	Status
4	Memory write	AB	=	Address of WR15
		DB	=	Contents of status register
5	ALU	AB	=	NC
		DB	=	PC
6	Memory write	AB	=	Address of WR14
		DB	=	PC + 2
7	ALU	AB	=	Address of WR13
		DB	=	SD
8	Memory write	AB	=	Address of workspace register 13
		DB	=	WP
9	ALU	AB	=	NC
		DB	=	SD
10	Memory read	AB	=	FFFE
		DB	=	New PC
11	ALU	AB	=	NC
		DB	=	SD

*Occurs immediately after last clock cycle of preceding instruction.

Psuedo Instructions

NOP

Same as JMP

RT

Same as B with indirect thru Register 11.

Interrupts

CYCLE	TYPE	DESCRIPTION		
1*	ALU	AB	=	NC
		DB	=	SD
2	Memory read	AB	=	Address of interrupt vector
		DB	=	WP
3	ALU	AB	=	NC
		DB	=	Status
4	Memory write	AB	=	Address of WR15
		DB	=	Status
5	ALU	AB	=	NC
		DB	=	PC
6	Memory write	AB	=	Address of WR 14
		DB	=	PC + 2
7	ALU	AB	=	Address of WR13
		DB	=	SD
8	Memory write	AB·	=	Address of WR 13
		DB	=	WP
9	ALU	AB	=	NC
		DB	=	SD
10	Memory read	AB	=	Address of second word of interrupt vector
		DB	=	New PC
11	ALU	AB	=	NC
		DB	=	SD

*Occurs immediately after last clock cycle of preceding instruction

TIMING

The timing of the ALU, CRU, and memory cycles is shown in *Figures 4-77, 78* and *79*. *Figure 4-80* shows the TMS9980A/81 memory cycle.

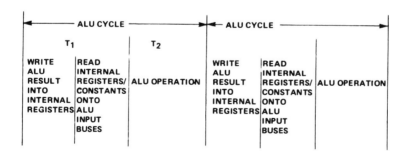

Figure 4-77. ALU Cycle

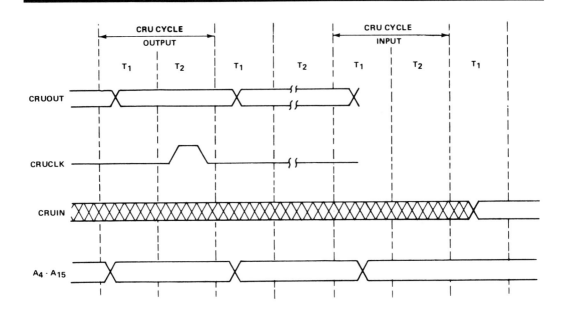

Figure 4-78. CRU Cycle.

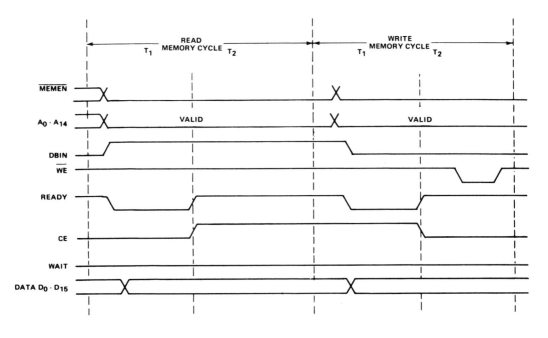

Figure 4-79. TMS 9900 Memory Cycle (No Wait States)

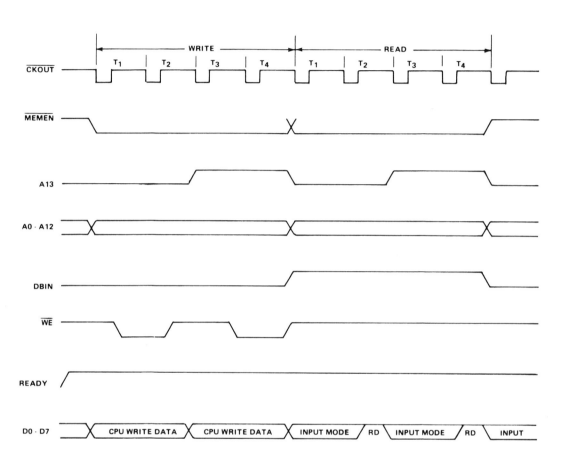

Figure 4-80. *TMS 9980A/81 Memory Cycle (No Wait States)*

CHAPTER 5

Software Design: Programming Methods and Techniques

9900 ARCHITECTURE

The 9900 system is illustrated in *Figure 5-1*. The major subsystems are the 9900 processor, the memory for program and data storage, and input and output devices for external communication and control. The processor controls the fetching of data and instructions from memory or input devices and the transferring of data from one location to another. The data and instructions are transferred 16 bits at a time in groups called words. These words are addressed or located by signals on the 15 address lines A_0 through A_{14} (called the address bus). A 15 binary bit address will select one of 32,768 memory words.

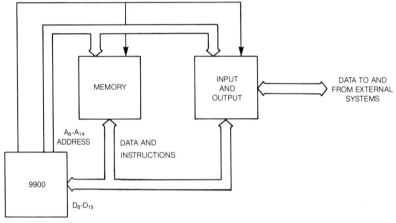

Figure 5-1. General 9900 System Structure

Internally, the processor generates a 16 bit address but the least significant bit, A_{15}, is not sent to the memory. Each word is further broken down into two 8 bit groups called bytes as shown in *Figure 5-2*. The first 8 bit byte of a word is located at an even address ($A_{15} = 0$). The second 8 bit byte is located at an odd address ($A_{15} = 1$). The byte selection is done internally in the processor once the full 16 bit data word is obtained from one of the 32,768 word locations in memory. Byte addressing is used only on instructions that perform byte operations; most 9900 instructions are word operations.

The processor contains certain basic elements as shown in *Figure 5-3*. The timing and control section is of primary interest to the hardware designer who must make certain that all system events occur in the correct order and at the correct time. The software designer is interested in what operations the ALU provides and the registers that determine the instruction and data addresses. These registers are the program counter, the status register, and the workspace pointer. In addition, the instruction register is of interest in understanding the basic instruction cycle of the processor. The 9900 contains other registers such as data address registers, ALU scratchpad registers, and so on. The processor also provides hardware to decode instructions, control the ALU operation, and to control the CRU input and outputs. These components all work together to provide the basic instruction fetch and execution cycle of the processor.

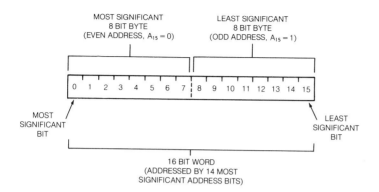

Figure 5-2. *9900 Words and Bytes*

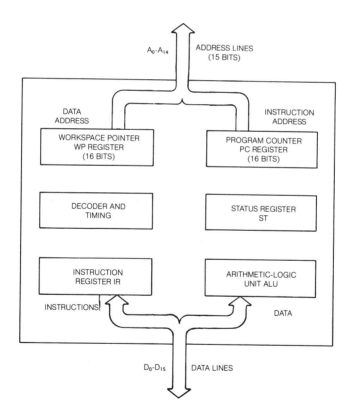

Figure 5-3. *Basic 9900 Elements.*

INSTRUCTION REGISTER AND CYCLE

The instruction cycle that is performed over and over again by the processor consists of the following basic operations:

1) *Instruction Fetch* — the contents of the program counter are sent out on the address lines and a memory read is performed. The 16 bit instruction operation code word is sent from the memory along the data lines D_0 through D_{15} and is latched in the processor instruction register.

2) *Instruction Execution* — The instruction is decoded and executed. Usually, the address of the data to be operated on (source data) is generated and a memory read cycle is performed to get the data into the processor. Then a destination address is generated and a memory write cycle is performed to store the result of the operation at a desired destination memory location.

3) The contents of the program counter are changed to indicate the address of the next instruction and the processor returns to the instruction fetch operation.

This sequence is repeated continually as long as power is supplied to the processor.

The number of memory references required in the instruction operation depends on the format that is used for the instruction. Instructions can have one of 9 such formats as illustrated in *Figure 5-4*. The instruction code indicates to the processor how many memory references are required to get all the information needed by the instruction. The first memory read obtains the instruction code which determines which operation is to be performed and how the data is located. A second and possibly a third memory read may be required to obtain values or addresses for the data to be used in this operation. An immediate instruction (format 8) consists of two successive memory words: the first for the instruction code and a second word that contains the data constant to be used. Other instruction formats contain a T_s and/or a T_d field to indicate the existence of data addresses as part of the instruction. If a T_s or T_d two bit field contains a 10_2, the address of the source or destination locations or both will be contained in the one or two memory locations immediately following the instruction code word as illustrated in *Figure 5-5*. In these cases, one or two additional memory reads are required to fetch these addresses for use by the instruction to locate data in memory. Obviously, the more memory references required to get all of the instruction, the longer the execution time for that instruction. The programmer also needs to be aware of the number of words of memory required for each instruction in order to estimate program memory requirements.

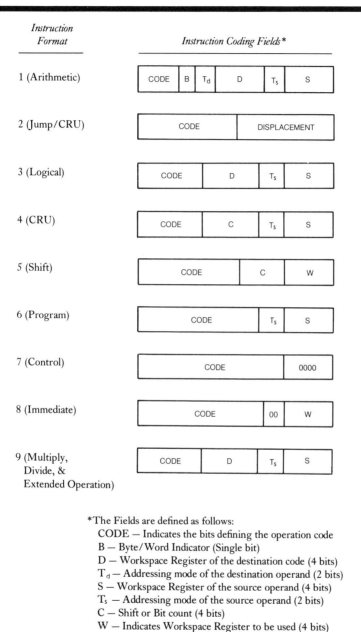

The Fields are defined as follows:

CODE — Indicates the bits defining the operation code
B — Byte/Word Indicator (Single bit)
D — Workspace Register of the destination code (4 bits)
T_d — Addressing mode of the destination operand (2 bits)
S — Workspace Register of the source operand (4 bits)
T_s — Addressing mode of the source operand (2 bits)
C — Shift or Bit count (4 bits)
W — Indicates Workspace Register to be used (4 bits)

***Figure 5-4.** 9900 Instruction Formats*

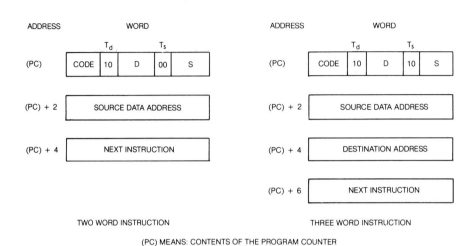

TWO WORD INSTRUCTION   THREE WORD INSTRUCTION

(PC) MEANS: CONTENTS OF THE PROGRAM COUNTER

Figure 5-5. Example Memory Requirements for Format 1 Instructions.

Program Counter (PC)

The program counter, abbreviated PC, contains the address of the instruction to be executed as illustrated in *Figure 5-6*. Normally, after executing an instruction, the contents of the program counter are incremented by two to locate the next instruction word in sequence in memory. The programmer can control the contents of the program counter (and thus control where the next instruction is to be found) by using branch or jump instructions. These instructions offer the alternatives of taking the next instruction in sequence or jumping to another part of program memory for the next instruction.

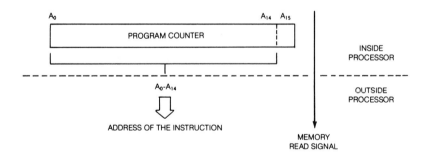

Figure 5-6. Purpose of the Program Counter

STATUS REGISTER (ST)

The purpose of the status register is to store the general arithmetic and logic conditions that result from the execution of each instruction. This information lets the programmer know if the last operation caused a result equal to or greater than some reference number (often zero). It includes the information regarding the sign of the result (was it a negative or a positive number), the parity of the result (an odd or even number of one bits), and if a carry or overflow occurred (indicating that the 16 bit word length was insufficient to hold the result). The status register also contains a 4 bit code known as the interrupt mask which defines which of 16 hardware subsystem interrupt signals will be recognized and responded to by the processor. The information contained in the status register is defined in *Figure 5-7.*

0	1	2	3	4	5	6	7 8 9 10 11	12 13 14 15
LGT	AGT	EQ	C	OV	OP	X		Interrupt Mask

Status
Register
Bit

0	LGT	— *Logical Greater Than* — set in a comparison of an unsigned number with a smaller unsigned number.
1	AGT	— *Arithmetic Greater Than* — set when one signed number is compared with another that is less positive (nearer to $-32,768$).
2	EQ	— *Equal* — set when the two words or two bytes being compared are equal.
3	C	— *Carry* — set by carry out of most significant bit of a word or byte in a shift or arithmetic operation.
4	OV	— *Overflow* — set when the result of an arthmetic operation is too large or too small to be correctly represented in 2's complement form. OV is set in addition if the most significant bit of the two operands are equal and the most significant bit of the sum is different from the destination operand most significant bit. OV is set in subtraction if the most significant bits of the operands are not equal and the most significant bit of the result is different from the most significant bit of the destination operand. In single operand instructions affecting OV, the OV is set if the most significant bit of the operand is changed by the instruction.
5	OP	— *Odd Parity* — set when there is an odd number of bits set to one in the result.
6	X	— *Extended Operation* — set when the PC and WP registers have been to set to values of the transfer vector words during the execution of an extended operation.
7-11		— Reserved for special Model 990/10 computer applications.
12-15		— *Interrupt Mask* — All interrupts of level equal to or less than mask value are enabled.

Figure 5-7. TMS9900 Status Register Contents

WORKSPACE POINTER (WP)

This register addresses the first word in a group of 16 consecutive memory words called a workspace as illustrated in *Figure 5-8*. These workspace words are called workspace registers and are treated by the processor as if they were registers on the processor chip. These workspace registers can be used as accumulators for arithmetic operations or for storage of often used data. When the workspace register contains the data used by the instruction, the T_s or T_d fields in the instruction format (see *Figure 5-4*) are 00. This way of locating instruction operands is an addressing mode called workspace register addressing. The workspace register can also be used to store the address of the data to be used instead of storing the data itself. In this case the T_s or T_d fields of the instruction code or format will be 01. This type of addressing (method of data location) is known as register indirect addressing. Workspace registers 1 through 15 can also be used to store the base address to which an offset will be added to determine a data address. This type of addressing is called indexed addressing and the T_s or T_d fields for this type of addressing will be a 10.

Some of the workspace registers are reserved for specific tasks as shown in *Figure 5-8*. If a certain type of subroutine branch called a branch and link (BL) is performed, register 11 is used to save the contents of the program counter at the time of the branch. In another type of subroutine branch, the branch and link workspace (BLWP) instruction, registers 13, 14, and 15, are used to save the values of WP, PC, and ST registers, respectively, that were in the processor at the time the branch instruction occurred. These registers then allow the programmer to return to the situation or program context that existed prior to the branch. Register 12 is used to form the address of certain input and output bits that make up part of the communications register unit (CRU) subsystem.

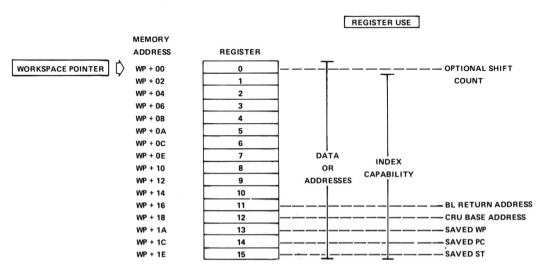

Figure 5-8. *9900 Workspace Structure*

The relationships between the workspace registers and the instruction operations must be understood by the programmer to effectively utilize the 9900. Much of the addressing of data involves the use of workspace registers and branch and input/output instructions must use the dedicated registers 11 through 15. The use of the workspace in performing the basic program functions offered by the 9900 will be covered in detail throughout this chapter.

PROGRAM ENVIRONMENT OR CONTEXT

The contents of the three processor registers (PC, WP, and ST) completely define the status of the system program at any given time. As illustrated in *Figure 5-9,* the program counter keeps track of that part of the system program currently being executed by specifying the current instruction location. The status register keeps track of the logical and arithmetic conditions that result from the execution of each instruction. The workspace pointer keeps track of the location in memory of the sixteen general purpose workspace registers currently being used by the program. The contents of the processor and workspace registers define the current program environment or *context* of the system. A change in the contents of these registers will change the environment to a new part of program memory and a new workspace area. Thus, the system will be switched to a new environment or program context by such a change. Similarly, by restoring the contents of PC, WP, and ST to original values, the program environment will be switched back to the original context and continue executing in the original program environment.

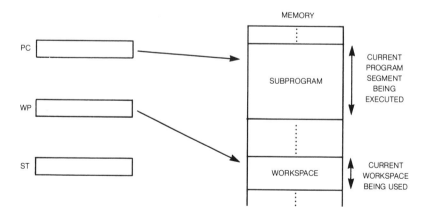

Figure 5-9. Program Context

MEMORY ORGANIZATION

The 9900 system memory must provide storage locations for the system program and subprograms and storage for system data. Since the physical devices used for storing instructions are often a different type of memory device from those used to store data, the program is usually stored in consecutive blocks of memory separate from the blocks of data. This is illustrated in *Figure 5-10*. Also shown in *Figure 5-10* are groups of memory locations that must be reserved for program and workspace addresses used by certain subprograms. Thus, the memory is subdivided into three types of storage locations: program memory, data memory, and reserved or dedicated memory.

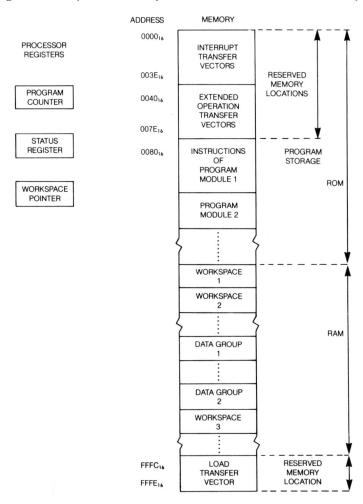

Figure 5-10. 9900 Memory Organization

RAM/ROM PARTITIONING

The program storage should be non-volatile so that the system program is not lost when the system power is turned off. Further, it is often desirable for the program memory to be a read-only memory or ROM. High volume read-only memory devices are mask programmable by the manufacturer. Alternatively, the program storage can be placed in a programmable read only memory (PROM). These devices may be economically programmed in smaller quantities. Programming may be performed by the user or by the distributor of the devices. Since both PROM and ROM devices provide word storage in consecutive addresses and the processor executes programs by going through instructions in sequence, the instructions that comprise a given subprogram should be placed in consecutive addresses in a block of memory words called a program module. It is not necessary that all program modules be adjacent to each other in memory, though certainly it is reasonable to do so.

System data storage, excluding input/output registers, provide storage for data being processed by the system program. These storage locations are usually located in consecutive blocks of memory. Since the data memory must provide both read and write capability, it is often called read-write memory. A more common terminology is random access memory or RAM, though this is somewhat misleading, since the program memory in ROM may also be randomly accessed.

The range of addresses that are assigned to the RAM storage locations and those that are assigned to the ROM locations are somewhat arbitrary. The reserved locations are the first locations in program memory, so that part of the ROM addresses are these reserved location areas. Often hardware considerations such as the simplification of the address decoding circuitry may decide the range of addresses that are used for each type of memory.

RESERVED MEMORY

The program modules, workspaces, and general data storage can generally be placed anywhere in memory, as long as the following reserved locations are preserved:

1) The first 32 words of memory (addresses 0 through $3E_{16}$) are reserved for interrupt transfer vectors.

2) The next 32 words of memory (addresses 40_{16} through $7E_{16}$) are reserved for extended operation transfer vectors.

3) The last two words of memory (addresses $FFFC_{16}$ and $FFFF_{16}$) are reserved for a load or reset transfer vector.

These transfer vectors provide storage for a value to be placed in the workspace pointer and a value to be placed in the program counter in order to switch the program context from its current environment to a subprogram and new workspace. This new subprogram and workspace context is used to respond to a hardware interrupt signal, a hardware reset signal, or an instruction called an extended operation (XOP).

WORKSPACE UTILIZATION

THE WORKSPACE CONCEPT AND USES

The advanced memory-to-memory architecture of the 9900 affords multiple register files in main memory for efficient data manipulation and flexible subroutine linkage. The usage of the workspace must follow certain constraints for optimum performance. Each workspace is a contiguous block of 16 words in main memory. All 16 general purpose registers are available to the programmer for use in any of four ways:

1) *Operand Registers* — to contain data for arithmetic and logical operations.
2) *Accumulators* — to store intermediate results of arithmetic operations.
3) *Address Registers* — to specify memory location of operands.
4) *Index Registers* — to provide an offset from a base address to define an operand location.

The workspace pointer in the processor contains the address of workspace register 0. The address of any workspace register R is:

Memory Address of Register $R = (WP) + 2R$

where (WP) means the contents of the workspace pointer.

When a workspace register is specified as an operand in an instruction, (workspace register addressing mode) the workspace register contains binary data for use by the instruction. As an example, consider the addition of the data in register 5 to the data in register 6. The instruction format is:

A   5,6

with address calculations of:

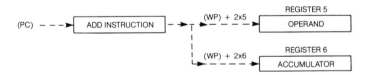

which is interpreted as follows:
1) The contents of the program counter addresses the instruction in ROM.
2) The instruction indicates workspace register addressing causing the calculation of the workspace addresses to locate the data to be used by the instruction (contained in registers 5 and 6) in RAM.

The resulting hardware operation with the data thus located is:

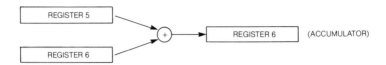

In this example, register 5 is functioning as an operand and register 6 is functioning as an accumulator. The difference between an operand and an accumulator register is that operands remain unchanged by an operation, while accumulators assume new values, the result of the operations.

The contents of a workspace register may be the address of an operand or an accumulator in main memory. Address registers are accessed through workspace register indirect addressing, with or without autoincrementing. If autoincrementing is not used, the content of the workspace register (the address of the data) is not changed by the operation. If autoincrementing is used, the address contained in the workspace register is incremented by one for byte operations and by two for word operations. An example of an addition instruction in which both the operand and the accumulator are specified by register indirect addressing is:

    A   *5,*6

with the address computations:

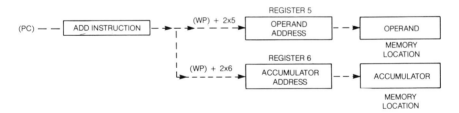

with the resulting hardware operation:

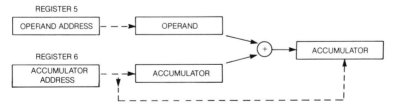

The contents of the address registers are not changed in execution since autoincrementing is not used.

Autoincrementing is often used when accessing structured data and data arrays. To add this feature to this example, the following format would be used:

A   *5+, *6+

which would result in the same events as described for standard workspace register indirect addressing with the addition of an incrementing by two of the contents of the address register 5 and 6:

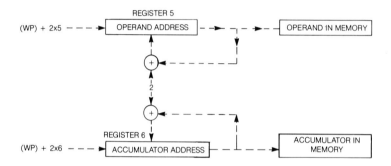

The addresses are modified (incremented by two) after the operand and accumulator addressing operations are completed.

When the workspace register is used as an index register, its contents specify an offset from a base address. The sum of this offset and the base address contained in the instruction defines the memory location of program data. Workspace registers act as index registers when the indexed addressing mode is used. The only restriction on the use of workspace registers as index registers is that register 0 cannot be used as an index register. An example of using register 5 as an indirect address register for the operand and register 6 as an index register for addressing the accumulator would be:

A   *5, @BASE (6)

The binary address BASE is the second word of the two word add instruction, with address calculations as follows:

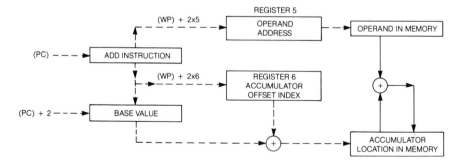

The operand data is added to the accumulator data and the sum is stored in the accumulator location.

DEDICATED AREAS OF WORKSPACES

Any register of a workspace may be used as a general purpose register (with the exception of register 0 not being available as an index register). A few of the registers are used by 9900 hardware in certain ways, and the software designer must observe these constraints to assure the integrity of stored data and program and hardware linkages. *Figure 5-11* shows the way the workspace is viewed by the hardware.

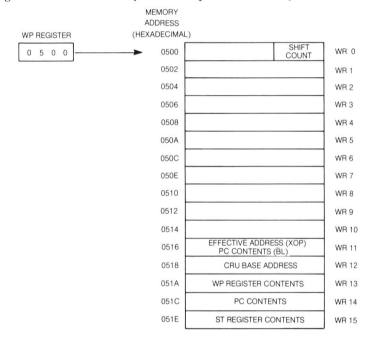

Figure 5-11. Reserved Areas of 9900 Workspaces

An examination of *Figure 5-11* reveals the following areas that may have to be reserved in a workspace:

Registers 13, 14, and 15 — Context Switches

These three workspace registers are loaded with current values of the workspace pointer, program counter, and status register with each context switch. A context switch occurs in response to an interrupt or in executing a BLWP or XOP instruction. When an RTWP return instruction is executed, the processor restores these values to the processor registers from the last three workspace registers. To insure that this return linkage is not destroyed, the programmer must insure that subprogram operations or subsequent context switches do not alter the contents of registers 13, 14, or 15.

Register 0 — Shift Instruction

Bits 12 through 15 of register 0 may specify a bit count for shift instructions. The 9900 shift instructions have the format:

OPCODE   R, SCNT

where the OPCODE is one of the shift instruction mnemonics SLA, SRC, SRL, or SRA, R is the operand register, and SCNT specifies the number of bit position to be shifted. When SCNT is zero, bits 12 through 15 of register 0 specifies the shift count. If both SCNT and bits 12 through 15 of register 0 are zero, a 16 bit shift will occur.

Register 11 — XOP and BL Instructions

Register 11 is used to save address information in extended operation instructions (XOP) and Branch and Link subroutine jump (BL) instructions. The BL instruction provides a means of subroutine linkage without the overhead of a context switch. Previous contents of register 11 are replaced with the program counter contents when a BL occurs. Return to the calling procedure is accomplished with the RT pseudo-instruction or by an indirect branch B *11. No critical data should be stored in register 11 if a BL instruction is to be executed.

In the case of the extended operation instruction, an address is passed to register 11 during the XOP context switch. For example:

XOP   VAR, OPNUM

OPNUM is the XOP number and locates the XOP transfer vector in main memory through the formula:

$$\text{Transfer Vector Address} = 40_{16} + 4 \times \text{OPNUM}$$

The effective address of the source operand VAR is placed into register 11 of the XOP workspace. Even if VAR is not provided, register 11 contents will be altered by executing an XOP instruction.

Register 12 — CRU Bit Addressing

The 9900 communications register unit (CRU) is a direct command-driven I/O interface. The five CRU instructions (SBO, SBZ, TB, LDCR, and STCR) all depend on the presence of a CRU hardware base address in bits 3 through 14 of workspace register 12. None of these instructions alter the content of register 12.

WORKSPACE LOCATION

Workspaces may be located anywhere in main memory. In practice, 66 words of memory are reserved to implement necessary hardware functions (transfer vectors). Workspaces and data may be stored in any other memory area, known as general memory. The memory locations reserved for 9900 transfer vectors for interrupts and extended operation instructions are memory addresses 0000_{16} through $007E_{16}$. The last two words of memory (addresses $FFFC_{16}$ and $FFFE_{16}$) are reserved for a load function transfer vector, so the last data or instruction word can occur at address $FFFA_{16}$.

Within general addresses 0080_{16} through $FFFA_{16}$, workspaces can be independent, or used in common by different program segments or subprograms. To reduce memory requirements of a software system, routines can share workspaces. The effect of a BL call to a subroutine is illustrated in Figure 5-12. The program counter is changed to fetch the instructions from the subroutine, but the *workspace pointer is not changed,* which results in a workspace shared by the called and the calling procedures.

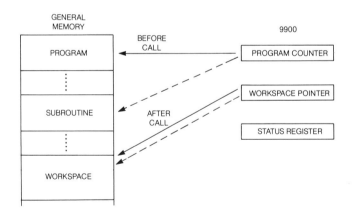

Figure 5-12. *Shared Workspace Subroutine Call*

When a routine requires the use of a large number of workspace registers, an independent workspace will be needed for that routine. In some cases, independent workspaces are used for routines when little common data is needed. When workspaces have no common memory words, parameter or data passing can be done by using the old program counter and workspace pointer. For example, in a context switch, which saves the old workspace pointer in the new workspace register 13, any of the old workspace registers can be accessed by referring to the contents of the new register 13. The contents of register 13 addresses the old workspace register 0. The use of register 13 as an index register allows the programmer access to any other of the old workspace registers. Thus, to access old register 0 as an operand in an add instruction, the following instruction would be used:

    A   *13,7

This instruction specifies the contents of old register 0 (addressed by the contents of new register 13) as an operand and new register 7 as an accumulator. To address old register 10, the following indexed addressing approach could be used:

    A   @20(13),7

This instruction adds 20 to the contents of new register 13 to generate the address of old workspace register 10, which is then used as an operand in the add operation. The effect of a context switch in providing an independent workspace is illustrated in *Figure 5-13.*

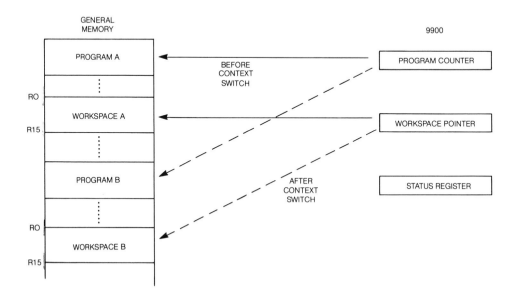

Figure 5-13. Independent Workspaces

SUBROUTINE TECHNIQUES

Software systems are implemented with a set of subprograms, usually subroutines. Subroutines offer several advantages over incorporation of all code into a large main program:

1) Repetition of code is reduced. Modular coding of repeated processes saves memory requirements of software.
2) Documentation is simplified. The clarity of complex programs is enhanced by breaking the overall task into manageable subsystems.
3) Debugging time is reduced. A complicated system can be made functional one module at a time.

These advantages point out the importance of understanding the characteristics of 9900 subroutine calls. The most important characteristics are the way the subroutine linkages back to the calling program are handled and the way parameters are passed between the calling program and the subroutine. The linkage procedures for the types of subroutine calls are discussed first.

TYPES OF SUBROUTINES

Three types of subroutine calls are used with the 9900. The following table summarizes the calls and returns for each type:

Call to Subroutine		Return to Calling Procedure	
Mnemonic	*Meaning*	*Mnemonic*	*Meaning*
BL	Branch & Link	RT or	Return
		B *11	
BLWP	Branch & Link Workspace Pointer	RTWP	Return with Workspace Pointer
XOP	Extended Operation	RTWP	Return with Workspace Pointer

The branch and link instruction is a fast transfer to a routine that shares the workspace with the calling procedure. Execution of a BL causes the contents of the program counter to be stored in workspace register 11. The new program counter value is the single argument of the BL instruction. An example of a typical BL instruction is:

```
PT       BL       @SUB1
```

SUB1 is the label of the first instruction of the subroutine being called. After execution of the BL instruction, program flow will continue at the symbolic address SUB1. Upon execution of the BL instruction, the update value of the program counter (address PT + 4) is stored in workspace 11 (PT is the symbolic address of the BL instruction). This process of a shared workspace subroutine call is illustrated in *Figure 5-14.* Return to the calling procedure is through the RT pseudo-instruction which is equivalent to the indirect branch;

```
B        *11
```

Since the BL instruction always reloads Workspace register 11, special steps must be taken to insure that the critical return address is not overstored. Generally, register 11 should not be used to save a variable whose value will be needed after a BL instruction occurs. Similarly, after a BL instruction has been executed (and before a RT instruction has been executed), register 11 cannot be used by any instruction that would change the contents of register 11, such as using register 11 as an accumulator or executing another BL instruction. If multiple levels of BL calls are to be used, a push-down stack must be established to save intermediate return linkage. Techniques for setting up a stack are discussed under the topics of multiple level subroutine calls and reentrancy.

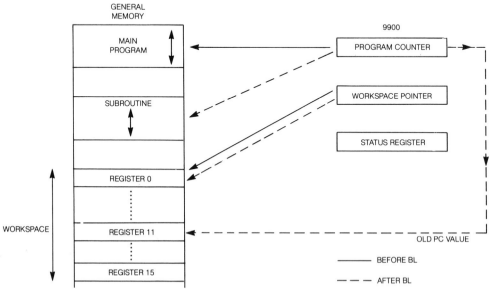

Figure 5-14. Effects of BL Instruction

The branch and load workspace pointer (BLWP) is a subroutine call that initiates a context switch. When a context switch occurs, the programming environment is changed to allow the subroutine to use a new register file (workspace). BLWP has the following effect as illustrated in *Figure 5-15:*

1) A transfer vector located by the argument of the BLWP instruction supplies a new workspace pointer value and program counter value.
2) The old values of WP, PC, and ST are saved in registers 13, 14, and 15, respectively, of the new workspace.
3) Execution proceeds in the subroutine using the new PC value.

The 9900 format for a typical BLWP using Symbolic addressing is:

      PCL   BLWP   @TVAL

where PCL is an arbitrary label and the symbolic address of the location of the BLWP instruction in general memory. TVAL is the symbolic address of the transfer vector, which in turn provides new values for the workspace pointer and the program counter. The contents of workspace register 13 through 15 of the new workspace are reserved for storage of the return linkage. Since the BLWP can store return linkage in an independent workspace, multiple subroutine levels may be implemented without a return stack as long as no two subroutines use the same workspace (transfer vector). Although the example in *Figure 5-15* uses symbolic addressing mode, other addressing modes can be used.

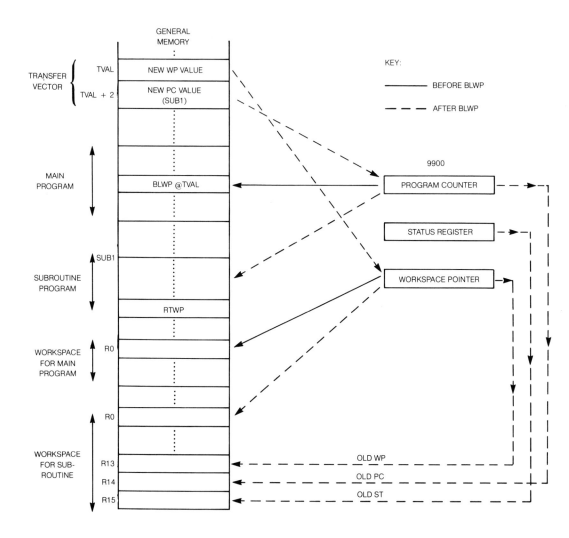

Figure 5-15. Execution of BLWP Instruction (BLWP @TVAL)

Extended operation instructions (XOP) offer a means of expanding the 9900 instruction set. The implementation of an XOP is similar to the execution of a BLWP; *the instructions differ only in the location of the transfer vector and in the parameter passing feature offered by the XOP.* The execution of an XOP is illustrated in *Figure 5-16* and consists of the following events:

1) Identify the XOP number (N) and locate a transfer vector in memory at the address $0040_{16} +_i 4 \times N$.
2) Use the transfer vector word one as the new workspace pointer value and the second word of the vector as the new program counter value.
3) Save the old contents of WP, PC, and ST in new workspace registers 13, 14, and 15, respectively.
4) Store the effective address of the source operand in new workspace register 11.

Thus, XOP initiates a context switch with the added benefit of direct passing of a parameter address to the new workspace (register 11). By using an assembler directive DXOP, the user can define a mnemonic string to present one of the 16 XOP transfer vectors. This mnemonic can then be used in the program as a user defined instruction, improving the clarity of the program coding. For example, to define XOP 15 as the mnemonic SAMPL, the following directive can be used:

         DXOP   SAMPL, 15

Then, instead of using the standard XOP entry in the program:

         XOP   @PARAM, 15

The programmer can insert the newly defined mnemonic:

         SAMPL   @PARAM

The XOP call is a software trap to a user-defined routine. It functions as though the routine were a single instruction added to the 9900 set of operation codes, hence the name "extended operation."

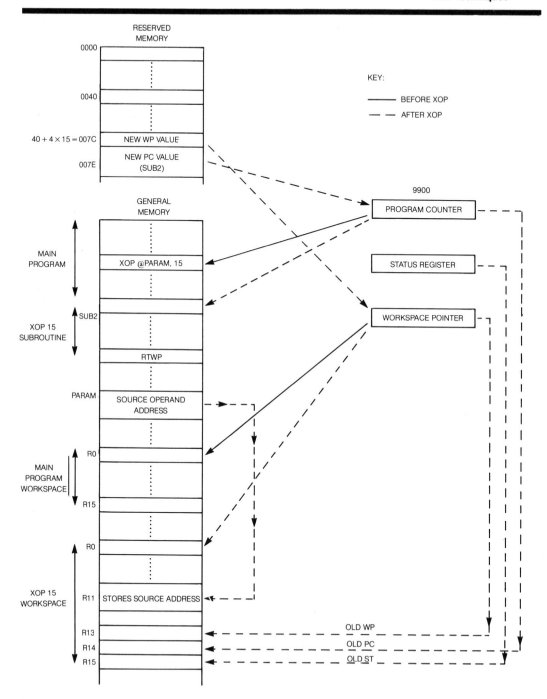

Figure 5-16. *Execution of XOP Instruction (XOP @PARAM, 15)*

PARAMETER PASSING

Most subroutines require access to data generated by the calling procedure. Different subroutine call types mandate different parameter passing techniques. All three types of subroutine calls, BL, BLWP, and XOP, *transfer the old contents of the program counter to the called procedure.* This return linkage provides a powerful tool for parameter passing as illustrated in *Figure 5-17.* A parameter list can be assembled in a block of words following the call and accessed through the old program counter by workspace register indirect autoincrement addressing. Regardless of the number of parameters used in any given call, the program counter must be incremented past the whole list, so that the return will be to the next instruction in the calling program. A subroutine call using only one of two passed parameters is shown in the following example:

```
0200              BL    @ANG       Call Subroutine ANG
0202   FLAG1   DATA  > 0         Parameter 1 is 0000₁₆
0204   FLAG2   DATA  > 1         Parameter 2 is 0001₁₆

0600   ANG     MOV   *11+,3     Move Parameter 1 into R3
0602           C     3,2        Compare Parameter 1 to contents of R2
0604           JEQ   FIRSTEQ    Try next test if equal
0606           INCT  R11        Move Return PC past parameter 2
0608           B     *11        Return
060A   FIRSTEQ
```

The subroutine ANG checks the first parameter against the contents of R2. If an inequality is found, the branch to continue the routine at FIRSTEQ is not taken. The move instruction which loaded parameter 1 into the workspace increments the program counter in R11 by 2 so that register 11 now points to parameter 2. The INCT instruction is required to increment the program counter value in R11 past parameter 2 to point to the next instruction in the calling program.

When parameters are passed in this way using the program counter, good programming practice dictates that they be constants or addresses only and not variables. Variable quantities should be stored in memory external to program code. To 'nest' variable data in program code causes in-line code modification, which would produce code that would be inoperative if stored in ROM.

The example above dealt with the BL subroutine call, though the same technique can be applied to BLWP or XOP calls. These calls store the program counter in workspace register 14, so the indirect address register must be 14 instead of 11.

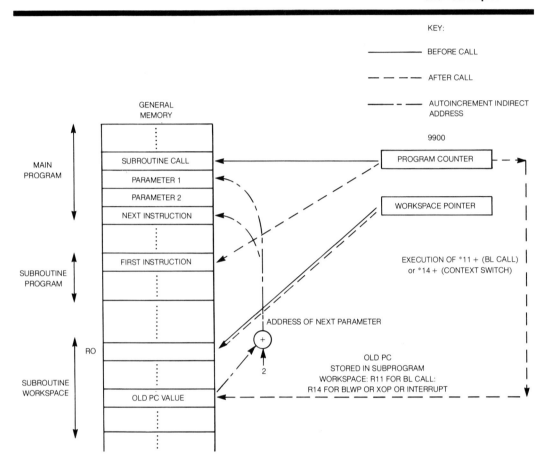

Figure 5-17. Parameter Passing Using Old Program Counter Value.

Another method of parameter passing is used when a context switch occurs. Both BLWP and XOP cause the old contents of the workspace pointer to be stored in the new workspace register 13. By using register 13 in the called procedure, access is gained to parameters in the old workspace as illustrated in *Figure 5-18*. Direct access to old register 0 is provided, but to use other parts of the old workspace, indexed addressing provides the most convenient access to old registers 1 through 15 without changing the old workspace pointer value. For example, to move the contents of old workspace register 2 to new workspace register 5, the following instruction can be used:

        MOV   @R2*2(13),R5

which causes the address of the operand to be the contents of register 13 plus 4, which is the address of old workspace register 2. Similarly, to move the contents of old workspace register 7 to old workspace register 6:

        MOV   @R7*2(13), @R6*2(13)

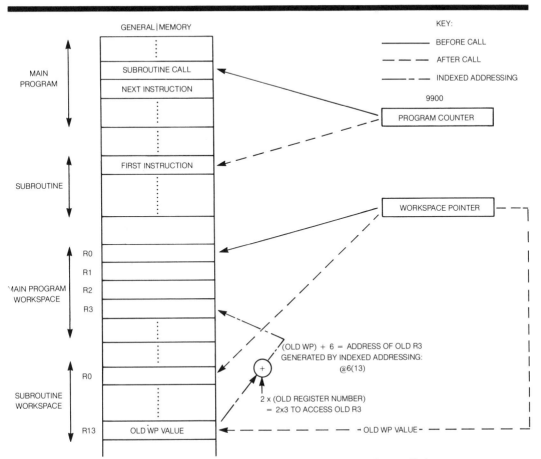

Figure 5-18. Parameter Passing through Old Workspace Pointer

A final type of parameter passing applies only to XOP context switches. The single argument of an XOP call specifies the effective address of a source operand. This form of parameter passing avoids the risk of changing the old PC and WP. The overhead of changing the WP and PC pointers is also avoided to increase execution speed. As an example, if XOP 9 has been defined as FADD by a DXOP directive, the call:

    FADD   @LIST

causes the address stored at location LIST to be placed in register 11 of the subroutine workspace. Then, workspace register indirect addressing can access the parameter. For example, if in the FADD subroutine it is desired that the parameter be incremented by two, the following instruction would be used.

    INCT   *11

The use of the parameter through its address in register 11 is straightforward and doesn't interfere with the return linkage. This type of parameter passing has already been illustrated in *Figure 5-16*.

MULTIPLE LEVEL SHARED WORKSPACE SUBROUTINES

Since the BL instruction always reloads the workspace register 11, special steps must be taken to insure that the information in register 11 is not overstored. In the case of multiple levels of BL called subroutines, routines which call other routines before returning to the main program, a pushdown stack should be established to save intermediate return linkage. To create a return linkage stack for multiple levels of subroutines which share a workspace, the following procedure is employed:

1) Allocate one workspace register to the stack pointer function.

2) For each subroutine, "push" the contents of workspace register 11 before the next call, and "pop" the stack to restore the register 11 contents after each call is complete.

An example of a stack manipulation code following this procedure to push and pop return linkage is as follows, with register 5 acting as a stack pointer:

```
        ┆    Subroutine code before next level call
        ┆

    DECT    5         Decrement Stack Pointer            ⎫
                                                         ⎬  Push Operation
    MOV     11, *5    Load return PC onto Stack          ⎭

    BL      @SUBNXT   Call next level of subroutine

    MOV     *5+, 11   After return, restore current      ⎫
                      return address and restore         ⎬  Pop Operation
        ┆             stack pointer                      ⎭
        ┆
```

This code allows the current subroutine to call subroutine SUBNXT without destroying the current subroutine's return linkage. The main program employs a standard BL call, and the lowest level routine would not use the stack, since its register 11 would not be replaced with a subsequent BL call. An example of this stack operation procedure with 3 nested subroutines is illustrated in *Figure 5-19*.

SHARED WORKSPACE MAPPING

Software systems for small computers must efficiently utilize available memory. This section presents an organized technique for sharing workspaces between subroutines to reduce system memory requirements.

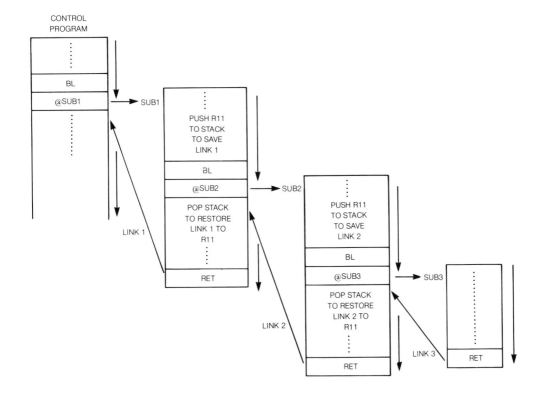

Figure 5-19. Stack Operations in Nested Subroutines.

The first step in system development is to write a main program and its associated subroutines with totally independent workspaces. Avoidance of shared workspaces at the start can prevent the undesirable aspect of destruction of critical data, including return linkage.

After independent software is written, the programmer begins the process of identifying potential shared workspaces. First, the relationship between called and calling procedures is summarized graphically as shown in *Figure 5-20.* This graph represents the fact that procedure A can call either procedure B or C. Procedure B may call D or E, while E can call D or G, and so on throughout the graph. Having identified routine relationships, *Figure 5-20* can be changed to a form that reflects subroutine levels. All procedures at the same level are called from a higher level and may call routines at a lower level.

Thus, *Figure 5-20* would be changed to the form illustrated in *Figure 5-21*. This information is equivalent to the information contained in *Figure 5-20*, but it clarifies the relationship between procedures. The routines on a particular level can never call another routine at the same or at a higher level. Thus, all routines at the same level can share a common workspace since return linkage will not be overstored by a subsequent call. Therefore, for the example described in *Figures 5-20 and 5-21*, five independent workspaces will suffice for a software system of eight procedures, saving 3 workspaces or 48 words of memory. By employing this simple technique, the software designer can write efficient code with an assurance of the integrety of return linkage.

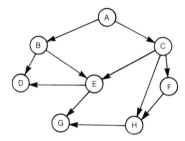

Figure 5-20. *Graphical Representation of Interrelation of Calls*

RE-ENTRANT PROGRAMMING

Re-entrant programming is a technique that allows one set of program code to be executed on multiple data sets concurrently. To be re-entrant, program code must have the following characteristics:
1) All data contained in a re-entrant routine must be common to all procedures which call it, and must be read-only to all using procedures.
2) All data unique to calling routines must be stored and used in a workspace unique to the calling procedure.
3) Re-entrant code must not alter data or instructions within its code during execution.

Re-entrant coding is a general programming technique that has many applications. Device service routines which control the operations of several similar units should be re-entrant. By passing a CRU base address with other unique data to a re-entrant service subprogram, any one of a group of calling procedures can access such a multi-purpose I/O routine, thereby saving system memory requirements. This is a case in which one routine is used for several applications at random time intervals. A re-entrant subroutine is so loosely coupled to its calling procedure that a re-entrant routine can be interrupted during execution, used on different data, and return to complete the original process without losing data integrity. Since re-entrant code is immune to problems with data resulting from interrupts, it finds application in interrupt service routines, commonly called procedures, in a multiprogramming environment such as assemblers or in real-time control applications.

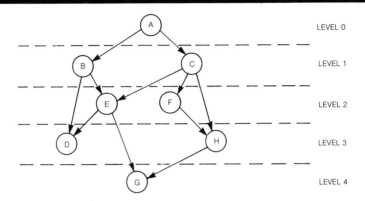

Figure 5-21. Levels of Subroutine Calls

Figure 5-22 illustrates a program flow in which subroutine A must be re-entrant. The alternative to writing subroutine A in re-entrant code is to make two copies of A, one for each time A can be executed concurrently. The re-entrant approach is more efficient in memory usage than is the multiple copy approach. In this program flow, the main program calls its first level subroutine which in turn calls subroutine A as a second level subroutine. During execution of routine A, an interrupt occurs, which in this example the interrupt handler program sequence calls several routines, including routine A. If A employs re-entrant programming, the same words of code can implement routine A for both parts of the program flow.

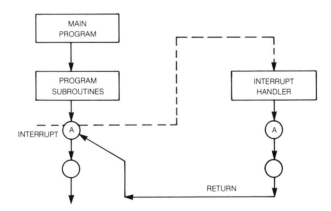

Figure 5-22. Interrupt Requiring Re-entrant Programming

As an example of re-entrant coding, consider the problem of forming a starting and an ending address for a block of data to be operated on by a subroutine. Register 1 is to hold the starting address, register 2 is to hold the ending address, and register 3 is to hold the current data address within the block.

This structure is in a subroutine that must be re-entrant, i.e., one that can be called concurrently by two different program segments as illustrated in *Figure 5-22*. Different program segments that use this subroutine will probably be dealing with blocks at different starting addresses and of different sizes. For example, the main program stream may be operating on a block of 10 words starting at address 1000_{16} while the interrupt handler may have to operate on a 32 word block starting at address 2000_{16}. Forming the starting and ending addresses as follows:

```
BLKLN   EQU   32
        LI    1,>1000       Load R1 with starting address
        LI    2,2*BLKLN     Load R2 with 2x (words in block)
        A     1,2           Form end address for block (1014₁₆)
```

would not result in re-entrant code. This sequence would be correct for the main program stream but is not correct for the interrupt handler stream. The code can be made to work for both streams by not placing the load immediates in the subroutine itself but by placing them in the program stream that calls the subroutine. Then, when either the main program or the interrupt handler gets ready to call the subroutine, the starting address and ending address can be established within the workspace for that environment. The subroutine can then concentrate on performing its manipulations, without being concerned with the address initialization process. Suppose that this addressing scheme is used in a subroutine that clears a block of memory words. *Figure 5-23* shows the re-entrant and non-re-entrant forms of this subroutine. The re-entrant form can be used in the situation of *Figure 5-22* since execution depends on the workspace being used. The subroutine can be executing with the registers 1 through 3 of the main program when an interrupt occurs. The interrupt handler uses a different workspace so when it calls the CLEAR subroutine, new starting and ending addresses are used, without affecting where the subroutine was in the main program execution. Then, when the subroutine and interrupt handler have been executed and the context is switched back to the main program, the subroutine will continue executing with the values in registers 2 and 3 of the main program environment.

This is not true of the non-re-entrant code. By moving the contents of the interrupt register 1 to the FIN location, the number of blocks to be cleared by the main program execution CLEAR subroutine could be changed, if the interrupt occurs after the MOV   1, @FIN instruction. Because the value FIN is unique for each calling program or computed in the subroutine, the code may not properly be re-entered. That is, it should not be used when an interrupting procedure may execute the same code. The re-entrant version could be used by any number of interrupting procedures without affecting execution results in either the main program or the interrupting program environments. Entrance to the routine would be performed by executing a BL @ CLRLUP.

Re-Entrant Coding

	MOV	1,3	Set R3 at first address of block
	A	1,2	Compute end address and place in R2
COM	C	3,2	Address past end?
	JH	PRET	If so, return
	CLR	*3+	Else, clear word and go to next address
	JMP	COM	Jump to continue clearing
PRET	B	*11	Return

Non-Re-entrant Coding

CLRLUP	MOV	1,3	Set R3 at first address of block
	MOV	1,@FIN	Set up first address in FIN
	A	2,@FIN	Compute final address and store at FIN
COM	C	3,@FIN	Address past end?
	JH	PRET	If so, return
	CLR	*3+	Else, clear word and go to next address
	JMP	COM	Jump to continue clearing
PRET	B	*11	Return

Figure 5-23. Subroutine Example of Re-entrant Coding.

PROGRAMMING TASKS

The programming techniques of workspace and subroutine usage, program loops, macros, and data representation must be applied to the development of programs and subprograms to perform the basic system functions of state initialization, pattern recognition, arithmetic, and input/output. Each of these system functions represents a programming task that involves programming structures peculiar to each function. This section discusses the basic requirements of the software for each function and presents some of the programming approaches that are used to meet those requirements.

INITIALIZATION

When the system is first turned on, the first few instructions encountered must initialize the state of the system to a desired predetermined starting state. The system initialization procedure is usually started by the RESET or LOAD functions. Similarly, as the system enters a subprogram or a new program sequence, the state of certain memory locations must be initialized to a desired starting state. Further, in developing the software, the transfer vectors and other program constants must be initialized by the assembly language software. The assembly language directives available for this purpose include the equate (EQU) and the data (DATA) directives. The application of these directives to the problem of initializing the reserved memory locations and program constants are covered in detail under the assembler directive discussion in Chapter 7.

Usually the first part of any program is the initialization of the system. The LWPI instruction is used to initialize the workspace pointer (WP register) to define the location of the 16 workspace registers. If the workspace of a program sequence is to be located at a starting address of 400_{16}, the following instruction will initialize the workspace pointer to that value:

    LWPI   >0400

Under the interrupts discussion the use of the LIMI (load interrupt mask immediate) instruction to establish which interrupts would be responded to was covered. For example, if the programmer wants to disable all interrupts above level 7 for a program segment, the following instruction must be used at the first of the segment:

    LIMI   7

Similarly, the load immediate (LI) instruction is used to initialize values in workspace registers. The LI can be followed by MOV instructions to further initialize other memory locations. As an example, to initialize register 3 and memory location TEST to the value $00FF_{16}$, the following instructions can be used:

    LI   3, >00FF
    MOV   3, @TEST

In some initialization sequences several registers have to be initialized to the same value, such as zero. For example, if 10 consecutive memory words starting at location 1000_{16} are to be cleared (zeroed) then a program loop is suggested. One possible implementation of this initialization task would be:

	LI	2,>1000	Set R2 to the starting address 1000_{16}
	LI	3,>100A	Set R3 to the address past the last data location to be cleared
LOOP	CLR	*2+	Clear data, increment the address by two
	C	2,3	Is address past the 10th data location
	JNE	LOOP	If not jump to LOOP to continue clears else go the next sequence of instructions

In this data initialization program segment, like most program segments, registers must be initialized to establish program limits, addresses, and other conditions. In this sequence register 2 was initialized to the starting data address and register 3 was initialized to indicate the first word address after the 10th data word to be cleared. Had this loop been implemented with a loop counter, the register acting as a loop counter would have been initialized to 10.

Generally, most program initialization tasks can be handled by using a combination of the techniques presented in this section. The immediate load instructions are the most commonly used operations in performing the initialization operation, followed by the use of assembler initialization directives to establish vectors and other data constant initialization.

MASKING AND TESTING

In many cases only certain portions of a word are of interest. The program segment may be examining or modifying a single bit or a group of bits. The bits that are not involved in the operation must be masked off so that they will not affect status bits and thus affect program decisions. There are several ways of approaching this masking and single bit testing problem.

If a single I/O bit is to be examined or modified, the simplest approach is to use the CRU single bit instruction SBO, SBZ, or TB to perform the desired operation. This is possible only if the hardware has been set up to address the desired bit as a CRU bit. If the bit is not accessible through CRU addressing, one of the selective masking instructions must be used. The set to ones or zeroes instructions (SOC, SOCB, SZC, and SZCB) can be used to selectively set or clear bits. The compare ones or zeroes corresponding instructions (COC and CZC) can be used to test selected bits. Of course these instructions can be used to test or change single or multiple bits. An alternative single bit approach is to use the circulate instruction (SRC) to get the desired bit into the carry status bit for examination or changing.

To see how these non-CRU masking instructions are used, consider the task of examining the value of bit 12 of the data of workspace register 1. The mask is contained in location MASK which will contain all zeroes in all bits except for bit 12 which will contain a one. Thus, location MASK will contain 0008_{16}. Then, the instruction:

    CZC   @MASK, 1

will set the equal status bit if bit 12 of R1 contains a zero. The instruction:

    COC   @MASK, 1

will set the equal status bit if bit 12 of R1 contains a one. In these cases, the JEQ or JNE instructions can be used to test the equal status bit after the comparison.

Alternatively, the instruction:

    SRC   1,4

will cause bit 12 to be in the carry flip-flop. However, this instruction will change the contents of R1 by moving all bits to the right 4 positions. The JC or JNC instructions are used to test the bit value in the carry status bit.

To selectively set bit 12 of R1, any of the following instructions could be used:

    ORI   1,>0008
    SOC   @MASK,1

To selectively clear bit 12 of R1, either or the following instructions could be used:

    ANDI   1,>FFF7

or:

    SZC   @MASK,1

If groups of bits are to be changed or examined, the above techniques can be used if all bits are to be ones or zeroes. For example, if bit 13 of register 2 is to be tested, the following instructions would jump to point P1 in the program if bit 13 of R2 is one:

    ANDI 2,>0004   Zero all bits but bit 13 of R2; compare to 0

    JNE   P1   If EQ=0, bit 13 was one and jump to point P1

A more complicated test would be to check bits 13 and 15 of R3. A jump to P2 is to be made if both of these bits are one. The following instructions would accomplish this test and program decision:

H5   DATA   5
    .
    .
    .
    COC   @H5,3   Compare to 5 to see if both bits are one.
    JEQ   P2   If they are, jump to point P2.

Thus, a combination of masks (ANDI) compares, and conditional jumps can be used to examine all features of system words and react appropriately.

If a group of bits is to be examined or modified arithmetically, a slightly different approach may be used. If for example the least four bits of R1 are to be compared to 8, one approach would be to provide a copy of the R1 contents in R2. Then the first 12 bits of R2 are zeroed with:

    ANDI   2,>000F

or with: SZC @MASK1,2 where the contents of location MASK1 are $FFF0_{16}$. Then, the contents of R2 can be compared to 8. The entire sequence would then be:

```
MOV   1,2
ANDI  2,>F
CI    2,8
JLT   P1
      .
      .    Sequence of instructions
      .       to handle case where least
      .       four bits of R1 (and R2) are
      .       greater than or equal to 8
      .
P1    .    Sequence of instructions
      .       to handle case where least
      .       four bits of R1 (and R2) are
              less than 8
```

This technique is useful in Decimal to Binary or Binary to Decimal number conversion and in implementing BCD (Binary Coded Decimal) arithmetic.

Of the techniques that can be used in masking and testing, the ANDI, ORI, SOC, and SZC instructions change the word they operate on. The Compare techniques, CZC and COC, do not affect the words being operated on but they do affect the status bits. Often, when part of a word is modified (such as portion of the word is zeroed by an ANDI instruction) the word must later be reassembled after all bit group operations have been completed. The programmer should see that such operations are performed on copies of the word so that further masking operations use the original word. As an example, if a word is to be broken down into four bit groups (to implement BCD arithmetic), at least four copies of the word are required or four accumulators must be used. If register 1 contains the master copy, and registers 2 through 5 contain the four bit groups, the following sequence of instructions would generate the desired four bit groupings in the four accumulators from the master copy in register 1:

```
MOV   @MASTER,1   Move word to be separated into R1
MOV   1,2         Move a copy of the word into
MOV   1,3         accumulators R2 through R5
MOV   1,4
MOV   1,5
ANDI  2,>000F     Mask all but least four bits in R2
ANDI  3,>00F0     Mask all but next four bits in R3
ANDI  4,>0F00     Mask all but next four bits in R4
ANDI  5,>F000     Mask all but most significant four bits in R5
```

With this program sequence, the original word can be broken into bit groups for further testing and modification. R1 still contains the original word for reference and further manipulation. However, by using ANDI mask instructions, several memory words are required to hold intermediate results. This would not have been necessary if compare (selective bit) instructions had been used. The specific application usually dictates which approach is to be used.

ARITHMETIC OPERATIONS

Basic arithmetic can be performed with addition and subtraction, though certain operations such as multi-word arithmetic require the use of shift instructions and conditional branch instructions such as the jump on carry or jump on greater than.

Multi-Precision Arithmetic

The 9900 arithmetic instructions perform mathematical functions on 16 bit words. For applications that require a greater numerical accuracy or a larger number (the 16 bit word can hold a magnitude number from 0 to 65,535), multiple word numbers must be used. The basic arithmetic instructions must then be used in such a way as to implement the desired mathematical functions on these multiple word numbers. This section deals with techniques for treating several words as a single binary value, that is, extended precision arithmetic.

A 16 bit two's complement word can represent a signed value in the range $-32,768$ to $+32,767$. The negate (NEG) and absolute value (ABS) instructions provide fast conversion between positive and negative 16 bit words. For sign conversion on binary values represented by multiple words, special conversion techniques are required. The process for converting a three word positive value to its negative or two's complement value is shown in *Figure 5-24*. The three word number is stored in registers 0, 1, and 2 of the workspace. The complementing procedure is to form the one's complement of the three word number using the invert (INV) instruction and then to add 1 to the result. The JNC instructions in the program check to see if a carry is to be propagated from a less significant word to a more significant word in the process of adding one to the three word number. If carries occur, the addition is handled by the increment (INC) instruction. Conversion of a number to its absolute value is accomplished by checking the sign bit (most significant bit) and executing the negate routine (COMP) on negative values.

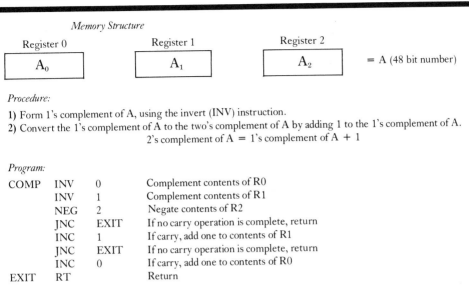

Memory Structure

Register 0	Register 1	Register 2	
A_0	A_1	A_2	= A (48 bit number)

Procedure:

1) Form 1's complement of A, using the invert (INV) instruction.
2) Convert the 1's complement of A to the two's complement of A by adding 1 to the 1's complement of A.

$$\text{2's complement of A} = \text{1's complement of A} + 1$$

Program:

```
COMP    INV     0       Complement contents of R0
        INV     1       Complement contents of R1
        NEG     2       Negate contents of R2
        JNC     EXIT    If no carry operation is complete, return
        INC     1       If carry, add one to contents of R1
        JNC     EXIT    If no carry operation is complete, return
        INC     0       If carry, add one to contents of R0
EXIT    RT              Return
```

Figure 5-24. *Process to form the Negative of A(−A).*

The process of adding or subtracting two multi-word numbers is to perform the operation on the least significant words, then on the next most significant words with the previous carry or borrow, and so on until the complete result is formed. Subtraction could be performed by first using the negate procedure of *Figure 5-24* on the value to be subtracted and then adding this two's complement result to the other number.

Multiple word multiplication can be handled by using the 9900 multiply (MPY) instruction to provide 32 bit partial products and then adding all partial products to achieve the final desired product. The procedure is illustrated in *Figure 5-25* for multiplication of one 32 bit number by a second 32 bit number. The multiplication of a 16 bit number by a second 16 bit number is performed by the MPY instruction. Thus, four applications of the MPY would form the required four partial products. Then, by adding these products in the correct positions, the 64 bit product is formed. The basic memory structure used by the example in *Figure 5-25* can be understood by looking at the operation of the MPY instruction. The accumulator or destination operand must be a workspace register. Then, the product is stored in two successive workspace registers, the most significant 16 bits in the destination workspace register and the least significant 16 bits in the next workspace register. The source operand which specifies the multiplier may be specified with any addressing mode, though the example of *Figure 5-25* uses register addressing for this operand. Thus, the instruction:

        MPY   1,8

multiples the contents of register 1 by the contents of register 8 and places the 32 bit product in registers 8 and 9. While the multiplier register 1 contents are unchanged, the multiplicand register 8 contents are changed to the most significant part of the product.

Thus, there must be several copies of each multiplicand to be able to form several partial products. In 32 bit by 32 bit multiplication, there are two multipliers (B_0 in register 0 and B_1 in register 1) and two multiplicands. Since each multiplicand is involved in two partial products, there must be two copies of each multiplicand. In *Figure 5-25* the copies of the A_0 multiplicand are saved in registers 4 and 6 and the copies of the A_1 multiplicand are saved in registers 2 and 8. Then, the following four MPY instructions form the four required partial products:

MULT	MPY	1,8	Form the $A_1 x B_1$ product in R8 and R9
	MPY	1,4	Form the $B_1 x A_0$ product in R4 and R5
	MPY	0,2	Form the $B_0 x A_1$ product in R2 and R3
	MPY	0,6	Form the $B_0 x A_0$ product in R6 and R7

Which can be followed by the additions to form the complete 64 bit product in registers 6 through 9:

	A	3,5	Add two of three 16 bit groups in positions 2^{16} to 2^{31}
	JNC	P0	If no carry, add in R8 contents
	INC	7	If carry, add one to R7 accumulator
P0	A	5,8	Finish adding 2^{16} to 2^{31} bits
	JNC	P1	If no carry, procede to next position adds
	INC	7	If carry, add one to R7 accumulator
P1	A	2,4	Add part of 2^{32} to 2^{47} bits in R2 and R4
	JNC	P2	If no carry, procede to rest of addition
	INC	6	If carry, add 1 to R6 accumulator
P2	A	4,7	Finish adding 2^{32} to 2^{47} bits
	JNC	FIN	If no carry, operation is complete
	INC	6	If carry, add one to R6 accumulator
FIN	RT	return	

The process illustrated by *Figure 5-25* is for multiplication of two 32 bit magnitude numbers. Multiplication of negative numbers can be handled with the same program by converting all numbers to their absolute value, saving the sign. Then, after the magnitude multiplication is complete, the sign of the product is the exclusive OR of the multiplier and multiplicand sign bits. If desired, the product can be complemented or negated and stored in two's complement form.

Basis of Procedure:

$A \times B = (A_0 \times 2^{16} + A_1) \times (B_0 \times 2^{16} + B_1) =$

$A \times B = A_0 \times B_0 \times 2^{32} + (A_1 \times B_0 + A_0 \times B_1) \times 2^{16} + A_1 \times B_1$

Where multiplying by 2^n implies shifting the number n positions to the left with respect to a number multiplied by 2^0 or 1.

Memory Structure:

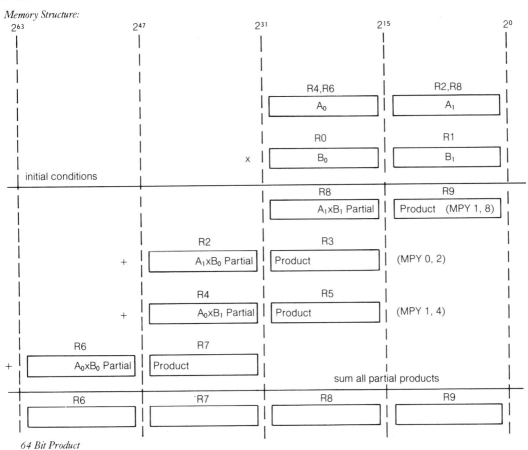

64 Bit Product

Figure 5-25. *Multiple Precision Multiplication*

Floating Point Arithmetic

If the system requires the ability to represent fractional numerical quantities instead of integer numbers, a method must be defined that will provide for the location of the radix point of such numbers. Just as the decimal point of 75.39 defines a quantity:

$$7x10^1 + 5x10^0 + 3x10^{-1} + 9x10^{-2}$$

the binary point in 101.01 defines a quantity:

$$1x2^2 + 0x2^1 + 1x2^0 + 0x2^{-1} + 1x2^{-2}$$

Although a group of bits can be configured in many ways to define a floating point number, most floating point representations share the following characteristics:

1) Floating point numbers are represented as a fraction and an exponent (mantissa and characteristic).
2) The fraction is by convention normalized to lie in the range $\frac{1}{2} \leq F < 1$, e.g., the binary point lies to the left of the first one bit.
3) The exponent defines the power of 2 by which the fraction is multiplied to evaluate the floating point number.

Possible floating point representatives include:

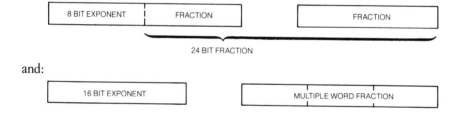

and:

When addition or subtraction of two floating point numbers is performed, the following operations must be performed:

1) Equalize exponents; increment the exponent of the smaller quantity until it is the same as the larger exponent. With each exponent increment, shift the corresponding fraction to the right with zero fill from the left.

2) Add or subtract the fractions as required. If a carry results from an addition, the sum fraction is shifted right, shifting the carry into the fraction, and the exponent is incremented. If the difference resulting from the subtraction is not normalized (zero in first bit position) the fraction must be shifted left until a one is in the leftmost position. With each left shift, the resultant exponent is decremented.

Floating point multiplication can be performed by multiplying the fractions and adding the exponents. Similarly, floating point division can be performed by dividing the fractions and subtracting the exponents. After such an operation the fraction must be normalized and the exponents must be checked for overflow or underflow. Signed numbers can be handled in the same way that the multiplication of signed integers is handled.

INPUT/OUTPUT

The most fundamental and necessary instructions of a processor are its input and output instructions and techniques. Without input and output, the system would not be able to control or communicate with the external world, and as a result would be of no use. There are two general ways of implementing input and output operations. One obvious approach is to use special input and output instructions that are interpreted by the hardware to apply to the input and output devices. The 9900 instructions that provide this capability are the CRU or communications register unit instructions (SBO, SBZ, TB, LDCR, and STCR) and the input and output hardware that respond to these instructions make up the communications register unit. Another approach to inputting and outputting information is to simply treat the input and output devices as one of the system memory locations, in which case any of the 9900 instructions can be used in accessing these locations. This approach is called memory mapped input/output, since the devices are assigned a portion of the available memory addresses, and the hardware must decode the appropriate address to activate a given device. Each of these approaches has its advantages and disadvantages, and the programmer must be aware of these trade-offs in order to provide an optimum approach to system input/output.

MEMORY MAPPED INPUT/OUTPUT

The principle advantages of using memory mapped input/output are:
1) The full instruction set is available for manipulating the data in the input/output device.
2) The hardware is straightforward, since address decoding and device timing signals are required for RAM and ROM memory anyway and these can be simply extended to handle the I/O subsystem as well.
3) Transfers of information are made 8 or 16 bits at a time, offering a high bit rate transfer.

The disadvantages of memory mapped I/O are:
1) Since some of the 'memory' locations are being used by input or output devices, less memory is available for instructions and general data storage.
2) Bit transfers must be made 8 or 16 bits at a time. This is wasteful if a given device can handle a single or a few bits at a time.
3) It is a more expensive technique in terms of pinouts, board space, and layout time.
4) The hardware interface must accomodate the full width memory bus.

The most commonly used instruction in memory mapped I/O operation is the MOV instruction to effect data transfers. However, it is quite possible to set up an input output subsystem as general purpose storage or as a workspace and perform shifts, additions, multiplications, logical operations, and so on, on the data contained in the I/O subsystem.

Generally, if I/O transfers are to be made 8 or 16 bits at a time and if the system is not memory bound (memory is needed for program and system data), memory mapped I/O is often used. Certainly, if performing arithmetic, logic, or other instructions directly on input/output data is required or advantageous, memory mapped I/O must be used. If single or multiple bit transfers are all that is required, and transfer rate is not critical, then memory mapped I/O has no advantage over CRU I/O. CRU I/O hardware is normally simpler and less expensive.

CRU Input/Output

The CRU instructions provide for single bit transfers with the SBO (set bit to one), SBZ (set bit to zero), and TB (test bit) instructions. Multiple bit transfers with the bits transferred one at a time are possible using the LDCR (load communications register) and STCR (store communications register) instructions. The advantages of the CRU instruction approach to I/O are:
1) Any number of bits (up to 16) can be transferred with the appropriate CRU instruction. Thus, the designer can set up the data transfer to exactly meet the requirements of the subsystem being serviced. This is especially useful in control situations where single sense bits are to be examined and single on-off output control signals are needed.
2) No memory locations are used by the subsystem. The CRU instructions can access 4096 input and 4096 output bits (which is equivalent to 256 data words) in addition to the 65,536 memory bytes.

The disadvantages of the CRU I/O are:
1) Only data transfers are provided. Arithmetic, logical or other operations must be performed on the data after it has been moved to one of the general data storage locations in RAM.
2) The hardware must include the capability to decode and implement the CRU transfers; however, the added IC complexity is more than offset by reduced package size.
3) Single bit transfer speed may be too slow for some applications.

INPUT/OUTPUT METHODS

There are three ways that an input/output transfer can be handled or initiated. The processor can be interrupted, causing the program to jump to a subroutine that handles the input/output task. The program can encounter an instruction to transfer data from an input location or to an output location, for the purpose of displaying results, actuating control elements, or inputting system status. The processor can be bypassed entirely and the data transferred directly to or from system memory, using direct memory access.

Interrupt Driver Input/Output

If the timing of input/output transfer is to be controlled by an external system, then the interrupt driven I/O method must be used. This approach is used in inputting data when the time of input is random. The external system inputs the data and signals the processor with an interrupt to indicate that data is in one of the 9900 system input registers. The 9900 responds by performing a context switch to a subprogram that will process the data in that register. The interrupt driven approach may also be used in outputting data when the processor needs to know when the data has been taken by an external system. Once the external system takes the data, it can signal the processor with an interrupt signal. The processor responds by performing a context switch to a subprogram that will then send more data to that output location.

The interrupt driven I/O procedure provides a mechanism of implementing a communications sequence known as handshaking. This communications protocol is illustrated in *Figure 5-26*. In the input mode, the data-present signal latches the 9900 system input register and serves as the interrupt signal. If desired the processor's reading of the contents of that register can be used to generate the data-taken signal. Upon receiving the data taken signal, the external system can then send more data to the 9900 system. In the output mode, the register write operation that sends data to the output register in the 9900 system can be used as a data-present signal to the external system. When the external system takes this data, it can use an interrupt signal to notify the 9900 that the register is ready to receive more data.

The interrupt driven approach has the main advantage of providing a means of setting up a handshaking communications with another system. It can handle data communications that occur at random or unpredictable times. The main disadvantage of this type of I/O is that it does involve the processor, slowing down its work on main system programs and subprograms. Further, since a context switch is involved in responding to an interrupt, such an approach may require more memory than one of the other two approaches.

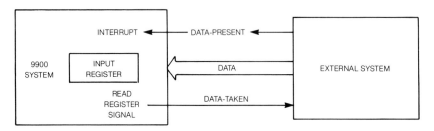

Figure 5-26a. Handshaking Input Transfer.

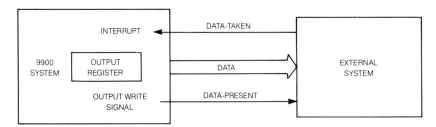

Figure 5-26b. Handshaking Output Transfer.

Programmed Input/Output

The simplest method of I/O is the programmed I/O. The times and conditions under which inputs and outputs are to occur are controlled by the system program. For example, the processor may update a display memory whenever the display is to be changed. The program determines the new information to be displayed and then outputs this information to the display storage locations. Similarly, the program may require information about the status of a subsystem in order to determine subsequent operations. Such status may be the condition of threshold detectors, the status of serial data transmission or reception, or some other system condition. When the program encounters a point at which it needs to check such status words, it simply inputs the desired word. Of course, as in all I/O methods, the input or output operations can be handled by either CRU instructions or through standard MOV or other instructions in memory mapped I/O devices.

The programmed input/output method is a high speed, low hardware cost approach to input/output, since no subroutine overhead is involved. However, it does not handle the random input situation very well, unless the program is devoted solely to waiting for the next signal input to occur. Even then, the program may not check for input occurrence and perform the desired input instruction before the external system sends new data, destroying the old data.

CHAPTER 6
Instruction Set

SOFTWARE FEATURES OF THE 9900

In order to understand the operation of the 9900 instructions, the basic software features of the 9900 must be understood. These features include the processor-memory interrelationships, the available addressing modes, the terminology and formats used in the 9900 assembly language, and the interrupt and subroutine procedures used by the 9900.

PROCESSOR REGISTERS AND SYSTEM MEMORY

There are three registers in the 9900 that are of interest to the programmer; their functions are illustrated in *Figure 6-1:*

Program Counter—This register contains the address of the instruction to be executed by the 9900. This instruction address can point to or locate an instruction anywhere in system memory, though instructions normally are not placed in the first 64 words of memory. These locations are reserved for interrupt and extended operation transfer vectors.

Workspace Pointer—This register contains the address of the first word of a group of 16 consecutive words of memory called a workspace. The workspace can be located anywhere in memory that is not already dedicated to transfer vector or program storage. These 16 workspace words are called workspace registers 0 through 15, and are treated by the 9900 processor as data registers much as other processors treat on-chip data registers for high access storage requirements.

Status Register—The status register stores the summary of the results of processor operations, including such information as the arithmetic or logical relation of the result to some reference data, whether or not the result can be completely contained in a 16-bit data word, and the parity of the result. The last bits of the status register contain the system interrupt mask which determines which interrupts will be responded to.

These three 16-bit registers completely define the current state of the processor: what part of the overall program is being executed, where the general purpose workspace is located in memory, and what the current status of operations and the interrupt system is. This information completely defines the current program environment or context of the system. A change in the program counter contents and workspace register contents switches the program environment or context to a new part of program memory with a new workspace area. Performing such a context switch or change in program environment is a very efficient method of handling subroutine jumps to subprograms that require the use of a majority of the workspace registers.

Program Counter

Figure 6-1 illustrates the use of the three processor registers. The program counter is the pointer which locates the instruction to be executed. All instructions require one or more 16-bit words and are always located at *even* addresses. Multiple word instructions include one 16-bit operation word and one or two 16-bit operand addresses. Two of the processors in the 9900 family (TMS9900, SBP9900) employ a 16-bit data bus and receive the instructions 16 bits at a time. The other processors (TMS9980A/81, TMS9985, TMS9940) use an 8-bit data bus and require extra memory cycles to fetch instructions. In both cases the even and odd bytes are located at even and odd addresses respectively as illustrated in *Figure 6-2*. In addition, data may be stored as 16-bit words located at even addresses or as 8-bit bytes at either even or odd addresses.

Workspace

The workspace is a set of 16 contiguous words of memory, the first of which is located by the workspace pointer. The individual 16-bit words, called workspace registers, are located at even addresses (see *Figure 6-1*). All of the registers are available for use as general registers; however, some instructions make use of certain registers as illustrated in *Figure 6-3*. Care should be exercised when using these registers for data or addresses not related to their special functions.

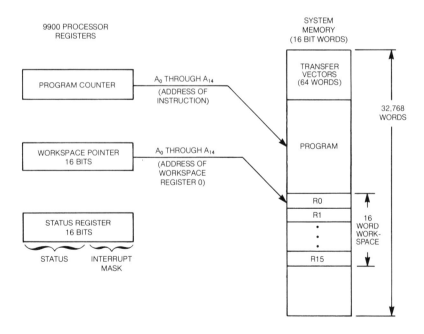

Figure 6-1. 9900 System Memory and Processor Registers.

Status Register

The status register contents for the 9900 are defined in *Figure 6-4.* The 9900 interrupt mask is a 4-bit code, allowing the specification of 16 levels of interrupt. Interrupt levels equal to or less than the mask value will be acknowledged and responded to by the 9900. The 9940 status register is similar, except the interrupt mask occupies bits 14 and 15 of the status register, providing for four interrupt levels in the 9940.

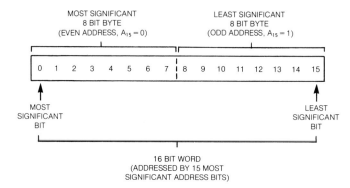

Figure 6-2. Word and Byte Definition.

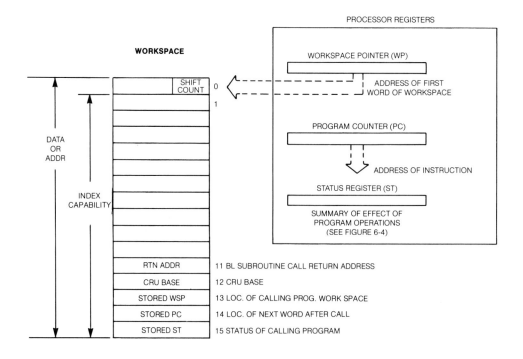

Figure 6-3. Workspace Register Utilization.

Status
Register
Bit

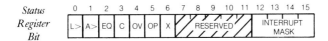

0   LGT —   *Logical Greater Than*—set in a comparison of an unsigned number with a smaller unsigned number.

1   AGT —   *Arithmetic Greater Than*—set when one signed number is compared with another that is less positive (nearer to −32,768).

2   EQ   —   *Equal*—set when the two words or two bytes being compared are equal.

3   C   —   *Carry*—set by carry out of most significant bit of a word or byte in a shift or arithmetic operation.

4   OV   —   *Overflow*—set when the result of an arithmetic; operation is too large or too small to be correctly represented in 2's complement form. OV is set in addition if the most significant bit of the two operands are equal and the most significant bit of the sum is different from the destination operand most significant bit. OV is set in subtraction if the most significant bits of the operands are not equal and the most significant bit of the result is different from the most significant bit of the destination operand. In single operand instructions affecting OV, the OV is set if the most significant bit of the operand is changed by the instruction.

5   OP   —   *Odd Parity*—set when there is an odd number of bits set to one in the result.

6   X   —   *Extended Operation*—set when the PC and WP registers have been to set to values of the transfer vector words during the execution of an extended operation.

7-11   Reserved for special Model 990/10 computer applications.

12-15   *Interrupt Mask*—All interrupts of level equal to or less than mask value are enabled.

Figure 6-4. 9900 Status Register Contents

ADDRESSING MODES

The 9900 supports five general purpose addressing modes or methods of specifying the location of a memory word:

Workspace Register Addressing

The data or address to be used by the instruction is contained in the workspace register number specified in the operand field of the instruction. For example, if the programmer wishes to decrement the contents of workspace register 2, the format of the decrement instruction would be:

DEC   2

The memory address of the word to be used by the instruction is computed as follows:

This type of addressing is used to access the often used data contained in the workspace.

Workspace Register Indirect Addressing

The address of the data to be used by the instruction is contained in the workspace register specified in the operand field (the workspace register number is preceded by an asterisk). This type of addressing is used to establish data counters so the programmer can sequence through data stored in successive locations in memory. If register 3 contains the address of the data word to be used, the following instruction would be used to clear (CLR) that data word:

CLR   *3

In this instruction the contents of register 3 would not be changed, but the data word addressed by the contents of register 3 would be cleared (set to all zeroes — 000_{16}). The word address is computed as follows for this type of addressing:

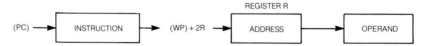

Workspace Register Indirect Addressing With Autoincrement—

This addressing mode locates the data word in the same way that workspace register indirect addressing does, with the added feature of incrementing the contents of the address register after the instruction has been completed. The address in the register is incremented by one if a byte operation is performed and by two if a word operation is performed. Thus, to set up a true data counter to clear a group of successive words in memory whose address will be contained in register 3, the following instruction would be used:

CLR   *3 +

where the asterisk (*) indicates the workspace register indirect addressing feature and the plus (+) indicates the autoincrementing feature. With this type of addressing, the following computations occur:

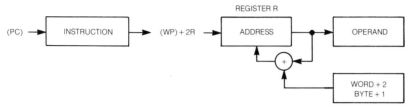

Symbolic or Direct Addressing

The address of the memory word is contained in the operand field of the instruction and is contained in program memory (ROM) in the word immediately following the operation code word for the instruction. For example, to clear the memory word at address 1000_{16}, the following format would be used:

CLR   @>1000

where the at sign (@) indicates direct addressing and the greater than (>) sign indicates a base 16 (hexadecimal) constant. Alternatively, the data word to be cleared could be named with a symbolic name such as COUNT and then the instruction would be:

CLR   @COUNT

and if COUNT is later equated to 1000_{16}, this instruction would clear the data word at address 1000_{16}. The instruction would occupy two words of program memory:

(PC) $04C0_{16}$ Operation Code for Clear

(PC) + 2 1000_{16} Address of Data

The address of the memory word is thus contained in the instruction itself and is located by the program counter. Since this address is part of the instruction, it cannot be modified by the program. As a result, this type of addressing is used for program variables that occupy a single memory word such as program counters, data masks, and so on. The address computations for direct addressing are as follows:

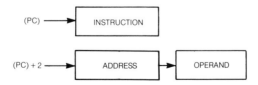

Indexed Addressing

Indexed addressing is a combination of symbolic and register indirect addressing. It provides for address modification since part of the address is contained in the workspace register used as an index register. Registers 1 through 15 can be used as index registers. The memory word address is obtained by adding the contents of the index register specified to the constant contained in the instruction:

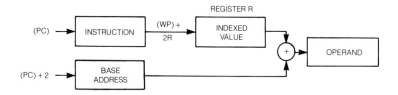

Thus, to locate the data word whose address is two words down from the address contained in register 5, and to clear this memory word, the following instruction is used:

    CLR   @4(5)

This instruction will cause the processor to add 4 to the contents of register 5 to generate the desired address. Alternatively, a symbolic name could be used for the instruction constant:

    CLR   @DISP(5)

with the value for the symbol DISP defined elsewhere in the assembly language program.

Special Addressing Modes

Three additional types of special purpose addressing are used by the 9900.

Immediate Addressing

Immediate addressing instructions contain the data to be used as a part of the instruction. In these instructions the first word is the instruction operation code and the second word of the instruction is the data to be used:

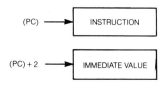

Program Counter Relative Addressing

Conditional branch or jump instructions use a form of program counter relative addressing. In such instructions the address of the instruction to be branched to is relative to the location of the branch instruction. The instruction includes a signed displacement with a value between -128 and $+127$. The branch address is the value of the program counter plus two plus twice the displacement. For example, if LOOP is the label at location 10_{16} and the instruction:

> JMP   LOOP

is at location 18_{16}, the displacement in the instruction machine code generated by the assembler will be -5 or FB_{16}. This value is obtained by adding two to the current program counter:

$$18_{16} + 2 = 1A_{16}$$

and subtracting from this result the location of LOOP:

$$1A_{16} - 10_{16} = A_{16} = 10 \text{ decimal.}$$

The displacement of 5 is one-half this value of 10 and it is negative since LOOP is 5 words prior to the $18_{16} + 2$ location.

CRU Addressing

CRU addressing uses the number contained in bits 3 through 14 of register 12 to form a hardware base address:

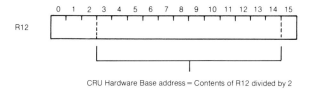

CRU Hardware Base address = Contents of R12 divided by 2

Thus if R12 contains 0400_{16} (the software base address), bits 3 through 14 will be 0200_{16}. This hardware base address is used to indicate the starting CRU bit address for multiple bit CRU transfer instructions (STCR and LDCR). It is added to the displacement contained in single bit CRU instructions (TB, SBO, SBZ) to form the CRU bit address for these instructions. For example, to set CRU bit 208 to a one, with register 12 containing 400_{16}, the following CRU instruction would be used:

> SBO   8

so that the CRU bit address is $200_{16} + 8. = 208_{16}$.

ASSEMBLY LANGUAGE PROGRAMMING INFORMATION †

In order to understand the instruction descriptions and applications the assembly language nomenclature must be understood. Assembly language is a readily understood language in which the 9900 instructions can be written. The machine code that results from the assembly of programs written in this language is called object code. Such object code may be absolute or relocatable, depending on the assembly language coding. Relocatable code is that which can be loaded into any block of memory desired, without reassembling or without changing program operation. Such code has its address information relative to the first instruction of the assembly language program so that once a loader program specifies the location of this first instruction, the address of all instructions are adjusted to be consistent with this location. Absolute code contains absolute addresses which cannot be changed by the loader or any operation other than reassembling the program. Generally, relocatable code is preferable since it allows the program modules to be located anywhere in memory of the final system.

ASSEMBLY LANGUAGE FORMATS

The general assembly language source statements consist of four fields as follows:

LABEL   MNEMONIC   OPERANDS   COMMENT

The first three fields must occur within the first 60 character positions of the source record. At least one blank must be inserted between fields.

Label Field

The label consists of from one to six characters, beginning with an alphabetic character in character position one of the source record. The label field is terminated by at least one blank. When the assembler encounters a label in an instruction it assigns the current value of the location counter to the label symbol. This is the value associated with the label symbol and is the address of the instruction in memory. If a label is not used, character position 1 may be a blank, or an asterisk.

Mnemonic or Opcode Field

This field contains the mnemonic code of one of the instructions, one of the assembly language directives, or a symbol representing one of the program defined operations. This field begins after the last blank following the label field. Examples of instruction mnemonics include A for addition and MOV for data movement. The mnemonic field is required since it identifies which operation is to be performed.

Operands Field

The operands specify the memory locations of the data to be used by the instruction. This field begins following the last blank that follows the mnemonic field. The memory locations can be specified by using constants, symbols, or expressions, to describe one of several addressing modes available. These are summarized in *Figure 6-5.*

†Excerpts from Model 990 computer TMS 9900 Microprocessor Assembly Language Programmer's Guide.

Type of Addressing	Operand Format	Memory Location Specified	MOV Instruction Example Coding	Result	T_d or T_s Field Code
Workspace Register	n	Workspace Register n Rn	MOV 3,5	R3 → R5	00
Workspace Register Indirect	*n	Address given by the contents of workspace register n M(Rn)	MOV *3,*5	M(R3) → M(R5)	01
Workspace Register Indirect, Autoincrement	*n+	As in register Indirect; address register Rn is incremented after the operation (by one for byte operations, by two for word operations)	MOV *3+,*5+	M(R3) → M(R5) R3 + 2 → R3 R5 + 2 → R5	11
Symbolic Memory	@exp	Address is given by value of exp. M(exp)	MOV @ONE,@10	M(ONE) → M(10)	10
Indexed Memory	@exp(n)	Address is the sum of the contents of Rn and the value of exp M(Rn + exp)	MOV @2(3), @DP(5)	M(R3 + 2) → M(R5 + DP)	10

Notes:

n is the number of the workspace register: $0 \le n \le 15$; n may not be 0 for indexed addressing.

exp is a symbol, number, or expression

The T_d and T_s fields are two bit portions of the instruction machine code. There are also S and D four bit fields, which are filled in with the four bit code for n. n is 0 for symbolic or direct addressing.

Figure 6-5. *Addressing Modes*

Comments Field

Comments can be entered after the last blank that follows the operands field. If the first character position of the source statement contains an asterisk (*), the entire source statement is a comment. Comments are listed in the source portion of the assembler listing, but have no affect on the object code.

TERMS AND SYMBOLS

Symbols are used in the label field, the operator field, and the operand field. A symbol is a string of alphanumeric characters, beginning with an alphabetic character.

Terms are used in the operand fields of instructions and assembler directives. A term is a decimal or hexadecimal constant, an absolute assembly-time constant, or a label having an absolute value. Expressions can also be used in the operand fields of instructions and assembler directives.

Constants

Constants can be decimal integers (written as a string of numerals) in the range of $-32,768$ to $+65,535$. For example:

> 257

Constants can also be hexadecimal integers (a string of hexadecimal digits preceded by >). For example:

> >09AF

ASCII character constants can be used by enclosing the desired character string in single quotes. For example:

> 'DX' $= 4458_{16}$ 'R' $+ 0052_{16}$

Throughout this book the subscript 16 is used to denote base 16 numbers. For example, the hexadecimal number 09AF will be written $09AF_{16}$.

Symbols

Symbols must begin with an alphabetic character and contain no blanks. Only the first six characters of a symbol are processed by the assembler.

The assembler predefines the dollar sign ($) to represent the current location in the program.

A given symbol can be used as a label only once, since it is the symbolic name of the address of the instruction. Symbols defined with the DXOP directive are used in the OPCODE field. Any symbol in the OPERANDS field must have been used as a label or defined by a REF directive.

Expressions

Expressions are used in the OPERANDS fields of assembly language statements. An expression is a term or a series of terms separated by the following arithmetic operations:

+ addition

− subtraction

* multiplication

/ division

The operator precedence is +, −, *, / (left to right).

The expression must not contain any imbedded blanks or extended operation defined (DXOP directive defined) symbols. Unary minus (a minus sign in front of a number or symbol) is performed first and then the expression is evaluated from left to right. An example of the use of the unary minus in an expression is:

LABEL + TABLE + (− INC)

which has the effect of the expression:

LABEL + TABLE − INC

The relocatability of an expression is a function of the relocatability of the symbols and constants that make up the expression. An expression is relocatable when the number of relocatable symbols or constants added to the expression is one greater than the number of relocatable symbols or constants subtracted from the expressions. All other expressions are absolute. The expression given earlier would be relocatable if the three symbols in the expression are all relocatable.

The following are examples of valid expressions.

BLUE + 1

2*16 + RED

440/2 − RED

SURVEY OF THE 9900 INSTRUCTION SET

The 9900 instructions can be grouped into the following general categories: data transfer, arithmetic, comparison, logical, shift, branch, and CRU input/output operations. The list of all instructions and their effect on status bits is given in *Figure 6-6.*

ASSEMBLY LANGUAGE PROGRAMMING INFORMATION

Mnemonic	L>	A>	EQ	C	OV	OP	X	Mnemonic	L>	A>	EQ	C	OV	OP	X
A	X	X	X	X	X	-	-	DIV	-	-	-	-	X	-	-
AB	X	X	X	X	X	X	-	IDLE	-	-	-	-	-	-	-
ABS	X	X	X	X	X	-	-	INC	X	X	X	X	X	-	-
AI	X	X	X	X	X	-	-	INCT	X	X	X	X	X	-	-
ANDI	X	X	X	-	-	-	-	INV	X	X	X	-	-	-	-
B	-	-	-	-	-	-	-	JEQ	-	-	-	-	-	-	-
BL	-	-	-	-	-	-	-	JGT	-	-	-	-	-	-	-
BLWP	-	-	-	-	-	-	-	JH	-	-	-	-	-	-	-
C	X	X	X	-	-	-	-	JHE	-	-	-	-	-	-	-
CB	X	X	X	-	-	X	-	JL	-	-	-	-	-	-	-
CI	X	X	X	-	-	-	-	JLE	-	-	-	-	-	-	-
CKOF	-	-	-	-	-	-	-	JLT	-	-	-	-	-	-	-
CKON	-	-	-	-	-	-	-	JMP	-	-	-	-	-	-	-
CLR	-	-	-	-	-	-	-	JNC	-	-	-	-	-	-	-
COC	-	-	X	-	-	-	-	JNE	-	-	-	-	-	-	-
CZC	-	-	X	-	-	-	-	JNO	-	-	-	-	-	-	-
DEC	X	X	X	X	X	-	-	JOC	-	-	-	-	-	-	-
DECT	X	X	X	X	X	-	-	JOP	-	-	-	-	-	-	-
LDCR	X	X	X	-	-	1	-	SBZ	-	-	-	-	-	-	-
LI	X	X	X	-	-	-	-	SETO	-	-	-	-	-	-	-
LIMI	-	-	-	-	-	-	-	SLA	X	X	X	X	X	-	-
LREX	-	-	-	-	-	-	-	SOC	X	X	X	-	-	-	-
LWPI	-	-	-	-	-	-	-	SOCB	X	X	X	-	-	X	-
MOV	X	X	X	-	-	-	-	SRA	X	X	X	X	-	-	-
MOVB	X	X	X	-	-	X	-	SRC	X	X	X	X	-	-	-
MPY	-	-	-	-	-	-	-	SRL	X	X	X	X	-	-	-
NEG	X	X	X	X	X	-	-	STCR	X	X	X	-	-	1	-
ORI	X	X	X	-	-	-	-	STST	-	-	-	-	-	-	-
RSET	-	-	-	-	-	-	-	STWP	-	-	-	-	-	-	-
RTWP	X	X	X	X	X	X	X	SWPB	-	-	-	-	-	-	-
S	X	X	X	X	X	-	-	SZC	X	X	X	-	-	-	-
SB	X	X	X	X	X	X	-	SZCB	X	X	X	-	-	X	-
SBO	-	-	-	-	-	-	-	TB	-	-	X	-	-	-	-
								X	2	2	2	2	2	2	2
								XOP	2	2	2	2	2	2	2
								XOR	X	X	X	-	-	-	-

Notes: 1. When an LDCR or STCR instruction transfers eight bits or less, the OP bit is set or reset as in byte instructions. Otherwise these instructions do not affect the OP bit.

2. The X instruction does not affect any status bit; the instruction executed by the X instruction sets status bits normally for that instruction. When an XOP instruction is implemented by software, the XOP bit is set, and the subroutine sets status bits normally.

Figure 6-6. Status Bits Affected by Instructions

Data Transfer Instructions

Load— used to initialize processor or workspace registers to a desired value.

Move— used to move words or bytes from one memory location to another.

Store— used to store the status or workspace pointer registers in a workspace register.

Arithmetic Instructions

*Addition and Subtraction—*perform addition or subtraction of signed or unsigned binary words or bytes stored in memory.

*Negate and Absolute Value—*changes the sign or takes the absolute value of data words in memory.

*Increment and Decrement—*Adds or subtracts 1 or 2 from the specified data words in memory.

*Multiply—*Performs unsigned integer multiplication of a word in memory with a workspace register word to form a 32 bit product stored in two successive workspace register locations.

*Divide—*Divides a 32 bit unsigned integer dividend (contained in two successive workspace registers) by a memory word with the 16 bit quotient and 16 bit remainder stored in place of the dividend.

Compare Instructions

These instructions provide for masked or unmasked comparison of one memory word or byte to another or a workspace register word to a 16 bit constant.

Logical Instructions

*OR and AND—*masked or unmasked OR and AND operations on corresponding bits of two memory words. A workspace register word can be ORed or ANDed with a 16 bit constant.

Complement and Clear — The bits of a selected memory word can be complemented, or cleared or set to ones.

*Exclusive OR—*A workspace register word can be exclusive ORed with another memory word on a bit by bit basis.

*Set Bits Corresponding—*Set bits to one (SOC) or to zero (SZC) whose positions correspond to one positions in a reference word.

Shift Instructions

A workspace register can be shifted arithmetically or logically to the right. The registers can be shifted to the left (filling in vacated positions with zeroes) or circulated to the right. The shifts and circulates can be from 1 to 16 bit positions.

Branch Instructions

The branch instructions and the JMP (jump) instruction unconditionally branch to different parts of the program memory. If a branch occurs, the PC register will be changed to the value specified by the operand of the branch instruction. In subroutine branching the old value of the PC is saved when the branch occurs and then is restored when the return instruction is executed. The conditional jump instructions test certain status bits to determine if jump is to occur. When a jump is made the PC is loaded with the sum of its previous value and a displacement value specified in the operand portion of the instruction.

Control/CRU Instructions

These instructions provide for transferring data to and from the communications register input/output unit (CRU) using the CRUIN, CRUOUT and CRUCLK pins of the 9900.

INSTRUCTION DESCRIPTIONS

The information provided for each instruction in the next section of this chapter is as follows:

> Name of the instruction.
>
> Mnemonic for the instruction.
>
> Assembly language and machine code formats.
>
> Description of the operation of the instruction.
>
> Effect of the instruction on the Status Bits.
>
> Examples.
>
> Applications.

The format descriptions and examples are written without the label or comment fields for simplicity. Labels and comments fields can be used in any instruction if desired.

Each instruction involves one or two operand fields which are written with the following symbols:

G—Any addressing mode is permitted except I (Immediate).

R—Workspace register addressing.

exp—A symbol or expression used to indicate a location.

value—a value to be used in immediate addressing.

cnt—A count value for shifts and CRU instructions.

CRU—CRU (Communications Register Unit) bit addressing.

The instruction operation is described in written and equation form. In the equation form, an arrow($\longrightarrow$) is used to indicate a transfer of data and a colon (:) is used to indicate a comparison. In comparisons, the operands are not changed. In transfers, the source operand (indicated with the subscript s) is not changed while the destination operand (indicated with the subscript d) is changed. For operands specified by the symbol G, the M(G) nomenclature is used to denote the memory word specified by G. MB(G) is used to denote the memory byte specified by G. Thus, transferring the memory word contents addressed by G_s to the memory word location specified by G_d and comparing the source (G_s) data to zero during the transfer, can be described as:

$$M(G_s) \longrightarrow M(G_d)$$

$$M(G_s):0$$

which is the operation performed by the MOV instruction:

MOV $\qquad G_s,G_d$

A specific example of this instruction could be:

MOV $\qquad$ @ONE,3

which moves the contents of the memory word addressed by the value of the symbol ONE to the contents of workspace register 3:

$$M(ONE) \longrightarrow R3$$

$$M(ONE) : 0$$

LI/LIMI

DATA TRANSFER INSTRUCTIONS

The MOV instructions are used to transfer data from one part of the system to another part. The LOAD instructions are used to initialize registers to desired values. The STORE instructions provide for saving the status register (ST) or the workspace pointer (WP) in a specified workspace register.

LOAD IMMEDIATE

LI

Format: **LI**   **R,value**

0	1	2	3	4	5	6	7	8	9	10	11	12	13	14	15
0	0	0	0	0	0	1	0	0	0	0	0		R		

(0200 + R)
$0 \leq R \leq 15$

Operation: The 16 bit data value in the word immediately following the instruction is loaded into the specified workspace register R.

value ⟶ R
immediate operand: 0

Affect on Status: **LGT, AGT, EQ**

Examples: **LI**   **7,5**   5 ⟶ R7

LI   **8, >FF** $00FF_{16}$ ⟶ R8

Applications: The LI instruction is used to initialize a workspace register with a program constant such as a counter value or data mask.

LOAD INTERRUPT MASK IMMEDIATE

LIMI

Format: **LIMI**   **value**

0	1	2	3	4	5	6	7	8	9	10	11	12	13	14	15
0	0	0	0	0	0	1	1	0	0	0	0	0	0	0	0

(0300)

Operation The low order 4 bit value (bits 12-15) in the word immediately following the instruction is loaded into the interrupt mask portion of the status register:

4 BIT VALUE

Affect on Status: Interrupt mask code only

Example: **LIMI   5**

Enables interrupt levels 0 through 5

Application: The LIMI instruction is used to initialize the interrupt mask to control which system interrupts will be recognized.

LOAD WORKSPACE POINTER IMMEDIATE

LWPI

Format: **LWPI   value**

0	1	2	3	4	5	6	7	8	9	10	11	12	13	14	15
0	0	0	0	0	0	1	0	1	1	1	0	0	0	0	0

(02E0)

Operation: The 16 bit value contained in the word immediately following the instruction is loaded into the workspace pointer (WP):

value ⟶ WP

Affect on Status: None

Example: **LWPI   >0500**

Causes 0500_{16} to be loaded into the WP.

Application: LWPI is used to establish the workspace memory area for a section of the program.

MOVE WORD

MOV

Format: **MOV   G$_s$,G$_d$**

0	1	2	3	4	5	6	7	8	9	10	11	12	13	14	15
1	1	0	0	T$_d$		D			T$_s$			S			

(C---)

Operation: The word in the location specified by G$_s$ is transferred to the location specified by G$_d$, without affecting the data stored in the G$_s$ location. During the transfer, the word (G$_s$ data) is compared to 0 with the result of the comparison stored in the status register:

M(G$_s$) ⟶ M(G$_d$)
M(G$_s$):0

Status Bits Affected: **LGT, AGT, and EQ**

Examples: **MOV   R1,R3**   R1 ⟶ R3,   R1:0
          MOV   *R1,R3   M(R1) ⟶ R3,   M(R1):0
          MOV   @ONES,*1   M(ONES) ⟶ M(R1),   M(ONES):0
          MOV   @2(5),3   M(R5 + 2) ⟶ R3,   M(R5 + 2):0
          MOV   *R1 + ,*R2 + M(R1) ⟶ M(R2),   M(R1):0,
                                  (R1) + 2 ⟶ R1,   (R2) + 2 ⟶ R2

Application: MOV is used to transfer data from one part of the system to another part.

MOVB

MOVE BYTE

MOVB

Format: **MOVB** G_s, G_d

0	1	2	3	4	5	6	7	8	9	10	11	12	13	14	15	
1	1	0	1	T_d		D				T_s		S				(D---)

Operation: The Byte addressed by G_s is transferred to the byte location specified by G_d. If G is workspace register addressing, the most significant byte is selected. Otherwise, even addresses select the most significant byte; odd addresses select the least significant byte. During the transfer, the source byte is compared to zero and the results of the comparison are stored in the status register.

$$MB(G_s) \longrightarrow MB(G_d)$$
$$MB(G_s):0$$

Status Bits Affected: **LGT, AGT, EQ, OP**

Examples: **MOVB   @>1C14,3**
           MOVB   *8,4

These instructions would have the following example affects:

Memory Location	Contents Initially	Contents After Transfer
1C14	2016	2016
R3	542B	202B
R8	2123	2123
2123	1040	1040
R4	0A0C	400C

The underlined data are the bytes selected.

Application: MOVB is used to transfer 8 bit bytes from one byte location to another.

Swap Bytes

SWPB

Format: **SWPB   G**

0	1	2	3	4	5	6	7	8	9	10	11	12 13 14 15	
0	0	0	0	0	0	1	1	0	1	1	T_s	S	(06C0 + T_s , S)

Operation: The most significant byte and the least significant bytes of the word at the memory location specified by G are exchanged.

Affect on Status: None

			Before	After
Example:	**SWPB 3**	R3 Contents:	F302	02F3

Application: Used to interchange bytes if needed for subsequent byte operations.

Store Status

STST

Format: **STST   R**

0	1	2	3	4	5	6	7	8	9	10	11	12 13 14 15	
0	0	0	0	0	0	1	0	1	1	0	0	R	(02C0 + R) 0≤R≤15

Operation: The contents of the status register are stored in the workspace register specified:

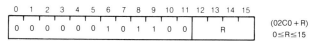

ST ⟶ R

Affect on Status: None

Example: **STST   3**   ST is transferred to R3

Application: STST is used to save the status for later reference.

STWP

S̲tore W̲orkspace P̲ointer

Format: **STWP R**

(02A0 + R)

$0 \leq R \leq 15$

Operation: The contents of the workspace pointer are stored in the workspace register specified:

WP⟶R

Affect on Status: None

Example: **STWP 3** WP is transferred into R3

Appliation: STWP is used to save the workspace pointer for later reference.

ARITHMETIC INSTRUCTIONS

These instructions perform the following basic arithmetic operations: addition (byte or word), subtraction (byte or word), multiplication, division, negation, and absolute value. More complicated mathematical functions must be developed using these basic operations. The basic instruction set will be adequate for many system requirements.

ADD WORDS

A

Format: **A** G_s, G_d

0	1	2	3	4	5	6	7	8	9	10	11	12	13	14	15	
1	0	1	0	T_d		D				T_s		S				(A---)

Operation: The data located at the address specified by G_s is added to the data located at the address specified by G_d. The resulting sum is placed in the G_d location and is compared to zero:

$$M(G_s) + M(G_d) \longrightarrow M(G_d)$$
$$M(G_s) + M(G_d):0$$

Status Bits Affected: **LGT, AGT, EQ, C, OV**

Examples: **A**   **5,@TABLE**   R5 + M(TABLE) $\longrightarrow$ M(TABLE)
                 A   **3,*2**   R3 + M(R2) $\longrightarrow$ M(R2)

with the sums compared to 0 in each case. Binary addition affects on status bits can be understood by studying the following examples:

$M(G_s)$	$M(G_d)$	*Sum*	*LGT*	*AGT***	*EQ*	*C*	*OV**
1000	0001	1001	1	1	0	0	0
F000	1000	0000	0	0	1	1	0
F000	8000	7000	1	1	0	1	1
4000	4000	8000	1	0	0	0	1

*OV (overflow) is set if the most significant bit of the sum is different from the most significant bit of $M(G_d)$ and the most significant bit of both operands are equal.

**AGT (arithmetic greater than) is set if the most significant bit of the sum is zero and if EQ (equal) is 0.

Application: Binary addition is the basic arithmetic operation required to generate many mathematical functions. This instruction can be used to develop programs to do multiword addition, decimal addition, code conversion, and so on.

AB

ADD BYTES

Format: **AB** G_s, G_d

Operation: The source byte addressed by G_s is added to the destination byte addressed by G_d and the sum byte is placed in the G_d byte location. Recall that even addresses select the most significant byte and odd addresses select the least significant byte. The sum byte is compared to 0.

$$MB(G_s) + MB(G_d) \longrightarrow MB(G_d)$$
$$MB(G_s) + MB(G_d):0$$

Status Bits Affected: **LGT, AGT, EQ, C, OV, OP**

Example: **AB**   **3,*4 +** $R3 + MB(R4) \longrightarrow MB(R4)$, $R4 + 2 \longrightarrow R4$
      AB   **@TAB,5** $MB(TAB) + R5 \longrightarrow R5$

To see how the AB works, the following example should be studied:
    AB   **@>2120,@>2123**

Memory Location	Data Before Addition	Data After Addition
2120	F320	F320
2123	2106	21F9

The underlined entries are the addressed and changed bytes.

Application: AB is one of the byte operations available on the 9900. These can be useful when dealing with subsystems or data that use 8 bit units, such as ASCII codes.

ADD IMMEDIATE

AI

Format: **AI**   **R,Value**

$(0220 + R)$
$0 \leq R \leq 15$

Operation: The 16 bit value contained in the word immediately following the instruction is added to the contents of the workspace register specified.

$R + Value \longrightarrow R, \quad R + Value:0$

Status Bits Affected: **LGT, AGT, EQ, C, OV**

Example: **AI**   **6,>C**
Adds C_{16} to the contents of workspace register 6. If R6 contains 1000_{16}, then the instruction will change its contents to $100C_{16}$, and the LGT and AGT status bits will be set.

Application: This instruction is used to add a constant to a workspace register. Such an operation is useful for adding a constant displacement to an address contained in the workspace register.

SUBTRACT WORDS

S

Format: **S**   **G$_s$,G$_d$**

0	1	2	3	4	5	6	7	8	9	10	11	12	13	14	15	
0	1	1	0	T$_d$		D			T$_s$			S				(6---)

Operation: The source 16 bit data (location specified by G_s) is subtracted from the destination data (location specified by G_d) with the result placed in the destination location G_d. The result is compared to 0.

$M(G_d) - M(G_s) \longrightarrow M(G_d)$
$M(G_d) - M(G_s):0$

Status Bits Affected: **LGT, AGT, EQ, C, OV**

Examples: **S**   **@OLDVAL,@NEWVAL**
would yield the following example results:

Memory Location	Before Subtraction Contents	After Subtraction Contents
OLDVAL	**1225**	**1225**
NEWVAL	**8223**	**6FFE (8223-1225)**

All status bits affected would be set to 1 except equal which would be reset to 0.

Application: Provides 16 bit binary subtraction.

SB

SUBTRACT BYTES

SB

Format: **SB**   **G$_s$G$_d$**

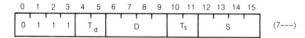

Operation: The source byte addressed by G$_s$ is subtracted from the destination byte addressed by G$_d$ with the result placed in byte location G$_d$. The result is compared to 0. Even addresses select the most significant byte and odd addresses select the least significant byte. If workspace register addressing is used, the most significant byte of the register is used.

$$MB(G_d) - MB(G_s) \longrightarrow MB(G_d)$$
$$MB(G_d) - MB(G_s):0$$

Status Bits Affected: **LGT, AGT, C, EQ, OV, OP**

Format: **SB**   ***6 + ,1** $R1 - MB(R6) \longrightarrow R1$
$R1 - MB(R6):0$
$R6 + 1 \longrightarrow R6$

This operation would have the following example result:

Memory Location	Contents Before Instruction	Contents After Instruction
R6	121D	121E
121D	3123	4123
R1	1344	F044

The underlined entries indicated the addressed and changed bytes. The LGT (logical greater than) status bit would be set to 1 while the other status bits affected would be 0.

Application: SB provides byte subtraction when 8 bit operations are required by the system.

INCREMENT

INC

Format: **INC** **G**

0	1	2	3	4	5	6	7	8	9	10	11	12	13	14	15	
0	0	0	0	0	1	0	1	1	0	T_s		S				(05--)

Operation: The data located at the address indicated by G is incremented and the result is placed in the G location and compared to 0.

$$M(G) + 1 \longrightarrow M(G)$$
$$M(G) + 1 : 0$$

Status Bits Affected: **LGT, AGT, EQ, C, OV**

Examples: **INC** **@TABL** $M(TABL) + 1 \longrightarrow M(TABL)$
INC **1** $(R1) + 1 \longrightarrow R1$

Application: INC is used to increment byte addresses and to increment byte counters. Autoincrementing addressing on byte instructions automatically includes this operation.

INCREMENT BY TWO

INCT

Format: **INCT G**

0	1	2	3	4	5	6	7	8	9	10	11	12	13	14	15	
0	0	0	0	0	1	0	1	1	1	T_s		S				(05--)

Operation: Two is added to the data at the location specified by G and the result is stored at the G location and is compared to 0:

$$M(G) + 2 \longrightarrow M(G)$$
$$M(G) + 2 : 0$$

Status Bits Affected: **LGT, AGT, EQ, C, OV**

Example: **INCT 5** $(R5) + 2 \longrightarrow R5$

Application: This can be used to increment word addresses, though autoincrementing on word instructions does this automatically.

DEC/DECT

DECREMENT

DEC

Format: **DEC** **G**

0	1	2	3	4	5	6	7	8	9	10 11	12 13 14 15
0	0	0	0	0	1	1	0	0	0	T_s	S

(06--)

Operation: One is subtracted from the data at the location specified by G, the result is stored at that location and is compared to 0:

$$M(G) - 1 \longrightarrow M(G)$$
$$M(G) - 1 : 0$$

Status Bits Affected: **LGT, AGT, EQ, C, OV**

Example: **DEC** **@TABL** $M(TABL) - 1 \longrightarrow M(TABL)$

Application: This instruction is most often used to decrement byte counters or to work through byte addresses in descending order.

DECREMENT BY TWO

DECT

Format: **DECT** **G**

0	1	2	3	4	5	6	7	8	9	10 11	12 13 14 15
0	0	0	0	0	1	1	0	0	1	T_s	S

(06--)

Operation: Two is subtracted from the data at the location specified by G and the result is stored at that location and is compared to 0:

$$M(G) - 2 \longrightarrow M(G)$$
$$M(G) - 2 : 0$$

Status Bits Affected: **LGT, AGT, EQ, C, OV**

Example: **DECT** **3** $(R3) - 2 \longrightarrow R3$

Application: This instruction is used to decrement word counters and to work through word addresses in descending order.

NEG/ABS

NEGATE

NEG

Format: **NEG**   **G**

0	1	2	3	4	5	6	7	8	9	10 11	12 13 14 15
0	0	0	0	0	1	0	1	0	0	T_s	S

(05--)

Operation: The data at the address specified by G is replaced by its two's complement. The result is compared to 0:

$$- M(G) \longrightarrow M(G)$$
$$- M(G) : 0$$

Status Bits Affected: **LGT, AGT, EQ, OV** (OV set only when operand = 8000_{16}).

Example: **NEG**   **5** $-(R5) \longrightarrow R5$

If R5 contained $A342_{16}$, this instruction would cause the R5 contents to changed to $5CBE_{16}$ and will cause the LGT and AGT status bits to be set to 1.

Application: NEG is used to form the 2's complement of 16 bit numbers.

ABSOLUTE VALUE

ABS

Format: **ABS**   **G**

0	1	2	3	4	5	6	7	8	9	10 11	12 13 14 15
0	0	0	0	0	1	1	1	0	1	T_s	S

(07---)

Operation: The data at the address specified by G is compared to 0. Then the absolute value of this data is placed in the G location:

$$M(G) : 0$$
$$|M(G)| \longrightarrow M(G)$$

Status Bits Affected: **LGT, AGT, EQ, OV** (OV set only when operand = 8000_{16})

Example: **ABS**   **@LIST(7)** $|M(R7 + LIST)| \longrightarrow M(R7 + LIST)$

If the data at R7 + LIST is $FF3C_{16}$, it will be changed to $00C4_{16}$ and LGT will be set to 1.

Application: This instruction is used to test the data in location G and then replace the data by its absolute value. This could be used for unsigned arithmetic algorithms such as multiplication.

MPY

MULTIPLY

Format: **MPY   G$_s$,R$_d$**

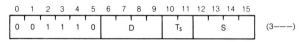

Operation: The 16 bit data at the address designated by G$_s$ is multiplied by the 16 bit data contained in the specified workspace register R. The unsigned binary product (32 bits) is placed in workspace registers R and R + 1:

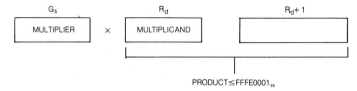

Affect on Status: None

Example: **MPY   @NEW,5**

If the data at location NEW is 0005_{16} and R5 contains 0012_{16}, this instruction will cause R5 to contain 0000_{16} and R6 to contain $005A_{16}$.

Application: MPY can be used to perform 16 bit by 16 bit binary multiplication. Several such 32 bit subproducts can be combined in such a way to perform multiplication involving larger multipliers and multiplicands such as a 32 bit by 32 bit multiplication.

DIVIDE

DIV

Format: **DIV**   **G$_s$,R$_d$**

0	1	2	3	4	5	6	7	8	9	10	11	12	13	14	15	
0	0	1	1	1	1		D			T$_s$			S			(3---)

Operation: The 32 bit number contained in workspace registers R$_d$ and R$_d$ + 1 is divided by the 16 bit data contained at the address specified by G$_s$. The workspace register R$_d$ then contains the quotient and workspace R$_d$ + 1 contains the 16 bit remainder. The division will occur only if the divisor at G is greater than the data contained in R$_d$:

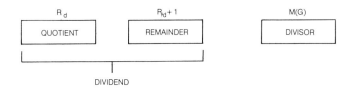

Affect on Status: Overflow (OV) is set if the divisor is less than the data contained in R$_d$. If OV is set, R$_d$ and R$_d$ + 1 are not changed.

Example: **DIV**   **@LOC,2**

If R2 contains 0 and R3 contains 000D$_{16}$ and the data at address LOC is 0005$_{16}$, this instruction will cause R2 to contain 0002$_{16}$ and R3 to contain 0003$_{16}$. OV would be 0.

Application: DIV provides basic binary division of a 32 bit number by a 16 bit number.

C

COMPARISON INSTRUCTIONS

These instructions are used to test words or bytes by comparing them with a reference constant or with another word or byte. Such operations are used in certain types of division algorithms, number conversion, and in recognition of input command or limit conditions.

COMPARE WORDS

C

Format: **C**   **G_s, G_d**

Operation: The 2's complement 16 bit data addressed by G_s is compared to the 2's complement 16 bit data addressed by G_d. The contents of both locations remain unchanged.

     $M(G_s) : M(G_d)$

Status Bits Affected: **LGT, AGT, EQ**

Example: **C**   **@T1,2**

This instruction has the following example results:

Data at Location T1	Data in R2	Results of Comparison LGT	AGT	EQ
FFFF	0000	1	0	0
7FFF	0000	1	1	0
8000	0000	1	0	0
8000	7FFF	1	0	0
7FFF	7FFF	0	0	1
7FFF	8000	0	1	0

Application: The need to compare two words occurs in such system functions as division, number conversion, and pattern recognition.

COMPARE BYTES

Format: **CB**   **G$_s$,G$_d$**

0	1	2	3	4	5	6	7	8	9	10	11	12	13	14	15	
1	0	0	1	T$_d$		D				T$_s$		S				(9---)

Operation: The 2's complement 8 bit byte addressed by G$_s$ is compared to the 2's complement 8 bit byte addressed by G$_d$:

   MB(G$_s$) : MB(G$_d$)

Status Bits Affected: **LGT, AGT,EQ,OP**

OP (odd parity) is based on the number of bits in the source byte.

Example: **CB**   **1,*2**

with the typical results of (assuming R2 addresses an odd byte):

			Results of Comparison		
R1 data	*M(R2) Data*	*LGT*	*AGT*	*EQ*	*OP*
FFFF	FF00	1	0	0	0
7F00	FF00	1	1	0	1
8000	FF00	1	0	0	1
8000	FF7F	1	0	0	1
7F00	007F	0	0	1	1

The underlined entries indicate the byte addressed.

Application: In cases where 8 bit operations are required, CB provides a means of performing byte comparisons for special conversion and recognition problems.

CI⁄COC

COMPARE IMMEDIATE

CI

Format: **CI R,Value**

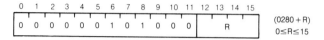

(0280 + R)
$0 \leq R \leq 15$

Operation: CI compares the specified workspace register contents to the value contained word immediately following the instruction:

R : Value

Status Bits Affected: **LGT, AGT, EQ**

Example: **CI   9,>F330**

If R9 contains 2183_{16}, the equal (EQ) and logical greater than (LGT) bits will be 0 and arithmetic greater than (AGT) will be set to 1.

Application: CI is used to test data to see if system or program limits have been met or exceeded or to recognize command words.

COMPARE ONES CORRESPONDING

COC

Format: **COC   Gₛ,R**

0	1	2	3	4	5	6	7	8	9	10	11	12	13	14	15
0	0	1	0	0	0	D			Tₛ		S				

(2---)

Operation: The data in the location addressed by G_s act as a mask for the bits to be tested in workspace register R. That is, only the bit position that contain ones in the G_s data will be checked in R. Then, if R contains ones in all the bit positions selected by the G_s data, the equal (EQ) status bit will be set to 1.

Status Bits Affected: **EQ**

Example: **COC   @TESTBIT, 8**

If R8 contains $E306_{16}$ and location TESTBIT contains $C102_{16}$,

TESTBIT Mask = 1100 0001 0000 0010
R8 = 1110 0011 0000 0110

equal (EQ) would be set to 1 since everywhere the test mask data contains a 1 (underlined positions), R8 also contains a 1.

Application: COC is used to selectively test groups of bits to check the status of certain sub-systems or to examine certain aspects of data words.

COMPARE ZEROES CORRESPONDING

CZC

Format: **CZC   G$_s$,R**

0	1	2	3	4	5	6	7	8	9	10	11	12	13	14	15	
0	0	1	0	0	1		D			T$_s$			S			(2---)

Operation: The data located in the address specified by G$_s$ act as a mask for the bits to be tested in the specified workspace register R. That is, only the bit positions that contain ones in the G$_s$ data are the bit positions to be checked in R. Then if R contains zeroes in all the selected bit positions, the equal (EQ) status bit will be set to 1.

Status Bits Affected: **EQ**

Examples: **CZC   @TESTBIT,8**

If the TESTBIT location contains the value C102$_{16}$ and the R8 location contains 2301$_{16}$,

$$\text{TESTBIT Data} = \underline{11}00\ 000\underline{1}\ 0000\ 00\underline{1}0$$
$$\text{R8} = \underline{00}10\ 001\underline{1}\ 0000\ 00\underline{0}1$$
$$\text{X}$$

the equal status bit would be reset to zero since not all the bits of R8 (note the X position) are zero in the positions that the TESTBIT data contains ones.

Application: Similar to the COC instruction.

ANDI

LOGIC INSTRUCTIONS

The logic instructions allow the processor to perform boolean logic for the system. Since AND, OR, INVERT, and Exclusive OR (XOR) are available, any boolean function can be performed on system data.

AND IMMEDIATE

ANDI

Format: **ANDI   R,Value**

0	1	2	3	4	5	6	7	8	9	10	11	12	13	14	15
0	0	0	0	0	0	1	0	0	1	0	0	R			

$(0240 + R)$
$0 \leq R \leq 15$

Operation: The bits of the specified workspace register R are logically ANDed with the corresponding bits of the 16 bit binary constant value contained in the word immediately following the instruction. The 16 bit result is compared to zero and is placed in the register R:

    R   AND   Value ——►R
    R   AND   Value : 0

Recall that the AND operation results in 1 only if *both* inputs are 1.

Status Bits Affected: **LGT, AGT, EQ**

Example: **ANDI 0,>6D03**

If workspace register 0 contains $D2AB_{16}$, then (D2AB) AND (6D03) is 4003_{16}:

Value =	0110	1101	0000	0011
R0 =	1101	0010	1010	1011
R0 AND Value =	0100	0000	0000	$0011 = 4003_{16}$

This value is placed in R0. The LGT and AGT status bits are set to 1.

Application: ANDI is used to zero all bits that are not of interest and leave the selected bits (those with ones in Value) unchanged. This can be used to test single bits or isolate portions of the word, such as a four bit group.

OR IMMEDIATE

ORI

Format: **ORI**   **R,Value**

0	1	2	3	4	5	6	7	8	9	10	11	12	13	14	15	
0	0	0	0	0	0	1	0	0	1	1	0		R			

(0260 + R)

$0 \le R \le 15$

Operation: The bits of the specified workspace register R are ORed with the corresponding bits of the 16 bit binary constant contained in the word immediately following instruction. The 16 bit result is placed in R and is compared to zero:

     R   OR   Value ——→ R
     R   OR   Value : 0

Recall that the OR operation results in a 1 if *either* of the inputs is a 1.

Status Bits Affected: **LGT, AGT, EQ**

Example: **ORI**   **5,>6D03**

If R5 contained $D2AB_{16}$, then R5 will be changed to $FFAB_{16}$:

         R5 = 1101   0010   1010   1011
     Value = 0110   1101   0000   0011
               1111   1111   1010   1011 = $FFAB_{16}$ = R5 OR Value

with LGT being set to 1.

Application: Used to implement the OR logic in the system.

XOR/INV

EXCLUSIVE OR

XOR

Format: **XOR**   **G$_s$R$_d$**

0	1	2	3	4	5	6	7	8	9	10	11	12	13	14	15	
0	0	1	0	1	0		D			T$_s$			S			(2————)

Operation: The exclusive OR is performed between corresponding bits of the data addressed by G$_s$ and the contents of workspace register R$_d$. The result is placed in workspace register R$_d$ and is compared to 0:

$$M(G_s) \text{ XOR } R_d \longrightarrow R_d$$
$$M(G_s) \text{ XOR } R_d : 0$$

Status Bits Affected: **LGT, AGT, EQ**

Example: **XOR**   **@CHANGE,2**

If location CHANGE contains $6D03_{16}$ and R2 contains $D2AA_{16}$, R2 will be changed to $BFA9_{16}$:

```
      CHANGE Data = 0110    1101    0000    0011
               R2 = 1101    0010    1010    1010
  M(CHANGE) XOR R2 = 1011    1111    1010    1001 = BFA9₁₆
```

and the LGT status bit will be set to 1. Note that the exclusive OR operation will result in a 1 if *only one* of the inputs is a 1.

Application: XOR is used to implement the exclusive OR logic for the system.

INVERT

INV

Format: **INV**   **G**

0	1	2	3	4	5	6	7	8	9	10	11	12	13	14	15	
0	0	0	0	0	1	0	1	0	1	T$_s$			S			(05——)

Operation: The bits of the data addressed by G are replaced by their complement. The result is compared to 0 and is stored at the G location:

$$\overline{M(G)} \longrightarrow M(G)$$
$$\overline{M(G)} : 0$$

Status Bits Affected: **LGT, AGT, EQ**

Example: **INV**   **11**

If R11 contains $00FF_{16}$, the instruction would change the contents to $FF00_{16}$, causing the LGT status bit to set to 1.

Application: INV is used to form the 1's complement of 16 bit binary numbers, or to invert system data.

CLR/SETO

CLEAR

CLR

Format: **CLR   G**

0	1	2	3	4	5	6	7	8	9	10	11	12	13	14	15	
0	0	0	0	0	1	0	0	1	1	T_s		S				(04 – –)

Operation: 0000_{16} is placed in the memory location specified by G.

$$0000_{16} \longrightarrow M(G)$$

Affect on Status: None

Example: **CLR   *11**

would clear the contents of the location addressed by the contents of R11, that is:

$0000_{16} \longrightarrow M(R11)$

Application: CLR is used to set problem arguments to 0 and to initialize memory locations to zero during system start-up operations.

SET TO ONE
Format: **SETO   G**

SETO

0	1	2	3	4	5	6	7	8	9	10	11	12	13	14	15	
0	0	0	0	0	1	1	1	0	0	T_s		S				(07 – –)

Operation: $FFFF_{16}$ is placed in the memory location specified by G: $FFFF_{16} \longrightarrow M(G)$

Affect on Status: None

Example: **SETO   11**

would cause all bits of R11 to be 1.

Application: Similar to CLR

SET ONES CORRESPONDING

SOC

Format: **SOC**   **G$_s$,G$_d$**

0	1	2	3	4	5	6	7	8	9	10	11	12	13	14	15	
1	1	1	0	T$_d$		D				T$_s$		S				(E———)

Operation: This instruction performs the OR operation between corresponding bits of the data addressed by G$_s$ and the data addressed by G$_d$. The result is compared to 0 and is placed in the G$_d$ location:

$$M(G_s) \ \ OR \ \ M(G_d) \longrightarrow M(G_d)$$
$$M(G_s) \ \ OR \ \ M(G_d) : 0$$

Status Bits Affected: **LGT, AGT, EQ**

Example: **SOC**   **3,@NEW**

If location NEW contains AAAA$_{16}$ and R$_3$ contains FF00$_{16}$, the contents at location NEW will be changed to FFAA$_{16}$ and the LGT status bit will be set to 1.

Application: Provides the OR function between any two words in memory.

SET ONES CORRESPONDING, BYTE

SOCB

Format: **SOCB**   **G$_s$,G$_d$**

0	1	2	3	4	5	6	7	8	9	10	11	12	13	14	15	
1	1	1	1	T$_d$		D				T$_s$		S				(F———)

Operation: The logical OR is performed between corresponding bits of the byte addressed by G$_s$ and the byte addressed by G$_d$ with the result compared to 0 and placed in location G$_d$:

$$MB(G_s) \ \ OR \ \ MB(G_d) \longrightarrow MB(G_d)$$
$$MB(G_s) \ \ OR \ \ MB(G_d) : 0$$

Status Bits Affected: **LGT, AGT, EQ, OP**

Example: **SOCB**   **5,8**

If R5 contains F013$_{16}$ and R8 contains AA24$_{16}$, the most significant byte of R8 will be changed to FA$_{16}$ so that R8 will contain FA24$_{16}$ and the LGT status bit will be set to 1.

Application: The SOCB provides the logical OR function on system bytes.

Set to Zeroes Corresponding

SZC

Format: **SZC** G_s, G_d

0	1	2	3	4	5	6	7	8	9	10	11	12	13	14	15	
0	1	0	0	T_d		D				T_s		S				(4———)

Operation: The data addressed by G_s forms a mask for this operation. The bits in the destination data (addressed by G_d) that correspond to the one bits of the source data (addressed by G_s) are cleared. The result is compared to zero and is stored in the G_d location.

$$\overline{M(G_s)} \quad \text{AND} \quad M(G_d) \longrightarrow M(G_d)$$
$$\overline{M(G_s)} \quad \text{AND} \quad M(G_d) : 0$$

Status Bits Affected: **LGT, AGT, EQ**

Example: **SZC**   **5,3**

If R5 contains $6D03_{16}$ and R3 contains $D2AA_{16}$, this instruction will cause the R3 contents to change to $92A8_{16}$:

```
R5 (Mask) = 0110 1101 0000 0011
       R3 = 1101 0010 1010 1010
   Result = 1001 0010 1010 1000 = 92A8₁₆
```

with the LGT status bit set. The underlined entries indicate which bits are to be cleared.

Application: SZC allows the programmer to selectively clear bits of data words. For example, when an interrupt has been serviced, the interrupt request bit can be cleared by using the SZC instruction.

SZCB

SET TO ZEROES CORRESPONDING, BYTES

Format: **SZCB   G_sG_d**

```
0  1  2  3  4  5  6  7  8  9  10 11 12 13 14 15

0  1  0  1    T_d        D        T_s        S           | (5---)
```

Operation: The byte addressed by G_s will provide a mask for clearing certain bits of the byte addressed by G_d. The bits in the G_d byte that will be cleared are the bits that are one in the G_s byte. The result is compared to zero and is placed in the G_d byte:

$$\overline{MB(G_s)} \quad AND \quad MB(G_d) \longrightarrow MB(G_d)$$
$$\overline{MB(G_s)} \quad AND \quad MB(G_d) : 0$$

Status Bits Affected: **LGT, AGT, EQ, OP**

Example: **SZCB   @BITS,@TEST**

If location BITS is an *odd* address which locates the data $18\underline{F0}_{16}$, and location TEST contains an *even* address which locates the data $\underline{AA}24_{16}$, the instruction will clear the first four bits of TEST data changing it to $0A24_{16}$.

Application: Provides selective clearing of bits of system bytes.

SHIFT INSTRUCTIONS

These instructions are used to perform simple binary multiplication and division on words in memory and to rearrange the location of bits in the word in order to examine a given bit with the carry (C) status bit.

SHIFT RIGHT ARITHMETIC

SRA

Format: **SRA   R,Cnt**

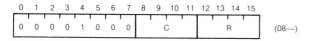

(08--)

Operation: The contents of the specified workspace register R are shifted right Cnt times, filling the vacated bit position with the sign (most significant bit) bit: The shifted number is compared to zero:

Status Bits Affected: **LGT, AGT, EQ, C**

Number of Shifts: Cnt (number contained in the instruction from 0 to 15) specifies the number of bits shifted unless Cnt is zero in which case the shift count is taken from the four least significant bits of workspace register 0. If both Cnt and these four bits are 0, a 16 bit position shift is performed.

Example: **SRA   5,2**   *Shift R5 2 bit positions right*
         SRA   7,0

If R0 least four bits contain 6_{16}, then the second instruction will cause register 7 to be shifted 6 bit positions (Cnt in that instruction is 0):

```
If R7 Before Shift| = 1011 1010 1010 1010 = BAAA₁₆
   R7 After Shift   = 1111 1110 1110 1010 = FEEA₁₆
If R5 Before Shift| = 0101 0101 0101 0101 = 5555₁₆
   R5 After Shift   = 0001 0101 0101 0101 = 1555₁₆
After the R7 shift the LGT would be set, and Carry = 1
After the R5 shift LGT and AGT would be set and Carry = 0
```

Application: SRA provides binary division by 2^{Cnt}.

SLA

SMALL CAPS: Shift Left Arithmetic

SHIFT LEFT ARITHMETIC

Format: **SLA** **R,Cnt**

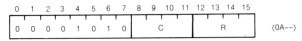

(0A--)

Operation: The contents of workspace register R are shifted left Cnt times (or if Cnt = 0, the number of times specified by the least four bits of R0) filling the vacated positions with zeroes. The carry contains the value of the last bit shifted out to the left and the shifted number is compared to zero:

Status Bits Affected: **LGT, AGT, EQ, C, OV**

Example: **SLA** **10,5**

If workspace register 10 contains 1357_{16} the instruction would change its contents to $6AE0_{16}$, causing the arithmetic greater than (AGT), logical greater than (LGT), and overflow (OV) bits to set. Carry would be zero, the value of the last bit shifted.

Application: SLA performs binary multiplication by 2^{Cnt}

SHIFT RIGHT LOGICAL

SRL

Format: **SRL   R,Cnt**

0	1	2	3	4	5	6	7	8	9	10	11	12	13	14	15	
0	0	0	0	1	0	0	1		C				R			(09--)

Operation: The contents of the workspace register specified by R are shifted right Cnt times (or if Cnt = 0, the number of times specified by the least four bits or R0) filling in the vacated positions with zeroes. The carry contains the value of the last bit shifted out to the right and the shifted number is compared to zero:

Status Bits Affected: **LGT, AGT, EQ, C**

Example: **SRL   0,3**

If R0 contained $FFEF_{16}$, the contents would become $1FFD_{16}$ with the AGT, LGT, and C bits set to 1:

```
R0 Before Shift = 1111 1111 1110 1111 = FFEF₁₆
R0 After Shift  = 0001 1111 1111 1101 = 1FFD₁₆
```

Application: Performs binary division by 2^{Cnt}

SHIFT RIGHT CIRCULAR

SRC

Format: **SRC   R,Cnt**

0	1	2	3	4	5	6	7	8	9	10	11	12	13	14	15	
0	0	0	0	1	0	1	1		C				R			(0B--)

Operation: On each shift the bit shifted out of bit 15 is shifted back into bit 0. Carry contains the value of the last bit shifted and the shifted number is compared to 0. The number of shifts to be performed is the number Cnt, or if Cnt = 0, the number contained in the least significant four bits of R0:

Status Bits Affected: **LGT, AGT, EQ, C**

Example: **SRC   2,7**

If R2 initially contains $FFEF_{16}$, then after the shift it will contain $DFFF_{16}$ with LGT and C set to 1.

```
R2 Before Shift = 1111 1111 1110 1111 = FFEF₁₆
R2 After Shift  = 1101 1111 1111 1111 = DFFF₁₆
```

Application: SRC can be used to examine a certain bit in the data word, change the location of 4 bit groups, or swap bytes.

B

UNCONDITIONAL BRANCH INSTRUCTIONS

These instructions give the programmer the capability of choosing to perform the next instruction in sequence or to go to some other part of the memory to get the next instruction to be executed. The branch can be a subroutine type of branch, in which case the programmer can return to the point from which the branch occurred.

<u>BRANCH</u>

B

Format: **B**   **G$_s$**

Operation: The G$_s$ address is placed in the program counter, causing the next instruction to be obtained from the location specified by G$_s$.

Affect on Status: None

Example: **B**   ***3**

If R3 contains 21CC$_{16}$, then the next instruction will be obtained from location 21CC$_{16}$.

Application: This instruction is used to jump to another part of the program when the current task has been completed.

BL

BL

BRANCH AND LINK

Format: **BL** G_s

0	1	2	3	4	5	6	7	8	9	10 11	12 13 14 15
0	0	0	0	0	1	1	0	1	0	T_s	S

(06--)

Operation: The source address G_s is placed in the program counter and the address of the instruction following the BL instruction is saved in workspace register 11.

$$G_s \longrightarrow PC$$
$$(Old\ PC) \longrightarrow R11$$

Affect on Status: None

Example: **BL**   **@TRAN**

Assume the BL instruction is located at 3200_{16} and the value assigned to TRAN is 2000_{16}. PC will be loaded with the value 2000_{16} (TRAN) and R11 will be loaded with the value 3202_{16} (old PC value).

Application: This is a shared workspace subroutine jump. Both the main program and the subroutine use the same workspace registers. To get back to the main program at the branch point, the following branch instruction can be used at the end of the subroutine:

      B   *11

which causes the R11 contents (old PC value) to be loaded into the program counter.

BLWP

BRANCH AND LOAD WORKSPACE POINTER

Format: **BLWP G$_s$**

0	1	2	3	4	5	6	7	8	9	10 11	12 13 14 15	
0	0	0	0	0	1	0	0	0	0	T$_s$	S	(04--)

Operation: The word specified by the source G$_s$ is loaded into the workspace pointer (WP) and the next word in memory (G$_s$ + 2) is loaded into the program counter (PC) to cause the branch. The old workspace pointer is stored in the new workspace register 13, the old PC value is stored in the new workspace register 14, and the status register is stored in new workspace register 15:

$$M(G_s) \longrightarrow WP$$
$$M(G_s + 2) \longrightarrow PC$$
$$(\text{Old WP}) \longrightarrow \text{New R13}$$
$$(\text{Old PC}) \longrightarrow \text{New R14}$$
$$(\text{Old ST}) \longrightarrow \text{New R15}$$

Affect on Status: None

Example: **BLWP *3**

Assuming that R3 contains 2100_{16} and location 2100_{16} contains 0500_{16} and location 2102_{16} contains 0100_{16}, this instruction causes WP to be loaded with 0500_{16} and PC to be loaded with 0100_{16}. Then, location $051A_{16}$ will be loaded with the old WP value, the old PC value will be saved in location $051C_{16}$, and the status (ST) will be saved in location $051E_{16}$. The next instruction will be taken from address 0100_{16} and the subroutine workspace will begin at 0500_{16} (R0). BLWP and XOP do not test IREQ at the end of instruction execution.

Application: This is a context switch subroutine jump with the transfer vector location specified by G$_s$. It uses a new workspace to save the old values of WP, PC, and ST (in the last three registers). The advantage of this subroutine jump over the BL jump is that the subroutine gets its own workspace and the main program workspace contents are not disturbed by subroutine operations.

EXTENDED OPERATION

Format: **XOP**   **G_s,n**

0	1	2	3	4	5	6	7	8	9	10	11	12	13	14	15
0	0	1	0	1	1		D			T_s			S		

(2---)

Operation: n specifies which extended operation transfer vector is to be used in the context switch branch from XOP to the corresponding subprogram. The effective address G_s is placed in R11 of the subprogram workspace in order to pass an argument or data location to the subprogram:

$$M(n \times 4 + 0040_{16}) \longrightarrow WP$$
$$M(n \times 4 + 0042_{16}) \longrightarrow PC$$
$$(\text{Old WP}) \longrightarrow \text{New R13}$$
$$(\text{Old PC}) \longrightarrow \text{New R14}$$
$$(\text{Old ST}) \longrightarrow \text{New R15}$$
$$G_s \longrightarrow \text{New R11}$$

Affect on Status: Extended Operation (X) bit is set.

Example: **XOP   *1,2**

Assume R1 contains 0750_{16}. WP is loaded with the word at address 48_{16} (first part of transfer vector for extended operation 2) and PC is loaded with the word at address $4A_{16}$. If location 48_{16} contains 0200_{16}, this will be the address of R0 of the subprogram workspace. Thus, location 0236_{16} (new R11) will be loaded with 0750_{16} (contents of R1 in main program), location $023A_{16}$ (new R13) will be loaded with the old WP value, location $023C_{16}$ will be loaded with the old PC value, and location $023E_{16}$ (new R15) will be loaded with the old status value:

$$M(48_{16}) \longrightarrow WP$$
$$M(4A_{16}) \longrightarrow PC$$
$$(\text{Old WP}) \longrightarrow M(023A_{16}) \quad \text{New R13}$$
$$(\text{Old PC}) \longrightarrow M(023C_{16}) \quad \text{New R14}$$
$$(\text{Old ST}) \longrightarrow M(023E_{16}) \quad \text{New R15}$$
$$0750_{16} \longrightarrow M(0236_{16}) \quad \text{New R11}$$

Application: This can be used to define a subprogram that can be called by a single instruction. As a result, the programmer can define special purpose instructions to augment the standard 9900 instruction set.

RTWP/JMP

RETURN WITH WORKSPACE POINTER

RTWP

Format: **RTWP**

0	1	2	3	4	5	6	7	8	9	10	11	12	13	14	15	
0	0	0	0	0	0	1	1	1	0	0	0	0	0	0	0	(0380)

Operation: This is a return from a context switch subroutine. It occurs by restoring the WP, PC, and ST register contents by transferring the contents of subroutine workspace registers R13, R14, and R15, into the WP, PC, and ST registers, respectively.

$$R13 \longrightarrow WP$$
$$R14 \longrightarrow PC$$
$$R15 \longrightarrow ST$$

Status Bits Affected: **All (ST receives the contents of R15)**

Application: This is used to return from subprograms that were reached by a transfer vector operation such as an interrupt, extended operation, or BLWP instruction.

UNCONDITIONAL JUMP

JMP

Format: **JMP   EXP**

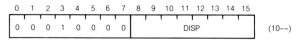

0	1	2	3	4	5	6	7	8	9	10	11	12	13	14	15	
0	0	0	1	0	0	0	0				DISP					(10--)

Operation: The signed displacement defined by EXP is added to the current contents of the program counter to generate the new value of the program counter. The location jumped to must be within -128 to $+127$ words of the present location.

Affect on Status: None

Example: **JMP   THERE**

If this instruction is located at 0018_{16} and THERE is the label of the instruction located at 0010_{16}, then the Exp value placed in the object code would be FB (for -5). Since the Assembler makes this computation, the programmer only needs to place the appropriate label or expression in the operand field of the instruction.

Application: If the subprogram to be jumped to is within 128 words of the JMP instruction location, the unconditional JMP is preferred over the unconditional branch since only one memory word (and one memory reference) is required for the JMP while two memory words and two memory cycles are required for the B instruction. Thus, the JMP instruction can be implemented faster and with less memory cost than can the B instruction.

EXECUTE

Format: **X**   **G$_s$**

0	1	2	3	4	5	6	7	8	9	10 11	12 13 14 15	
0	0	0	0	0	1	0	0	1	0	T$_s$	S	(04--)

Operation: The instruction located at the address specified by G$_s$ is executed.

Status Bits Affected: **Depends on the instruction executed**

Example: **X**   ***11**

If R11 contains 2000_{16} and location 2000_{16} contains the instruction for CLR 2 then this execute instruction would clear the contents of register 2 to zero.

Application: X is useful when the instruction to be executed is dependent on a variable factor.

CONDITIONAL JUMP INSTRUCTIONS

JH

JL

JHE

JLE

JGT

JLT

JEQ

JNE

JOC

JNC

JNO

JOP

These instructions perform a branching operation only if certain status bits meet the conditions required by the jump. These instructions allow decision making to be incorporated into the program. The conditional jump instruction mnemonics are summarized in *Table 6-1* along with the status bit conditions that are tested by these instructions.

Format: **Mnemonic   Exp**

```
  0   1   2   3   4   5   6   7   8   9  10  11  12  13  14  15
+-----------+-----------------+---------------------------+
| 0   0   0   1 |     CODE     |          DISP         | (1---)
+-----------+-----------------+---------------------------+
```

Operation: If the condition indicated by the branch mnemonic is true, the jump will occur using relative addressing as was used in the unconditional JMP instruction. That is, the Exp defines a displacement that is added to the current value of the program counter to determine the location of the next instruction, which must be within 128 words of the jump instruction.

Effect on Status Bits: None

Example: **C   R1, R2**
              JNE   LOOP

The first instruction compares the contents of registers one and two. If they are not equal, EQ = 0 and the JNE instruction causes the branch to LOOP to be taken. If R1 and R2 are equal, EQ = 1 and the branch is not taken.

Table 6-1. *Status Bits Tested by Instructions*

Mnemonic	L>	A>	EQ	C	OV	OP	Jump if:	CODE*
JH	X	—	X	—	—	—	L> $\bullet$ $\overline{EQ}$ = 1	B
JL	X	—	X	—	—	—	L> + EQ = 0	A
JHE	X	—	X	—	—	—	L> + EQ = 1	4
JLE	X	—	X	—	—	—	$\overline{L>}$ + EQ = 1	2
JGT	—	X	—	—	—	—	A> = 1	5
JLT	—	X	X	—	—	—	A> + EQ = 0	1
JEQ	—	—	X	—	—	—	EQ = 1	3
JNE	—	—	X	—	—	—	EQ = 0	6
JOC	—	—	—	X	—	—	C = 1	8
JNC	—	—	—	X	—	—	C = 0	7
JNO	—	—	—	—	X	—	OV = 0	9
JOP	—	—	—	—	—	X	OP = 1	C

Note: In the Jump if column, a logical equation is shown in which $\bullet$ means the AND operation, + means the OR operation, and a line over a term means negation or inversion.

*CODE is entered in the CODE field of the OPCODE to generate the machine code for the instruction.

Application: Most algorithms and programs with loop counters require these instructions to decide which sequence of instructions to do next.

CRU INSTRUCTIONS

The communications register unit (CRU) performs single and multiple bit programmed input/output for the microcomputer. All input consists of reading CRU line logic levels into memory, and all output consists of setting CRU output lines to bit values from a word or byte of memory. The CRU provides a maximum of 4096 input and 4096 output lines that may be individually selected by a 12 bit address which is located in bits 3 through 14 of workspace register 12. This address is the hardware base address for all CRU communications.

SET BIT TO LOGIC ONE

SBO

Format: **SBO**   **disp**

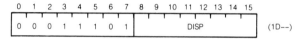

0	1	2	3	4	5	6	7	8	9	10	11	12	13	14	15
0	0	0	1	1	1	0	1				DISP				

(1D--)

Operation: The CRU bit at disp plus the hardware base address is set to one. The hardware base address is bits 3 through 14 of workspace register 12. The value disp is a signed displacement.

        1 ——▶ Bit (disp + base address)

Affect on Status: None

Example: **SBO**   **15**

If R12 contains a software base address of 0200_{16} so that the hardware base address is 0100_{16} (the hardware base address is one-half the value of the contents of R12 excluding bits 0, 1 and 2), the above instruction would set CRU line $010F_{16}$ to a 1.

Application: Output a one on a single bit CRU line.

SBZ/TB

SBZ

SET BIT TO LOGIC ZERO

SBZ

Format: **SBZ   disp**

0	1	2	3	4	5	6	7	8	9	10	11	12	13	14	15	
0	0	0	1	1	1	1	0				DISP					(1E--)

Operation: The CRU bit at disp plus the base address is reset to zero. The hardware base address is bits 3 through 14 of workspace register 12. The value disp is a signed displacement.

$$0 \longrightarrow \text{Bit (disp + hardware base address)}$$

Affect on Status: None

Example: **SBZ   2**

If R12 contains 0000_{16}, the hardware base address is 0 so that the instruction would reset CRU line 0002_{16} to zero.

Application: Output a zero on a single bit CRU line.

TEST BIT

TB

Format: **TB   disp**

0	1	2	3	4	5	6	7	8	9	10	11	12	13	14	15	
0	0	0	1	1	1	1	1				DISP					(1F--)

Operation: The CRU bit at disp plus the base address is read by setting the value of the equal (EQ) status bit to the value of the bit on the CRU line. The hardware base address is bits 3 through 14 of workspace register 12. The value disp is a signed displacement.

$$\text{Bit (disp + hardware base address)} \longrightarrow \text{EQ}$$

Status Bits Affected: **EQ**

Example: **TB   4**

If R12 contains 0140_{16}, the hardware base address is $A0_{16}$ (which is one-half of 0140_{16}):

R12 Contents = 0000 0001 0100 0000

Note that the underlined hardware base address is $0A0_{16}$. Equal (EQ) would be made equal to the logic level on CRU line $0A0_{16} + 4 = $ CRU line $0A4_{16}$.

Application: Input the CRU bit selected.

LOAD CRU

LDCR

Format: **LDCR G$_s$,Cnt**

0	1	2	3	4	5	6	7	8	9	10	11	12	13	14	15	
0	0	1	1	0	0		C			T$_s$			S			(3---)

Operation: Cnt specifies the number of bits to be transferred from the data located at the address specified by G$_s$, with the first bit transferred from the least significant bit of this data, the next bit from the next least significant bit and so on. If Cnt = 0, the number of bits transferred is 16. If the number of bits to be transferred is one to eight, the source address is a byte address. If the number of bits to be transferred is 9 to 16, the source address is a word address. The source data is compared to zero before the transfer. The destination of the first bit is the CRU line specified by the hardware base address, the second bit is transferred to the CRU line specified by the hardware base address + 1, and so on.

Status Bits Affected: **LGT, AGT, EQ**
　　　　　　　　　　　　OP   (odd parity) with transfer of 8 or less bits.

Example: **LDCR @TOM,8**

Since 8 bits are transferred, TOM is a byte address. If TOM is an even number, the most significant byte is addressed. If R12 contains 0080_{16}, the hardware base address is 0040_{16} which is the CRU line that will receive the first bit transferred. 0041_{16} will be the address of the next bit transferred, and so on to the last (8th) bit transferred to CRU line 0047_{16}. This transfer is shown in *Figure 6-7.*

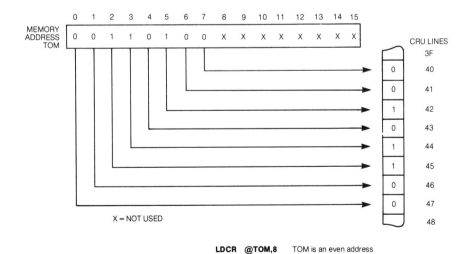

LDCR @TOM,8   TOM is an even address

Figure 6-7. LDCR byte transfer

LDCR

Application: The LDCR provides a number of bits (from 1 to 16) to be transferred from a memory word or byte to successive CRU lines, starting at the hardware base address line; the transfer begins with the least significant bit of the source field and continues to successively more significant bits. A further example of word versus byte transfers is given in *Figure 6-8*, in which a 9 bit (word addressed source) transfer is shown.

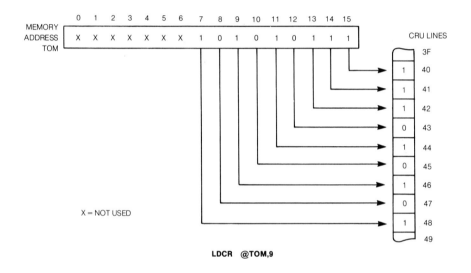

LDCR   @TOM,9

Figure 6-8. LDCR Word transfer

STORE CRU

STCR

Format: **STCR   G$_s$,Cnt**

0	1	2	3	4	5	6	7	8	9	10	11	12	13	14	15	
0	0	1	1	0	1		C			T$_s$			S			(3---)

Operation: Cnt specifies the number of bits to be transferred from successive CRU lines (starting at the hardware base address) to the location specified by G$_s$, beginning with the least significant bit position and transferring successive bits to successively more significant bits. If the number of bits transferred is 8 or less, G$_s$ is a byte address. Otherwise, G$_s$ is a word address. If Cnt=0, 16 bits are transferred. The bits transferred are compared to zero. If the transfer does not fill the entire memory word, the unfilled bits are reset to zero.

Status Bits Affected: **LGT, AGT, EQ**
                          OP for transfers of 8 bits or less

Example: **STCR   2,7**

Since 7 bits are to be transferred this is a byte transfer so that the bits will be transferred to the most significant byte of R2. *Figure 6-9* illustrates this transfer assuming that R12 contains 90_{16} so that the hardware base address is 48_{16} for the first bit to be transferred.

Note: Bits 8-15 are unchanged if transfer is less than 8 bits.

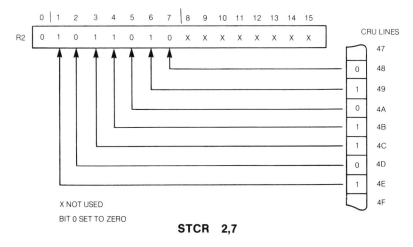

STCR   2,7

Figure 6-9. STCR Example

CONTROL INSTRUCTIONS

The control instructions are primarily applicable to the Model 990 Computer. These instructions are RSET (Reset), IDLE, CKOF (Clock off), CKON (Clock on), LREX (restart). The Model 990/10 also supports the long distance addressing instructions: LDS (Load long distance source) and LDD (Long distance destination). The use of these instructions are covered in the appropriate Model 990 computer programmer's manuals.

The control instructions have an affect on the 9900 signals on the address lines during the CRU Clock as shown below:

Instruction	A₀	A₁	A₂	OP CODE	
LREX	H	H	H	0 0 0 0 0 0 1 1 1 1 1 0 0 0 0 0	(03E0)
CKOF	H	H	L	0 0 0 0 0 0 1 1 1 1 0 0 0 0 0 0	(03C0)
CKON	H	L	H	0 0 0 0 0 0 1 1 1 0 1 0 0 0 0 0	(03A0)
RSET	L	H	H	0 0 0 0 0 0 1 1 0 1 1 0 0 0 0 0	(0360)
IDLE	L	H	L	0 0 0 0 0 0 1 1 0 1 0 0 0 0 0 0	(0340)
CRU	L	L	L		

(OP CODE bit positions: 0 1 2 3 4 5 6 7 8 9 10 11 12 13 14 15)

The IDLE instruction puts the 9900 in the idle condition and causes a CRUCLK output every six clock cycles to indicate this state. The processor can be removed from the idle state by 1) a $\overline{RESET}$ signal, 2) any interrupt that is enabled, or 3) a $\overline{LOAD}$ signal.

For the 9900 the above instructions are referred to as external instructions, since external hardware can be designed to respond to these signals. The address signals A_0, A_1, and A_2 can be decoded and the instructions used to control external hardware.

SPECIAL FEATURES OF THE 9940

The 9940 instruction set includes the instructions already presented. Two of these instructions are slightly different for the 9940. These are the extended operation and the load interrupt mask immediate instructions. There are two new arithmetic instructions that provide for binary coded decimal (BCD) addition and subtraction. The 9940 uses extended operations 0 through 3 to generate the load interrupt mask and the decimal arithmetic instructions. Thus, the 9940 extended operations 4 through 15 are available to the programmer.

LOAD IMMEDIATE INTERRUPT MASK

LIIM

Format: **LIIM   n**

$0 \leq n \leq 3$

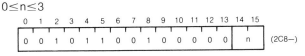

Operation: The interrupt mask bits 14 and 15 of the status register are loaded with n. Subsequent to this instruction, interrupt levels greater than n will be ignored by the processor, and interrupts of level n or less will be responded to by the processor.

Status Bits Affected: **Interrupt Mask (Bits 14 and 15)**

Example: **LIIM   2**

This operation will load the interrupt mask with 2, that is bit 14 would be set to a 1 and bit 15 would be reset to zero. This would disable interrupts of level 3, but would enable other interrupt levels.

Application: This instruction is used to control the 9940 interrupt system.

XOP

EXTENDED OPERATION

Format: **XOP**   **G$_s$,n**

0	1	2	3	4	5	6	7	8	9	10	11	12	13	14	15	
0	0	1	0	1	1	D				T$_s$		S				(2----)

Operation: n specifies the extended operation transfer vector to be used in the context switch to the extended operation subprogram. The TMS9940 restricts the range of n ($4 \leq n \leq 15$) so that there are only 12 XOP's available. This is because the first four are used by the processor to implement the LIIM, DCA, and DCS instructions. The transfer vector procedure for the programmer-defined extended operations is:

$$M(40_{16} + 4xn) \longrightarrow (WP)$$
$$M(42_{16} + 4xn) \longrightarrow (PC)$$
$$G_s \longrightarrow (New\ WR11)$$
$$(Old\ WP) \longrightarrow (New\ WR13)$$
$$(Old\ PC) \longrightarrow (New\ WR14)$$
$$(Old\ ST) \longrightarrow (New\ WR15)$$

Status Bits Affected: **None**

Example and Applications: **XOP**   ***1,4**

This instruction will cause an extended operation 4 to occur with the new workspace register 11 containing the address found in workspace register 1. The new WP value will be obtained from $40_{16} + 4 \times 4 = 50_{16}$ and the new PC value will be obtained from 52_{16}.

DCA

DECIMAL CORRECT ADDITION

Format: **DCA**   G$_s$

0	1	2	3	4	5	6	7	8	9	10 11	12 13 14 15	
0	0	1	0	1	1	0	0	0	0	T$_s$	S	(2C——)

Operation: The byte addressed by G$_s$ is corrected according to the table given in *Figure 6-10.* This operation is a processor defined extended operation with n = 0 so that the sequence of events described under the XOP discussion will occur in executing this instruction.

Status Bits Affected: **LGT, AGT, EQ, C, P, and DC (Digit Carry).**

Example: **DCA**   *10

This instruction would cause the byte addressed by the contents of the current workspace register 10 to be decimal adjusted in accordance with the truth table of *Figure 6-10.*

Application: This instruction is used immediately after the binary addition of two bytes (AB instruction) to correct any decimal digits outside the BCD code range of 0000_2 through 1001_2. It also keeps decimal addition accurate by responding to digit carries. For example, if 8_{16} is added to 8_{16} in BCD addition, 16_{16} should be generated. However, if this operation is performed with binary addition, 10_{16} results:

```
    0 0 0 0    1 0 0 0
 +  0 0 0 0    1 0 0 0
    0 0 0 1    0 0 0 0    Digit Carry = 1
```

The DCA detects the digit carry and adds 0110_2 to the least significant digit to get the correct 16_{16}.

DCS

DECIMAL CORRECT SUBTRACTION

DCS

Format: **DCS** **G**$_s$

0	1	2	3	4	5	6	7	8	9	10 11	12 13 14 15	
0	0	1	0	1	1	0	0	0	1	T$_s$	S	(2C——)

Operation: The byte addressed by G$_s$ is corrected according to the table given in *Figure 6-10.* This instruction is a processor defined extended operation with n = 1, so that the sequence of events described under extended operation will occur in executing this instruction.

Status Bits Affected: **LGT, AGT, EQ, C, P, and DC**

Example: **DCS** **3**

This instruction would cause the most significant byte of register 3 to be corrected in accordance with the truth table of *Figure 6-10.*

Application: As in the DCA instruction, this instruction extends the 9940 capability to include decimal subtraction. The programmer first performs binary subtraction on bytes (the SB instruction) and then immediately performs the DCS operation on the result byte to correct the result so that it is within the BCD code range 0000$_2$ through 1001$_2$.

0			7	
	X	:	Y	
	MSB		LSB	

} 8-BIT BYTE CONTAINING RESULT OF BINARY ADD OR SUBTRACT OF 2 BCD DIGITS

BYTE BEFORE EXECUTION				BYTE AFTER DCA				BYTE AFTER DCS			
C	X	DC	Y	C	X	DC	Y	C	X	DC	Y
0	X<10	0	Y<10	0	X	0	Y	—	—	—	—
0	X<10	1	Y<10	0	X	0	Y+6	—	—	—	—
0	X<9	0	Y≥10	0	X+1	1	Y+6	—	—	—	—
1	X<10	0	Y<10	1	X+6	0	Y	—	—	—	—
1	X<10	1	Y<10	1	X+6	0	Y16	—	—	—	—
1	X<10	0	Y≥10	1	X+7	1	Y+6	—	—	—	—
0	X≥10	0	Y<10	1	X+6	0	Y	—	—	—	—
0	Z≥10	1	Y<10	1	X+6	0	Y+6	—	—	—	—
0	X≥9	0	Y≥10	1	X+7	1	Y+6	—	—	—	—
0	X	0	Y	—	—	—	—	0	X+10	1	Y+10
0	X	1	Y	—	—	—	—	0	X+10	0	Y
1	X	0	Y	—	—	—	—	1	X	1	Y+10
1	X	1	Y	—	—	—	—	1	X	0	Y

Figure 6-10. *Result of DCA and DCS Instructions of the 9940.*

CHAPTER 7

Program Development: Software Commands— Descriptions and Formats

INTRODUCTION

The purpose of this chapter is to provide reference data for the various software development systems available for the 9900 family of microprocessors and microcomputers.

Table 7-1 lists the sections in the chapter. One or more cards are made for those sections marked with a bullet. The section on Assembly Language programming describes the basic format for coding instructions and assembler directives. It is a general topic, applicable to all of the programming systems.

The 9900 reference card will come in handy for product design and programming activities for any of the processors. Explanation of the terms, mnemonics instruction execution rules, etc. can be found in Chapters 4, 5, and 6.

The complete TM 990/402 Line-by-Line Assembler User's Guide is included because this EPROM resident software is used in Chapter 8. It should serve as an illustration of the need for some form of an assembler in writing even the simplest programs. Contrast the programming efforts of Chapter 3 with the programming efforts for the extended applications of Chapter 8, and you will appreciate the power of this LBL assembler.

Reference material for the other programming systems is in the form of lists of commands and their syntax. These pages are not stand-alone documents. Software documentation is supplied with each of the programming systems and is required for full explanations of the commands and their use. Experienced designers always need assistance in recalling exact command mnemonics and their formats. Thus, this chapter supports you in any programming environment by appropriate reminders.

Table 7-1

Assembly language programming and assembler directives
- 9900 Reference Data
TM 990/402 Line-by-Line Assembler
- TIBUG Monitor
- TM 990/302 Software Development board

- TXDS Commands for the FS 990 PDS
- AMPL Reference data
- POWER BASIC Commands
- Cross Support reference data
    Assembler
    Simulator
    Utilities

Assembly Language Programming: Formats and Directives

ASSEMBLY LANGUAGE PROGRAMMING

An assembly language is a computer oriented language for writing programs. The TMS9900 recognizes instructions in the form of 16 bit (or longer) binary numbers, called instruction or operation codes (Opcodes). Programs could be written directly in these binary codes, but it is a tedious effort, requiring frequent reference to code tables. It is simpler to use names for the instructions, and write the programs as a sequence of these easily recognizable names (called mnemonics). Then, once the program is written in mnemonic or assembly language form, it can be converted to the corresponding binary coded form (machine language form). The assembler programs described here indicate parts of PX9ASM, TXMIRA and SDSMAC, which operate on cassette, floppy disc, and moving head disc systems respectively. Several other assemblers are available from TI which provide fewer features, but operate with much smaller memory requirements.

ASSEMBLY LANGUAGE APPLICATION

The assembly language programming and program verification through simulation or execution are the main elements involved in developing microprocessor programs. The overall program development effort consists of the following steps:

- Define the problem.
- Flowchart the solution to the problem.
- Write the assembly language program for the flowchart.
- Execute the Assembler to generate the machine code.
- Correct any format errors indicated by the Assembler.
- Execute the corrected machine code program on a TMS9900 computer or on a Simulator to verify program operation.

This program development sequence is defined in flowchart form in *Figure 7-1.*

ASSEMBLY LANGUAGE FORMATS

The general assembly language source statements consists of four fields as follows:

LABEL   MNEMONIC   OPERANDS   COMMENT

The first three fields must occur within the first 60 character positions of the source record. At least one blank must be inserted between fields.

Label Field

The label consists of from one to six characters, beginning with an alphabetic character in character position one of the source record. The label field is terminated by at least one blank. When the assembler encounters a label in an instruction it assigns the current value of the location counter to the label symbol. This is the value associated with the label symbol and is the address of the instruction in memory. If a label is not used, character position 1 must be a blank.

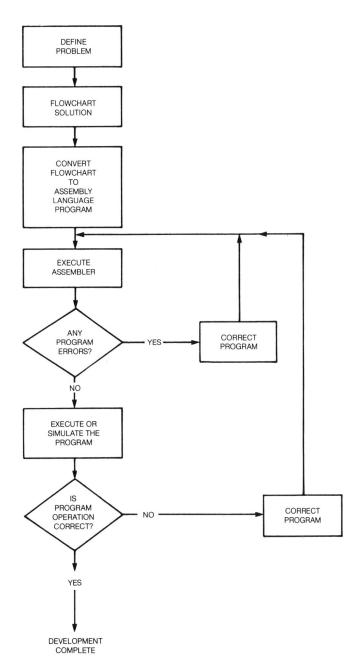

Figure 7-1. Program Development Flowchart

Mnemonic or Opcode Field

This field contains the mnemonic code of one of the instructions, one of the assembly language directives, or a symbol representing one of the program defined operations. This field begins after the last blank following the label field. Examples of instruction mnemonics include A for addition and MOV for data movement. The mnemonic field is required since it identifies which operation is to be performed.

Operands Field

The operands specify the memory locations of the data to be used by the instruction. This field begins following the last blank that follows the mnemonic field. The memory locations can be specified by using constants, symbols, or expressions, to describe one of several addressing modes available.

Comment Field

Comments can be entered after the last blank that follows the operands field. If the first character position of the source statement contains an asterisk (*), the entire source statement is a comment. Comments are listed in the source portion of the Assembler listing, but have no affect on the object code.

TERMS AND SYMBOLS

Symbols are used in the label field, the operator field, and the operand field. A symbol is a string of alphanumeric characters, beginning with an alphabetic character.
Terms are used in the operand fields of instructions and assembler directives. A term is a decimal or hexadecimal constant, an absolute assembly-time constant, or a label having an absolute value. Expressions can also be used in the operand fields of instructions and assembler directives.

Constants

Constants can be decimal integers (written as a string of numerals) in the range of $-32,768$ to $+65,535$. For example:

> 257

Constants can also be hexadecimal integers (a string of hexadecimal digits preceded by $>$). For example:

> >09AF

ASCII character constants can be used by enclosing the desired character string in single quotes. For example:

> 'DX'

Throughout this book the subscript 16 is used to denote base 16 numbers. For example, the hexadecimal number 09AF is written $09AF_{16}$.

Symbols

Symbols must begin with an alphabetic character and contain no blanks. Only the first six characters of a symbol are processed by the Assembler.

The Assembler predefines the dollar sign ($) to represent the current location in the program. The symbols R0 through R15 are used to represent workspace registers 0 through 15, respectively.

A given symbol can be used as a label only once, since it is the symbolic name of the address of the instruction. Symbols defined with the DXOP directive are used in the OPCODE field. Any symbol in the OPERANDS field must have been used as a label or defined by a REF directive.

Expressions

Expressions are used in the OPERANDS fields of assembly language statements. An expression is a constant, a symbol, or a series of constants and symbols separated by the following arithmetic operators:

+ addition
− subtraction
* multiplication
/ division

Unary minus is performed first and then the expression is evaluated from left to right. A unary minus is a minus sign (negation) in front of a number or a symbol.

The expression must not contain any imbedded blanks or extended operation defined (DXOP directive) symbols.

The multiplication and division operations must be used on absolute code symbols. The result of evaluating the expression up to the multiplication or division operator must be an absolute value. There must not be more than one more relocatable symbol added to an expression than are subtracted from it.

The following are examples of valid expressions:

BLUE + 1	The sum of the value of symbol BLUE plus 1.
GREEN − 4	The result of subtracting 4 from the value of symbol GREEN.
2*16 + RED	The sum of 32 and the value of symbol RED.
440/2 − RED	220 minus the value of symbol RED.

ASSEMBLER DIRECTIVES

GENERAL INFORMATION

The assembler directives are used to assign values to program symbolic names, address locations, and data. There are directives to set up linkage between program modules and to control output format, titles, and listings.

The assembler directives take the general form of:

LABEL   DIRECTIVE   EXPRESSION   COMMENT

The LABEL field begins in column one and extends to the first blank. It is optional on all directives except the EQU directive which requires a label. There is no label in the OPTION directive. When no label is present, the first character position in the field must be a blank. When a label is used (except in an EQU directive) the label is assigned the current value of the location counter.

The two required directives are:

IDT	Assign a name to the program
END	Terminate assembly

The most commonly used optional directives are:

EQU	Assign a value to a label or a data name.
RORG	Relocatable Origin
BYTE	Assign values to successive bytes of memory
DATA	Assign 16 bit values to successive memory words
TEXT	Assign ASCII values to successive bytes of memory

Other directives include:

AORG	Absolute (non-relocatable) Origin
DORG	Dummy Origin
BSS	Define bytes of storage beginning with symbol
BES	Define bytes of storage space ending with symbol
DXOP	Define an extended operation
NOP	No operation Pseudo-instruction
RT	Return from subroutine Pseudo-instruction
PAGE	Skip to new page before continuing listing
TITL	Define title for page headings
LIST	Allows listing of source statements
UNL	Prevents listing of source statements
OPTION	Selects output option to be used
DEF	Define symbol for external reference
REF	Reference to an external source

REQUIRED DIRECTIVES

Two directives must be supplied to identify the beginning and end of the assembly language program. The IDT directive must be the first statement and the END directive must be the last statement in the assembly language program.

Program Identifier   IDT

This directive assigns a name to the program and must precede any directive that generates object code. The basic format is:

    IDT   'Name'

The name is the program name consisting of up to 8 characters. As an example, if a program is to be named Convert, the basic directive would be:

    IDT   'CONVERT'

The name is printed only when the directive is printed in the source listing.

Program End   END

This directive terminates the assembly. Any source statement following this directive is ignored. The basic format is:

    END

INITIALIZATION DIRECTIVES

These directives are used to establish values for program symbols and constants.

Define Assembly-Time Constant   EQU

Equate is used to assign values to program symbols. The symbol to be defined is placed in the label field and the value or expression is placed in the Expression field:

    Symbol   EQU   Expression

The symbol can represent an address or a program parameter. This directive allows the program to be written in general symbolic form. The equate directive is used to set up the symbol values for a specific program application.

The following are examples of the use of the Equate directive:

```
TIME    EQU    HOURS + 5
N       EQU    8
VAR     EQU    > 8000
```

BYTE
DATA
TEXT

Initialize Memory

These directives provide for initialization of successive 8 bit bytes of memory with numerical data (BYTE directive) or with ASCII character codes (TEXT directive). The DATA directive provides for the initialization of successive 16 bit words with numerical data.

The formats are the same for all three directives:

    Directive   Expression-list

The Label and Comment are optional. The expression or value list contains the data entries for the 8 bit bytes (BYTE directive), or the 16 bit words (DATA directive), or a character string enclosed in quotes (TEXT directive).

Examples of the use and effects of these directives are shown in *Figure 7-2.*

PROGRAM LOCATION DIRECTIVES

These directives affect the location counter by causing the instructions to be located in specified areas of memory.

AORG
RORG
DORG

Origin Directives

These directives set the address of the next instruction to the value listed in the expression field of the directive:

    Directive   Expression

The expression field is required on all except the RORG directive. It is a value or an expression (containing only previously defined symbols). This value is the address of the next instruction and is the value that is assigned to the label (if any) and to the location counter. The AORG and DORG expressions must result in an absolute value and contain no character constants.

Example Directives:

   KONS   BYTE $>10, -1$, 'A', 'B', N + 3

   WD1   DATA $>01FF, 3200, -'AF', 8, N + >1000$

   MSG1   TEXT 'EXAMPLE'

AFFECTS ON MEMORY LOCATION	MEMORY DATA: DIRECTIVE ENTRY	RESULTING DATA (BINARY FORM)				RESULTING DATA (HEXADECIMAL)
KONS	$>10,-1$	0001	0000	1111	1111	1 0FF
KONS + 2	'A', 'B'	0100	0001	0100	0010	.4142
KNOS + 4	N + 3	0000	1011	X	X	0B--
.	.	.	.	.	.	.
.	.	.	.	.	.	.
WD1	$>01FF$	0000	0001	1111	1111	01FF
WD1 + 2	3200	0000	1100	1000	0000	0C80
WD1 + 4	$-'AF'$	1011	1110	1011	1010	BEBA
WD1 + 6	8	0000	0000	0000	1000	0008
WD1 + 8	N + >1000	0001	0000	0000	1000	1008
.	.	.	.	.	.	.
.	.	.	.	.	.	.
.	.	.	.	.	.	.
MSG1	'EX'	0100	0101	0101	1000	4558
MSG1 + 2	'AM'	0100	0001	0101	1101	414D
MSG1 + 4	'PL'	0101	0000	0100	1100	504C
MSG1 + 6	'E'	0100	0101	X	X	4E--

XX (--) is original unaltered data in this location. N is assumed to be previously defined as 8.

Figure 7-2. Initialization Directive Examples

The AORG directive causes this value to be absolute and fixed. For example:

   AORG $> 1000 + X$

If X has been previously defined to have an absolute value of 6, the next instruction would be unalterably located at the address 1006_{16}. If a label had been included, it would have been assigned this same value.

The RORG directive causes this value to be relative or relocatable so that subsequent operations by the assembler or simulator can relocate the block of instructions to any desired area of memory. Thus, a relocatable block of instructions occupying memory locations 1000_{16} to 1020_{16} could be moved by subsequent simulator (or other software) operations to locations 2000_{16} to 2020_{16}. An example RORG statement is:

   SEG1   RORG > 1000

This directive would cause SEG1 and the value of the location counter (address of the next instruction) to be set to 1000_{16}. This and all subsequent locations are relocatable.

> SEG2   RORG

This directive would cause subsequent instructions to be at relocatable addresses. SEG2 and the address of the next instruction would be set to the value of the location counter.

The DORG directive causes the instructions to be listed but the assembler does not generate object code that can be passed on to simulators or other subsystems. However, symbols defined in the dummy section would then be legitimate symbols for use in the AORG or RORG program sections. For example:

> DORG 0

The labels with the subsequent dummy section of instructions will be assigned values relative to the start of the section (the instruction immediately following this directive). No object code would be generated for this section.

An RORG directive is used after a DORG or AORG section to cause the subsequent instructions to be relocatable object code. If no origin directives are included in the assembly language program, all object code is relocatable starting at (referenced to) an address of 0.

BES
BSS

STORAGE ALLOCATION DIRECTIVES

These directives reserve a block of memory (range of addresses) for data storage by advancing the location counter by the amount specified in the expression field. Thus, the instruction after the directive will be at an address equal to the expression value plus the address of the instruction just before the directive.

Basic Formats:

> BES   Expression
>
> BSS   Expression

If a label is included in the BSS directive it is assigned the value of the location counter at the *first byte* if the storage block. If the label is included in the BES directive it is assigned the value of the location counter for the instruction *after* the block.

The Expression designates the number of bytes to be reserved for storage. It is a value or an expression containing no character constants. Expressions must contain only previously defined symbols and result in an absolute value.

Examples:

    BUFF1 BES >10

A 16 byte buffer is provided. Had the location counter contained the value 100_{16} (FF_{16} was the address of the previous instruction), the new value of the location counter would be 110_{16}, and this would be the value assigned to the symbol BUFF1. The next instruction after the buffer would be at address 110_{16}.

    BUFF2 BSS 20

If the previous instruction is located at FF_{16}, BUFF2 will be assigned the value 100_{16}, and the next instruction will be located at 114_{16}. A 20 byte area of storage with addresses 100_{16} through 113_{16} has been reserved.

Word Boundary   **EVEN**

This directive causes the location counter to be set to the next even address (beginning of the next word) if it currently contains an odd address. The basic format is:

    EVEN

The label is assigned the value of the location counter prior to the EVEN directive.

PROGRAM LISTING CONTROL DIRECTIVES

These directives control the printer, titling, and listing provided by the assembler.

Output Options   **OPTION**

The basic format of this directive is:
    OPTION   Keyword-list

No label is permitted. The keywords control the listing as follows:'

Keyword	*Listing*
XREF	Print a cross reference listing.
OBJ	Print a hexadecimal listing of the object code.
SYMT	Print a symbol table with the object code.

Example:

OPTION XREF,SYMT
Print a cross reference listing and the symbol table with the object code.

Advance Page

PAGE

This directive causes the assembly listing to continue at the top of the next page. The basic format is:

PAGE

Page Title

TITL

This directive specifies the title to be printed at the top of each page of the assembler listing. The basic format is:

TITL   'String'

The String is the title enclosed in single quotes. For example:

TITL   'REPORT GENERATOR'

LIST
UNL

Source Listing Control

These directives control the printing of the source listing. UNL inhibits the printing of the source listing: LIST restores the listing. The basic formats are:

UNL

LIST

Extended Operation Definition

DXOP

This directive names an extended operation. Its format is:

DXOP   SYMBOL, Term

The symbol is the desired name of the extended operation. Term is the corresponding number of the extended operation. For example:

DXOP   DADD,13

defines DADD as extended operation 13. Once DADD has been so defined, it can be used as the name of a new operation, just as if it were one of the standard instruction mnemonics.

Program Linkage Directives

These directives enable program modules to be assembled separately and then integrated into an executable program.

External Definition   DEF

This directive makes one or more symbols available to other programs for reference. Its basic format is:

      DEF   Symbol-list

Symbol-list contains the symbols to be defined by the program being assembled. For example:

      DEF   ENTER, ANS

causes the assembler to include the Symbols ENTER and ANS in the object code so that they are available to other programs. When DEF does not precede the source statements that contain the symbols, the assembler identifies the symbols as multi-defined symbols.

External Reference   REF

This directive provides access to symbols defined in other programs. The basic format is:

      REF   Symbol-list

The Symbol-list contains the symbols to be included in the object code and used in the operand fields of subsequent source statements. For example:

      REF   ARG1,ARG2

causes the symbols ARG1 and ARG2 to be included in the object code so that the corresponding address can be obtained from other programs.

Note: If a REF symbol is the first operand of a DATA directive causing the value of the symbol to be in 0 absolute location, the symbol will not be linked correctly in location 0.

ASSEMBLER OUTPUT

INTRODUCTION

The types of information provided by Assemblers include:

Source Listing	— Shows the source statements and the resulting object code.
Error Messages	— Errors in the assembly language program are indicated.
Cross Reference	— Summarizes the label definitions and program references.
Object Code	— Shows the object code in a tagged record format to be passed on to a computer or simulator for execution.

SOURCE LISTING

Assemblers produce a source listing showing the source statements and the resulting object code. A typical listing is shown in *Figure 7-3.*

0229			*		
0230			*		DEMONSTRATE EXTERNAL REFERENCE LINKING
0231			*		
0232				REF	EXTR
0233	028C			RORG	
0234	028C	C820		MOV	@EXTR, @EXTR
	028E	0000			
	0290	028E'			
0235	0292	28E0		XDR	@EXTR, 3
	0294	0290'			
0236	B000			AORG	>B000
0237	B000	3220		LDCR	@EXTR, 8
	B002	0294'			
0238	B004	0420		BLWP	@EXTR
	B006	B002			
0239	B008	0223		AI	3, EXTR
	B00A	B006			
0240	B00C	38A0		MPY	@EXTR, 2
	B00E	B00A			
0241	0296			RORG	
0242	0296	C820		MOV	@EXTR, @EXTR
	0298	B00E			
	029A	0298'			
0243	029C	28E0		XOR	@EXTR, 3
	029E	029A'			
0244	C000			AORG	>C000
0245.	C000	3220		LDCR	@EXTR, 8
	C002	029E'			
0246	C004	0420		BLWP	@EXTR
	C006	C002			
0247	C008	0223		AI	3, EXTR
	C00A	C006			
0248	C00C	38A0		MPY	@EXTR, 2
	C00E	C00A			

Figure 7-3. Typical Source Listing.

The first line available in a listing is the title line which will be blank unless a TITL directive has been used. After this line, a line for each source statement is printed. For example:

0018	0156	C820	MOV	@INIT + 3,@3
	0158	012B'		
	015A	0003		

In this case the source statement:

    MOV   @INIT + 3,@3

produces 3 lines of object code. The source statement number 18 applies to the entire 3 line entry. Each line has its own location counter value (0156, 0158, and 015A). C820 is the OPCODE for MOV with symbolic memory addressing.

012B' is the value for INIT + 3. 0003 is for the direct address 3. The apostrophe (') after 012B indicates this address is program-relocatable. Source statements are numbered sequentially, whether they are listed or not (listing could be prevented by using the UNLIST directive).

9900
Reference Data

INSTRUCTION FORMAT

FORMAT (USE)	0	1	2	3	4	5	6	7	8	9	10	11	12	13	14	15
1 (ARITH)	OP CODE		B	T_D			D				T_S		S			
2 (JUMP)										SIGNED DISPLACEMENT*						
3 (LOGICAL)	OP CODE					D			T_S		S					
4 (CRU)	OP CODE				C				T_S		S					
5 (SHIFT)	OP CODE						C				W					
6 (PROGRAM)	OP CODE							T_S		S						
7 (CONTROL)	OP CODE								NOT USED							
	OP CODE						NU		W							
8 (IMMEDIATE)	IMMEDIATE VALUE															
9 (MPY,DIV,XOP)	OP CODE					D			T_S		S					

KEY

B = BYTE INDICATOR
  (1 = BYTE, 0 = WORD)
T_D = D ADDR, MODIFICATION
D = DESTINATION ADDR.
T_S = ADDR. MODIFICATION

S = SOURCE ADDR.
C = XFR OR SHIFT LENGTH (COUNT)
W = WORKSPACE REGISTER NO.
* = SIGNED DISPLACEMENT OF − 128 TO + 127 WORDS
NU = NOT USED

T_D / T_S FIELD

CODE		EFFECTIVE ADDRESS	MNEMONIC
00:	REGISTER	WP + 2 · [S OR D]	Rn
01:	INDIRECT	(WP + 2 · [S OR D])	*Rn
10:	INDEXED (S OR D ≠ 0)	(WP + 2 · [S OR D]) + (PC); PC ← PC + 2	NUM (Rn)
10:	SYMBOLIC (DIRECT, S OR D = 0)	(PC); PC ← PC + 2	NUM
11:	INDIRECT WITH AUTO INCREMENT	(WP + 2 · [S OR D]); INCREMENT EFF. ADDR.	*Rn+

STATUS REGISTER

0	1	2	3	4	5	6	7	11	12	15
L>	A>	=	C	O	P	X	RESERVED		INTERRUPT MASK	

0 — LOGICAL GREATER THAN
1 — ARITHMETIC GREATER THAN
2 — EQUAL/TB INDICATOR
3 — CARRY FROM MSB
4 — OVERFLOW

5 — PARITY (ODD NO. OF BITS SET)
6 — XOP IN PROGRESS

INTERRUPT MASK
F = ALL INTERRUPTS ENABLED
0 = ONLY LEVEL 0 ENABLED

INTERRUPTS

TRAP ADDR	WP
TRAP ADDR + 2	PC

LEVEL	ID	TRAP ADDR	LEVEL	ID	TRAP ADDR
0	RESET	0000	8	EXTERNAL	0020
1	EXTERNAL	0004	9	EXTERNAL	0024
2	EXTERNAL	0008	10	EXTERNAL	0028
3	EXTERNAL	000C	11	EXTERNAL	002C
4	EXTERNAL	0010	12	EXTERNAL	0030
5	EXTERNAL	0014	13	EXTERNAL	0034
6	EXTERNAL	0018	14	EXTERNAL	0038
7	EXTERNAL	001C	15	EXTERNAL	003C

NOTES: 1) XOP VECTORS 0—15 OCCUPY MEMORY LOCATIONS 0040-007C
2) LOAD VECTOR OCCUPIES MEMORY LOCATIONS FFFC–FFFF

BLWP TRANSFERS	RTWP TRANSFERS	BL TRANSFER	XOP TRANSFER
WP → NEW W13	CURRENT W13 → WP	PC → W11	EFF. ADDR. → NEW W11
PC → NEW W14	CURRENT W14 → PC		WP → NEW W13
ST → NEW W15	CURRENT W15 → ST		PC → NEW W14
			ST → NEW W15
			1 → ST6

INSTRUCTIONS BY MNEMONIC

MNEMONIC	OP CODE	FORMAT	RESULT COMPARED TO ZERO	STATUS AFFECTED	INSTRUCTIONS
A	A000	1	Y	0-4	ADD(WORD)
AB	B000	1	Y	0-5	ADD(BYTE)
ABS	0740	6	Y	0-4	ABSOLUTE VALUE
AI	0220	8	Y	0-4	ADD IMMEDIATE
ANDI	0240	8	Y	0-2	AND IMMEDIATE
B	0440	6	N	—	BRANCH
BL	0680	6	N	—	BRANCH AND LINK (W11)
BLWP	0400	6	N	—	BRANCH LOAD WORKSPACE POINTER
C	8000	1	N	0-2	COMPARE (WORD)
CB	9000	1	N	0-2,5	COMPARE (BYTE)
CI	0280	8	N	0-2	COMPARE IMMEDIATE
CKOF	03C0	7	N	—	EXTERNAL CONTROL
CKON	03A0	7	N	—	EXTERNAL CONTROL
CLR	04C0	6	N	—	CLEAR OPERAND
COC	2000	3	N	2	COMPARE ONES CORRESPONDING
CZC	2400	3	N	2	COMPARE ZEROES CORRESPONDING
DEC	0600	6	Y	0-4	DECREMENT (BY ONE)
DECT	0640	6	Y	0-4	DECREMENT (BY TWO)
DIV	3C00	9	N	4	DIVIDE
IDLE	0340	7	N	—	COMPUTER IDLE
INC	0580	6	Y	0-4	INCREMENT (BY ONE)
INCT	05C0	6	Y	0-4	INCREMENT (BY TWO)
INV	0540	6	Y	0-2	INVERT (ONES COMPLEMENT)
JEQ	1300	2	N	—	JUMP EQUAL (ST2 = 1)

INSTRUCTIONS BY MNEMONIC

JGT	1500	2	N	—	JUMP GREATER THAN (ST1 = 1)
JH	1B00	2	N	—	JUMP HIGH (STO = 1 AND ST2 = 0)
JHE	1400	2	N	—	JUMP HIGH OR EQUAL (STO OR ST2 = 1)
JL	1A00	2	N	—	JUMP LOW (STO AND ST2 = 0)
JLE	1200	2	N	—	JUMP LOW OR EQUAL (STO = 0 OR ST2 = 1)
JLT	1100	2	N	—	JUMP LESS THAN (ST1 AND ST2 = 0)
JMP	1000	2	N	—	JUMP UNCONDITIONAL
JNC	1700	2	N	—	JUMP NO CARRY (ST3 = 0)
JNE	1600	2	N	—	JUMP NOT EQUAL (ST2 = 0)
JNO	1900	2	N	—	JUMP NO OVERFLOW (ST4 = 0)
JOC	1800	2	N	—	JUMP ON CARRY (ST3 = 1)
JOP	1C00	2	N	—	JUMP ODD PARITY (ST5 = 1)
LDCR	3000	4	Y	0-2,5	LOAD CRU
LI	0200	8	N	0-2	LOAD IMMEDIATE
LIMI	0300	8	N	12-15	LOAD IMMEDIATE TO INTERRUPT MASK
LREX	03E0	7	N	12-15	EXTERNAL CONTROL
LWPI	02E0	8	N	—	LOAD IMMEDIATE TO WORKSPACE POINTER
MOV	C000	1	Y	0-2	MOVE (WORD)
MOVB	D000	1	Y	0-2,5	MOVE (BYTE)
MPY	3800	9	N	—	MULTIPLY
NEG	0500	6	Y	0-4	NEGATE (TWO'S COMPLEMENT)
ORI	0260	8	Y	0-2	OR IMMEDIATE
RSET	0360	7	N	12-15	EXTERNAL CONTROL
RTWP	0380	7	N	0-6,12-15	RETURN WORKSPACE POINTER
S	6000	1	Y	0-4	SUBTRACT (WORD)
SB	7000	1	Y	0-5	SUBTRACT (BYTE)
SBO	1D00	2	N	—	SET CRU BIT TO ONE
SBZ	1E00	2	N	—	SET CRU BIT TO ZERO
SETO	0700	6	N	—	SET ONES
SLA	0A00	5	Y	0-4	SHIFT LEFT (ZERO FILL)
SOC	E000	1	Y	0-2	SET ONES CORRESPONDING (WORD)
SOCB	F000	1	Y	0-2,5	SET ONES CORRESPONDING (BYTE)
SRA	0800	5	Y	0-3	SHIFT RIGHT (MSB EXTENDED)
SRC	0800	5	Y	0-3	SHIFT RIGHT CIRCULAR
SRL	0900	5	Y	0-3	SHIFT RIGHT (LEADING ZERO FILL)
STCR	3400	4	Y	0-2,5	STORE FROM CRU
STST	02C0	8	N	—	STORE STATUS REGISTER
STWP	02A0	8	N	—	STORE WORKSPACE POINTER
SWPB	06C0	6	N	—	SWAP BYTES
SZC	4000	1	Y	0-2	SET ZEROES CORRESPONDING (WORD)
SZCB	5000	1	Y	0-2,5	SET ZEROS CORRESPONDING (BYTE)
TB	1F00	2	N	2	TEST CRU BIT
X	0480	6	N	—	EXECUTE
XOP	2C00	9	N	6	EXTENDED OPERATION
XOR	2800	3	Y	0-2	EXCLUSIVE OR
DCA	2C00	9	N	0-3,5,7	DECIMAL CORRECT ADD
DCS	2C00	9	N	0-3,5,7	DECIMAL CORRECT SUB
LIIM	2C00	9	N	14,15	LOAD INTERRUPT MASK

ILLEGAL OP CODES 0000-01FF;0320-033F;0780-07FF;0C00-0FFF

INSTRUCTIONS BY OP CODE

OP CODE	MNEMONIC	OP CODE	MNEMONIC
0000-01FF	ILLEGAL	1000	JMP
0200	LI	1100	JLT
0220	AI	1200	JLE
0240	ANDI	1300	JEQ
0260	ORI	1400	JHE
02A0	CI	1500	JGT
0240	STWP	1600	JNE
02C0	STST	1700	JNC
02E0	LWPI	1800	JOC
0300	LIMI	1900	JNO
0320-033F	ILLEGAL	1A00	JL
0340	IDLE	1B00	JH
0360	RSET	1C00	JOP
0380	RTWP	1D00	SBO
03A0	CKON	1E00	SBZ
03C0	CKOF	1F00	TB
03E0	LREX	2000	COC
0400	BLWP	2400	CZC
0440	B	2800	XOR
0480	X	2C00	XOP
04C0	CLR	3000	LDCR
0500	NEG	3400	STCR
0540	INV	3800	MPY
0580	INC	3C00	DIV
05C0	INCT	4000	SZC
0600	DEC	5000	SZCB
0640	DECT	6000	S
0680	BL	7000	SB
06C0	SWPB	8000	C
0700	SETO	9000	CB
0740	ABS	A000	A
0780-07FF	ILLEGAL	B000	AB
0800	SRA	C000	MOV
0900	SRL	D000	MOVB
0A00	SLA	E000	SOC
0B00	SRC	F000	SOCB
0C00	ILLEGAL		

PSEUDO-INSTRUCTIONS

MNEMONIC	PSEUDO-INSTRUCTIONS	CODE GENERATED
NOP	NO OPERATION	1000
RT	RETURN	045B

PIN DESCRIPTIONS

PIN #	FUNCTION	PIN #	FUNCTION	PIN #	FUNCTION
1	V_{BB}	23	A1	44	D3
2	V_{CC}	24	A0	45	D4
3	WAIT	25	$\phi4$	46	D5
4	$\overline{LOAD}$	26	V_{SS}	47	D6
5	HOLDA	27	V_{DD}	48	D7
6	$\overline{RESET}$	28	$\phi3$	49	D8
7	IAQ	29	DBIN	50	D9
8	$\phi1$	30	CRUOUT	51	D10
9	$\phi2$	31	CRUIN	52	D11
10	A14	32	$\overline{INTREQ}$	53	D12
11	A13	33	IC3	54	D13
12	A12	34	IC2	55	D14
13	A11	35	IC1	56	D15
14	A10	36	IC0	57	NC
15	A9	37	NC	58	NC
16	A8	38	NC	59	NC
17	A7	39	NC	60	CRUCLK
18	A6	40	NC	61	$\overline{WE}$
19	A5	41	D0	62	READY
20	A4	42	D1	63	$\overline{MEMEN}$
21	A3	43	D2	64	$\overline{HOLD}$
22	A2				

ASSEMBLER DIRECTIVES

MNEMONIC	DIRECTIVE
AORG	ABSOLUTE ORIGIN
BES	BLOCK ENDING WITH SYMBOL
BSS	BLOCK STARTING WITH SYMBOL
BYTE	INITIALIZE BYTE
DATA	INITIALIZE WORD
DEF	EXTERNAL DEFINITION
DORG	DUMMY ORIGIN
DXOP	DEFINE EXTENDED OPERATION
END	PROGRAM END
EQU	DEFINITE ASSEMBLY — TIME CONSTANT
EVEN	WORD BOUNDARY
IDT	PROGRAM IDENTIFIER
LIST	LIST SOURCE
PAGE	PAGE EJECT
REF	EXTERNAL REFERENCE
RORG	RELOCATABLE ORIGIN
TEXT	INITIALIZE TEXT
TITL	PAGE TITLE
UNL	NO SOURCE LIST

USASCII/HOLLERITH CHARACTER CODE

CHAR.	USASCII (HEXADECIMAL)	HOLLERITH*	CHAR.	USASCII (HEXADECIMAL)	HOLLERITH*
NUL	00		3	33	3
SOH	01		4	34	4
STX	02		5	35	5
ETX	03		6	36	6
EOT	04		7	37	7
ENQ	05		8	38	8
ACK	06		9	39	9
BEL	07		:	3A	2-8
BS	08		;	3B	11-6-8
HT	09		<	3C	12-4-8
LF	0A		=	3D	6-8
VT	0B		>	3E	0-6-8
FF	0C		?	3F	0-7-8
CR	0D		@	40	4-8
S0	0E		A/a	41/61	12-1
SI	0F		B/b	42/62	12-2
DLE	10		C/c	43/63	12-3
DC1	11		D/d	44/64	12-4
DC2	12		E/e	45/64	12-5
DC3	13		F/f	46/66	12-6
DC4	14		G/g	47/67	12-7
NAK	15		H/h	48/68	12-8
SYN	16		I/i	49/69	12-9
ETB	17		J/j	4A/6A	11-1
CAN	18		K/k	4B/6B	11-2
EM	19		L/l	4C/6C	11-3
SUB	1A		M/m	4D/6D	11-4
ESC	1B		N/n	4E/6E	11-5
FS	1C		O/o	4F/6F	11-6
GS	1D		P/p	50/70	11-7
RS	1E		Q/q	51/71	11-8
US	1F		R/r	52/72	11-9
SPACE	20	BLANK	S/s	53/73	0-2
!	21	11-2-8	T/t	54/74	0-3
''	22	7-8	U/u	55/75	0-4
#	23	3-8	V/v	56/76	0-5
$	24	11-3-8	W/w	57/77	0-6
%	25	0-4-8	X/x	58/78	0-7
&	26	12	Y/y	59/79	0-8
'	27	5-8	Z/z	5A/7A	0-9
(	28	12-5-8	[	5B	12-2-8
)	29	11-5-8	\	5C	
*	2A	11-4-8	]	5D	12-7-8
+	2B	12-6-8	∧	5E	11-7-8
,	2C	0-3-8	—	SF	0-5-8
-	2D	11	`	60	
.	2E	12-3-8	{	7B	
/	2F	0-1	>	7C	
0	30	0	}	7D	
1	31	1	~	7E	
2	32	2	DEL	7F	

*PUNCH IN CARD ROWS

HEX-DECIMAL TABLE

EVEN BYTE				ODD BYTE			
HEX	DEC	HEX	DEC	HEX	DEC	HEX	DEC
0	0	0	0	0	0	0	0
1	4,096	1	256	1	16	1	1
2	8,192	2	512	2	32	2	2
3	12,288	3	768	3	48	3	3
4	16,384	4	1,024	4	64	4	4
5	20,480	5	1,280	5	80	5	5
6	24,576	6	1,536	6	96	6	6
7	28,672	7	1,792	7	112	7	7
8	32,766	8	2,048	8	128	8	8
9	36,864	9	2,304	9	144	9	9
A	40,960	A	2,560	A	160	A	10
B	45,066	B	2,816	B	176	B	11
C	49,152	C	3,072	C	192	C	12
D	53,248	D	3,328	D	208	D	13
E	57,344	E	3,584	E	224	E	14
F	61,440	F	3,840	F	240	F	15

OBJECT RECORD FORMAT AND CODE

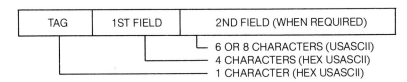

TAG	1ST FIELD	2ND FIELD (WHEN REQUIRED)

6 OR 8 CHARACTERS (USASCII)
4 CHARACTERS (HEX USASCII)
1 CHARACTER (HEX USASCII)

TAG	FIRST FIELD	SECOND FIELD	MEANING
0	LENGTH OF ALL RELOCATABLE CODE	PROGRAM ID (8-CHARACTER)	PROGRAM START
1	ADDRESS	(NOT USED)	ABSOLUTE ENTRY ADDRESS
2	ADDRESS	(NOT USED)	RELOCATABLE ENTRY ADDRESS
3	LOCATION OF LAST APPEARANCE OF SYMBOL	6 CHARACTER SYMBOL	EXTERNAL REFERENCE LAST USED IN RELOCATABLE CODE
4	LOCATION OF LAST APPEARANCE OF SYMBOL	6 CHARACTER SYMBOL	EXTERNAL REFERENCE LAST USED IN ABSOLUTE CODE
5	LOCATION	6 CHARACTER SYMBOL	RELOCATABLE EXTERNAL DEFINITION
6	LOCATION	6 CHARACTER SYMBOL	ABSOLUTE EXTERNAL DEFINITION
7	CHECKSUM FOR CURRENT RECORD	(NOT USED)	CHECKSUM
8	ANY VALUE	(NOT USED)	IGNORE CHECKSUM VALUE
9	LOAD ADDRESS	(NOT USED)	ABSOLUTE LOAD ADDRESS
A	LOAD SDDRESS	(NOT USED)	RELOCATABLE LOAD ADDRESS
B	DATA	(NOT USED)	ABSOLUTE DATA
C	DATA	(NOT USED)	RELOCATABLE DATA
D	LOAD BIAS	(NOT USED)	LOAD BIAS OR OFFSET (NOT A PART OF ASSEMBLER OUTPUT)
E			ILLEGAL
F	(NOT USED)	(NOT USED)	END OF RECORD

TM990/402
Line-by-Line
Assembler
User's Guide

GENERAL

The TM 990/402 Line-By-Line Assembler (LBLA) is a standalone program that assembles into object code the 69 instructions used by the TM 990/100M/101M/180M microcomputers. Comments can be a part of the source statement; however, assembler directives are not recognized. Assembler TM 990/402-1 consists of two EPROM's and supports the TM 990/100M microcomputer. TM 990/402-2 consists of one EPROM and supports the TM 990/180M microcomputer.

INSTALLATION

Remove the TMS 2708 chip(s) from the package and install as follows (see *Figure 1*):

(1) Turn off power to the TM 990/1XXM microcomputer.

(2) Place the chip(s) into the proper socket(s) as shown in *Figure 1*. The shaded components in *Figure 1* denote the LBLA EPROM's correctly placed in their sockets. The corresponding socket number (UXX number) is marked on the EPROM.

NOTES

1. Place the TMS 2708(s) into the socket(s) with pin 1 in the lower left corner as denoted by a 1 on the board and on the EPROM. Be careful to prevent bending of the pins.

2. Do not remove EPROM's containing the monitor as shown in *Figure 1*. The monitor is used by the assembler.

(3) Verify proper positioning in the sockets. Apply power to the microcomputer board.

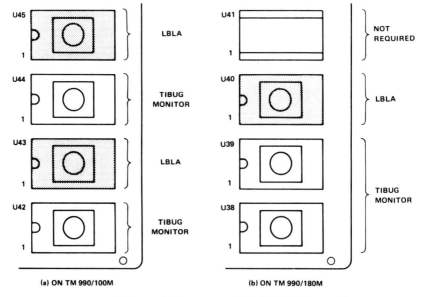

(a) ON TM 990/100M   (b) ON TM 990/180M

Figure 1. *Placement of TMS 2708 Eprom's*

OPERATION

SETUP

NOTE

The examples in this guide use memory addresses obtainable in RAM on the TM 990/
100M microcomputer. To exemplify the TM 990/180M addressing scheme, the reader
should substitute a 3 for the F in the most significant digit (left most) of a four-digit
memory address in the following examples (e.g., $3EE0_{16}$ for $FEE0_{16}$).

- With the Line-By-Line Assembler EPROMs installed, call up the monitor by pressing
the RESET switch in the upper left corner of the board and then pressing the A key at
the terminal.

- Invoke the R keyboard command and set the Program Counter (PC) to $09E6_{16}$. This is
the memory address entry point for the Line-By-Line Assembler.

- Invoke the E (execute) command. The assembler will execute and print the memory
address (M.A.) $FE00_{16}$ for the TM 990/100 or $3E00_{16}$ for the TM 990/180M. The
printhead will space to the assembly language opcode input column and wait for input
from the keyboard.

```
?R
W=0BA4
P=000F        9E6 ◄─────────── LBLA ENTRY ADDRESS
?E
FE00
```

INPUTS TO ASSEMBLER

The Line-By-Line Assembler accepts assembly language inputs from a terminal. As each
instruction is input, the assembler interprets it, places the resulting machine code in an
absolute address, and prints the machine code (in hexadecimal) next to its absolute address:

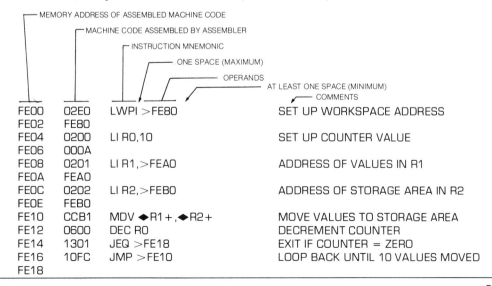

```
     ┌─ MEMORY ADDRESS OF ASSEMBLED MACHINE CODE
     │   ┌─ MACHINE CODE ASSEMBLED BY ASSEMBLER
     │   │   ┌─ INSTRUCTION MNEMONIC
     │   │   │      ┌─ ONE SPACE (MAXIMUM)
     │   │   │      │        ┌─ OPERANDS
     │   │   │      │        │      AT LEAST ONE SPACE (MINIMUM)
     │   │   │      │        │        ┌─ COMMENTS
FE00  02E0   LWPI >FE80               SET UP WORKSPACE ADDRESS
FE02  FE80
FE04  0200   LI R0,10                 SET UP COUNTER VALUE
FE06  000A
FE08  0201   LI R1,>FEA0              ADDRESS OF VALUES IN R1
FE0A  FEA0
FE0C  0202   LI R2,>FEB0              ADDRESS OF STORAGE AREA IN R2
FE0E  FEB0
FE10  CCB1   MDV ◆R1+,◆R2+            MOVE VALUES TO STORAGE AREA
FE12  0600   DEC R0                   DECREMENT COUNTER
FE14  1301   JEQ >FE18                EXIT IF COUNTER = ZERO
FE16  10FC   JMP >FE10                LOOP BACK UNTIL 10 VALUES MOVED
FE18
```

Use only one space between the mnemonic and the operand. If you use the comment field, use at least one space between the operand and comment. If no comment is used, complete the instruction with a space and carriage return. If a comment is used, only a carriage return is required.

No loader tags are created; code is loaded in contiguous memory addresses by the assembler. The location can be changed as desired (explained in paragraph 3.2.2). Labels cannot be used. Addressing is by byte displacement (jump instructions) or by absolute memory address.

NOTE

Be aware that the workspace for the TIBUG monitor begins in RAM at address $FFB0_{16}$ for the TM 990/100M and begins at address $3FB0_{16}$ for the TM 990/180M. Understand that assembled object code should not be entered at or above these addresses.

Program Preparation

Set up your program using flow charts with code written on a coding pad. Do not use assembler directives.

Changing Absolute Load Address

Code is located at the address written on the assembler output. When initialized, the assembler loads code contiguously starting at M.A. $FE00_{16}$ ($3E00_{16}$ for TM 990/180M). This address can be changed at any time during assembly by typing a slash (/) followed by the desired M.A.:

```
FE80    8081    C R1,R2              COMPARE VALUES
FE82    1301    JEQ >FE86            IF EQUAL, SKIP ERROR ROUTINE
FE84    06A0    BL @>FF20            OTHERWISE DO ERROR ROUTINE
FE86    FF20
FE88            /FF20        ◄──────── CHANGE ADDRESS
FF20    2FA0    XOP @>FF26,14        SEND ERROR MESSAGE (See TIBUG Monitor)
FF22    FF26
FF24    045B    B ◆R11               RETURN TO CALLING PROGRAM
FF26    0A0D    +>0A0D
FF28    4552    $ERROR FOUND
FF2A    524F
FF2C    5220
FF2E    464F
FF30    554E
FF32    4420
FF34    0000    +0000
FF36            /FE86        ◄─────── CHANGE ADDRESS
FE86
```

Note that this is similar to using an AORG (absolute origin) 990 assembler directive.

Entering Instructions

Any of the 69 instructions applicable to the TM 990/1XXM microcomputers can be interpreted by the Line-By-Line Assembler. The following apply:

(1) Place one space between instruction mnemonic and operand.

(2) Terminate entire instruction with a space and a carriage return. Lines with comments need only a carriage return. Character strings require two carriage returns.

(3) Do not use labels; addressing is through byte displacement (jump instructions) or absolute addresses:

```
FE8C    1607    JNE    $+16
FC8E    10E8    JMP    >FE60
FE90    C8A2    MOV    @>FD20(R2), @>FE10(R2)
FE92    FD20
FE94    FE10
FE96
```

(4) Register numbers are in decimal and can be predefined (preceded by an R):

```
FE96    020C    LI 12,>D00
FE98    0D00
FE9A    020D    LI R13,>FFFF
FE9C    FFFF
FE9E
```

(5) Jump instruction operand can be $+n, $−n, or >M where n is a decimal value of bytes (+256≥n≥ −254) and M is a memory address in hexadecimal. The dollar sign must be followed by a sign and number (JMP $ is not allowed).

```
FE20    1304    JEQ    $+10              EXIT
FE22    1304    JEQ    $+>A              EXIT
FE24    1304    JEQ    $+%1010           EXIT
FE26    1304    JEQ    >FE30             EXIT
FE28    10FF    JMP    $+0               LOOP AT THIS ADDRESS (>FE28)
FE2A    10FF    JMP    $−0               LOOP AT THIS ADDRESS
```

(6) Absolute numerical values can be in binary, decimal, or hexadecimal.

- Binary values are preceded by a percent sign (%). One to 16 ones and zeroes can follow; unspecified bits on the left will be zero filled:

```
FE58    0204    LI R4,%10101010          >AA IN R4
FE5A    00AA
FE5C    000A    +%1010                   DATA STATEMENT
FE5E    FFF6    −%1010                   DATA STATEMENT
FE60
```

- Decimal values have no prefix in an operand:

```
FE6C    0205    LI R5,100                    LOAD COUNTER
FE6E    0064
FE70    0206    LI R6,32768                  SET LIMIT
FE72    8000
FE74    8000    +32768
FE76    8000    −32768
FE78    7FFF    +32767
FE7A    8001    −32767
FE7C    FFFF    −1
FE7E
```

- Hexadecimal values are preceded by the greater-than sign (>):

```
FE7E    02E0    LWPI>FF00                    SET WP ADDRESS
FE80    FF00
FE82    FFFF    +>FFFF                       DATA STATEMENT
FE84    0001    ÷>FFFF                       DATA STATEMENT
FE86
```

NOTE

In operands, absolute value must be unsigned values only. However, there is a method for using the assembler to compute and assemble a negative value; this method is especially useful with the immediate instructions (e.g., AI, CI, LI). Enter the instruction using the negative value. The assembled value will be all zeroes in the last assembled word. Use the slash command (paragraph 3.2.2) to assemble at the previous address, then enter the negative value as a data statement as shown in the following example:

```
FE1A    0201    LI R1,−>100          ←—USE SIGNED OPERAND
FE1C    0000                         ←—SIGNED NUMBER ASSEMBLIES AS 0000 (IN M.A.>FE1C)
FE1E            /FE1C                ←—SET OBJECT LOAD ADDRESS TO PREVIOUS ADDRESS
FE1C    FF00    −>100                ←—−>100(>FF00) NOW IN M.A.>FE1C
FE1E
```

(7) Absolute addresses are used instead of labels:

```
FEA0    C820    MOV    @>FE10,@>FED0         MOVE TO STORAGE
FEA2    FE10
FEA4    FED0
FEA6    16FC    JNE    >FEA0                 LOOP BACK TO MOVE INSTRUCTION
FEA8
```

(8) Character strings are preceded by a dollar sign and are terminated with two carriage returns.

```
FF10    4142    $ABCD        1233
FF12    4344
FF14    2020
FF16    2031
FF18    3233
FF1A    3320              ◄— UNUSED RIGHT BYTE FILLED WITH >20 (SPACE)
```

(9) Character strings of one or two characters can be designated by encoding the string in quotes. If not part of an operand, a plus or minus sign must precede the value. If the string is larger than two characters, the last two characters are interpreted.

```
FEAA    3132    +'12'         CHARACTERS ONE AND TWO
FEAC    000C    +12           VALUE OF POSITIVE TWELVE
FEAE    FFF4    −12           VALUE OF NEGATIVE TWELVE
FEB0    0000    +             + FOLLOWED BY CTRL KEY AND NULL KEY PRESSED
FEB2    0202    LIR2, 'ABCD'  ASSEMBLED LAST TWO CHARACTERS (C AND D)
FEB4    4344
FEB6    0202    LI R2, 'E'    CHARACTER E IN RIGHT BYTE
FEB8    0045
FEBA    0202    LI R2, >E     VALUE >E IN RIGHT BYTE
FEBC    000E
FEBE
```

(10) Signed numerical values of up to 16 bits can be designated by preceding the value with a plus or minus sign. If more than 16 bits are entered in binary or hexadecimal, the last 16 bits entered are used. If more than 16 bits are entered in decimal, the assembled value is the same as the remainder had the number between divided by 2^{15} ($65,536_{10}$).

```
FE18    00FF    +%1111111100000000111111111
FE1A    FF01    −%1111111100000000011111111
FE1C    AAEE    +>AAAAAAEE
FE1E    8000    +32768
FE20    8001    +32769
FE22    0000    +65536
FE24    FFFF    +131071
FE26    0000    +131072
FE28    8000    −32768
FE2A    8001    −32767
FE2C    7FFF    −32769
FE2E
```

ERRORS

When the assembler detects an error, it types an error symbol and readies the terminal for re-entering data at the same memory address. The following error symbols are used:

- D (Displacement error). The jump instruction destination is more than $+256$ or -254 bytes away.

```
FF38            JNC    $+300◆D
FF38            JNC    >F000◆D
FF38    170B    JNC    >FF50
FF3A
```

- R (Range error). The operand is out of range for its field:

```
FF30            LI     R44,◆R
FE30    0204    LI     R4,200
FF32    00C8
```

- S (Syntax error). The instruction syntax was incorrect:

```
FF34            MOZ◆S  }
FF34            MOS◆S  }  INCORRECT MNEMONICS
FF34    C802    MOV R2, @>FE90
FF36    FE90
```

EXITING TO THE MONITOR

Return control to monitor by pressing the escape (ESC) key.

PSEUDO-INSTRUCTIONS

The TM 990/402 also interprets two pseudo-instructions. These pseudo-instructions are not additional instructions but actually are additional mnemonics that conveniently represent two members of the instruction set:

- The NOP mnemonic can be used in place of a JMP $+2$ instruction which is essentially a no-op (no operation). This can be used to replace an existing instruction in memory, or it can be included in code to force additional execution time in a routine. Both NOP and JMP $+2$ assemble to the machine code 1000_{16}.

- The RT mnemonic can be used in place of a B *R11 instruction which is a common return from a branch and link (BL) subroutine. Both RT and B *R11 assemble to the machine code $045B_{16}$.

Note the following examples:

```
FE00 1000 JMP $+2            JUMP TO NEXT INSTRUCTION
FE02 1000 NOP               ALSO ASSEMBLES TO >1000
FE04 045B B ◆R11            RETURN COMMAND
FE06 045B RT                ALSO A RETURN COMMAND
```

TIBUG
Monitor

TIBUG COMMANDS

INPUT	RESULTS
B	Execute under Breakpoint
C	CRU Inspect/Change
D	Dump Memory to Cassette/Paper Tape
E	Execute
F	Find Word/Byte in Memory
H	Hex Arithmetic
L	Load Memory from Cassette/Paper Tape
M	Memory Inspect/Change
R	Inspect/Change User WP, PC, and ST Registers
S	Execute in Step Mode
T	1200 Baud Terminal
W	Inspect/Change Current User Workspace

COMMAND SYNTAX CONVENTIONS

CONVENTION SYMBOL	EXPLANATION
< >	Items to be supplied by the user. The term.within the angle brackets is a generic term.
[ ]	Optional Item — May be included or omitted at the user's discretion. Items not included in brackets are required.
{ }	One of several optional items must be chosen.
(CR)	Carriage Return
∧	Space Bar
LF	Line Feed
R or Rn	Register (n = 0 to 15)
WP	Current User Workspace Pointer contents
PC	Current User Program Counter contents
ST	Current User Status Register contents

USER ACCESSIBLE UTILITIES

XOP	FUNCTION
8	Write 1 Hexadecimal Charter to Terminal
9	Read Hexadecimal Word from Terminal
10	Write 4 Hexadecimal Characters to Terminal
11	Echo Character
12	Write 1 Character to Terminal
13	Read 1 Character from Terminal
14	Write Message to Terminal
	NOTE All characters are in ASCII code.

TIBUG ERROR MESSAGES

ERROR	CONDITION
0	Invalid tag detected by the loader.
1	Checksum error detected by the loader.
2	Invalid termination character detected.
3	Null input field detected by the dump routine.
4	Invalid command entered.

COMMAND

SYNTAX

Execute under Breakpoint (B)

B<address><(CR)>

CRU Inspect/Change (C)

C<base address>{$\wedge$,}<count><(CR)>

Dump Memory to Cassette/Paper Tape (D)

┌─MONITOR PROMPT

D<start address>{$\wedge$,}<stop address>{$\wedge$,}<entry address>{$\wedge$,}IDT = <name><$\wedge$>

Execute Command (E)

E

Find Command (F)

F<start address>{$\wedge$,}<stop address>{$\wedge$,}<value>{(C̄R̄)}

Hexadecimal Arithmetic (H)

H<number 1>{$\wedge$,}<number 2><(CR)>

Load Memory from Cassette or Paper Tape (L)

L<bias><(CR)>

Memory Inspect/Change, Memory Dump (M)

Memory Inspect/Change Syntax
  M<address><(CR)>
Memory Dump Syntax
  M<start address>{$\wedge$,}<stop address><(CR)>

Inspect/Change User WP,PC, and ST Registers (R)

R<(CR)>

Execute In Single Step Mode (S)

S

TI 733 ASR Baud Rate (T)

T

Inspect/Change User Workspace (W)

W [Register Number] <(CR)>

TM 990/302
Software Development Board

EPROM's which may be programmed by the '302

2708
2716
2516
2532
9940

SOFTWARE COMPONENTS

	Access Command
Executive	(CR)
Text Editor	TE
Symbolic Assembler	SA
Debug Package	DP
EPROM Programmer	EP
Relocating Loader	RL
EIA Interface	EI
I/O Scheduler/Handler	SR

LUNO ASSIGNMENTS

Device	Logical Unit No.
Dummy	0
Terminal (LOG)	1
Audio Cassette 1	2
Audio Cassette 2	3
Second EIA Connector	4
Memory	5

SOFTWARE COMPONENT CALLS

Text Editor   TEØ(input device),(output device)

Symbolic Assembler   SAØ(source device), (object device), (listing device)

Debug Package   DPØ(output device)

EPROM Programmer   EP

Relocating Loader   RLØ(input device)

Set Baud Rate   SRØ(nnnn)

Escape   ESC (return to executive)

TEXT EDITOR COMMANDS

D Delete lines n thru m

I Insert at line n with optional auto increment by m

K Keep buffer and print new top line in the buffer

G Get buffer and print new bottom line in the buffer

P Print lines n thru m

Q Flush the input file until end of input file and return to executive

R Resequence input to output, n is initialized line # and m is the increment

COMMAND	SYNTAX
Delete Lines n thru m (Rn,m)	D (starting line #)[,(ending line #)]
Insert After Line n with optional auto increment by m (In,m)	I (line number after which new data is entered) [,(auto increment value)]
Get Buffer (G)	G
Keep Buffer (K)	K
Print lines n thru m (Pn,m)	P (first line # to be printed) [,(last line # to be printed)]
Quit Text Editor (Q)	Q
Resequence Output (Rn,m)	R (initial line number) [,(increment value)]

ASSEMBLER DIRECTIVES

AORG	[label]ϕAORGϕ(value)ϕ[comment]
BSS	[label]ϕBSSϕ(value)ϕ[comment]
BYTE	[label]ϕBYTEϕ(value),(value),(value),....ϕ[comment]
DXOP	[label]ϕDXOPϕ(symbol),(value)ϕ[comment]
END	[label]ϕENDϕ(symbol)ϕ[comment]
EQU	[label]ϕEQUϕ(expression)ϕ[comment]
DATA	[label]ϕDATAϕ(exp),(exp),...ϕ[comment]
EVEN	[label]ϕEVENϕ[comment]
IDT	[label]ϕIDTb(string)ϕ[comment]
TEXT	[label]ϕTEXTϕ(−),'string'ϕ[comment)

DEBUG Package

Verb	Command
SB	Set Software Breakpoint and Execute
IM	Inspect/Change Memory
IC	Inspect/Change CRU
IR	Inspect/Change MPU Registers
ST	Set Software Trace
RU	Single Step for 1 or more instructions with or without trace
DM	Dump Memory

DEBUG COMMANDS

Set Breakpoint and Execute	SBϕ(address)
Inspect/Change Memory	IMϕ(address)
Inspect/Change CRU	ICϕ(CRU base addr.)(no. of bits)
Inspect/Change MPU registers	IR
Set Software Trace	STϕ(0 or 1)
Run 1 or more Instructions	RUϕ(no. of instructions in decimal)
Dump Memory	DMϕ(starting addr.),(ending addr.)

EPROM PROGRAMMING CRU ASSIGNMENTS

CRU BASE ADDRESS$_{16}$	INPUT/OUTPUT	FUNCTION
1710	I/O	EPROM DATA BIT 0
1712	I/O	:
1714	I/O	:
1716	I/O	:
1718	I/O	:
171A	I/O	:
171C	I/O	:
171E	I/O	EPROM DATA BIT 7
1720	O	EPROM ADDRESS LSB
1722	O	:
1724	O	:
1726	O	:
1728	O	:
172A	O	:
172C	O	:
172E	O	:
1730	O	:
1732	O	:
1734	O	:
1736	O	:
1738	O	EPROM ADDRESS MSB
173A	O	EPROM PROGRAM ENABLE
173E	O	EPROM PROGRAMMING PULSE

EPROM PROGRAMMING RESPONSES

PP = Program EPROM

RE = Read EPROM to Memory

CE = Compare EPROM to Memory

Memory Bounds: MEM BDS? (start addr.),(stop addr.)

EPROM Start addr: EPROM START? (start addr.)

Programming Mode: MODE? P(parallel) or I(in line)

Starting Byte: ST byte ? (0 or 1 if P above)

PREDEFINED CRU ADDRESSES FOR I/O DEVICES

Device	CRU Address
Users Terminal (9902)	80_{16}
Timer (9901)	100_{16}
EIA Interface (9902)	180_{16}
Recorder 1 Forward	1700_{16}
Recorder 2 Forward/9940 Flag 1	1702_{16}
Recorder 2 Write Data/9940 Flag 2	1704_{16}
Recorder 1 Read Data/9940 Flag 3	1706_{16}
Personality Card Code Bit 0	1708_{16}
Personality Card Code Bit 1	$170A_{16}$
Personality Card Code Bit 2	$170C_{16}$
Switch Code Bit	$170E_{16}$
EPROM Data	$1710_{16} - 171E_{16}$
EPROM Address	$1720_{16} - 1738_{16}$
EPROM Program Enable	$173A_{16}$
EPROM Programming Pulse	$173C_{16}$

TXDS Commands
for FS 990 Software
Development System

Examples of manuals available in support of the TXDS System:

TXDS PROGRAMMER'S GUIDE (#946258-9701)

This manual enables the user to employ the Terminal Executive Development System (TXDS) in conjunction with the TX990 Operating System and the Model 990/4 and 990/10 Computer System hardware configuration to develop, improve, change, or maintain (1) the user's customized Operating System and the user's applications programs or (2) any other type of user-produced programs (e.g., the user's own supervisor call processors or the user's own utility programs). It is assumed the reader is familiar with the Model 990 Computer System assembly language and the concepts of the TX990 Operating System.

The sections and appendixes of this manual are organized as follows:

I   Introduction — Provides a general description of the TXDS utility programs and their capabilities. Also includes a description of the control functions of the TXDS Control Program.

II   Loading and Executing a Program — Provides a step-by-step procedure for loading and executing (1) each of the TXDS and TX990 Operating System utility programs and (2) a user program. Also describes the TXDS Control Program and how to correctly respond to its prompts.

III   Verification of Operation — Provides several short step-by-step procedures to checkout proper operation of the TXDS software.

IV   Creating and Editing Program Source Code — Describes the capabilities of the TXEDIT utility program and how the user can employ those capabilities to edit or generate the text of source programs and object programs.

V   Assembling Source Programs — Describes how the user can employ the TXMIRA utility program to assemble source files (i.e., source code programs).

VI   TX990 Cross Reference (TXXREF) Utility Program — Describes how the user can employ the TXXREF utility program to produce a listing of each user-defined symbol in a 990 assembly source program along with the line numbers on which the symbol is defined and all of the line numbers on which the symbol is referenced.

VII   Linking Object Modules — Describes how the user can employ the TXDS Linker utility program to form a single object module from a set of independently assembled object modules (in the form of object code or compressed object code.)

VIII   TXDS Copy Concatenate (TXCCAT) Utility Program — Describes how the user can employ the TXCCAT utility program to copy one to three files to a single output file.

IX   TXDS Standalone Debug Monitor (TXDBUG) Utility Program — Describes how the user can employ the TXDBUG utility program to debug programs which have been designed to operate in a "standalone" situation without support of an operating system.

X   TXDS PROM (TXPROM) Programmer Utility Program — Describes how the user can employ the TXPROM programming utility program to control the Programming Module (PROM) hardware to make customized ROMs containing user-created data or programs.

XI   TXDS BNPF/High Low (BNPFHL) Dump Utility Program — Describes how the user can employ the BNPFHL utility program to produce a BNPF or high/low file format.

XII   TXDS IBM Diskette Conversion Utility (IBMUTL) Program — Describes how the user can employ the IBMUTL utility program to transfer standard IBM-formatted diskette datasets to TX990 Operating System files and to transfer TX990 Operating System files to standard IBM-formatted diskette datasets.

XIII   TXDS Assign and Release LUNO Utility Program — Describes how the operator can assign and release LUNOs in systems which do not include OCP.

A   Glossary — Clarifies selected words used in this TX990 Operating System Programmer's Guide.

B   Compressed Object Code Format — Describes the compressed object code format.

C   Task State Codes — Lists and describes the task state codes.

D   I/O Error Codes — List and describes the I/O error codes available to the user, when coding a program, for printout or display on a terminal device.

The following documents contain additional information related to the TX990 Operating System and are referenced herein this manual:

TITLE	PART NUMBER
Model 990 Computer TX990 Operating System Programmer's Guide	946259-9701
Model 990 Computer TMS9900 Microprocessor Assembly Language Programmer's Guide	943441-9701
Model 990 Computer Model FD800 Floppy Disc System Installation and Operation	945253-9701
Model 990 Computer Model 913 CRT Display Terminal Installation and Operation	943457-9701
Model 990 Computer Model 911 Video Display Terminal Installation and Operation	943423-9701
Model 990 Computer Model 733 ASR/KSR Data Terminal Installation and Operation	945259-9701
Model 990 Computer Model 804 Card Reader Installation and Operation	945262-9701
Model 990 Computer Models 306 and 588 Line Printers Installation and Operation	945261-9701
Model 990 Computer PROM Programming Module Installation and Operation	945258-9701
990 Computer Family Systems Handbook	945250-9701
Model 990 Computer Communications Systems Installation and Operation	945409-9701

List of Commands and Special Keys/Characters

COMMAND SYNTAX	DESCRIPTION

SETUP COMMANDS

SL — Start Line Numbers (SL) command causes line numbers to be printed with each line of text.

SN — Stop Line Numbers (SN) comman causes line numbers not to be printed.

SP — Set Print Margin (SP) command sets the right boundary for print display.

SM — Set Margin (SM) for Find command sets the left and right boundaries for the Find command.

ST — Set Tabs (ST) command sets up to five tab stops.

PRINTER-MOVEMENT COMMANDS

D — Down (D) command moves the pointer down toward the bottom of the buffer.

U — Up (U) command moves the pointer up towards the first line in the buffer.

T — Top (T) command moves the pointer to the first line in the buffer.

B — Bottom (B) command moves the pointer to the last line in the buffer.

EDIT COMMANDS

C — Change (C) command removes lines from the buffer and inserts new ones in their place. The new lines are input from the terminal.

I — Insert (I) command takes input from the terminal and places the new lines into the buffer.

M — Move (M) command moves lines from one place in the buffer to another.

R — Remove (R) command deletes lines from the buffer.

F — Find string (F) command searches for the first occurrence of a character string in a line and replaces it with another string of characters.

PRINT COMMANDS

L — Limits (L) command causes the first line and the last line to be displayed.

P — Print (P) command displays lines of text.

List of Commands and Special Keys/Characters (Continued)

COMMAND SYNTAX	DESCRIPTION
	OUTPUT COMMANDS
K	Keep (K) command takes lines of text out of the buffer and puts them in the output file.
Q	Quit (Q) command takes lines of text out of the buffer or the input files and puts them in the output file.
E	An (E) command terminates without writing an EOF to the output file.
	TERMINATE-SEQUENCE COMMANDS
T or C	Allows the user to make multiple single directional editing passes on a source or object program.
	SPECIAL KEYS/CHARACTERS
CTRL-H	Pressing the control key and the H key simultaneously on the hard copy terminal causes the terminal to backspace a character to enable rewriting over an entered character-error.
RUB OUT	The RUB OUT key causes the line just entered to be deleted so that a new line can replace it.
CTRL-I	Pressing the control (CTRL) key and the I key simultaneously on a hard-copy terminal causes a tab stop to be entered in the input string, although only one space will be echoed on the terminal.
ESC/RESET	Pressing the ESCape or RESET key on the system console causes a display to be aborted.
position keys	When using a VDT, only the left position key (←) and the right (→) position key are recognized. The up and down position keys cause garbage to be entered into the input string. The left position key causes characters to be deleted from the character string; a right position key causes whatever was under the cursor to be entered.
DELETE LINE	DELETE LINE on a VDT acts the same as a RUB OUT on a hardcopy terminal.
TAB	A SPACE character is echoed. The TAB is interpreted by the text editor and spaces are inserted to fill the text line to the next TAB setting.

TXMIRA Options

OPTION   DESCRIPTION

Mnnnnn   Overrides memory size default; default is 2400 bytes
X   Produce cross-reference
L   Produce assembly listing
T   Expand TEXT code on listing
S   Produce sorted symbol list
C   Produce compressed object output where n is a decimal digit

TXLINK Options

OPTION   DESCRIPTION

Mnnnnn   Override default memory size, default is 11800 bytes.
C   Compressed object output.
Iaaaaaaaa   IDT for linked object.
P   Partial link desired.
L   Print load map and symbol list.

Note: n is a decimal digit and a is an alphanumeric character.

TXCCAT Options

OPTION   DESCRIPTION

TRnnnn   Truncate record to length nnnn.
FLnnnn   Fix records to size nnnn by padding with blanks or by
                truncation.
SKnnnn   Skip nnnn input records, prior to output.
LFnn   List file, page length = nn, default = 55.
SLnn   Space lines on listing, nn = space count, default = 0.
NL   Number lines on listing.
RI   Do not rewind input on open.
RO   Do not rewind output on open.

Note: n is a decimal digit and the maximum field size is given by the number of n's.

TXDBUG Keyboard Commands

DEBUG Commands

IC	Inspect Communications Register Unit (CRU)
IM	Inspect Memory
IR	Inspect AU Register (WP, PC, ST)
IS	Inspect Snapshot
IW	Inspect Workspace Registers
MC	Modify Communications Register Unit (CRU)
MM	Modify Memory
MR	Modify Registers
MW	Modify Workspace Registers
SB	Set Breakpoint
SP	Set H/W Write Protect Option
SR	Set Trace Region
SS	Set Snapshot
ST	Set Trace
CB	Clear Breakpoint
CP	Clear H/W Write Protect Option
CR	Clear Trace Region
CS	Clear Snapshot

AMPL
Reference Data

EXPLANATION OF THE NOTATION USED IN THIS CARD

	Notation	Explanation
Optional Items	[item]	Bracketed item may be omitted.
	$\begin{cases} \text{item 1} \\ \text{item 2} \end{cases}$	Exactly one item must be selected. from the items in braces.
Substitution	expr 'file'	Any expression may be used. File or device name required.
Repetition	item . . .	A list of items may be used.
Required	<item>	Replace with item.

CHARACTER SET

Type	Characters	Use
Special	RETURN SPACE ! " $ / ( ) * + , − . / : ; < = > ? @	Any printable character may be used in a quoted string. RETURN terminates line and statement. ";" may separate statements. SPACE separates adjacent numbers and identifiers.
Numerals	0 − 9	
Letters	A − Z,a − z	

NOTE: All AMPL reserved words use only upper case (UPPER CASE LOCK).

SYMBOL NAMES

Type	Example	Definition
System	RO ETRC	Up to four alphanumeric characters; all system symbols are predefined.
User-defined	USRVAR X3 BRKADR GO	Up to six alphanumeric characters; assignment defines a variable. ARRAY statement defines an array. PROC/FUNC statement defines a procedure/function.
Program label	IDT. .DEF	Up to six alphanumeric characters. Period after IDT and before DEF labels, defined by LOAD command.

CONSTANTS

Type	Example	Range
Decimal	10833	1 . . . 32767
Hexadecimal	02A51, >2A51	>0 . . . >FFFF
Octal	125121	!0 . . . !177777
Binary	<10101001010001	<0 . . . <1111111111111111
ASCII	" *Q "	
Instruction	# XOR *R1,R9 #	
Keyword	IAQ	See keyword constant table.

EXPRESSIONS

Type	Example	Definition
Subexpression	(expr)	
Identity	+ expr	Value of <expr>.
Negation	− expr	Two's complement of <expr>.
Target memory	@addr	<addr> used as word address into emulator or target memory.
Proc/Func Argument	ARG expr	Argument in position <expr> of call list; ARG 0 is number of arguments in list.
Proc/Func local variable	LOC expr	Word <expr> of local variable array; LOC 0 is length of local variable array.
Multiplication	expr1*expr2	Signed product (warning on overflow).
Division	expr1/expr2	Signed quotient (warning on divide by zero).
Remainder	expr1 MOD EXPR2	Signed remainder of division (warning on divide by zero).
Addition	expr1 + expr2	Signed sum.
Subtraction	expr1 - expr2	Signed difference.

NOTE: Result of relational operator is either FALSE (0) or TRUE (-1).

Equality	expr1 EQ expr2 expr1 NE expr2	16-bit comparison.
Arithmetic inequality	expr1 LT expr2 expr1 LE expr2 expr1 GT expr2 expr1 GE expr2	Signed, 16-bit comparison.
Logical inequality	expr1 LO expr2 expr1 LOE expr2 expr1 HI expr2 expr1 HIE expr2	Unsigned, 16-bit comparison.
Complement	NOT expr	16-bit one's complement.
Conjunction	expr1 AND expr2 expr 1 NAND expr2	16-bit boolean AND. 16-bit boolean not AND.
Disjunction	expr1 OR expr2 expr1 XOR expr2	16-bit boolean OR. 16-bit boolean exclusive OR.

NOTE: Operators are given in order of precedence, highest to lowest. Solid lines separate precedence groups; within each group, precedence is equal and evaluation is left to right. Evaluation results in a 16-bit integer value.

UNSIGNED ARITHMETIC

Syntax

Definition

MPY (expr1, expr2)

Low-order 16 bits of unsigned product. $<expr1>$ * $<expr2>$; high order 16 in MDR.

DIV (divisor, dividend)

Unsigned quotient of 32-bit number (MDR, $<dividend>$) over $<divisor>$; remainder in MDR.

MDR

High-order 16-bits of MPY product and of DIV dividend; remainder of DIV; unsigned carry of + and-.

ARRAY DEFINITION

ARRAY name(expr1[,expr2]), . . .

User $<name>$ (previously undefined or name of deleted array) is defined as one- or two-dimension array.

DISPLAY STATEMENTS

expr[:f . . . f]	Value of expression
'LITERAL STRING'	Literal string
add1 [TO addr2] [:f . . . f] ? [:f . . . f]	Target memory

Format specification /[:f . . . f]

ASCII	A	set default	G	octal	O[i]
binary	B[i]	hexadecimal	H[i]	symbolic	S
decimal	D[i]	instruction	I	unsigned	U[i]
name =	E	newline	N[j]	space	X[j]

Note:

1< =i< =9	field width 'i' digits, then two blanks
i = 0	default field width, no trailing blanks
1< =j< =9	repeat 'j' times
j = 0	repeat 10 times

Response to display/modify mode(?):

forward step	RETURN, +	replace contents	$<expr>$
back step	—	open new address	$@<addr>$
exit	;	change display	:f . . . f

DISASSEMBLER

Instruction	DST	Destination address.
operands	SRC	Source address.

NOTE: Additional instructions of the TMS9940 (DCA, DCS, LIIM, SM) will assemble correctly (#DCA *RC1 #) but will disassemble as XOP instructions. See TMS9940 specifications for details.

ASSIGNMENT STATEMENTS

Type	Example	Definition
Variable	sym = expr	User-defined or writable system symbol or REF program label.
Target memory	@addr = expr	Put value of <expr> at target <addr>
Proc/Func argument	ARG n = expr	Local copy of argument in position <n> of call list.
Command local	LOC n = expr	Word <n> of local storage array.
Array	A[(i1[,i2])] = e	User defined array name; zero, one, or two index expressions.

NOTE: Precedence of @, ARG, and LOC may require parenthesis around following expression.

COMPOUND STATEMENTS

Syntax	Definition
BEGIN statements END	Statements are executed sequentially. Use in place of any single statement syntax.

CONTROL STATEMENTS

IF expr
  THEN s1
  [ELSE s2]
	<s1> is executed if <expr> is TRUE (nonzero). Otherwise, <s2> is executed, if included.

CASE expr OF
  expr 1::s1;
  . . . .
  exprn::sn
  [ELSE s]
END
	Statement <si> at first label expression <expr> equal to <expr> is executed. If none, statement <s> is executed, if included.

WHILE expr DO statement	While <expr> is TRUE (nonzero), <statement> is executed.
REPEAT statement UNTIL expr	<statement> is executed. If <expr> FALSE (zero), <statement> is executed until <expr> is TRUE.
FOR var = expr1 TO expr 2[BY expr3] DO statement	Value of <expr1> is assigned to <var>. <statement> is executed until <var> is equal to <expr2>; <expr3> is added to <var>, and <statement> repeated. Default value of <exp3> is 1.
ESCAPE	Exit from innermost enclosing WHILE, REPEAT, or FOR statement.

PROCEDURE/FUNCTION/FORM DEFINITION

PROC name [(args[,locs])] statements END
FUNC name [(args[,locs])] statements END

User-defined <name> (previously
undefined or deleted procedure/function)
is bound to <statements>.
<args> is the required number of
arguments.
<locs> is the size of local storage array.

RETURN [expr]

Pass control back to calling statement. In a
procedure, <expr> is ignored. In a
function, value of <expr> replaces the
function call in the calling expression.

FORM name 'prompt' [= [{ constant / 'string' }]]; . . .

END

<name> must be a previously defined
procedure or function, semicolon required
between prompts.

PROCEDURE/FUNCTION CALLS

proc name [(expr, . . .)]

func name [(expr, . . .)]

User-defined or system procedure/function
with list of argument expressions.

Command definition determines number of
arguments required. Some system
commands require quoted strings as
arguments.

NOTE: Procedure/functions with defined FORM when called with no arguments will prompt
for arguments using the FORM.

example FORM:

COMMENTARY ENTRY

comment, not a prompt required argument,
with default value required argument, must
enter value default given if value not
entered

    PROMPT 1 = default value
    PROMPT 2 =
    PROMPT 3* =

FORM control function keys:

Next prompt:	TAB,↓,→FIELD, SKIP, RETURN
Previous prompt:	↑,←FIELD
First prompt:	HOME
Erase value:	ERASE FIELD, ERASE INPUT
Redisplay default:	INSERT LINE
Duplicate previous value:	F4
Complete form:	ENTER
Abort form:	CMD

INPUT/OUTPUT COMMANDS

Syntax	**Definition**
HCRB	Host computer CRU base address.
HCRR (offset,width)	Read host computer CRU field.
HCRW (offset,width,value)	Write <value> into host CRU field.

$$\text{COPY} \begin{pmatrix} \text{'file'} \\ \text{edit id} \end{pmatrix}$$

AMPL input from 'file'
AMPL input from edit buffer

$$\text{LIST} \begin{pmatrix} \begin{Bmatrix} \text{'file'} \\ \text{OFF} \\ \text{ON} \\ \text{EOF} \end{Bmatrix} \end{pmatrix}$$

Initialize listing device or file. Disable listing output.
Enable listing output. Close listing device or file with EOF.

NL   Print newline.

$$\text{unit} = \text{OPEN} \left[\left(\begin{Bmatrix} \text{'file'} \\ \text{edit id} \end{Bmatrix} \left[, \begin{Bmatrix} 0 \\ \text{IN} \\ \text{OUT} \\ \text{IO} \end{Bmatrix} \left[, \begin{Bmatrix} 0 \\ \text{REWIND} \\ \text{EXTEND} \end{Bmatrix} \left[\begin{Bmatrix} \text{SEQ} \\ \text{REL} \end{Bmatrix} \right] \right] \right] \right) \right]$$

no arguments — list all open units and edit buffers.
initialize 'file'/<edit id> I/O unit
    0 — device IO, file IN only
    IN — for input only
    OUT — for output only
    IO — for input/output
    REWIND — position to beginning of file
    EXTEND — position to end of file
    SEQ — auto-create sequential file
    REL — auto-create rel-rec file

$$\text{event-READ} \left[\left(\text{unit} \left[, \begin{Bmatrix} 0 \\ \text{DIRECT} \end{Bmatrix} \left[, \begin{Bmatrix} 0 \\ \text{GRAPH} \end{Bmatrix} \right. \right. \right. \right.$$

$$\left. \left. \left. \left[, \begin{Bmatrix} \text{VDT} \\ \text{SEQ} \\ \text{REL} \end{Bmatrix} \begin{Bmatrix} 0 \\ \text{f row} \\ [, \text{rec \#}] \end{Bmatrix} \left[, \begin{Bmatrix} 0 \\ \text{f col} \end{Bmatrix} [, \text{s col}] \right] \right] \right] \right) \right]$$

no arguments — read console
Read record from (unit)
    0 — issue read ASCII
    DIRECT — issue read direct
    GRAPH — read graphics on 922 VDT
    VDT — read in cursor positioning mode
      f row — field start row
      f col — field start column
      s col — cursor start column

INPUT/OUTPUT COMMANDS (continued)

SEQ — read sequentially
REL — read sepecified record
rec # — record number to read
<event>/256 = cursor column after read if VDT
<event> AND 255 = event key value if VDT,
else >OD for end of record,
>13 for end of file.

value = EVAL [(unit)]　　　Evaluate expression in <unit>'s buffer;
　　　　　　　　　　　　　　if no <unit>, READ/EVAL the console.

DPLY [(unit)]　　　　　　　AMPL display unit for output to <unit>;
　　　　　　　　　　　　　　if no <unit>, to console.

okay = MOVE　　　　　　　Move contents of <from unit>'s buffer to <to unit>'s buffer
(from unit,　　　　　　　　　<okay> = 0 if moved
to unit)　　　　　　　　　　　　　　 = >FFFF if too big and not moved.

REW[(unit)]　　　　　　　　Rewind (unit) — repositions, file clears console
　　　　　　　　　　　　　　no argument — clears console

$$\text{Cursor} = \text{WRIT} \left(\text{unit} \left[, \left\{ {0 \atop \text{DIRECT}} \right\} \left[, \left\{ {0 \atop \text{GRAPH}} \right\} \right] \right. \right.$$

$$\left. \left. \left[, \left\{ {\text{VDT} \atop {\text{SEQ} \atop \text{REL}}} , \left\{ {0 \atop \text{f row}} \right\} \begin{array}{c} [, [\text{f col}]] \\ [, \text{rec} \#] \end{array} \right\} \right] \right] \right)$$

no arguments — write console
Write record to (unit),
　　0 — issue write ASCII
　　DIRECT — issue write direct
　　GRAPH — write graphics on 911 VDT
　　VDT — write in cursor positioning mode
　　　f row — field start row
　　　f col — field start column
　　SEQ — write sequentially
　　REL — read specified record
　　rec # — record number to read
　　<cursor>/256 = cursor column after write if VDT

$$\text{CLSE} \left(\text{unit} \left[, \left\{ {\text{EOF} \atop \text{UNLOAD}} \right\} \right] \right.$$ 　Release I/O <unit>,
　　　　　　　　　　　　　　　　EOF — write end-of-file mark
　　　　　　　　　　　　　　　　UNLOAD — unload unit

SYSTEM SYMBOLS

V — variable   F — function   P — procedure

CLR	P — clear	MDEL	P — symbols
CLSE	P — I/O close	MDR	V — arithmetic
COPY	P — copy	MIN	V — minutes
CRUB	V — CRU base	MOVE	F — I/O buffer
CRUR	F — CRU read	MPY	F — multiply
CRUW	P — CRU write	MSYM	P — symbols
DAY	V — day	NL	P — newline
DBUF	P — delete buffer	OPEN	F — I/O open
DELE	P — delete symbol	PC	V — registers
DIV	F — divide	R0-R15	V — registers
DPLY	P — display	READ	F — I/O read
DR	P — registers	REW	P — I/O rewind
DST	V — destination	RSTR	P — restore
DUMP	P — dump	SAVE	P — save
EBRK	P — emulator	SEC	V — seconds
ECLK	V — emulator	SRC	V — source
EDIT	F — edit	ST	V — register
EHLT	F — emulator	TBRK	P — trace module
EINT	P — emulator	TEVT	P — trace module
EMEM	V — emulator	THLT	F — trace module
ERUN	P — emulator	TINT	P — trace module
EST	F — emulator	TNCE	V — trace module
ETB	F — emulator	TNE	V — trace module
ETBH	F — emulator	TRUN	P — trace module
ETBO	V — emulator	TST	F — trace module
ETRC	P — emulator	TTB	F — trace module
ETYP	V — emulator	TTBH	F — trace module
EVAL	F — evaluate	TTBN	V — trace module
EXIT	P — exit AMPL	TTBO	V — trace module
HCRB	V — host CRU	TTRC	P — trace module
HCRR	F — CRU read	USYM	P — user symbols
HCRW	P — CRU write	VRFY	P — verify
HR	V — hour	WAIT	F — delay AMPL
IOR1	V — I/O	WP	V + register
KEEP	P — keep edit	WRIT	P — I/O write
LIST	P — list	YR	V — year
LOAD	P — load object		

EDIT

Syntax

$$\text{edit id} = \text{EDIT}[(\begin{Bmatrix} \text{'file'} \\ \text{edit id} \end{Bmatrix} [\text{,record}])]$$

KEEP (edit id, 'file')

DBUF (edit id)

Definition

Create edit buffer with 'file'. Edit existing buffer. No argument creates an empty buffer.

Save edit buffer onto 'file' and delete edit buffer.

Delete edit buffer.

EDIT CONTROL FUNCTION KEYS

Function	911 KEY	913 KEY	CONTROL CHARACTER
edit/compose mode	F7	F7	V
quit edit mode	CMD	HELP	X
roll up	F1	F1	A
roll down	F2	F2	B
set tab	F3	F3	C
clear tab	F4	F4	D
tab	TAB (shift SKIP)	TAB	I
back tab	FIELD	BACK TAB	T
newline	RETURN	NEWLINE	RETURN
insert line	unlabeled gray	INSERT LINE	O
delete line	ERASE INPUT	DELETE LINE	N
erase line	ERASE FIELD	CLEAR	W
truncate line	SKIP	SET	K
insert character	INS CHAR	INSERT CHAR	
delete character	DEL CHAR	DELETE CHAR	
cursor up	↓	↓	U
cursor down	↓	↓	J
cursor right	→	→	R
cursor left	←	←	H
top of screen	HOME	HOME	

GENERAL COMMANDS

Syntax	Definition
USYM	List all user symbols, procedures, functions, and arrays.
DELE ('name'....)	Delete user procedure, function, or array.
SAVE ('file')	Save all user defined symbols, functions, and arrays on 'file'.
RSTR ('file')	Restore user defined symbols, procedures, functions, and arrays from 'file'.
CLR	Delete all user symbols, procedures, functions and arrays.
MSYM	List object program labels.
MDEL	Delete all object program labels.
EXIT	Exit from AMPL back to operating system.

TIMING

YR	Year (1976 to 1999)
DAY	Julian day (1 to 366)
HR	Hour (0 to 23)
MIN	Minute (0 to 59)
SEC	Second (0 to 59)
WAIT (expr)	Suspend AMPL for $<expr>*50$ milliseconds ($<expr> = 20$ is one second).

TARGET MEMORY COMMANDS

EMEM	Emulator memory mapping: 9900/9980 map 8K bytes (0->1FFF) 9940 define RAM and ROM sizes.
LOAD ('file'[,bias[,IDT] [+ DEF] [+ REF]]]):	Load object program by bias and enter program labels into table.
VRFY ('file' [,bias])	Verify object program, listing differences between object and target memory.
DUMP ('file',low,high[,start])	Dump program from target $<low>$ to $<high>$ in nonrelocatable format.

EMULATOR CONTROL COMMANDS

Syntax	Definition
EINT ('EM0n' [,$\begin{Bmatrix} 1 \\ 0 \end{Bmatrix}$[,'TM0n']])	Initialize Emulator device, clock 0 = prototype/ 1 = emulator.
ECLK	Processor clock.
ETYP	Processor type: -1 = TMS9940, 0 = SBP9900, 1 = TMS9900, 2 = TMS9980.
ETRC ($\begin{Bmatrix} MA \\ IAQX \\ IAQ \end{Bmatrix}$ [,count[,low,high]])	Trace qualifier, completion break count (OFF-255), address range.
EBRK ($\begin{Bmatrix} MA \\ IAQ \\ MR \\ MW \end{Bmatrix}$ [+ ILLA] [,address]...)	Address breakpoint(s) (ILLA only valid for TMS9940).
ERUN	Run emulation at PC, WP, ST.
EST	Emulation status (3 LSBits): HOLD, IDLE, Running
EHLT	Halt emulation, return status.
ETBH (index[,$\begin{Bmatrix} MR \\ MW \\ IAQ \end{Bmatrix}$])	Indexed bus signal from buffer. (TRUE if expression matches).
ETB (index)	Indexed address from trace buffer.
ETBO, ETBN	Emulator Trace buffer limits: Oldest, Newest sample indices.

TRACE MODULE CONTROL

Syntax	Definition

Syntax | **Definition**

TINT ('TM0n')   Initialize trace module.

TTRC   ([INT] { OFF / [±Q0] [±Q1][±Q2][±Q3] / [±IAQ][±DBIN] } [,count[, {ON / OFF}]])

Qualify data samples, trace completion counter (OFF-255), latch option on D0-D3.

TEVT ({ OFF / [±D0] [±D1] [±D2] [±D3] / [±IAQ] [±DBIN) / EXT } [,value[,mask]])

Qualify D0-D3 event (or EXTernal), <value> and <mask> for D4-D19.

TBRK (count [,<delay>[,INV] [+ EDGE]]])

Set event counter (OFF-FFFF), set delay counter (OFF-244), count INVerted/EDGE events.

TRUN   Start Trace module tracing.

TST   Trace module status (3 LSB's), event occurred, trace full, tracing.

THLT   Halt trace module, return status.

TNE   Number of events since last TRUN.

TNCE   Number of event count overflows.

TTBH (index[, { [±D0] [±D1][±D2] [±D3] / [±IAQ][±DBIN] }])

D0-D3 of indexed samples, (TRUE if expression matches).

TTB (<index>)   D4-D19 indexed samples (data bus)

TTBO, TTBN   Trace module trace buffer limits: Oldest, Newest sample indices.

TRACE MODULE INTERCONNECT TO EMULATOR

Q0	Memory address bit 15 (TMS9940 only).
D0	Byte memory cycle (TMS9940 only).
Q1,D1, IAQ	Instruction Acquisition.
Q2,D2,DBIN	DataBusIN = MR(read), MW = -DBIN(write).
Q3	Emulator trace qualifier and range (ETRC).
D3, External Event	Emulator address breakpoint (EBRK).
D4-D19	Emulator data bus (bits 0-15).
External Clock	Emulator memory cycle clock.
Control Cable	Synchronizes emulation and tracing. Trace module will halt emulator for EINT ('EM0n', clock 'TM0n').

TARGET REGISTERS

PC,WP,ST	Processor registers.
R0-R15	Workspace registers.
DR	Display all registers.

CRU READ/WRITE

CRUB	CRU interface base address.
CRUR (offset,width)	Read target CRU field.
CRUW (offset,width,value);	Write <value> into target CRU field

KEYWORDS

ARG	FORM	THEN	GE
ARRAY	FUNC	TO	GT
BEGIN	IF	UNTIL	HI
BY	LOC	WHILE	HIE
CASE	MOD	AND	LE
DO	NULL	NAND	LO
ELSE	OF	OR	LOE
END	PROC	XOR	LT
ESCAPE	REPEAT	NOT	NE
FOR	RETURN	EQ	

KEYWORD CONSTANTS

D0	EXT	IO	Q2
D1	EXTEND	MA	Q3
D2	GRAPH	MR	REF
D3	IAQ	MW	REL
DBIN	IAQX	N	REWIND
DEF	IDT	OFF	SEQ
DIRECT	ILLA	ON	UNLOAD
EDGE	IN	OUT	VDT
EOF	INT	Q0	Y
ETBN	INV	Q1	

ERROR MESSAGES

0 — ! UNDEFINED ERROR CODE !

1 — I/O ERROR, OS ERROR CODE RETURNED

2 — INSUFFICIENT MEMORY TO CONTINUE

3 — ! SEGMENT VIOLATION !

4 — I/O ERROR: INVALID UNIT ID

5 — I/O ERROR: READ/WRITE VIOLATION

6 — I/O ERROR: INSUFFICIENT MEMORY FOR OPEN

7 — ! DELETE UNIT CONTROL BLOCKS ERROR !

8 — TOO MANY IDT DEF/REF SYMBOLS IN LOAD

9 — EXCEEDED 15 LOAD OPERATIONS SINCE LAST CLR

10 — CANNOT ALLOCATE MEMORY FOR USER SYMBOL TABLE

11 — ! ERROR IN I/O UNIT CHAIN POINTERS !

12 — OVERLAY ERROR

101 — VARIABLE CANNOT BE READ

102 — VARIABLE CANNOT BE WRITTEN

103 — SYMBOL IS UNDEFINED

104 — ! INVALID CODEGEN BRANCH TABLE INDEX !

105 — INSUFFICIENT MEMORY TO COMPILE STATEMENT

106 — SYMBOL IS DEFINED; CANNOT BE REDEFINED

107 — INSUFFICIENT MEMORY TO COMPILE PROC/FUNC

108 — INPUT RECORD CANNOT BE CLASSIFIED

109 — INPUT STRING EXCEEDS MAXIMUM ALLOWED LENGTH

110 — ! INVALID SCANNER BRANCH TABLE INDEX !

111 — UNRECOGNIZABLE INPUT ITEM

112 — ! UNDEFINED OPERATOR !

114 — SYMBOL NOT AN IDT/DEF/REF LOAD SYMBOL

115 — USER SYMBOL TABLE FULL

116 — CONSTANT EXCEEDS 16 BITS

117 — SYNTAX ERROR

118 — ! INVALID KEYWORD STRING LENGTH !

119 — SYNTAX ERROR IN ONE-LINE-ASSEMBLY STATEMENT

120 — INCORRECT NUMBER OF ARRAY SUBSCRIPTS

121 — ESCAPE SPECIFIED OUTSIDE A LOOP CONSTRUCT

122 — ARRAY REDEFINED WITH INCORRECT SUBSCRIPTS

NOTE: A hexadecimal number is also printed with some error messages. Refer to the AMPL System Operation Guide for complete explanation.

ERROR MESSAGES

201 — SYMBOL NOT FOUND TO DELETE

202 — SYMBOL CANNOT BE DELETED

203 — INVALID DISPLAY FORMAT CHARACTER FOLLOWING:

204 — NO LIST DEVICE ASSIGNED

205 — EMULATOR I/O ERROR CODE RETURNED

209 — INVALID INDEX INTO EMULATOR TRACE BUFFER

210 — !CANNOT ALLOCATE FORM CURRENT VALUE SEGMENT!

211 — INSUFFICIENT MEMORY TO SAVE FORM PARAMETERS

214 — INVALID RESTORE FILE

215 — INSUFFICIENT MEMORY TO COMPLETE THE RESTORE

216 — BAD TRACE OR COMPARISON MODE SELECTED

219 — TRACE MODULE I/O ERROR CODE RETURNED

220 — CANNOT EDIT ON THIS DEVICE TYPE

 221 — TRACE INTERFACE CHANGE ILLEGAL WHILE TRACING

222 — INVALID INDEX INTO TRACE MODULE BUFFER

223 — INSUFFICIENT ARGUMENTS IN PROC/FUNC CALL

224 — STACK OVERFLOW; DELETE PROC/FUNC/ARRAY

225 — DELETED PROC/FUNC/ARRAY REFERENCED

226 — INSUFFICIENT ARGUMENTS IN FORM FOR PROC/FUNC

227 — ! INVALID FORM SEGMENT ID !

228 — ! INVALID FORM CURRENT VALUE SEGMENT ID !

229 — INVALID CHARACTER IN LOAD FILE

230 — CHECKSUM ERROR IN LOAD FILE

231 — ARITHMETIC OVERFLOW

233 — PROC/FUNC CALL ARGUMENT OUT OF RANGE

234 — INVALID "ARG" OR "LOC" INDEX FOR WRITING

235 — INVALID "ARG" OR "LOC" INDEX FOR READING

237 — ARRAY ALREADY DEFINED

238 — INVALID ARRAY DIMENSION

240 — REFERENCE TO UNDECLARED ARRAY

241 — INVALID ARRAY SUBSCRIPT

242 — ! ERROR ARRAY SEGMENT LENGTH !

243 — DELETED IDT/DEF/REF LOAD SYMBOL REFERENCED

244 — ALL IDT/DEF/REF LOAD SYMBOLS DELETED

245 — INVALID DEVICE TYPE TO "EINT" OR "TINT"

NOTE: Error messages withing exclamation marks (!) are AMPL internal system errors.

Contact Texas Instruments if problem persists.

POWER BASIC
MP 307

REFERENCE CARD FOR DEVELOPMENT AND EVALUATION BASIC

This card contains a summary of all POWER BASIC† statements and commands for Development and Evaluation BASIC. An explanation preceded by an asterisk (*) indicates the statement or command is not supported by Evaluation BASIC. A ★ indicates the statement is supported only by the Development BASIC software enhancement package.

COMMANDS

CONtinue

 *Execution continues from last break.

LIST

 LIST the user's POWER BASIC program. In LIST will list from specified line number through end of program or until ESC key is struck.

LOAD

 Reads a previously recorded POWER BASIC program from an auxiliary device or configures POWER BASIC to execute a BASIC program in EPROM.
 LOAD reads program from 733ASR digital cassette.
 LOAD 1 or LOAD 2 ★ reads program from audio cassette drive No. 1 or No. 2.
 LOAD <address>★ configures POWER BASIC to execute BASIC program in EPROM at specified address.

NEW

 Prepare for entry of NEW POWER BASIC program or set the lower RAM memory bound after auto-sizing.
 NEW clears pointers of POWER BASIC and prepares for entry of new program.
 NEW <address>* sets the lower RAM memory bound used by POWER BASIC after auto-sizing or power-up.

PROGRAM

 Program current POWER BASIC application program into EPROM.

RUN

 Begin program execution at the lowest line number.

SAVEn (n is interpreted as in LOADn command)

 Record current user program on auxiliary device.

SIZE

 Display current program size, variable space allocated, and available memory in bytes.

†*Trademark of Texas Instruments*

EDITING

The phrase "(ctrl)" indicates that the user holds down the control key while depressing the key corresponding to the character immediately following.

(CR)	Enter edited line.
(ctrl)In	*Insert n blanks.
(ctrl)Dn	*Delete n characters.
(ctrl)H	Backspace one character.
(ctrl)F	Forward space one character.
In(ctrl)E	Display for editing source line indicated by line number (In).
(ctrl)T	Toggle from one partition to the other partition (only in Evaluation BASIC).
(esc)	Cancel input line or break program execution.
(Rubout) or (DEL)	Backspace and delete character.

STATEMENTS

InBAUD <exp 1,> <exp 2>

    *sets baud rate of serial I/O port(s).

InBASE <(exp)>

    Sets CRU base address for subsequent CRU operations

InCALL <subroutine address>[, <var 1>, <var 2>, <var 3>, <var 4>]

    *Transfers to external subroutines. If variable is contained in parentheses, the address will be passed; otherwise, the value will be passed.

InDATA $\left\{ \begin{array}{l} <exp> \\ <string\ const> \end{array} \right\} \left[\left\{ \begin{array}{l} <exp> \\ <string\ const> \end{array} \right\} \right] \cdots$

    defines internal data block. Strings excluded from DATA statements in Evaluation BASIC.

In DEF FN<x>[(<arg 1> [, arg 2] [, arg 3])] = <exp>

    *Defines user arithmetic function.

InDIM <var (dim[, dim] . . .)> [, ...)

    Allocates user variable space for dimensioned or array variables.

InEND

    Terminates program execution and returns to edit mode.

In ERROR<In>

    *Specifies a subroutine that will be called via a GOSUB statement when an error occurs.

In ESCAPE
InNOESC

    *Enables or disables the excape key to interrupt program execution (always enabled in Evaluation BASIC).

lnFOR <sim-var> = <exp> TO <exp> [STEP <exp>]
lnNEXT <sim-var>

Open and close program loop. Both identify the same control variable. FOR assigns starting, ending, and optionally stepping values.

lnGOSUB<ln>

Transfer of control to an internal subroutine beginning at the specified line.

lnPOP

*Removal of most previous return address from GOSUB stack without an execution transfer.

lnRETURN

Return from external subroutine.

lnGOTO<ln>

Transfers program execution to specified line number.

lnIF<exp>THEN<statement>
lnELSE<statement>

Causes conditional execution of the statement following THEN. *ELSE statements execute when IF condition is false.

lnIMASK<LEVEL>

*Set interrupt mask of TMS 9900 processor to specified level.

lnTRAP<level>TO<ln>

*Assign interrupt level to interrupt subroutine.

lnIRTN

*Return from BASIC interrupt service routine.

$$\text{lnINPUT}<\text{var}> \left[\begin{Bmatrix} \cdot \\ ; \end{Bmatrix} <\text{var}> \right] \cdots \left[\begin{Bmatrix} \cdot \\ ; \end{Bmatrix} \right]$$

Accesses numeric constants and strings from the keyboard into variables in the INPUT list.

ln [LET] <var> = <exp>

Evaluates and assigns values to variables or array elements.

$$\text{lnON} \begin{Bmatrix} <\text{var}> \\ <\text{exp}> \end{Bmatrix} \text{ THEN GOTO ln [,ln]} \dots$$

$$\text{lnON} \begin{Bmatrix} <\text{var}> \\ <\text{exp}> \end{Bmatrix} \text{ THEN GOSUB ln [,ln]} \dots$$

*Transfers execution to the line number specified by the expression or variable.

lnPRINT <exp> [,exp] . . .

Print (format free) the evaluated expressions.

lnRANDOM [exp]

*Set the seed to the specified expression value.

$$\text{lnREAD} \begin{Bmatrix} <\text{numeric var}> \\ <\text{string var}> \end{Bmatrix} \left[, \begin{Bmatrix} <\text{numeric var}> \\ <\text{string var}> \end{Bmatrix} \right] \dots$$

Assigns values from the internal data list to variables or array elements.

lnREM [text]

Inserts comments.

lnRESTOR [exp]

Without an argument, resets pointer to beginning of data sequence; with an argument, resets pointer to line number specified.

lnSTOP

Terminates program execution and returns to Edit mode.

lnTIME

Sets, displays, or stores the 24 hour time of day clock.
lnTIME <exp>, <exp>, <exp>
Sets and starts clock.
lnTIME <string-var>
Enables storing clock time into a string variable.
lnTIME
Prints clock time as HR:MN:SD.

lnUNIT <exp>

*Designates device(s) to receive all printed output.

FUNCTIONS

ABS <(exp)>	*Absolute value of expression.
ASC <(string var)>	*Returns decimal ASCII code for first character of string variable.
ATN <(exp)>	Arctangent of expression in radians.
BIT <(var, exp)>	*Reads or modifies any bit within a variable.
BIT <(var, exp 1)> = <exp 2>	Returns a 1 if bit is set and 0 if not set. Selected bit is set to 1 if assigned value is non-zero and to zero if the assigned value is zero.
COS >(exp)>	Cosine of the expression in radians.
CRB <(exp)>	Reads CRU bit as selected by CRU base + exp. Exp is valid for − 127 thru 128.
CRB <(exp 1)> = <(exp 2)>	Sets or resets CRU bit as selected by CRU base + exp 1. If exp 2 is non-zero, the bit will be set, else reset. Exp 1 is valid for − 127 thru 128.
CRF <(exp)>	Reads n CRU bits as selected by CRU base where exp evaluates to n. Exp·is valid for 0 thru 15. If exp = 0, 16 bits will be read.
CRF <(exp 1)> = <(exp 2)>	Stores exp 1 bits of exp 2 to CRU lines as selected by CRU BASE. Exp 1 if valid for 0 thru 15. If exp 1 = 0, 16 bits will be stored.
EXP <(exp)>	*Raise the constant e to the power of the evaluated expression.
INP <(exp)>	Returns the signed integer portion of the expression.

LOG <(exp)>.	*Returns natural logarithm of the expression.
MEM <(exp)>	Reads byte from user memory at address specified by exp. Exp must be in the integer range, (0 to 65535).
MEM >(exp 1)> = <(exp 2)>	Stores byte exp 2 into user memory specified by exp 1. Exp 1 and exp 2 must be in the integer range.
MCH <(string 1), (string 2)>	*Returns the number of characters to which the two strings agree.
NYK <(exp)>	Conditionally samples the keyboard in run time mode. If exp <>0, return decimal value of last key struck and clear key register. (0 if no key struck.) If exp = 0, return a 1 if the last key struck has the same decimal value as the expression. Clear key register if TRUE, else return 0 if FALSE.
RND	Returns a random number between 0 and 1.
SIN <(exp)>	Sine of the expression in radians.
SQR <(exp)>	Square root of expression.
SRH <(string 1), (string 2)>	*Return the position of string 1 in string 2, 0 if not found.
SYS <(exp)>	*Obtains system parameters generated during program execution. Example: SYS(0) = INPUT control character, SYS(1) = Error code number, SYS(2) = error line number.
TIC <(exp)>	Returns the number of time tics less the expression value. One TIC equals 40 milliseconds (1/25 second).

STRINGS

ASCII Character Conversion Function	ASC (string-var) *Convert first character of string to ASCII numeric representation.
Assignment	$<\text{string-var}> = \begin{Bmatrix} <\text{string-var}> \\ <\text{string-constant}> \end{Bmatrix}$ Store string into string-var ending with a null.
Character Match Function	MCH (<string 1>, <string 2>) *Return the number of characters to which the 2 strings agree.
Character Search Function	SRH (<string 1>, <string 2>) *Return the position of string 1 in string 2. Zero is returned if not found.
Concatenate	<string-var> = $\begin{Bmatrix} <\text{string-var}> \\ <\text{string-constant}> \end{Bmatrix} + \begin{Bmatrix} <\text{string-var}> \\ <\text{string-constant}> \end{Bmatrix} \begin{bmatrix} + \{...\} \end{bmatrix}$

Convert to ASCII	<string-var> = <exp> <string-var> = # <string>, <exp> *Convert exp to ASCII characters ending with a null. # string specifies a formatted conversion.
Convert to Binary	<var 1> = <string>, <var 2> *Convert string into binary equivalent. Var 2 receives the delimiting non-numeric character in first byte.
Deletion	<String-var> = / <exp> *Delete exp characters from string-var.
Insertion	<string-var> = / <string> *Pick byte into string-var.
Pick	$<string\text{-}var> = \begin{Bmatrix} <string\text{-}var> \\ <string\text{-}constant> \end{Bmatrix}, <exp>$ Pick number of characters specified by exp into string-var ending with a null.
Replace	$<string\text{-}var> = \begin{Bmatrix} <string\text{-}var> \\ <string\text{-}constant> \end{Bmatrix}; <exp>$ Replace number of characters specified by exp of string-var with string.
String Length Function	<var> = LEN <(string-var)> <var> = LEN "string" *Return the length of string.

INPUT OPTIONS

string-var	Prompt with colon and input character data. Example: INPUT $A
,	Delimit expressions. Example A, B
;	Suppress prompting or CR LF if at end of line. Examples: INPUT ;A INPUT A;
# exp	Allow a maximum of exp characters to be entered. Example: INPUT # 1"Y or N"$1
%exp	*Must enter exactly exp number of characters. Example: INPUT %4"CODE"C
?<ln>	*Upon an invalid input or entry of a control character, a GOSUB is performed to the line # . SYS(0) will be equal to − 1 if there was an invalid input. Otherwise, SYS(0) will equal the decimal equivalent of the control character. Example: INPUT ?100;A

OUTPUT OPTIONS

;	Delimit expressions or suppress CR LF if at end of line. Examples: PRINT A;B PRINT A;
,	Tab to next print field. Example: PRINT A, B
TAB <(exp)>	Tab to exp column. Example: PRINT TAB (50);A
string	Print string or string-var. Example: PRINT ''HI'';$A(0)
# exp	*Print exp as hexadecimal in free format. Example: PRINT # 123
# ,exp	*Print exp as hexadecimal in byte format. Example: PRINT # ,50
# ;exp	*Print exp as hexadecimal in word format. Example: PRINT # ,A
<hex value>	*Direct output of ASCII codes. Example: PRINT ''<OD> <OA>''
# string	★Print under specified format where: PRINT # ''9999''I 9 = digit holder
	PRINT # ''000-00-0000''SS 0 = digit holder or force 0
	PRINT # ''$$$,$$$.00''DLR $ = digit holder and floats $
	PRINT # ''SSS.0000''4*ATN1 S = digit holder and floats sign
	PRINT # ''<<<.00>''I < = digit holder. and float on negative >number
	PRINT # ''990.99E''N E = sign holder after decimal
	PRINT # ''990.99''N = decimal point specifier
	PRINT # ''999,990.99''N , = suppressed if before significant digit
	PRINT # ''999,990 ∧ 00''I ∧ = translates to decimal point
	PRINT # ''HI = 99''I any other character is printed.

GENERAL INFORMATION

ARITHMETIC OPERATIONS

A + B	Assignment
A − B	Negation or subtraction
A + B, $A + $B	Addition or string concatenation
A*B	Multiplication
A / B	Division
A∧B	Exponentiation
− A	Unary Minus
+ A	Unary Plus

LOGICAL OPERATORS

LNOT A	# 1's complement of integer.
A LAND B	*Bit wise AND.
A LOR B	*Bit wise OR.
A LXOR B	*Bit wise exclusive OR.

RELATIONAL OPERATORS

1 if TRUE and 0 if FALSE

A = B	TRUE if equal, else FALSE.
A = = B	*TRUE if approximately equal (1E-7), else FALSE
A<B	TRUE if less than, else FALSE.
A< = B	TRUE if less than or equal, else FALSE.
A>B	TRUE if greater than, else FALSE.
A> = B	TRUE if greater than or equal, else FALSE.
A<>B	TRUE if not equal, else FALSE.
NOT A	*TRUE if zero, else FALSE.
A AND B	*TRUE if both non-zero, else FALSE.
A OR B	*TRUE if either non-zero, else FALSE.

OPERATOR PRECEDENCE

1.	Expressions in parentheses	7.	= ,>
2.	Exponentiation and negation	8.	= , LXOR
3.	*,/	9.	NOT, LNOT
4.	+ ,−	10.	AND, LAND
5.	< = ,<>	11.	OR, LOR
6.	> = ,<	12.	(=)ASSIGNMENT

SPECIAL CHARACTERS

::   Separates statements typed on same line.

!   Tail remark used for comments after program statement

;   Equivalent to PRINT.

ERROR CODES

1 =	SYNTAX ERROR	37 =	ILLEGAL DELIMITER
2 =	UNMATCHED PARENTHESIS	38 =	UNDEFINED FUNCTION
3 =	INVALID LINE NUMBER	39 =	UNDIMENSIONED VARIABLE
4 =	ILLEGAL VARIABLE NAME	40 =	UNDERFINED VARIABLE
5 =	ILLEGAL CHARACTER	41 =	EXPANSION EPROM NOT INSTALLED
		42 =	INTERRUPT W/O TRAP
7 =	EXPECTING OPERATOR	43 =	INVALID BAUD RATE
8 =	ILLEGAL FUNCTION NAME	44 =	TAPE READ ERROR
9 =	ILLEGAL FUNCTION ARGUMENT	45 =	EPROM VERIFY ERROR
10 =	STORAGE OVERFLOW	46 =	INVALID DEVICE NUMBER
11 =	STACK OVERFLOW		
12 =	STACK UNDERFLOW		
13 =	NO SUCH LINE NUMBER		
14 =	EXPECTING STRING VARIABLE		
15 =	INVALID SCREEN COMMAND		
16 =	EXPECTING DIMENSIONED VARIABLE		
17 =	SUBSCRIPT OUT OF RANGE		
18 =	TWO FEW SUBSCRIPTS		
19 =	TOO MANY SUBSCRIPTS		
20 =	EXPECTING SIMPLE VARIABLE		
21 =	DIGITS OUT OF RANGE (0< # of digits <12)		
22 =	EXPECTING VARIABLE		
23 =	READ OUT OF DATA		
24 =	READ TYPE DIFFERS FROM DATA TYPE		
25 =	SQUARE ROOT OF NEGATIVE NUMBER		
26 =	LOG OF NON-POSITIVE NUMBER		
27 =	EXPRESSION TOO COMPLEX		
28 =	DIVISION BY ZERO		
29 =	FLOATING POINT OVERFLOW		
30 =	FIX ERROR		
31 =	FOR WITHOUT NEXT		
32 =	NEXT WITHOUT FOR		
33 =	EXP FUNCTION HAS INVALID ARGUMENT		
34 =	UNNORMALIZED NUMBER		
35 =	PARAMETER ERROR		
36 =	MISSING ASSIGNMENT OPERATOR		

Cross Support

The Cross Assembler data base which is assigned to PUNIT, is read by the FORTRAN program as the first file at execution time. It is the actual Cross Assembler program written in internal code, and it is suggested that it be assigned to a permanent disk file.

INTERNAL NAME	DEFAULT UNIT	DEVICE TYPE	RECORD LENGTH	FUNCTION
IUNIT	5	CR,CS MT,DF	80	TMS 9900 Source Input
LUNIT	6	CS,MT	80	Listing Output
OUNIT	7	CS,MT	80	TMS9900 Object Output
SUNIT	10	MT,DF	80	Assembly Scratch
PUNIT	11	CR,CS	80	Data Base INPUT

CR—CARD READER; CS—CASSETTE TAPE; MT—MAGNETIC TAPE; DF—DISKFILE; CP—CARD PUNCH; LP—LINE PRINTER

CROSS ASSEMBLER SYSTEM FILES

AORG places the expression value in the location counter, and defines the succeeding locations as absolute. ·

ABSOLUTE ORIGIN

AORG

Syntax Definition:

[<label>]ɸ . . . AORGɸ . . . <wd-exp>ɸ . . .[<comment>]

RORG places the expression value in the location counter, and defines the succeeding locations as relocatable.

RELOCATABLE ORIGIN

RORG

Syntax Definition:

[<label>ɸ . . . RORGɸ . . . [<exp>]ɸ . . .[<comment>]

DORG places the expression value in the location counter, and defines the succeeding locations as a dummy section. No object code is generated in a dummy section.

DUMMY ORIGIN

DORG

Syntax Definition:

<label>ɸ . . . DORGɸ . . . <exp>ɸ . . .[<comment>]

BSS first assigns the label, if present, and increments the location counter by the value of the expression.

BLOCK STARTING WITH SYMBOL

BSS

Syntax Definition:

[<label>]ɸ . . . BSSɸ . . . <wd-exp>ɸ . . .[<comment>]

BSS first increments the location counter by the value of the expression, and then assigns the label, if present.

BLOCK ENDING WITH SYMBOL

BES

Syntax Definition:

[<label>]ɸ . . . BESɸ . . . <wd-exp>ɸ . . .[<comment>]

EQU assigns an assembly-time constant to the label.

DEFINE ASSEMBLY-TIME CONSTANT

EQU

Syntax Definition:

<label>ɸ . . . EQUɸ . . . <exp>ɸ . . .[<comment>]

EVEN first assigns the label, if present, and then aligns the location counter on a word boundary (even address).

WORD BOUNDARY

EVEN

Syntax Definition:

[<label>]ɸ . . . EVENɸ . . .[<comment>]

OPTIONS allows cross referencing when XREF is specified, and allows printing of the symbol table when SYMT is present.

OUTPUT OPTIONS

OPTION

Syntax Definition:

ɸ , . . OPTIONɸ . . . <keyword>[,<keyword>] . . . ɸ . . . [<comment>]

IDT assigns a name to the program, and must precede any code-generating directive or instruction.

PROGRAM IDENTIFIER   **IDT**

Syntax Definition:

[<label>]β . . . IDTβ . . . <string>β . . .[<comment>]

TITL supplies a string to be printed at the top of each subsequent source listing page.

PAGE TITLE   **TITL**

Syntax Definition:

[<label>]β . . . TITLβ . . . <string>β . . . [<comment>]

LIST restores printing of the source listing.

LIST SOURCE   **LIST**

Syntax Definition:

[<label>]β . . . LISTβ . . . [<comment>]

UNL inhibits printing of the source listing.

NO SOURCE LIST   **UNL**

Syntax Definition:

[<label>]β . . . UNLβ . . . [<comment>]

PAGE directs the assembler to continue the source listing on the next page.

PAGE EJECT   **PAGE**

Syntax Definition:

[<label>]β . . . PAGEβ . . . [<comment>]

BYTE places expressions in successive bytes, optionally assigning the label the address of the first byte.

INITIALIZE BYTE   **BYTE**

Syntax Definition:

[<label>]β . . . BYTEβ . . . <exp>[,<exp>] . . . β . . . [<comment>]

DATA places expressions in successive words, optionally assigning the label the address of the first word.

INITIALIZE WORD   **DATA**

Syntax Definition:

[<label>]β . . . DATAβ . . . <exp>[,<exp>] . . . β . . . [<comment>]

TEXT places characters in successive bytes, arithmetically negating the last character, and optionally assigns the label the address of the first character.

INITIALIZE TEXT   **TEXT**

Syntax Definition:

[<label>]β . . . TEXTβ . . . [−]<string>β . . . [<comment>]

DEF makes symbols available to other programs as external references.

EXTERNAL DEFINITION **DEF**

Syntax Definition:

[<label>]∅ . . . DEF∅ . . . <symbol>[,<symbol>] . . . ∅ . . . [<comment>]

REF directs the assembler to look externally for symbols.

EXTERNAL REFERENCE **REF**

Syntax Definition:

[<label>]∅ . . . REF∅ . . . <symbol>[,<symbol>] . . . ∅ . . . [<comment>]

DXOP assigns an extended operation to a symbol.

DEFINE EXTENDED OPERATIONS **DXOP**

Syntax Definition:

[<label>]∅ . . . DXOP∅ . . . <symbol>,<term>∅ . . . [<comment>]

END terminates the assembly

PROGRAM END **END**

Syntax Definition:

[<label>]∅ . . . END∅ . . . [<symbol>]∅ . . . [<comment>]

NOP places a no-operation code in the object file.

NO OPERATION **NOP**

Syntax Definition:

[<label>]∅ . . . NOP∅ . . . [<comment>]

RT assembles as a return from subroutine by substituting a branch through register 11.

RETURN **RT**

Syntax Definition:

[<label>]∅ . . . RT∅ . . . [<comment>]

SIMULATOR FILES

INTERNAL NAME	DEFAULT UNIT	DEVICE TYPE	RECORD LENGTH	FUNCTION	WHERE USED
INCOPY	4	MT,DF	80	Batch copy file	C
INCOM	5	TE,CR MT,DF	80	Simulation command	C
OUTPRT OUTTRC	6	MT,DF TE,CR	80 or 136	Listing output	L,C,R
INLOD	10	TE,CR MT,DF	80	Linker commands	L
OUTCOM	11	TE,LP	80 or 136	Prompts and error msg. for linker output	L
OUTSAV	17	MT,CP DF	80	Absolute object	L,S
INSCR	20	MT,DF	136	Input scratch file	C,R,S
OUTSCR	21	MT,DF	136	Output scratch file	L,C,R

Device type legend
TE—terminal; CR—card reader; MT—magnetic tape; DF—disk file; CP—card punch

Where used legend
L—link processor; C—command processor; R—run processor; S-save processor

In addition to the above unit number assignments, the user must also assign unique FORTRAN logical unit numbers to each TMS9900 object code module to be included in the LINK processor.

SIMULATOR DIRECTIVES

ORIGIN COMMAND. The "ORIGIN" command can be used to specify where relocatable code is to be loaded.

ORIGIN hex-number

INCLUDE COMMAND. The "INCLUDE" command directs the loader to load an object module from a data set (e.g., card reader, disc, tape). The data set must be a sequential data set and may contain one or more object modules. At least one "INCLUDE" command should be used in the LINK processor command stream. The format for the command is as follows:

INCLUDE n

ENTRY COMMAND. The "ENTRY" command specifies the program entry point to the loader. The format for the command is as follows:

ENTRY name

SUMMARY OF CONTROL LANGUAGE STATEMENTS

The formats of the control statements for the "COMMAND" processor are shown below, with a brief description following:

[label] $\begin{Bmatrix} R \\ RUN \end{Bmatrix}$ [*] $\begin{Bmatrix} F \\ FOR \end{Bmatrix}$ n $\left[\begin{Bmatrix} FR \\ FROM \end{Bmatrix} i1\right]\left[\begin{Bmatrix} T \\ TO \end{Bmatrix}\right]$i2 [,label]

Specifies where to start and stop simulation. Control passes to statement at label operand when a breakpoint occurs.

[label] $\begin{Bmatrix} T \\ TRACE \end{Bmatrix}$ [list] Specifies locations to be traced.

[label] $\begin{Bmatrix} NOT \\ NOTRACE \end{Bmatrix}$ [list] Disables trace for specified locations.

[label] $\begin{Bmatrix} RE \\ REFER \end{Bmatrix}$ [list] Specifies locations for reference breakpoint.

[label] $\begin{Bmatrix} NOR \\ NOREFER \end{Bmatrix}$ [list] Disables reference breakpoint at specified locations.

[iabel] $\begin{Bmatrix} A \\ ALTER \end{Bmatrix}$ [list] Specifies locations for alteration breakpoint.

[label] $\begin{Bmatrix} NOA \\ NOALTER \end{Bmatrix}$ [list] Disables alteration breakpoint at specified locations.

[label] $\begin{Bmatrix} P \\ PROTECT \end{Bmatrix}$ [list] Specifies areas for memory protection.

[label] IF (logical expression) label Conditional transfer of control program.

[label] $\begin{Bmatrix} J \\ JUMP \end{Bmatrix}$ label Unconditional transfer of control program.

[label] $\begin{Bmatrix} TI \\ TIME \end{Bmatrix}$ [n] Prints the value of 9900 time and optionally sets a new value.

[label] $\begin{Bmatrix} D \\ DISPLAY \end{Bmatrix}$ [D] $\begin{Bmatrix} CP \\ CPU \end{Bmatrix}$ [register list] Prints contents of registers.

[label] $\begin{Bmatrix} D \\ DISPLAY \end{Bmatrix} \begin{bmatrix} D \\ C \end{bmatrix} \begin{Bmatrix} M \\ MEMORY \end{Bmatrix}$ list Prints contents of memory.

[label] $\begin{Bmatrix} D \\ DISPLAY \end{Bmatrix}$ $\begin{Bmatrix} S \\ SYMBOL \end{Bmatrix}$ $\begin{bmatrix} \$ \\ symbol \\ number \end{bmatrix}$ Prints values from symbol table.

[label] $\begin{Bmatrix} D \\ DISPLAY \end{Bmatrix}$ $\begin{Bmatrix} CR \\ CRU \end{Bmatrix}$ $\begin{Bmatrix} I \\ INPUT \\ O \\ OUTPUT \end{Bmatrix}$ list   Prints CRU values.

[label] $\begin{Bmatrix} S \\ SET \end{Bmatrix}$ $\begin{Bmatrix} C \\ CPU \end{Bmatrix}$ register-value list   Places values into registers.

[label] $\begin{Bmatrix} S \\ SET \end{Bmatrix}$ $\begin{Bmatrix} M \\ MEMORY \end{Bmatrix}$ location-value list   Places values into memory.

[label] $\begin{Bmatrix} S \\ SET \end{Bmatrix}$ $\begin{Bmatrix} I \\ INT \end{Bmatrix}$ level, n_1 [,n_2,n_3]   Sets up one or more interrupts.

[label] $\begin{Bmatrix} E \\ END \end{Bmatrix}$ Disables breakpoints and traces, and initializes simulation. Passes control to next control statement.

[label $\begin{Bmatrix} I \\ INPUT \end{Bmatrix}$ $\begin{Bmatrix} n \\ n_1 \ TO \ n_2 \end{Bmatrix}$ $\begin{bmatrix} F \\ FIRST \\ L \\ LAST \\ A \\ ALL \end{bmatrix}$ [data]   Defines input lines and fields, and supplies data for program being simulated.

[label] $\begin{Bmatrix} O \\ OUTPUT \end{Bmatrix}$ $\begin{Bmatrix} n \\ n_1 \ TO \ n_2 \end{Bmatrix}$ Defines output lines and fields, or prints output of program being simulated.

[label] $\begin{Bmatrix} CONN \\ CONNECT \end{Bmatrix}$ list   Connects input CRU lines to output CRU lines.

[label] $\begin{Bmatrix} C \\ CONVERT \end{Bmatrix}$ expression   list   Evaluates and prints values of expressions in decimal and hexadecimal form.

$\begin{Bmatrix} B \\ BATCH \end{Bmatrix}$ Specifies batch mode.

[label] $\begin{Bmatrix} L \\ LOAD \end{Bmatrix}$ Loads Wp and PC from locations $FFFC_{16}$ and $FFFE_{16}$.

[label] $\begin{Bmatrix} CL \\ CLOCK \end{Bmatrix}$ t   Specify clock period.

[label] $\begin{Bmatrix} M \\ MEMORY \end{Bmatrix}$ $\begin{Bmatrix} RA \\ RAM \\ RO \\ ROM \end{Bmatrix}$ $\begin{Bmatrix} R \\ READ \end{Bmatrix} = n_1$ $\begin{bmatrix} W \\ WRITE \end{bmatrix} = n_2$ list

Define available memory. Default is 32K RAM.

[label] $\begin{Bmatrix} SA \\ SAVE \end{Bmatrix}$ Create absolute object module.

[label] $\begin{Bmatrix} W \\ WIDTH \end{Bmatrix}$ n   Specifies number of columns available for printing.

MONITOR COMPLETION CODES

The simulator signals completion by executing and writing an appropriate STOP I statement, where I takes on one of the following values:

CODE	MEANING
0	Normal completion
1	Abnormal completion from LNKPRC
2	Premature EOF
	—If this error occurs it indicates that a premature EOF was encountered while attempting to reposition the BATCH command file.
3	Internal error; invalid label value
4	Roll memory overflow
5	Loader error
	—If this error occurs it means an attempt was made to load an object file into simulated memory and it failed causing termination of the link processor.
8	Abnormal completion from LOADER
9	Abnormal completion from CMDPRC
99	Internal error
	—Illegal completion from CMDPRC
	Internal error
999	Internal error
	—Illegal parameter passed to WRITER

If an error of 99 or 999 results, an internal error has occurred and the error should be reported to TEXAS INSTRUMENTS INC.

LINK PROCESSOR ERRORS

CODE	MESSAGE
L01	Load not completed
L02	Multiply defined external symbol (name)
L03	Empty object file on unit
L04	Attempt to load undefined memory
L05	Tag D follows tag 0
L06	Invalid tag character
L09	Undefined external memory
L13	Empty memory on save
L14	(name) not in external symbol table
L18	Maximum memory size exceeded
L19	Missing end
L21	Checksum error (computed value)
L22	Odd origin value specified—even value used
L24	Ref chain loop
L25	Object module does not start with tag 0
L26	Odd value (value) specified for tag (tag) even value used
L27	Missing F tag in record (number)
L28	Bad REF chain for (name)
L29	Bad object format in object module
L30	Illegal hex digit in field (digit)

COMMAND PROCESSOR ERRORS

CODE NUMBER	NAME	MESSAGE	CODE NUMBER	NAME	MESSAGE
1	BADCHR	Bad character	18	RANGE	Range error
2	BADCMD	Unrecognizable command	19	SYNTAX	Syntax error
3	BADIGT	Bad digit	20	TOOMNY	Too many values
4	BADMOD	Bad module name	21	UNDEF	Undefined symbol
5	BADREG	Bad register mnemonic			
6	BADVAL	Bad value			
7	CRUSPC	CRU specification error			
8	FLDCNT	Too few/many fields			
9	HITEOF	Hit EOF			
10	HITEOL	Hit end-of-line			
11	MEMDEF	Undefined			
12	MISSEQ	Missing equal sign			
13	NODATA	No data found			
14	NOROL	No data rolls available			
15	NOSET	Set not performed			
16	NOTIMP	Command not implemented			
17	ORDER	Command out of order			

RUN PROCESSOR ERRORS

CODE	MESSAGE
1	PC interrupt vector entry in undefined memory
2	WP interrupt vector entry in undefined memory
3	Register out of address space (WP 65502)
4	Registers in undefined memory
5	Registers in ROM
6	PC interrupt vector refer breakpoint
7	WP interrupt vector refer breakpoint
8	Register alter breakpoint
9	Register protect breakpoint
10	Register refer breakpoint
11	Undefined opcode
12	Undefined memory reference
13,14	Unused
15	PC refer breakpoint
16	Unimplemented opcode
17,18,19	Unused
20	Destination address in undefined memory
21	Destination refer breakpoint
22	Destination alter breakpoint
23	Destination ROM breakpoint
24	Unused
25	Source address in undefined memory
26	Source refer breakpoint
27	Source alter breakpoint
28	Source ROM breakpoint

TMSUTL

CONCEPT

TMSUTL is a general purpose ultility program that accepts as input TI microprocessor object format, PROM manufacturing formats, or ROM manufacturing formats. This data is syntax checked, output options are gathered, the input data converted and an output file is produced.

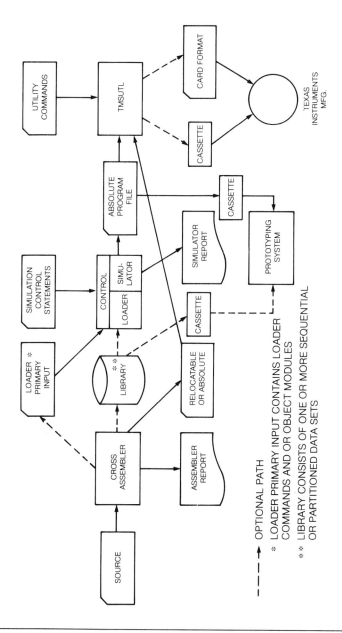

INPUT, OUTPUT CONTROL CARD FORMATS

GENERAL DESCRIPTION

INPUT frmt [addr1 addr2] [WIDTH = x] [PARTITION = y]

frmt	— is the format number (integer 1-12).
addr1	— is the starting address where input data is to be stored.
addr2	— is the maximum address where data is to be stored.
x	— is the bit width of the input words.
y	— is the number of input data set partitions 1 Y 4

OUTPUT num addr1 addr2 WIDTH = x PARTITION = y

num	— is the format number (integer 1-12).
addr1	— is the minimum address to be output.
addr2	— is the maximum address to be output.
x	— is the bit width of an output word.
y	—

EOF—End of COMMAND FILE indicator

AVAILABLE FORMATS

FORMAT #	FORMAT	INPUT	OUTPUT
1	Hexadecimal #1 (PROM)	X	X
2	Hexadecimal #2 (ROM)	X	X
3	BNPF	X	X
4	271 & 371 ROM/HILO of prototyping System	X	X
5	TMS8080/TMS1000 Absolute Object from SIM8080/SIM1000 Loader/Simulator	X	X
6	TMS1000 Absolute ROM Object from Assembler	X	X
7	TMS1000 Listed Absolute Object	X	X
8	TMS1000 OPLA Data	X	
9	TMS9900 Standard Absolute Object of Cross Support System (Assembler or Loader/Simulator) & Prototyping System	X	X
10	TMS9900 Compressed Absolute Object of Prototyping System	X	X
11	TI4700 ROM	X	X
12	TI4800 ROM	X	X

TMSUTL FORMAT PATHS

Output Format →	1	2	3	4	5	6	7	8	9	10	11	12
1) Hexadecimal #2 (PROM)	YES	YES	YES	YES	NO	NO	YES	NO	NO	NO	YES	YES
2) Hexadecimal #2 (ROM)	YES	YES	YES	YES	NO	NO	YES	NO	NO	NO	YES	YES
3) BNPF	YES	YES	YES	YES	YES	YES	YES	NO	YES	YES	YES	YES
4) 271 & 371 ROM/ HILO of Prototyping System	YES	YES	YES	YES	NO	NO	YES	NO	NO	NO	YES	YES
5) TMS1000 / TMS8080 Absolute Object from Loader/Simulator	YES	YES	YES	YES	YES	YES	YES	NO	NO	NO	YES	YES
6) TMS1000 Absolute ROM Objects from Assembler for masking	YES	YES	YES	YES	YES	YES	YES	NO	NO	NO	YES	YES
7) TMS1000 Listed Absolute Object	YES	YES	YES	YES	YES	YES	YES	NO	NO	NO	YES	YES
8) TMS1000 OPLA Data	YES	YES	YES	NO	NO	NO	NO	NO	NO	NO	NO	NO
9) TMS9900 Standard Absolute Object of Cross Support System (Assembler or Loader/Simulator) & Prototyping System	YES	YES	YES	YES	NO	NO	NO	NO	YES	YES	YES	YES
10) TMS9900 Compressed Absolute Object of Protoyping System	YES	YES	YES	YES	NO	NO	NO	NO	YES	YES	YES	YES
11) TI4700 ROM	YES	YES	YES	YES	YES	NO	YES	NO	NO	NO	YES	YES
12) TI4800 ROM	YES	YES	YES	YES	YES	NO	YES	NO	NO	NO	YES	YES

DATA DELIMITERS

The following is a table of data delimiters or end-of-module records for Input Data.

FORMAT #	TYPES
1. Hex format 1	End of file record (:00)
2. Hex format 2	Trailer record — "END OF TEXT" (hollerith code 12-9-3) character followed by 79 non-blank characters (without asterisks)
3. BNPF	End of file record ($ in column 1)
4. 271/371 ROM and HILO of Prototyping System	End of file record ($END)
5. TMS8080/TMS1000 Absolute Object from Loader/Simulator	End record (+ END)
6. TMS1000 Absolute ROM Object	End of file record ($END)
7. TMS1000 Listed Absolute Object	End of file record ($END)
8. TMS1000 OPLA Data	End of file record ($END)
9. TMS9900 Standard Absolute Object	End of module record (:)
10. TMS9900 Binary Compressed Absolute Object	End of file record ($END)
11. TI4700 ROM	End of file record ($END)
12. TI4800 ROM	End of file record ($END)

ADDRESS RANGES FOR FORMATS

FORMAT#	FORMAT	ADDRESS RANGE
1	Hexadecimal # 1 (PROM)	(0-FFFF)$_H$
2	Hexadecimal # 2 (ROM)	None
3	BNPF	None
4	271 & 371 ROM/HILO of Prototyping System	None
5	TMS8080/TMS1000 Absolute Object from Loader/Simulator	(0-255)
6	TMS1000 Absolute ROM Object	(0-800)$_H$
7	TMS1000 Listed Absolute Object	(0-1 Chapter 0-15 page 0-3F location)$_H$
8	TMS1000 OPLA Data	(0-1F)$_H$
9	TMS9900 Standard Absolute Object	(0-FFFF)$_H$
10	TMS9900 Compressed Absolute Object	(0-FFFF)$_H$
11	TI4700 ROM	(0-400)$_H$
12	TI4800 ROM	(0-400)$_H$

INPUT AND OUTPUT WIDTHS FOR FORMATS

FORMAT#	FORMAT	WIDTH (BITS)
1	Hexadecimal #1 (PROM)	8
2	Hexadecimal #2 (ROM)	8
3	BNPF	2 or 4 or 8 or 16
4	271 & 371 ROM/HILO of Prototyping System	4 or 8
5	TMS8080/TMS1000 Absolute Object from Loader/Simulator	8
6	TMS1000 Object from Assembler	8
7	TMS1000 Listed Absolute Object	8
8	TMS1000 OPLA Data	8 or 16
9	TMS9900 Standard Absolute Object	16
10	TMS9900 Compressed Absolute Object	16
11	TI4700 ROM	8
12	TI4800 ROM	4 or 8

FILES DEFINITIONS & DESCRIPTIONS

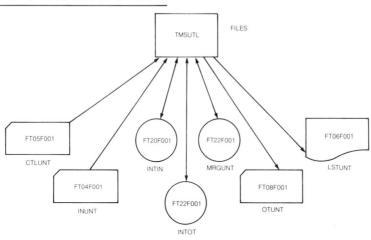

CTLUNT — Input file for control cards.

INUNT — Input file for data.

INTIN — Intermediate file for storage of input data. It must be a rewindable file with a logical record length of 80 bytes.

INTOT — Intermediate file for storage of internal data. It must be a rewindable file with a logical record length of 80 bytes.

OTUNT — Output file for translated data.

LSTUNT — Print file for listing of data and error messages.

MRGUNT — Intermediate file for storage of internal data. It must be a rewindable file with a logical record length of 80 bytes.

TMSUTL ERROR MESSAGES

··· INPUT CONTROL CARD MISSING. Input control card missing or misplaced; it should be the first control card.

··· INVALID CONTROL CARD FIELD. Control card has an invalid field. Dollar signs point to the beginning and the end of the field.

··· OUTPUT FORMAT INCOMPATIBLE WITH INPUT FORMAT. The output format specified can not be converted from the input format specified.

··· OUTPUT FORMAT MISSING. Output control card missing or misplaced; it should follow the Input card.

··· ADDR2 ADDR1 OR BOTH NOT SPECIFIED. Either minimum or maximum address is invalid. Addr1 must be less than or equal to Addr2.

··· WIDTH INVALID FOR I/O FORMAT SPECIFIED. For the format specified the bit width is invalid.

··· PARTITION ERR. The Input bit width times the number of input partitions is not equal to the width times the number of output partitions.

··· ERROR DETECTED ON INPUT CARD. The format of a data card is invalid, check the field pointed to by the dollar signs.

··· INPUT OUT OF SEQUENCE. The addresses of the input data are not in sequential order.

··· # OF WORDS INPUT FOR CURRENT PARTITION NOT EQUAL TO THAT IN PREVIOUS PARTITION. The number of words input for each partition is not equal. Check the input data.

··· ADDRESS OUT OF RANGE. Either Addr1 or Addr2 is out of range or the address read on the input data is out of range of the format specified.

STOP CODES	ERROR
1	Input data error. (A message describing the error is output before this is issued.)
2	Format not implemented yet in EOF.
3	Format not implemented yet in TRANS.

STOP CODES	ERROR
90	DECHEX unable to find H or blank.
91	Data will not fit in card field passed to AFORMT.
92	Invalid format number in EOF.
93	Invalid width passed to INWORD.
94	SHFTR called with invalid arguments.
95	TRANS called with an invalid format number.

CHAPTER 8
Applications

This chapter is devoted to examples of applications of the 9900 family of components. Throughout this book many details of the 9900 family of CPU's, peripherals, microcomputer modules, software and software development system support have been discussed. However, these have been somewhat isolated general discussions and not directed to a particular application. This chapter has solutions of specific problems — from the beginning concept to the final machine code — to give you examples of how someone else has approached the problem and to help you understand the concepts behind the approach and the details of the solution.

Three applications are included. They are:

1. A SIMULATED INDUSTRIAL CONTROL APPLICATION

A 9900 microprocessor based microcomputer is used in a system simulating the control of industrial manufacturing processes. Solutions to the problems of interfacing between industrial power levels and computer logic levels, both at the input and the output, are demonstrated, as well as basic concepts of computer control.

2. A LOW-COST DATA TERMINAL

Direct comparison is made showing how the characteristics of the 9940 single chip 16-bit microcomputer are used to significantly reduce the package count of an intelligent terminal designed with an 8080 8-bit processor. At the same time the performance-cost ratio of the end equipment is improved.

3. A FLOPPY DISK CONTROLLER

The design of a complex system used for the control of a floppy diskette memory is described. All the details of how a 9900 family microprocessor is used to arrive at a problem solution are included.

A Simulated Industrial
Control Application

INTRODUCTION

Controlling motors, relays, solenoids, actuators; sensing limit switches, photo-electric outputs, push-button switches are real world problems encountered in controlling industrial manufacturing. This application simulates such conditions. It develops the application of a TMS9900 microprocessor (using the 990/100M microcomputer module of Chapter 3) and interconnecting hardware to automating industrial control requirements. This example includes the description of interface hardware to couple industrial power levels to and from the microcomputer system. It illustrates the use of an EIA/TTY terminal for interactive program entry and control, a line-by-line assembler for inexpensive program assembly, and the techniques of interrupt driven processing.

No motors, actuators, or solenoids are actually being controlled, but by sensing switches for logical voltage inputs and by turning lights on and off, the industrial control inputs and loads are simulated and the means demonstrated to accomplish the control.

As a logical extension of the first encounter application of Chapter 3, this application is written for "hands-on" operation to develop basic concepts and show that the 9900 family of microprocessors is ideally suited for industrial control applications. Each program step is described as the subprograms are developed and the total program is assembled into machine code.

Excitement comes from actually getting a microprocessor system doing useful things. This application is designed for that purpose. Let it demonstrate how easy it is to begin applying the 9900 family of microprocessors.

INITIAL SYSTEM SETUP WITH AN EIA TERMINAL

To begin, look at *Figures 1* and *6.* The system uses the same TM990/100M-1 microcomputer module shown in *Figure 3-12* and interconnected in *Figure 3-14.* It is a complete microcomputer with 256 16-bit words of RAM, 1024 16-bit words of ROM, and interface circuits to handle parallel and serial I/O. In *Figure 3-14* it has power supplied to it through P1, the 100 pin edge connector as specified in *Figure 3-17.* P2 interconnects the TM990/301 microterminal which is being used as an input terminal for programming, editing, and debugging. The output board *(Figure 3-9)* with a 7 segment LED display is connected to the microcomputer through P4. The program *(Table 3-2)* sequenced the elements f, b, e and c of the LED display on and off, either fast or slow, depending on the position of the control switch.

Table 3-2 was "assembled-by-hand." In the examples that follow, a ROM resident "line-by-line" assembler will be used. This is a low-cost, effective way of providing machine code. However, a different terminal is required so that print out of the code can be obtained. Therefore, in this application the microterminal attached to the TM990/100M microcomputer is replaced with a keyboard terminal with EIA/TTY interconnection. Refer to *Figure 1.*

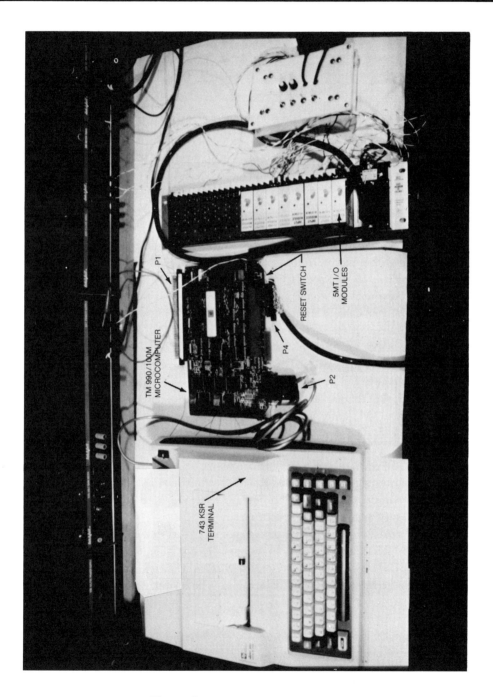

Figure 1. Picture of System Set-up

A 743 KSR terminal is chosen for this purpose. A special cable is required to interface the terminal to the microcomputer through P2. The cable connections are as follows:

TM 990/100M-1 P2 Pin	743 Terminal P1 Pin	Description
1	9	Protective Gnd
2	13	Transmit data
3	12	Receive data
7	1	Signal Gnd
8	11	Request to send
20	15	Data Terminal Ready

If a preassembled cable is desired, a TM990/503 can be purchased for the purpose.

If the TM990/100M-1 microcomputer was used for the Chapter 3 First Encounter, power was supplied to the microterminal from the TM990/100M module by jumpers installed across the pins J13, J14 and J15 *(Figure 3-12* and *3-13)*. These should now be removed; the microterminal disconnected from P2; and the 743 KSR terminal connected to P2 with the referenced cable. Connect ac power to the 743 terminal with a separate cord. Return the jumpers to the spare positions on the board J16, J17, and J18 *(Figure 3-13)*. If P1 is to be wired to supply power, use *Figure 3-17* for the connections. *Figure 1* shows the 743 terminal in place instead of the microterminal. It also shows the I/O interface components that will be used for this application connected to P4. If familiar with a 743 terminal, skip the next discussion and go on to the description of the I/O interface components (5MT interface modules).

For those not familiar with the operation of a 743 terminal, reconnect the output board of *Figure 3-9* to P4 and proceed thru the following steps:

1. Turn on the power supplies, the $-12V$, $+12V$ and $+5V$, in that order.
2. Turn on the terminal and place it "on line."
3. The system is now ready to receive a program.
4. The terminal uses the TIBUG interactive monitor (TM990/401-1) resident on the TM990/100M-1 in the U42 and U44 sockets. It must be initialized. To do this, press the RESET toggle switch on the TM990/100M *(Figure 1)* and the character "A" or a carriage return (CR) on the terminal. The terminal responds:

   ```
   TIBUG REV.A
   ?
   ```

5. The question mark is the TIBUG prompt symbol saying "what's next?" To enter code or data into memory, press the M (Memory Inspect and Change) command key followed by the address in Memory where the program or routine is to start followed by a (CR). The terminal printout looks like this:

   ```
   ?M FE00 (CR)
   ```

6. TIBUG responds with the address and the data located at that address such as:

    FE00=ABCD

If the data is not correct and is to be changed, type in the correct data and press either of these options:

A. (CR) to return to TIBUG
B. The space bar to increment to the next memory word location.
C. A minus (−) character to return to the previous word location.

The complete sequence is illustrated here:

    ?M FE00   (CR)
    FE00=ABCD   02E0 (Space)
    FE02=3D04   FF20 (Space)
    FE04=FC36   −   (minus)*
    FE02=FF20   (Space)
    FE04=FC36   0201 (Space)
    FE06=0032   (CR)
    ?   *requires pressing "NUM" key

7. After an M and the starting address FE00 and a (CR), the total program of *Table 3-2,* should be entered by entering the correct machine code at each address and then pressing the space bar. At the end of the program, exit the memory inspect and change mode by pressing (CR). The terminal responds with the familiar "?". If an error occurs, press (CR), then M and the address at which the error occurred; then repeat the input code.

8. Now the program is ready to run. However, the workspace pointer and the program counter may have to be set; at least the program counter, because it controls where the program starts. The register inspect and change command R is pressed. TIBUG responds with the contents of the workspace pointer. Press the space bar and TIBUG comes back with the program counter contents. Either of these can be changed in the same manner as memory.

Change the contents of the PC to the first address of the program to be run, then type a (CR) and the program is ready to be executed. The total routine looks like this:

    ?R
    W=0020 (Space)
    P=0846 FE00 (CR)
    ?

The program counter is now set at the starting address of the program of *Table 3-2,* FE00. Usually as the program proceeds, it will set the workspace pointer as needed; thus, no change is made to W in the above routine.

9. The Execute Command, E, runs the program:

?E

It runs until the RESET switch is pressed. After RESET, the program counter must be reset to FE00. This is done with a (CR), then R, then (Space), then FE00, then (CR), then E to start again.

The necessary details of interfacing and operating the 743 KSR have now been covered. Further information on commands may be obtained by referring to the TM990/100M user's guide. Operation with a 745 KSR acoustical terminal is possible but an EIA/auxiliary coupler cable kit (Part #983856) must be obtained from a TI Digital Systems Division distributor.

SIMULATING CONTROL OF AN ASSEMBLY LINE

Coupling the KSR-745 terminal to the TM990/100M microcomputer provides a more interactive terminal than the 301 microterminal so that the hardware can be expanded to simulate general kinds of input and output requirements encountered in light-manufacturing assembly lines. In addition, the "assembling" of the program is made easier by using a "line-by-line" assembler, which requires an EIA compatible terminal for this interaction.

Now, obviously, the output board shown in *Figure 3-9,* which contained only simple logic level inverters and an LED display, will not be adequate to provide the reaction power levels that are required for the simulated application. Therefore, new interface modules are needed.

5MT INTERFACE MODULES

A means must be provided in the system to change input signals from push buttons, limit switches, cam switches, or transducers that are at voltage levels of 90-132 volts ac or 3 to 28 volts dc to standard TTL low-level logic signals between 0 and +5 volts.

In like fashion, means must also be provided in the hardware system to change the low-level logic output signals into power signals up to 28 volts dc or 90 to 132 volts ac. The concept is shown in *Figure 2.*

Texas Instruments supplies modules which meet these requirements. They are called the 5MT I/O modules that are part of a 5TI Control system. A simplified set of specifications for the basic modules is contained in *Table I.*

The I/O modules are solid-state devices incorporating optical coupler isolation between input and output of 1500 volts for excellent noise immunity. Internal protection is provided to guard against external voltage transients. Each module has an LED status indicator located at the low-level logic side of the module to help in set-up and troubleshooting. The I/O modules operate from 0-60° C and are designed for 100 million operations. The modules are shown in *Figure 3* with a 5MT43 mounting base which accepts 16 plug-in modules and provides all of the wiring terminals. A logic interface module which mounts on the 5MT mounting base is also shown in *Figure 3*. It provides a serial interface between the 5MT mounting base and a 5TI sequencer. It is not necessary for this application, but is very necessary if other 5TI components are interconnected in the system.

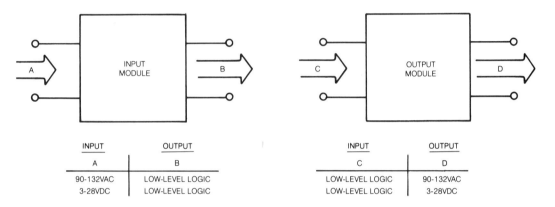

INPUT	OUTPUT
A	B
90-132VAC	LOW-LEVEL LOGIC
3-28VDC	LOW-LEVEL LOGIC

INPUT	OUTPUT
C	D
LOW-LEVEL LOGIC	90-132VAC
LOW-LEVEL LOGIC	3-28VDC

Figure 2. Input/Output Modules

CATALOG NO.	TYPE OF DEVICE	RATING		TURN ON TIME (ms)	TURN OFF TIME (ms)
		VOLTAGE	CURRENT		
5MT11-A05L	AC Input	90-132 Vac Input Voltage	35 mA Max	8 Typ. 8.3 Max	12 Typ. 8.3 Max
5MT12-40AL	AC Output	90-132 Vac Output Voltage	3 Amps Continuous (40°C)	4 Max	4 Max
5MT13-D03L	DC Input	3-28 Vdc Input Voltage	30 mA Max	2 Max	2 Max
5MT14-30CL	DC Output	10-28 Vdc Output Voltage	1 Amp Continuous (60°C)		
5MT43	Mounting Base Holds Up to 16 Modules				

Table 1. 5MT Module Selection Table

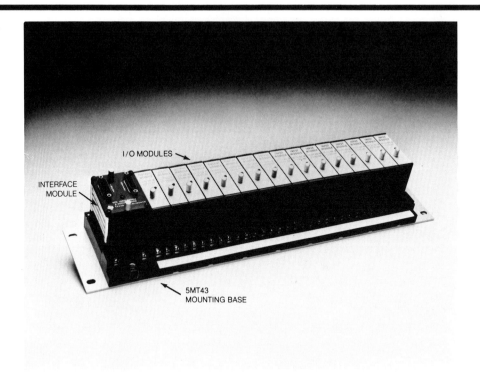

Figure 3. I/O Modules and Mounting Base

The 5MT43 mounting base interfaces with the TM 990/100M-1 microcomputer with a cable to P4, the same 40 pin edge connector that was used for the output board of *Figure 3-9.* The cable connections and hardware required are shown in *Figure 4.* This cable may be wired from scratch or a TM 990/507 cable can be purchased for the purpose. With this cable in place (J1 to the 5MT43 base and J4 to P4 on the TM 990/100M microcomputer module), the major components will be ready to simulate the industrial application. Of course, the additional parts must be purchased:

       1 — 5MT43 Mounting Base
       2 — 5MT11-A05L Input Modules
       2 — 5MT12-40AL Output Modules
       2 — 5MT13-D03L Input Modules
       2 — 5MT14-30CL Output Modules
       1 — TM990/507 Cable (or this can be fabricated as per *Figure 4*)

(Equivalent circuits of 5MT modules are provided in *Figure 5* in case these are to be simulated.)

WIRE LIST

J1	J4	SIGNAL
1	10	MODULE 5
2	18	MODULE 4
3	14	MODULE 2
4	20	MODULE 0
5	24	MODULE 7
6	28	MODULE 9
7	32	MODULE 11
8	36	MODULE 13
9	40	MODULE 15
10	13	GROUND 2
11	19	GROUND 0
12	9	GROUND 5
13	23	GROUND 7
14	27	GROUND 9
15	31	GROUND 11
16	35	GROUND 13
17	39	GROUND 15
21	16	MODULE 3
22	22	MODULE 1
23	12	MODULE 6
24	26	MODULE 8
25	30	MODULE 10
26	34	MODULE 12
27	38	MODULE 14
28	15	GROUND 3
29	21	GROUND 1
30	17	GROUND 4
31	11	GROUND 6
32	25	GROUND 8
33	29	GROUND 10
34	33	GROUND 12
35	37	GROUND 14
36	#24 GA., STRANDED FOR MODULE V_{CC} $(7-9V_{dc} @.6A)$ TERMINATION CAN BE #6 SPADE LUG, BANANA PLUG, ETC.	

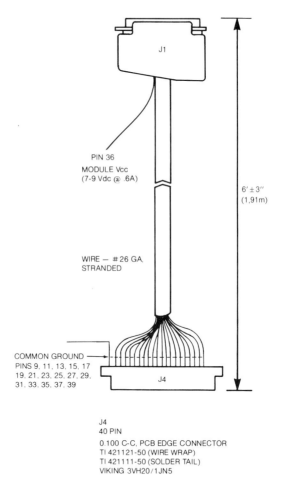

J1
37 PIN "D" TYPE CONNECTOR, FEMALE TYPE
AMP 205-209-1
TRW 6 INCH DC375

J1

PIN 36
MODULE Vcc
(7-9 Vdc @ .6A)

6' ± 3"
(1,91m)

WIRE — #26 GA,
STRANDED

COMMON GROUND →
PINS 9, 11, 13, 15, 17
19, 21, 23, 25, 27, 29,
31, 33, 35, 37, 39

J4

J4
40 PIN
0.100 C-C, PCB EDGE CONNECTOR
TI 421121-50 (WIRE WRAP)
TI 421111-50 (SOLDER TAIL)
VIKING 3VH20/1JN5

Figure 4. 5MT Interface Cable

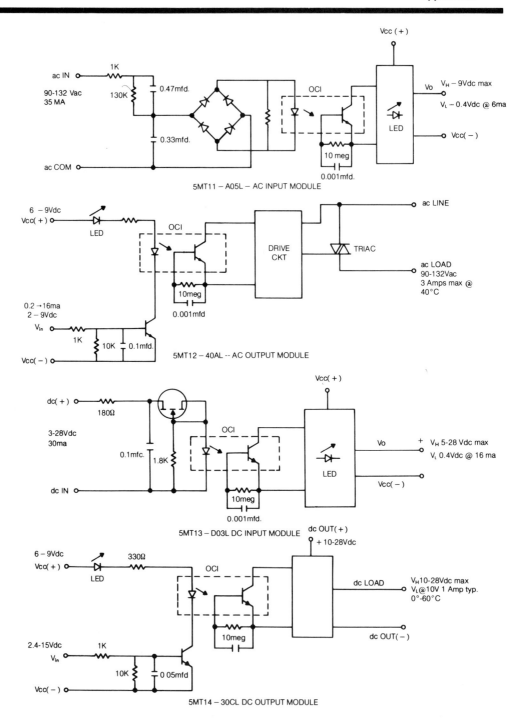

Figure 5. *Equivalent Circuits for 5MT Modules*

DEMONSTRATION EXAMPLE

The industrial control example, shown in concept form in the block diagram of *Figure 6*
is intended to give the reader an insight into the use of a microcomputer based system.
Even though no motors, actuators, solenoids, positioning valves, etc. are actually
energized, the application demonstrates the means to do it. It also uses real world
control voltages in its operation. There will be three modes of operation. To add
interest, the system will be programmed so that the user can select the mode of
operation.

In the first mode of operation *(Figure 6)*, the system is to be programmed to accept
inputs and switch a corresponding output according to the state of the input. Switches
are going to apply input industrial level dc voltages to the dc input modules and input
industrial level ac voltages to the ac input modules. Output lights powered by industrial
level dc and ac voltages will be activated corresponding to the state of the input signal.
Such a mode of operation simulates switch closures on the assembly line requesting an
output reaction.

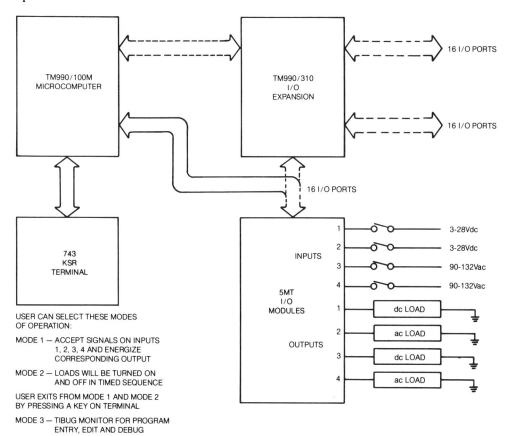

Figure 6. Application Block Diagram

The second mode of operation is very similar to the light sequence of Chapter 3. However, with the 5MT modules controlling either + 12Vdc light bulbs or 110Vac light bulbs, it demonstrates a different means of timed sequence control. It uses the real time clock in the TMS9901 in the microcomputer module for a much greater precision. The system is to be programmed so the time can be varied easily. There is to be an added feature in the first and second mode. The system has a routine that allows the user to choose the mode of operation by selecting a key on the keyboard.

A third mode returns the system to the TIBUG interactive monitor. In this mode, the program can be edited, debugged or added to and initial conditions can be changed.

Lets see how this can be accomplished.

The TM990/100M Microcomputer Module

Figure 7 is a much more detailed block diagram of the TM990/100M microcomputer. Four areas are of particular interest:

1. More details on the TMS9901;
2. Details on the TMS9902—this device was not discussed at all in Chapter 3;
3. The addition of a TM990/310 module to the system to obtain I/O expansion; and
4. Expansion of resident RAM and ROM.

Note in particular that the TM990/100M-1 comes populated with 256 words of RAM and 1K words of ROM (which is the TIBUG EPROM resident monitor). Also note the address bus goes to the I/O interface units. Thus, I/O is selected with addresses in the same fashion as memory words. In addition, the four busses—address, control, data and CRU are available for off-board expansion. This is the way I/O expansion through the TM990/310 module is controlled. 512 words of RAM can be provided on the board. Further expansion is possible with off-board memory. Additional ROM, expandable on the board to 4K, will be used when the line-by-line assembler (LBLA) is used.

TMS9901

The TMS9901, programmable system interface, shown in *Figure 7* was previously shown in the block diagram of *Figure 3-17*. Only one portion of it was used to control output signals and detect an input signal. Now all of the functions will be examined in more detail.

The block diagram of the TMS9901 in *Figure 8* will be used to identify the major functions.

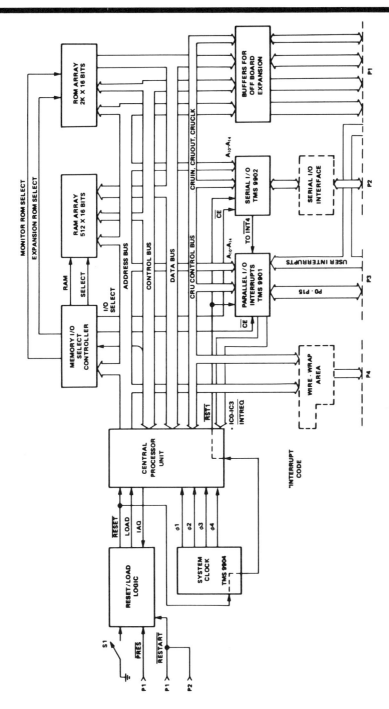

Figure 7. TM 990/100M Block Diagram

First of all, since the TMS9901 is a programmable systems interface, as shown in *Figure 7*, it is designed to handle parallel input and output signals. The input signals are either data inputs or special signals called interrupts. Interrupts are special signals because they interrupt the main program routine of the microcomputer and ask for service from the microcomputer to do some selected priority subroutine or subprogram. In *Figure 8*, the data output paths and input paths and the interrupt paths are identified. The 22 pins are programmable and divide into three groups as follows:

Table 1. Programmable Pin Functions

GROUP	NAME	IN	OUT	INT	COMMENT
1.	$\overline{\text{INT}}$ 1	X		X	Principally inputs but may be used
	$\overline{\text{INT}}$ 2	X		X	as interrupts
	$\overline{\text{INT}}$ 3	X		X	
	$\overline{\text{INT}}$ 4	X		X	
	$\overline{\text{INT}}$ 5	X		X	
	$\overline{\text{INT}}$ 6	X		X	
2.	$\overline{\text{INT}}$ 7/P15	X	X	X	Fully programmable as inputs,
	$\overline{\text{INT}}$ 8/P14	X	X	X	outputs or interrupts
	$\overline{\text{INT}}$ 9/P13	X	X	X	
	$\overline{\text{INT}}$ 10/P12	X	X	X	
	$\overline{\text{INT}}$ 11/P11	X	X	X	
	$\overline{\text{INT}}$ 12/P10	X	X	X	
	$\overline{\text{INT}}$ 13/P9	X	X	X	
	$\overline{\text{INT}}$ 14/P8	X	X	X	
	$\overline{\text{INT}}$ 15/P7	X	X	X	
3.	P6	X	X		Programmable as inputs or outputs.
	P5	X	X		
	P4	X	X		
	P3	X	X		
	P2	X	X		
	P1	X	X		
	P0	X	X		

In addition to the input/output function, the TMS9901 also has incorporated a clock function. This was identified in *Figure 8*, but is further detailed in *Figure 9*. This real time clock will be used in this application as an interval timer for the Mode 2 light sequence. To provide this function, the clock register is loaded with a value, (just like in Chapter 3); however, now the register automatically decrements after it is loaded. When it has decremented to zero, an interrupt signal is sent out to be processed by the interrupt path of the TMS9901. It won't be used for this application, but an elapsed time counter can be implemented by reading the value of the clock read register (*Figure 9*) periodically to determine how much time has elapsed from an established start.

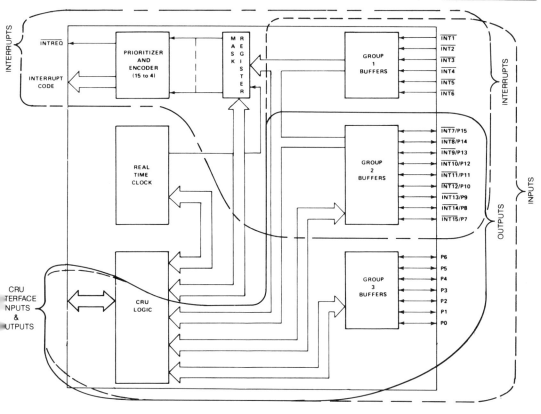

Figure 8. *TMS 9901 Block Diagram*

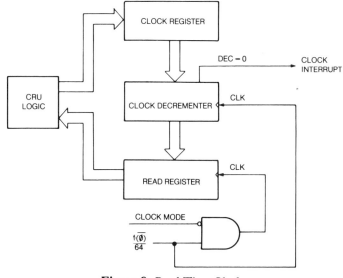

Figure 9. *Real Time Clock*

INTERFACE WITH THE 9900

It is important to understand the communications channels between the TMS 9901 and the 9900 microprocessor in the microcomputer. Basic concepts need to developed to understand how the algorithm for this application is programmed.

The communications channels are shown in *Figure 10*. They are presented in somewhat different form than shown previously in Chapter 3.

The main data link between the 9900 and the 9901 and subsequent inputs and outputs is via a serial data link. The line CRUIN transfers data from the 9901 to the 9900 in serial format. Again in serial format, the line CRUOUT transfers data from the 9900 to the 9901. The transfer of data out is synchronized by the signal CRUCLK, which comes from the 9900 and specifies that data is valid on the CRUOUT line. Remember that CRU means Communications Register Unit.

In order to manipulate data from the CRU to and from the inputs and outputs and the real time clock of the 9901, five CRU instructions are included in the instruction set. They are:

1.	SBO	Set bit to one
2.	SBZ	Set bit to zero
3.	TB	Test bit
4.	LDCR	Load CRU Register
5.	STCR	Store CRU Register

In Chapter 3, it was demonstrated how individual bits could be selected and set to a "1" or a "0" by using the SBO and SBZ instructions. If this hasn't been reviewed, it would be helpful to do so.

Not only can individual bits be manipulated, but data can also be transferred in blocks of from one to 16 bits. The multiple bit instructions LDCR, "Load CRU Register", and STCR, "Store CRU Register", are used for this purpose. Since this application requires the use of these multiple-bit instructions, further time will be spent explaining them in more detail.

Basic Concepts

Figure 11 summarizes the basic concept of the programmable input-output capability of the 9900 family. In this example, a microcomputer, the TM990/100M, which contains a 9901, and a TM990/310 module, which contains 3 additional 9901's are used. Such an arrangement expands the I/O capabilities by 48 inputs or outputs.

Industrial control applications like the one that is being simulated normally require many inputs and outputs. Much more capability is available because I/O could be expanded to 4096 ports by adding more units and continuing the example of *Figure 11*.

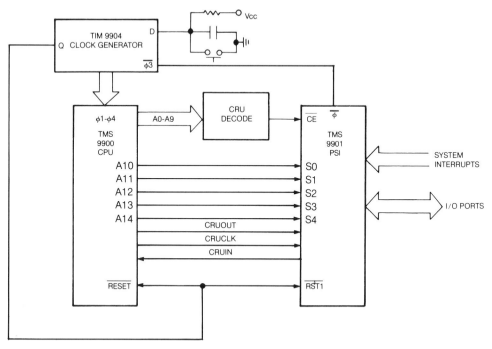

Figure 10. TMS 9900-TMS 9901 Interface

As shown, the data moves over CRUIN and CRUOUT in a serial format from the 9900 to the 9901, or vice versa. When the instruction LDCR is used, the data is flowing from the 9900 to the 9901 over CRUOUT. The first bit to arrive serially (the least significant bit) is latched in the zero bit position of the 9901 determined by the CRU select bit, subsequent bits that arrive are then placed in bits, 1, 2, 3-12, 13, 14, 15 at each CRUCLK pulse. Such is the case if 16-bits are being processed. Any number of bits from 1 to 16 may be processed at the user's discretion. When flowing out on CRUOUT, the transfer rate is determined by CRUCLK. When flowing in on CRUIN, the 9900 microprocessor transfers the data present on the inputs during ϕ_1 of clock cycle 2 of the machine cycles.

What determines where the bit position starts? The select bits on S_0-S_4 in the 9901 (*Figure 10* and *11*) are distributed as A_{10} thru A_{14} from the 9900. Since this address is distributed to each 9901 shown, and since CRUOUT goes to each 9901, the data out would tend to be latched in each 9901. This is prevented by the chip enable (CE) signal. The only CE that is active low is the one decoded from the corresponding base address for the correct 9901. Bits A_0 thru A_9 provide the additional address information. For example, if in *Figure 11* the 9901 on the TM990/100M board is to be used for the I/O, then hardware base address 0080_{16} is used. If the second 9901 on the TM990/310 module is used, the hardware base address is 0140_{16}.

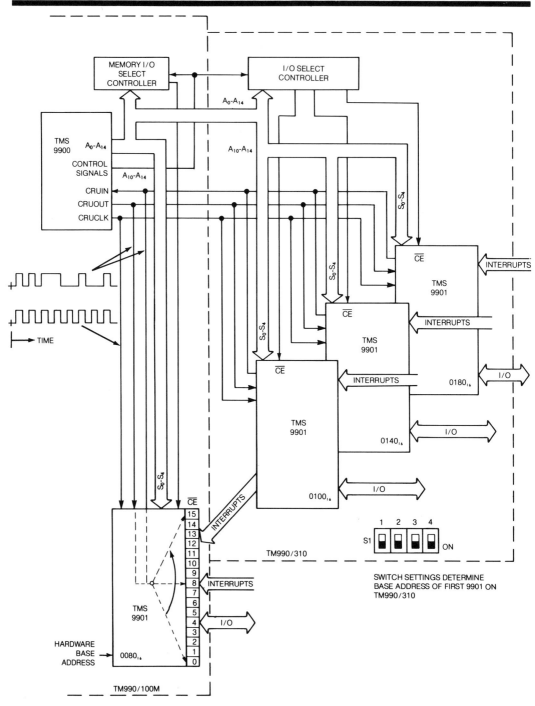

Figure 11. *Basic Concept of Programmable I/O*

In *Figure 3-23,* for the single bit instructions SBO, SBZ, and TB, the effective CRU bit address is obtained by adding a signed displacement to the 9901 base address. For the multiple bit instructions, the effective CRU bit address is computed in the same way; however, the base address is the address of the first bit. From there, the address is incremented by the number of multiple bits to be transferred. The LDCR instruction format contains a C field which specifies the number of multiple bits to be transferred. For example:

LDCR   R1,9

would instruct the microcomputer to send out (output) the 9 least significant bits of register R1. The 9 would be in the C field of the instruction format. Before the LDCR instruction in the program, there is an instruction that loaded the software base address of the particular 9901 to be used into the correct workspace register 12. Recall that WR12 is the register where the software base address is always located for a CRU instruction. This will become clearer as a specific example is discussed later. What is important is that the software base address for the 9901 must be loaded into workspace register 12. However, this is not completely straightforward. For example, if the 9901 on the TM990/100M microcomputer is to be addressed with a LDCR or STCR instruction, the 0080_{16} hardware base address must be displaced to the software base address 0100_{16} when it is loaded into WR12. This is necessary because bit 15 of WR12 is not used in the calculation of the effective CRU bit address. The concept, described in *Figure 3-23,* is shown again in *Figure 12.*

It is probably obvious that the STCR instruction operates in the reverse of the LDCR. The data from the input pins on the selected 9901 is incremented bit by bit and sent to the CRU in the 9900 over CRUIN. The final result of a STCR instruction is that the 9900 processor stores the input data in RAM in a specified location called out in the instruction. In like fashion, when LDCR is used the data transferred to the output is obtained from a RAM location called out in the instruction. This is a distinct advantage in that it need not be a register. The specifics on the data transfers are shown in *Figure 13.*

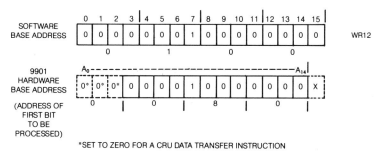

Figure 12. 9901 Base Address

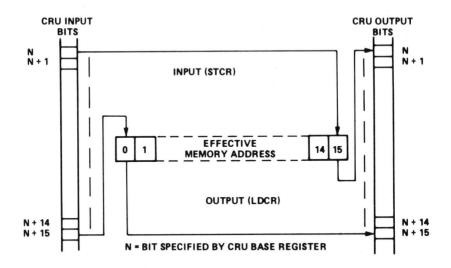

Figure 13. LDCR/STCR Data Transfers

Interrupts

Another form of input is the special one called interrupt, so named because it asks the microcomputer to interrupt the program routine presently in process.

In *Figure 8,* it was pointed out that there are only certain lines on which an interrupt is accepted. Group 1 of the 9901 pins may be used for 6 interrupts. Up to 15 interrupt signals can be programmed by using Group 2 pins.

What value do interrupts have? First, they allow external events to interrupt the current program so that the program can provide service to an external device. In so doing certain pieces of data must be saved in order to return to the same point in the program that was interrupted. This allows the program to continue correctly after the interrupt has been serviced. Secondly, interrupts provide quick response. Third, they provide a priority to be established for time critical events. Certain interrupts are more important than others. The user decides the priority. To set up priorities for interrupt signals, a means is provided to honor the priority established. In the 9900 system family, this is called enabling a valid interrupt through a "masking" of interrupts.

Masking means to enable or disable. *Figure 14* shows that the TM990/100M microcomputer module has two levels of masking. One mask must be enabled to pass the interrupt signals through the 9901 and another must be enabled at the 9900 microprocessor. The value in bits 12, 13, 14 and 15 of the status register set the priority level of the interrupt mask in the 9900. Any interrupt equal to or higher than the priority level is enabled and allowed to interrupt the microcomputer.

Masking

Figure 15 is a block diagram of the 9901 control logic illustrating how the masking is accomplished. In order to enable an interrupt, MASK must equal 1 for the particular interrupt pin. When several interrupts are present at the same time, the control logic encodes the enabled interrupt inputs and sends to the 9900 microprocessor a code that represents the highest level of interrupt that has been enabled. $\overline{\text{INT}}$ 1 is the highest level, $\overline{\text{INT}}$ 2 is next and so on down to 15. In addition, an $\overline{\text{INTREQ}}$ active low signal is also sent to the 9900. The code sent on lines IC0 through IC3 is shown in *Table 2*. Level zero is used by $\overline{\text{RESET}}$ and will be covered later.

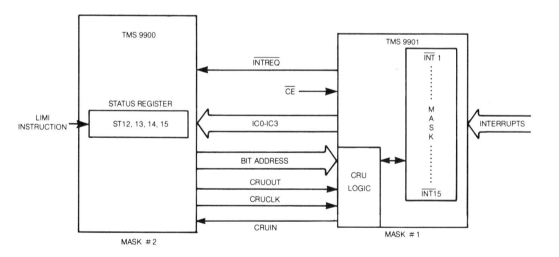

Figure 14. Interrupt Masking

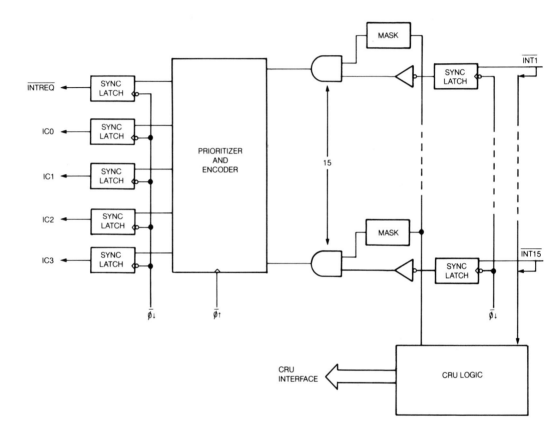

Figure 15. Interrupt Control Logic

The code on IC0 thru IC3 is compared to the status bits ST12, 13, 14 and 15 in the status register of the 9900. The priority level loaded into the interrupt mask of the 9900 enables that level and all higher priority levels as well. If the interrupt level set up in ST12, 13, 14 and 15 is higher than the interrupt level received, the interrupt is not enabled. If the interrupt received is higher in level than the priority level, then the interrupt is enabled and all higher level interrupts as well. This is shown in *Figure 16*.

The code on IC0-IC3 is as follows:

Table 2. Interrupt Code Generation

INTERRUPT/STATE	PRIORITY	IC0	IC1	IC2	IC3	INTREQ
INT 1	1 (HIGHEST)	0	0	0	1	0
INT 2	2	0	0	1	0	0
INT 3/CLOCK	3	0	0	1	1	0
INT 4	4	0	1	0	0	0
INT 5	5	0	1	0	1	0
INT 6	6	0	1	1	0	0
INT 7	7	0	1	1	1	0
INT 8	8	1	0	0	0	0
INT 9	9	1	0	0	1	0
INT 10	10	1	0	1	0	0
INT 11	11	1	0	1	1	0
INT 12	12	1	1	0	0	0
INT 13	13	1	1	0	1	0
INT 14	14	1	1	1	0	0
INT 15	15 (LOWEST)	1	1	1	1	0
NO INTERRUPT		1	1	1	1	1

The output signals will remain valid until the corresponding interrupt input is removed, or an interrupt service routine disables (MASK = 0), or a higher priority enabled interrupt becomes active. When the highest priority enabled interrupt is removed, the code corresponding to the next highest priority enabled interrupt is output. If no enabled interrupt is active, all CPU interface lines (INTREQ, IC0-IC3) are held high.

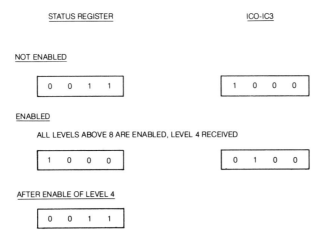

Figure 16. Interrupt Mask at 9900

Remember to enable an interrupt, say $\overline{\text{INT}}$ 1, a "1" must be placed in the latch (MASK = 1) for the CRU bit (pin) associated with that interrupt. Likewise, to disable an interrupt, a "0" must be placed in the latch (MASK = 0) associated with the pin receiving the particular interrupt.

To mask any of the interrupts from 1 through 15, the 9901 must be in the interrupt mode. The zero select bit of the 9901 is the control bit for this. As shown in *Figure 23*, if this control bit is a zero, the 9901 is in the interrupt mode. If it is a "1", the 9901 is in the clock mode.

Enabling or disabling the mask in the 9901 for the interrupts may be accomplished by individual bit instructions SBO and SBZ or by a multiple bit LDCR instruction.

All masks can be disabled simultaneously by performing a hardware ($\overline{\text{RESET}}$) or software ($\overline{\text{RST}}$ 2) reset.

Signals appearing on the inputs to the 9901 will be accepted as interrupt signals by the 9901 if the masks are enabled. The priority code for the highest priority level interrupt simultaneously received will be sent to the 9900 via the code lines, IC0-IC3, as well as the signal $\overline{\text{INTREQ}}$. If the interrupt mask in the 9900 has the level enabled, the interrupt is accepted and serviced.

Saving Items on Interrupt

When an interrupt occurs, data pertinent to the "state of the machine" must be saved. This provides a return to the interrupted program so that the program can continue to execute properly. For example, when an interrupt occurs, the CPU suspends its current program routine to do the subroutine called for by the interrupt. How does it do this? As any program executes, the "state of the machine" at any time is determined by the value in the program counter, the value in the workspace pointer, the value in the status register, and the contents of the registers in the workspace register file. Each of these is saved through a "context switch" when an interrupt occurs. Full details are available in Chapter 4. A brief summary will be covered here for convenience.

Interrupt Vectors — Context Switching

To execute an interrupt, here's what happens. There are special places in memory reserved for the address that contains a new workspace pointer for a given interrupt. In addition, in the next word following there is a new program counter value. These special places in memory are called interrupt vector traps and the two addresses — one for workspace and the other for the program counter — have the name "interrupt vector."

Figure 17 illustrated the process. A valid interrupt is received and its level points to its vector. The vector contains a new workspace pointer and a new program counter value. The program shifts and points to the new workspace. In the new workspace, the microprocessor stores the old workspace pointer in R13, the old program counter in R14 and the old status register in R15. These old contents are always put in the same place in the new workspace — R13, R14 and R15.

After all this occurs, the program counter with its new value executes the interrupt subroutine. The last instruction in this subroutine, RTWP, is an instruction to return to the interrupted routine. RTWP — "Return with Workspace Pointer" — returns to the interrupted routine by loading the contents of R13 into the workspace pointer (R13→WP), R14 into the program counter (R14→PC), and R15 into the status register (R15→ST) and then executes the instruction pointed to by the program counter. In so doing, the system has returned to the interrupted program at the point of interruption and begins execution using the old workspace. This is illustrated in *Figure 18.*

Note: When the interrupt priority level comes into the 9900 and the interrupt is enabled, a number one less than the interrupt level received is placed in the interrupt mask in the status register as shown in *Figure 16* to prevent lower level interrupts from occurring during the servicing of the present interrupt. If a higher priority interrupt occurs, a second interrupt context switch takes place after at least one instruction is executed for the first interrupt routine. This means that an interrupt service routine may begin with a LIMI instruction which can load an interrupt mask in the 9900 which disables other interrupts. Completion of the second interrupt passes control back to the first interrupt using the RTWP instruction.

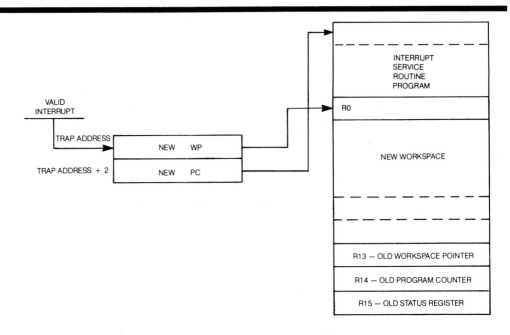

*Figure 17. Interrupt Context Switch — New Workspace
and Saving Old WP, PC, and ST Data*

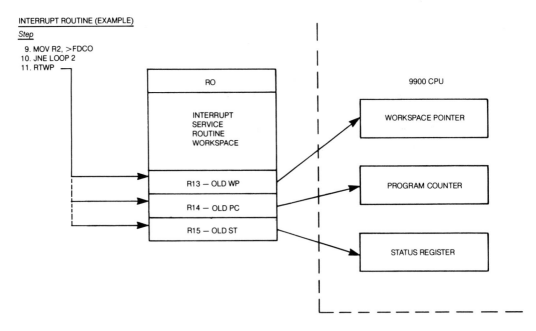

Figure 18. Interrupt Context Switch Returning to Interrupted Program

Memory Map and Interrupt Vectors

In *Figure 19,* the memory map of the TM990/100M microcomputer module is shown. Note that the first words of memory from hexadecimal addresses 0000_{16} to $07FE_{16}$ are dedicated memory. Addresses 0000_{16} to $003E_{16}$ are reserved for the 16 interrupt transfer vectors. These are detailed further in Figure 20. Each interrupt vector has two words of memory — one for the workspace pointer, one for the program counter.

There are two interrupt vectors, $\overline{INT}$ 3 and $\overline{INT}$ 4 that will be of particular interest for they have important use in the program for this application.

Notice that interrupt 0 in *Figure 20* is used for $\overline{RESET}$ and that values have already been placed in the vector locations for interrupt 3 and interrupt 4.

When an $\overline{INT}$ 3 level is received, it points to the interrupt 3 vector. The context switch occurs and at $000C_{16}$ it obtains the value $FF68_{16}$ for the workspace pointer and at $000E_{16}$ the value $FF88_{16}$ for the program counter. The context switch operations store the old context registers in the new workspace pointed to by $FF68_{16}$. Then the interrupt service routine begins by executing the instruction pointed to by $FF88_{16}$. Since there are valid reserved locations for only two memory words at the $FF88_{16}$ location, the instruction pointed to by $FF88_{16}$ and $FF8A_{16}$ must branch to another section of memory where the remaining interrupt service routine is located.

A similar sequence of events occurs when an $\overline{INT}$ 4 level interrupt signal is received, except that the workspace pointer value is $FF8C_{16}$ and the program counter value is $FFAC_{16}$.

The remaining interrupt vectors do not have values. These would be programmed into EPROM locations by the user as the need arises.

For the interrupt 3 and 4 service routines, 16-word workspaces are provided, pointed to by $FF68_{16}$ and $FF8C_{16}$. These are reserved and must be noted by the programmer.

The microcomputer must always start from initial conditions. These are usually started by a reset. The vector space required for the initial value of the workspace pointer and the program counter resides in the reserved memory spaces 0000_{16} for WP and 0002_{16} for PC, as shown in *Figure 20.* The 16 interrupt vectors at 0000_{16} to $003E_{16}$ are in read only memory and cannot be changed unless the read only memory is reprogrammed.

As the extended application program is written, it must be remembered that the TIBUG monitor needs workspaces. The space from $FFB0_{16}$ to $FFFB_{16}$ is reserved for this purpose. This is noted because this space cannot be used for data or program memory in the application.

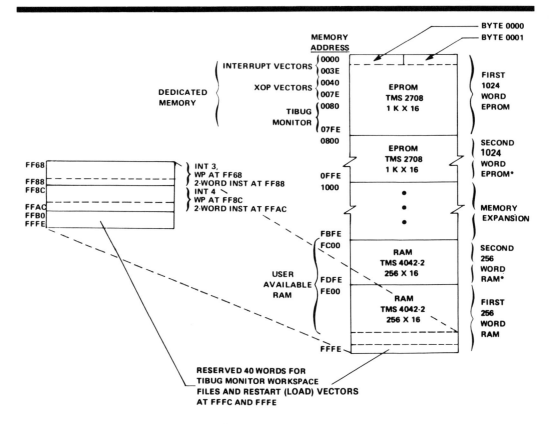

Figure 19. Memory Map

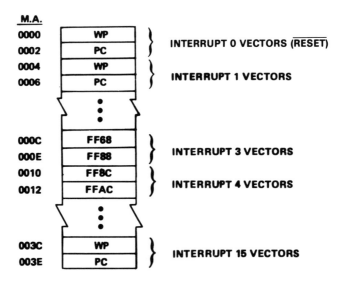

Figure 20. Interrupt Trap Locations

Extended Operations (XOP's)

Refer to *Figure 19* which shows the read-only memory space reserved for software interrupt vectors. Memory words from 0040_{16} to $007E_{16}$ are XOP vectors. As with interrupts, each XOP vector has a word containing a workspace pointer value and a next word containing a program counter value.

XOP instructions point to XOP vectors which point to new workspace pointer and program counter values in a similar way to what was just described for interrupts.

An instruction calling for an XOP (extended operation) is a means of switching from the main program to a subroutine. It has a special calling sequence and it functions as though the routine were a single instruction added to the 9900 set of operation codes, hence the name "extended operation".

For example, the TIBUG monitor in the microcomputer contains seven XOP routines that perform input/output functions with the terminal. These are as follows:

XOP Description
   8   Write one hexadecimal character to terminal
   9   Read hexadecimal word from terminal
  10   Write 4 hexadecimal characters to terminal
  11   Echo character
  12   Write one character to terminal
  13   Read one character from terminal
  14   Write message to terminal

Two of these XOPs are used in the extended application example. XOP 11 is used to read a character from the terminal and at the same time print it at the terminal. XOP 14 is used to print out instructions to explain how the program operates. Some of these XOPs call other XOPs. Further detail on XOPs can be obtained in Chapter 5 and 6.

Printing a Message

A message at the beginning of the program which will be developed for this application tells the user to select the mode of operation. XOP 14 is used to write the message. The instruction

XOP @MSG1,14

is used. XOP 14 identifies that the subtask is "Write message to terminal". A context switch takes place. The vector at location 14 of the reserved XOP vector memory space provides the WP and the PC values. The PC value provides the first subtask instruction and the subroutine continues until the subtask is complete and the program returns to the main program.

Suppose the message identified with the label MSG1 is "THIS IS A SAMPLE." Its coding would look like the following:

LINE	ADDRESS	CODE	MESSAGE		ASCI I CODE
0	MSG1	5448	$THIS IS A SAMPLE.	A	41
				E	45
1		4953		H	48
				I	49
2		2049		L	4C
				M	4D
3		5320		P	50
				S	53
4		4120		T	54
5		5341			
6		4D50		SPACE (SP)	20
7		4C45		LINE FEED (LF)	0A
8		2E20			
9		0D0A	+>0D0A	CARRIAGE RETURN (CR)	0D
10		0000	+>0000	· (PERIOD)	2E

Note that line 9 contains a carriage return and a line feed and has the code 0D0A. The message beginning at location MSG1 is preceded by a dollar sign and terminated with a byte containing all binary zeroes. The + > 0D0A is a code recognized by the line-by-line assembler that is loaded directly into memory. It is initiated by typing the (+) before the desired number. The dollar sign indicates that a comment is being entered. Such XOPs are very useful in calling subroutines prepared to accomplish specific terminal functions.

Selecting a Mode

XOP 11 will be used to make the choice of the mode of operation. ECHO CHARACTER means that whatever key is pressed on the terminal will be read into a designated workspace register and then sent back from the register and printed on the terminal.

The one instruction,

XOP R5,11

accomplishes this. If a key is pressed, the terminal reads the character, places it in workspace register 5 and then prints the character on the terminal. The XOP subroutine was provided by the TIBUG monitor but it all was accomplished with one instruction — thus, the "extended operation."

TMS9902

The TMS9902, asynchronous communications controller provides an interface between the EIA terminal (serial asynchronous communications channel) and the 9900 in the TM990/100M microcomputer module. The block diagram of the microcomputer was shown in *Figure 7*. A simplified one is shown in *Figure 21a*. Note that the interface to the CPU (TMS9900) is the same as for the 9901. Note also the line $\overline{INT}$ 4 going from the 9902 to the 9901; this interrupt line will be important in this application.

All of the discussion that pertained to the 9901 and the addressing of the I/O bits also applies to the 9902. It has the same address bits $A_{10}-A_{14}$ used for addressing the CRU bits inside the 9902 through S_0-S_4. It has the same CRU control bus signals for communication over the CRU serial data link.

A base address and $\overline{CE}$ select the 9902 over other I/O units that might be available in the system (in this case, only 9901s are present). The hardware base address 0040_{16} identifies the 9902 contained in the microcomputer. The software base address of 0080_{16} is loaded into WR12. This is added to the appropriate displacement to arrive at the effective CRU bit address desired as described for the 9901.

In this extended application, pressing a key on the terminal while the system is in mode 1 or mode 2 will switch the system back to the command mode. The user then selects a new mode of operation. This is a common way to use a terminal and the 9902 must be programmed to accomplish it. The arrangement is as shown in *Figure 21a*.

First, the 9902 must recognize that a character has been generated by the terminal and received by the 9902. Second, the output signal line $\overline{INT}$ from the 9902 must be enabled so it can pass the signal to the 9901 input $\overline{INT}$ 4. Since the 9901 receives this signal as an interrupt, then interrupt masks at the 9901 and the 9900 must be enabled. With these steps accomplished, the main program of the processor is interrupted and the operation mode is shifted.

Figure 21b shows that $\overline{INT}$ will be active in the receive mode if RBRL = 1 and RIENB = 1. RBRL will be a "1" when the Receive Buffer Register has received a character and stored it. This happens when a key is pressed. The 9902 is enabled by making RIENB (Receiver Interrupt Enable) a "1". *Figure 22* identifies that CRU bit 18 must be made a "1" to make RIENB = 1. A CRU SBO instruction with a displacement of 18 will set CRU bit 18 to a "1" if the software base address has previously been loaded in WR12.

Since $\overline{INT}4$ is the desired interrupt level, it is enabled in the 9900 by placing this level in its interrupt mask. This is accomplished with an instruction LIMI 4 which loads the value 4 into the status register.

With the $\overline{\text{INT}}4$ enabled at the 9901 by placing a "1" in the CRU bit mask corresponding to the input for $\overline{\text{INT}}4$, the 9901 sends the interrupt code to the 9900 over IC0-IC3 when the $\overline{\text{INT}}$ signal is received from the 9902. Since $\overline{\text{INT}}4$ is enabled in the 9900, the signal path is complete and the operating mode shifts.

$\overline{\text{INT}}4$ executes a context switch and finds its new workspace pointer is $FF8C_{16}$ and its new PC is $FFAC_{16}$.

In all the discussion, only the enabling of interrupts has been covered. It must be stressed that similar instructions in many cases must be included in the programming to disable an interrupt once it has been enabled.

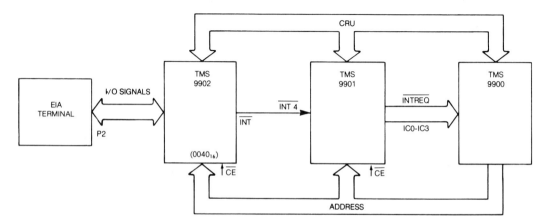

Figure 21a. Simplified Block Diagram Showing TMS 9902 Interface

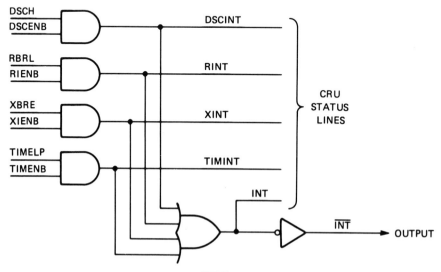

Figure 21b. $\overline{\text{INT}}$ Output Generation

ADDRESS$_2$					ADDRESS$_{10}$	NAME	DESCRIPTION
S0	S1	S2	S3	S4			
1	1	1	1	1	31	RESET	Reset device.
					30-22		Not used.
1	0	1	0	1	21	DSCENB	Data Set Status Change Interrupt Enable.
1	0	1	0	0	20	TIMENB	Timer Interrupt Enable
1	0	0	1	1	19	XBIENB	Transmitter Interrupt Enable
1	0	0	1	0	18	RIENB	Receiver Interrupt Enable
1	0	0	0	1	17	BRKON	Break On
1	0	0	0	0	16	RTSON	Request to Send On
0	1	1	1	1	15	TSTMD	Test Mode
0	1	1	1	0	14	LDCTRL	Load Control Register
0	1	1	0	1	13	LDIR	Load Interval Register
0	1	1	0	0	12	LRDR	Load Receiver Data Rate Register
0	1	0	1	1	11	LXDR	Load Transmit Data Rate Register
					10-0		Control, Interval, Receive Data Rate, Transmit Data Rate, and Transmit Buffer Registers

Figure 22. TMS 9902 ACC Output Bit Address Assignments

PROGRAMMING THE 9901 I/O

The discussion, previously quite general, now gets more specific, focusing on how the program will have to be written to satisfy the requirements of the application. Since all input and output signals must go through the 9901, let's begin there. Refer to *Figure 23*.

Note that there are multiple functions for the pins on the 9901. The pins are referenced to establish the link between Group 1, Group 2 and Group 3 which were mentioned previously in the text. Note that all the functions are referenced to a select bit number from 0 to 31. Select bit zero is addressed when the 9901 base address is called. For example, the instruction:

SBO 0

addresses select bit zero in the 9901 and will set this bit, called the control bit, to a "1". Because it was bit zero, there was no additional displacement value added to the base address. However, as was done in Chapter 3, 10_{16} will be added to the 9901 hardware base address in the microcomputer when P_0 thru P_{15} are being used as data inputs and data outputs. This makes the base address point to select bit 16 as indicated in *Figure 23*. It makes the assignment of I/O bit 0 correspond to P_0, bit 1 to P_1, bit 2 to P_2, etc.

Figure 23 shows how select bit zero, the control bit, controls the mode of the 9901. When it is a "0", the 9901 is in the interrupt mode; when it is a "1", the 9901 is in the clock mode. The 9901 must be in the interrupt mode to mask interrupt inputs; it must be in the clock mode to use the internal clock.

NOTES	SELECT BIT	S0 S1 S2 S3 S4	PIN NO.	PIN FUNCTION WHEN BEING READ BY A CRU INSTRUCTION		PIN FUNCTION WHEN BEING SET OR "WRITTEN TO" BY A CRU INSTRUCTION	
9901	MODE			INTERRUPT	CLOCK	INTERRUPT	CLOCK
Base Address	0 (control bit)	0 0 0 0 0		0	1	0	1
	1	0 0 0 0 1	17	INT 1	CLK 1	MASK 1	CLK 1
	2	0 0 0 1 0	18	INT 2	CLK 2	MASK 2	CLK 2
	3	0 0 0 1 1	9	INT 3	CLK 3	MASK 3	CLK 3
	4	0 0 1 0 0	8	INT 4	CLK 4	MASK 4	CLK 4
	5	0 0 1 0 1	7	INT 5	CLK 5	MASK 5	CLK 5
	6	0 0 1 1 0	6	INT 6	CLK 6	MASK 6	CLK 6
	7	0 0 1 1 1	*34	INT 7	CLK 7	MASK 7	CLK 7
	8	0 1 0 0 0	*33	INT 8	CLK 8	MASK 8	CLK 8
	9	0 1 0 0 1	*32	INT 9	CLK 9	MASK 9	CLK 9
	10	0 1 0 1 0	*31	INT 10	CLK 10	MASK 10	CLK 10
	11	0 1 0 1 1	*30	INT 11	CLK 11	MASK 11	CLK 11
	12	0 1 1 0 0	*29	INT 12	CLK 12	MASK 12	CLK 12
	13	0 1 1 0 1	*28	INT 13	CLK 13	MASK 13	CLK 13
	14	0 1 1 1 0	*27	INT 14	CLK 14	MASK 14	CLK 14
	15	0 1 1 1 1	*23	INT 15	△INTREQ	MASK 15	RST 2
I/O Ports → Address	16	1 0 0 0 0	38	P0 INPUT		P0 OUTPUT	
	17	1 0 0 0 1	37	P1 INPUT		P1 OUTPUT	
	18	1 0 0 1 0	26	P2 INPUT		P2 OUTPUT	
	19	1 0 0 1 1	22	P3 INPUT		P3 OUTPUT	
	20	1 0 1 0 0	21	P4 INPUT		P4 OUTPUT	
	21	1 0 1 0 1	20	P5 INPUT		P5 OUTPUT	
	22	1 0 1 1 0	19	P6 INPUT		P6 OUTPUT	
	23	1 0 1 1 1	*23	P7 INPUT		P7 OUTPUT	
	24	1 1 0 0 0	*27	P8 INPUT		P8 OUTPUT	
	25	1 1 0 0 1	*28	P9 INPUT		P9 OUTPUT	
	26	1 1 0 1 0	*29	P10 INPUT		P10 OUTPUT	
	27	1 1 0 1 1	*30	P11 INPUT		P11 OUTPUT	
	28	1 1 1 0 0	*31	P12 INPUT		P12 OUTPUT	
	29	1 1 1 0 1	*32	P13 INPUT		P13 OUTPUT	
	30	1 1 1 1 0	*33	P14 INPUT		P14 OUTPUT	
	31	1 1 1 1 1	*34	P15 INPUT		P15 OUTPUT	

*COMMON
△ INVERTED FROM INTREQ

Figure 23. 9901 Select Bit Assignments

INTERRUPT MODE

Select bit outputs 1 through 15 become MASK bits 1 through 15 when writing to these bits to enable (MASK = 1) or disable (MASK = 0) interrupts. Enabled interrupts received on the inputs will be decoded by the prioritizer and encoder of *Figure 15.*

CLOCK MODE

To set or read the self-contained clock, the 9901 must be in the clock mode. Using the CRU, the clock is set to a total count by writing a value to select bits 1 through 14.

Reading the clock is accomplished by a CRU instruction to read select bits 1 through 14. Another read instruction without switching the 9901 out of the clock mode will read the same value.

The clock is reset by writing a zero value to the clock or by a system reset.

In the clock mode, select bits 1 through 14 become CLK bits 1 through 14.

DATA INPUTS AND OUTPUTS

Select bits 16 through 31 are used for data inputs and outputs. All I/O pins are set to the input mode by a reset. To set a select bit as an output, just write data to that pin. The data will be latched and can be read with a CRU read instruction without affecting the data. Once an I/O port is programmed to be an output, it can only be programmed as an input by a hardware or software reset. This can be done two ways.

1. Receiving a hardware reset, $\overline{\text{RESET}}$.
   (Operating the RESET switch on the microcomputer.)
2. Writing a "0" to select bit 15 of the 9901 while in the clock mode will cause a software $\overline{\text{RST2}}$ and force all I/O ports to the input mode.

The status of the 9901 can be evaluated by checking (reading) the control bit. Testing select bit 15 in the interrupt mode can indicate if an interrupt has been received. If one has, INTREQ will be high because $\overline{\text{INTREQ}}$ is low.

After a hardware $\overline{\text{RESET}}$, or a software reset $\overline{\text{RST2}}$, all interrupts $\overline{\text{INT1}}$ through $\overline{\text{INT15}}$ are disabled, all I/O ports will be in the input mode, the code on IC0-IC3 will be 0000, $\overline{\text{INTREQ}}$ will be high and the 9901 will be in the interrupt mode.

EXAMPLES OF PROGRAMMING

Setting the Control Bit

If the interrupt and clock modes of the 9901 are to be controlled, load the base address in WR12 (100_{16} for 9901 on microcomputer board) and set select bit zero to the respective value:

```
LI  R12,>100        LOADS>100 INTO WR12
SBZ  0              9901 TO INTERRUPT MODE
SBO  0              9901 TO CLOCK MODE
```

Enabling or Disabling Interrupt Level

Interrupt levels are enabled or disabled by setting the MASK to a "1" or a "0" value, respectively. As an example, after a reset, the 9901 would be in the interrupt mode. Now interrupts 2, 5, 6 and 8 are to be enabled. The instruction:

> LDCR R2,9

will do this as shown in *Figure 24.* The contents of workspace register 2, 0164_{16} from bit 15 thru 7 are read into select bits 0 thru 8 to enable interrupt levels 2, 5, 6 and 8. Of course, WR12 had to be loaded with the software base address using a

> LI   R12,>100

instruction, as an example, and WR2 would have been loaded in a similar fashion.

In like fashion, the same levels could be disabled by writing "0" to bits 2, 5, 6 and 8 with an LDCR instruction, or programming a software $\overline{RST2}$, or by using the single bit CRU instructions.

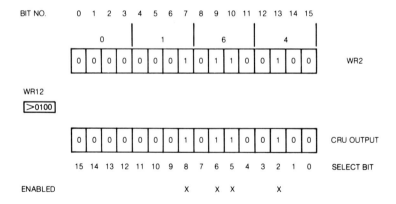

Figure 24. Enabling Interrupt Levels 2, 5, 6 and 8 with an LDCR Instruction

For example,

SBZ 2
SBZ 5
SBZ 6
SBZ 8

would set each bit to a "0". Previously WR12 was set to 0100_{16} to reference the 9901 on the microcomputer module.

Setting the Output Bits

Similar single bit or LDCR CRU instructions can be used to set the output bits.

LDCR R2, 0 would read out the value of WR2 to the output pins P_0 through P_{15} (the 0 in the LDCR R2, 0 means all 16 bits will be written to the output). WR12 has previously been loaded with 0120_{16}. This is shown in *Figure 25.*

A routine of loading 9901 I/O INPUTS and storing 9901 I/O OUTPUTS with a 743 KSR terminal would look like the following, after pressing the RESET toggle switch on the microcomputer module and a carriage return on the terminal:

```
TIBUG REV A
?M FE00 (CR)
```

ADDRESS	OP CODE		MNEMONIC	COMMENT
FE00 = XXXX	02E0	(SP)	LWPI >FF20	;WP = >FF20
FE02 = XXXX	FF20	(SP)		
FE04 = XXXX	020C	(SP)	LI R12,>120	;9901, SOFTWARE BASE ADDRESS = >120
FE06 = XXXX	0120	(SP)		
FE08 = XXXX	0200	(SP)	LI R0,>F0F0	;CRU DATA
FE0A = XXXX	F0F0	(SP)		
FE0C = XXXX	3000	(SP)	LDCR R0,0	LOAD 9901 I/O PORTS WITH R0
FE0E = XXXX	3400	(SP)	STCR R0,0	STORE 9901 I/O PORTS IN R0
FE10 = XXXX	0460	(SP)	B @>80	;RETURN TO TIBUG
FE12 = XXXX	0080	(CR)		
?				

The XXXX shown are don't care contents at the respective memory addresses which are changed as the op codes are entered. (SP) is a space bar command and (CR) is a carriage return.

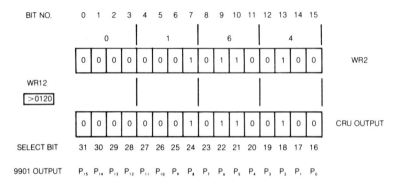

Figure 25. Output From WR 2 with LDCR Instruction

PROGRAMMING THE 9901 CLOCK

In *Figure 9,* the clock function of the 9901 was described. The clock register must be loaded with a value to set its total count and enable the clock. When the register is decremented to zero, it generates a level 3 interrupt (INT 3) as the elapsed time signal.

Access is gained to the clock by setting select bit zero to a "1" which puts the 9901 in the clock mode. All select bits 1 thru 15 are then in the clock mode and become the access for setting the clock count. CLK bit 15 is used for software reset. Therefore, the clock count is set by the value on select bits 1 through 14. An example is shown in *Figure 26.* The maximum value that can be loaded into 14 bits (all ones) would be 16,383. The rate at which the clock decrements the value is $f(\phi)/64$. If f is 3 MHz, then the rate is approximately 46,875 Hz. The time interval is equal to the value in the clock register times 1/46,875. With the maximum value, the maximum interval is 349 milliseconds.

If 25 millisecond intervals are required, then the clock register would have to be loaded with $46,875 \times 0.025 = 1172$. This is equivalent to 0494_{16}. The least significant bit of the register value must be a 1 to set the control bit, therefore 0494_{16} is moved over a bit position and the register is loaded with 0929_{16}. A LDCR instruction is used for loading the value and the sequence of steps is shown in *Figure 26.*

The software is as follows:

```
LI  R12,>0100        ;SET 9901 ON MODULE SOFTWARE ADDRESS=>0100
LI  R1,>0929         ;LOAD CLOCK VALUE INTO R1, SET CLOCK MODE
LDCR  R1,15          ;MOVE TIMER VALUE AND CONTROL BIT TO 9901
```

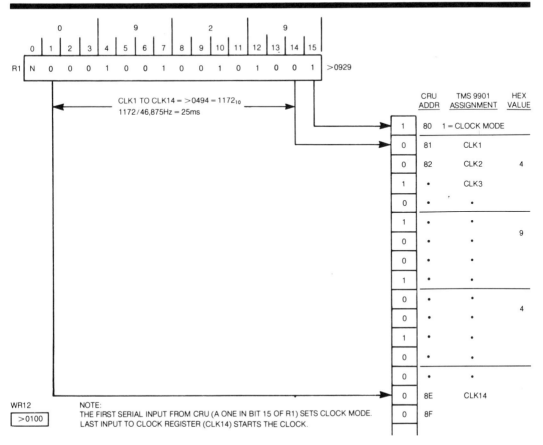

Figure 26. Enabling and Triggering TMS 9901 Interval Timer

Enabling Clock Interrupt

When the clock decrements to zero, a level 3 interrupt is given. The interrupt level 3 mask needs to be enabled on the 9901 and the 9900 CPU. The interrupt mask on the 9901 is enabled by setting the control bit to a logical "0" (interrupt mode) and then setting select bit 3 to a "1" (write a "1" to bit 3). The interrupt mask on the 9900 is enabled by loading the appropriate value (in this case, 3) into the interrupt mask. When 3 is loaded into the 9900 with a LIMI 3 instruction, all higher priority levels are also enabled.

The software is:

```
LI  R12,>0100        ;SET BASE ADDRESS TO 9901 ON BOARD, >0100
SBZ 0                ;9901 TO INTERRUPT MODE
SBO 3                ;ENABLE INTERRUPT 3 AT 9901
LIMI 3               ;LOAD 9900 INTERRUPT MASK
```

PUTTING SOME PIECES TOGETHER

Some of the pieces can now be combined to provide a larger program. It looks like this:

```
          LI  R12,>0100        ;SET SOFTWARE BASE ADDRESS OF 9901=0100
          CLR R0              ;INITIALIZE INTERRUPT INDICATOR, R0 SET TO ZERO
          LI  R1,>0929         ;CLOCK COUNT 0494 AND CLOCK MODE IN R1
          LDCR R1,15          ;SET CLOCK COUNT ENABLE TIMER
          SBZ 0               ;9901 TO INTERRUPT MODE
          SBO 3               ;ENABLE INT 3 AT 9901
          LIMI 3              ;LOAD 9900 INTERRUPT MASK
LOOP 2    CI  R0, >FFFF        ;HAS INT 3 OCCURED?
          JNE LOOP 2          ;IF NO, GO TO LOOP 2
```

When the timer gives an interrupt 3, a context switch occurs; the interrupt 3 vector PC points to $FF88_{16}$ which contains an instruction to get to the interrupt routine:

```
          B   @CLKINT          ;BRANCH TO INTERRUPT ROUTINE IDENTIFIED BY CLK INT
```

The branch then takes the program to:

```
CLKINT    LI  R12,>0100        ;SET SOFTWARE BASE ADDRESS OF 9901=0100
          SBZ 3               ;DISABLE INTERRUPT 3
          SETO *R13           ;SET PREVIOUS R0 TO FFFF
          RTWP               ;RETURN TO PROGRAM
```

Thus, if an interrupt 3 has not occured, the program remains in Loop 2 until it does. When $\overline{INT}$ 3 occurs a context switch to the interrupt subroutine causes R0 to be changed from all zeros to all ones. R0 will now equal $FFFF_{16}$ and the program proceeds to the step after JNE Loop 2, which, as will be seen later, is a count down.

FROM BASIC CONCEPTS TO PROGRAM

As with the Chapter 3 application, converting the idea to program starts with solidifying the basic concept, then developing acceptable flow charts, and then programming the algorithm for the problem solution. As with hard-wired logic design, the place to start is with a block diagram. The one used in *Figure 6* will be expanded with a bit more detail and will be the concept diagram *(Figure 27)*.

The terminal, the microcomputer module and the interface modules with their respective inputs and outputs will constitute the system. Later on the TM900/310 module will be added to show the I/O expansion capability. This will only involve plugging the interface modules into one of the additional 9901 outputs on the 310 board (P4 in this case) and changing the CRU base address to select the chosen 9901. It will be assumed that the power and all interconnections have also been made through P1 to the microcomputer and 310 module as shown in *Figure 27*. There is a special power supply required for supplying the interface modules. This is the $+8V$ shown in *Figure 27.* 110Vac is supplied separately for the terminal and the industrial level voltages of 12 volts dc and 110Vac are supplied separately, as they would be in a user facility.

The physical arrangement of the interface modules is important to the program for the problem solution. Therefore, I/O positions 0 thru 7 are identified. Positions 0 thru 3 are input positions; positions 4 thru 7 are output positions. Signals received on input position 0 will cause reaction at output position 4. Correspondingly for input 1 and output 5, input 2 and output 6, and input 3 and output 7. Thus, the program will be written to sense input 1 and set output 5 to correspond.

Switches S1 through S4 represent industrial level input voltages, either dc or ac. Lights L1 and L3 represent industrial dc loads; L2 and L4 represent industrial ac loads.

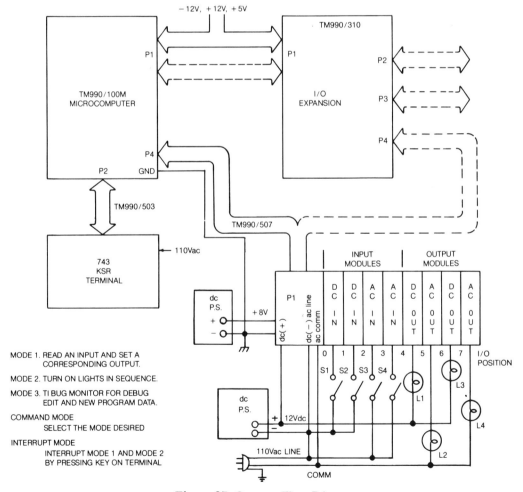

Figure 27. *Concept Flow Diagram*

Flow Charts for the Program

Software design is really little different from hardware design in the execution of good engineering practice.

The task from overall concept stage is divided into subsystems — in the case of software, subprograms or subroutines. *Figure 28* identifies subprograms for the extended application which are detailed in flow charts so that basic functions can be identified.

The flow charts are separated according to the functions that are to be implemented. Operation in Mode 1 simulates sensing four industrial level inputs 0 through 3 and reacting to these inputs by providing output voltages to four corresponding loads, 4 through 7. The flow chart identifies that inputs will be sensed and a corresponding output will be set to match the input state or value.

The four output loads, in this case light bulbs, will be turned on and off in sequence and held in each of these states for a set time (variable by the program). This is Mode 2 operation. The flow chart shows the major functions. After all four lights are turned off and on, the sequence starts over. The clock in the 9901 will be used to provide the time interval.

There is an operating Mode 3 but it will be contained in the mode called the COMMAND Mode. In Mode 3 the operation of the system is under the control of the TIBUG Monitor which is contained in the 1K words of EPROM resident in the microcomputer. It is used for inputting the original program and editing and changing the program as the need may be.

The flow chart for the Command Mode starts with initial setup of the system. Certain registers and certain locations in memory are loaded with data used throughout the program. A print-out of general information and specific instructions follows. Since the user will make a choice, instructions identify that a one (1) key is to be pressed on the terminal to operate in Mode 1; a two (2) key to operate in Mode 2; and a Q for Mode 3. The character pressed by the user is then examined and the appropriate operating mode selected. If none of the operating mode characters are received the system waits in the command mode until one is received.

On the flow chart for the COMMAND mode A and B connect with the respective points on the MODE 1 and MODE 2 flow charts.

Recall that the system is to have a provision for the user to command an escape from the continuous operation in Mode 1 or Mode 2. This happens by interrupting Mode 1 or Mode 2 operation by pressing a key on the terminal. The first blocks in the flowcharts of MODE 1 and MODE 2 provide the means for accomplishing the interrupt. When a key is pressed on the terminal, this initiates an interrupt signal output from the 9902. This interrupt must be enabled to pass to the 9901 and the 9900 so that it will cause the return to the COMMAND MODE. The generation of the signal in the 9902 is flowcharted under the heading INTERRUPT MODE of *Figure 28*.

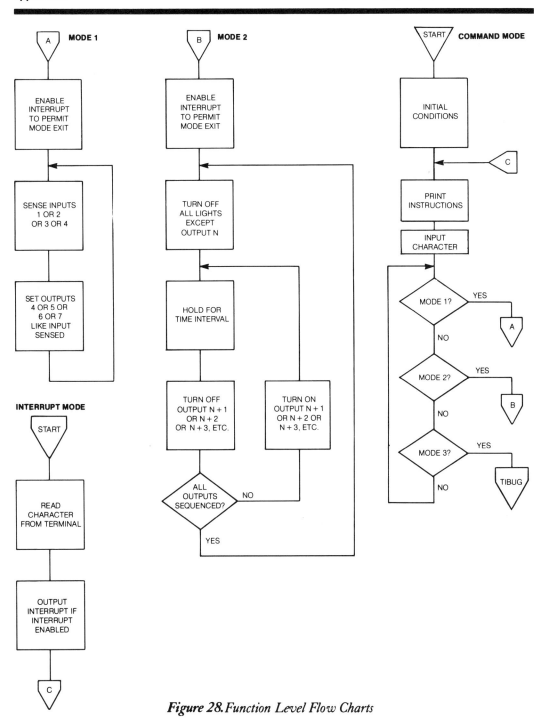

Figure 28. Function Level Flow Charts

WRITING THE PROGRAM

Memory Space

All elements are now in place to write the program. First, it is necessary to decide what locations are to be used in memory for the program, for the workspace and for data. Refer to *Figure 29*.

For this application more memory space is required than for Chapter 3's First Encounter. Thus, additional RAM units are installed on the microcomputer board at locations U33, U35, U37 and U39 (4042 Units). This expands the available RAM space to $FC00_{16}$ and this is the location for the start of the program.

Incidentally, while available memory is being discussed, note the address of the TIBUG monitor, 0080_{16}. This memory location must be referenced when returning to the TIBUG Monitor in Mode 3. The TIBUG workspace located at $FFB0_{16}$ has already been discussed. This space must be reserved.

One more point — the second 1K of EPROM starting at location 0800_{16} will be populated with the Line-by-Line Assembler (LBLA) resident in EPROM. This will be used for assembly of the program. The socket locations on the board are U43 and U45 and the product number is TM990/402-1. Normally, the LBLA would start assemblying at address $FE00_{16}$, however, by using a /FC00 command the start location is changed to $FC00_{16}$.

The Command Mode

A more complete flow chart is shown in *Figure 30* for the Command Mode. The program begins with initialization of registers. When writing the first draft of the program, labels are used for ease of writing. For later drafts and when a LBLA is used, the labels are replaced with actual addresses. INPUT1 will be the label for the start of Mode 1. BLINKR will be the label for the start of Mode 2. COMODE labels the message that asks the user to select the mode.

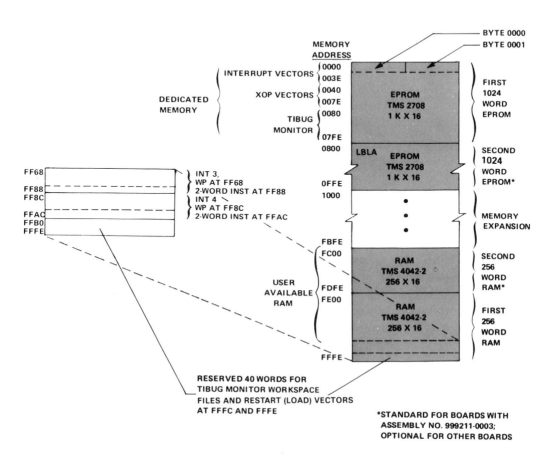

DEDICATED MEMORY

ADDRESS (HEX)	PURPOSE
0000-0003	Level zero interrupt vector (RESET)
000C-000F	INT3 vectors (TMS 9901 timer)
0010-0013	INT4 vectors (TMS9902 timer)
0040-0047	Vectors for XOP's 0 and 1 (Microterminal I/O)
0060-007F	Vectors for XOP's 8 to 15 (TIBUG utilities)
0080-07FF	TIBUG monitor
FFB0-FFFB	Four overlapping monitor workspaces
FFFC-FFFF	Restart (load) vector

Figure 29. Memory Map with Fully Populated 990/100M-1 Module

The Command Mode program is as follows:

```
COUNT      +>929                 ;SET UP 9901 CLOCK
BASE1      +>100                 ;SET UP 9901 CRU BASE
BASE2      +>120                 ;SET UP 9901 I/O BASE
START      LWPI >FF20            ;SET WP AT FF20
           LI  R1,>1E00          ;SBZ OP CODE TO R1
           LI  R2,>1D00          ;SBO OP CODE TO R2
           LI  R3,>1F00          ;TB OP CODE TO R3
           XOP @MSG1, 14         ;PRINT HEADER @MSG1
COMODE     XOP @MSG2, 14         ;ASK FOR MODE WITH MSG2
           XOP  R7, 11           ;READ CHAR FROM TER TO R7
           CI  R7,>3100          ;IS CHAR A 1?
           JEQ INPUT1            ;IF YES GO TO MODE 1
           CI  R7,>3200          ;IS CHAR A 2?
           JEQ BLINKR            ;IF YES TO TO MODE 2
           CI  R7,>5100          ;IS CHAR A Q?
           JNE COMODE            ;IF NO KEEP LOOPING
           B  @>80               ;IF YES GO TO TIBUG
```

To initialize registers, the values for the TMS 9901 clock interval, TMS 9901 CRU software base address and TMS 9901 I/O software base address are loaded directly into memory spaces by using a ($+$) in front of the data. 0929_{16} is placed in the 9901 for a 25ms interval. Recall that the module 9901 has a base address of 0100_{16} for select bit zero and 0120_{16} so that select bit 16 activates P0 when input or output bit 0 is addressed, as discussed previously. Note that the workspace is set up at $FF20_{16}$.

The machine codes for SBZ, SBO and TB are loaded into workspace registers one, two and three, respectively. As discussed previously, an XOP 14 is used to print the header and instructions for use of the program. The messages are labeled with MSG1 and MSG2 and are located at the end of the program and will be discussed later. Next an XOP is used to read a character from the terminal and load the ASCII code into R7. This is then compared with the ASCII codes for the number one, two and the letter Q to determine the character. Depending on what character is received, the program jumps to the proper area in memory to execute the correct mode of operation. The entry point to the TIBUG monitor is 0080_{16} and a branch to this location will execute the monitor.

Mode 1 Operation

Figure 31 shows the flow chart for Mode 1 Operation. The label INPUT1 begins the operation. The first function sets up the system so that the 9902 will generate an interrupt when a received character fills the receiver buffer (RBRL = 1). Recall that the interrupt generated by the 9902 must be enabled by making RIENB = 1. This is accomplished by making the 9902 select bit 18 equal to "1". The enabled interrupt from the 9902 is wired to the $\overline{INT}4$ input of the 9901. Thus, as previously discussed, level 4 interrupts must be enabled both at the 9901 and the 9900.

The software looks like this:

```
INPUT1    RSET              ; PUT 9901 INTO INPUT MODE
          LIMI  4           ; ENABLE 9900 INT1-INT4
          LI  R12,>80       ; LOAD R12 W/9902 BASE ADDR
          STCR  R7,0        ; CLEAR 9902 RCV BUFFER
          SBO  18           ; ENABLE 9902 RCV INT
          MOV  @BASE1,R12   ; SET 9901 BASE ADDR TO  >100
          SBO  4            ; ENABLE 9902 INT AT 9901
```

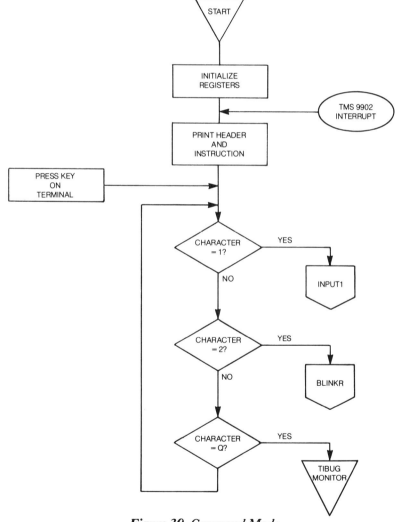

Figure 30. Command Mode

First the 9901 is reset to put it into the input mode. Then the 9900 interrupt mask is set to 4 to allow interrupts 1 thru 4 to be acknowledged. To enable select bit 18 of the 9902, the software base address is loaded into WR12 and an SBO 18 instruction sets the bit to "1" for the enable. The 9902 receiver buffer is read into R7 with the STCR instruction which resets the buffer for receipt of a character. WR12 is set with the software base address for the 9901, and then select bit 4 is set to a "1". These steps enable the 9901 interrupt level 4 to clear the complete path for generating an interrupt when a character is received from the terminal.

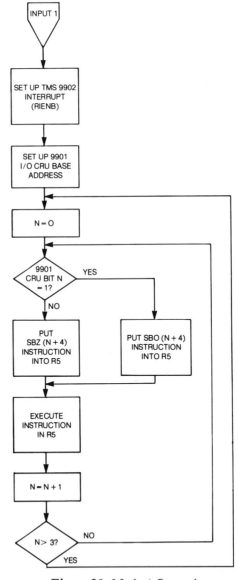

Figure 31. Mode 1 Operation

CHECKING THE INPUTS—SETTING THE OUTPUTS

Figure 31 shows that with $N = 0$ the CRU is testing the zero input bit of the 9901. If it is a "1", then the $N + 4$ bit (I/O bit 4) will be set to a "1" to correspond. One will be added to N $(0 + 1 = 1)$, which will be less than 3 and the cycle is repeated: the second time with $N = 1$, the next time with $N = 2$ and the next with $N = 3$. With $N = 3$, $N + 1$ will be greater than three and everything is reinitialized and the sequence starts over with input bit zero again. So the procedure is to check each input bit and set the corresponding output bit. The software is as follows:

```
        MOV  @BASE2,R12    ; SET 9901 BASE ADDR TO >120
INIT1   CLR  R4            ; R4 CONTAINS CRU BIT TO BE
                           ; TESTED
INDEX1  MOV  R4,R5         ; MOVE CRU BIT TO R5
        SOC  R3,R4         ; R4 CONTAINS TB INST (R3)
        X    R4            ; EXECUTE TB SPECIFIED BY R4
        JEQ  HIGH          ; IF CRU BIT=1 GO TO HIGH
LOW     MOV  R5,R4         ; RELOAD CRU BIT INTO R4
        AI   R5,>4         ; SHIFT CRU BIT OVER BY 4
        SOC  R1,R5         ; R5 CONTAINS SBZ OP CODE (R1)
XECUTE  X    R5            ; EXECUTE OP CODE SPECIFIED BY R5
        INC  R4            ; INCREMENT TO NEXT CRU BIT
        CI   R4,>3         ; IS CRU BIT >3?
        JGT  INIT1         ; IF YES REINITIALIZE
        JMP  INDEX1        ; START TESTING NEXT CRU BIT
HIGH    MOV  R5,R4         ; RELOAD CRU BIT INTO R4
        AI   R5,>4         ; SHIFT CRU BIT OVER 4
        SOC  R2,R5         ; R5 CONTAINS SBO OP CODE (R2)
        JMP  XECUTE        ; GO EXECUTE SBO INST
```

Input bits 0-3 correspond to output bits 4-7 respectively. R4 contains the value of the select bit to be tested (the program starts with bit zero). R4 is moved to R5 to preserve the contents of R4. R3 contains the machine code for TB. Actually it contains the machine code for the instruction TB 0 (Test bit 0). By doing a set ones correspondence (SOC) between R3 and R4, the machine code for the TB instruction is combined with the value of the select bit to be tested so that R4 contains the instruction — "test the select bit previously specified by R4." More specifically, $R4 = TB$ (R4).

An X of R4 will execute this instruction. Using this procedure allows R4 to contain the bit position separate from the TB instruction which is in R3. The bit position in R4 or R5 can also be combined with the SBO and SBZ op codes located in R2 and R1 to allow execution of the SBO or SBZ instructions on the select bits specified by R4 or R5. The procedure is the same as for the TB instruction.

If the bit tested is a zero, R4 is reloaded from R5 with the original value of the select bit to be tested, which is still in R5. R5 plus 4 is combined with R1 using a SOC R1, R5 instruction. The selected output bit will be set to zero when the resulting SBZ instruction in R5 is executed. Thus, an $N + 4$ output is set to zero, if the corresponding N bit was a zero.

R4 is incremented to the next bit and is tested to determine if its value is greater than 3. When it is not, the program jumps to label INDEX1 and tests the next bit in the same sequence as the first and sets the corresponding output bit. Now, suppose this bit is a "1" instead of a "0" as for the preceding bit. The program jumps to the label HIGH, reloads R4, adds 4 to R5, and now executes an SOC R2, R5 to set the N + 4 output to one when the SBO instruction in R5 is executed.

When input bit 3 is tested, the test of R4 + 1 will show its value is greater than 3 and the program is reinitialized and the procedure starts over. To exit the loop, any key on the keyboard is pressed which produces a level 4 interrupt. The level 4 interrupt comes from the 9902 and the system enters the command mode as shown in *Figure 30*.

Mode 2 Operation *(Figure 32)*

Mode 2 operation sequences the loads simulated by light bulbs. The flowchart is shown in *Figure 32*. It has a time interval of 25ms set up by the 9901 real time clock. A program loop multiples the 25ms times R6 to obtain the total time interval; with R6 = 4, each total time interval is 100ms. The time interval can also be varied by changing the initial value 0929_{16} set into the clock register of the 9901. The value in R4 determines the number of light bulbs (loads) that are going to be turned on, held for 100ms, turned off, and started through the sequence again. As with mode 1, pressing a key on the terminal causes a return to the Command Mode.

It is worthy to note, even though the 9901 is in the input mode when reset, outputs 4,5,6 and 7 are such that all light bulbs are on. Thus, the function of turning off outputs 5, 6 and 7 and leaving 4 on starts the program after the CRU base address is set. In actual industrial applications it may be necessary to put additional inverters between the output of the microcomputer and the 5MT modules so that the reset condition has all loads off.

Recall that when the 9901 clock register is decremented to zero it puts out a $\overline{INT3}$ signal. This interrupt causes a context switch to occur and sets the old workspace R0 to $FFFF_{16}$. When this happens the time interval has ended.

Interrupt 4 from TMS 9902

The software for Mode 2 starts as follows to set up the interrupt 4 from the 9902:

```
BLINKR      RSET            ; SET 9901 TO THE INPUT MODE
            LIMI  4         ; ENABLE 9900 INT1-INT4
            LI  R12,>80     ; SET UP 9902 BASE ADDR
            STCR  R7,0      ; CLEAR 9902 RCV BUFFER
            SBO  18         ; ENABLE 9902 RCV INT
```

The reset at BLINKR sets the 9901 to the input mode and turns on the loads on outputs 4, 5, 6 and 7.

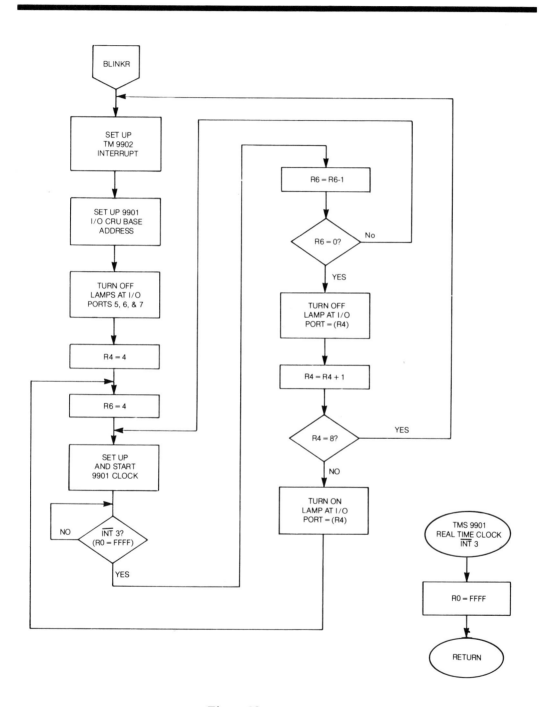

Figure 32. *Mode 2 Operation*

The next 7 instructions after the 9901 software base address is set at 0120_{16} are concerned with turning off outputs 5, 6 and 7. These start with INT2 and continue through the next 6 instructions after LOOP 1.

```
              MOV  @BASE2, R12      ; SET 9901 BASE ADDR=>120
    INT2      LI   R4,>5            ; R4 CONTAINS CRU BIT POS 5
    LOOP1     MOV  R4,R5            ; MOV POS 5 TO R5
              SOC  R1,R5            ; R5 CONTAINS SBZ OP CODE (R1)
              X    R5               ; EXECUTE SBZ SPECIFIED BY (R5)
              INC  R4               ; R4=R4+1
              CI   R4,>8            ; HAS CRU BIT 7 BEEN SET=0?
              JNE  LOOP1            ; IF NO GO TO LOOP 1
```

Lamp 4 remains on.

Register 4 must now be loaded with the output position from which the sequence starts—in this case 4.

```
              LI   R4,>4            ; SET OUTPUT BASE BIT
```

Timing Loop

R6 is set equal to 4 so that the overall time interval is 100ms. This starts the timing loop at INDEX2. The 5 instructions following TIMER set up the 9901 clock to count a 25ms interval and then cause a level 3 interrupt. Note that the 9901 must be put into the interrupt mode and the level 3 interrupt enabled. Since the 9902 interrupt signal comes in on interrupt level 4, it is convenient to enable it at this same time. The loop is such that it loops 4 times. Each loop is controlled by the interval timer of the TMS9901. The TMS9901 timer is set and started when loaded with the value at the label COUNT. The clock decrements until it hits zero and then it gives a level 3 interrupt. The interrupt service routine begins at $FF88_{16}$ as directed by the level 3 vector. It sets R0 to $FFFF_{16}$ and returns to the program. The program will be in a continuous loop (Loop 2) checking R0 for an indication that an interrupt has occured. When the time interval is complete, the I/O bit dictated by R4 is turned off. R4 is incremented and checked to see if it is equal to 8. If not, the I/O bit position of the new R4 is turned on and the sequence restarts. If R4+1=8, then the program jumps back to BLINKR and starts over causing R4 to be reset to 4 and to restart the sequence.

The software looks like this:

```
INDEX 2     LI   R6,>4          ; OVERALL LOOP COUNT=100ms
TIMER       MOV  @BASE1,R12     ; SET CRU BASE ADDR OF 9901=>100
            CLR  R0             ; INITIALIZE INT3 INDICATOR
            LDCR @COUNT,15      ; LOAD TIMER AND START COUNT
            SBZ  0              ; 9901 TO INTERRUPT MODE
            SBO  3              ; ENABLE INT3 AT 9901
            SBO  4              ; ENABLE 9902 INT AT 9901
LOOP2       CI   R0,>FFFF       ; HAS INT3 OCCURRED?
            JNE  LOOP2          ; IF NO GO TO LOOP2
            DEC  R6             ; R6=R6-1
            JNE  TIMER          ; IF R6=0 GO TO TIMER
            MOV  @BASE2,R12     ; SET 9901 BASE ADDR=>120
            MOV  R4,R5          ; MOV CRU BIT TO R5
            SOC  R1,R5          ; (R5)=SBZ (R5)
            X    R5             ; EXECUTE SBZ SPECIFIED BY (R5)
            INC  R4             ; R4=R4+1
            CI   R4,>9          ; IS R4=9?
            JEQ  BLINKR         ; IF YES RESTART SEQUENCE
            MOV  R4,R5          ; R4=R5
            SOC  R2,R5          ; (R5)=SBO (R5)
            X    R5             ; EXECUTE SBO SPECIFIED BY (R5)
            JMP  INDEX2         ; RESTART TIMING CYCLE AT INDEX 2
```

9902 Interrupt Service Routing

This interrupt service routine is the one resulting from a level 4 interrupt generated by the 9902. It starts at INTREC. As discussed previously, when the interrupt occurs, the program counter points to $FFAC_{16}$, the reserved space, where it finds an instruction directing it to INTREC. This instruction looks like this:

```
ADDRESS     INSTRUCTION

FFAC        B @INTREC              ; GO TO INT4 SERVICE ROUTINE
```

The routine first disables the 9901 timer interrupt level 3, then disables the 9902 interrupt at the 9902 (Set select bit 18 = 0) and finally loads the address of COMODE into the old PC, so that when an RTWP (return with workspace pointer) is executed, the program returns to the command mode. The software is as follows:

```
INTREC      MOV  @BASE1,R12     ; SET 9901 BASE ADDR=>100
            SBZ  3              ; DISABLE INT3 AT 9901
            SRL  R12, 1         ; SET BASE ADDR=>80 FOR 9902
            SBZ  18             ; DISABLE 9902 INT
            STOR R7, 0          ; READ 9902 RCV BUFFER (CLEARS)
            LI   R14, COMODE    ; LOAD ADDR OF COMODE INTO PC
            RTWP               ; RETURN TO 5MT ROUTINE
```

9901 Clock Interrupt Service Routine

When the clock decrements to zero it generates a level 3 interrupt. The routine to service this interrupt starts at CLKINT. The level 3 interrupt context switch provides a new PC at $FF88_{16}$ which directs the program to CLKINT. This instruction looks like this:

```
ADDRESS    INSTRUCTION

FF88       B  @CLKINT              ; GO TO INT3 SERVICE ROUTINE
```

Here, after setting the software base address of the 9901 to 0100_{16}, $\overline{\text{INT3}}$ is disabled and R0 of the previous workspace is set to $FFFF_{16}$. A RTWP instruction then returns the processor to the interrupted routine.

The software is as follows:

```
CLKINT     LI   R12,>100          ; SET 9901 BASE ADDR
           SBZ  3                  ; DISABLE INT3 AT 9901
           SETO *R13               ; SET PREVIOUS R0=>FFFF
           RTWP                    ; RETURN TO INTERRUPTED ROUTINE
```

Message Routines

The remaining routines that must be included in the program are the messages at MSG1 and MSG2. In order to program the message, a $ sign is used at the beginning of each line and each message is terminated with a zero byte. The ASCII code for a carriage return — line feed is $0D0A_{16}$ and is included in the instruction format.

Each character must be coded with the appropriate ASCII code and placed into bytes of memory. A typical example is shown; however, the individual character codes have not been listed. This can be seen on the LBLA listing.

```
MSGI       $5MT I/O DEMONSTRATION ROUTINE
           +>0D0A
           $MODE 1 — INPUTS 0-3 SWITCH OUTPUTS
           $4-7 RESPECTIVELY
           +>0D0A
           $MODE 2 — OUTPUTS 4-7 ARE SWITCHED SEQUENTIALLY
           +>0D0A
           $A Q RETURNS CONTROL TO THE TIBUG MONITOR
           +>0D0A
           $A CARRIAGE RETURN DURING MODE 1 OR 2
           $OPERATION RETURNS THE USER TO THE
           +>0D0A
           $CONTROL MODE
           +>0D0A
           +>0000
           +>0D0A
           $SELECT MODE 1, 2 or Q
           +>0D0A
           +>0000
```

SYSTEM OPERATION

With program in hand, it is time to connect the hardware to prove out the complete program. Refer to the block diagram of *Figure 27*.

The terminal and its cable have been previously connected to P2 of the microcomputer module. P1 has the same power supply connections as for Chapter 3 supplying − 12V, + 12V, + 5V and ground. The full connections will be added to P1 to interface with P1 on the TM990/310 I/O expansion board. However, for now, operations will be only with the microcomputer and the 5MT I/O modules. Connection to the modules is made through the cable of *Figure 4* and P4 on the microcomputer and P1 on the 5MT43 module base. There is a separate wire from the J1 connector to provide + 8 volts to the 5MT modules. This + 8 volts must supply 0.6A worst case if all the positions in the 5MT43 base are populated. *This supply ground must be common with the microcomputer module ground and isolated from the + 12V industrial control voltage supply ground.*

The + 12V for the industrial control level voltages must supply 200mA. *This must have a minus terminal free of chassis ground, otherwise its case will be at ac line voltage when the 5MT I/O module ac power cord is connected.*

Light bulbs that are rated at 80 mA at 14 Vdc are used for the dc loads. Standard 110 Vac light bulbs and sockets are used for the ac loads. A separate ac power cord is connected to the 5MT43 base for the ac power. The industrial level power *(both dc and ac) is and must be isolated from the dc power for the microcomputer module and low-level logic + 8V power source of the 5MT interface modules.*

A summary of the parts list and power supply requirements follows:

System Parts List

- TM990/100M-1 board
- TM990/310 48 I/O board (optional)
- 5MT43 base*
- 2 − 5MT11-A05L AC input modules*
- 2 − 5MT12-40AL AC output modules*
- 2 − 5MT13-D03L DC input modules*
- 2 − 5MT14-30CL DC output modules*
- 5MT interface cable-TM990/507
- 743 KSR terminal
- TM 990/503 cable assembly for Terminal
- 4 − TMS 4042-2 (or 2111-1) 256 x 4 RAM's

*In case your local distributor does not have these parts, the address from which they can be ordered is:

    Industrial Controls Order Entry
    M/S 12-38
    34 Forrest St.
    Attleboro, Mass. 02703
    Phone: (617) 222-2800

- Line-by-line assembler TM990/402-1 (in two TMS 2708 EPROM's)
- Power supplies for Microcomputer and I/O Expansion (TM990/518)

Voltage	REG	/100M Current	w/310 Module Current
+5V	±3%	1.3A	2.1A
+12V	±3%	0.1A	0.1A
−12V	±3%	0.2A	0.2A

- Industrial Control Level Power Supplies

Voltage	REG	Current
+8Vdc	±5%	0.6A
+12Vdc	±5%	0.2A
110Vac		1A

- 4 Toggle switches, SPST
- 2 dc lamps and sockets (14V — 80mA)
- 2 ac lamps and sockets (130V — 30 W)

- Power cord
- 14 and 18 AWG insulated stranded wire

Equipment Hookup

Follow these steps in making the system interconnections;

Step 1 — Verify that the power supply connections to P1 are correct for − 12V, + 12V and + 5V. Refer to *Figure 3-11* or to the TM990/ 100M user's guide *Figure 2-1*. Don't turn on any power supplies. It may be desirable to make all the connections from P1 of the TM990/100M to P1 of the TM990/310 at this time. Refer to *Table 6* for these connections. Some reprogramming because of power shutdown will be required if this is not done.

Step 2 — Verify that the 743 KSR terminal is connected to P2 with the TM990/503 cable. AC power is supplied to the terminal with a separate cord.

Step 3 — Special connections must now be made at the jumpers on the TM990/100M microcomputer. The jumper positions are shown in Chapter 3, *Figures 12* and *13*. Make sure of the following jumper connections.

JUMPERS	INTERCONNECTION	COMMENT
J15	Disconnected	Power for TM990/301
J14	Disconnected	Microterminal, not
J13	Disconnected	required for 743 KSR
J12	N.A.	For multiple boards
J11	Disconnected	For ASR 745
J10,9,8	N.A.	For multiple boards
J7	EIA position	
J6,5	N.A.	For multiple boards
J4,3,2	In 08, or 2708 Position	For 2708 EPROMS
J1	9902	This will likely need to be positioned

Step 4 —   As mentioned previously, the RAM on the TM990/100M should be fully populated for this example. Make sure that 4-TMS 4042-2's have been inserted in U33, U35, U37 and U39 with the #1 pin towards the TMS 9900. The LBLA which is in two TMS 2708 EPROM's should have also been inserted in U43 and U45 with the #1 pin towards the TMS 9900. The higher order byte (bits 0-7) must be in U45. It is quite difficult to insert these packages in the sockets the first time so it must be done carefully. Rocking the packages will help.

Step 5 —   Install the 5MT modules in the 5MT43 base as shown in *Figure 33.* Be sure modules are in the proper order. This arrangement will show dc input controlling dc output, dc input—ac output, ac input—dc output and ac input — ac output. Connect the wiring as shown. Be sure to use heavy gage (14 AWG) insulated wire for the ac connections. 18 AWG can be used for dc power connections. *NOTE THAT AC LINE IS CONNECTED TO DC COMMON.* Two screw connections on the base are available for each module as shown in *Figure 33.* All connections to the 5MT modules are to the right-hand leads when facing the terminals and P1 is on the left. Be sure to screw down the locking screw to ensure good connections.

Step 6 —   Connect J1 of the cable of *Figure 4* to the 5MT43 base. Connect the + 8V lead to the power supply and its ground to the common ground lead on J4 of the cable of *Figure 4. DO NOT CONNECT THIS GROUND TO THE DC COMMON OF THE INDUSTRIAL CONTROL LEVEL POWER SUPPLY OF FIGURE 33.*

Step 7 —   Connect the + 12Vdc industrial power supply. Don't plug in the 110Vac power cord.

Step 8 —   Turn on the + 8V and + 12V supply and verify that the dc input and output 5MT modules are connected correctly. Use J4 for test voltages.

Step 9 —   Plug-in the ac power cord for the 5MT modules and verify that the ac input and output modules are interconnected correctly. The LED's on the modules will be useful for this.

Step 10 —   Unplug ac cord, turn off + 12V and + 8V supplies.

Step 11 —   Connect J4 of the cable from the 5MT43 base to P4 on the TM990/100M module.

Step 12 —   Turn on the power supplies for the microcomputer *in this order:* − 12V, + 12V, + 5V.

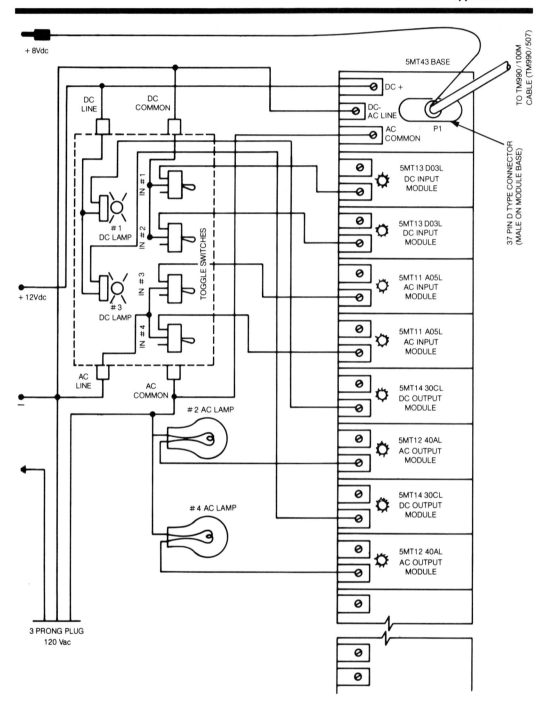

Figure 33. 5MT I/O Module Wiring

Step 13 —   Turn on the terminal. Make sure it is "ON LINE."

Step 14 —   Turn on the +8V supply for the 5MT modules; then the industrial level +12Vdc and then plug in the power cord for the 110Vac.

Step 15 —   Press the RESET switch on the microcomputer. All the light bulbs will be lit since a RESET latches I/O pins on the microcomputer in the "1" state.

                  The microcomputer system is now ready to be programmed.

LOADING THE PROGRAM

The program as it was developed will now be loaded into RAM in the microcomputer. Instead of assembling the program by hand, the line-by-line assembler contained in EPROM will be used. It works with the EIA terminal and the TIBUG monitor.

The LBLA is a stand alone program that assembles into object code the 69 instructions used by the TM 990/100M microcomputer. To initialize the LBLA, the TIBUG monitor must first be brought up. This is done by switching the reset switch on the TM 990/100M module and pressing the carriage return (CR) on the terminal. The terminal will respond with:

```
TIBUG REV. A.
?
```

The question mark is the TIBUG prompt.

Now an R is typed to inspect/change the WP, PC and ST registers. The LBLA program begins at location $09E6_{16}$* so this is the value that is to be loaded into the PC. After typing an R the terminal prints out the value of the WP. This can be changed by typing the new value and a space or it can be left alone by typing just a space. The terminal will then print the value of the PC. The same procedure as for the WP applies except that ST is printed if a space is typed. A CR after the WP or PC value will cause the TIBUG prompt to be printed, or a space or CR after the ST is printed will do the same.

Loading $09E6_{16}$ into the PC looks like this:

```
?R                      (CR)
W=FFC6                  (SP)
P=01A6      09E6        (CR)
?
```

Once the PC has been loaded, executing the program will initialize the LBLA. Pressing the E key accomplishes this. The LBLA responds with an address. That address can be changed to the starting address of the program by typing a slash (/) and the new address and a CR.

```
?E
FE00                /FC00        (CR)
FC00
```

*This value may change depending on the version of LBLA. Early versions had $09E8_{16}$ as entry point.

The program can then be entered using the machine instructions. The LBLA accepts assembly language inputs from a terminal. As each instruction is input, the assembler interprets it, places the resulting machine code in an absolute address, and prints the machine code (in hexadecimal) next to its absolute address as shown in Figure 34.

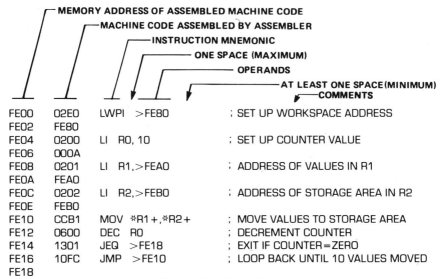

MEMORY ADDRESS OF ASSEMBLED MACHINE CODE
MACHINE CODE ASSEMBLED BY ASSEMBLER
INSTRUCTION MNEMONIC
ONE SPACE (MAXIMUM)
OPERANDS
AT LEAST ONE SPACE (MINIMUM)
COMMENTS

FE00	02E0	LWPI >FE80	; SET UP WORKSPACE ADDRESS
FE02	FE80		
FE04	0200	LI R0, 10	; SET UP COUNTER VALUE
FE06	000A		
FE08	0201	LI R1,>FEA0	; ADDRESS OF VALUES IN R1
FE0A	FEA0		
FE0C	0202	LI R2,>FEB0	; ADDRESS OF STORAGE AREA IN R2
FE0E	FEB0		
FE10	CCB1	MOV *R1+,*R2+	; MOVE VALUES TO STORAGE AREA
FE12	0600	DEC R0	; DECREMENT COUNTER
FE14	1301	JEQ >FE18	; EXIT IF COUNTER=ZERO
FE16	10FC	JMP >FE10	; LOOP BACK UNTIL 10 VALUES MOVED
FE18			

Figure 34. LBLA Format

Only one space is used between the mnemonic and the operand. If comments are used, use at least one space between the operand and the start of the comment. If no comment is used complete the instruction *with a space and a carriage return.* If a comment is used, only a carriage return is required.

Note that to load a hex value directly into a memory location a (+) is used. (see Start of Program, *Table 4.*) Also a string of characters is preceded by a dollar sign ($) and *terminated with two carriage returns*—CR (Example shown under—Message Routines). To change the address location being loaded, type a slash (/) and the address desired. To exit from the LBLA and return to the TIBUG monitor, press the ESC key on the terminal. The terminal will then give the TIBUG prompt—a question mark.

Labels cannot be used with the LBLA. However, in the program of *Table 4,* the left side is the assembled program with LBLA and the right side is for a comparison to the labels and the comments that were previously used on each of the pieces of the program as it was developed on the preceding pages.

Remember to press the ESC when the last program address location is reached. This returns control to the TIBUG monitor.

Table 4. *Final Program*

LBLA			Labels	Comments
?R				
W = FFB0				
P = 0168	09E6			
?E				
FD00		/FC00		
FC00	0929	+ > 929	COUNT	; SET UP 9901 CLOCK
FC02	0100	+ > 100	BASE 1	; SET UP 9901 CRU BASE
FC04	0120	+ > 120	BASE 2	; SET UP 9901 I/O BASE
FC06	02E0	LWPI > FF20	START	; SET WP AT FF20
FC08	FF20			
FC0A	0201	LI R1, > 1E00		; SBZ OP CODE TO R1
FC0C	1E00			
FC0E	0202	LI R2, > 1D00		; SBO OP CODE TO R2
FC10	1D00			
FC12	0203	LI R3, > 1F00		; TB OP CODE TO R3
FC14	1F00			
FC16	2FA0	XOP @ > FCF2,14		; PRINT HEADER @MSG1
FC18	FCF2			
FC1A	2FA0	XOP @ > FE00,14	COMODE	; ASK FOR MODE WITH MSG2
FC1C	FE00			
FC1E	2EC7	XOP R7,11		; READ CHAR FROM TER TO R7
FC20	0287	CI R7, > 3100		; IS CHAR A 1?
FC22	3100			
FC24	1308	JEQ > FC36		; IF YES GO TO MODE 1
FC26	0287	CI R7, > 3200		; IS CHAR A 2?
FC28	3200			
FC2A	1325	JEQ > FC76		; IF YES GO TO MODE 2
FC2C	0287	CI R7, > 5100		; IS CHAR A Q?
FC2E	5100			
FC30	16F4	JNE > FC1A		; IF NO KEEP LOOPING
FC32	0460	B @ > 0080		; IF YES GO TO TIBUG
FC34	0080			
FC36	0360	RSET	INPUT1	; PUT 9901 INTO INPUT MODE
FC38	0300	LIMI 4		; ENABLE 9900 INT1-INT4
FC3A	0004			
FC3C	020C	LI R12, > 0080		; LOAD R12 W/9902 BASE ADDR
FC3E	0080			
FC40	3407	STCR R7,0		; CLEAR 9902 RCV BUFFER
FC42	1D12	SBO 18		; ENABLE 9902 RCV INT
FC44	C320	MOV @ > FC02,R12		; SET 9901 BASE ADDR TO > 100
FC46	FC02			
FC48	1D04	SBO 4		; ENABLE 9902 INT AT 9901
FC4A	C320	MOV @ > FC04,R12		; SET 9901 BASE ADDR TO > 120
FC4C	FC04			
FC4E	04C4	CLR R4	INIT1	; R4 CONTAINS CRU BIT TO BE TESTED
FC50	C144	MOV R4,R5	INDEX1	; MOVE CRU BIT TO R5
FC52	E103	SOC R3,R4		; R4 CONTAINS TB INST [R3]
FC54	0484	X R4		; EXECUTE TB SPECIFIED BY R4
FC56	130A	JEQ > FC6C		; IF CRU BIT = 1 GO TO HIGH
FC58	C105	MOV R5,R4	LOW	; RELOAD CRU BIT INTO R4
FC5A	0225	AI R5, > 4		; SHIFT CRU BIT OVER BY 4
FC5C	0004			
FC5E	E141	SOC R1,R5		; R5 CONTAINS SBZ OP CODE [R1]
FC60	0485	X R5	XECUTE	; EXECUTE OP CODE SPECIFIED BY R5
FC62	0584	INC R4		; INCREMENT TO NEXT CRU BIT
FC64	0284	CI R4, > 3		; IS CRU BIT > 3?
FC66	0003			

FC68	15F2	JGT >FC4E		; IF YES REINITIALIZE
FC6A	10F2	JMP >FC50		; START TESTING NEXT CRU BIT
FC6C	C105	MOV R5,R4	HIGH	; RELOAD CRU BIT INTO R4
FC6E	0225	AI R5,>4		; SHIFT CRU BIT OVER 4
FC70	0004			
FC72	E142	SOC R2,R5		; R5 CONTAINS SBO OP CODE [R2]
FC74	10F5	JMP >FC60		; GO EXECUTE SBO INST
FC76	0360	RSET	BLINKR	; SET 9901 TO INPUT MODE
FC78	0300	LIMI 4		; ENABLE 9900 INT1-INT4
FC7A	0004			
FC7C	020C	LI R12,>80		; SET UP 9902 BASE ADDR
FC7E	0080			
FC80	3407	STCR R7,0		; CLEAR 9902 RCV BUFFER
FC82	1D12	SBO 18		; ENABLE 9902 RCV INT
FC84	C320	MOV @>FC04,R12		; SET 9901 BASE ADDR=>120
FC86	FC04			
FC88	0204	LI R4,>5	INT2	; R4 CONTAINS CRU BIT POS 5
FC8A	0005			
FC8C	C144	MOV R4,R5	LOOP1	; MOV POS 5 TO R5
FC8E	E141	SOC R1,R5		; R5 CONTAINS SBZ OP CODE [R1]
FC90	0485	X R5		; EXECUTE SBZ SPECIFIED BY [R5]
FC92	0584	INC R4		; R4=R4+1
FC94	0284	CI R4,>8		; HAS CRU BIT 7 BEEN SET=0?
FC96	0008			
FC98	16F9	JNE >FC8C		; IF NO GO TO LOOP1
FC9A	0204	LI R4,>4		; SET OUTPUT BASE BIT
FC9C	0004			
FC9E	0206	LI R6,>4	INDEX2	; OVERALL LOOP COUNT=100MS
FCA0	0004			
FCA2	C320	MOV @>FC02,R12	TIMER	; SET CRU BASE ADDR OF 9901=>100
FCA4	FC02			
FCA6	04C0	CLR R0		; INITIALIZE INT3 INDICATOR
FCA8	33E0	LDCR @>FC00,15		; LOAD TIMER AND START COUNT
FCAA	FC00			
FCAC	1E00	SBZ 0		; 9901 TO INTERRUPT MODE
FCAE	1D03	SBO 3		; ENABLE INT3 AT 9901
FCB0	1D04	SBO 4		; ENABLE 9902 INT AT 9901
FCB2	0280	CI R0,>FFFF	LOOP2	; HAS INT3 OCCURRED?
FCB4	FFFF			
FCB6	16FD	JNE >FCB2		; IF NO GO TO LOOP2
FCB8	0606	DEC R6		; R6=R6-1
FCBA	16F3	JNE >FCA2		; IF R6=0 GO TO TIMER
FCBC	C320	MOV @>FC04,R12		; SET 9901 BASE ADDR=>120
FCBE	FC04			
FCC0	C144	MOV R4,R5		; MOV CRU BIT TO R5
FCC2	E141	SOC R1,R5		; [R5]=SBZ [R5]
FCC4	0485	X R5		; EXECUTE SBZ SPECIFIED BY [R5]
FCC6	0584	INC R4		; R4=R4+1
FCC8	0284	CI R4,>9		; IS R4=9?
FCCA	0009			
FCCC	13D4	JEQ >FC76		; IF YES RESTART SEQUENCE
FCCE	C144	MOV R4,R5		; R4=R5
FCD0	E142	SOC R2,R5		; [R5]=SBO [R5]
FCD2	0485	X R5		; EXECUTE SBO SPECIFIED BY [R5]
FCD4	10E4	JMP >FC9E		; RESTART TIMING CYCLE AT INDEX2
FCD6	C320	MOV @>FC02,R12	INTREC	; SET 9901 BASE ADDR=>100
FCD8	FC02			
FCDA	1E03	SBZ 3		; DISABLE INT3 AT 9901
FCDC	091C	SRL R12,1		; SET BASE ADDR=>80 FOR 9902
FCDE	1E12	SBZ 18		; DISABLE 9902 INT

FCE0	3407	STCR R7,0		; READ 9902 RCV BUFFER [CLEARS]
FCE2	020E	LI R14,>FC1A		; LOAD ADDR OF COMODE INTO PC
FCE4	FC1A			
FCE6	0380	RTWP		; RETURN TO 5MT ROUTINE
FCE8	020C	LI R12,>100	CLKINT	; SFT 9901 BASE ADDR
FCEA	0100			
FCEC	1E03	SBZ 3		; DISABLE INT3 AT 9901
FCEE	071D	SETO *R13		; SET PREVIOUS R0=>FFFF
FCF0	0380	RTWP		; RETURN TO INTERRUPTED ROUTINE
FCF2		/FF88		
FF88	0460	B @>FCE8		; GO TO INT3 SERVICE ROUTINE @CLKINT
FF8A	FCE8			
FF8C		/FFAC		
FFAC	0460	B @>FCD6		; GO TO INT4 SERVICE ROUTINE @INTREC
FFAE	FCD6			
FFB0		/FCF2		
FCF2	354D	$5MT I/O DEMONSTRATION ROUTINE		
FCF4	5420			
FCF6	492F			
FCF8	4F20			
FCFA	4445			
FCFC	4D4F			
FCFE	4E53			
FD00	5452			
FD02	4154			
FD04	494F			
FD06	4E20			
FD08	524F			
FD0A	5554			
FD0C	494E			
FD0E	4520			
FD10	0D0A	+>0D0A		
FD12	4D4F	$MODE 1 — INPUTS 0-3 SWITCH OUTPUTS		
FD14	4445			
FD16	2031			
FD18	202D			
FD1A	2049			
FD1C	4E50			
FD1E	5554			
FD20	5320			
FD22	302D			
FD24	3320			
FD26	5357			
FD28	4954			
FD2A	4348			
FD2C	204F			
FD2E	5554			
FD30	5055			
FD32	5453			
FD34	2020			
FD36	342D	$4-7 RESPECTIVELY.		
FD38	3720			
FD3A	5245			
FD3C	5350			
FD3E	4543			
FD40	5449			
FD42	5645			
FD44	4C59			
FD46	2E20			
FD48	0D0A	+>0D0A		

```
FD4A   4D4F   $MODE 2 — OUTPUTS 4-7 ARE SWITCHED SEQUENTIALLY.
FD4C   4445
FD4E   2032
FD50   202D
FD52   204F
FD54   5554
FD56   5055
FD58   5453
FD5A   2034
FD5C   2D37
FD5E   2041
FD60   5245
FD62   2053
FD64   5749
FD66   5443
FD68   4845
FD6A   4420
FD6C   5345
FD6E   5155
FD70   454E
FD72   5449
FD74   414C
FD76   4C59
FD78   2E20
FD7A   0D0A   + >0D0A
FD7C   4120   $A Q RETURNS CONTROL TO THE TIBUG MONITOR
FD7E   5120
FD80   5245
FD82   5455
FD84   524E
FD86   5320
FD88   434F
FD8A   4E54
FD8C   524F
FD8E   4C20
FD90   544F
FD92   2054
FD94   4845
FD96   2054
FD98   4942
FD9A   5547
FD9C   204D
FD9E   4F4E
FDA0   4954
FDA2   4F52
FDA4   0D0A   + >0D0A
FDA6   4120   $A CARRIAGE RETURN DURING MODE 1 OR 2 OPERATION
FDA8   4341
FDAA   5252
FDAC   4941
FDAE   4745
FDB0   2052
FDB2   4554
FDB4   5552
FDB6   4E20
FDB8   4455
FDBA   5249
FDBC   4E47
FDBE   204D
```

```
FDC0   4F44
FDC2   4520
FDC4   3120
FDC6   4F52
FDC8   2032
FDCA   204F
FDCC   5045
FDCE   5241
FDD0   5449
FDD2   4F4E
FDD4   5245    $RETURNS THE USER TO THE
FDD6   5455
FDD8   524E
FDDA   5320
FDDC   5448
FDDE   4520
FDE0   5553
FDE2   4552
FDE4   2054
FDE6   4F20
FDE8   5448
FDEA   4520
FDEC   0D0A    +>0D0A
FDEE   434F    $CONTROL MODE.
FDF0   4E54
FDF2   524F
FDF4   4C20
FDF6   4D4F
FDF8   4445
FDFA   2E20
FDFC   0D0A    +>0D0A,
FDFE   0000    +>0000
FE00   0D0A    +>0D0A
FE02   5345    $SELECT MODE 1, 2 OR Q
FE04   4C45
FE06   4354
FE08   204D
FE0A   4F44
FE0C   4520
FE0E   312C
FE10   2032
FE12   204F
FE14   5220
FE16   5120
FE18   0D0A    +>0D0A
FE1A   0000    +>0000
FE1C
```

I/O EXPANSION
WITH THE TM990/310

RUNNING THE PROGRAM

To execute the program, the PC needs to be set to the starting address. This is done by typing an R to enter the inspect/change mode of TIBUG. The WP will be printed. A space will give the PC and here the new PC should be entered. A CR will return to TIBUG and the prompt will be given. Typing an E will cause the program to begin executing. The following is an example of this:

```
?R
W=FFFE  (SP)
P=006C  FC00  (CR)
?E
```

The program will begin by requesting a mode of operation from the user. Typing a "1" will get mode 1 and the state of outputs can be changed by changing the input toggle switches. Pressing a key will cause a return to the command mode. Pressing a 2, switches to mode 2 and the light sequence. Pressing a key returns to the command mode. Pressing a Q on the terminal returns the system to the TIBUG and specific address locations could be inspected for contents, etc.

Debugging

Because of the hard copy given by the terminal, looking for mistakes is made easier. If the program is stuck in a loop, the reset switch on the TM990/100M board can be switched. When in the LBLA use a slash (/) and a new address to change the address. When in TIBUG use the memory inspect/change (M) command to change the address. The TM990/100M user's guide gives the TIBUG commands and the TM990/402 LBLA user's guide gives the LBLA commands. These are also given in Chapter 7.

I/O EXPANSION WITH THE TM990/310

What remains now is to show the I/O expansion through the use of the TM990/310 module. As shown in *Figure 35,*there are three additional 9901's on the /310 module. The 9901's signals are connected to edge connections P2, P3, and P4, respectively, and are shown in *Table 5.*

All of the pins on the connector to P1 on the 900/100M-1 microcomputer module must now be connected to P1 on the TM990/310 module (if not made previously). These are shown in *Table 6.* Such a power down requires the program to be re-entered.

Table 5. 9901 Pin-Outs on TM990/310.

P2, P3, P4 Pin Number	Signature
20	P0
22	P1
14	P2
16	P3
18	P4
10	P5
12	P6
24	INT15/P7
26	INT14/P8
28	INT13/P9
30	INT12/P10
32	INT11/P11
34	INT10/P12
36	INT9/P13
38	INT8/P14
40	INT7/P15
6	Neg. Edge Triggered INT5
8	Pos. Edge Triggered INT6
1	+12V
2	−12V
3	+5V
4	Spare
All remaining pins	Ground

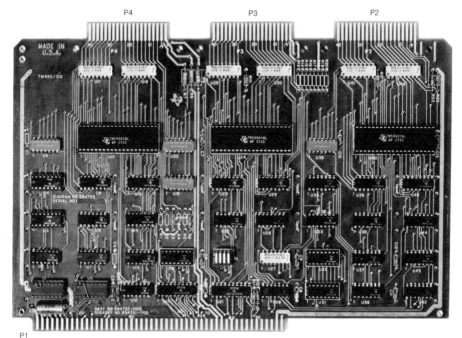

Figure 35. TM 990/310 I/O Expansion Module

Table 6. P1 Connections

P1 PIN	SIGNAL	P1 PIN	SIGNAL	P1 PIN	SIGNAL
33	D0	71	A14	12	INT13
34	D1	72	A15	11	INT14
35	D2	22	φ1	14	INT15
36	D3	24	φ3	28	EXTCLK
37	D4	92	HOLD	3	+5V
38	D5	86	HOLDA	4	+5V
39	D6	82	DBIN	97	+5V
40	D7	26	CLK	98	+5V
41	D8	80	MEMEN	75	+12V
42	D9	84	MEMCYC	76	+12V
43	D10	78	WE	73	−12V
44	D11	90	READY	74	−12V
45	D12	87	CRUCLK	1	GND
46	D13	30	CRUOUT	2	GND
47	D14	29	CRUIN	21	GND
48	D15	19	IAQ	23	GND
57	A0	94	PRES	25	GND
58	A1	88	IORST	27	GND
59	A2	16	INT1	31	GND
60	A3	13	INT2	77	GND
61	A4	15	INT3	79	GND
62	A5	18	INT4	81	GND
63	A6	17	INT5	83	GNG
64	A7	20	INT6	85	GND
65	A8	6	INT7	89	GND
66	A9	5	INT8	91	GND
67	A10	8	INT9	99	GND
68	A11	7	INT10	100	GND
69	A12	10	INT11	93	RESTART
70	A13	9	INT12		

USING THE TM990/310 BOARD

The TMS 9901s on the TM990/310 board are accessed in the same manner as the TMS9901 on the TM990/100M board except the CRU base addresses differ. These hardware base addresses are user selectable by a DIP switch that is on the TM990/310 board. The position of the switch and the corresponding addresses are given in *Figure 36*. The first column of addresses are the actual CRU hardware addresses and the second column is the software address that is to be loaded into workspace register 12 to access the appropriate TMS 9901. The addresses shown correspond to the first TMS 9901 on the TM990/310 board and the positions on the DIP switch. The addresses to be loaded into workspace register 12 for the second TMS9901 are obtained by adding 80_{16} to the addresses of the first TMS 9901. The addresses for the third TMS 9901 are obtained by adding 80_{16} to the addresses of the second TMS 9901 (or 100_{16} to the addresses of the first TMS 9901). For example, if S1 was set to binary 4, workspace register 12 would be loaded with: 0800_{16} to access the first TMS 9901, 0880_{16} to access the second TMS 9901, or 0900_{16} to access the third TMS 9901. The first TMS 9901 corresponds to the P2 pins, the second to the P3 pins, and the third to the P4 pins.

Switch all S1 positions on so the hardware base address 0100 is used for the /310 to correspond to the example in *Figure 11*. The third 9901 will be used so the software base address to be loaded in the program will be 0300_{16} and the I/O software base address will be 0320_{16}. The connection to the 5MT I/O modules will be thru P4 on the TM990/310 as shown in *Figures 27* and *35*. This connection should be made at this time.

CHANGING THE PROGRAM

To change the program, the software address at the labels BASE 1 and BASE 2 needs to be changed. In the assembled program, these are at FC02 and FC04. The TIBUG monitor mode is obtained. A memory inspect/change (M) command to address FC02 will allow a change of the contents at that address to 0300_{16}. A space obtains address FC04 and its contents can be changed to 0320_{16}. However, when this change is made, the 9901 in the TM990/100M module no longer is enabled to receive the keyboard interrupt from the 9902 and, thus, the mode operation cannot be interrupted. Additional program changes must be made at $FC44_{16}$, $FCA2_{16}$, and $FCD6_{16}$ to continue to enable the 9901 INT4 in the module.

More sophisticated program changes could be made but one pattern that can be used for such changes is as follows:

```
1. (CR)                    ; CARRIAGE RETURN TO MONITOR
2. R                       ; OBTAIN WORKSPACE POINTER
3. (SP)                    ; OBTAIN PROGRAM COUNTER
4. 09E6 (CR)               ; SET PC FOR LBLA
5. E                       ; EXECUTE LBLA
6. /FC44 (SP) (CR)         ; GO TO FC44
7. LI R12,>0100   (SP) (CR) ; LOAD SOFTWARE BASE ADDRESS FOR
                             9901 ON MODULE
```

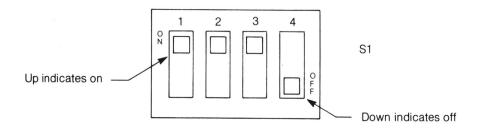

S1 Switch Settings				Binary Equal	TM990/310 Module CRU Base Address (Hex)	Register 12 Contents (Hex)
1	2	3	4			
ON	ON	ON	ON	0	0100	0200
ON	ON	ON	OFF	1	01C0	0380
ON	ON	OFF	ON	2	0280	0500
ON	ON	OFF	OFF	3	0340	0680
ON	OFF	ON	ON	4	0400	0800
ON	OFF	ON	OFF	5	04C0	0980
ON	OFF	OFF	ON	6	0580	0B00
ON	OFF	OFF	OFF	7	0640	0C80
OFF	ON	ON	ON	8	0700	0E00
OFF	ON	ON	OFF	9	07C0	0F80
OFF	ON	OFF	ON	A	0880	1100
OFF	ON	OFF	OFF	B	0940	1280
OFF	OFF	ON	ON	C	0A00	1400
OFF	OFF	ON	OFF	D	0AC0	1580
OFF	OFF	OFF	ON	E	NOT USED	NOT USED
OFF	OFF	OFF	OFF	F	NOT USED	NOT USED

Figure 36. Programming Base Address of TM 990/310 Module

On the terminal the routine looks like this:

```
Q
?R
W=FF20
P=FC1A 09E6
?E
FE00    /FC44
FC44    020C    LI  R12,>100
FC46    0100
FC48
```

The same program change must be made at FCA2 and FCD6. When these are made, return to TIBUG by pressing the ESC key. The memory location just changed can be checked with the M command and the memory location.

To run the program, press the R key (it gives the WP) then (SP) to get the PC. Change the PC to $FC00_{16}$ and execute the program by pressing (CR) and the E key.

Incidentally, after these program changes, the only thing that needs to be done to change the 5MT I/O to the microcomputer module connector P4 is to change the original software base addresses at FC02 = >0100 and FC04 = >0120. No other changes need be made.

FUTURE EXTENSIONS

Now that the system is available there are endless variations that can be accomplished. Here are some that come to mind immediately:

1. Change the time interval on Mode 2 by:
    a. Changing the value in R6
    b. Changing the value loaded into the clock register

2. Add more modules to the 5MT43 and program a different input-output relationship.

3. Reprogram so that the program itself shifts the 5MT I/O to the /310 module if a /310 is present. Otherwise, the interface would remain on P4 of the microcomputer module.

4. Expand to more modules thru the TM990/310 modules.

5. Investigate how interrupts come through the TM990/310 module to the processor. There are some special linkages that must be connected on the /310 module to choose the interrupts that will come through the /310 to the processor.

CONCLUSION

CONCLUSION

It has been quite an experience starting at the first encounter and proceeding to
the point where a microcomputer system is up and running and capable of being
programmed to sense and control real-world industrial level energy. Components are
available to easily apply the systems to many varieties of problem solutions.

Continue the learning process by finding real things to do with the system. Build on it to
use it to its full capability and then add to it or replace it with a larger system to expand
the applications. And remember, all the software that has been learned will be applicable
to the new system applications, to different 9900 family members, and to new family
members to be added in the future. Common compatible software is a real advantage.
It's built into the 9900 family, so build on it. Good Luck.

A Low Cost
Data Terminal

ABSTRACT

The architecture of the TMS 9940 Microcomputer is briefly reviewed. The microcomputer portion of a data terminal which currently employs the TMS 8080A Microprocessor is described. An equivalent design, which significantly reduces the chip count by using the TMS 9940 Microcomputer, is discussed in detail. Software comparisons between the two systems are made. A cost analysis of the two designs is discussed.

INTRODUCTION

As the complexity of LSI (large scale integration) electronics continues to increase, the system designer gains more and more freedom in designing low cost systems. One example of this capability is the Texas Instruments (TI) Model 745 Electronic Data Terminal, first introduced by TI in 1975. The Model 745 is a self-contained compact, telecommunications terminal which uses the thermal printing technique to achieve silent operation. The Model 745 features a 58 key, TTY33-compatible modular keyboard with integral numeric keypad, carrier detect indicator, two-key rollover, and key debounce circuitry. The Model 745 is capable of operating in full or half duplex modes at 10 or 30 characters per second, using a character set and code compatible with the American Standard Code for Information Interchange (ASCII).

The particular design of the Model 745 Data Terminal was made possible by the use of a microcomputer system as its controller. The Model 745 incorporates a TMS 8080A Microprocessor as the CPU of the Microcomputer. The purpose of this paper is to show how the Model 745 Terminal could be simplified even further by utilizing the newest addition to the 990/9900 Computer family: the TMS 9940 Microcomputer.

MICROCOMPUTER ARCHITECTURES

TMS 8080A MICROPROCESSOR

The TMS 8080A is an eight-bit general purpose Microprocessor *(Figure 1)*. The TMS 8080A chip contains seven registers and has a 78-instruction repertoire. The chip requires three power supplies (+ 12, ± 5Vdc) and accepts a two-phase high-level clock input. The TMS 8080A features 64K byte addressing of off-chip memory, and is packaged in a 40-pin package.

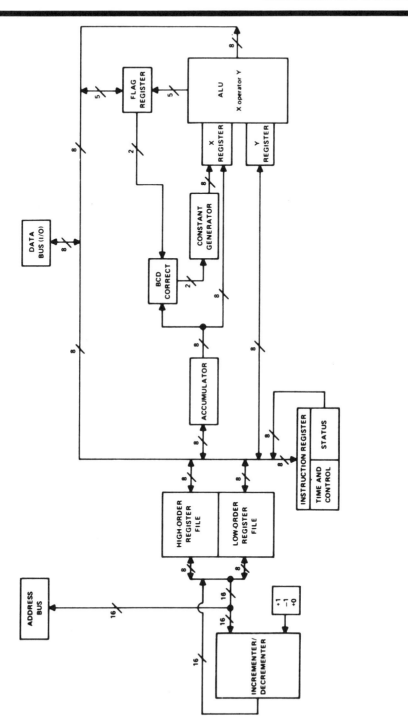

Figure 1. *TMS 8080A Functional Block Diagram*

MICROCOMPUTER
ARCHITECTURE

TMS 9940 MICROCOMPUTER

The TMS 9940 is a 16-bit general purpose, single-chip microcomputer *(Figure 2)*.
The TMS 9940 contains 2K bytes of ROM (or EPROM) and 128 bytes of RAM, along
with a programmable timer/event counter. The 9940 is software-compatible with the
990/9900 family of microprocessors/minicomputers, and executes 68 instructions. The
TMS 9940 requires a single 5-volt power supply and incorporates an (external) crystal-
controlled oscillator on the chip. The circuit has 32 bits of general purpose I/O
(expandable to 256 bits), and is housed in a 40-pin package.

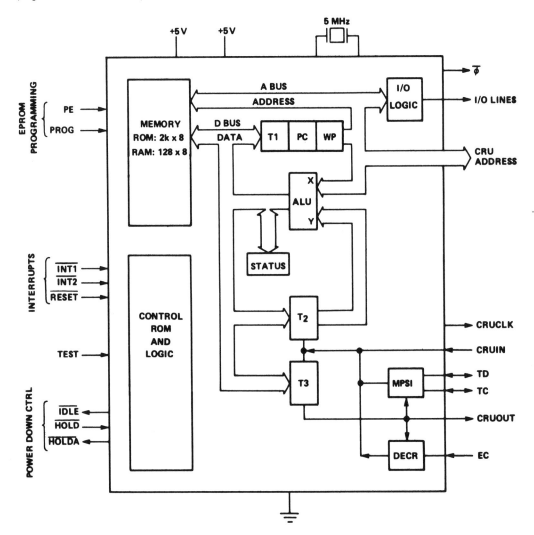

Figure 2. TMS 9940 Functional Block Diagram

HARDWARE DESIGN

A functional block diagram of the Model 745 Data Terminal is shown in *Figure 3*. The control electronics monitor all terminal inputs and generate all necessary timing and control signals to effect data transfers, cause printhead and paper motion, and create printable characters through the thermal printhead. Each block of the diagram is discussed separately below.

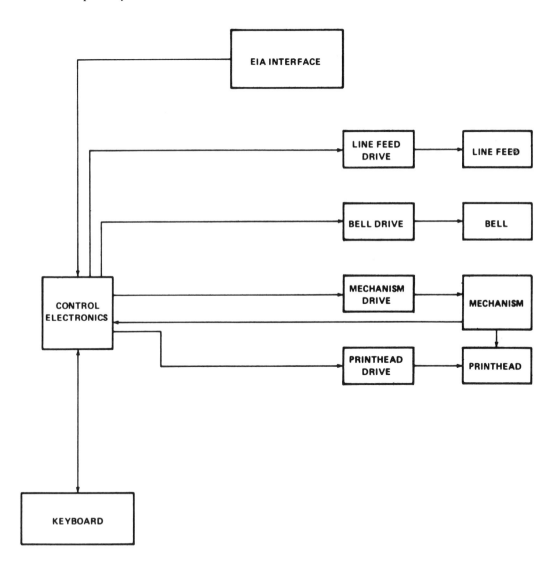

Figure 3. Model 745 Data Terminal Functional Block Diagram

KEYBOARD

The Model 745 keyboard is a TTY33-compatible, alphanumeric keyboard with an integral numeric keypad. The keyboard is equipped with 54 single-action keys, four alternate action switches, and an indicator lamp which signals that the data carrier signal is being received by the terminal. The control electronics must generate control signals to scan the keyboard and debounce key switch depressions. When a key depression is detected during a scan, the character is encoded and the appropriate action is taken by the terminal. Each scan is total so as to detect possible multiple key depressions. When simultaneous depressions are detected during a scan, neither key is acted upon. This scanning/debounce technique effects a two-key rollover with lockout.

PRINTHEAD

The printhead consists of a five by seven dot matrix of 35 heating elements *(Figure 4)* mounted on a monolithic chip. The chip is mounted on a heatsink, and is connected to the printhead drive electronics through a flexible ribbon cable. Upon receipt of a character from the keyboard or the communications line, the control electronics must generate the appropriate control signals to form the selected character utilizing the five by seven dot matrix format. The PRINT signal is switched on; then the matrix data is transferred to the printhead one column at a time. Each of the 35 heating elements on the printhead contains an SCR which controls the heating current. When both X and Y inputs are positive to a given element, the SCR energizes and remains on (approximately 10 msec) until PRINT is switched off.

The X and Y address drivers are implemented on two SN98614 linear integrated circuits, each of which consists of six driver circuits. Each driver circuit has a low power TTL-AND input stage and a totem-pole, power transistor output stage. The drivers are enabled by the signal LDPRHD.

PRINTHEAD LIFT

The printhead is lifted to relieve pressure upon the paper during line feed and carriage return operations. The control electronics must generate a signal (LFTHD) to control the solenoid which lifts the printhead.

MECHANISM

Horizontal movement of the printhead is controlled by a three-phase 15-degree stepping motor. An optical sensor is mounted on the motor shaft to provide feedback for the control of stepping motion during printing and slew motion during carriage return. The print/step cycle operates synchronously up to 35 characters per second. The control electronics must output five signals to control the motor. The STEP and FAST signals are used to control the current in the motor windings; and PHA, PHB, and PHC are drive signals for the three motor phases. The mechanism drive electronics converts these TTL logic level signals into the closed loop controller dc current required by the motor.

The optical sensor provides data on motor position so that the control electronics "know" when to apply braking to change phases, or to make other decisions concerning motion of the printhead carriage. The sensor consists of a 24-position slotted wheel which interrupts a light path between an IR emitting diode and a photosensitive transistor. The sensor issues pulses to the control electronics as the slots interrupt the light path.

BELL

A buzzer (a piezoelectric disc) produces an audible signal at a nominal frequency of 3.2 kHz. Upon receipt of the BEL character from the keyboard or communications line, the control electronics must generate a timed signal (250 ± 25 msec) to produce the sound.

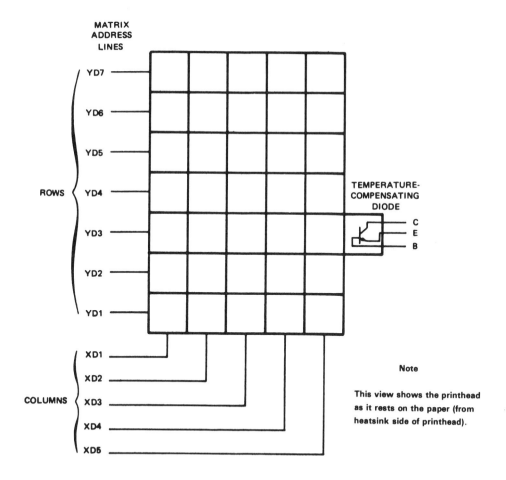

Figure 4. Printhead Matrix Address Lines

LINE FEED

Vertical movement of the paper is controlled by the line feed solenoid which is mechanically coupled to a rachet mechanism. To advance the paper one line, the control electronics must lift the printhead and output a timed signal (15 msec) followed by an off period of 16.8 msec to the line feed solenoid.

EIA INTERFACE

The control electronics must transmit and receive asynchronous serial data in accord with *ANSI Standard for Character Structure and Parity Sense,* X3.16-1966 and *ANSI Standard for Bit Sequence,* X3.15-1967. The TTL-level signals RCVD and XD are converted to standard EIA RS-232-C levels in the EIA interface.

CONTROL ELECTRONICS

The control electronics function is performed by an interrupt driven, stored program microcomputer. As aforementioned the system requirements for the microcomputer I/O consist of:

Keyboard:	Matrix scan lines
Printhead:	Print data (12),LDPRHD,PRINT,LFTHD
Mechanism:	Step,FAST,PHA,PHB,PHC,SENSOR
Bell:	BELL
Linefeed:	LNFD
EIA Interface:	RCVD,XD

The microcomputer must generate these signals in the specified times and sequences to control the system.

TMS 8080A MICROCOMPUTER SYSTEM

A schematic of the microcomputer design using the TMS 8080A Microprocessor is shown in *Figure 5.* The complete design requires 17 integrated circuits, 41 resistors, one crystal, and one capacitor. The memory consists of 2K bytes of ROM (two TMS 4700's) and 64 bytes of RAM (one TMS 4036). The TMS 5501 is an 8080A peripheral I/O controller which contains a universal asynchronous receiver/transmitter, programmable timers, interrupt prioritization and control, an eight-bit input port, and an eight-bit output port. The eight-bit output port is expanded by using TTL components (7406, 74174, 74175) to provide the necessary number of direct outputs for the keyboard and latched outputs for the static outputs. The input port is expanded using 2-to-1 multiplexers (74157) to permit elimination of diodes from the keyboard matrix. Data is sent to the printhead over 12 bits of the address bus by loading the data into the HL registers, and then executing a dummy MOVM instruction while the 74109 JK flip-flop outputs the LDPRHD strobe signal. The 74S138, 3-to-8 decoder generates the required chip selects for the various components. The SENSOR input feeds into the TMS 5501 interrupt logic to interface to the TMS 8080A.

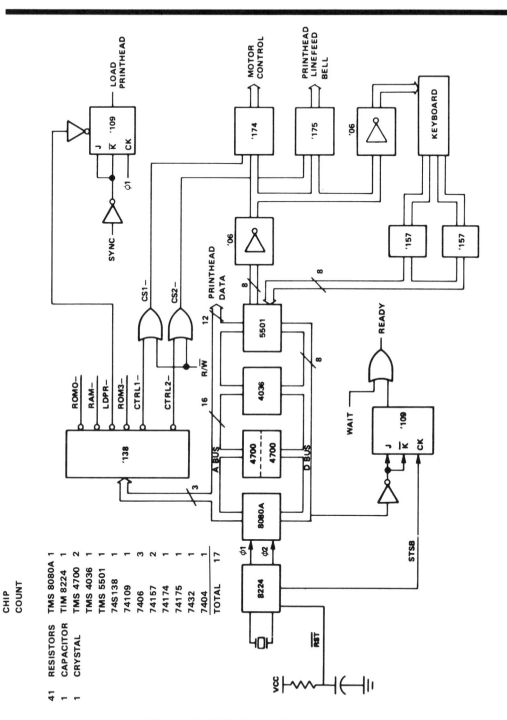

Figure 5. TMS 8080A Microcomputer System

TMS 9940 MICROCOMPUTER SYSTEM

A schematic of the microcomputer design using the TMS 9940 Microcomputer is shown in *Figure 6.* The complete design requires two integrated circuits, 18 resistors, one crystal, one capacitor and 16 diodes. The internal memory of the TMS 9940 provides 2K bytes of ROM and 128 bytes of RAM. The TMS 9902 Asynchronous Communications Controller is a TMS 9900-family peripheral which contains a universal asynchronous receiver/transmitter and a programmable timer. The 32 I/O lines provided by the TMS 9940 interface to all the I/O functions with 10 lines software-multiplexed between the keyboard scan, TMS 9902 control, and printhead data. When P14 through P20 are in the input mode, the keyboard is scanned by sequentially raising P1 through P10 *high* (with the others being held *low*) while switching P14 through P20 to the output mode and outputting *high* signals, isolates P1 through P10 so that they can be used for other purposes. The LDPRHD signal is divided into two signals (LDPRHD1 and LDPRHD2) to obtain an output current sink needed for the SN98614's. The two interrupt inputs are used by the SENSOR input (highest priority) and the $\overline{\text{INT}}$ output from the TMS 9902.

FIRMWARE DESIGN

A block diagram of the Model 745 firmware, *Figure 7,* shows that the system firmware can be divided into three major sections: (1) keyboard scanning and encoding, (2) printhead control, and (3) internal data control. The keyboard and printhead routines represent the major portion of the system: the data control routine is used to direct character processing between the keyboard, the printhead, and the EIA interface.

KEYBOARD ROUTINE

The keyboard is viewed by the control electronics as a matrix of key switches, with all keyboard scanning, debouncing, and encoding done by the microcomputer. The keyboard is scanned once each 4.3 msec. When a key depression is detected, the character is encoded by the addition of a constant number to the row/column number of the key to provide the ASCII code, and the appropriate action is taken by the terminal. (*Note:* In the numeric mode a look-up table is used to provide the ASCII code).

After a depression is detected, 12 msec are allowed for all contact-make bounce to settle out and then scanning resumes at 4.3-msec intervals. No other key depressions are processed by the terminal until the first depression is released. When this occurs, 12 msec are allowed for contact-break bounce, then the keyboard scan again resumes at 4.3-msec intervals. Each scan is a complete scan so that multiple key depressions may be detected. When simultaneous depressions are detected, neither key is acted upon, thus effecting a two-key-rollover-with-lockout operation.

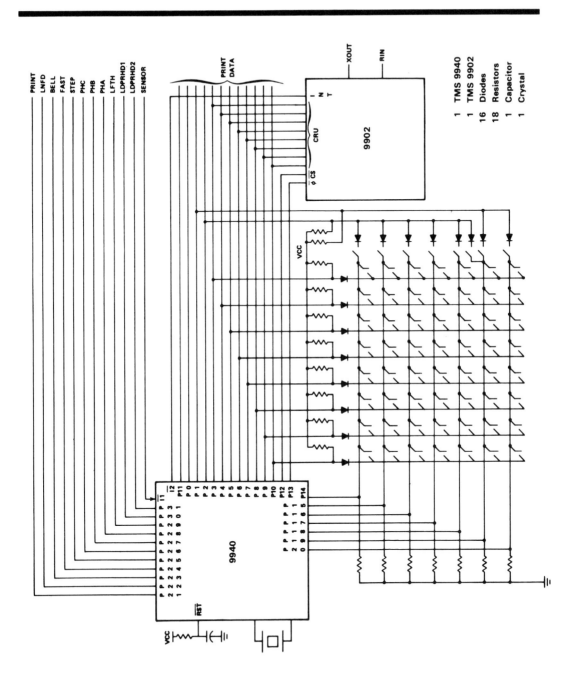

Figure 6. TMS 9940 Microcomputer System

PRINTHEAD CONTROL

The microcomputer positions the printhead horizontally by timing different levels of current through the phase windings of the stepping motor. The print/step cycle operates asynchronously up to 35 CPS, with the cycle time divided into three basic segments: settle (11.3 msec), print (10 msec), and step (7.2 msec). Slew time for a full 80 columns is a maximum of 195 msec with backspace operations performed in one character-time. An automatic carriage return/line feed is executed upon receipt of the 81st character in a line. Upon applying power the printhead is backspaced to the left margin.

Fault detection methods are used by the microcomputer to prevent damage during power cycling conditions, obstruction of printhead motion, or loss of optical sensor signal. During the print segment, the microcomputer energizes the printhead voltage (PRINT), indexes into the dot matrix table (part of the 2K of ROM) by the ASCII character value, chooses the appropriate dot pattern, and loads the printhead one column at a time. The printhead is loaded during the first 200 μsec of PRINT; the PRINT signal remains on for 10 msec to allow the thermal sensitive paper to convert.

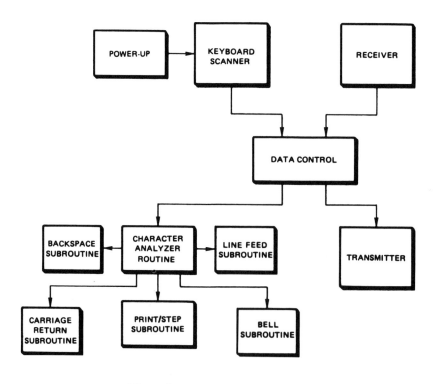

Figure 7. *Model 745 Firmware Structure*

The step segment steps the printhead one column by using two timers and the sensor. One timer is used to control pulse widths for the FAST and STEP pulses. These pulses control the amount of current in both the leading and lagging winding of the stepper motor, thus controlling the torque generated by the motor. The sensor signals the beginning of braking. The second timer is used to time the total step and is divided into two segments: The first verifies that the sensor occurred, and the second segment defines the end of the step. The use of the second timer makes the step time independent of when the sensor interrupt occurs so that the microcomputer can compensate for varying friction loads on the printhead.

The carriage return operation will slew the head to column one under control of the microcomputer using two timers and the sensor input. The step current remains on during the entire carriage return to develop high torques in the motor. One timer is used to control the fast pulse, thus controlling the current in the lagging phase of the stepper motor. The second timer is used as a reference to which to compare the sensor information, and this comparison results in the microcomputer accelerating or decelerating the motor to maintain control of printhead speed.

FIRMWARE IMPLEMENTATION

Table 1 lists the number of instructions and memory bytes required to implement the system firmware for both the TMS 8080A and the TMS 9940. The three major sections [(1) keyboard routine, (2) printhead control, and (3) data control] are listed separately, along with the dot pattern table for the five by seven printhead matrix. The number of memory bytes required for each system is 2048 (the number available) and the number of instructions required is 867 for the TMS 8080A and 584 for the TMS 9940.

Table 1. System Firmware Implementation

Routine	TMS 8080A Microprocessor		TMS 9940 Microcomputer	
	Number of Instructions	Bytes	Number of Instructions	Bytes
Keyboard	260	486	178	472
Printhead	411	855·	291	884
Control	196	367	115	352
Dot Pattern	–	340	–	340
TOTAL	867	2048	584	2048

COST ANALYSIS

Table 2 illustrates the component cost for the two microcomputer systems, assuming a production level of 10,000 units. The component cost of the TMS 8080A System is $48.81, and the cost of the TMS 9940 System is $22.78. In addition, other cost reductions will be realized from savings in incoming test (17 IC's versus two IC's), PC board area (approximately 45 square inches versus 6 square inches), and associated assembly labor and overhead. In total a significant overall cost savings will be realized in the recurring cost of the end product.

Table 2. Component Cost Analysis

TMS 8080A System	$48.81
TMS 9940 System	$22.78

TMS 9900
Floppy Disk Controller

SECTION I

INTRODUCTION

This application report describes a TMS 9900 microprocessor system which controls a floppy disk drive and interfaces to an RS-232C type terminal. In addition to providing useful information for the design of a similar system, this application report also shows many of the design considerations for any TMS 9900 microprocessor system design.

The floppy disk is rapidly becoming the most widely accepted bulk storage medium for microprocessor systems. Using standard encoding techniques, a single floppy disk will contain in excess of 400K bytes of unformatted data. Access time to a random record of data is vastly superior to serial media such as cassettes and cartridges, and the medium is both non-volatile and removable.

The use of a microprocessor in the floppy-disk controller or "formatter" is desirable for a number of reasons. The number and cost of components is reduced: this design contains 24 integrated circuits, while random-logic designs typically contain more than 100. The commands from the user interface (in this case, the terminal) to the controller may be more sophisticated, relying on the microprocessor to intrepret the commands. The microprocessor also enables the controller to perform diagnostic functions, both on the controller itself and on its associated drives, not available with a random-logic system.

The Texas Instruments TMS 9900 microprocessor is particularly well-suited to this application. The TMS 9900 is a 16-bit microprocessor capable of performing operations on single bits, bytes, and words. The CRU provides an economical port for bit-oriented input/output, while the parallel memory bus is available for high-speed data. The speed of operation of the TMS 9900 minimizes additional hardware requirements. The powerful memory-to-memory instruction set and large number of available registers simplify software, both in terms of number of assembly language statements and total program memory requirements.

SECTION II

SYSTEM DESCRIPTION

Figure 1 illustrates the relationship of the system elements. Commands are entered by the user at the terminal. These commands are serially transmitted to the controller. The controller interprets the commands and performs the operations specified, such as stepping the read/write head of the drive to a particular track, and reading or writing selected data.

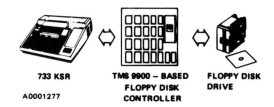

733 KSR

A0001277

**TMS 9900 — BASED
FLOPPY DISK
CONTROLLER**

**FLOPPY DISK
DRIVE**

**Figure 1. TMS 9900 Floppy Disk
Controller System**

2.1 DATA TERMINAL

The terminal used in this design is the Texas Instruments 733 KSR Silent Electronic Data Terminal (see Figure 2). Slight modifications to the software will allow the use of virtually any RS-232 terminal.

A0001278

Figure 2. TI 733 KSR Terminal

The 733 KSR consists of a keyboard, printer, and a serial-communication line to the controller. The keyboard enables the operator to enter control commands and data for storage on floppy disc. The printer is used for echoing operator entries, data printout, and reporting of operational errors. The serial interface is full duplex, allowing data transmission both to and from the data terminal simultaneously.

Characters entered on the keyboard are transmitted to the controller in 7-bit ASCII code using asynchronous format, and characters to be printed are sent from the controller to the terminal in the same way. Transmission speed is 300 baud. The format for data transmission is shown in Figure 3.

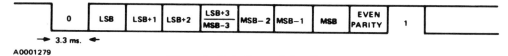

Figure 3. Data Transmission Format

The line idle condition is represented by a logic one. When a character is to be transmitted, the ASCII character is preceded by a zero bit, followed by the 7-bit ASCII code, even parity bit, and the logic-one stop bit. Any amount of idle time may separate consecutive characters by maintaining the logic-one level. Reading data is accomplished by continuously monitoring the line for the one-to-zero transition at the beginning of the start bit. After delaying one-half bit time (1.67 ms) the line is again sampled to ensure that the start bit is valid. If so, the line is sampled each bit time (3.33 ms) until all of the bits of the character have been sampled. The initial one-half bit delay causes subsequent samples to be taken at the theoretical center of each bit, thus providing a margin for distortion due to time base differences between the transmitter and receiver.

The control signals for the terminal are shown in Figure 4.

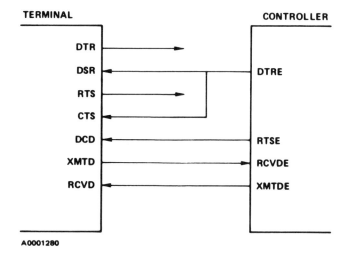

Figure 4. Terminal Interface

Detailed description of the signals is provided in *Electronics Industries Association Standard RS-232C*. The signals used in this design are briefly described below.

DTRE – Data Terminal Ready is always on when power is applied to the controller, enabling operation of the serial interface by the terminal.

RTSE – Request to Send is on when a character is transmitted from the controller to the terminal.

XMTDE – Transmitted Data from the controller to the terminal.

RCVDE – Received Data from the terminal to the controller.

Signal levels conform to EIA Standard RS-232C, as shown in Table 1.

Table 1. RS-232C Signal Levels

Voltage Level	Data (XMTDE,RCVDE)	Control (DTRE,RTSE)
−25 to −3 VDC	1	OFF
+3 to +25 VDC	0	ON

The other important parameter for interfacing to the terminal is the amount of time required for a carriage return by the printer, which is 200 ms maximum for the 733 KSR.

2.2 FLOPPY-DISK DRIVE

The floppy-disk drive (Figure 5) is the electromechanical unit in which the recording medium, the floppy disk is inserted. The drive contains the electronics which control the rotation of the floppy disk, the reading and writing of data, and the positioning of the read/write head to select a particular track on the diskette.

2.2.1 Floppy Disk

The floppy disk, or diskette, is the recording medium (see Figure 6). It is enclosed in a plastic protective envelope which keeps foreign particles away from the recording surface. The inner material of the envelope is specially treated to minimize friction and static electricity discharge. The read/write head opening enables the head to come in contact with the recording surface. The index-access hole enables detection of the index hole.

When the index hole in the diskette becomes aligned with the index-access hole, an optical sensor generates the index pulse, providing a reference point for the beginning of each track. There are 77 concentric tracks for recording data. A particular track is accessed by moving the read/write head radially until the desired track is located.

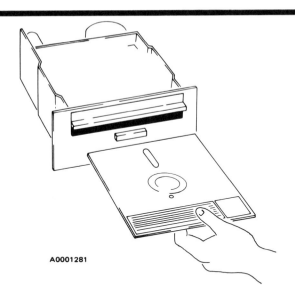

A0001281

Figure 5. Floppy Disk Drive

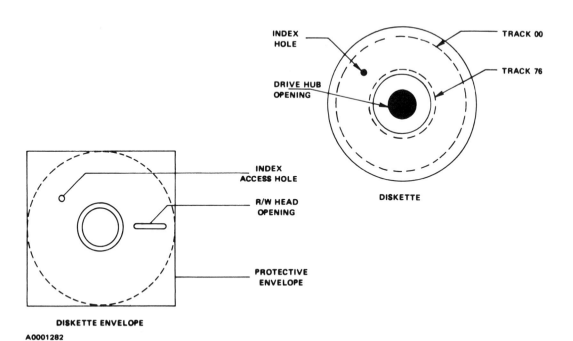

INDEX
HOLE

TRACK 00

DRIVE HUB
OPENING

TRACK 76

INDEX
ACCESS HOLE

R/W HEAD
OPENING

DISKETTE

PROTECTIVE
ENVELOPE

DISKETTE ENVELOPE

A0001282

Figure 6. Diskette Envelope and Diskette

2.2.2 Physical Data Structure

The 77 tracks on a diskette are numbered from 00 (outermost) to 76 (innermost). Each track is subdivided into 26 sectors, or records, numbered sequentially from 1 to 26. Each sector consists of two fields: the ID field, which contains sector identification (track and sector number) and the data field, which contains 128 bytes of data.

2.2.3 Encoding Technique

The encoding technique used for representation of data on the diskette is a form of frequency modulation (FM), as shown in Figure 7. Each bit period is 4 microseconds long, resulting in a data-transfer rate of 250K bits per second. A pulse occurs at the beginning of each normal bit period. This pulse is called the clock pulse. If the data bit is a one, a pulse will occur also in the middle of the bit period, 2 μs after the clock bit. If the data bit is a zero, no pulse occurs in the middle of the bit period.

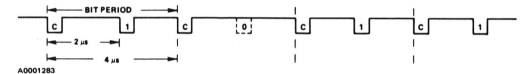

A0001283

Figure 7. FM Data Pattern   1011

Selected clock bits are deleted in special characters called marks. The absence of the clock bits results in unique sequences, used for synchronization at the beginning of fields.

2.2.4 Track Format

Each track is formatted to provide 26 "soft" sectors. The term soft sectoring means that the beginning of each sector is encoded on the medium through a unique bit sequence. Each of the sectors is separated by a gap of dummy data. Each of the two fields (ID and data) in each sector are also separated by a gap. The first byte of each field is a mark in which the clock pattern for the byte is $C7_{16}$ rather than FF_{16}. The organization of data and clock bits on each track is shown in Figure 8.

2.2.5 Cyclic Redundancy Check Character

The last two bytes at the end of each ID and data field comprise the 16-bit cyclic redundancy check character (CRC). The CRC is generated by performing modulo-2 division on the data portion of the entire field (including the mark) by the polynomial $X^{16} + X^{12} + X^5 + 1$. Before generation of the CRC begins, the initial value is $FFFF_{16}$.

The analogous hardware operation is illustrated in Figure 9. All flip-flops are initially set to one. Each data bit in the field, beginning with the MSB of the mark byte, is shifted into the logic at DATAIN. The previous

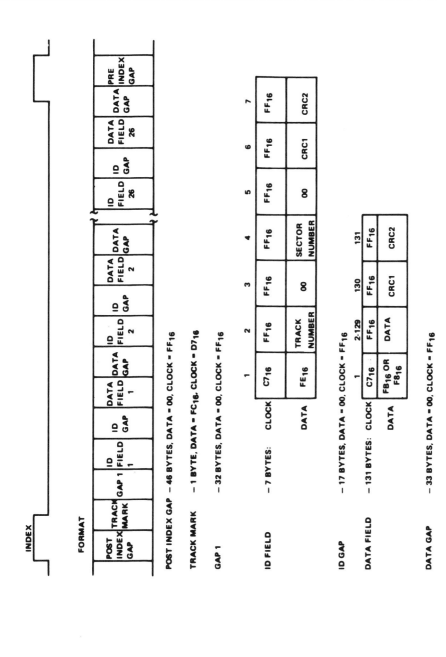

Figure 8. Track Recording Format

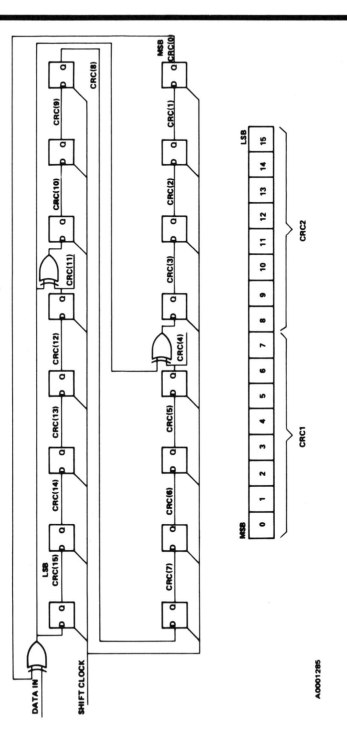

Figure 9. Hardware CRC Generation

A0001285

MSB is exclusive ORed with the new input bit to generate a feedback term. This feedback term is stored in the LSB of the register, and is also exclusive ORed with other terms of the CRC. After all data bits of the field have been shifted in, the value in the register is the CRC. The most-significant byte is CRC1 and the least-significant byte is CRC2.

When reading the field, the identical operation is performed, presetting all flip-flops and shifting in all data bits. When reading, it is convenient to also shift in the CRC, causing the resultant value in the register to finally become all zeroes.

In this design, the CRC is calculated by software; however, the algorithm is identical.

2.2.6 Reading Data

The procedure for reading diskette data is as follows:

1. Search the serial-bit string for the ID mark (clock = $C7_{16}$, data = FE_{16}).

2. Read the next four bytes to determine if the desired sector has been located. If not, return to 1.

3. Read the CRC for the ID field and compare it to the expected value. If incorrect, report error and/or return to 1.

4. Search the serial-bit string for either the data mark (clock = $C7_{16}$, data = FB_{16}) or the deleted-data mark (clock = $C7_{16}$, data = $F8_{16}$).

5. Read the next 128 bytes and save.

6. Read the CRC for the data field and compare it to the expected value. If incorrect, report error and/or return to 1.

Normally, if the process is not completed before two index pulses are detected, indicating a complete diskette revolution, the try has failed. Either a retry will be performed, or an error is reported.

2.2.7 Writing Data

When writing data, the sector is located as in steps 1 through 3 above. Then, the ID gap. the data field complete with CRC, and a pad byte (data = 0, clock = FF_{16}) are written.

2.2.8 Track Formatting

The formatting process consists of writing all of the gaps, track mark, ID fields, and data fields, putting dummy data into the data bytes of the data field. After a track is formatted, only the ID gap, data field, and the first byte of the data gap are altered when updating sectors. The number of bytes in the pre-index gap will possibly vary slightly, due to variations in the speed of revolution of the diskette.

2.2.9 Floppy-Disk Timing

Several important timing parameters pertain to the operation of the disk drive:

Bit transfer rate	250,000 bits/second
Track-to-track stepping time	10 milliseconds
Settling time (before read/write)	10 milliseconds
Rotational speed	360 RPM ±2%
Head load time (before read/write)	35 milliseconds

Thus, data is transferred at a rate of 250K bits/second, or 31.25K bytes/second ±2%. Stepping the head each track position requires 10 ms. An additional 10 ms delay must be observed after the final step before reliable data may be written or read. A delay of 35 ms must occur after the head is loaded ($\overline{RDY} = 0$) before reliable data may be written or read.

SECTION III

HARDWARE DESCRIPTION

A complete logic diagram of the system is contained in the center of this report. The operation of each section is described separately.

3.1 CLOCK GENERATION AND RESET

The TIM 9904 is used to generate the 4-phase MOS clocks for the TMS 9900 (see Figure 10). Ten ohm resistors are connected in series to the clock lines for damping. The TIM 9904 should always be located physically close to the TMS 9900 to minimize the length of the conductor run for the MOS clocks. The $\overline{\phi 3}$ TTL-level output is used in the synchronous disk read/write control logic.

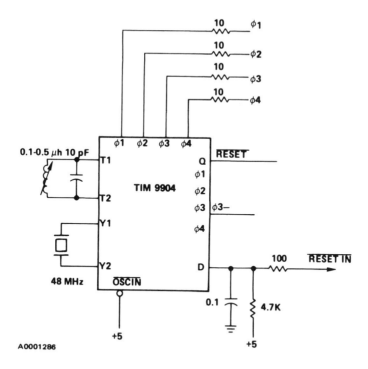

Figure 10. Clock Generation and Reset

A 48 MHz, third overtone crystal causes the clock frequency to be 3 MHz. The inductor of the LC tank circuit need not be variable; however, in wire-wrap prototypes the capacitance due to interconnect is difficult to predict. The $\overline{\text{OSCIN}}$ input is held high to disable the external clock input.

The RC input to the Schmitt-D input provides power-on detection. The $\overline{\text{RESETIN}}$ input is connected to an external pushbutton. The 100 ohm series resistor reduces contact arcing, thereby extending switch life.

3.2 CPU

The TMS 9900 requires a minimum of external logic. Note that both the data and address buses are connected directly to the memory and disk read/write control logic without buffering as shown in Figure 11. This is due to the ability of the TMS 9900 outputs to sink up to 3.2 mA with 200 pF capacitive load.

The READY input is used to synchronize data transfers to and from the disk read/write control logic, eliminating the need for buffer registers. The $\overline{\text{HOLD}}$, $\overline{\text{LOAD}}$, and interrupt functions are not used in this design and are tied to their inactive (high) level.

3.3 MEMORY CONTROL

Memory control logic, shown in Figure 12, consists of a simple decode of the high-order address lines, enabled by $\overline{\text{MEMEN}}$. Memory enabling signals are generated for EPROM (ROMSEL−), RAM (RAM-SEL−), and the disk interface (DISKSEL−). Table 2 shows the memory address assignments.

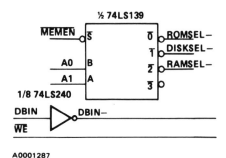

A0001287

Figure 12. Memory Control

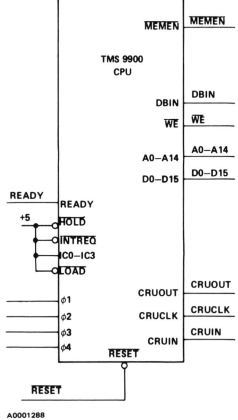

A0001288

Figure 11. TMS 9900 CPU

Table 2. Memory Address Assignments

Signal	A0	A1	Address Space	Function	Actually Used
ROMSEL–	0	0	000-3FFF	EPROM	000-07FF
DISKSEL–	0	1	4000-7FFF	Disk	7F8E-7FFE
RAMSEL–	1	0	8000-BFFF	RAM	8000-81FF
	1	1	C000-FFFF	Not Used	

Each of the enabling signals will be active when a memory cycle is being performed ($\overline{\text{MEMEN}}$ = 0) accessing its address space.

3.4 DISK READ/WRITE SELECT

The DISKSEL signal is further decoded to generate separate select lines for disk read (DISKRD–) and disk write (DISKWT–) operations.

$$\text{DISKRD–} = \overline{(\text{DISKSEL}) \, (\text{DBIN}) \, (\text{A14–})}, \text{ and}$$
$$\text{DISKWT–} = \overline{(\text{DISKSEL}) \, (\text{DBIN–}) \, (\text{A14})}.$$

Disk read and write operations are specified by different addresses, and are selected only when the DBIN signal is at the proper level for the direction of transfer (see Figure 13). This is required because of the sequence of machine cycles performed by the TMS 9900 when performing a memory-write operation. In the MOV instruction, the CPU first fetches the contents of the memory location to be altered, then replaces this value with the source operand. In this design, the disk read and write

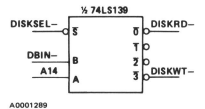

A0001289

Figure 13. Disk Read/Write Select

operations are controlled by the READY line to synchronize data transfers. If read and write signals were not generated separately, there would be ambiguity with respect to the type of operation desired.

This applies to all memory-mapped interfaces in TMS 9900 systems, i.e., the MOV instruction will cause a read operation to precede the write operation to the specified destination address.

3.5 STORAGE MEMORY

Storage memory, shown in Figure 14, is used for implementing workspace registers, maintenance of software pointers and counters, and buffering of a full sector of data.

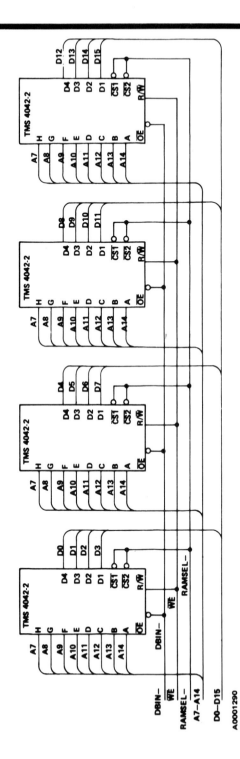

Figure 14. Storage Memory

A0001290

This design utilizes four TMS 4042-2 RAMs, resulting in a 256-word array of RAM for temporary storage. This 256-word array may be addressed at locations 8000-BFFF, causing each memory location to be multiply defined (e.g., memory address 8000 selects the same word as memory address 8200). For simplificity, RAM will be referred to only as locations 8000-81FF.

Access times for the TMS 4042-2 are sufficiently fast to allow the TMS 9900 to access RAM without any wait states, thus READY will always be true when RAM is addressed. The output enable ($\overline{OE}$) inputs require that the DBIN output from the TMS 9900 be inverted to gate RAM onto the data bus. The $\overline{WE}$ output from the TMS 9900 is directly compatible with the R/$\overline{W}$ input. Data and address lines are connected directly to the CPU.

3.6 PROGRAM MEMORY

Program memory (Figure 15) is used for storage of the machine code program to be executed by the TMS 9900. Also, constants, the RESET vector and XOP vectors are contained in this space.

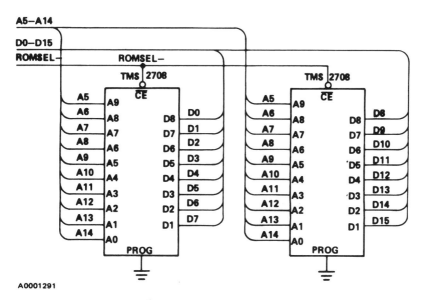

A0001291

Figure 15. Program Memory

Two TMS 2708 erasable programmable read-only memories (EPROMs) comprise the program memory for this design, resulting in 1024 words of EPROM. EPROM is addressed at memory locations 0000-3FFF. Since these addresses are multiply defined, EPROM will be described only as memory addresses 0000-07FF. Access times for the TMS 2708 are such that no wait states are required.

3.7 CONTROL I/O

All of the control and status signals which require individual testing, setting, or resetting are implemented on the CRU, the bit addressable I/O port for the TMS 9900.

The benefits of using the CRU for these functions is twofold. First, eight bits of input and eight bits of output can be implemented with two 16-pin devices, which are substantially smaller and lower in cost than if these functions were implemented on the parallel-data bus. The second benefit is increased software efficiency. Control and status testing operations can be performed with single one-word instructions, rather than the ORing, ANDing, and maintenance of software images necessary when performing single-bit I/O on the memory bus.

Eight bits of output are implemented with the TIM 9906 8-bit addressable latch. The CRUCLK line must be inverted for input to the TIM 9906. The eight input bits are implemented using the TIM 9905 8-to-1 multiplexer. Individual I/O bits are selected using the three least-significant address lines, A12–A14. The control I/O is illustrated in Figure 16.

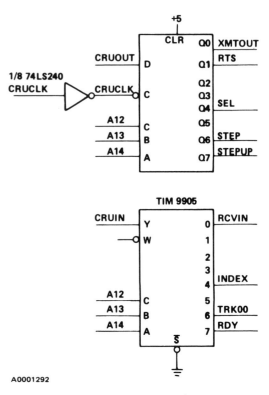

Figure 16. Control I/O

3.8 FLOPPY-DISK-DRIVE INTERFACE

All outputs to the drive are 7406 open-collector, high-voltage and current drivers. Pullups for the output signals are provided in the drive electronics. All inputs are terminated by 150 ohm pullup resistors to +5 volts, and are buffered and inverted. All input and output signals are active low.

$\overline{\text{SEL}}$ – Active when a stepping operation or a data transfer is being performed.

$\overline{\text{RDY}}$ – Active when the disk is ready to perform a stepping or transfer operation (i.e., $\overline{\text{SEL}} = 0$, diskette is in place, door is closed, power is furnished to the drive).

$\overline{\text{STEP}}$ – A minimum 10 µs pulse causes the read/write head to move one track position in the direction selected by $\overline{\text{STEPUP}}$.

$\overline{\text{STEPUP}}$ — When $\overline{\text{STEPUP}}$ = 0, the read/write head moves in one track position. When $\overline{\text{STEPUP}}$ = 1, the head will move out (toward track 00).

$\overline{\text{TRK00}}$ — Active when the read/write head is located on the outermost track (track 00).

$\overline{\text{INDEX}}$ — As the diskette rotates in the drive, the index pulse occurs once per revolution, providing a reference point for the beginning of each track.

$\overline{\text{WRITE ENABLE}}$ — This signal must be active a minimum of 4 μs before a write operation begins, and must be maintained active during the entire write operation.

$\overline{\text{WRITE DATA}}$ — This signal contains a series of pulses representing the data to be written to the disk in the FM format previously described.

$\overline{\text{READ DATA}}$ — This signal contains a series of pulses representing the data to be read from the disk in the FM format previously described.

Figure 17 illustrates the floppy-disk-drive interface.

3.9 INDEX PULSE SYNCHRONIZATION

Since the index pulse is a term in some of the expressions that are sampled by the CPU, it must be synchornous to the CPU. The circuit shown in Figure 18 generates a signal one $\phi3$ clock cycle long at the beginning of each index pulse from the drive. RDY will be inactive when the drive is turned off or the door is open, thus connection of RDY to the preset input of the flip-flop shown causes INDSYN to be active as long as RDY = 0 (see Figure 19). Forcing INDSYN to be one when RDY = 0 prevents the CPU from remaining in a wait state when the drive is disabled during data transfer.

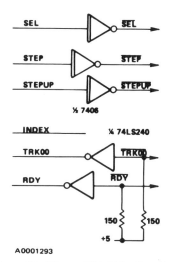

Figure 17. Floppy-Disk Drive Interface

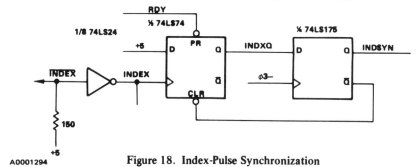

Figure 18. Index-Pulse Synchronization

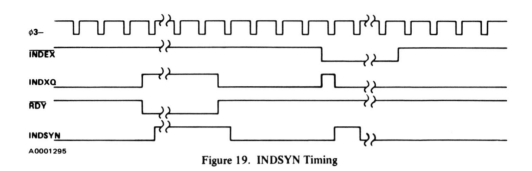

A0001295

Figure 19. INDSYN Timing

3.10 READ PULSE SYNCHRONIZATION

The read-pulse synchronization logic, Figure 20, generates an active signal, BITIN, one clock cycle long each time a read pulse is detected during read operations. During write operations BITIN is maintained at a logic-one level.

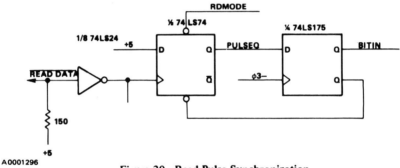

A0001296

Figure 20. Read-Pulse Synchronization

3.11 BIT DETECTOR

The bit detector, Figure 21, consists of a 74LS163 counter and random logic contained in PROM. During write operations, the counter is used to time the 2 μs spacing between clock bits and data bits. During read operations the bit detector is used to determine the time interval between successive read pulses. The key signal generated by the bit detector is BITTIME, which is active for one clock cycle every 2 μs during disk writing, and which is active each time a one or zero bit is detected during read operations.

3.12 BIT COUNTER

The bit counter, Figure 22, is a 74LS163 used to count the number of bits currently read or written during disk-data transfers. Each time a clock or data bit is detected or written (BITTIME = 1) the bit counter is

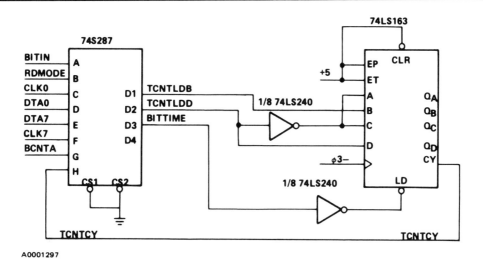

A0001297

Figure 21. Bit Detector

incremented. The two key outputs are BCNTA and BCNT = 15. BCNTA is the least-significant bit of the counter and is used to alternately select clock (BCNTA = 0) and data (BCNTA = 1) bits as the counter increments. BCNTA = 15 is active when a complete byte has been read or written. This signal establishes byte boundaries for the data and is used to synchronize the parallel data from the CPU to the serial-bit string and from the disk.

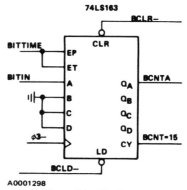

A0001298

Figure 22. Bit Counter

3.13 WRITE CONTROL AND DATA

Writing to the diskette is controlled by $\overline{\text{WRITE ENABLE}}$, which is the inverted and buffered WTMODE signal. WTMODE is active when a write operation has been initiated by the CPU. The $\overline{\text{WRITE DATA}}$ signal is a series of negative pulses representing FM data to be recorded on the diskette. Figure 23 illustrates write control and data.

3.14 DATA SHIFT REGISTER

The data shift register, see Figure 24, is used for accumulation of data bits during read operations and storage of data bits to be shifted out during write operations. Data is transferred to and from the CPU via the eight most-significant data lines (D0−D7). The data shift register is device type 74LS299.

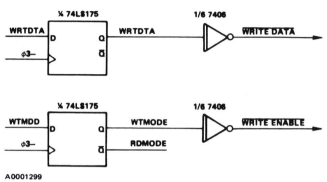

Figure 23. Write Control and Data

3.15 CLOCK SHIFT REGISTER

The clock shift register, Figure 25, is used for accumulation of clock bits during read operations and storage of clock bits to be shifted out during write operations. The clock shift register is device type 74198, which has separate parallel inputs and outputs. Three address lines, A9—A11, are connected to the parallel inputs. As data is loaded into the data shift register during write operations, these three address lines select the clock pattern for that byte (i.e., C7 for ID and data marks, D7 for track mark, FF for normal data). The parallel outputs (CLK0-CLK7) are used to detect mark clock patterns during read operations.

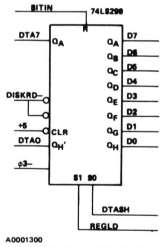

Figure 24. Data Shift Register

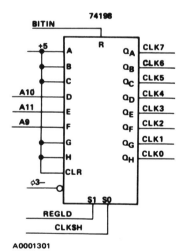

Figure 25. Clock Shift Register

SECTION IV

DISKETTE DATA TRANSFER

The previous section described the various functional blocks in the TMS 9900 floppy-disk controller. However, detailed information was not provided with respect to the logical relationships and timing of the control signal in the read/write control logic.

Most of the read/write control logic varies in function depending on the direction of transfer. This section will describe the operation of the logic separately for read and write operations. After both operations have been completely described, the combined operation will be explained.

4.1 DISK-WRITE OPERATIONS

Disk writing is initiated by executing an instruction which writes data to the data shift register (i.e., when DISKWT$-$ = 0). When this transfer occurs, READY is held low until a byte boundary occurs (BCNT = 15), then READY becomes active, permitting completion of the write cycle. In this way, the data transfers are synchronized to the serial bit string.

To complete the transfer, READY must be active to the CPU, and the CLKSH, DTASH, and REGLD signals to the clock and data shift registers must be active to permit loading. READY = CLKSH = DTASH = REGLD = (DISKWT) (A13) (BCNT = 15) + . . .

The preceding equation indicates that the disk write must be performed with A13 = 1 for data transfer on byte boundaries. When formatting a track, the write operation must be synchronized with the index pulse, and the bit counter must be cleared regardless of its current state. When this type of write operation is to be performed, A13 must be 0.

READY = CLKSH = DTASH = REGLD = (DISKWT) (A13) (BCNT = 15) + (DISKWT) (A13$-$)
(INDSYN) + . . .

BCLR$-$ = $\overline{\text{(DISKWT) (A13}-\text{) (INDSYN)}}$ + . . .

As the data byte is loaded into the data shift register, address lines A9, A10, and A11 select the clock pattern to be loaded into the clock shift register (see Table 3).

Table 3. Write Clock Patterns

A9	A10	A11	Clock Pattern
0	0	0	C7 (ID and Data Mark)
0	0	1	D7 (Track Mark)
1	1	1	FF (Normal Data)

When the transfer is complete to the clock and data shift registers, the write mode (WTMODE) flip flop is set, causing $\overline{\text{WRITE ENABLE}}$ to become active. If another byte is not written at the next byte boundary, WTMODE is reset, causing the control logic to revert to the read mode (RDMODE = 1). Also, control reverts to read mode and the bit counter is cleared when the index pulse occurs and when no write operation synchronized to the index pulse is being performed. This is useful when formatting a track, since $\overline{\text{WRITE ENABLE}}$ will automatically be turned off when the second index pulse occurs. If an index pulse occurs during a write operation with A13 = 1, the CPU proceeds, but no data transfer takes place.

WTMDD = (WTMODE) (BCNT = 15−) (INDSYN−) + (DISKWT) (A13) (BCNT = 15) + (DISKWT) (A13−) INDSYN)

BCLR− = $\overline{\text{INDSYN} + \ldots}$

READY = (DISKWT) [(A13) (BCNT = 15) + INDSYN)] + . . .

While WTMODE = 1, write data is generated by alternately shifting out bits from the clock and data shift register every two microseconds. Shifting of the clock shift register occurs when CLKSH = 1, and shifting of the data shift register when DTASH = 1. The shift is enabled by BITTIME, which is active for one clock cycle every 2 μs by loading the counter with 10_{10} each time TCNTCY = 1.

BITTIME = (WTMODE) (TCNTCY) + . . .

TCNTLDD = TCNTLDB = WTMODE + . . .

CLKSH = (DISKWT) [(A13) (BCNT = 15) + (A13−) (INDSYN)] + (WTMODE) (BCNTA−) (BITTIME) + . . .

DTASH = (DISKWT) [(A13) (BCNT = 15) + (A13−) (INDSYN)] + (WTMODE) (BCNTA) (BITTIME) + . . .

WRTDTAD = (WTMODE) (BITTIME) [(CLK0) (BCNTA−) + (DTA0) (BCNTA)]

On even bit counts (BCNTA = 0) clock bits are shifted, and on odd bits (BCNTA = 1) data bits are shifted, producing the desired interleaving of clock and data bits. (See Figure 26.)

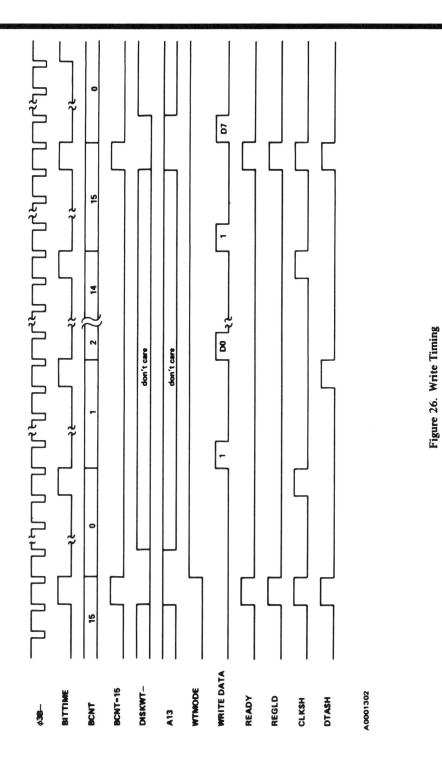

Figure 26. Write Timing

4.2 DISK READ OPERATIONS

Any time disk write operations are not being performed, the read/write control logic defaults to the read mode (RDMODE = 1). The following functions are performed to enable the CPU to read diskette data:

1.   Conversion of FM to digital data;

2.   Separation of clock and data bits;

3.   Byte synchronization of the bit string;

4.   Assembly of the seria data into bytes to be ready by CPU.

4.2.1 Clock and Data Bit Detection

Clock and data bits read from the disk are represented as a series of pulses. Each logic one clock or data bit is simply a pulse. Logic zero data and clock bits are indicated by the absence of a pulse between two pulses separated by a full data period (4 μs). Under ideal circumstances, detection of zero bits could be achieved by simply measuring the time between pulses. If $t_{p2}-t_{p1} = 2\,\mu$s, no zero bit is present; and if $t_{p2}-t_{p1} = 4\,\mu$s, a zero bit occurs between the two pulses.

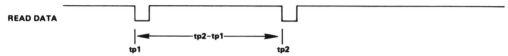

Three phenomena make zero-bit detection more complex:

1.   Variations in rotational speed of the disk;

2.   Uncertainty of measured delays when using synchronous counters;

3.   Apparent positional distortion or "bit-shifting" resulting from the tendency of pulses to move away from adjacent pulses.

Disk speed variations are typically specified at ±2% by diskette drive manufacturers. Figure 27 illustrates the bit shifting phenomenon:

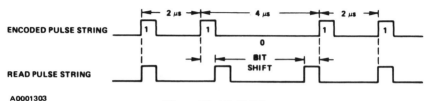

A0001303

Figure 27. Bit Shifting

Pulses in the string have a tendency to move away from each other, and the closer together the pulses, the stronger the tendency to separate. A zero bit causes contiguous pulses to move toward each other, reducing pulse separation and complicating zero detection.

The bit detector is used to generate the synchronous signal BITTIME, which is active when a one or zero bit has been detected.

$$BITTIME = (RDMODE) (BITIN) + \ldots$$

Detection of zero bits is accomplished by measuring the time between successive pulses. When TCNTCY = 1 and BITIN = 0, a zero bit is detected.

$$BITTIME = (RDMODE) (BITIN + TCNTCY) + \ldots$$

Data and clock bits could be detected by measuring the time between read pulses, and if this time is greater than 3 μs, a zero bit is present; otherwise, no zero bit is present. Since the read pulse is asynchronous to the system, the time between pulses can only be measured to an accuracy of 333 ns ($\pm$1 clock cycle). For example, if the counter in Figure 28 is loaded with seven, no zero will be detected if the time between pulses ($t_{P2} - t_{P1}$) is less than 3.0 μs, and a zero will always be detected if $t_{P2} - t_{P1} > 3.333$ μs. If 3.0 μs $< t_{P2} - t_{P1} < 3.333$ μs, an ambiguity occurs in that a zero may or may not be detected. Similarly, if the counter is loaded with eight rather than seven, no zero bit will be detected if $t_{P2} - t_{P1} < 2.667$ μs, a zero bit will be detected if $t_{P2} - t_{P1} > 3.0$ μs, and the result is indeterminate if 2.667 μs $< t_{P2} - t_{P1} < 3.0$ μs. Most floppy-disk drive manufacturers specify that the maximum shift for any bit is 500 ns. Thus, two consecutive 1 bits may be separated by nearly 3.0 μs, and two 1 bits separated by a zero bit may shift toward each other to result in a minimum separation of nearly 3.0 μs. The combined distortion of consecutive 1 bits never fully reaches 1 μs, but the 667 ns margin provided by loading the counter with either seven or eight does not provide for reliable, accurate reading of data. (See Figure 28.)

As stated previously, adjacent 1 bits affect the direction of distortion of a particular 1 bit, with the closest pulses having the greatest effect. Empirical observation indicates that only the two bit positions on either side of a pulse have significant effect on a pulse, as shown in Table 4.

Table 4. Bit Shift Direction

Bit n-2	Bit n-1	Bit n	Direction of Distortion For Bit n	Bit n+1	Bit n+2
0	1	1	→	0	1
0	1	1	−	1	0
0	1	1	←	1	1
1	0	1	−	0	1
1	0	1	←	1	0
1	0	1	←	1	1
1	1	1	→	0	1
1	1	1	→	1	0
1	1	1	−	1	1

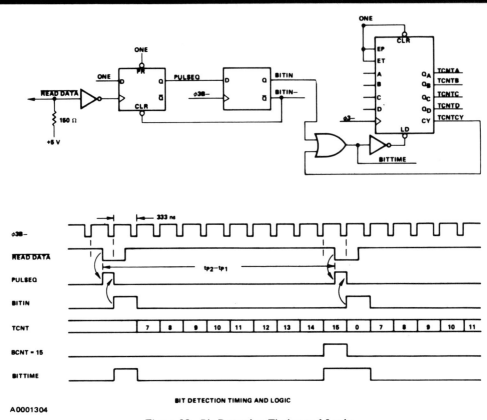

A0001304

BIT DETECTION TIMING AND LOGIC

Figure 28. Bit Detection Timing and Logic

The most difficult detection problem is that of differentiating between two contiguous 1 bits which are shifted away from each other (worst case 11) and two 1 bits separated by a zero bit where the 1 bits move toward each other (worst case 101). The worst case 11 occurs in the patterns

			←	→			
Pattern A	0	1	1	1	1	0	, and
Pattern B	1	0	1	1	0	1	
			→	←			

The worst case 101 occurs in the patterns

			→		←		
Pattern C	0	1	1	0	1	1	, and
Pattern D	1	1	1	0	1	1	.
			→		←		

The timing logic is such that the period of uncertainty does not lie in the area where a severely distorted pulse will occur; that is, when the worst case 11 can occur, and $t_{p2} - t_{p1} < 3.0 \, \mu s$, the logic always indicates that no zero was detected; when the worst case 101 can occur and $t_{p2} - t_{p1} > 3.0\,\mu s$, a zero is always detected. To accomplish this, the value loaded into the counter is shown in Table 5.

Table 5. Worst Case Pattern Load Values

Pattern	Bit n−2	Bit n−1	Bit n	Bit n+1	Bit n+2	Bit n+3	Load Value
A	0	1	1	1	1	0	7
B	1	0	1	1	0	1	7
C	0	1	1	0	1	1	8
D	1	1	1	0	1	1	8

When bit n is detected, the counter is loaded with the value shown, dependent upon the data pattern.

Accommodation of patterns B and D are simple, since bits following that being sampled don't matter. Patterns A and C present the problem that, as the serial pulses are being read, the logic does not know what bits n+1, n+2, and n+3 are going to be.

Further analysis of the data format reveals that patterns A and C occur only when an ID or data mark are being read, see Table 6.

Table 6. Data Mark

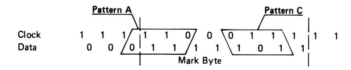

Pattern A can only occur at the beginning of an ID, data, or deleted data mark, and pattern C can only occur in a data mark. With pattern A, the first 0 is a data bit, and with pattern C, the first 0 is a clock bit. BCNTA selects whether the current 1 bit is to be shifted into the clock or data shift register. The previous two bits are CLK7 and DTA7, the LSB's of the clock and data shift registers, and the order of these bits is determined by BCNTA. Using this information, the values loaded into the counter are as shown in Table 7.

$$TCNTLDD = (RDMODE)\ ](CLK7)\ (DTA7) + (BCNTA-)\ (DTA7)] + \ldots$$

$$TCNTLDB = (RDMODE)\ [(DTA7-) + (BCNTA)\ (CLK7-)] + \ldots$$

The bit detector will thus adjust its count interval to accommodate the worst-case distortion which can occur for the anticipated data pattern.

Table 7. Bit Detector Counter Load Values

BCNTA	CLK7	DTA7	Load Value
0	0	0	Illegal
0	0	1	8
0	1	1	8
0	1	0	7
1	1	0	7
1	1	1	8
1	0	1	7
1	0	0	Illegal

4.2.2 Clock/Data Separation

Each time BITTIME is active, a new clock or data bit is shifted in. The value of the clock or data bit is BITIN. Since clock and data bits are interleaved, the value of BITIN will be alternately shifted into the clock or data shift register each time BITTIME is active. This is accomplished by incrementing the bit counter each time BITTIME is active, causing BCNTA to toggle. The equations for shifting the clock and data shift registers are:

$$CLKSH = (BITTIME)\,(BCNTA-)\,(RDMODE) + \ldots$$

$$DTASH = (BITTIME)\,(BCNTA)\,(RDMODE) + \ldots$$

When four consecutive zeroes are detected in the clock shift register, the order in which bits go to the clock and data shift registers is reversed, since four consecutive zero clock bits never occur in the recording format used. This is accomplished by the control signal:

$$BCLD- = \overline{(CLK4-)\,(CLK5-)\,(CLK6-)\,(CLK7-)}.$$

When this signals becomes active, the bit counter is cleared to zero, and remains cleared until the next 1 bit is detected. This 1 bit is directed to the clock shift register, causing BCLD− to become inactive and normal operation is resumed. Synchronization is thus assured at the beginning of each ID and data field because each field is preceded by several bytes with all zero data bits and all one clock bits.

The timing for clock/data separation is shown in Figure 29.

4.2.3 Byte Synchronization

Initial byte synchronization is achieved when reading an ID or data field by detecting the unique clock pattern of $C7_{16}$ which occurs only in ID and data marks. The mark detect signal is expressed by the equation:

$$MRKDT = (CLK0)\,(CLK1)\,(CLK2-)\,(CLK3-)\,(CLK4-)\,(CLK5)\,(CLK6)\,(CLK7)$$

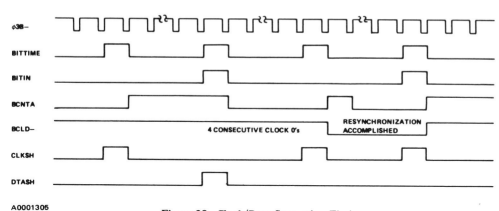

A0001305

Figure 29. Clock/Data Separation Timing

After the mark is detected, one additional BITTIME must occur, allowing the data bit to be shifted into the data shift register.

4.2.4 Reading Disk Data

Two types of disk reads may be performed. When reading an ID or data field, the first byte read is always the ID or data mark. This is accomplished by performing a disk read with A13 = 0. The READY input signal will not become active until MRKDT = 1 and BITTIME = 1. After the mark is read, byte synchronization is established and subsequent disk reads are performed with A13 = 1. In this case, READY becomes true at each byte boundary when BCNT = 15.

$$READY = (DSKRD) [(BCNTA) (MRKDT) (BITTIME) (A13-) + (BCNT = 15) (A13) + INDSYN] + ...$$

The addresses for the two types of disk reads are $7FF8_{16}$ for reading marks, and $7FFC_{16}$ for reading normal data. The INDSYN term of the above equation causes the read operation to be completed any time the index pulse is detected or when the disk becomes not ready. (See Figure 30.)

4.3 READ/WRITE LOGIC COMBINATION

This subsection summarizes the equations for the control lines resulting from the combination of the read and write control functions.

BCLD–
$$BCLD- = \overline{(CLK4-) (CLK5-) (CLK6-) (CLK7-)}$$

BCLR–
$$BCLR- = \overline{(RDMODE) (MRKDT) (BCNTA) (BITTIME) + (INDSYN)}$$

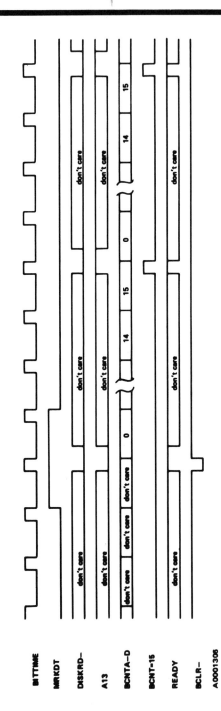

Figure 30. Disk Read Timing

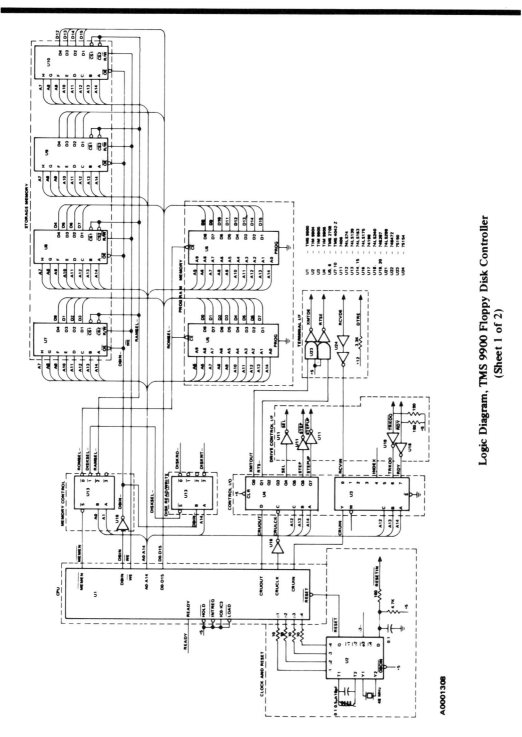

**Logic Diagram, TMS 9900 Floppy Disk Controller
(Sheet 1 of 2)**

A0001308

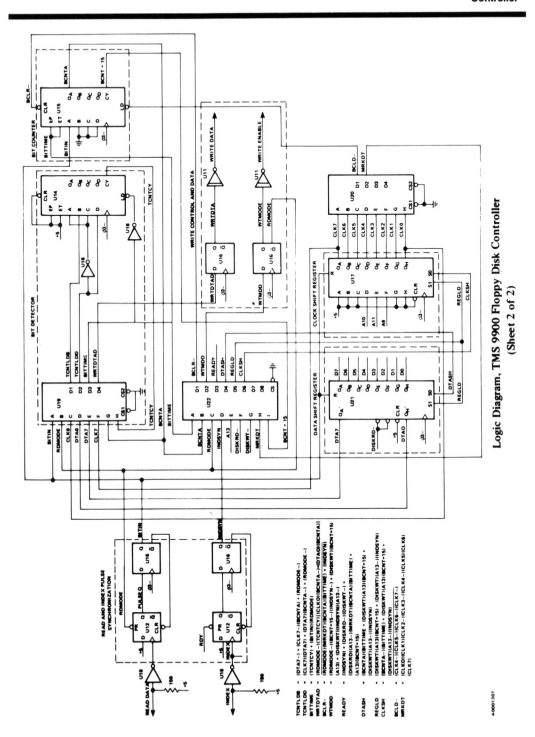

Logic Diagram, TMS 9900 Floppy Disk Controller
(Sheet 2 of 2)

BITTIME

BITTIME = (WTMODE) (TCNTCY) + (RDMODE) [(BITIN) + (TCNTCY)]
$\qquad$ = (TCNTCY) + (RDMODE) (BITIN)

CLKSH

CLKSH = (DISKWT) [(A13) (BCNT = 15) + (A13−) (INDSYN)] + (WTMODE) (BCNTA−)
$\quad$ (BITTIME) + (RDMODE) (BCNTA−) (BITTIME)
$\qquad$ = (DISKWT) [(A13) (BCNT = 15) + (A13−) (INDSYN)] + (BCNTA−) (BITTIME)

DTASH

DTASH = (DISKWT) [(A13) (BCNT = 15) + (A13−) (INDSYN)] + (WTMODE) (BCNTA) (BITTIME)
$\quad$ + (RDMODE) (BCNTA) (BITTIME)
$\qquad$ = (DISKWT) [(A13) (BCNT = 15) + (A13−) (INDSYN)] + (BCNTA) (BITTIME)

MRKDT

MRKDT = (CLK0) (CLK1) (CLK2−) (CLK3−) (CLK4−) (CLK5) (CLK6) (CLK7)

READY

READY = (DISKWT) [(A13) (BCNT = 15) + (INDSYN)] + (DISKWT−) (DISKRD−) + (DISKRD)
$\quad$ [(A13) (BCNT = 15) + (INDSYN) + (A13−) (MRKDT) (BCNTA) (BITTIME)]
$\qquad$ = (DISKWT−) (DISKRD−) + (A13) (BCNT = 15) + (INDSYN) + (DISKRD) (A13−)
$\quad$ (MRKDT) (BCNTA) (BITTIME)

REGLD

REGLD = (DISKWT) [(A13) (BCNT = 15) + (A13−) (INDSYN)]

TCNTLDB

TCNTLDB = (WTMODE) + (RDMODE) [(DTA7−) + (BCNTA) (CLK7−)]
$\qquad$ = (WTMODE) + (DTA7−) + (BCNTA) (CLK7−)

TCNTLDD

TCNTLDD = (WTMODE) + (RDMODE) [(CLK7) (DTA7) + (BCNTA−) (DTA7)]
$\qquad$ = (WTMODE) + (CLK7) (DTA7) + (BCNTA−) (DTA7)

WRTDTAD

WRTDTAD = (WTMODE) (BITTIME) [(CLK0) (BCNTA−) +(DTA0) (BCNTA)]
$\qquad$ = (WTMODE) (TCNTCY) [(CLK0) (BCNTA−) + (DTA0) (BCNTA)]

WTMDD

WTMDD = (WTMODE) (BCNT = 15−) (INDSYN−) + (DISKWT) [(A13) (BCNT = 15) + (A13−)
$\quad$ (INDSYN)]

SECTION V

SOFTWARE

The software design of a microprocessor system is as important as its hardware design. In this system, several functions which are normally performed by hardware are instead done in software in order to reduce device count. Examples of hardware/software tradeoffs include timing, transmit/receive, and CRC calculation.

5.1 SOFTWARE INTERFACE SUMMARY

The memory map in Figure 31 shows the memory address assignments for program memory, storage memory and the floppy-disk interface.

The CRU bit address assignments are summarized in Table 8 below.

Table 8. CRU Address Assignments

Bit Address	Output	Input
0	XMTOUT	RCVIN
1	RTS–	
2		
3		
4	SEL	INDEX
5		
6	STEP	TRK00
7	STEPUP	RDY

5.2 CONTROL SOFTWARE

Rather than providing individual examples of each individual control and data transfer function, all of the functions are combined to demonstrate complete system operation. The control software is modular, and the various subroutines may easily be adapted to different configurations of a TMS 9900 floppy-disk controller.

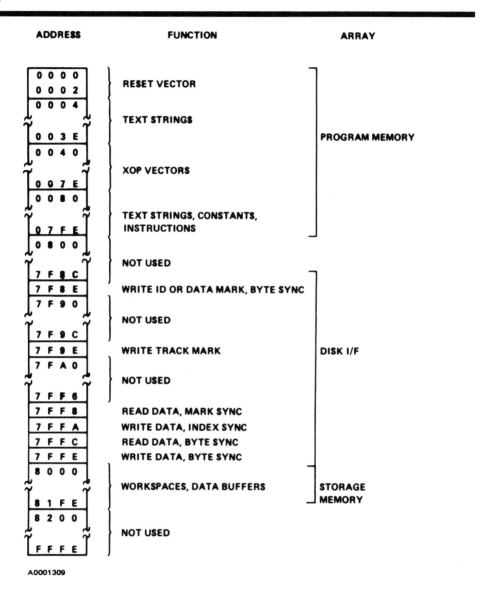

ADDRESS	FUNCTION	ARRAY

A0001309

Figure 31. Memory Address Assignments

5.2.1 Floppy-Disk Control Program

This program contains the complete software for interfacing the TMS 9900 floppy-disk controller to both the RS-232 terminal and the floppy-disk drive.

5.2.2 Operator Commands

The commands listed in Table 9 are available to the terminal operator. These commands enable the user to write and read data to and from the diskette, format tracks, display and enter data from memory, and execute from a selected address. The user is able to load and execute diagnostics in addition to performing normal data transfer operations. When errors are encountered, error information is reported at the terminal.

Table 9. Operator Commands

?WA	TRACK = ct st,	SECTOR = cs ss,	NUMBER = sn
?WH	TRACK = ct st,	SECTOR = cs ss,	NUMBER = sn
?WD	TRACK = ct st,	SECTOR = cs ss,	NUMBER = sn
?RA	TRACK = ct st,	SECTOR = cs ss,	NUMBER = sn
?RH	TRACK = ct st,	SECTOR = cs ss,	NUMBER = sn
?FM	TRACK = ct st	END TRACK = st et	
?MD	sadd eadd		
?ME	sadd		
?MX	sadd		

Underscored characters are entered by the user. All others are supplied by the controller. The lower case fields are hexadecimal values. If the users enters a blank into these fields, the default value is used by the controller. Entry of any non-printable character (e.g., Carriage Return, ESCape) during command entry causes the command to be aborted. Entry of a non-hexadecimal value in hexadecimal fields causes the command to be aborted.

Table 10 lists the command entry parameters and Table 11 gives a summary of the commands.

Table 10. Command Entry Parameters

Parameter	Definition	Default Value	Range
ct	Current track number	—	$00 \leqslant ct \leqslant 4C\ (76_{10})$
st	Starting track number	ct	$00 \leqslant st \leqslant 4C$
cs	Current sector number	—	$01 \leqslant cs \leqslant 1A\ (26_{10})$
ss	Starting sector number	cs	$01 \leqslant ss \leqslant 1A$
sn	Number of sectors	01	$01 \leqslant sn \leqslant FF(255_{10})$
et	Ending track number	st	$st \leqslant et \leqslant 4C$
sadd	Starting address	8000	$0 \leqslant sadd \leqslant FFFF$
eadd	Ending address	sadd	$0 \leqslant eadd \leqslant FFFF$

Table 11. Command Summary

Command	Description
WA	Write ASCII. The ASCII character strings entered by the user are written sequentially onto the diskette. Each sector may be terminated, filling remaining bytes with 00, by entry of any non-printable character. (ASCII code $< 20_{16}$) other than ESCape. Entry of ESCape aborts the command.
WH	Write Hexadecimal. Hexadecimal bytes entered by the user are written sequentially onto the diskette. Sector termination and abort are performed in the same way as for the WA command.
WD	Write Deleted Data. Same as WH command, except the Deleted Data Mark (Clock = $C7_{16}$ Data = $F8_{16}$) rather than the Data Mark (Clock = $C7_{16}$, Data = FB_{16}) is written at the beginning of the Data Field.
RA	Read ASCII. The specified sectors are read and printed out as ASCII character strings. Each sector is printed beginning at a new line, and printing continues until the end of the sector, or until a non-printable ASCII character is encountered. When more than 80 characters are printed, the controller prints the eighty-first character in the first position of the next line. The command may be aborted at the end of any sector by depressing the BREAK key before the last character of the sector is printed. If a Deleted Data field is encountered, it is reported, and normal operation continues.
RH	Read Hexadecimal. The specified sectors are read and printed out as hexadecimal bytes, 16 bytes per line. The command may be aborted by depressing the BREAK key before the last character of any line is printed. If a Deleted Data field is encountered, it is reported and normal operation continues.
FM	Format Track. The specified tracks are completely rewritten with gaps, Track Marks, ID fields, and Data fields. All zero data is written into the 128 bytes of the data field.
MD	Memory Display. The contents of the specified memory addresses are printed out in hexadecimal byte format. The address of the first word of each line is printed, followed by 16 bytes. The command may be aborted by depressing the BREAK key before the last character of any line is printed.
ME	Memory Enter. Beginning with the selected location, the memory address and contents are printed. If it is to be modified, the user enters a hexadecimal byte value which will be stored at that address. If the value is not to be changed, the user enters a blank character (SPACE bar). The address is then incremented and the process is repeated until a non-hex character is entered; terminating the command.
MX	The CPU begins execution at the selected memory location.

Figure 32 shows the control software for the system described in this application report.

SECTION VI

SUMMARY

This application report has provided a thorough discussion of the TMS 9900 floppy-disk controller hardware and software system design. The economy of the CRU and the high throughput capability of the memory bus result in an economical, powerful system. The memory-to-memory architecture of the TMS 9900, along with its powerful instruction set and addressing capability, make the TMS 9900 ideally suited for applications where large amounts of data manipulation are necessary. Also, software development time is optimized by the minimization of lines of code resulting from the memory-to-memory instructions and large number of working registers.

It is likely that the designer using this application report will have requirements that are not addressed in this design. Variations in the sector length are accommodated with slight software modification. Higher density recording formats such as MFM and M^2FM require changes in the bit detector and data-separation logic. Higher throughput can be achieved by using an LSI terminal interface such as the TMS 9902 asynchronous communication controller and hardware CRC generation. Controlling multiple disks requires only the addition of drive select control lines. In short, variations on this design are easily implemented through slight hardware and software modifications.

```
FLOPPY DISK CONTROL PROGRAM                              PAGE 0001

  0002                          IDT   'FDCTRL'
  0003                  ◆◆◆◆◆◆◆◆◆◆◆◆◆◆◆◆◆◆◆◆◆◆◆◆◆◆◆◆◆◆◆◆◆◆◆◆◆◆◆◆◆◆◆◆◆◆◆◆◆◆◆◆◆◆◆◆◆◆◆◆◆◆◆
  0004                  ◆
  0005                  ◆           FLOPPY DISK CONTROL PROGRAM
  0006                  ◆
  0007                  ◆           DECEMBER 21, 1976
  0008                  ◆
  0009                  ◆       THIS PROGRAM CONTAINS THE CONTROL SOFTWARE FOR THE
  0010                  ◆       SYSTEM DESCRIBED IN THE "TMS 9900 FLOPPY DISK
  0011                  ◆       CONTROL SYSTEM" APPLICATION REPORT.  THE PROGRAM
  0012                  ◆       ALLOWS THE USER TO READ, WRITE, AND FORMAT DATA ON
  0013                  ◆       FLOPPY DISK.  ADDITIONALLY, THE USER MAY ENTER,
  0014                  ◆       DISPLAY, AND INITIATE EXECUTION FROM
  0015                  ◆       ANY LOCATION IN MEMORY.  IT IS ASSUMED THAT THE
  0016                  ◆       CONSOLE USED FOR COMMAND ENTRY AND DATA DISPLAY IS
  0017                  ◆       A 300 BAUD, RS-232C TYPE TERMINAL.  THE COMMANDS
  0018                  ◆       USED IN INTERFACING THE TERMINAL OPERATOR
  0019                  ◆       INTERFACE TO THE CONTROLLER ARE FULLY
  0020                  ◆       DESCRIBED IN SECTION 5.3 OF THE "TMS 9900
  0021                  ◆       FLOPPY DISK CONTROL SYSTEM" APPLICATION
  0022                  ◆       REPORT.
  0023                  ◆
  0024                  ◆◆◆◆◆◆◆◆◆◆◆◆◆◆◆◆◆◆◆◆◆◆◆◆◆◆◆◆◆◆◆◆◆◆◆◆◆◆◆◆◆◆◆◆◆◆◆◆◆◆◆◆◆◆◆◆◆◆◆◆◆◆◆
  0025                  ◆
  0026                  ◆       DISK TRANSFER ADDRESSES
  0027                  ◆
  0028       7F8E   MRKWT   EQU   >7F8E              DATA MARK WRITE
  0029       7F9E   TKMWT   EQU   >7F9E              TRACK MARK WRITE
  0030       7FFA   INDXWT  EQU   >7FFA              INDEX SYNC WRITE
  0031       7FFE   DTAWT   EQU   >7FFE              BYTE SYNC WRITE
  0032       7FF8   MRKRD   EQU   >7FF8              MARK SYNC READ
  0033       7FFC   DTARD   EQU   >7FFC              BYTE SYNC READ
  0034                  ◆◆◆◆◆◆◆◆◆◆◆◆◆◆◆◆◆◆◆◆◆◆◆◆◆◆◆◆◆◆◆◆◆◆◆◆◆◆◆◆◆◆◆◆◆◆◆◆◆◆◆◆◆◆◆◆◆◆◆◆◆◆◆
  0035                  ◆
  0036                  ◆       RAM EQUATES
  0037                  ◆
  0038       80C0   SECBUF  EQU   >80C0              CRC BUFFER FOR FORMATTING
  0039       80F7   IDFLD   EQU   >80F7              ID FIELD IMAGE
  0040       80F8   TKNUM   EQU   >80F8              TRACK NUMBER
  0041       80FA   SECNUM  EQU   >80FA              SECTOR NUMBER
  0042       80FC   IDCRC   EQU   >80FC              CRC FOR ID FIELD
  0043       80FF   DTAFLD  EQU   >80FF              DATA FIELD IMAGE
  0044       8100   DTABUF  EQU   >8100              128 BYTE DATA BUFFER
  0045       8180   DTACRC  EQU   >8180              CRC FOR DATA FIELD
  0046       8170   FDWP5   EQU   >8170              WORKSPACE 5
  0047       8190   FDWP4   EQU   >8190              WORKSPACE 4
  0048       81A0   FDWP3   EQU   >81A0              WORKSPACE 3
  0049       81C0   FDWP2   EQU   >81C0              WORKSPACE 2
  0050       81E0   FDWP1   EQU   >81E0              WORKSPACE 1
```

Figure 32. Floppy Disk Control Program (Sheet 1 of 28)

FLOPPY DISK CONTROL PROGRAM   PAGE 0002

```
0052            ◆◆◆◆◆◆◆◆◆◆◆◆◆◆◆◆◆◆◆◆◆◆◆◆◆◆◆◆◆◆◆◆◆◆◆◆◆◆◆◆◆◆◆◆◆◆◆◆◆◆◆◆◆◆◆◆◆◆◆◆
0053            ◆
0054            ◆        CRU EQUATES
0055            ◆
0056    0000  RIN    EQU  0                 RECEIVE IN
0057    0004  INDEX  EQU  4                 INDEX PULSE
0058    0006  TRK00  EQU  6                 TRACK 00 INDICATOR
0059    0007  RDY    EQU  7                 DRIVE READY
0060    0000  XOUT   EQU  0                 TRANSMIT OUT
0061    0001  RTS    EQU  1                 REQUEST TO SEND
0062    0004  SEL    EQU  4                 DRIVE SELECT
0063    0006  STEP   EQU  6                 HEAD STEP CONTROL
0064    0007  STEPUP EQU  7                 STEP DIRECTION CONTROL
0065            ◆◆◆◆◆◆◆◆◆◆◆◆◆◆◆◆◆◆◆◆◆◆◆◆◆◆◆◆◆◆◆◆◆◆◆◆◆◆◆◆◆◆◆◆◆◆◆◆◆◆◆◆◆◆◆◆◆◆◆◆
0066            ◆
0067            ◆        XOP  EQUATES
0068            ◆
0069          DXOP ERPT,1              ERROR REPORT
0070          DXOP IDRD,2              READ ID FIELD
0071          DXOP TKST,3              SET TRACK
0072          DXOP SINC,4              INCREMENT SECTOR
0073          DXOP DSON,5              SELECT DRIVE ON
0074          DXOP AXMT,6              ASCII DATA TRANSMIT
0075          DXOP CRCI,7              ID FIELD CRC CALCULATION
0076          DXOP CRCD,8              DATA FIELD CRC CALCULATION
0077          DXOP TINC,9              INCREMENT TRACK
0078          DXOP HRC2,10             RECEIVE HEX BYTE
0079          DXOP HXM2,11             TRANSMIT HEX BYTE
0080          DXOP NLIN,12             NEW LINE
0081          DXOP PECV,13             RECEIVE CHARACTER
0082          DXOP XMIT,14             TRANSMIT CHARACTER
0083          DXOP DLAY,15             SOFTWARE TIME DELAY
0084            ◆◆◆◆◆◆◆◆◆◆◆◆◆◆◆◆◆◆◆◆◆◆◆◆◆◆◆◆◆◆◆◆◆◆◆◆◆◆◆◆◆◆◆◆◆◆◆◆◆◆◆◆◆◆◆◆◆◆◆◆
0085            ◆
0086            ◆        TIME CONSTANTS
0087            ◆
0088    00FA  HBDLY  EQU  250               HALF BIT (1.667 MS.)
0089    01F4  FBDLY  EQU  500               FULL BIT (3.333 MS.)
0090    03E8  B2DLY  EQU  1000              2 BITS (6.667 MS.)
0091    7530  B30DLY EQU  30000             CARRIAGE RETURN
0092            ◆                            (200 MS.)
0093    05DC  HSDLY  EQU  1500              HEAD STEP (10 MS.)
0094    1482  HDLDLY EQU  5250              HEAD LOAD (35 MS.)
0095            ◆◆◆◆◆◆◆◆◆◆◆◆◆◆◆◆◆◆◆◆◆◆◆◆◆◆◆◆◆◆◆◆◆◆◆◆◆◆◆◆◆◆◆◆◆◆◆◆◆◆◆◆◆◆◆◆◆◆◆◆
0096            ◆
0097            ◆        POWER ON RESET VECTOR
0098            ◆
0099  0000  81E0  RSETVC DATA FDWP1,START
      0002  ----
```

Figure 32. Floppy Disk Control Program (Sheet 2 of 28)

```
0101                    ◆◆◆◆◆◆◆◆◆◆◆◆◆◆◆◆◆◆◆◆◆◆◆◆◆◆◆◆◆◆◆◆◆◆◆◆◆◆◆◆◆◆◆◆◆◆◆◆◆◆◆◆◆◆
0102                    ◆
0103                    ◆       ERROR MESSAGES
0104                    ◆
0105   0004    49   NIDMSG TEXT 'ID NOT FOUND'
0106   0010    00          BYTE 0
0107   0011    44   NDMMSG TEXT 'DATA MARK NOT FOUND'
0108   0024    00          BYTE 0
0109   0025    44   NRDYMS TEXT 'DRIVE NOT READY'
0110   0034    00          BYTE 0
0111   0035    43   CRCMSG TEXT 'CRCC ERROR'
0112   003F    00          BYTE 0
0113                    ◆◆◆◆◆◆◆◆◆◆◆◆◆◆◆◆◆◆◆◆◆◆◆◆◆◆◆◆◆◆◆◆◆◆◆◆◆◆◆◆◆◆◆◆◆◆◆◆◆◆◆◆◆◆
0114                    ◆
0115                    ◆       XOP VECTORS
0116                    ◆
0117   0040   FFFF         DATA -1,-1
       0042   FFFF
0118   0044   81E0         DATA FDWP1,ERPTPC
       0046   ----
0119   0048   31C0         DATA FDWP2,IDRDPC
       004A   ----
0120   004C   8180         DATA FDWP4,TKSTPC
       004E   ----
0121   0050   31C0         DATA FDWP2,SINCPC
       0052   ----
0122   0054   8180         DATA FDWP4,DSONPC
       0056   ----
0123   0058   81C0         DATA FDWP2,AXMTPC
       005A   ----
0124   005C   31A0         DATA FDWP3,CRCIPC
       005E   ----
0125   0060   31A0         DATA FDWP3,CRCDPC
       0062   ----
0126   0064   31A0         DATA FDWP3,TINCPC
       0066   ----
0127   0068   81A0         DATA FDWP3,HRC2PC
       006A   ----
0128   006C   31A0         DATA FDWP3,HXM2PC
       006E   ----
0129   0070   81A0         DATA FDWP3,NLINPC
       0072   ----
0130   0074   8180         DATA FDWP4,RECVPC
       0076   ----
0131   0078   8190         DATA FDWP4,XMITPC
       007A   ----
0132   007C   8170         DATA FDWP5,DLAYPC
       007E   ----
```

Figure 32. Floppy Disk Control Program (Sheet 3 of 28)

FLOPPY DISK CONTROL PROGRAM   PAGE 0004

```
0134              ◆◆◆◆◆◆◆◆◆◆◆◆◆◆◆◆◆◆◆◆◆◆◆◆◆◆◆◆◆◆◆◆◆◆◆◆◆◆◆◆◆◆◆◆◆◆◆◆◆◆◆◆◆◆◆◆◆
0135              ◆
0136              ◆          ASCII VALUES
0137              ◆
0138   0080   41  ASCIIA TEXT 'A'
0139   0081   46  ASCIIF TEXT 'F'
0140   0082   4D  ASCIIM TEXT 'M'
0141   0083   1B  ESC    BYTE  >1B
0142   0084   20  BLANK  BYTE  >20
0143   0085   3F  QUEST  BYTE  >3F
0144   0086   07  BELL   BYTE  >07
0145   0087   08  BACKSP BYTE  >08
0146   0088   0D  CARRET BYTE  >0D
0147   0089   0A  LINEFD BYTE  >0A
0148              ◆◆◆◆◆◆◆◆◆◆◆◆◆◆◆◆◆◆◆◆◆◆◆◆◆◆◆◆◆◆◆◆◆◆◆◆◆◆◆◆◆◆◆◆◆◆◆◆◆◆◆◆◆◆◆◆◆
0149              ◆
0150              ◆          ADDITIONAL TEXT MESSAGES
0151              ◆
0152   008A   20  TKMSG  TEXT '   TRACK ='
0153   0093   00         BYTE 0
0154   0094   20  ENDMSG TEXT '   END'
0155   0099   00         BYTE 0
0156   009A   2C  SCTMSG TEXT ', SECTOR ='
0157   00A4   00         BYTE 0
0158   00A5   2C  NUMMSG TEXT ', NUMBER ='
0159   00AF   00         BYTE 0
0160   00B0   20  ADDMSG TEXT '   ADDRESS ='
0161   00BB   00         BYTE 0
0162   00BC   44  DLDMSG TEXT 'DELETED DATA FIELD'
0163   00CE   00         BYTE 0
0164              ◆◆◆◆◆◆◆◆◆◆◆◆◆◆◆◆◆◆◆◆◆◆◆◆◆◆◆◆◆◆◆◆◆◆◆◆◆◆◆◆◆◆◆◆◆◆◆◆◆◆◆◆◆◆◆◆◆
0165              ◆
0166              ◆          DISK MARK CONSTANTS
0167              ◆
0168   00CF   F8  DLDMRK BYTE  >F8
0169   00D0   FE  IDMRK  BYTE  >FE
0170   00D1   FB  DTMRK  BYTE  >FB
0171   00D2   FC  TKMRK  BYTE  >FC
0172              EVEN
0173              ◆◆◆◆◆◆◆◆◆◆◆◆◆◆◆◆◆◆◆◆◆◆◆◆◆◆◆◆◆◆◆◆◆◆◆◆◆◆◆◆◆◆◆◆◆◆◆◆◆◆◆◆◆◆◆◆◆
0174              ◆
0175              ◆          SUBROUTINE:  DLAY
0176              ◆
0177              ◆          CALLING SEQUENCE:  DLAY @COUNT
0178              ◆
0179              ◆          A SOFTWARE LOOP WILL BE EXECUTED THE NUMBER
0180              ◆          OF TIMES SPECIFIED BY THE CALLING PROGRAM.
0181              ◆          EACH ITERATION OF THE LOOP RESULTS IN A
0182              ◆          DELAY OF 6.67 MICROSECONDS.
0183              ◆
0184   00D4  060B DLAYPC DEC. R11              DECREMENT COUNT
       007E◆◆00D4'
0185   00D6  16FE        JNE  DLAYPC           LOOP IF NOT 0
0186   00D8  0380        RTWP                  RETURN
```

Figure 32. Floppy Disk Control Program (Sheet 4 of 28)

FLOPPY DISK CONTROL PROGRAM   PAGE 0005

```
0188                     ◆◆◆◆◆◆◆◆◆◆◆◆◆◆◆◆◆◆◆◆◆◆◆◆◆◆◆◆◆◆◆◆◆◆◆◆◆◆◆◆◆◆◆◆◆◆◆◆◆◆◆◆◆
0189                     ◆
0190                     ◆        SUBROUTINE:   RECV
0191                     ◆
0192                     ◆        CALLING SEQUENCE:   RECV @LOCATN
0193                     ◆
0194                     ◆        AN ASCII CHARACTER WITH CORRECT FORMATTING
0195                     ◆        IS RECEIVED AND THEN RETRANSMITTED
0196                     ◆        AT 300 BAUD.   THE RECEIVED CHARACTER IS STORED
0197                     ◆        AT THE SPECIFIED LOCATION.
0198                     ◆
0199   00DA   04CC   RECVPC CLR   R12               SET CRU BASE
       0076◆◆00DA
0200   00DC   1F00   RCV    TB    RIN               TEST RECEIVE INPUT
0201   00DE   13FE          JEQ   RCV               LOOP UNTIL RIN = 0
0202   00E0   2FE0          DLAY  @HBDLY            DELAY HALF BIT TIME
       00E2   00FA
0203   00E4   1F00          TB    RIN               TEST RECEIVE INPUT
0204   00E6   13FA          JEQ   RCV               IF RIN = 0, VALID 'START BIT
0205   00E8   020A          LI    R10,>3F           INITIALIZE ACCUMULATOR
       00EA   003F
0206   00EC   2FE0   RCVLP  DLAY  @FBDLY            DELAY FULL BIT TIME
       00EE   01F4
0207   00F0   1F00          TB    RIN               TEST RECEIVE INPUT
0208   00F2   16--          JNE   RCVOFF            SET MSB OF ACCUMULATOR
0209   00F4   026A          ORI   R10,>8000         IF RIN = 1
       00F6   8000
0210   00F8   091A   RCVOFF SRL   R10,1             SHIFT ACCUMULATOR
       00F2◆◆1602
0211   00FA   18F8          JOC   RCVLP             IF CARRY, RECEIVE NEXT BIT
0212   00FC   2FE0          DLAY  @B2DLY            DELAY 2 BIT TIMES
       00FE   03E8
0213   0100   1F00          TB    RIN               TEST RECEIVE INPUT
0214   0102   16EC          JNE   RCV               IF RIN = 0, FRAMING ERROR
0215   0104   D6CA          MOVB  R10,◆R11          MOVE RECEIVED CHARACTER
0216                     ◆                          TO SPECIFIED LOCATION AND
0217                     ◆                          RETRANSMIT.
```

Figure 32. Floppy Disk Control Program (Sheet 5 of 28)

FLOPPY DISK CONTROL PROGRAM   PAGE 0006

```
0219                        ◆◆◆◆◆◆◆◆◆◆◆◆◆◆◆◆◆◆◆◆◆◆◆◆◆◆◆◆◆◆◆◆◆◆◆◆◆◆◆◆◆◆◆◆◆◆◆◆◆◆◆◆◆◆◆◆◆◆◆◆
0220                        ◆
0221                        ◆       SUBROUTINE:  XMIT
0222                        ◆
0223                        ◆       CALLING SEQUENCE:  XMIT @LOCATN
0224                        ◆
0225                        ◆       AN ASCII CHARACTER WITH CORRECT FORMATTING
0226                        ◆       AND EVEN PARITY IS TRANSMITTED AT 300 BAUD.
0227                        ◆       THE LOCATION OF THE CHARACTER TO BE TRANS-
0228                        ◆       MITTED IS SPECIFIED AS THE CALLING PARAMETER.
0229                        ◆
0230    0106   04CC  XMITPC  CLR   R12                INITIALIZE CRU BASE
        007A◆◆0106'
0231    0108   020A          LI    R10,3              INITIALIZE ACCUMULATOR
        010A   0003
0232    010C   0209          LI    R9,>8000           INITIALIZE PARITY MASK
        010E   8000
0233    0110   D29B          MOVB  ◆R11,R10           FETCH CHARACTER
0234    0112   1C--          JOP   PARADJ             IF ODD PARITY INVERT MSB
0235    0114   04C9          CLR   R9                 ELSE, CLEAR PARITY MASK
0236    0116   2A89  PARADJ  XOR   R9,R10             XOR PARITY MASK
        0112◆◆1C01
0237                        ◆                         WITH CHARACTER
0238    0118   1E01          SBZ   RTS                TURN ON RTS
0239    011A   0B8A          SRC   R10,8              ROTATE CHARACTER
0240    011C   18--  XMTLP1  JOC   XOUTON             TEST TRANSMIT BIT
0241    011E   1E00          SBZ   XOUT               IF 0, RESET XOUT
0242    0120   10--          JMP   XFBDLY             AND SKIP
0243    0122   1D00  XOUTON  SBO   XOUT               ELSE, SET XOUT
        011C◆◆1802
0244    0124   2FE0  XFBDLY  DLAY  @FBDLY             DELAY FULL BIT TIME
        0126   01F4
        0120◆◆1001
0245    0128   091A          SRL   R10,1              SHIFT ACCUMULATOR 1 BIT
0246    012A   16F8          JNE   XMTLP1             IF NOT ZERO, TRANSMIT NEXT BIT
0247    012C   1D01          SBO   RTS                TURN OFF RTS
0248    012E   0380          RTWP                     RETURN
```

Figure 32. Floppy Disk Control Program (Sheet 6 of 28)

FLOPPY DISK CONTROL PROGRAM   PAGE 0007

```
0250                    ◆◆◆◆◆◆◆◆◆◆◆◆◆◆◆◆◆◆◆◆◆◆◆◆◆◆◆◆◆◆◆◆◆◆◆◆◆◆◆◆◆◆◆◆◆◆◆◆◆◆◆◆◆
0251                    ◆
0252                    ◆     SUBROUTINE:  DSON
0253                    ◆
0254                    ◆     CALLING SEQUENCE:  DSON 0
0255                    ◆
0256                    ◆     THE FLOPPY DISK CRIVE IS SELECTED AND
0257                    ◆     THE SELECT DELAY PERIOD IS EXECUTED.   IF THE
0258                    ◆     DEVICE IS NOT READY, AN ERROR MESSAGE IS
0259                    ◆     PRINTED AND THE OPERATION IS ABORTED.
0260                    ◆     OTHERWISE, CONTROL RETURNS TO THE CALLING
0261                    ◆     PROGRAM.
0262                    ◆
0263   0130  04CC   DSONPC CLR  R12              INITIALIZE CRU BASE
       0056◆◆0130'
0264   0132  1D04       SBO  SEL              SELECT DRIVE
0265   0134  2FE0       DLAY @HDLDLY          DELAY FOR HEAD LOAD
       0136  1482
0266   0138  1F07       TB   RDY              TEST DRIVE STATUS
0267   013A  13--       JEQ  DSONRT           IF READY, NORMAL RETURN
0268   013C  2C60       ERPT @NRDYMS          ELSE, ABORT AND PRINT
       013E  0025'
0269                  ◆                        ERROR MESSAGE.
0270   0140  0380   DSONRT RTWP                NORMAL RETURN
       013A◆◆1302
0271                    ◆◆◆◆◆◆◆◆◆◆◆◆◆◆◆◆◆◆◆◆◆◆◆◆◆◆◆◆◆◆◆◆◆◆◆◆◆◆◆◆◆◆◆◆◆◆◆◆◆◆◆◆◆
0272                    ◆
0273                    ◆     SUBROUTINE:  HRC2
0274                    ◆
0275                    ◆     CALLING SEQUENCE:  HRC2 @LOCATN
0276                    ◆
0277                    ◆     A BLANK IS TRANSMITTED AND 2 CHARACTERS
0278                    ◆     ARE RECEIVED.  IF EITHER CHARACTER IS A
0279                    ◆     BLANK, NO OPERATION IS PERFORMED AND THE
0280                    ◆     NORMAL RETURN IS EXECUTED.  IF TWO HEXADEC-
0281                    ◆     IMAL VALUES ARE ENTERED, THE HEXADECIMAL
0282                    ◆     BYTE IS STORED AT THE LOCATION SPECIFIED
0283                    ◆     AS THE CALLING PARAMETER.  IF EITHER CHARACTER
0284                    ◆     IS AN ESCAPE, CONTROL IS RETURNED TO THE MAIN
0285                    ◆     PROGRAM AT THE POINT WHERE OPERATOR COMMANDS
0286                    ◆     ARE REQUESTED.  IF ANY OTHER CHARACTER IS
0287                    ◆     RECEIVED, NO OPERATION IS PERFORMED AND THE
0288                    ◆     RETURN PC VALUE WILL BE THE CONTENTS OF REG-
0289                    ◆     ISTER 10 OF THE CALLING PROGRAM.
0290                    ◆
0291   0142  81E0   RTRNVC DATA FDWP1,TOP      RETURN VECTOR
       0144  ----
0292   0146  2FA0   HRC2PC XMIT @BLANK         TRANSMIT BLANK
       0148  0084
       006A◆◆0146
0293   014A  04CA       CLR  R10              CLEAR HEX ACCUMULATOR
0294   014C  0708       SETO R8               INITIALIZE CHARACTER COUNTER
0295   014E  2F49   HRC2LP RECV R9            FETCH CHARACTER
0296   0150  9309       CB   R9,@ESC          COMPARE TO ESCAPE
```

Figure 32. Floppy Disk Control Program (Sheet 7 of 28)

FLOPPY DISK CONTROL PROGRAM   PAGE 0008

```
        0152  0083'
0297    0154  16--        JNE   NOTESC        IF NOT,CONTINUE
0298    0156  0420        BLWP  @RTRNVC       ELSE, ABORT COMMAND
        0158  0142'
0299    015A  9809  NOTESC CB   R9,@BLANK     COMPARE TO BLANK
        015C  0084'
        0154**1602
0300    015E  13--        JEQ   HRC2RT        IF = BLANK, RETURN
0301                 *                        ELSE, CONVERT TO HEXADECIMAL
0302    0160  0229        AI    R9,->3000     SUBTRACT ASCII BIAS
        0162  D000
0303    0164  11--        JLT   HRC2AB        IF LESS THAN >30, ABORT
0304    0166  0289        CI    R9,>A00       TEST FOR NUMERIC
        0168  0A00
0305    016A  11--        JLT   NOHAJ         IF NUMERIC, SKIP
0306    016C  0229        AI    R9,->700      ELSE, SUBTRACT ALPHA BIAS
        016E  F900
0307    0170  0289        CI    R9,>A00       IF LESS THAN >41, ABORT
        0172  0A00
0308    0174  11--        JLT   HRC2AB
0309    0176  0289        CI    R9,>FFF       COMPARE TO ASCII F
        0178  0FFF
0310    017A  15--        JGT   HRC2AB        IF GREATER THAN, ABORT
0311    017C  F289  NOHAJ SOCB  R9,R10        STORE HEX VALUE IN
        016A**1109
0312                 *                        ACCUMULATOR
0313    017E  0588        INC   R8            INCREMENT CHARACTER COUNT
0314    0180  16--        JNE   HRC2ND        IF NOT 0, SKIP
0315    0182  0A4A        SLA   R10,4         SHIFT HEX ACCUMULATOR
0316    0184  10E4        JMP   HRC2LP        FETCH SECOND CHARACTER
0317    0186  D6CA  HRC2ND MOVB R10,*R11      STORE HEX VALUE
        0180**1602
0318                 *                        AT SPECIFIED LOCATION
0319    0188  0380  HRC2RT RTWP                RETURN
        015E**1314
0320    018A  C3AD  HRC2AB MOV  @20(R13),R14  MODIFY RETURN PC
        018C  0014
        0164**1112
        0174**110A
        017A**1507
0321    018E  10FC        JMP   HRC2RT        RETURN
```

Figure 32. Floppy Disk Control Program (Sheet 8 of 28)

FLOPPY DISK CONTROL PROGRAM   PAGE 0009

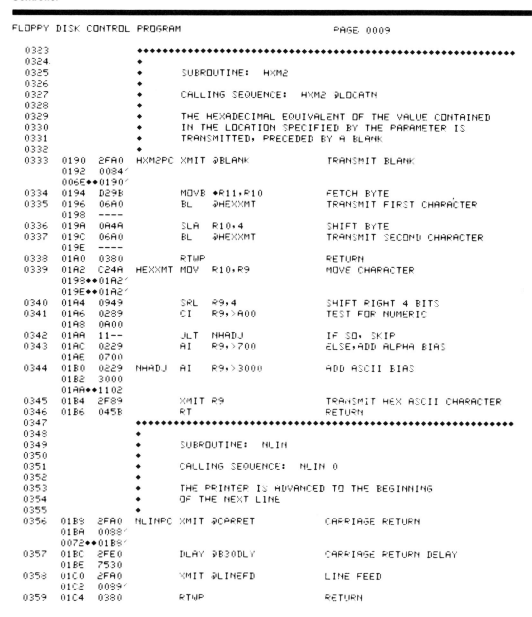

Figure 32. Floppy Disk Control Program (Sheet 9 of 28)

8-137

```
0361                   ◆◆◆◆◆◆◆◆◆◆◆◆◆◆◆◆◆◆◆◆◆◆◆◆◆◆◆◆◆◆◆◆◆◆◆◆◆◆◆◆◆◆◆◆◆◆◆◆◆◆◆◆◆◆◆◆◆◆
0362                   ◆
0363                   ◆        SUBROUTINE:   IDRD
0364                   ◆
0365                   ◆        CALLING SEQUENCE:   IDRD 0
0366                   ◆
0367                   ◆        EACH ID FIELD OF THE CURRENT DISKETTE TRACK
0368                   ◆        IS READ UNTIL THE ID FIELD WITH THE CORRECT
0369                   ◆        TRACK, SECTOR, AND CRC IS FOUND, AT WHICH
0370                   ◆        TIME THE ROUTINE IS EXITED.  IF THE CORRECT
0371                   ◆        FIELD IS NOT FOUND WITHIN A COMPLETE DISK
0372                   ◆        REVOLUTION (IE BEFORE 2 INDEX PULSES ARE
0373                   ◆        DETECTED), THE OPERATION IS ABORTED AND AN
0374                   ◆        ERROR MESSAGE IS REPORTED.
0375                   ◆
0376     01C6   2DC0   IDRDPC CRCI  0                   UPDATE ID FIELD IMAGE CRC
         004A◆◆01C6
0377     01C8   2D40          DSON  0                   TURN ON DRIVE
0378     01CA   0209          LI    R9,2               INITIALIZE INDEX PULSE COUNT
         01CC   0002
0379     01CE   020A   IDMRD  LI    R10,IDFLD           SET POINTER TO ID FIELD
         01D0   30F7
0380     01D2   9EA0          CB    @MRKRD,◆R10+        COMPARE DISK BYTE TO
         01D4   7FF8
0381                   ◆                                MARK CHARACTER
0382     01D6   13--          JEQ   MRKFND             IF MARK, CONTINUE
0383     01D8   1F04          TB    INDEX              ELSE, TEST FOR INDEX SIGNAL
0384     01DA   16F9          JNE   IDMRD              IF NO INDEX, REREAD DISK
0385     01DC   0609          DEC   R9                 IF INDEX,DECREMENT INDEX COUNT
0386     01DE   16F7          JNE   IDMRD              IF NOT 0, REREAD DISK
0387     01E0   2C60          ERPT  @NIDMSG            ELSE, REPORT ID READ ERROR
         01E2   0004
0388     01E4   0209   MRKFND LI    R9,6               LOAD BYTE COUNT
         01E6   0006
         01D6◆◆1306
0389     01E8   983A   IDRDLP CB    ◆R10+,@DTARD       COMPARE DISK DATA
         01EA   7FFC
0390                   ◆                                TO ID FIELD IMAGE
0391     01EC   16F0          JNE   IDMRD              IF NOT EQUAL, START OVER
0392     01EE   0609          DEC   R9                 DECREMENT BYTE COUNT
0393     01F0   16FB          JNE   IDRDLP             IF NOT 0, READ NEXT BYTE
0394     01F2   0380          RTWP                     ELSE, ID FOUND, RETURN
```

Figure 32. Floppy Disk Control Program (Sheet 10 of 28)

```
FLOPPY DISK CONTROL PROGRAM                          PAGE 0011
 0396                    ◆◆◆◆◆◆◆◆◆◆◆◆◆◆◆◆◆◆◆◆◆◆◆◆◆◆◆◆◆◆◆◆◆◆◆◆◆◆◆◆◆◆◆◆◆◆◆◆◆◆◆
 0397                    ◆
 0398                    ◆      SUBROUTINE:   ERPT
 0399                    ◆
 0400                    ◆      CALLING SEQUENCE:   ERPT @MESSAGE
 0401                    ◆
 0402                    ◆      THE MESSAGE WHOSE ADDRESS IS CONTAINED IN R11
 0403                    ◆      WHEN THE ROUTINE IS ENTERED IS PRINTED,
 0404                    ◆      FOLLOWED BY THE CURRENT TRACK AND SECTOR
 0405                    ◆      NUMBER.  THE DRIVE IS TURNED OFF AND CONTROL
 0406                    ◆      IS RETURNED TO THE COMMAND ENTRY PROGRAM.
 0407                    ◆
 0408   01F4  2F00  ERPTPC NLIN 0                    NEW LINE
        0046◆◆01F4'
 0409   01F6  2D9B         AXMT ◆R11                 PRINT SELECTED MESSAGE
 0410   01F8  2DA0         AXMT @TKMSG               PRINT TRACK MESSAGE
        01FA  008A'
 0411   01FC  2EE0         HXM2 @TKNUM               PRINT TRACK NUMBER
        01FE  80F8
 0412   0200  2DA0         AXMT @SCTMSG              PRINT SECTOR MESSAGE
        0202  009A'
 0413   0204  2EE0         HXM2 @SECNUM              PRINT SECTOR NUMBER
        0206  80FA
 0414   0208  1E04         SBZ  SEL                  TURN OFF DISK DRIVE
 0415   020A  0420         BLWP @RTRNVC              RETURN TO COMMAND
        020C  0142'
 0416                    ◆                           ENTRY PROGRAM
```

Figure 32. Floppy Disk Control Program (Sheet 11 of 28)

FLOPPY DISK CONTROL PROGRAM   PAGE 0012

```
0418                ◆◆◆◆◆◆◆◆◆◆◆◆◆◆◆◆◆◆◆◆◆◆◆◆◆◆◆◆◆◆◆◆◆◆◆◆◆◆◆◆◆◆◆◆◆◆◆◆◆◆◆◆◆◆◆◆◆
0419                ◆
0420                ◆       SUBROUTINE:   AXMT
0421                ◆
0422                ◆       CALLING SEQUENCE:   AXMT @MESSAGE
0423                ◆
0424                ◆       THE ASCII CHARACTER STRING, THE
0425                ◆       BEGINNING ADDRESS OF WHICH IS CONTAINED
0426                ◆       IN R11, IS TRANSMITTED.  THE END OF THE
0427                ◆       STRING IS INDICATED BY A NON-PRINTABLE
0428                ◆       CHARACTER (IE LESS THAN HEX 20)
0429                ◆
0430   020E  020A  AXMTPC LI    R10,80            LOAD MAX CHARACTERS
       0210  0050
       005A◆◆020E
0431                ◆                             PER LINE
0432   0212  D27B  AXMTLP MOVB  ◆R11+,R9          FETCH CHARACTER
0433   0214  9809         CB    R9,@BLANK         PRINTABLE CHARACTER?
       0216  0084
0434   0218  11--         JLT   AXMTRT            IF NOT, RETURN
0435   021A  2F89         XMIT  R9                ELSE, PRINT CHARACTER
0436   021C  060A         DEC   R10               DECREMENT MAX CHAR COUNT
0437   021E  16F9         JNE   AXMTLP            IF NOT 0, FETCH NEXT CHAR
0438   0220  981B         CB    ◆R11,@BLANK       ELSE, IS NEXT CHAR
       0222  0084
0439                ◆                             PRINTABLE?
0440   0224  11--         JLT   AXMTRT            IF NOT, RETURN
0441   0226  2F00         NLIN  0                 NEW LINE
0442   0228  10F4         JMP   AXMTLP            PRINT REST OF STRING
0443   022A  0380  AXMTRT RTWP                    STRING PRINTED, RETURN
       0218◆◆1108
       0224◆◆1102
```

Figure 32. Floppy Disk Control Program (Sheet 12 of 28)

FLOPPY DISK CONTROL PROGRAM   PAGE 0013

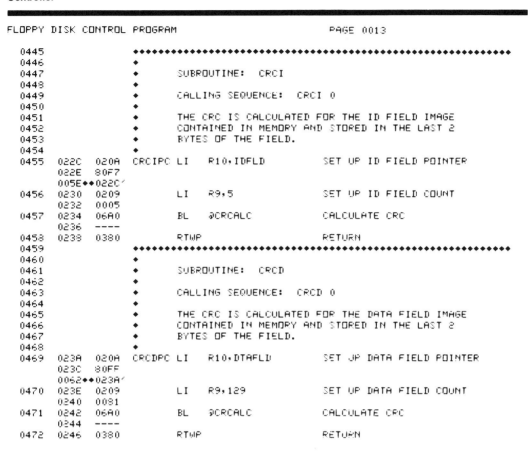

```
0445          ◆◆◆◆◆◆◆◆◆◆◆◆◆◆◆◆◆◆◆◆◆◆◆◆◆◆◆◆◆◆◆◆◆◆◆◆◆◆◆◆◆◆◆◆◆◆◆◆◆◆◆◆◆
0446          ◆
0447          ◆        SUBROUTINE:  CRCI
0448          ◆
0449          ◆        CALLING SEQUENCE:  CRCI 0
0450          ◆
0451          ◆        THE CRC IS CALCULATED FOR THE ID FIELD IMAGE
0452          ◆        CONTAINED IN MEMORY AND STORED IN THE LAST 2
0453          ◆        BYTES OF THE FIELD.
0454          ◆
0455  022C  020A  CRCIPC LI   R10,IDFLD      SET UP ID FIELD POINTER
      022E  80F7
      005E◆◆022C
0456  0230  0209         LI   R9,5           SET UP ID FIELD COUNT
      0232  0005
0457  0234  06A0         BL   @CRCALC        CALCULATE CRC
      0236  ----
0458  0238  0380         RTWP                RETURN
0459          ◆◆◆◆◆◆◆◆◆◆◆◆◆◆◆◆◆◆◆◆◆◆◆◆◆◆◆◆◆◆◆◆◆◆◆◆◆◆◆◆◆◆◆◆◆◆◆◆◆◆◆◆◆
0460          ◆
0461          ◆        SUBROUTINE:  CRCD
0462          ◆
0463          ◆        CALLING SEQUENCE:  CRCD 0
0464          ◆
0465          ◆        THE CRC IS CALCULATED FOR THE DATA FIELD IMAGE
0466          ◆        CONTAINED IN MEMORY AND STORED IN THE LAST 2
0467          ◆        BYTES OF THE FIELD.
0468          ◆
0469  023A  020A  CRCDPC LI   R10,DTAFLD     SET UP DATA FIELD POINTER
      023C  80FF
      0062◆◆023A
0470  023E  0209         LI   R9,129         SET UP DATA FIELD COUNT
      0240  0031
0471  0242  06A0         BL   @CRCALC        CALCULATE CRC
      0244  ----
0472  0246  0380         RTWP                RETURN
```

Figure 32. Floppy Disk Control Program (Sheet 13 of 28)

FLOPPY DISK CONTROL PROGRAM   PAGE 0014

```
0474                      ◆◆◆◆◆◆◆◆◆◆◆◆◆◆◆◆◆◆◆◆◆◆◆◆◆◆◆◆◆◆◆◆◆◆◆◆◆◆◆◆◆◆◆◆◆◆◆◆◆◆◆◆
0475                      ◆
0476                      ◆      SUBROUTINE:   CRCALC
0477                      ◆
0478                      ◆      CALLING SEQUENCE:   LI   R10,FLDADD
0479                      ◆                          LI   R9,FLDCNT
0480                      ◆                          BL   @CRCALC
0481                      ◆
0482                      ◆      THE CYCLIC REDUNDANCY CHECK CHARACTER (CRC) FOR
0483                      ◆      THE FIELD ADDRESSED BY R10 IS CALCULATED
0484                      ◆      AND STORED IN THE LAST 2 BYTES OF THE
0485                      ◆      FIELD.   THE LENGTH OF THE FIELD (EXCLUDING CRC)
0486                      ◆      IS SPECIFIED BY R9.   THE CRC POLYNOMIAL IS
0487                      ◆      X◆◆16+X◆◆12+X◆◆5+1.   BEFORE CRC CALCULATION
0488                      ◆      BEGINS, THE PARTIAL CRC IS PRESET TO ALL ONES.
0489                      ◆      R7, R8, R9, AND R10 ARE DESTROYED.
0490                      ◆
0491   0248   0708  CRCALC SETO R8                    PRESET PARTIAL CRC
       0236◆◆0248'
       0244◆◆0248'
0492   024A   04C7  CRCLP  CLR  R7                    CLEAR SCRATCH REGISTER
0493   024C   D1FA         MOVB ◆R10+,R7              FETCH NEXT BYTE
0494   024E   2A07         XOR  R7,R8                 XOR NEW BYTE WITH CRC
0495   0250   C1C8         MOV  R8,R7                 MOVE TO SCRATCH REG
0496   0252   0947         SRL  R7,4                  SHIFT SCRATCH RIGHT 4
0497   0254   29C8         XOR  R8,R7                 XOR CRC WITH SCRATCH
0498   0256   0247         ANDI R7,>FF00              MASK OFF LOWER BYTE
       0258   FF00
0499   025A   0947         SRL  R7,4                  SHIFT SCRATCH RIGHT 4
0500   025C   2A07         XOR  R7,R8                 XOR SCRATCH WITH CRC
0501   025E   0B77         SRC  R7,7                  ROTATE SCRATCH RIGHT 7
0502   0260   2A07         XOR  R7,R8                 XOR SCRATCH WITH CRC
0503   0262   06C8         SWPB R8                    REVERSE BYTES IN CRC
0504   0264   0609         DEC  R9                    DECREMENT BYTE COUNT
0505   0266   16F1         JNE  CRCLP                 IF NOT 0, FETCH NEXT BYTE
0506   0268   DE88         MOVB R8,◆R10+              ELSE, TRANSFER
0507   026A   06C8         SWPB R8                    CRC TO THE END
0508   026C   D688         MOVB R8,◆R10               OF THE FIELD
0509   026E   045B         RT                         RETURN
```

Figure 32. Floppy Disk Control Program (Sheet 14 of 28)

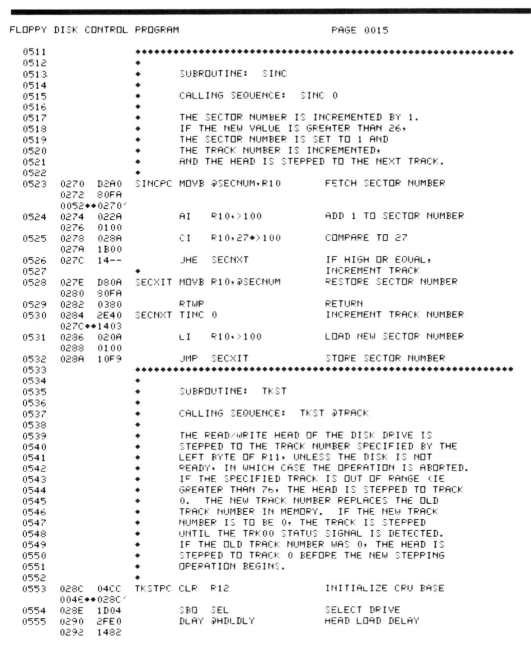

```
FLOPPY DISK CONTROL PROGRAM                           PAGE 0015
0511                    ◆◆◆◆◆◆◆◆◆◆◆◆◆◆◆◆◆◆◆◆◆◆◆◆◆◆◆◆◆◆◆◆◆◆◆◆◆◆◆◆◆◆◆◆◆◆◆◆◆◆◆◆◆◆◆
0512                    ◆
0513                    ◆       SUBROUTINE:  SINC
0514                    ◆
0515                    ◆       CALLING SEQUENCE:  SINC 0
0516                    ◆
0517                    ◆       THE SECTOR NUMBER IS INCREMENTED BY 1.
0518                    ◆       IF THE NEW VALUE IS GREATER THAN 26,
0519                    ◆       THE SECTOR NUMBER IS SET TO 1 AND
0520                    ◆       THE TRACK NUMBER IS INCREMENTED,
0521                    ◆       AND THE HEAD IS STEPPED TO THE NEXT TRACK.
0522                    ◆
0523   0270  D2A0  SINCPC MOVB @SECNUM,R10      FETCH SECTOR NUMBER
       0272  80FA
       0052◆◆0270´
0524   0274  022A      AI    R10,>100          ADD 1 TO SECTOR NUMBER
       0276  0100
0525   0278  028A      CI    R10,27◆>100       COMPARE TO 27
       027A  1B00
0526   027C  14--      JHE   SECNXT            IF HIGH OR EQUAL,
0527                   ◆                        INCREMENT TRACK
0528   027E  D80A  SECXIT MOVB R10,@SECNUM      RESTORE SECTOR NUMBER
       0280  80FA
0529   0282  0380      RTWP                    RETURN
0530   0284  2E40  SECNXT TINC 0                INCREMENT TRACK NUMBER
       027C◆◆1403
0531   0286  020A      LI    R10,>100          LOAD NEW SECTOR NUMBER
       0288  0100
0532   028A  10F9      JMP   SECXIT            STORE SECTOR NUMBER
0533                    ◆◆◆◆◆◆◆◆◆◆◆◆◆◆◆◆◆◆◆◆◆◆◆◆◆◆◆◆◆◆◆◆◆◆◆◆◆◆◆◆◆◆◆◆◆◆◆◆◆◆◆◆◆◆◆
0534                    ◆
0535                    ◆       SUBROUTINE:  TKST
0536                    ◆
0537                    ◆       CALLING SEQUENCE:  TKST @TRACK
0538                    ◆
0539                    ◆       THE READ/WRITE HEAD OF THE DISK DRIVE IS
0540                    ◆       STEPPED TO THE TRACK NUMBER SPECIFIED BY THE
0541                    ◆       LEFT BYTE OF R11, UNLESS THE DISK IS NOT
0542                    ◆       READY, IN WHICH CASE THE OPERATION IS ABORTED.
0543                    ◆       IF THE SPECIFIED TRACK IS OUT OF RANGE (IE
0544                    ◆       GREATER THAN 76, THE HEAD IS STEPPED TO TRACK
0545                    ◆       0.  THE NEW TRACK NUMBER REPLACES THE OLD
0546                    ◆       TRACK NUMBER IN MEMORY.  IF THE NEW TRACK
0547                    ◆       NUMBER IS TO BE 0, THE TRACK IS STEPPED
0548                    ◆       UNTIL THE TRK00 STATUS SIGNAL IS DETECTED.
0549                    ◆       IF THE OLD TRACK NUMBER WAS 0, THE HEAD IS
0550                    ◆       STEPPED TO TRACK 0 BEFORE THE NEW STEPPING
0551                    ◆       OPERATION BEGINS.
0552                    ◆
0553   028C  04CC  TKSTPC CLR  R12              INITIALIZE CRU BASE
       004E◆◆028C´
0554   028E  1D04      SBO   SEL               SELECT DRIVE
0555   0290  2FE0      DLAY  @HDLDLY           HEAD LOAD DELAY
       0292  1482
```

Figure 32. Floppy Disk Control Program (Sheet 15 of 28)

```
FLOPPY DISK CONTROL PROGRAM                                PAGE 0016

0556  0294  1F07            TB    RDY           CHECK DRIVE STATUS
0557  0296  13--            JEQ   TKCNTU        IF READY, CONTINUE
0558  0298  2C60            ERPT  @NRDYMS       ELSE, REPORT ERROR
      029A  0025'
0559  029C  C24B  TKCNTU MOV    R11,R9          SAVE NEW TRACK NUMBER
      0296♦♦1302
0560  029E  0989            SRL   R9,8          TO RIGHT BYTE OF R9
0561  02A0  13--            JEQ   TKTOO         IF 0, CLEAR TRACK
0562  02A2  0289            CI    R9,76         NEW TRACK NUMBER IN RANGE?
      02A4  004C
0563  02A6  12--            JLE   TKNZRO        IS SO, SKIP
0564  02A8  04C9            CLR   R9            ELSE, CLEAR NEW TRACK NUMBER
0565  02AA  06A0  TKTOO  BL    @TKCLR          STEP TO TRACK 00
      02AC  ----
      02A0♦♦1304
0566  02AE  10--            JMP   TKSTRT        RETURN
0567  02B0  D2A0  TKNZRO MOVB  @TKNUM,R10      FETCH OLD TRACK NUMBER
      02B2  80F8
      02A6♦♦1204
0568  02B4  098A            SRL   R10,8         MOVE TO RIGHT BYTE
0569  02B6  16--            JNE   TKNZR1        IF NOT 00, CONTINUE
0570  02B8  06A0            BL    @TKCLR        ELSE, STEP TO TRACK 00
      02BA  ----
0571  02BC  8289  TKNZR1 C     R9,R10          COMPARE NEW TRACK
      02B6♦♦1602
0572                        ♦                   TO OLD TRACK NUMBER
0573  02BE  11--            JLT   STPOUT        IF LESS THAN, STEP OUT 1 TRACK
0574  02C0  13--            JEQ   TKSTRT        IF EQUAL, RETURN
0575  02C2  1D07            SBO   STEPUP        ELSE, STEP IN 1 TRACK
0576  02C4  058A            INC   R10           INCREMENT OLD TRACK
0577  02C6  10--            JMP   TKGO          STEP HEAD
0578  02C8  1E07  STPOUT SBZ   STEPUP          SELECT STEP OUT
      02BE♦♦1104
0579  02CA  060A            DEC   R10           DECREMENT OLD TRACK
0580  02CC  06A0  TKGO   BL    @TKSTEP         STEP HEAD
      02CE  ----
      02C6♦♦1002
0581  02D0  10F5            JMP   TKNZR1        REPEAT FOR NEXT STEP
0582  02D2  06C9  TKSTRT SWPB  R9              MOVE NEW TRACK NUMBER
      02AE♦♦1011
      02C0♦♦1308
0583                        ♦                   TO LEFT BYTE
0584  02D4  D809            MOVB  R9,@TKNUM     UPDATE TRACK NUMBER
      02D6  80F8
0585  02D8  0380            RTWP                RETURN
```

Figure 32. Floppy Disk Control Program (Sheet 16 of 28)

FLOPPY DISK CONTROL PROGRAM   PAGE 0017

```
0587              ◆◆◆◆◆◆◆◆◆◆◆◆◆◆◆◆◆◆◆◆◆◆◆◆◆◆◆◆◆◆◆◆◆◆◆◆◆◆◆◆◆◆◆◆◆◆◆◆◆◆◆◆
0588              ◆
0589              ◆        SUBROUTINE:   TKCLR
0590              ◆
0591              ◆        CALLING SEQUENCE:   BL   ∂TKCLR
0592              ◆
0593              ◆        THE READ/WRITE HEAD IS STEPPED OUT UNTIL
0594              ◆        THE TRK00 STATUS SIGNAL BECOMES ACTIVE.
0595              ◆        THE CONTENTS OF R8 AND R11 ARE DESTROYED.
0596              ◆
0597   02DA  C20B  TKCLR   MOV   R11,R8            SAVE RETURN LINKAGE
       02AC◆◆02DA´
       02BA◆◆02DA´
0598   02DC  1F07  TKCLP   TB    RDY               TEST DRIVE STATUS
0599   02DE  16--          JNE   TKCABT            IF NOT READY, ABORT
0600   02E0  1F06          TB    TRK00             TEST TRACK 00 STATUS SIGNAL
0601   02E2  16--          JNE   TKICNT            IF NOT ACTIVE,CONTINUE
0602   02E4  0458          B     ◆R8               ELSE, RETURN
0603   02E6  1E07  TKICNT  SBZ   STEPUP            SET TO STEP OUT
       02E2◆◆1601
0604   02E8  06A0          BL    ∂TKSTEP           STEP HEAD
       02EA  ----
0605   02EC  10F7          JMP   TKCLP             CONTINUE LOOP
0606   02EE  04C8  TKCABT  CLR   R8                SET TRACK
       02DE◆◆1607
0607   02F0  D808          MOVB  R8,∂TKNUM         NUMBER TO 00
       02F2  80F8
0608   02F4  2C60          ERPT  ∂NRDYMS           REPORT ERROR AND ABORT
       02F6  0025´
0609              ◆◆◆◆◆◆◆◆◆◆◆◆◆◆◆◆◆◆◆◆◆◆◆◆◆◆◆◆◆◆◆◆◆◆◆◆◆◆◆◆◆◆◆◆◆◆◆◆◆◆◆◆
0610              ◆
0611              ◆        SUBROUTINE:   TKSTEP
0612              ◆
0613              ◆        CALLING SEQUENCE:   BL   ∂TKSTEP
0614              ◆
0615              ◆        THE STEP PULSE IS GENERATED FOR 11.3
0616              ◆        MICROSECONDS AND THE HEAD STEP DELAY
0617              ◆        IS OBSERVED.
0618              ◆
0619   02F8  1D06  TKSTEP  SBO   STEP              SET STEP SIGNAL
       02CE◆◆02F8´
       02EA◆◆02F8´
0620   02FA  1000          NOP                     DUMMY DELAY
0621   02FC  1E06          SBZ   STEP              RESET STEP SIGNAL
0622   02FE  2FE0          DLAY  ∂HSDLY            DELAY FOR HEAD STEP
       0300  05DC
0623   0302  045B          RT                      RETURN
```

Figure 32. Floppy Disk Control Program (Sheet 17 of 28)

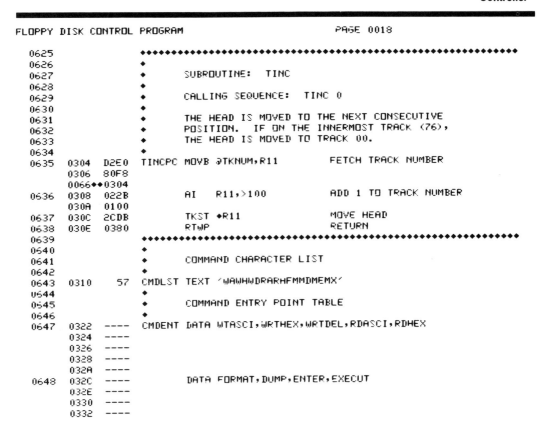

```
FLOPPY DISK CONTROL PROGRAM                                    PAGE 0018

  0625              ◆◆◆◆◆◆◆◆◆◆◆◆◆◆◆◆◆◆◆◆◆◆◆◆◆◆◆◆◆◆◆◆◆◆◆◆◆◆◆◆◆◆◆◆◆◆◆◆◆◆◆◆◆◆◆◆◆◆◆
  0626              ◆
  0627              ◆        SUBROUTINE:   TINC
  0628              ◆
  0629              ◆        CALLING SEQUENCE:   TINC 0
  0630              ◆
  0631              ◆        THE HEAD IS MOVED TO THE NEXT CONSECUTIVE
  0632              ◆        POSITION.   IF ON THE INNERMOST TRACK (76),
  0633              ◆        THE HEAD IS MOVED TO TRACK 00.
  0634              ◆
  0635   0304  D2E0  TINCPC MOVB  @TKNUM,R11        FETCH TRACK NUMBER
         0306  80F8
         0066◆◆0304
  0636   0308  022B         AI    R11,>100         ADD 1 TO TRACK NUMBER
         030A  0100
  0637   030C  2CDB         TKST  ◆R11             MOVE HEAD
  0638   030E  0380         RTWP                   RETURN
  0639              ◆◆◆◆◆◆◆◆◆◆◆◆◆◆◆◆◆◆◆◆◆◆◆◆◆◆◆◆◆◆◆◆◆◆◆◆◆◆◆◆◆◆◆◆◆◆◆◆◆◆◆◆◆◆◆◆◆◆◆
  0640              ◆
  0641              ◆        COMMAND CHARACTER LIST
  0642              ◆
  0643   0310   57  CMDLST TEXT  'WAWHWDRARHFMMDMEMX'
  0644              ◆
  0645              ◆        COMMAND ENTRY POINT TABLE
  0646              ◆
  0647   0322  ----  CMDENT DATA  WTASCI,WRTHEX,WRTDEL,RDASCI,RDHEX
         0324  ----
         0326  ----
         0328  ----
         032A  ----
  0648   032C  ----         DATA  FORMAT,DUMP,ENTER,EXECUT
         032E  ----
         0330  ----
         0332  ----
```

Figure 32. Floppy Disk Control Program (Sheet 18 of 28)

FLOPPY DISK CONTROL PROGRAM   PAGE 0019

```
0650              ◆◆◆◆◆◆◆◆◆◆◆◆◆◆◆◆◆◆◆◆◆◆◆◆◆◆◆◆◆◆◆◆◆◆◆◆◆◆◆◆◆◆◆◆◆◆◆◆◆◆◆◆◆◆◆
0651              ◆
0652              ◆     POWER-ON RESET ENTRY POINT
0653              ◆
0654  0334  04CC  START  CLR   R12            INITIALIZE CRU BASE
      0002◆◆0334´
0655  0336  020B         LI    R11,>300       LOAD CRU INITIALIZATION VALUE
      0338  0300
0656  033A  320B         LDCR  R11,8          AND OUTPUT TO CRU
0657  033C  020B         LI    R11,IDFLD      SET ID FIELD IMAGE POINTER
      033E  80F7
0658  0340  020A         LI    R10,>100       SET INITIAL SECTOR VALUE
      0342  0100
0659  0344  DEE0         MOVB  @IDMRK,◆R11+   ID MARK DATA PATTERN TO
      0346  00D0´
0660              ◆                           FIRST BYTE OF ID FIELD IMAGE
0661  0348  DECC         MOVB  R12,◆R11+      0 TO SECOND BYTE
0662              ◆                           (TRACK NUMBER)
0663  034A  DECC         MOVB  R12,◆R11+      0 TO THIRD BYTE
0664  034C  DECA         MOVB  R10,◆R11+      01 TO FOURTH BYTE
0665              ◆                           (SECTOR NUMBER)
0666  034E  D6CC         MOVB  R12,◆R11       0 TO FIFTH BYTE
0667  0350  2CDC         TKST  ◆R12           SET READ/WRITE HEAD TO TRACK 0
0668  0352  1E04         SBZ   SEL            TURN OFF DRIVE
0669              ◆◆◆◆◆◆◆◆◆◆◆◆◆◆◆◆◆◆◆◆◆◆◆◆◆◆◆◆◆◆◆◆◆◆◆◆◆◆◆◆◆◆◆◆◆◆◆◆◆◆◆◆◆◆◆
0670              ◆
0671              ◆     OPERATOR COMMAND REQUEST ENTRY POINT
0672              ◆
0673  0354  2F00  TOP    NLIN  0              NEW LINE
      0144◆◆0354´
0674  0356  2FA0         XMIT  @QUEST         PRINT PROMPTING MESSAGE
      0358  0085´
0675  035A  2FA0         XMIT  @BELL          (QUESTION MARK, BELL)
      035C  0086´
0676  035E  2F4A         RECV  R10            READ FIRST CHARACTER
0677              ◆                           OF COMMAND
0678  0360  06CA         SWPB  R10            SAVE IN RIGHT BYTE
0679  0362  2F4A         RECV  R10            READ SECOND CHARACTER
0680              ◆                           OF COMMAND
0681  0364  06CA         SWPB  R10            REVERSE CHARACTERS IN R10
0682  0366  0208         LI    R8,CMDLST      SET COMMAND LIST POINTER
      0368  0310´
0683  036A  0209         LI    R9,CMDENT-2    SET COMMAND ENTRY POINTER
      036C  0320´
0684  036E  C1F8  CMDLP  MOV   ◆R8+,R7        FETCH COMMAND IN LIST
0685  0370  13F1         JEQ   TOP            IF LIST VALUE = 0, NOT
0686              ◆                           A LEGAL COMMAND
0687  0372  05C9         INCT  R9             INCREMENT ENTRY POINTER
0688  0374  81CA         C     R10,R7         COMPARE ENTERED COMMAND
0689              ◆                           TO LIST
0690  0376  16FB         JNE   CMDLP          IF NOT EQUAL, REPEAT
0691  0378  C259         MOV   ◆R9,R9         ELSE, COMMAND FOUND,
0692              ◆                           FETCH ENTRY POINT
0693  037A  020A         LI    R10,TOP        COMMAND PROGRAM RETURN
```

Figure 32. Floppy Disk Control Program (Sheet 19 of 28)

FLOPPY DISK CONTROL PROGRAM   PAGE 0020

```
            037C   0354'
     0694                      ◆                             ADDRESS
     0695   037E   9807         CB    R7,@ASCIIM            TEST FOR MD,ME, OR
            0380   0092'
     0696                      ◆                             MX COMMANDS
     0697   0382   13--         JEQ   ADDFCH                IF SO, FETCH ADDRESS ENTRY
     0698   0384   2DA0         AXMT  @TKMSG                PRINT TRACK MESSAGE
            0386   008A'
     0699   0388   D220         MOVB  @TKNUM,R8             FETCH CURRENT TRACK
            038A   80F8
     0700                      ◆                             NUMBER
     0701   038C   2EC8         HXM2  R8                    PRINT TRACK NUMBER
     0702   038E   2E88         HRC2  R8                    READ NEW TRACK NUMBER
     0703   0390   0288         CI    R8,77◆256             NEW TRACK NUMBER LEGAL?
            0392   4D00
     0704   0394   14DF         JHE   TOP                   IF NOT, ABORT
     0705   0396   2CD8         TKST  ◆R8                   STEP HEAD TO NEW TRACK
     0706   0398   1E04         SBZ   SEL                   TURN OFF DRIVE
     0707   039A   9807         CB    R7,@ASCIIF            FORMAT COMMAND?
            039C   0081'
     0708   039E   16--         JNE   SECFCH                IF NOT, CONTINUE
     0709   03A0   0459         B     ◆R9                   ELSE, EXECUTE COMMAND
     0710   03A2   2DA0  SECFCH AXMT  @SCTMSG               PRINT SECTOR MESSAGE
            03A4   009A'
            039E◆◆1601
     0711   03A6   D1A0         MOVB  @SECNUM,R6            FETCH CURRENT SECTOR
            03A8   80FA
     0712   03AA   2EC6         HXM2  R6                    PRINT CURRENT SECTOR
     0713   03AC   2E86         HRC2  R6                    READ NEW SECTOR NUMBER
     0714   03AE   0286         CI    R6,>100               LESS THAN 1
            03B0   0100
     0715   03B2   11D0         JLT   TOP                   IF SO, ABORT
     0716   03B4   0286         CI    R6,27◆256             GREATER THAN 26?
            03B6   1B00
     0717   03B8   14CD         JHE   TOP                   IF SO, ABORT
     0718   03BA   D806         MOVB  R6,@SECNUM            UPDATE SECTOR NUMBER
            03BC   80FA
     0719   03BE   2DA0         AXMT  @NUMMSG               PRINT NUMBER MESSAGE
            03C0   00A5'
     0720   03C2   0205         LI    R5,>100               LOAD DEFAULT NUMBER
            03C4   0100
     0721   03C6   2E85         HRC2  R5                    READ NUMBER
     0722   03C8   0985         SRL   R5,8                  MOVE TO RIGHT BYTE
     0723   03CA   13C4         JEQ   TOP                   IF NUMBER = 0, ABORT
     0724   03CC   0459         B     ◆R9                   EXECUTE COMMAND
     0725   03CE   0208  ADDFCH LI    R8,>8000              LOAD DEFAULT ADDRESS
            03D0   8000
            0382◆◆1325
     0726   03D2   2E88         HRC2  R8                    READ FIRST BYTE OF ADDRESS
     0727   03D4   06C8         SWPB  R8                    SAVE IN RIGHT BYTE
     0728   03D6   2FA0         XMIT  @BACKSP               BACKSPACE PRINTER
            03D8   0087'
     0729   03DA   2E88         HRC2  R8                    READ SECOND BYTE OF ADDRESS
     0730   03DC   06C8         SWPB  R8                    CORRECT ADDRESS BYTES
     0731   03DE   0459         B     ◆R9                   EXECUTE COMMAND
```

Figure 32. Floppy Disk Control Program (Sheet 20 of 28)

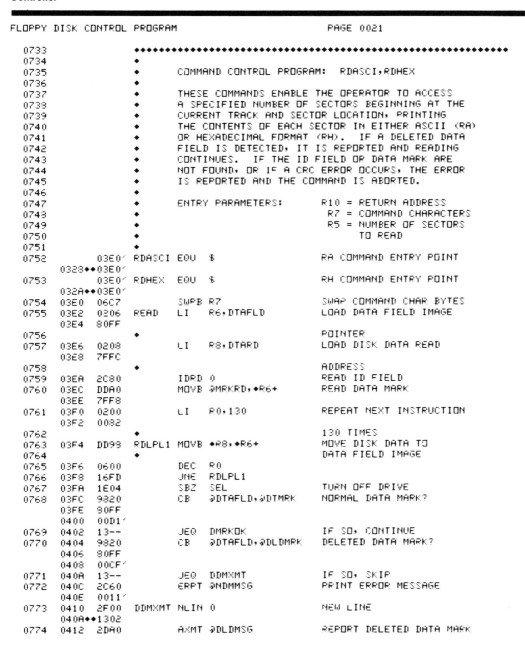

FLOPPY DISK CONTROL PROGRAM   PAGE 0021

```
0733          ◆◆◆◆◆◆◆◆◆◆◆◆◆◆◆◆◆◆◆◆◆◆◆◆◆◆◆◆◆◆◆◆◆◆◆◆◆◆◆◆◆◆◆◆◆◆◆◆◆◆◆
0734          ◆
0735          ◆      COMMAND CONTROL PROGRAM:  RDASCI,RDHEX
0736          ◆
0737          ◆      THESE COMMANDS ENABLE THE OPERATOR TO ACCESS
0738          ◆      A SPECIFIED NUMBER OF SECTORS BEGINNING AT THE
0739          ◆      CURRENT TRACK AND SECTOR LOCATION, PRINTING
0740          ◆      THE CONTENTS OF EACH SECTOR IN EITHER ASCII (RA)
0741          ◆      OR HEXADECIMAL FORMAT (RH).  IF A DELETED DATA
0742          ◆      FIELD IS DETECTED, IT IS REPORTED AND READING
0743          ◆      CONTINUES.  IF THE ID FIELD OR DATA MARK ARE
0744          ◆      NOT FOUND, OR IF A CRC ERROR OCCURS, THE ERROR
0745          ◆      IS REPORTED AND THE COMMAND IS ABORTED.
0746          ◆
0747          ◆      ENTRY PARAMETERS:      R10 = RETURN ADDRESS
0748          ◆                             R7 = COMMAND CHARACTERS
0749          ◆                             R5 = NUMBER OF SECTORS
0750          ◆                                  TO READ
0751          ◆
0752      03E0′ RDASCI EQU   $              RA COMMAND ENTRY POINT
     0328◆◆03E0′
0753      03E0′ RDHEX  EQU   $              RH COMMAND ENTRY POINT
     032A◆◆03E0′
0754 03E0 06C7       SWPB R7               SWAP COMMAND CHAR BYTES
0755 03E2 0206 READ  LI   R6,DTAFLD        LOAD DATA FIELD IMAGE
     03E4 80FF
0756          ◆                            POINTER
0757 03E6 0208       LI   R8,DTARD         LOAD DISK DATA READ
     03E8 7FFC
0758          ◆                            ADDRESS
0759 03EA 2C80       IDRD 0                READ ID FIELD
0760 03EC DDA0       MOVB @MRKRD,◆R6+      READ DATA MARK
     03EE 7FF8
0761 03F0 0200       LI   R0,130           REPEAT NEXT INSTRUCTION
     03F2 0082
0762          ◆                            130 TIMES
0763 03F4 DD98 RDLPL1 MOVB ◆R8,◆R6+        MOVE DISK DATA TO
0764          ◆                            DATA FIELD IMAGE
0765 03F6 0600       DEC  R0
0766 03F8 16FD       JNE  RDLPL1
0767 03FA 1E04       SBZ  SEL              TURN OFF DRIVE
0768 03FC 9820       CB   @DTAFLD,@DTMRK   NORMAL DATA MARK?
     03FE 80FF
     0400 00D1′
0769 0402 13--       JEQ  DMRKOK           IF SO, CONTINUE
0770 0404 9820       CB   @DTAFLD,@DLDMRK  DELETED DATA MARK?
     0406 80FF
     0408 00CF′
0771 040A 13--       JEQ  DDMXMT           IF SO, SKIP
0772 040C 2C60       ERPT @NDMMSG          PRINT ERROR MESSAGE
     040E 0011′
0773 0410 2F00 DDMXMT NLIN 0               NEW LINE
     040A◆◆1302
0774 0412 2DA0       AXMT @DLDMSG          REPORT DELETED DATA MARK
```

Figure 32. Floppy Disk Control Program (Sheet 21 of 28)

```
        0414  00BC'
0775    0416  C220   DMRKOK MOV   @DTACRC,R8       FETCH READ CRC
        0418  8180
        0402**1309
0776    041A  2E00          CRCD  0                RECALCULATE CRC
0777    041C  8220          C     @DTACRC,R8       CRC CORRECT?
        041E  8180
0778    0420  13--          JEQ   RDPRT            IF SO CONTINUE
0779    0422  2C60          ERPT  @CRCMSG          ELSE, REPORT ERROR
        0424  0035'
0780    0426  2F00   RDPRT  NLIN  0                NEW LINE
        0420**1302
0781    0428  04E0          CLR   @DTACRC          CLEAR END OF DATA
        042A  3180
0782          *                                    FIELD IMAGE
0783    042C  0206          LI    R6,DTABUF        LOAD FIELD IMAGE
        042E  8100
0784          *                                    POINTER
0785    0430  9807          CB    R7,@ASCIIA       RA COMMAND?
        0432  0080'
0786    0434  13--          JEQ   ASCIRD           IF SO, PRINT IN ASCII
0787          *                                    FORMAT
0788    0436  0209          LI    R9,8             LOAD LINE COUNT
        0438  0008
0789    043A  0208   HXPTLP LI    R8,16            LOAD BYTE COUNT
        043C  0010
0790    043E  2F00          NLIN  0                NEW LINE
0791    0440  2ED6   HXPLP1 HXM2  *R6              PRINT DATA BYTE
0792    0442  0586          INC   R6               INCREMENT DATA POINTER
0793    0444  0608          DEC   R8               DECREMENT BYTE COUNT
0794    0446  16FC          JNE   HXPLP1           IF NOT 0, PRINT NEXT BYTE
0795    0448  1F00          TB    RIN              OPERATOR INTERRUPT?
0796    044A  16--          JNE   READRT           IF SO, ABORT
0797    044C  0609          DEC   R9               DECREMENT LINE COUNT
0798    044E  16F5          JNE   HXPTLP           IF NOT 0, PRINT NEXT LINE
0799    0450  10--          JMP   NXTSCT           CONTINUE
0800    0452  2D96   ASCIRD AXMT  *R6              PRINT DATA FIELD
        0434**130E
0801          *                                    IN ASCII
0802    0454  2D00   NXTSCT SINC  0                UPDATE SECTOR NUMBER
        0450**1001
0803    0456  1F00          TB    RIN              OPERATOR INTERRUPT?
0804    0458  16--          JNE   READRT           IF SO, ABORT
0805    045A  0605          DEC   R5               DECREMENT SECTOR COUNT
0806    045C  16C2          JNE   READ             IF NOT 0, READ NEXT SECTOR
0807    045E  1E04   READRT SBZ   SEL              TURN OFF DRIVE
        044A**1609
        0458**1602
0808    0460  045A          B     *R10             RETURN
```

Figure 32. Floppy Disk Control Program (Sheet 22 of 28)

FLOPPY DISK CONTROL PROGRAM   PAGE 0023

```
0310               ◆◆◆◆◆◆◆◆◆◆◆◆◆◆◆◆◆◆◆◆◆◆◆◆◆◆◆◆◆◆◆◆◆◆◆◆◆◆◆◆◆◆◆◆◆◆◆◆◆◆◆◆◆◆◆◆◆◆
0311               ◆
0312               ◆       COMMAND CONTROL PROGRAM:  WRTHEX,WTASCI,WTDDTA
0313               ◆
0314               ◆       THESE COMMANDS ENABLE THE OPERATOR TO WRITE
0315               ◆       A SPECIFIED NUMBER OF SECTORS OF DATA BEGINNING
0316               ◆       AT THE CURRENT TRACK AND SECTOR LOCATION, IN
0317               ◆       EITHER ASCII (WA) OR HEXADECIMAL (WD,WH) FORMAT.
0318               ◆       THE WD COMMAND CAUSES A DELETED DATA MARK TO
0319               ◆       PRECEDE THE DATA, AND THE WA AND WH COMMANDS
0320               ◆       WRITE THE DATA MARK.  IF THE ID FIELD OF
0321               ◆       ANY SECTOR IS NOT FOUND, AN ERROR IS
0322               ◆       REPORTED.
0323               ◆
0324               ◆       ENTRY PARAMETERS:    R10 = RETURN ADDRESS
0325               ◆                            R7 = COMMAND CHARACTERS
0326               ◆                            R5 = NUMBER OF SECTORS
0327               ◆                                 TO WRITE
0328               ◆
0329   0462  D820  WRTDEL MOVB @DLDMRK,@DTAFLD  LOAD DELETED DATA MARK
       0464  00CF'
       0466  80FF
       0326◆◆0462'
0330   0468  10--         JMP  WRITE            CONTINUE
0331       046A' WRTHEX EQU  $                  WH COMMAND ENTRY POINT
       0324◆◆046A'
0332   046A  D820  WTASCI MOVB @DTMRK,@DTAFLD   LOAD DATA MARK
       046C  00D1'
       046E  80FF
       0322◆◆046A'
0333   0470  06C7  WRITE  SWPB R7               MOVE SECOND COMMAND
       0468◆◆1003
0334               ◆                            CHARACTER TO LEFT BYTE
0335   0472  0208  WRITLP LI   R8,DTABUF        LOAD DATA FIELD
       0474  8100
0336               ◆                            IMAGE POINTER
0337   0476  0200         LI   R0,64            REPEAT 64 TIMES
       0478  0040
0338   047A  04F8  WTLPL1 CLR  *R8+             CLEAR DATA BUFFER
0339   047C  0600         DEC  R0
0340   047E  16FD         JNE  WTLPL1
0341   0480  0208         LI   R8,DTABUF        LOAD DATA BUFFER POINTER
       0482  8100
0342   0484  9807         CB   R7,@ASCIIH       WH COMMAND?
       0486  0030
0343   0488  13--         JEQ  WRTASC           IF SO, READ ASCII STRING
0344   048A  C10A         MOV  R10,R4           SAVE RETURN ADDRESS
0345   048C  020A         LI   R10,WTBRDY       LOAD HRC2 SUBROUTINE
       048E  ----
0346               ◆                            RETURN ADDRESS
0347   0490  0209         LI   R9,8             LOAD LINE COUNT
       0492  0008
0348   0494  0206  WTHLP1 LI   R6,16            LOAD BYTE COUNT
       0496  0010
```

Figure 32. Floppy Disk Control Program (Sheet 23 of 28)

FLOPPY DISK CONTROL PROGRAM   PAGE 0024

```
0849   0498   2F00           NLIN   0              NEW LINE
0850   049A   2E98    WTHLP2 HRC2   *R8            READ BYTE
0851   049C   0588           INC    R8             INCREMENT BUFFER POINTER
0852   049E   0606           DEC    R6             DECREMENT BYTE COUNT
0853   04A0   16FC           JNE    WTHLP2         IF NOT 0, READ NEXT BYTE
0854   04A2   0609           DEC    R9             DECREMENT LINE COUNT
0855   04A4   16F7           JNE    WTHLP1         IF NOT 0, READ NEXT LINE
0856   04A6   C284    WTBRDY MOV    R4,R10         RESTORE RETURN ADDRESS
       048E**04A6'
0857   04A8   10--           JMP    WTCRCD         CONTINUE
0858   04AA   0206    WRTASC LI     R6,128         LOAD CHARACTER COUNT
       04AC   0080
       04B8**1310
0859   04AE   2F00           NLIN   0              NEW LINE
0860   04B0   2F58    WTASLP RECV   *R8            READ CHARACTER
0861   04B2   9818           CB     *R8,@ESC       ESCAPE CHARACTER?
       04B4   0083'
0862   04B6   13--           JEQ    WRITRT         IF SO, RETURN
0863   04B8   9838           CB     *R8+,@BLANK    NON-PRINTABLE?
       04BA   0084'
0864   04BC   11--           JLT    WTCRCD         IF SO, END OF SECTOR
0865   04BE   0606           DEC    R6             DECREMENT CHARACTER COUNT
0866   04C0   16F7           JNE    WTASLP         IF NOT 0, READ NEXT CHAR
0867   04C2   2E00    WTCRCD CRCD   0              GENERATE DATA FIELD CRC
       04A8**100C
       04BC**1102
0868   04C4   0209           LI     R9,DTAWT       DISK DATA WRITE ADDRESS
       04C6   7FFE
0869   04C8   0208           LI     R8,DTAFLD      DATA FIELD IMAGE POINTER
       04CA   80FF
0870   04CC   2C80           IDRD   0              READ ID FIELD
0871   04CE   0200           LI     R0,16          REPEAT 16 TIMES
       04D0   0010
0872   04D2   04D9    WTLPL2 CLR    *R9            WRITE LAST 16 BYTES OF
0873                  *                            ID GAP (FIRST BYTE SKIPPED FOR
0874                  *                            BYTE SYNCHRONIZATION)
0875   04D4   0600           DEC    R0
0876   04D6   16FD           JNE    WTLPL2
0877   04D8   D833           MOVB   *R8+,@MRKWT     WRITE DATA MARK
       04DA   7F8E
0878   04DC   0200           LI     R0,130         REPEAT 130 TIMES
       04DE   0082
0879   04E0   D678    WTLPL3 MOVB   *R8+,*R9        WRITE DATA FIELD
0880   04E2   0600           DEC    R0
0881   04E4   16FD           JNE    WTLPL3
0882   04E6   04D9           CLR    *R9            REWRITE FIRST BYTE OF
0883                  *                            DATA GAP
0884   04E8   2D00           SINC   0              UPDATE SECTOR NUMBER
0885   04EA   1E04           SBZ    SEL            TURN OFF DRIVE
0886   04EC   0605           DEC    R5             DECREMENT SECTOR COUNT
0887   04EE   16C1           JNE    WRITLP         IF NOT 0, WRITE NEXT SECTOR
0888   04F0   045A    WRITRT B      *R10           ELSE, RETURN
       04B6**131C
```

Figure 32. Floppy Disk Control Program (Sheet 24 of 28)

```
0890                 ◆◆◆◆◆◆◆◆◆◆◆◆◆◆◆◆◆◆◆◆◆◆◆◆◆◆◆◆◆◆◆◆◆◆◆◆◆◆◆◆◆◆◆◆◆◆◆◆◆◆◆◆◆◆◆◆◆◆◆◆
0891                 ◆
0892                 ◆      COMMAND CONTROL PROGRAM:   FORMAT
0893                 ◆
0894                 ◆      THIS COMMAND ENABLES THE OPERATOR TO FORMAT
0895                 ◆      A NUMBER OF TRACKS BEGINNING AT THE CURRENT TRACK
0896                 ◆      AND SPECIFYING THE LAST TRACK.   ALL GAPS,
0897                 ◆      TRACK, ID, AND DATA MARKS, AND TRACK AND
0898                 ◆      SECTOR NUMBERS ARE WRITTEN.   THE DATA IN THE
0899                 ◆      DATA FIELDS IS ALL ZEROES.
0900                 ◆
0901                 ◆      ENTRY PARAMETERS:      R10 = RETURN ADDRESS
0902                 ◆
0903   04F2   2DA0   FORMAT AXMT  ƏENDMSG          PRINT END MESSAGE
       04F4   0094´
       032C◆◆04F2´
0904   04F6   2DA0          AXMT  ƏTKMSG           PRINT TRACK MESSAGE
       04F8   008A´
0905   04FA   D260          MOVB  ƏTKNUM,R9        FETCH TRACK NUMBER
       04FC   80F8
0906   04FE   2EC9          HXM2  R9               PRINT TRACK NUMBER
0907   0500   2E89          HRC2  R9               READ LAST TRACK NUMBER
0908   0502   0289          CI    R9,77◆256        LEGAL VALUE?
       0504   4D00
0909   0506   14--          JHE   FRMTRT           IF NOT, RETURN
0910   0508   0208          LI    R8,DTAFLD        LOAD DATA FIELD POINTER
       050A   80FF
0911   050C   DE20          MOVB  ƏDTMRK,◆R8+      LOAD DATA MARK
       050E   00D1´
0912   0510   0200          LI    R0,64            REPEAT 64 TIMES
       0512   0040
0913   0514   04F8   FFLPL1 CLR   ◆R8+             CLEAR DATA BUFFER
0914   0516   0600          DEC   R0
0915   0518   16FD          JNE   FFLPL1
0916   051A   2E00          CRCD  0                CALCULATE THE CRC FOR THE
0917                 ◆                             DATA FIELD
0918   051C   9809   FRMTLP CB    R9,ƏTKNUM        LAST TRACK LESS
       051E   80F8
0919                 ◆                             THAN CURRENT TRACK?
0920   0520   11--          JLT   FRMTRT           IF SO, RETURN
0921   0522   0208   FPMT1  LI    R8,>100          LOAD INITIAL SECTOR
       0524   0100
0922                 ◆                             VALUE
0923   0526   0207          LI    R7,SECBUF        LOAD SECTOR BUFFER
       0528   80C0
0924                 ◆                             POINTER
0925   052A   D808   FRIDBL MOVB  R8,ƏSECNUM       UPDATE SECTOR
       052C   80FA
0926                 ◆                             NUMBER
0927   052E   2DC0          CRCI  0                CALCULATE CRC FOR ID FIELD
0928   0530   CDE0          MOV   ƏIDCRC,◆R7+      SAVE CRC IN BUFFER
       0532   80FC
0929   0534   0228          AI    R8,>100          INCREMENT SECTOR NUMBER
       0536   0100
```

Figure 32. Floppy Disk Control Program (Sheet 25 of 28)

FLOPPY DISK CONTROL PROGRAM   PAGE 0026

```
0930    0538    0288            CI      R8,27*256       LAST SECTOR?
        053A    1B00
0931    053C    16F6            JNE     FRIDBL          IF NOT, REPEAT FOR
0932                    ♦                               NEXT SECTOR
0933    053E    0207            LI      R7,SECBUF       LOAD SECTOR BUFFER
        0540    80C0
0934                    ♦                               POINTER
0935    0542    0208            LI      R8,>100         LOAD INITIAL SECTOR
        0544    0100
0936                    ♦                               NUMBER
0937    0546    2D40            DSON    0               TURN ON DRIVE
0938    0548    0206    FMINDX  LI      R6,DTAWT        DISK DATA WRITE
        054A    7FFE
0939    054C    04E0            CLR     @INDXWT         WRITE 0 AT INDEX PULSE
        054E    7FFA
0940    0550    0200            LI      R0,45           REPEAT 45 TIMES
        0552    002D
0941    0554    04D6    FFLPL2  CLR     ♦R6             WRITE REST OF POST-INDEX
0942                    ♦                               GAP
0943    0556    0600            DEC     R0
0944    0558    16FD            JNE     FFLPL2
0945    055A    D820            MOVB    @TKMRK,@TKMWT   WRITE TRACK MARK
        055C    00D2
        055E    7F9E
0946    0560    0200    SECTLP  LI      R0,32           REPEAT 32 TIMES
        0562    0020
0947    0564    04D6    FFLPL3  CLR     ♦R6             WRITE 32 BYTE GAP
0948    0566    0600            DEC     R0
0949    0568    16FD            JNE     FFLPL3
0950    056A    D820            MOVB    @IDMRK,@MRKWT   WRITE ID MARK
        056C    00D0
        056E    7F8E
0951    0570    D5A0            MOVB    @TKNUM,♦R6      WRITE TRACK NUMBER
        0572    80F8
0952    0574    D58C            MOVB    R12,♦R6         WRITE SECOND BYTE
0953    0576    D588            MOVB    R8,♦R6          WRITE SECTOR NUMBER
0954    0578    0228            AI      R8,>100         INCREMENT SECTOR NUMBER
        057A    0100
0955    057C    D58C            MOVB    R12,♦R6         WRITE FOURTH BYTE
0956    057E    D5B7            MOVB    ♦R7+,♦R6        WRITE CRC1
0957    0580    D5B7            MOVB    ♦R7+,♦R6        WRITE CRC2
0958    0582    0200            LI      R0,17           REPEAT 17 TIMES
        0584    0011
0959    0586    04D6    FFLPL4  CLR     ♦R6             WRITE ID GAP
0960    0588    0600            DEC     R0
0961    058A    16FD            JNE     FFLPL4
0962    058C    0204            LI      R4,DTAFLD       LOAD DATA FIELD
        058E    80FF
0963                    ♦                               IMAGE POINTER
0964    0590    D834            MOVB    ♦R4+,@MRKWT     WRITE DATA MARK
        0592    7F8E
0965    0594    0200            LI      R0,130          REPEAT 130 TIMES
        0596    0082
0966    0598    D5B4    FFLPL5  MOVB    ♦R4+,♦R6        WRITE DATA AND CRC
0967    059A    0600            DEC     R0
```

Figure 32. Floppy Disk Control Program (Sheet 26 of 28)

FLOPPY DISK CONTROL PROGRAM   PAGE 0027

```
0968   059C   16FD         JNE    FFLPL5
0969   059E   04D6         CLR    ◆R6              WRITE PAD BYTE
0970   05A0   0288         CI     R8,>27◆256       LAST BYTE?
       05A2   2700
0971   05A4   16DD         JNE    SECTLP           IF NOT, FORMAT NEXT SECTOR
0972   05A6   04D6  PREILP CLR    ◆R6              WRITE PRE-INDEX GAP
0973   05A8   1F04         TB     INDEX            UNTIL INDEX
0974   05AA   16FD         JNE    PREILP           PULSE OCCURS
0975   05AC   2E40         TINC   0                STEP HEAD TO NEXT TRACK
0976   05AE   10B6         JMP    FRMTLP           FORMAT NEXT TRACK
0977   05B0   1E04  FRMTRT SBZ    SEL              TURN OFF DRIVE
       0506◆◆1454
       0520◆◆1147
0978   05B2   045A         B      ◆R10             RETURN
0979                ◆◆◆◆◆◆◆◆◆◆◆◆◆◆◆◆◆◆◆◆◆◆◆◆◆◆◆◆◆◆◆◆◆◆◆◆◆◆◆◆◆◆◆◆◆◆◆◆◆◆◆◆◆◆◆◆◆◆◆
0980                ◆
0981                ◆      COMMAND CONTROL PROGRAM:   EXECUT
0982                ◆
0983                ◆      THIS COMMAND ENABLES THE OPERATOR TO BEGIN
0984                ◆      EXECUTION OF A PROGRAM AT ANY LOCATION
0985                ◆      IN MEMORY.
0986                ◆
0987                ◆      ENTRY PARAMETERS:     R8 = ENTRY POINT
0988                ◆
0989   05B4   0458  EXECUT B      ◆R8              BRANCH TO ENTRY POINT
       0332◆◆05B4´
0990                ◆◆◆◆◆◆◆◆◆◆◆◆◆◆◆◆◆◆◆◆◆◆◆◆◆◆◆◆◆◆◆◆◆◆◆◆◆◆◆◆◆◆◆◆◆◆◆◆◆◆◆◆◆◆◆◆◆◆◆
0991                ◆
0992                ◆      COMMAND CONTROL PROGRAM:   ENTER
0993                ◆
0994                ◆      THIS COMMAND ENABLES THE OPERATOR TO ENTER
0995                ◆      DATA INTO SEQUENTIAL MEMORY LOCATIONS.
0996                ◆
0997                ◆      CALLING PARAMETERS:    R8 = BEGINNING MEMORY
0998                ◆                                  LOCATION
0999                ◆
1000   05B6   0209  ENTER  LI     R9,8             LOAD BYTE COUNT
       05B8   0008
       0330◆◆05B6´
1001   05BA   2F00         NLIN   0                NEW LINE
1002   05BC   2EC8         HXM2   R8               PRINT FIRST BYTE OF ADDRESS
1003   05BE   06C8         SWPB   R8               REVERSE BYTES
1004   05C0   2FA0         XMIT   @BACKSP          BACKSPACE
       05C2   0087´
1005   05C4   2EC8         HXM2   R8               PRINT SECOND BYTE OF ADDRESS
1006   05C6   06C8         SWPB   R8               RESTORE BYTES
1007   05C8   2ED8  ENTLP  HXM2   ◆R8              PRINT MEMORY CONTENTS
1008   05CA   2E98         HRC2   ◆R8              READ AND STORE NEW VALUE
1009   05CC   0588         INC    R8               UPDATE ADDRESS POINTER
1010   05CE   0609         DEC    R9               DECREMENT BYTE COUNT
1011   05D0   13F2         JEQ    ENTER            IF 0, NEW LINE
1012   05D2   10FA         JMP    ENTLP            ELSE, FETCH NEXT BYTE
```

Figure 32. Floppy Disk Control Program (Sheet 27 of 28)

SUMMARY

TMS 9900
Floppy Disk
Controller

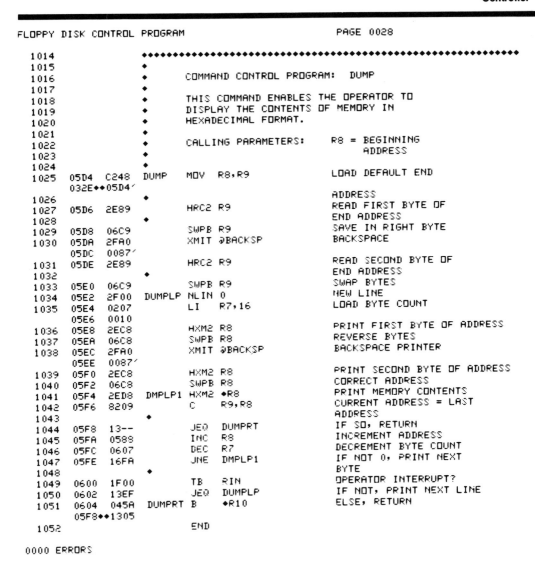

```
1014                    ••••••••••••••••••••••••••••••••••••••••••••••••••••••
1015                    •
1016                    •        COMMAND CONTROL PROGRAM:   DUMP
1017                    •
1018                    •        THIS COMMAND ENABLES THE OPERATOR TO
1019                    •        DISPLAY THE CONTENTS OF MEMORY IN
1020                    •        HEXADECIMAL FORMAT.
1021                    •
1022                    •        CALLING PARAMETERS:    R8 = BEGINNING
1023                    •                                    ADDRESS
1024                    •
1025    05D4  C248  DUMP    MOV  R8,R9            LOAD DEFAULT END
        032E••05D4•                              ADDRESS
1026                    •                        READ FIRST BYTE OF
1027    05D6  2E89          HRC2 R9              END ADDRESS
1028                    •                        SAVE IN RIGHT BYTE
1029    05D8  06C9          SWPB R9              BACKSPACE
1030    05DA  2FA0          XMIT ƏBACKSP
        05DC  0087•
1031    05DE  2E89          HRC2 R9              READ SECOND BYTE OF
1032                    •                        END ADDRESS
1033    05E0  06C9          SWPB R9              SWAP BYTES
1034    05E2  2F00  DUMPLP  NLIN 0               NEW LINE
1035    05E4  0207          LI   R7,16           LOAD BYTE COUNT
        05E6  0010
1036    05E8  2EC8          HXM2 R8              PRINT FIRST BYTE OF ADDRESS
1037    05EA  06C8          SWPB R8              REVERSE BYTES
1038    05EC  2FA0          XMIT ƏBACKSP         BACKSPACE PRINTER
        05EE  0087•
1039    05F0  2EC8          HXM2 R8              PRINT SECOND BYTE OF ADDRESS
1040    05F2  06C8          SWPB R8              CORRECT ADDRESS
1041    05F4  2ED8  DMPLP1  HXM2 •R8             PRINT MEMORY CONTENTS
1042    05F6  8209          C    R9,R8           CURRENT ADDRESS = LAST
1043                    •                        ADDRESS
1044    05F8  13--          JEQ  DUMPRT          IF SO, RETURN
1045    05FA  0588          INC  R8              INCREMENT ADDRESS
1046    05FC  0607          DEC  R7              DECREMENT BYTE COUNT
1047    05FE  16FA          JNE  DMPLP1          IF NOT 0, PRINT NEXT
1048                    •                        BYTE
1049    0600  1F00          TB   RIN             OPERATOR INTERRUPT?
1050    0602  13EF          JEQ  DUMPLP          IF NOT, PRINT NEXT LINE
1051    0604  045A  DUMPRT  B    •R10            ELSE, RETURN
        05F8••1305
1052                        END

0000 ERRORS

ASM/TERM? T
```

Figure 32. Floppy Disk Control Program (Sheet 28 of 28)

Appendix and Glossary

GLOSSARY

absolute address: 1. An address that is permanently assigned by the machine designer to a storage location. 2. A pattern of characters that identifies a unique storage location without further modification. 3. Synonymous with machine address, specific address.

access time: The time interval between the request for information and the instant this information is available.

accumulator: A device which stores a number and which, on receipt of another number, adds the two and stores the sum.

address: An expression, usually numerical, which designates a specific location in a storage or memory device.

address format: 1. The arrangement of the address parts of an instruction. The expression "plus-one" is frequently used to indicate that one of the addresses specifies the location of the next instruction to be executed, such as one-plus-one, two-plus-one, three-plus-one, four-plus-one. 2. The arrangement of the parts of a single address, such as those required for identifying channel, module, track, etc., in a disc system.

address register: A register in which an address is stored.

ALGOL: ALGOrithmic Language. A language primarily used to express computer programs by algorithms.

algorithm: A term used by mathematicians to describe a set of procedures by which a given result is obtained.

alphanumeric: Pertaining to a character set that contains letters, digits, and usually other characters such as punctuation marks.

ALU: Arithmetic Logic Unit, a computational subsystem which performs the mathematical operations of a digital system.

analog: Electric analog information is information represented by a variable property of electricity, such as voltage, current, amplitude of waves or pulses, or frequency of waves or pulses. Analog circuitry, also called "linear" circuitry, is circuitry that varies certain properties of electricity continuously and smoothly over a certain range, rather than switching suddenly between certain levels.

AND: A logic operator having the property that if P is a statement, Q is a statement, R is a statement . . . , then the AND of P, Q, R . . . is true if all statements are true, false if any statement is false. P AND Q is often represented by P·Q or PQ. Synonymous with logical multiply.

arithmetic shift: 1. A shift that does not affect the sign position. 2. A shift that is equivalent to the multiplication of a number by a positive or negative integral power of the radix.

ASCII: (American National Standard Code for Information Interchange, 1968) The standard code, using a coded character set consisting of 7-bit coded characters (8 bits including parity check), used for information interchange among data processing systems, communication systems, and associated equipment. The ASCII set consists of control characters and graphic characters. Synonymous with USASCII.

assemble: To prepare a machine language program from a symbolic language program by substituting absolute operation codes for symbolic operation codes and absolute or relocatable addresses for symbolic addresses.

assembler: A computer program that assembles.

asynchronous device: A device in which the speed of operation is not related to any frequency in th system to which it is connected.

base: 1. a reference value. 2. A number that is multiplied by itself as many times as indicated by an exponent. 3. Same as radix.

base address: A given address from which an absolute address is derived by combination with a relative address.

baud: A unit of signaling speed equal to the number of discrete conditions or signal events per second. For example, one baud equals one-half dot cycle per second in Morse code, one bit per second in a train of binary signals, and one 3-bit value per second in a train of signals each of which can assume one of eight different states.

BCD: Binary coded decimal notation.

GLOSSARY

benchmark problem: A problem used to evaluate the performance of hardware or software or both.

binary: 1. Pertaining to a characteristic or property involving a selection, choice, or condition in which there are two possibilities. 2. Pertaining to the number representation system with a radix of two.

binary coded decimal (BCD): A binary numbering system for coding decimal numbers in groups of 4 bits. The binary value of these 4-bit groups ranges from 0000 to 1001, and codes the decimal digits "0" through "9". To count to 9 takes 4 bits; to count to 99 takes two groups of 4 bits; to count to 999 takes three groups of 4 bits, etc.

block diagram: A diagram of a system, instrument, or computer in which the principal parts are represented by suitable associated geometrical figures to show both the basic functions and the functional relationships among the parts.

block transfer: The process of transmitting one or more blocks of data where the data are organized in such blocks.

bootstrap: A technique or device designed to bring itself into a desired state by means of its own action, e.g., a machine routine whose first few instructions are sufficient to bring the rest of itself into the computer from an input device.

borrow: An arithmetically negative carry.

branch: 1. A set of instructions that is executed between two successive decision instructions. 2. To select a branch as in definition 1. 3. A direct path joining two nodes of a network or graph. 4. Loosely, a conditional jump.

branching: A method of selecting, on the basis of results, the next operation to execute while the program is in progress.

breakpoint: A place in a routine specified by an instruction, instruction digit, or other condition, where the routine may be interrupted by external intervention or by a monitor routine.

buffer: An isolating circuit used to avoid reaction of a driven circuit on the corresponding driver circuit. Also, a storage device used to compensate for a difference in the rate of flow of information or the time of occurrence of events when transmitting information from one device to another.

bus: One or more conductors used for transmitting signals or power.

byte: A sequence of adjacent binary digits operated upon as a unit and usually shorter than a computer word. Usually 8 bits.

carry: One or more digits, produced in connection with an arithmetic operation on one digit place of two or more numerals in positional notation, that are forwarded to another digit place for processing there.

CCD: Charge-coupled device. A means for very dense serial-access storage of bits as tiny packets of electric charge moving along the surface of a semiconductor chip.

central processor unit (CPU): Part of a computer system which contains the main storage, arithmetic unit, and special register groups. It performs arithmetic operations, controls instruction processing, and provides timing signals and other housekeeping operations.

character: A letter, digit, or other symbol that is used as part of the organization, control, or representation of data. A character is often in the form of a spatial arrangement of adjacent or connected strokes.

character check: A check that verifies the observance of rules for the formation of characters.

check bit: A binary check digit, e.g., a parity bit.

check digit: A digit used for purpose of performing a check.

checkpoint: A place in a routine where a check or a recording of data for restart purposes, is performed.

chip-enable input: A control input that when active permits operation of the integrated circuit for input, internal transfer, manipulation, refreshing, and/or output of data and when inactive causes the integrated circuit to be in a reduced-power standby mode.

GLOSSARY

circulating register: A shift register in which data moved out of one end of the register are reentered into the other end as in a closed loop.

clock: 1. A device that generates periodic signals used for synchronization. 2. A register whose content changes at regular intervals in such a way as to measure time.

COBOL: (Common Business Oriented Language) A business data processing language.

code: 1. A set of unambiguous rules specifying the way in which data may be represented, e.g., the set of correspondences in the standard code for information interchange. Synonymous with coding scheme. 2. In telecommunications, a system of rules and conventions according to which the signals representing data can be formed, transmitted, received, and processed. 3. In data processing, to represent data or a computer program in a symbolic form that can be accepted by a data processor.

communication link: The physical means of connecting one location to another for the purpose of transmitting and receiving data.

compile: To prepare a machine language program from a computer program written in another programming language by making use of the overall logic structure of the program, or generating more than one machine instruction for each symbolic statement, or both, as well as performing the function of an assembler.

compiler: A program that compiles.

complement: A number that can be derived from a specified number by subtracting it from a second specified number. For example, in radix notation, the second specified number may be a given power of the radix or one less than a given power of the radix. The negative of a number is often represented by its complement.

computer: A data processor that can perform substantial computation, including numerous arithmetic or logic operations, without intervention by a human operator during the run.

conditional jump: A jump that occurs if specified criteria are met.

controller: Digital subsystem responsible for implementing "how" a system is to function. Not to be confused with "timing" as timing tells the system "when" to perform its function.

counter: A circuit which counts input pulses and will give an output pulse after receiving a predetermined number of input pulses.

CRU: Communications Register Unit: a command-driven bit addressable I/O interface. The processor instruction can set, reset, or test any bit in the CRU array or move data between the memory and CRU data fields.

cycle: 1. An interval of space or time in which one set of events or phenomena is completed. 2. Any set of operations that is repeated regularly in the same sequence. The operations may be subject to variations on each repetition.

data: 1. A representation of facts, concepts, or instructions in a formalized manner suitable for communication, interpretation, or processing by humans or automatic means. 2. Any representations such as characters or analog quantities to which meaning is or might be assigned.

data bus: One method of input-output for a system where data are moved into or out of the digital system by way of a common bus connected to several subsystems.

data processing: The execution of a systematic sequence of operations performed upon data. Synonymous with information processing.

data selector: A combinational building-block that routes data from one of several inputs to a single output, according to control signals. Also called "multiplexer." Two or more such one-bit selectors operating in parallel would be called a "two-bit data selector," etc.

debug: To detect, locate, and remove mistakes from a routine or malfunctions from a computer. Synonymous with troubleshoot.

decimal: 1. Pertaining to a characteristic or property involving a selection, choice, or condition in which there are ten possibilities. 2. Pertaining to the number representation system with a radix of ten.

decimal digit: In decimal notation, one of the characters 0 through 9.

decoder: A conversion circuit that accepts digital input information — in the memory case, binary address information — that appears as a small number of lines and selects and activates one line of a large number of output lines.

digital: 1. Pertaining to data in the form of digits. 2. Contrast with analog. 3. Information in discrete or quantized form; not continuous.

direct access: Pertaining to the process of obtaining data from, or placing data into, storage where the time required for such access is independent of the location of the data most recently obtained or placed in storage.

direct addressing: Method of programming that has the address pointing to the location of data or the instruction that is to be used.

direct memory access channel (DMA): A method of input-output for a system that uses a small processor whose sole task is that of controlling input-output. With DMA, data are moved into or out of the system without program intervention.

double precision: Pertaining to the use of two computer words to represent a number

dump: 1. To copy the contents of all or part of a storage, usually from an internal storage into an external storage. 2. A process as in definition 1 above. 3. The data resulting from the process as in definition 1 above.

duplex: In communications, pertaining to a simultaneous two-way independent transmission in both directions. Contrast with half duplex. Synonymous with full duplex.

edge triggering: Activation of a circuit at the edge of the pulse as it begins its change. Circuits then trigger at the edge of the input pulse rather than sensing a level change.

edit: To modify the form or format of data, e.g., to insert or delete characters such as page numbers or decimal points.

effective address: The address that is derived by applying any specified indexing or indirect addressing results to the specified address and that is actually used to identify the current operand.

emulate: To imitate one system with another such that the imitating system accepts the same data, executes the same programs, and achieves the same results as the imitated system.

encode: To apply a set of unambiguous rules specifying the way in which data may be represented such that a subsequent decoding is possible. Synonymous with code.

entry point: In a routine, any place to which control can be passed.

EPROM: Eraseable and programmable read-only memory. An IC memory chip whose stored data can be read at random. The data can be erased and new data can be stored, but only by a special system other than the one in which the memory is used.

erase: To obliterate information from a storage medium, e.g., to clear, to overwrite.

error: Any discrepancy between a computed, observed, or measured quantity and the true, specified, or theoretically correct value or condition.

exclusive-OR function: A modified form of the OR function which has a logic equation equal to the sum output of the half-adder.

execute: That portion of a computer cycle during which a selected control word or instruction is accomplished.

exponent: In a floating-point representation, the numeral, of a pair of numerals representing a number, that indicates the power to which the base is raised.

GLOSSARY

family: A family of digital integrated circuits is a group of ICs that use the same general design style for all gates, and processed during manufacture in much the same way, and whose input and output signals are all "compatible" with one another so that one can transmit to another.

fetch: That portion of a computer cycle during which the next instruction is retrieved from memory.

field: In a record, a specified area used for a particular category of data, e.g., a group of card columns used to represent a wage rate, a set of bit locations in a computer word used to express the address of the operand.

first-in first-out (FIFO) memory: A memory from which data bytes or words can be read in the same order, but not necessarily at the same rate, as that of the data entry.

fixed-point representation: A positional representation in which each number is represented by a single set of digits, the position of the radix point being fixed with respect to one end of the set, according to some convention.

flag: 1. Any of various types of indicators used for identification, e.g., a wordmark. 2. A character that signals the occurrence of some condition, such as the end of a word. 3. Synonymous with mark, sentinel, tag.

flip-flop (storage element): A circuit having two stable states and the capability of changing from one state to another with the application of a control signal and remaining in that state after removal of signals.

flow chart: A graphical representation for definition, analysis, or solution of a problem, in which symbols are used to represent operations, data, flow, equipment, etc.

format: The arrangement of data.

FORTRAN: (FORmula TRANslating system) A language primarily used to express computer programs by arithmetic formulas.

function: 1. A specific purpose of an entity, or its characteristic action. 2. In communications, a machine action such as a carriage return or line feed.

gate: 1. A device having one output channel and one or more input channels, such that the output channel state is completely determined by the input channel states, except during switching transients. 2. A combinational logic element having at least one input channel. 3. An AND gate. 4. An OR gate.

general-purpose computer: A computer that is designed to handle a wide variety of problems.

generate: To produce a program by selection of subsets from a set of skeletal coding under the control of parameters.

half duplex: In communications, pertaining to an alternate, one way at a time, independent transmission. Contrast with duplex.

hardware: Physical equipment, as opposed to the computer program or method of use, e.g., mechanical, magnetic, electrical, or electronic devices.

hold time: Hold time, t_h. The interval during which a signal is retained at a specified input terminal after an active transition occurs at another specified input terminal.

immediate address: Pertaining to an instruction in which an address part contains the value of an operand rather than its address. Synonymous with zero-level address.

indexed address: An address that is modified by the content of an index register prior to or during the execution of a computer instruction.

indexing: In computers, a method of address modification that is implemented by means of index registers.

index register: A register whose content may be added to or subtracted from the operand address prior to or during the execution of a computer instruction.

indirect addressing: Programming method that has the initial address being the storage location of a word that contains another address. This indirect address is then used to obtain the data to be operated upon.

input/output devices (I/O): Computer hardware by which data is entered into a digital system or by which data are recorded for immediate or future use.

instruction: A statement that specifies an operation and the values or locations of its operands.

instruction cycle: The period of time during which a programmed system obeys a particular instruction.

instruction register: A register that stores an instruction for execution.

interface: A shared boundary. An interface might be a hardware component to link two devices or it might be a portion of storage or registers accessed by two or more computer programs.

interrupt: To stop a process in such a way that it can be resumed.

jump: A departure from the normal sequence of executing instructions in a computer.

jump conditions: Conditions defined in a transition table that determine the changes of flip-flops from one state to another state.

label: One or more characters used to identify a statement or an item of data in a computer program.

language: A set of representations, conventions, and rules used to convey information.

large scale integration (LSI): The simultaneous realization of large area chips and optimum component packing density, resulting in cost reduction by maximizing the number of system connections done at the chip level. Circuit complexity above 100 gates.

level: The degree of subordination in a hierarchy.

linkage: In programming, coding that connects two separately coded routines.

load: In programming, to enter data into storage or working registers.

location: Any place in which data may be stored.

logic diagram: A diagram that represents a logic design and sometimes the hardware implementation.

logic shift: A shift that affects all positions.

logic symbol: 1. A symbol used to represent a logic element graphically. 2. A symbol used to represent a logic operator.

loop: A sequence of instructions that is executed repeatedly until a terminal condition prevails.

LSB: Least significant bit.

machine code: An operation code that a machine is designed to recognize. Usually expressed in ones and zeros.

macroinstruction: An instruction in a source language that is equivalent to a specified sequence of machine instructions.

macroprogramming: Programming with macroinstructions.

magnetic bubble: A tiny moveable magnetized region formed under certain conditions in a thin film of magnetic garnet crystal fabricated similar to an IC. Such bubbles provide very dense serial-access storage of bits.

magnetic drum: A right circular cylinder with a magnetic surface on which data can be stored by selective magnetization of portions of the curved surface.

main storage: The general-purpose storage of a computer. Usually, main storage can be accessed directly by the operating registers. Contrast with auxiliary storage.

mask: 1. A pattern of characters that is used to control the retention or elimination of portions of another pattern of characters. 2. A filter.

microprocessor: An IC (or set of a few ICs) that can be programmed with stored instructions to perform a wide variety of functions, consisting at least of a controller, some registers, and some sort of ALU (that is, the basic parts of a simple CPU.)

GLOSSARY

mnemonic symbol: A symbol chosen to assist the human memory, e.g., an abbreviation such as "mpy" for "multiply".

modem: (MOdulator — DEModulator) A device that modulates and demodulates signals transmitted over communication facilities.

MSB: Most significant bit.

multiplex: To interleave or simultaneously transmit two or more messages on a single channel.

multiprocessing: 1. Pertaining to the simultaneous execution of two or more computer programs or sequences of instructions by a computer or computer network. 2. Loosely, parallel processing.

multiprocessor: A computer employing two or more processing units under integrated control.

multiprogramming: Pertaining to the concurrent execution of two or more programs by a computer.

MUX: Multiplexer.

NAND: A logic operator having the property that if P is a statement, Q is a statement, R is a statement, . . . , then the NAND of P, Q, R, . . . is true if at least one statement is false, false if all statements are true. Synonymous with NOT-AND, Sheffer stroke.

nest: To imbed subroutines or data in other subroutines or data at a different hierarchical level such that the different levels of routines or data can be executed or accessed recursively.

noise: Any signal that isn't supposed to be there. Electrical noise may be caused by small, irregular sparks when a switch is opened or closed. Or it may be caused by radio waves or by electric or magnetic fields generated by one wire and picked up by another.

NOR: A logic operator having the property that if P is a statement, Q is a statement, R is a statement, . . . , then the NOR of P, Q, R, . . . is true if all statements are false, false if at least one statement is true. P NOR Q is often represented by a combination of "OR" and "NOT" symbols, such as $\overline{(P+Q)}$. P NOR Q is also called "neither P nor Q". Synonymous with NOT-or.

NOT: A logic operator having the property that if P is a statement, then the NOT of P is true if P is false, false if P is true. The NOT of P is often represented by $\overline{P}$.

object code: Output from a compiler or assembler which is itself executable machine code or is suitable for processing to produce executable machine code.

object language: The language to which a statement is translated.

operand: That which is operated upon. An operand is usually identified by an address part of an instruction.

operating system: Software which controls the execution of computer programs and which may provide scheduling, debugging, input/output control, accounting, compilation, storage assignment, data management, and related services.

operation: 1. A defined action, namely, the act of obtaining a result from one or more operands in accordance with a rule that completely specifies the result for any permissible combination of operands. 2. The set of such acts specified by such a rule, or the rule itself. 3. The act specified by a single computer instruction. 4. A program step undertaken or executed by a computer, e.g., addition, multiplication, extraction, comparison, shift, transfer. The operation is usually specified by the operator part of an instruction. 5. The specific action performed by a logic element.

pack: To compress data in a storage medium by taking advantage of known characteristics of the data, in such a way that the original data can be recovered, e.g., to compress data in a storage medium by making use of bit or byte locations that would otherwise go unused.

parallel operation: The organization of data manipulating within circuitry wherein all the digits of a word are transmitted simultaneously or separate lines in order to speed up operation.

parity check: A check that tests whether the number of ones (or zeros) in an array of binary digits is odd or even. Synonymous with odd-even check.

PC: Program counter.

peripheral equipment: Units which work in conjunction with a computer but are not part of it.

phase: The time interval for each clock "cycle" in a system may be divided into two or more "phases". The phases are defined by pulses in a separate network of wires for each phase. During a particular phase, the signal in that clock network is in the state defined as "active". The clock cycles are repeated over and over again, phase by phase. The phases provide a method of making several things happen in the proper order during one clock cycle.

PLA (programmable logic array): An integrated circuit that employs ROM matrices to combine sum and product terms of logic networks.

positive logic: Logic in which the more-positive voltage represents the "1" state; the less positive voltage represents the "0" state.

priority interrupt: Designation given to method of providing some commands to have precedence over others thus giving one condition of operation priority over another.

problem oriented language: A programming language designed for the convenient expression of a given class of problems.

processor: 1. In hardware, a data processor. 2. In software, a computer program that includes the compiling, assembling, translating, and related functions for a specific programming language, COBOL processor, or FORTRAN processor.

program: 1. A series of actions proposed in order to achieve a certain result. 2. Loosely, a routine. 3. To design, write, and test a program as in definition 1 above. 4. Loosely, to write a routine.

programmable read only memory (PROM): A fixed program, read only, semiconductor memory storage element that can be programmed after packaging.

PROM: Programmable read only memory.

propagation delay: The time required for a change in logic level to be transmitted through an element or a chain of elements.

pulse width: Pulse width, t_w The time interval between specified reference points on the leading and trailing edges of the pulse waveform.

pushdown list: A list that is constructed and maintained so that the item to be retrieved is the most recently stored item in the list, i.e., last in, first out.

pushdown stack: A set of registers which implement a pushdown list.

RAM: Random access memory.

random access memory (RAM): A memory from which all information can be obtained at the output with approximately the same time delay by choosing an address randomly and without first searching through a vast amount of irrelevant data.

read only memory (ROM) A fixed program semiconductor storage element that has been preprogrammed at the factory with a permanent program.

real time: 1. Pertaining to the actual time during which a physical process transpires. 2. Pertaining to the performance of a computation during the actual time that the related physical process transpires, in order that results of the computation can be used in guiding the physical process.

recovery time: Sense Recovery time, t_{sR} The time interval needed to switch a memory from a write mode to a read mode and to obtain valid data signals at the output.

refresh: Method which restores charge on capacitance which deteriorates because of leakage.

GLOSSARY

register: Temporary storage for digital data.

Relative address: The number that specifies the difference between the absolute address and the base address.

relocate: In computer programming, to move a routine from one portion of storage to another and to adjust the necessary address references so that the routine, in its new location, can be executed.

ROM: Read only memory.

routine: An ordered set of instructions that may have some general or frequent use.

sequencing: Control method used to cause a set of steps to occur in a particular order.

sequential logic systems: Digital system utilizing memory elements.

serial: 1. Pertaining to the sequential or consecutive occurrence of two or more related activities in a single device or channel. 2. Pertaining to the sequencing of two or more processes. 3. Pertaining to the sequential processing of the individual parts of a whole such as the bits of a character or the characters of a word, using the same facilities of successive parts. 4. Contrast with parallel.

serial operation: The organization of data manipulation within circuitry wherein the digits of a word are transmitted one at a time along a single line. The serial mode of operation is slower than parallel operation, but utilizes less complex circuitry.

set-up time: The minimum amount of time that data must be present at an input to ensure data acceptance when the device is clocked.

shift: A movement of data to the right or left.

shift register: A register in which the stored data can be moved to the right or left.

sign and magnitude notation: A system of notation where binary numbers are represented by a sign-bit and one or more number bits:

significant digit: A digit that is needed for a certain purpose, particularly one that must be kept to preserve a specific accuracy or presicion.

sign position: A position, normally located at one end of a number, that contains an indication of the algebraic sign of the number.

simulate: 1. To represent certain features of the behavior of a physical or abstract system by the behavior of another system. 2. To represent the functioning of a device, system, computer program by another, e.g., to represent the functioning of one computer by another, to represent the behavior of a physical system by the execution of a computer program, to represent a biological system by a mathematical model.

simulator: A device, system, or computer program that represents certain features of the behavior of a physical or abstract system.

software: A set of computer programs, procedures, and possibly associated documentation concerned with the operation of a data processing system, e.g., compilers, library routines, manuals, circuit diagrams.

source language: The language from which a statement is translated.

source program: A computer program written in a source language.

state: The condition of an input or output of a circuit as to whether it is a logic "1" or a logic "0". The state of a circuit (gate or flip-flop) refers to its output. A flip-flop is said to be in the "1" state when its Q output is "1". A gate is in the "1" state when its output is "1".

static storage elements: Storage elements which contain storage cells that retain their information as long as power is applied unless the information is altered by external excitation.

stored program: A set of instructions in memory specifying the operations to be performed.

stored program computer: A computer controlled by internally stored instructions that can synthesize, store, and in some cases alter instruction as though they were data and that can subsequently execute these instructions.

subroutine: A routine that can be part of another routine.

synchronous: Refers to two or more things made to happen in a system at the same time, by means of a common clock signal.

temporary storage: In programming, storage locations reserved for intermediate results. Synonymous with working storage.

terminal: A point in a system or communication network at which data can either enter or leave.

transmit: To send data from one location and to receive the data at another location. Synonymous with transfer definition 2, move.

TTL: Bipolar semiconductor transistor-transistor coupled logic circuits.

USASCII: United States of America Standard Code for Information Interchange. The standard code used by the United State for transmission of data. Sometimes simply referred to as the "as'ki" code.

variable: A quantity that can assume any of a given set of values.

volatile storage: A storage device in which stored data are lost when the applied power is removed.

word: A character string or a bit string considered as an entity

working storage: Same as temporary storage.

WR: Working register.

workspace: In the 9900, a set of 16 consecutive words of memory referred to by many of the instructions.

write: To record data in a storage device or a data medium. The recording need not be permanent, such as the writing on a cathode ray tube display device.

APPENDIX

Table K-1. Hexadecimal Arithmetic

ADDITION TABLE

0	1	2	3	4	5	6	7	8	9	A	B	C	D	E	F
1	02	03	04	05	06	07	08	09	0A	0B	0C	0D	0E	0F	10
2	03	04	05	06	07	08	09	0A	0B	0C	0D	0E	0F	10	11
3	04	05	06	07	08	09	0A	0B	0C	0D	0E	0F	10	11	12
4	05	06	07	08	09	0A	0B	0C	0D	0E	0F	10	11	12	13
5	06	07	08	09	0A	0B	0C	0D	0E	0F	10	11	12	13	14
6	07	08	09	0A	0B	0C	0D	0E	0F	10	11	12	13	14	15
7	08	09	0A	0B	0C	0D	0E	0F	10	11	12	13	14	15	16
8	09	0A	0B	0C	0D	0E	0F	10	11	12	13	14	15	16	17
9	0A	0B	0C	0D	0E	0F	10	11	12	13	14	15	16	17	18
A	0B	0C	0D	0E	0F	10	11	12	13	14	15	16	17	18	19
B	0C	0D	0E	0F	10	11	12	13	14	15	16	17	18	19	1A
C	0D	0E	0F	10	11	12	13	14	15	16	17	18	19	1A	1B
D	0E	0F	10	11	12	13	14	15	16	17	18	19	1A	1B	1C
E	0F	10	11	12	13	14	15	16	17	18	19	1A	1B	1C	1D
F	10	11	12	13	14	15	16	17	18	19	1A	1B	1C	1D	1E

MULTIPLICATION TABLE

1	2	3	4	5	6	7	8	9	A	B	C	D	E	F
2	04	06	08	0A	0C	0E	10	12	14	16	18	1A	1C	1E
3	06	09	0C	0F	12	15	18	1B	1E	21	24	27	2A	2D
4	08	0C	10	14	18	1C	20	24	28	2C	30	34	38	3C
5	0A	0F	14	19	1E	23	28	2D	32	37	3C	41	46	4B
6	0C	12	18	1E	24	2A	30	36	3C	42	48	4E	54	5A
7	0E	15	1C	23	2A	31	38	3F	46	4D	54	5B	62	69
8	10	18	20	28	30	38	40	48	50	58	60	68	70	78
9	12	1B	24	2D	36	3F	48	51	5A	63	6C	75	7E	87
A	14	1E	28	32	3C	46	50	5A	64	6E	78	82	8C	96
B	16	21	2C	37	42	4D	58	63	6E	79	84	8F	9A	A5
C	18	24	30	3C	48	54	60	6C	78	84	90	9C	A8	B4
D	1A	27	34	41	4E	5B	68	75	82	8F	9C	A9	B6	C3
E	1C	2A	38	46	54	62	70	7E	8C	9A	A8	B6	C4	D2
F	1E	2D	3C	4B	5A	69	78	87	96	A5	B4	C3	D2	E1

Table K-2. Table of Powers of 16_{10}

16^n	n	16^{-n}		
1	0	0.10000 00000 00000 00000	x	10
16	1	0.62500 00000 00000 00000	x	10^{-1}
256	2	0.39062 50000 00000 00000	x	10^{-2}
4 096	3	0.24414 06250 00000 00000	x	10^{-3}
65 536	4	0.15258 78906 25000 00000	x	10^{-4}
1 048 576	5	0.95367 43164 06250 00000	x	10^{-6}
16 777 216	6	0.59604 64477 53906 25000	x	10^{-7}
268 435 456	7	0.37252 90298 46191 40625	x	10^{-8}
4 294 967 296	8	0.23283 06436 53869 62891	x	10^{-9}
68 719 476 736	9	0.14551 91522 83668 51807	x	10^{-10}
1 099 511 627 776	10	0.90949 47017 72928 23792	x	10^{-12}
17 592 186 044 416	11	0.56843 41886 08080 14870	x	10^{-13}
281 474 976 710 656	12	0.35527 13678 80050 09294	x	10^{-14}
4 503 599 627 370 496	13	0.22204 46049 25031 30808	x	10^{-15}
72 057 594 037 927 936	14	0.13877 78780 78144 56755	x	10^{-16}
1 152 921 504 606 846 976	15	0.86736 17379 88403 54721	x	10^{-18}

Table K-3. Table of Powers of 10_{16}

10^n	n	10^{-n}		
1	0	1.0000 0000 0000 0000		
A	1	0.1999 9999 9999 999A		
64	2	0.28F5 C28F 5C28 F5C3	x	16^{-1}
3E8	3	0.4189 374B C6A7 EF9E	x	16^{-2}
2710	4	0.68DB 8BAC 710C B296	x	16^{-3}
1 86A0	5	0.A7C5 AC47 1B47 8423	x	16^{-4}
F 4240	6	0.10C6 F7A0 B5ED 8D37	x	16^{-4}
98 9680	7	0.1AD7 F29A BCAF 4858	x	16^{-5}
5F5 E100	8	0.2AF3 1DC4 6118 73BF	x	16^{-6}
3B9A CA00	9	0.44B8 2FA0 9B5A 52CC	x	16^{-7}
2 540B E400	10	0.6DF3 7F67 5EF6 EADF	x	16^{-8}
17 4876 E800	11	0.AFEB FF0B CB24 AAFF	x	16^{-9}
E8 D4A5 1000	12	0.1197 9981 2DEA 1119	x	16^{-9}
918 4E72 A000	13	0.1C25 C268 4976 81C2	x	16^{-10}
5AF3 107A 4000	14	0.2D09 370D 4257 3604	x	16^{-11}
3 8D7E A4C6 8000	15	0.480E BE7B 9D58 566D	x	16^{-12}
23 86F2 6FC1 0000	16	0.734A CA5F 6226 F0AE	x	16^{-13}
163 4578 5D8A 0000	17	0.B877 AA32 36A4 B449	x	16^{-14}
DE0 B6B3 A764 0000	18	0.1272 5DD1 D243 ABA1	x	16^{-14}
8AC7 2304 89E8 0000	19	0.1D83 C94F B6D2 AC35	x	16^{-15}

APPENDIX

Table K-4. Table of Powers of Two

2^n	n	2^{-n}							
1	0	1.0							
2	1	0.5							
4	2	0.25							
8	3	0.125							
16	4	0.062	5						
32	5	0.031	25						
64	6	0.015	625						
128	7	0.007	812	5					
256	8	0.003	906	25					
512	9	0.001	953	125					
1 024	10	0.000	976	562	5				
2 048	11	0.000	488	281	25				
4 096	12	0.000	244	140	625				
8 192	13	0.000	122	070	312	5			
16 384	14	0.000	061	035	156	25			
32 768	15	0.000	030	517	578	125			
65 536	16	0.000	015	258	789	062	5		
131 072	17	0.000	007	629	394	531	25		
262 144	18	0.000	003	814	697	265	625		
524 288	19	0.000	001	907	348	632	812	5	
1 048 576	20	0.000	000	953	674	316	406	25	
2 097 152	21	0.000	000	476	837	158	203	125	
4 194 304	22	0.000	000	238	418	579	101	562	5
8 388 608	23	0.000	000	119	209	289	550	781	25
16 777 216	24	0.000	000	059	604	644	775	390	625
33 554 432	25	0.000	000	029	802	322	387	695	312 5
67 108 864	26	0.000	000	014	901	161	193	847	656 25
134 217 728	27	0.000	000	007	450	580	596	923	828 125
268 435 456	28	0.000	000	003	725	290	298	461	914 062 5
536 870 912	29	0.000	000	001	862	645	149	230	957 031 25
1 073 741 824	30	0.000	000	000	931	322	574	615	478 515 625
2 147 483 648	31	0.000	000	000	465	661	287	307	739 257 812 5

**Table K-5. Hexadecimal–Decimal Integer
Conversion Table**

The table appearing on the following pages provides a means for direct conversion of decimal integers in the range of 0 to 4095 and for hexadecimal integers in the range of 0 to FFF.

To convert numbers above those ranges, add table values to the figures below:

Hexadecimal	Decimal	Hexadecimal	Decimal
01 000	4 096	20 000	131 072
02 000	8 192	30 000	196 608
03 000	12 288	40 000	262 144
04 000	16 384	50 000	327 680
05 000	20 480	60 000	393 216
06 000	24 576	70 000	458 752
07 000	28 672	80 000	524 288
08 000	32 768	90 000	589 824
09 000	36 864	A0 000	655 360
0A 000	40 960	B0 000	720 896
0B 000	45 056	C0 000	786 432
0C 000	49 152	D0 000	851 968
0D 000	53 248	E0 000	917 504
0E 000	57 344	F0 000	983 040
0F 000	61 440	100 000	1 048 576
10 000	65 536	200 000	2 097 152
11 000	69 632	300 000	3 145 728
12 000	73 728	400 000	4 194 304
13 000	77 824	500 000	5 242 880
14 000	81 920	600 000	6 291 456
15 000	86 016	700 000	7 340 032
16 000	90 112	800 000	8 388 608
17 000	94 208	900 000	9 437 184
18 000	98 304	A00 000	10 485 760
19 000	102 400	B00 000	11 534 336
1A 000	106 496	C00 000	12 582 912
1B 000	110 592	D00 000	13 631 488
1C 000	114 688	E00 000	14 680 064
1D 000	118 784	F00 000	15 728 640
1E 000	122 880	1 000 000	16 777 216
1F 000	126 976	2 000 000	33 554 432

Table K-5. Hexadecimal—Decimal Integer Conversion Table (Cont.)

	0	1	2	3	4	5	6	7	8	9	A	B	C	D	E	F
000	0000	0001	0002	0003	0004	0005	0006	0007	0008	0009	0010	0011	0012	0013	0014	0015
010	0016	0017	0018	0019	0020	0021	0022	0023	0024	0025	0026	0027	0028	0029	0030	0031
020	0032	0033	0034	0035	0036	0037	0038	0039	0040	0041	0042	0043	0044	0045	0046	0047
030	0048	0049	0050	0051	0052	0053	0054	0055	0056	0057	0058	0059	0060	0061	0062	0063
040	0064	0065	0066	0067	0068	0069	0070	0071	0072	0073	0074	0075	0076	0077	0078	0079
050	0080	0081	0082	0083	0084	0085	0086	0087	0088	0089	0090	0091	0092	0093	0094	0095
060	0096	0097	0098	0099	0100	0101	0102	0103	0104	0105	0106	0107	0108	0109	0110	0111
070	0112	0113	0114	0115	0116	0117	0118	0119	0120	0121	0122	0123	0124	0125	0126	0127
080	0128	0129	0130	0131	0132	0133	0134	0135	0136	0137	0138	0139	0140	0141	0142	0143
090	0144	0145	0146	0147	0148	0149	0150	0151	0152	0153	0154	0155	0156	0157	0158	0159
0A0	0160	0161	0162	0163	0164	0165	0166	0167	0168	0169	0170	0171	0172	0173	0174	0175
0B0	0176	0177	0178	0179	0180	0181	0182	0183	0184	0185	0186	0187	0188	0189	0190	0191
0C0	0192	0193	0194	0195	0196	0197	0198	0199	0200	0201	0202	0203	0204	0205	0206	0207
0D0	0208	0209	0210	0211	0212	0213	0214	0215	0216	0217	0218	0219	0220	0221	0222	0223
0E0	0224	0225	0226	0227	0228	0229	0230	0231	0232	0233	0234	0235	0236	0237	0238	0239
0F0	0240	0241	0242	0243	0244	0245	0246	0247	0248	0249	0250	0251	0252	0253	0254	0255
100	0256	0257	0258	0259	0260	0261	0262	0263	0264	0265	0266	0267	0268	0269	0270	0271
110	0272	0273	0274	0275	0276	0277	0278	0279	0280	0281	0282	0283	0284	0285	0286	0287
120	0288	0289	0290	0291	0292	0293	0294	0295	0296	0297	0298	0299	0300	0301	0302	0303
130	0304	0305	0306	0307	0308	0309	0310	0311	0312	0313	0314	0315	0316	0317	0318	0319
140	0320	0321	0322	0323	0324	0325	0326	0327	0328	0329	0330	0331	0332	0333	0334	0335
150	0336	0337	0338	0339	0340	0341	0342	0343	0344	0345	0346	0347	0348	0349	0350	0351
160	0352	0353	0354	0355	0356	0357	0358	0359	0360	0361	0362	0363	0364	0365	0366	0367
170	0368	0369	0370	0371	0372	0373	0374	0375	0376	0377	0378	0379	0380	0381	0382	0383
180	0384	0385	0386	0387	0388	0389	0390	0391	0392	0393	0394	0395	0396	0397	0398	0399
190	0400	0401	0402	0403	0404	0405	0406	0407	0408	0409	0410	0411	0412	0413	0414	0415
1A0	0416	0417	0418	0419	0420	0421	0422	0423	0424	0425	0426	0427	0428	0429	0430	0431
1B0	0432	0433	0434	0435	0436	0437	0438	0439	0440	0441	0442	0443	0444	0445	0446	0447
1C0	0448	0449	0450	0451	0452	0453	0454	0455	0456	0457	0458	0459	0460	0461	0462	0463
1D0	0464	0465	0466	0467	0468	0469	0470	0471	0472	0473	0474	0475	0476	0477	0478	0479
1E0	0480	0481	0482	0483	0484	0485	0486	0487	0488	0489	0490	0491	0492	0493	0494	0495
1F0	0496	0497	0498	0499	0500	0501	0502	0503	0504	0505	0506	0507	0508	0509	0510	0511
200	0512	0513	0514	0515	0516	0517	0518	0519	0529	0521	0522	0523	0524	0525	0526	0527
210	0528	0529	0530	0531	0532	0533	0534	0535	0536	0537	0538	0539	0540	0541	0542	0543
220	0544	0545	0546	0547	0548	0549	0550	0551	0552	0553	0554	0555	0556	0557	0558	0559
230	0560	0561	0562	0563	0564	0565	0566	0567	0568	0569	0570	0571	0572	0573	0574	0575
240	0576	0577	0578	0579	0580	0581	0582	0583	0584	0585	0586	0587	0588	0589	0590	0591
250	0592	0593	0594	0595	0596	0597	0598	0599	0600	0601	0602	0603	0604	0605	0606	0607
260	0608	0609	0610	0611	0612	0613	0614	0615	0616	0617	0618	0619	0620	0621	0622	0623
270	0624	0625	0626	0627	0628	0629	0630	0631	0632	0633	0634	0635	0636	0637	0638	0639
280	0640	0641	0642	0643	0644	0645	0646	0647	0648	0649	0650	0651	0652	0653	0654	0655
290	0656	0657	0658	0659	0660	0661	0662	0663	0664	0665	0666	0667	0668	0669	0670	0671
2A0	0672	0673	0674	0675	0676	0677	0678	0679	0680	0681	0682	0683	0684	0685	0686	0687
2B0	0688	0689	0690	0691	0692	0693	0694	0695	0696	0697	0698	0699	0700	0701	0702	0703
2C0	0704	0705	0706	0707	0708	0709	0710	0711	0712	0713	0714	0715	0716	0717	0718	0719
2D0	0720	0721	0722	0723	0724	0725	0726	0727	0728	0729	0730	0731	0732	0733	0734	0735
2E0	0736	0737	0738	0739	0740	0741	0742	0743	0744	0745	0746	0747	0748	0749	0750	0751
2F0	0752	0753	0754	0755	0756	0757	0758	0759	0760	0761	0762	0763	0764	0765	0766	0767

Table K-5. Hexadecimal–Decimal Integer Conversion Table (Cont.)

	0	1	2	3	4	5	6	7	8	9	A	B	C	D	E	F
300	0768	0769	0770	0771	0772	0773	0774	0775	0776	0777	0778	0779	0780	0781	0782	0783
310	0784	0785	0786	0787	0788	0789	0790	0791	0792	0793	0794	0795	0796	0797	0798	0799
320	0800	0801	0802	0803	0804	0805	0806	0807	0808	0809	0810	0811	0812	0813	0814	0815
330	0816	0817	0818	0819	0820	0821	0822	0823	0824	0825	0826	0827	0828	0829	0830	0831
340	0832	0833	0834	0835	0836	0837	0838	0839	0840	0841	0842	0843	0844	0845	0846	0847
350	0848	0849	0850	0851	0852	0853	0854	0855	0856	0857	0858	0859	0860	0861	0862	0863
360	0864	0865	0866	0867	0868	0869	0870	0871	0872	0873	0874	0875	0876	0877	0878	0879
370	0880	0881	0882	0883	0884	0885	0886	0887	0888	0889	0890	0891	0892	0893	0894	0895
380	0896	0897	0898	0899	0900	0901	0902	0903	0904	0905	0906	0907	0908	0909	0910	0911
390	0912	0913	0914	0915	0916	0917	0918	0919	0920	0921	0922	0923	0924	0925	0926	0927
3A0	0928	0929	0930	0931	0932	0933	0934	0935	0936	0937	0938	0939	0940	0941	0942	0943
3B0	0944	0945	0946	0947	0948	0949	0950	0951	0952	0953	0954	0955	0956	0957	0958	0959
3C0	0960	0961	0962	0963	0964	0965	0966	0967	0968	0969	0970	0971	0972	0973	0974	0975
3D0	0976	0977	0978	0979	0980	0981	0982	0983	0984	0985	0986	0987	0988	0989	0990	0991
3E0	0992	0993	0994	0995	0996	0997	0998	0999	1000	1001	1002	1003	1004	1005	1006	1007
3F0	1008	1009	1010	1011	1012	1013	1014	1015	1016	1017	1018	1019	1020	1021	1022	1023
400	1024	1025	0126	0127	1028	1029	1030	1031	1032	1033	1034	1035	1036	1037	1038	1039
410	1040	1041	1042	1043	1044	1045	1046	1047	1048	1049	1050	1051	1052	1053	1054	1055
420	1056	1057	1058	1059	1060	1061	1062	1063	1064	1065	1066	1067	1068	1069	1070	1071
430	1072	1073	1074	1075	1076	1077	1078	1079	1080	1081	1082	1083	1084	1085	1086	1087
440	1088	1089	1090	1091	1092	1093	1094	1095	1096	1097	1098	1099	1100	1101	1102	1103
450	1104	1105	1106	1107	1108	1109	1110	1111	1112	1113	1114	1115	1116	1117	1118	1119
460	1120	1121	1122	1123	1124	1125	1126	1127	1128	1129	1130	1131	1132	1133	1134	1135
470	1136	1137	1138	1139	1140	1141	1142	1143	1144	1145	1146	1147	1148	1149	1150	1151
480	1152	1153	1154	1155	1156	1157	1158	1159	1160	1161	1162	1163	1164	1165	1166	1167
490	1168	1169	1170	1171	1172	1173	1174	1175	1176	1177	1178	1179	1180	1181	1182	1183
4A0	1184	1185	1186	1187	1188	1189	1190	1191	1192	1193	1194	1195	1196	1197	1198	1199
4B0	1200	1201	1202	1203	1204	1205	1206	1207	1208	1209	1210	1211	1212	1213	1214	1215
4C0	1216	1217	1218	1219	1220	1221	1222	1223	1224	1225	1226	1227	1228	1229	1230	1231
4D0	1232	1233	1234	1235	1236	1237	1238	1239	1240	1241	1242	1243	1244	1245	1246	1247
4E0	1248	1249	1250	1251	1252	1253	1254	1255	1256	1257	1258	1259	1260	1261	1262	1263
4F0	1264	1265	1266	1267	1268	1269	1270	1271	1272	1273	1274	1275	1276	1277	1278	1279
500	1280	1281	1282	1283	1284	1285	1286	1287	1288	1289	1290	1291	1291	1293	1294	1295
510	1296	1297	1298	1299	1399	1301	1302	1303	1304	1305	1306	1307	1308	1309	1310	1311
520	1312	1313	1314	1315	1316	1317	1318	1319	1329	1321	1322	1323	1324	1325	1326	1327
530	1328	1329	1330	1331	1332	1333	1334	1335	1336	1337	1338	1339	1340	1341	1342	1343
540	1344	1345	1346	1347	1348	1349	1350	1351	1352	1353	1354	1355	1356	1367	1358	1359
550	1360	1361	1362	1363	1364	1365	1366	1367	1368	1369	1370	1371	1372	1373	1374	1375
560	1376	1377	1378	1379	1380	1381	1382	1383	1384	1385	1386	1387	1388	1389	1390	1391
570	1392	1393	1394	1395	1396	1397	1398	1399	1400	1401	1402	1403	1404	1405	1406	1407
580	1408	1409	1410	1411	1412	1413	1414	1415	1416	1417	1418	1419	1429	1421	1422	1423
590	1324	1425	1426	1427	1428	1429	1430	1431	1432	1433	1434	1435	1436	1437	1438	1439
5A0	1440	1441	1442	1443	1444	1445	1446	1447	1448	1449	1450	1451	1452	1453	1454	1455
3B0	1456	1457	1458	1459	1460	1461	1462	1463	1464	1465	1466	1467	1468	1469	1470	1471
5C0	1472	1473	1474	1475	1476	1477	1478	1479	1480	1481	1482	1483	1484	1485	1486	1487
5D0	1488	1489	1490	1491	1492	1493	1494	1495	1496	1497	1498	1499	1500	1501	1502	1503
5E0	1504	1505	1506	1507	1508	1509	1510	1511	1512	1513	1514	1515	1516	1517	1518	1519
5F0	1520	1521	1522	1523	1524	1515	1526	1527	1528	1529	1530	1531	1532	1533	1534	1535

Table K-5. Hexadecimal–Decimal Integer Conversion Table (Cont.)

	0	1	2	3	4	5	6	7	8	9	A	B	C	D	E	F
600	1536	1537	1538	1539	1540	1541	1542	1543	1544	1545	1546	1547	1548	1549	1550	1551
610	1552	1553	1554	1555	1556	1557	1558	1559	1560	1561	1562	1563	1564	1565	1566	1567
620	1568	1569	1570	1571	1572	1573	1574	1575	1576	1577	1578	1579	1580	1581	1582	1583
630	1584	1585	1586	1587	1588	1589	1590	1591	1592	1592	1594	1595	1596	1597	1598	1599
640	1600	1601	1602	1603	1604	1605	1606	1607	1608	1609	1610	1611	1612	1613	1614	1615
650	1616	1617	1618	1619	1620	1621	1622	1623	1624	1625	1626	1627	1628	1629	1630	1631
660	1632	1633	1634	1635	1636	1637	1638	1639	1640	1641	1642	1643	1644	1645	1646	1647
670	1648	1649	1650	1651	1652	1653	1654	1655	1656	1657	1658	1659	1660	1661	1662	1663
680	1664	1665	1666	1667	1668	1669	1670	1671	1672	1673	1674	1675	1676	1677	1678	1679
690	1680	1681	1682	1683	1684	1685	1686	1687	1688	1689	1690	1691	1692	1693	1694	1695
6A0	1696	1697	1698	1699	1700	1701	1702	1703	1704	1705	1706	1707	1708	1709	1710	1711
6B0	1712	1713	1714	1715	1716	1717	1718	1719	1720	1721	1722	17231	1724	1725	1726	1727
6C0	1728	1729	1730	1731	1732	1733	1734	1735	1736	1737	1738	1739	1740	1741	1742	1743
6D0	1744	1745	1746	1747	1748	1749	1750	1751	1752	1753	1754	1755	1756	1757	1758	1759
6E0	1760	1761	1762	1763	1764	1765	1766	1767	1768	1769	1770	1771	1772	1773	1774	1775
6F0	1776	1777	1778	1779	1780	1781	1782	1783	1784	1785	1786	1787	1788	1789	1790	1791
700	1792	1793	1794	1795	1796	1797	1798	1799	1800	1801	8102	1803	1804	1805	1806	1807
710	1808	1809	1810	1811	1812	1813	1814	1815	1816	1817	1818	1819	1820	1821	1822	1823
720	1824	1825	1826	1827	1818	1829	1830	1831	1832	1833	1834	1835	1836	1837	1838	1839
730	1840	1841	1842	1843	1844	1845	1846	1847	1848	1849	1850	1851	1852	1853	1854	1855
740	1856	1857	1858	1859	1860	1861	1862	1863	1864	1865	1866	1867	1868	1869	1870	1871
750	1872	1873	1874	1875	1876	1877	1878	1879	1880	1881	1882	1883	1884	1885	1886	1887
760	1888	1889	1890	1891	1892	1893	1894	1895	1896	1897	1898	1899	1900	1909	1902	1903
770	1904	1905	1906	1907	1908	1909	1910	1911	1912	1913	1914	1915	1916	1917	1918	1919
780	1920	1921	1922	1923	1924	1925	1926	1927	1928	1929	1930	1931	1932	1933	1934	1935
790	1936	1937	1938	1939	1940	1941	1942	1943	1944	1945	1946	1947	1948	1949	1950	1951
7A0	1952	1953	1954	1955	1956	1957	1958	1959	1960	1961	1962	1963	1964	1965	1966	1967
7B0	1968	1969	1970	1971	1972	1973	1974	1975	1976	1977	1978	1979	1980	1981	1982	1983
7C0	1984	1985	1986	1987	1988	1989	1990	1991	1992	1993	1994	1995	1996	1997	1998	1999
7D0	2000	2001	2002	2003	2004	2005	2006	2007	2008	2009	2010	2011	2012	2013	2014	2015
7E0	2016	2017	2018	2019	2020	2021	2022	2023	2024	2025	2026	2027	2028	2029	2030	2031
7F0	2032	2033	2034	2035	2036	2037	2038	2039	2040	2041	2042	2043	2044	2045	2046	2047
800	2048	2049	2050	2051	2052	2053	2054	2055	2056	2057	2058	2059	2060	2061	2062	2063
810	2064	2065	2066	2067	2068	2069	2070	2071	2072	2073	2074	2075	2076	2077	2078	2079
820	2080	2081	2082	2083	2084	2085	2086	2087	2088	2089	2090	2091	2092	2093	2094	2095
830	2096	2097	2098	2099	2100	2101	2102	2103	2104	2105	2106	2107	2108	2109	2110	2111
840	2112	2113	2114	2115	2116	2117	2118	2119	2120	2121	2122	2123	2124	2125	2126	2127
850	2128	2129	2130	2131	2132	2133	2134	2135	2136	2137	2138	2139	2140	2141	2142	2143
860	2144	2145	2146	2147	2148	2149	2150	2151	2152	2153	2154	2155	2156	2157	2158	2159
870	2160	2161	2162	2163	2164	2165	2166	2167	2168	2169	2170	2171	2172	2173	2174	2175
880	2176	2177	2178	2179	2180	2181	2182	2183	2184	2185	2186	2187	2188	2189	2190	2191
890	2192	2193	2194	2195	2196	2197	2198	2199	2200	2201	2202	2203	2204	2205	2206	2207
8A0	2208	2209	2210	2211	2212	2213	2214	2215	2216	2217	2218	2219	2220	2221	2222	2223
8B0	2224	2225	2226	2227	2228	2229	2230	2231	2232	2233	2234	2235	2236	2237	2238	2239
8C0	2240	2241	2242	2243	2244	2245	2246	2247	2248	2249	2250	2251	2252	2253	2254	2255
8D0	2256	2257	2258	2259	2260	2261	2262	2263	2264	2265	2266	2267	2268	2269	2270	2271
8E0	2272	2273	2274	2275	2276	2277	2278	2279	2280	2281	2282	2283	2284	2285	2286	2287
8F0	2288	2289	2290	2291	2292	2293	2294	2295	2296	2297	2298	2299	2300	2301	2302	2303

Table K-5. Hexadecimal–Decimal Integer Conversion Table (Cont.)

	0	1	2	3	4	5	6	7	8	9	A	B	C	D	E	F
900	2304	2305	2306	2307	2308	2309	2310	2311	2312	2313	2314	2315	2316	2317	2318	2319
910	2320	2321	2322	2323	2324	2325	2326	2327	2328	2329	2330	2331	2332	2333	2334	2335
920	2336	2337	2338	2339	2340	2341	2342	2343	2344	2345	2346	2347	2348	2349	2350	2351
930	2352	2353	2354	2355	2356	2357	2358	2359	2360	2361	2362	2363	2364	2365	2366	2367
940	2368	2369	2370	2371	2372	2373	2374	2375	2376	2377	2378	2379	2380	2381	2382	2383
950	2384	2385	2386	2387	2388	2389	2390	2391	2392	2393	2394	2395	3496	2397	2398	2399
960	2400	2401	2402	2403	2404	2405	2406	2407	2408	2409	2410	2411	2412	2413	2414	2415
970	2416	2417	2418	2419	2420	2421	2422	2423	2424	2425	2426	2427	2428	2429	2430	2431
980	2432	2433	2434	24351	2436	2437	2438	2439	2440	2441	2442	2443	2444	2445	2446	2447
990	2448	2449	2450	2451	2452	2453	2454	2455	2456	2457	2458	2459	2460	2461	2462	2463
9A0	2464	2465	2466	2467	2468	2469	2479	2471	2472	2473	2474	2475	2476	2477	2478	2479
9B0	2480	2481	2482	2483	2484	2485	2486	2487	2488	2489	2490	2491	2492	2493	2494	2495
9C0	2496	2497	2498	2499	2500	2501	2502	2503	2504	2505	2506	2507	2508	2509	2510	2511
9D0	2512	2513	2514	2515	2516	2517	2518	2519	2520	2521	2522	2523	2524	2525	2526	2527
9E0	2528	2529	2530	2531	2532	2533	2534	2535	2536	2537	2538	2539	2540	2541	2542	2543
9F0	2544	2545	2546	2547	2548	2549	2550	2551	2552	2553	2554	2555	2556	2557	2558	2559
A00	2560	2561	2562	2563	2564	2565	2566	2567	2568	2569	2570	2571	2572	2573	2574	2575
A10	2576	2577	2578	2579	2580	2581	2582	2583	2584	2585	2586	2587	2588	2589	2590	2591
A20	2592	2593	2594	2595	2596	2597	2598	2599	2600	2601	2602	2603	2604	2605	2606	2607
A30	2608	2609	2610	2611	2612	2613	2614	2615	2626	2617	2618	2619	2620	2621	2622	2623
A40	2624	2625	2626	2627	2628	2629	2630	2631	2632	2633	2634	2635	2636	2637	2638	2639
A50	2640	2641	2642	2643	2644	2645	2646	2647	2648	2649	2650	2651	2652	2653	2654	2655
A60	2656	2657	2658	2659	2660	2661	2662	2663	2664	2665	2666	2667	2668	2669	2670	2671
A70	2672	2673	2674	2675	2676	2677	2678	2679	2680	2681	2682	2683	2684	2685	2686	2687
A80	2688	2689	2690	2691	2692	2693	2694	2695	2696	2697	2698	2699	2700	2701	2702	2703
A90	2704	2705	2706	2707	2708	2709	2710	2711	2712	2713	2714	2715	2716	2717	2718	2719
AA0	2720	2721	2722	2723	2724	2725	2726	2727	2728	2729	2730	2731	2732	2733	2734	2735
AB0	2736	2737	2738	2739	2740	2741	2742	2743	2744	2745	2746	2747	2748	2749	2750	2751
AC0	2752	2753	2754	2755	2756	2757	2758	2759	2760	2761	2762	2763	2764	2765	2766	2767
AD0	2768	2769	2770	2771	2772	2773	2774	2775	2776	2777	2778	2779	2780	2781	2782	2783
AE0	2784	2785	2786	2787	2788	2789	2790	2791	2792	2793	2794	2795	2796	2797	2798	2799
AF0	2800	2801	2802	2803	2804	2805	2806	2807	2808	2809	2810	2811	2812	2813	2814	2815
B00	2816	2817	2818	2819	2820	2821	2822	2823	2824	2825	2826	2827	2828	2829	2830	2831
B10	2832	2833	2834	2835	2836	2837	2838	2839	2840	2841	2842	2843	2844	2845	2846	2847
B20	2848	2849	2850	2851	2852	2853	2854	2855	2856	2857	2858	2859	2860	2861	2862	2863
B30	2864	2865	2866	2867	2868	2869	2870	2871	2872	2873	2874	2875	2876	2877	2878	2879
B40	2880	2881	2882	2883	2884	2885	2886	2887	2888	2889	2890	2891	2892	2893	2894	2895
B50	2896	2897	2898	2899	2900	2901	2902	2903	2904	2905	2906	2907	2908	2909	2910	2911
B60	2912	2913	2914	2915	2916	2917	2918	2919	2920	2921	2922	2923	2924	2925	2926	2927
B70	2928	2929	2930	2931	2932	2933	2934	2935	2936	2937	2938	2939	2940	2941	2942	2943
B80	2944	2945	2946	2947	2948	2949	2950	2951	2952	2953	2954	2955	2956	2957	2958	2959
B90	2960	2961	2962	2963	2964	2965	2966	2967	2968	2969	2970	2971	2972	2973	2974	2975
BA0	2976	2977	2978	2979	2980	2981	2982	2983	2984	2985	2986	2987	2988	2989	2990	2991
BB0	2992	2993	2994	2995	2996	2997	2998	2999	3000	3001	3002	3003	3004	3005	3006	3007
BC0	3008	3009	3010	3011	3012	3013	3014	3015	3016	3017	3018	3019	3020	3021	3022	3023
BD0	3024	3025	3026	3027	3028	3029	3030	3031	3032	3033	3034	3035	3036	3037	3038	3039
BE0	3040	3041	3042	3043	3044	3045	3046	3047	3048	3049	3050	3051	3052	3053	3054	3055
BF0	3056	3057	3058	3059	3060	3061	3062	3063	3064	3065	3066	3067	3068	3069	3070	3071

Table K-5. Hexadecimal–Decimal Integer Conversion Table (Cont.)

	0	1	2	3	4	5	6	7	8	9	A	B	C	D	E	F
C00	3072	3073	3074	3075	3076	3077	3078	3079	3080	3081	3082	3083	3084	3085	3086	3087
C10	3088	3089	3090	3091	3092	3093	3094	3095	3096	3097	3098	3099	3100	3101	3102	3103
C20	3104	3105	3106	3107	3108	3109	3110	3111	3112	3113	3114	3115	3116	3117	3118	3119
C30	3120	3121	3122	3123	3124	3125	3126	3127	3128	3129	3130	3131	3132	3133	3134	3135
C40	3136	3137	3138	3139	3140	3141	3142	3143	3144	3145	3146	3147	3148	3149	3150	3151
C50	3152	3153	3154	3155	3156	3157	3158	3159	3160	3161	3162	3163	3164	3165	3166	3167
C60	3168	3169	3170	3171	3172	3173	3174	3175	3176	3177	3178	3179	3180	3181	3182	3183
C70	3184	3185	3186	3187	3188	3189	3190	3191	3192	3193	3194	3195	3196	3197	3198	3199
C80	3200	3201	3202	3203	3204	3205	3206	3207	3208	3209	3210	3211	3212	3213	3214	3215
C90	3216	3217	3218	3219	3220	3221	3222	3223	3224	3225	3226	3227	3228	3229	3230	3231
CA0	3232	3233	3234	3235	3236	3237	3238	3239	3240	3241	3242	3243	3244	3245	3246	3247
CB0	3248	3249	3250	3251	3252	3253	3254	3255	3256	3257	3258	3259	3260	3261	3262	3263
CC0	3264	3265	3266	3267	3268	3269	3270	3271	3272	3273	3274	3275	3276	3277	3278	3279
CD0	3280	3281	3282	3283	3284	3285	3286	3287	3288	3289	3290	3291	3292	3293	3294	3295
CE0	3296	3297	3298	3299	3300	3301	3302	3303	3304	3305	3306	3307	3308	3309	3310	3311
CF0	3312	3313	3314	3315	3316	3317	3318	3319	3320	3321	3322	3323	3324	3325	3326	3327
D00	3328	3329	3330	3331	3332	3333	3334	3335	3336	3337	3338	3339	3340	3341	3342	3343
D10	3344	3345	3346	3347	3348	3349	3350	3351	3352	3353	3354	3355	3356	3357	3358	3359
D20	3360	3361	3362	3363	3364	3365	3366	3367	3368	3369	3370	3371	3372	3373	3374	3375
D30	3376	3377	3378	3379	3380	3381	3382	3383	3384	3385	3386	3387	3388	3389	3390	3391
D40	3392	3393	3394	3395	3396	3397	3398	3399	3400	3401	3402	3403	3404	3405	3406	3407
D50	3408	3409	3410	3411	3412	3413	3414	3415	3416	3417	3418	3419	3420	3421	3422	3423
D60	3424	3425	3426	3427	3428	3429	3430	3431	3432	3433	3434	3435	3436	3437	3438	3439
D70	3440	3441	3442	3443	3444	3445	3446	3447	3448	3449	3450	3451	3452	3453	3454	3455
D80	3456	3457	3458	3459	3460	3461	3462	3463	3464	3465	3466	3467	3468	3469	3470	3471
D90	3472	3473	3474	3475	3476	3477	3478	3479	3480	3481	3482	3483	3484	3485	3486	3487
DA0	3488	3489	3490	3491	3492	3493	3494	3495	3496	3497	3498	3499	3500	3501	3502	3503
DB0	3504	3505	3506	3507	3508	3509	3510	3511	3512	3513	3514	3515	3516	3517	3518	3519
DC0	3520	3521	3522	3523	3524	3525	3526	3527	3528	3529	3530	3531	3532	3533	3534	3535
DD0	3536	3537	3538	3539	3540	3541	3542	3543	3544	3545	3546	3547	3548	3549	3550	3551
DE0	3552	3553	3554	3555	3556	3557	3558	3559	3560	3561	3562	3563	3564	3565	3566	3567
DF0	3568	3569	3570	3571	3572	3573	3574	3575	3576	3577	3578	3579	3580	3581	3582	3583
E00	3584	3585	3586	3587	3588	3589	3590	3591	3592	3593	3594	3595	3596	3597	3598	3599
E10	3600	3601	3602	3603	3604	3605	3606	3607	3608	3609	3610	3611	3612	3613	3614	3615
E20	3616	3617	3618	3619	3620	3621	3622	3623	3624	3625	3626	3627	3628	3629	3630	3631
E30	3632	3633	3634	3635	3636	3637	3638	3639	3640	3641	3642	3643	3644	3645	3646	3647
E40	3648	3649	3650	3651	3652	3653	3654	3655	3656	3657	3658	3659	3660	3661	3662	3663
E50	3664	3665	3666	3667	3668	3669	3670	3671	3672	3673	3674	3675	3676	3677	3678	3679
E60	3680	3681	3682	3683	3684	3685	3686	3687	3688	3689	3690	3691	3692	3693	3694	3695
E70	3696	3697	3698	3699	3700	3701	3702	3703	3704	3705	3706	3707	3708	3709	3710	3711
E80	3712	3713	3714	3715	3716	3717	3718	3719	3720	3721	3722	3723	3724	3725	3726	3727
E90	3728	3729	3730	3731	3732	3733	3734	3735	3736	3737	3738	3739	3740	3741	3742	3743
EA0	3744	3745	3746	3747	3748	3749	3750	3751	3752	3753	3754	3755	3756	3757	3758	3759
EB0	3760	3761	3762	3763	3764	3765	3766	3767	3768	3769	3770	3771	3772	3773	3774	3775

Table K-5. Hexadecimal–Decimal Integer Conversion Table (Cont.)

	0	1	2	3	4	5	6	7	8	9	A	B	C	D	E	F
EC0	3776	3777	3778	3779	3780	3781	3782	3783	3784	3785	3786	3787	3788	3789	3790	3791
ED0	3792	3793	3794	3795	3796	3797	3798	3799	3800	3801	3802	3803	3804	3805	3806	3807
EE0	3808	3809	3810	3811	3812	3813	3814	3815	3816	3817	3818	3819	3820	3821	3822	3823
EF0	3824	3825	3826	3827	3828	3829	3830	3831	3832	3833	3834	3835	3836	3837	3838	3839
F00	3840	3841	3842	3843	3844	3845	3846	3847	3848	3849	3850	3851	3852	3853	3854	3855
F10	3856	3857	3858	3859	3860	3861	3862	3863	3864	3865	3866	3867	3868	3869	3870	3871
F20	3872	3873	3874	3875	3876	3877	3878	3879	3880	3881	3882	3883	3884	3885	3886	3887
F30	3888	3889	3890	3891	3892	3893	3894	3895	3896	3897	3898	3899	3900	3901	3902	3903
F40	3904	3905	3906	3907	3908	3909	3910	3911	3912	3913	3914	3915	3916	3917	3918	3919
F50	3920	3921	3922	3923	3924	3925	3926	3927	3928	3929	3930	3931	3932	3933	3934	3935
F60	3936	3937	3938	3939	3940	3941	3942	3943	3944	3945	3946	3947	3948	3949	3950	3951
F70	3952	3953	3954	3955	3956	3957	3958	3959	3960	3961	3962	3963	3964	3965	3966	3967
F80	3968	3969	3970	3971	3972	3973	3974	3975	3976	3977	3978	3979	3980	3981	3982	3983
F90	3984	3985	3986	3987	3988	3989	3990	3991	3992	3993	3994	3995	3996	3997	3998	3999
FA0	4000	4001	4002	4003	4004	4005	4006	4007	4008	4009	4010	4011	4012	4013	4014	4015
FB0	4016	4017	4018	4019	4020	4021	4022	4023	4024	4025	4026	4027	4028	4029	4030	4031
FC0	4032	4033	4034	4035	4036	4037	4038	4039	4040	4041	4042	4043	4044	4045	4046	4047
FD0	4048	4049	4050	4051	4052	4053	4054	4055	4056	4057	4058	4059	4060	4061	4062	4063
FE0	4064	4065	4066	4067	4068	4069	4070	4071	4072	4073	4074	4075	4076	4077	4078	4079
FF0	4080	4081	4082	4083	4084	4085	4086	4087	4088	4089	4090	4091	4092	4093	4094	4095

APPENDIX

Table K-6. Hexadecimal–Decimal Fraction Conversion Table

Hexadecimal	Decimal	Hexadecimal	Decimal	Hexadecimal	Decimal	Hexadecimal	Decimal
.00 00 00 00	.00000 00000	.40 00 00 00	.25000 00000	.80 00 00 00	.50000 00000	.C0 00 00 00	.75000 00000
.01 00 00 00	.00390 62500	.41 00 00 00	.25390 62500	.81 00 00 00	.50390 62500	.C1 00 00 00	.75390 62500
.02 00 00 00	.00781 25000	.42 00 00 00	.25781 25000	.82 00 00 00	.50781 25000	.C2 00 00 00	.75781 25000
.03 00 00 00	.01171 87500	.43 00 00 00	.26171 87500	.83 00 00 00	.51171 87500	.C3 00 00 00	.76171 87500
.04 00 00 00	.01562 50000	.44 00 00 00	.26562 50000	.84 00 00 00	.51562 50000	.C4 00 00 00	.76562 50000
.05 00 00 00	.01953 12500	.45 00 00 00	.26953 12500	.85 00 00 00	.51953 12500	.C5 00 00 00	.76953 12500
.06 00 00 00	.02343 75000	.46 00 00 00	.27343 75000	.86 00 00 00	.52343 75000	.C6 00 00 00	.77343 75000
.07 00 00 00	.02734 37500	.47 00 00 00	.27734 37500	.87 00 00 00	.52734 37500	.C7 00 00 00	.77734 37500
.08 00 00 00	.03125 00000	.48 00 00 00	.28125 00000	.88 00 00 00	.53125 00000	.C8 00 00 00	.78125 00000
.09 00 00 00	.03515 62500	.49 00 00 00	.28515 62500	.89 00 00 00	.53515 62500	.C9 00 00 00	.78515 62500
.0A 00 00 00	.03906 25000	.4A 00 00 00	.28906 25000	.8A 00 00 00	.53906 25000	.CA 00 00 00	.78906 25000
.0B 00 00 00	.04296 87500	.4B 00 00 00	.29296 87500	.8B 00 00 00	.54296 87500	.CB 00 00 00	.79296 87500
.0C 00 00 00	.04687 50000	.4C 00 00 00	.29687 50000	.8C 00 00 00	.54687 50000	.CC 00 00 00	.79687 50000
.0D 00 00 00	.05078 12500	.4D 00 00 00	.30078 12500	.8D 00 00 00	.55078 12500	.CD 00 00 00	.80078 12500
.0E 00 00 00	.05468 75000	.4E 00 00 00	.30468 75000	.8E 00 00 00	.55468 75000	.CE 00 00 00	.80468 75000
.0F 00 00 00	.05859 37500	.4F 00 00 00	.30859 37500	.8F 00 00 00	.55859 37500	.CF 00 00 00	.80859 37500
.10 00 00 00	.06250 00000	.50 00 00 00	.31250 00000	.90 00 00 00	.56250 00000	.D0 00 00 00	.81250 00000
.11 00 00 00	.06640 62500	.51 00 00 00	.31640 62500	.91 00 00 00	.56640 62500	.D1 00 00 00	.81640 62500
.12 00 00 00	.07031 25000	.52 00 00 00	.32031 25000	.92 00 00 00	.57031 25000	.D2 00 00 00	.82031 25000
.13 00 00 00	.07421 87500	.53 00 00 00	.32421 87500	.93 00 00 00	.57421 87500	.D3 00 00 00	.82421 87500
.14 00 00 00	.07812 50000	.54 00 00 00	.32812 50000	.94 00 00 00	.57812 50000	.D4 00 00 00	.82812 50000
.15 00 00 00	.08203 12500	.55 00 00 00	.33203 12500	.95 00 00 00	.58203 12500	.D5 00 00 00	.83203 12500
.16 00 00 00	.08593 75000	.56 00 00 00	.33593 75000	.96 00 00 00	.58593 75000	.D6 00 00 00	.83593 75000
.17 00 00 00	.08984 37500	.57 00 00 00	.33984 37500	.97 00 00 00	.58984 37500	.D7 00 00 00	.83984 37500
.18 00 00 00	.09375 00000	.58 00 00 00	.34375 00000	.98 00 00 00	.59375 00000	.D8 00 00 00	.84375 00000
.19 00 00 00	.09765 62500	.59 00 00 00	.34765 62500	.99 00 00 00	.59765 62500	.D9 00 00 00	.84765 62500
.1A 00 00 00	.10156 25000	.5A 00 00 00	.35156 25000	.9A 00 00 00	.60156 25000	.DA 00 00 00	.85156 25000
.1B 00 00 00	.10546 87500	.5B 00 00 00	.35546 87500	.9B 00 00 00	.60546 87500	.DB 00 00 00	.85546 87500
.1C 00 00 00	.10937 50000	.5C 00 00 00	.35937 50000	.9C 00 00 00	.60937 50000	.DC 00 00 00	.85937 50000
.1D 00 00 00	.11328 12500	.5D 00 00 00	.36328 12500	.9D 00 00 00	.61328 12500	.DD 00 00 00	.86328 12500
.1E 00 00 00	.11718 75000	.5E 00 00 00	.36718 75000	.9E 00 00 00	.61718 75000	.DE 00 00 00	.86718 75000
.1F 00 00 00	.12109 37500	.5F 00 00 00	.37109 37500	.9F 00 00 00	.62109 37500	.DF 00 00 00	.87109 37500
.20 00 00 00	.12500 00000	.60 00 00 00	.37500 00000	.A0 00 00 00	.62500 00000	.E0 00 00 00	.87500 00000
.21 00 00 00	.12890 62500	.61 00 00 00	.37890 62500	.A1 00 00 00	.62890 62500	.E1 00 00 00	.87890 62500
.22 00 00 00	.13281 25000	.62 00 00 00	.38281 25000	.A2 00 00 00	.63281 25000	.E2 00 00 00	.88281 25000
.23 00 00 00	.13671 87500	.63 00 00 00	.38671 87500	.A3 00 00 00	.63671 87500	.E3 00 00 00	.88671 87500
.24 00 00 00	.14062 50000	.64 00 00 00	.39062 50000	.A4 00 00 00	.64062 50000	.E4 00 00 00	.89062 50000
.25 00 00 00	.14453 12500	.65 00 00 00	.39453 12500	.A5 00 00 00	.64453 12500	.E5 00 00 00	.89453 12500
.26 00 00 00	.14843 75000	.66 00 00 00	.39843 75000	.A6 00 00 00	.64843 75000	.E6 00 00 00	.89843 75000
.27 00 00 00	.15234 37500	.67 00 00 00	.40234 37500	.A7 00 00 00	.65234 37500	.E7 00 00 00	.90234 37500
.28 00 00 00	.15625 00000	.68 00 00 00	.40625 00000	.A8 00 00 00	.65625 00000	.E8 00 00 00	.90625 00000
.29 00 00 00	.16015 62500	.69 00 00 00	.41015 62500	.A9 00 00 00	.66015 62500	.E9 00 00 00	.91015 62500
.2A 00 00 00	.16406 25000	.6A 00 00 00	.41406 25000	.AA 00 00 00	.66406 25000	.EA 00 00 00	.91406 25000
.2B 00 00 00	.16796 87500	.6B 00 00 00	.41796 87500	.AB 00 00 00	.66796 87500	.EB 00 00 00	.91796 87500
.2C 00 00 00	.17187 50000	.6C 00 00 00	.42187 50000	.AC 00 00 00	.67187 50000	.EC 00 00 00	.92187 50000
.2D 00 00 00	.17578 12500	.6D 00 00 00	.42578 12500	.AD 00 00 00	.67578 12500	.ED 00 00 00	.92578 12500
.2E 00 00 00	.17968 75000	.6E 00 00 00	.42968 75000	.AE 00 00 00	.67968 75000	.EE 00 00 00	.92968 75000
.2F 00 00 00	.18359 37500	.6F 00 00 00	.43359 37500	.AF 00 00 00	.68359 37500	.EF 00 00 00	.93359 37500
.30 00 00 00	.18750 00000	.70 00 00 00	.43750 00000	.B0 00 00 00	.68750 00000	.F0 00 00 00	.93750 00000
.31 00 00 00	.19140 62500	.71 00 00 00	.44140 62500	.B1 00 00 00	.69140 62500	.F1 00 00 00	.94140 62500
.32 00 00 00	.19531 25000	.72 00 00 00	.44531 25000	.B2 00 00 00	.69531 25000	.F2 00 00 00	.94531 25000
.33 00 00 00	.19921 87500	.73 00 00 00	.44921 87500	.B3 00 00 00	.69921 87500	.F3 00 00 00	.94921 87500
.34 00 00 00	.20312 50000	.74 00 00 00	.45312 50000	.B4 00 00 00	.70312 50000	.F4 00 00 00	.95312 50000
.35 00 00 00	.20703 12500	.75 00 00 00	.45703 12500	.B5 00 00 00	.70703 12500	.F5 00 00 00	.95703 12500
.36 00 00 00	.21093 75000	.76 00 00 00	.46093 75000	.B6 00 00 00	.71093 75000	.F6 00 00 00	.96093 75000
.37 00 00 00	.21484 37500	.77 00 00 00	.46484 37500	.B7 00 00 00	.71484 37500	.F7 00 00 00	.96484 37500
.38 00 00 00	.21875 00000	.78 00 00 00	.46875 00000	.B8 00 00 00	.71875 00000	.F8 00 00 00	.96875 00000
.39 00 00 00	.22265 62500	.79 00 00 00	.47265 62500	.B9 00 00 00	.72265 62500	.F9 00 00 00	.97265 62500
.3A 00 00 00	.22656 25000	.7A 00 00 00	.47656 25000	.BA 00 00 00	.72656 25000	.FA 00 00 00	.97656 25000
.3B 00 00 00	.23046 87500	.7B 00 00 00	.48046 87500	.BB 00 00 00	.73046 87500	.FB 00 00 00	.98046 87500
.3C 00 00 00	.23437 50000	.7C 00 00 00	.48437 50000	.BC 00 00 00	.73437 50000	.FC 00 00 00	.98437 50000
.3D 00 00 00	.23828 12500	.7D 00 00 00	.48828 12500	.BD 00 00 00	.73828 12500	.FD 00 00 00	.98828 12500
.3E 00 00 00	.24218 75000	.7E 00 00 00	.49218 75000	.BE 00 00 00	.74218 75000	.FE 00 00 00	.99218 75000
.3F 00 00 00	.24609 37500	.7F 00 00 00	.49609 37500	.BF 00 00 00	.74609 37500	.FF 00 00 00	.99609 37500

Table K-6. Hexadecimal–Decimal Fraction Conversion Table (Cont.)

Hexadecimal	Decimal	Hexadecimal	Decimal	Hexadecimal	Decimal	Hexadecimal	Decimal
.00 00 00 00	.00000 00000	.00 40 00 00	.00097 65625	.00 80 00 00	.00195 31250	.00 C0 00 00	.00292 96875
.00 01 00 00	.00001 52587	.00 41 00 00	.00099 18212	.00 81 00 00	.00196 83837	.00 C1 00 00	.00294 49462
.00 02 00 00	.00003 05175	.00 42 00 00	.00100 70800	.00 82 00 00	.00198 36425	.00 C2 00 00	.00296 02050
.00 03 00 00	.00004 57763	.00 43 00 00	.00102 23388	.00 83 00 00	.00199 89013	.00 C3 00 00	.00297 54638
.00 04 00 00	.00006 10351	.00 44 00 00	.00103 75976	.00 84 00 00	.00201 41601	.00 C4 00 00	.00299 07226
.00 05 00 00	.00007 62939	.00 45 00 00	.00105 28564	.00 85 00 00	.00202 94189	.00 C5 00 00	.00300 59814
.00 06 00 00	.00009 15527	.00 46 00 00	.00106 81152	.00 86 00 00	.00204 46777	.00 C6 00 00	.00302 12402
.00 07 00 00	.00010 68115	.00 47 00 00	.00108 33740	.00 87 00 00	.00205 99365	.00 C7 00 00	.00303 64990
.00 08 00 00	.00012 20703	.00 48 00 00	.00109 86328	.00 88 00 00	.00207 51953	.00 C8 00 00	.00305 17578
.00 09 00 00	.00013 73291	.00 49 00 00	.00111 38916	.00 89 00 00	.00209 04541	.00 C9 00 00	.00306 70166
.00 0A 00 00	.00015 25878	.00 4A 00 00	.00112 91503	.00 8A 00 00	.00210 57128	.00 CA 00 00	.00308 22753
.00 0B 00 00	.00016 78466	.00 4B 00 00	.00114 44091	.00 8B 00 00	.00212 09716	.00 CB 00 00	.00309 75341
.00 0C 00 00	.00018 31054	.00 4C 00 00	.00115 96679	.00 8C 00 00	.00213 62304	.00 CC 00 00	.00311 27929
.00 0D 00 00	.00019 83642	.00 4D 00 00	.00117 49267	.00 8D 00 00	.00215 14892	.00 CD 00 00	.00312 80517
.00 0E 00 00	.00021 36230	.00 4E 00 00	.00119 01855	.00 8E 00 00	.00216 67480	.00 CE 00 00	.00314 33105
.00 0F 00 00	.00022 88818	.00 4F 00 00	.00120 54443	.00 8F 00 00	.00218 20068	.00 CF 00 00	.00315 85693
.00 10 00 00	.00024 41406	.00 50 00 00	.00122 07031	.00 90 00 00	.00219 72656	.00 D0 00 00	.00317 38281
.00 11 00 00	.00025 93994	.00 51 00 00	.00123 59619	.00 91 00 00	.00221 25244	.00 D1 00 00	.00318 90869
.00 12 00 00	.00027 46582	.00 52 00 00	.00125 12207	.00 92 00 00	.00222 77832	.00 D2 00 00	.00320 43457
.00 13 00 00	.00028 99169	.00 53 00 00	.00126 64794	.00 93 00 00	.00224 30419	.00 D3 00 00	.00321 96044
.00 14 00 00	.00030 51757	.00 54 00 00	.00128 17382	.00 94 00 00	.00225 83007	.00 D4 00 00	.00323 48632
.00 15 00 00	.00032 04345	.00 55 00 00	.00129 69970	.00 95 00 00	.00227 35595	.00 D5 00 00	.00325 01220
.00 16 00 00	.00033 56933	.00 56 00 00	.00131 22558	.00 96 00 00	.00228 88183	.00 D6 00 00	.00326 53808
.00 17 00 00	.00035 09521	.00 57 00 00	.00132 75146	.00 97 00 00	.00230 40771	.00 D7 00 00	.00328 06396
.00 18 00 00	.00036 62109	.00 58 00 00	.00134 27734	.00 98 00 00	.00231 93359	.00 D8 00 00	.00329 58984
.00 19 00 00	.00038 14697	.00 59 00 00	.00135 80322	.00 99 00 00	.00233 45947	.00 D9 00 00	.00331 11572
.00 1A 00 00	.00039 67285	.00 5A 00 00	.00137 32910	.00 9A 00 00	.00234 98535	.00 DA 00 00	.00332 64160
.00 1B 00 00	.00041 19873	.00 5B 00 00	.00138 85498	.00 9B 00 00	.00236 51123	.00 DB 00 00	.00334 16748
.00 1C 00 00	.00042 72460	.00 5C 00 00	.00140 38085	.00 9C 00 00	.00238 03710	.00 DC 00 00	.00335 69335
.00 1D 00 00	.00044 25048	.00 5D 00 00	.00141 90673	.00 9D 00 00	.00239 56298	.00 DD 00 00	.00337 21923
.00 1E 00 00	.00045 77636	.00 5E 00 00	.00143 43261	.00 9E 00 00	.00241 08886	.00 DE 00 00	.00338 74511
.00 1F 00 00	.00047 30224	.00 5F 00 00	.00144 95849	.00 9F 00 00	.00242 61474	.00 DF 00 00	.00340 27099
.00 20 00 00	.00048 82812	.00 60 00 00	.00146 48437	.00 A0 00 00	.00244 14062	.00 E0 00 00	.00341 79687
.00 21 00 00	.00050 35400	.00 61 00 00	.00148 01025	.00 A1 00 00	.00245 66650	.00 E1 00 00	.00343 32275
.00 22 00 00	.00051 87988	.00 62 00 00	.00149 53613	.00 A2 00 00	.00247 19238	.00 E2 00 00	.00344 84863
.00 23 00 00	.00053 40576	.00 63 00 00	.00151 06201	.00 A3 00 00	.00248 71826	.00 E3 00 00	.00346 37451
.00 24 00 00	.00054 93164	.00 64 00 00	.00152 58789	.00 A4 00 00	.00250 24414	.00 E4 00 00	.00347 90039
.00 25 00 00	.00056 45751	.00 65 00 00	.00154 11376	.00 A5 00 00	.00251 77001	.00 E5 00 00	.00349 42626
.00 26 00 00	.00057 98339	.00 66 00 00	.00155 63964	.00 A6 00 00	.00253 29589	.00 E6 00 00	.00350 95214
.00 27 00 00	.00059 50927	.00 67 00 00	.00157 16552	.00 A7 00 00	.00254 82177	.00 E7 00 00	.00352 47802
.00 28 00 00	.00061 03515	.00 68 00 00	.00158 69140	.00 A8 00 00	.00256 34765	.00 E8 00 00	.00354 00390
.00 29 00 00	.00062 56103	.00 69 00 00	.00160 21728	.00 A9 00 00	.00257 87353	.00 E9 00 00	.00355 52978
.00 2A 00 00	.00064 08691	.00 6A 00 00	.00161 74316	.00 AA 00 00	.00259 39941	.00 EA 00 00	.00357 05566
.00 2B 00 00	.00065 61279	.00 6B 00 00	.00163 26904	.00 AB 00 00	.00260 92529	.00 EB 00 00	.00358 58154
.00 2C 00 00	.00067 13867	.00 6C 00 00	.00164 79492	.00 AC 00 00	.00262 45117	.00 EC 00 00	.00360 10742
.00 2D 00 00	.00068 66455	.00 6D 00 00	.00166 32080	.00 AD 00 00	.00263 97705	.00 ED 00 00	.00361 63330
.00 2E 00 00	.00070 19042	.00 6E 00 00	.00167 84667	.00 AE 00 00	.00265 50292	.00 EE 00 00	.00363 15917
.00 2F 00 00	.00071 71630	.00 6F 00 00	.00169 37255	.00 AF 00 00	.00267 02880	.00 EF 00 00	.00364 68505
.00 30 00 00	.00073 24218	.00 70 00 00	.00170 89843	.00 B0 00 00	.00268 55468	.00 F0 00 00	.00366 21093
.00 31 00 00	.00074 76806	.00 71 00 00	.00172 42421	.00 B1 00 00	.00270 08056	.00 F1 00 00	.00367 73681
.00 32 00 00	.00076 29394	.00 72 00 00	.00173 95019	.00 B2 00 00	.00271 60644	.00 F2 00 00	.00369 26269
.00 33 00 00	.00077 81982	.00 73 00 00	.00175 47607	.00 B3 00 00	.00273 13232	.00 F3 00 00	.00370 78857
.00 34 00 00	.00079 34570	.00 74 00 00	.00177 00195	.00 B4 00 00	.00274 65820	.00 F4 00 00	.00372 31445
.00 35 00 00	.00080 87158	.00 75 00 00	.00178 52783	.00 B5 00 00	.00276 18408	.00 F5 00 00	.00373 84033
.00 36 00 00	.00082 39746	.00 76 00 00	.00180 05371	.00 B6 00 00	.00277 70996	.00 F6 00 00	.00375 36621
.00 37 00 00	.00083 92333	.00 77 00 00	.00181 57958	.00 B7 00 00	.00279 23583	.00 F7 00 00	.00376 89208
.00 38 00 00	.00085 44921	.00 78 00 00	.00183 10546	.00 B8 00 00	.00280 76171	.00 F8 00 00	.00378 41796
.00 39 00 00	.00086 97509	.00 79 00 00	.00184 63134	.00 B9 00 00	.00282 28759	.00 F9 00 00	.00379 94384
.00 3A 00 00	.00088 50097	.00 7A 00 00	.00186 15722	.00 BA 00 00	.00283 81347	.00 FA 00 00	.00381 46972
.00 3B 00 00	.00090 02685	.00 7B 00 00	.00187 68310	.00 BB 00 00	.00285 33935	.00 FB 00 00	.00382 99560
.00 3C 00 00	.00091 55273	.00 7C 00 00	.00189 20898	.00 BC 00 00	.00286 86523	.00 FC 00 00	.00384 52148
.00 3D 00 00	.00093 07861	.00 7D 00 00	.00190 73486	.00 BD 00 00	.00288 39111	.00 FD 00 00	.00386 04736
.00 3E 00 00	.00094 60449	.00 7E 00 00	.00192 26074	.00 BE 00 00	.00289 91699	.00 FE 00 00	.00387 57324
.00 3F 00 00	.00096 13037	.00 7F 00 00	.00193 78662	.00 BF 00 00	.00291 44287	.00 FF 00 00	.00389 09912

Table K-6. Hexadecimal–Decimal Fraction Conversion Table (Cont.)

Hexadecimal	Decimal	Hexadecimal	Decimal	Hexadecimal	Decimal	Hexadecimal	Decimal
.00 00 00 00	.00000 00000	.00 00 40 00	.00000 38146	.00 00 80 00	.00000 76293	.00 00 C0 00	.00001 14440
.00 00 01 00	.00000 00596	.00 00 41 00	.00000 38743	.00 00 81 00	.00000 76889	.00 00 C1 00	.00001 15036
.00 00 02 00	.00000 01192	.00 00 42 00	.00000 39339	.00 00 82 00	.00000 77486	.00 00 C2 00	.00001 15633
.00 00 03 00	.00000 01788	.00 00 43 00	.00000 39935	.00 00 83 00	.00000 78082	.00 00 C3 00	.00001 16229
.00 00 04 00	.00000 02384	.00 00 44 00	.00000 40531	.00 00 84 00	.00000 78678	.00 00 C4 00	.00001 16825
.00 00 05 00	.00000 02980	.00 00 45 00	.00000 41127	.00 00 85 00	.00000 79274	.00 00 C5 00	.00001 17421
.00 00 06 00	.00000 03576	.00 00 46 00	.00000 41723	.00 00 86 00	.00000 79870	.00 00 C6 00	.00001 18017
.00 00 07 00	.00000 04172	.00 00 47 00	.00000 42319	.00 00 87 00	.00000 80466	.00 00 C7 00	.00001 18613
.00 00 08 00	.00000 04768	.00 00 48 00	.00000 42915	.00 00 88 00	.00000 81062	.00 00 C8 00	.00001 19209
.00 00 09 00	.00000 05364	.00 00 49 00	.00000 43511	.00 00 89 00	.00000 81658	.00 00 C9 00	.00001 19805
.00 00 0A 00	.00000 05960	.00 00 4A 00	.00000 44107	.00 00 8A 00	.00000 82254	.00 00 CA 00	.00001 20401
.00 00 0B 00	.00000 06556	.00 00 4B 00	.00000 44703	.00 00 8B 00	.00000 82850	.00 00 CB 00	.00001 20997
.00 00 0C 00	.00000 07152	.00 00 4C 00	.00000 45299	.00 00 8C 00	.00000 83446	.00 00 CC 00	.00001 21593
.00 00 0D 00	.00000 07748	.00 00 4D 00	.00000 45895	.00 00 8D 00	.00000 84042	.00 00 CD 00	.00001 22189
.00 00 0E 00	.00000 08344	.00 00 4E 00	.00000 46491	.00 00 8E 00	.00000 84638	.00 00 CE 00	.00001 22785
.00 00 0F 00	.00000 08940	.00 00 4F 00	.00000 47087	.00 00 8F 00	.00000 85234	.00 0C CF 00	.00001 23381
.00 00 10 00	.00000 09536	.00 00 50 00	.00000 47683	.00 00 90 00	.00000 85830	.00 00 D0 00	.00001 23977
.00 00 11 00	.00000 10132	.00 00 51 00	.00000 48279	.00 00 91 00	.00000 86426	.00 00 D1 00	.00001 24573
.00 00 12 00	.00000 10728	.00 00 52 00	.00000 48875	.00 00 92 00	.00000 87022	.00 00 D2 00	.00001 25169
.00 00 13 00	.00000 11324	.00 00 53 00	.00000 49471	.00 00 93 00	.00000 87618	.00 00 D3 00	.00001 25765
.00 00 14 00	.00000 11920	.00 00 54 00	.00000 50067	.00 00 94 00	.00000 88214	.00 00 D4 00	.00001 26361
.00 00 15 00	.00000 12516	.00 00 55 00	.00000 50663	.00 00 95 00	.00000 88810	.00 00 D5 00	.00001 26957
.00 00 16 00	.00000 13113	.00 00 56 00	.00000 51259	.00 00 96 00	.00000 89406	.00 00 D6 00	.00001 27553
.00 00 17 00	.00000 13709	.00 00 57 00	.00000 51856	.00 00 97 00	.00000 90003	.00 00 D7 00	.00001 28149
.00 00 18 00	.00000 14305	.00 00 58 00	.00000 52452	.00 00 98 00	.00000 90599	.00 00 D8 00	.00001 28746
.00 00 19 00	.00000 14901	.00 00 59 00	.00000 53048	.00 00 99 00	.00000 91195	.00 00 D9 00	.00001 29342
.00 00 1A 00	.00000 15497	.00 00 5A 00	.00000 53644	.00 00 9A 00	.00000 91791	.00 00 DA 00	.00001 29938
.00 00 1B 00	.00000 16093	.00 00 5B 00	.00000 54240	.00 00 9B 00	.00000 92387	.00 00 DB 00	.00001 30534
.00 00 1C 00	.00000 16689	.00 00 5C 00	.00000 54836	.00 00 9C 00	.00000 92983	.00 00 DC 00	.00001 31130
.00 00 1D 00	.00000 17285	.00 00 5D 00	.00000 55432	.00 00 9D 00	.00000 93579	.00 00 DD 00	.00001 31726
.00 00 1E 00	.00000 17881	.00 00 5E 00	.00000 56028	.00 00 9E 00	.00000 94175	.00 00 DE 00	.00001 32322
.00 00 1F 00	.00000 18477	.00 00 5F 00	.00000 56624	.00 00 9F 00	.00000 94771	.00 00 DF 00	.00001 32918
.00 00 20 00	.00000 19073	.00 00 60 00	.00000 57220	.00 00 A0 00	.00000 95367	.00 00 E0 00	.00001 33514
.00 00 21 00	.00000 19669	.00 00 61 00	.00000 57816	.00 00 A1 00	.00000 95963	.00 00 E1 00	.00001 34110
.00 00 22 00	.00000 20265	.00 00 62 00	.00000 58412	.00 00 A2 00	.00000 96559	.00 00 E2 00	.00001 34706
.00 00 23 00	.00000 20861	.00 00 63 00	.00000 59008	.00 00 A3 00	.00000 97155	.00 00 E3 00	.00001 35302
.00 00 24 00	.00000 21457	.00 00 64 00	.00000 59604	.00 00 A4 00	.00000 97751	.00 00 E4 00	.00001 35898
.00 00 25 00	.00000 22053	.00 00 65 00	.00000 60200	.00 00 A5 00	.00000 98347	.00 00 E5 00	.00001 36494
.00 00 26 00	.00000 22649	.00 00 66 00	.00000 60796	.00 00 A6 00	.00000 98943	.00 00 E6 00	.00001 37090
.00 00 27 00	.00000 23245	.00 00 67 00	.00000 61392	.00 00 A7 00	.00000 99539	.00 00 E7 00	.00001 37686
.00 00 28 00	.00000 23841	.00 00 68 00	.00000 61988	.00 00 A8 00	.00001 00135	.00 00 E8 00	.00001 38282
.00 00 29 00	.00000 24437	.00 00 69 00	.00000 62584	.00 00 A9 00	.00001 00731	.00 00 E9 00	.00001 38878
.00 00 2A 00	.00000 25033	.00 00 6A 00	.00000 63180	.00 00 AA 00	.00001 01327	.00 00 EA 00	.00001 39474
.00 00 2B 00	.00000 25629	.00 00 6B 00	.00000 63776	.00 00 AB 00	.00001 01923	.00 00 EB 00	.00001 40070
.00 00 2C 00	.00000 26226	.00 00 6C 00	.00000 64373	.00 00 AC 00	.00001 02519	.00 00 EC 00	.00001 40666
.00 00 2D 00	.00000 26822	.00 00 6D 00	.00000 64969	.00 00 AD 00	.00001 03116	.00 00 ED 00	.00001 41263
.00 00 2E 00	.00000 27418	.00 00 6E 00	.00000 65565	.00 00 AE 00	.00001 03712	.00 00 EE 00	.00001 41859
.00 00 2F 00	.00000 28014	.00 00 6F 00	.00000 61661	.00 00 AF 00	.00001 04308	.00 00 EF 00	.00001 42455
.00 00 30 00	.00000 28610	.00 00 70 00	.00000 66757	.00 00 B0 00	.00001 04904	.00 00 F0 00	.00001 43051
.00 00 31 00	.00000 29206	.00 00 71 00	.00000 67353	.00 00 B1 00	.00001 05500	.00 00 F1 00	.00001 43647
.00 00 32 00	.00000 29802	.00 00 72 00	.00000 67949	.00 00 B2 00	.00001 06096	.00 00 F2 00	.00001 44243
.00 00 33 00	.00000 30398	.00 00 73 00	.00000 68545	.00 00 B3 00	.00001 06692	.00 00 F3 00	.00001 44839
.00 00 34 00	.00000 30994	.00 00 74 00	.00000 69141	.00 00 B4 00	.00001 07228	.00 00 F4 00	.00001 45435
.00 00 35 00	.00000 31590	.00 00 75 00	.00000 69737	.00 00 B5 00	.00001 07884	.00 00 F5 00	.00001 46031
.00 00 36 00	.00000 32186	.00 00 76 00	.00000 70333	.00 00 B6 00	.00001 08480	.00 00 F6 00	.00001 46627
.00 00 37 00	.00000 32782	.00 00 77 00	.00000 70929	.00 00 B7 00	.00001 09076	.00 00 F7 00	.00001 47223
.00 00 38 00	.00000 33378	.00 00 78 00	.00000 71525	.00 00 B8 00	.00001 09672	.00 00 F8 00	.00001 47819
.00 00 39 00	.00000 33974	.00 00 79 00	.00000 75121	.00 00 B9 00	.00001 10268	.00 00 F9 00	.00001 48415
.00 00 3A 00	.00000 34570	.00 00 7A 00	.00000 72717	.00 00 BA 00	.00001 10864	.00 00 FA 00	.00001 49011
.00 00 3B 00	.00000 35166	.00 00 7B 00	.00000 73313	.00 00 BB 00	.00001 11460	.00 00 FB 00	.00001 49607
.00 00 3C 00	.00000 35762	.00 00 7C 00	.00000 73909	.00 00 BC 00	.00001 12056	.00 00 FC 00	.00001 50203
.00 00 3D 00	.00000 36358	.00 00 7D 00	.00000 74505	.00 00 BD 00	.00001 12652	.00 00 FD 00	.00001 50799
.00 00 3E 00	.00000 36954	.00 00 7E 00	.00000 75101	.00 00 BE 00	.00001 13248	.00 00 FE 00	.00001 51395
.00 00 3F 00	.00000 37550	.00 00 7F 00	.00000 75697	.00 00 BF 00	.00001 13844	.00 00 FF 00	.00001 51991

Table K-6. Hexadecimal–Decimal Fraction Conversion Table (Cont.)

Hexadecimal	Decimal	Hexadecimal	Decimal	Hexadecimal	Decimal	Hexadecimal	Decimal
.00 00 00 00	.00000 00000	.00 00 00 40	.00000 00149	.00 00 00 80	.00000 00298	.00 00 00 C0	.00000 00447
.00 00 00 01	.00000 00002	.00 00 00 41	.00000 00151	.00 00 00 81	.00000 00300	.00 00 00 C1	.00000 00449
.00 00 00 02	.00000 00004	.00 00 00 42	.00000 00153	.00 00 00 82	.00000 00302	.00 00 00 C2	.00000 00451
.00 00 00 03	.00000 00006	.00 00 00 43	.00000 00155	.00 00 00 83	.00000 00305	.00 00 00 C3	.00000 00454
.00 00 00 04	.00000 00009	.00 00 00 44	.00000 00158	.00 00 00 84	.00000 00307	.00 00 00 C4	.00000 00456
.00 00 00 05	.00000 00011	.00 00 00 45	.00000 00160	.00 00 00 85	.00000 00309	.00 00 00 C5	.00000 00458
.00 00 00 06	.00000 00013	.00 00 00 46	.00000 00162	.00 00 00 86	.00000 00311	.00 00 00 C6	.00000 00461
.00 00 00 07	.00000 00016	.00 00 00 47	.00000 00165	.00 00 00 87	.00000 00314	.00 00 00 C7	.00000 00463
.00 00 00 08	.00000 00018	.00 00 00 48	.00000 00167	.00 00 00 88	.00000 00316	.00 00 00 C8	.00000 00465
.00 00 00 09	.00000 00020	.00 00 00 49	.00000 00169	.00 00 00 89	.00000 00318	.00 00 00 C9	.00000 00467
.00 00 00 0A	.00000 00023	.00 00 00 4A	.00000 00172	.00 00 00 8A	.00000 00321	.00 00 00 CA	.00000 00470
.00 00 00 0B	.00000 00025	.00 00 00 4B	.00000 00174	.00 00 00 8B	.00000 00323	.00 00 00 CB	.00000 00472
.00 00 00 0C	.00000 00027	.00 00 00 4C	.00000 00176	.00 00 00 8C	.00000 00325	.00 00 00 CC	.00000 00474
.00 00 00 0D	.00000 00030	.00 00 00 4D	.00000 00179	.00 00 00 8D	.00000 00328	.00 00 00 CD	.00000 00477
.00 00 00 0E	.00000 00032	.00 00 00 4E	.00000 00181	.00 00 00 8E	.00000 00330	.00 00 00 CE	.00000 00479
.00 00 00 0F	.00000 00034	.00 00 00 4F	.00000 00183	.00 00 00 8F	.00000 00332	.00 00 00 CF	.00000 00481
.00 00 00 10	.00000 00037	.00 00 00 50	.00000 00186	.00 00 00 90	.00000 00335	.00 00 00 D0	.00000 00484
.00 00 00 11	.00000 00039	.00 00 00 51	.00000 00188	.00 00 00 91	.00000 00337	.00 00 00 D1	.00000 00486
.00 00 00 12	.00000 00041	.00 00 00 52	.00000 00190	.00 00 00 92	.00000 00339	.00 00 00 D2	.00000 00488
.00 00 00 13	.00000 00044	.00 00 00 53	.00000 00193	.00 00 00 93	.00000 00342	.00 00 00 D3	.00000 00491
.00 00 00 14	.00000 00046	.00 00 00 54	.00000 00195	.00 00 00 94	.00000 00344	.00 00 00 D4	.00000 00493
.00 00 00 15	.00000 00048	.00 00 00 55	.00000 00197	.00 00 00 95	.00000 00346	.00 00 00 D5	.00000 00495
.00 00 00 16	.00000 00051	.00 00 00 56	.00000 00200	.00 00 00 96	.00000 00349	.00 00 00 D6	.00000 00498
.00 00 00 17	.00000 00053	.00 00 00 57	.00000 00202	.00 00 00 97	.00000 00351	.00 00 00 D7	.00000 00500
.00 00 00 18	.00000 00055	.00 00 00 58	.00000 00204	.00 00 00 98	.00000 00353	.00 00 00 D8	.00000 00502
.00 00 00 19	.00000 00058	.00 00 00 59	.00000 00207	.00 00 00 99	.00000 00356	.00 00 00 D9	.00000 00505
.00 00 00 1A	.00000 00060	.00 00 00 5A	.00000 00209	.00 00 00 9A	.00000 00358	.00 00 00 DA	.00000 00507
.00 00 00 1B	.00000 00062	.00 00 00 5B	.00000 00211	.00 00 00 9B	.00000 00360	.00 00 00 DB	.00000 00509
.00 00 00 1C	.00000 00065	.00 00 00 5C	.00000 00214	.00 00 00 9C	.00000 00363	.00 00 00 DC	.00000 00512
.00 00 00 1D	.00000 00067	.00 00 00 5D	.00000 00216	.00 00 00 9D	.00000 00365	.00 00 00 DD	.00000 00514
.00 00 00 1E	.00000 00069	.00 00 00 5E	.00000 00218	.00 00 00 9E	.00000 00367	.00 00 00 DE	.00000 00516
.00 00 00 1F	.00000 00072	.00 00 00 5F	.00000 00221	.00 00 00 9F	.00000 00370	.00 00 00 DF	.00000 00519
.00 00 00 20	.00000 00074	.00 00 00 60	.00000 00223	.00 00 00 A0	.00000 00372	.00 00 00 E0	.00000 00521
.00 00 00 21	.00000 00076	.00 00 00 61	.00000 00225	.00 00 00 A1	.00000 00374	.00 00 00 E1	.00000 00523
.00 00 00 22	.00000 00079	.00 00 00 62	.00000 00228	.00 00 00 A2	.00000 00377	.00 00 00 E2	.00000 00526
.00 00 00 23	.00000 00081	.00 00 00 63	.00000 00230	.00 00 00 A3	.00000 00379	.00 00 00 E3	.00000 00528
.00 00 00 24	.00000 00083	.00 00 00 64	.00000 00232	.00 00 00 A4	.00000 00381	.00 00 00 E4	.00000 00530
.00 00 00 25	.00000 00086	.00 00 00 65	.00000 00235	.00 00 00 A5	.00000 00384	.00 00 00 E5	.00000 00533
.00 00 00 26	.00000 00088	.00 00 00 66	.00000 00237	.00 00 00 A6	.00000 00386	.00 00 00 E6	.00000 00535
.00 00 00 27	.00000 00090	.00 00 00 67	.00000 00239	.00 00 00 A7	.00000 00388	.00 00 00 E7	.00000 00537
.00 00 00 28	.00000 00093	.00 00 00 68	.00000 00242	.00 00 00 A8	.00000 00391	.00 00 00 E8	.00000 00540
.00 00 00 29	.00000 00095	.00 00 00 69	.00000 00244	.00 00 00 A9	.00000 00393	.00 00 00 E9	.00000 00542
.00 00 00 2A	.00000 00097	.00 00 00 6A	.00000 00246	.00 00 00 AA	.00000 00395	.00 00 00 EA	.00000 00544
.00 00 00 2B	.00000 00100	.00 00 00 6B	.00000 00249	.00 00 00 AB	.00000 00398	.00 00 00 EB	.00000 00547
.00 00 00 2C	.00000 00102	.00 00 00 6C	.00000 00251	.00 00 00 AC	.00000 00400	.00 00 00 EC	.00000 00549
.00 00 00 2D	.00000 00104	.00 00 00 6D	.00000 00253	.00 00 00 AD	.00000 00402	.00 00 00 ED	.00000 00551
.00 00 00 2E	.00000 00107	.00 00 00 6E	.00000 00256	.00 00 00 AE	.00000 00405	.00 00 00 EE	.00000 00554
.00 00 00 2F	.00000 00109	.00 00 00 6F	.00000 00258	.00 00 00 AF	.00000 00407	.00 00 00 EF	.00000 00556
.00 00 00 30	.00000 00111	.00 00 00 70	.00000 00260	.00 00 00 B0	.00000 00409	.00 00 00 F0	.00000 00558
.00 00 00 31	.00000 00114	.00 00 00 71	.00000 00263	.00 00 00 B1	.00000 00412	.00 00 00 F1	.00000 00561
.00 00 00 32	.00000 00116	.00 00 00 72	.00000 00265	.00 00 00 B2	.00000 00414	.00 00 00 F2	.00000 00563
.00 00 00 33	.00000 00118	.00 00 00 73	.00000 00267	.00 00 00 B3	.00000 00416	.00 00 00 F3	.00000 00565
.00 00 00 34	.00000 00121	.00 00 00 74	.00000 00270	.00 00 00 B4	.00000 00419	.00 00 00 F4	.00000 00568
.00 00 00 35	.00000 00123	.00 00 00 75	.00000 00272	.00 00 00 B5	.00000 00421	.00 00 00 F5	.00000 00570
.00 00 00 36	.00000 00125	.00 00 00 76	.00000 00274	.00 00 00 B6	.00000 00423	.00 00 00 F6	.00000 00572
.00 00 00 37	.00000 00128	.00 00 00 77	.00000 00277	.00 00 00 B7	.00000 00426	.00 00 00 F7	.00000 00575
.00 00 00 38	.00000 00130	.00 00 00 78	.00000 00279	.00 00 00 B8	.00000 00428	.00 00 00 F8	.00000 00577
.00 00 00 39	.00000 00132	.00 00 00 79	.00000 00281	.00 00 00 B9	.00000 00430	.00 00 00 F9	.00000 00579
.00 00 00 3A	.00000 00135	.00 00 00 7A	.00000 00284	.00 00 00 BA	.00000 00433	.00 00 00 FA	.00000 00582
.00 00 00 3B	.00000 00137	.00 00 00 7B	.00000 00286	.00 00 00 BB	.00000 00435	.00 00 00 FB	.00000 00584
.00 00 00 3C	.00000 00139	.00 00 00 7C	.00000 00288	.00 00 00 BC	.00000 00437	.00 00 00 FC	.00000 00586
.00 00 00 3D	.00000 00142	.00 00 00 7D	.00000 00291	.00 00 00 BD	.00000 00440	.00 00 00 FD	.00000 00589
.00 00 00 3E	.00000 00144	.00 00 00 7E	.00000 00293	.00 00 00 BE	.00000 00442	.00 00 00 FE	.00000 00591
.00 00 00 3F	.00000 00146	.00 00 00 7F	.00000 00295	.00 00 00 BF	.00000 00444	.00 00 00 FF	.00000 00593

Index

INDEX

INDEX